Lecture Notes in Computer Science 15650

Founding Editors

Gerhard Goos
Juris Hartmanis

AF172589

The series Lecture Notes in Computer Science (LNCS), including its subseries Lecture Notes in Artificial Intelligence (LNAI) and Lecture Notes in Bioinformatics (LNBI), has established itself as a medium for the publication of new developments in computer science and information technology research, teaching, and education.

LNCS enjoys close cooperation with the computer science R & D community, the series counts many renowned academics among its volume editors and paper authors, and collaborates with prestigious societies. Its mission is to serve this international community by providing an invaluable service, mainly focused on the publication of conference and workshop proceedings and postproceedings. LNCS commenced publication in 1973.

Osvaldo Gervasi · Beniamino Murgante ·
Chiara Garau · Yeliz Karaca · David Taniar ·
Ana Maria A. C. Rocha · Bernady O. Apduhan
Editors

Computational Science and Its Applications – ICCSA 2025

25th International Conference
Istanbul, Turkey, June 30 – July 3, 2025
Proceedings, Part III

 Springer

Editors
Osvaldo Gervasi ⓘD
University of Perugia
Perugia, Italy

Beniamino Murgante ⓘD
University of Basilicata
Potenza, Italy

Chiara Garau ⓘD
University of Cagliari
Cagliari, Italy

Yeliz Karaca ⓘD
University of Massachusetts Chan Medical
Worcester, MA, USA

David Taniar ⓘD
Monash University
Clayton, VIC, Australia

Ana Maria A. C. Rocha ⓘD
University of Minho
Braga, Portugal

Bernady O. Apduhan
Kyushu Sangyo University
Fukuoka, Japan

ISSN 0302-9743   ISSN 1611-3349 (electronic)
Lecture Notes in Computer Science
ISBN 978-3-031-96961-4   ISBN 978-3-031-96962-1 (eBook)
https://doi.org/10.1007/978-3-031-96962-1

Preface

The compiled 3 volumes (LNCS volumes 15648–15650) consist of the peer-reviewed papers from the 6 Main Conference Tracks of the 2025 International Conference on Computational Science and Its Applications (ICCSA 2025), which was held between June 30 – July 3, 2025 in Istanbul (Türkiye). The peer-reviewed papers of the 68 Workshops are published in a separate set made up of fourteen volumes (LNCS 15886–15899).

The conference was held in a hybrid form, with the large majority of participants in presence, hosted by Galatasaray University, Istanbul, Türkiye. We enabled virtual participation for those who did not attend the event in person due to logistical, political and economic problems, by adopting a technological infrastructure via open-source software (jitsi + riot) and a commercial Cloud infrastructure.

With the 2025 edition, ICCSA celebrated its 25th anniversary, a quarter of a century as a memorable moment that is harmoniously aligned with Istanbul, an extraordinary city located at the crossroads and acting as a bridge connecting Asia and Europe, representing different cultures, beliefs as well as lifestyles, which highlights its intercultural fabric.

ICCSA 2025 marked another fruitful and thought-provoking academic event in the International Conferences on Computational Science and Its Applications (ICCSA) conference series, previously held in Hanoi, Vietnam (2024), Athens, Greece (2023), Málaga, Spain (2022), Cagliari, Italy (hybrid with a few participants in presence in 2021 and completely online in 2020), whilst earlier editions took place in Saint Petersburg, Russia (2019), Melbourne, Australia (2018), Trieste, Italy (2017), Beijing, China (2016), Banff, Canada (2015), Guimaraes, Portugal (2014), Ho Chi Minh City, Vietnam (2013), Salvador, Brazil (2012), Santander, Spain (2011), Fukuoka, Japan (2010), Suwon, South Korea (2009), Perugia, Italy (2008), Kuala Lumpur, Malaysia (2007), Glasgow, UK (2006), Singapore (2005), Assisi, Italy (2004), Montreal, Canada (2003), and (as ICCS) Amsterdam, the Netherlands (2002) and San Francisco, USA (2001).

Computational Science constitutes the main pillar of most present research, industrial and commercial applications, and plays a unique role in exploiting ICT innovative technologies, and the ICCSA conference series has, accordingly, provided ample opportunities to researchers and industry practitioners to discuss new ideas, to share complex problems and their solutions, and to shape new trends in Computational Science. As the conference mirrors society from a scientific point of view, this year's undoubtedly dominant theme was large language models, machine learning and Artificial Intelligence (AI) and their applications in the most diverse technological, economic and industrial fields, amongst the others.

The ICCSA 2025 conference was structured in six general tracks covering the fields of computational science and its applications: Computational Methods, Algorithms and Scientific Applications – High Performance Computing and Networks – Geometric Modeling, Graphics and Visualization – Advanced and Emerging Applications – Information Systems and Technologies – Urban and Regional Planning. In addition, the conference consisted of 68 workshops, focusing on topical issues of utmost importance to science, technology and society: from new computational approaches for earth science, to mathematical methods for image processing, new statistical and optimization methods, several Artificial Intelligence approaches, sustainability issues, smart cities and related technologies, to name some.

In the Main Conference Proceedings, we accepted 71 full papers, 6 short papers and 1 Ph.D. Showcase paper from 269 submissions to the General Tracks of the Conference (with an acceptance rate of 29.9%). In the Workshops proceedings, we accepted 362 full papers, 37 short papers and 2 Ph.D. Showcase papers from a total of 1043 submissions (Acceptance rate 38.4%). We would like to convey our sincere appreciation to the workshops' chairs and co-chairs and program committee members for their diligent work, commitment and dedication.

The success and consistent maintenance of the ICCSA conference series in general, and of ICCSA 2025 in particular, rely upon the support of many people: authors, presenters, participants, keynote speakers, workshop chairs, session chairs, organizing committee members, student volunteers, Program Committee members, Advisory Committee members, International Liaison chairs, reviewers and other individuals in various roles. Thus, we take this opportunity to wholehartedly thank each and everyone.

We additionally wish to thank publisher Springer for their agreement to publish the proceedings, besides sponsoring part of the best papers awards and for their kind assistance and cooperation during the editing process.

We would cordially like to invite you to refer to the ICCSA website https://iccsa.org, where you can find the relevant details regarding this academic endeavor and event of ours.

June 2025

Osvaldo Gervasi
Yeliz Karaca
Beniamino Murgante
Chiara Garau

A Welcome Message from the Organizers

The International Conference on Computational Science and Its Applications (ICCSA) reflects a culmination of meticulous and dedicated efforts and academic endeavors toward the progress of science and technology.

One of the most noteworthy aspects of ICCSA is its fostering of a collective spirit, bringing together a plethora of participants from all over the world. Correspondingly, this merging power manifests itself in the 25th anniversary of ICCSA, which is a quarter of a century, in Istanbul, Türkiye, which connects and acts as a bridge between two continents, namely Asia and Europe. This unique location in the world hosts the 25th year of ICCSA at Galatasaray University, located on Çırağan Avenue by Istanbul's Bosphorus, which is an established international university bestowed with a distinctive past of teaching tradition, research and education exceeding five centuries.

Istanbul, having served as the capital city of four empires, namely the Roman Empire (330–395), the Byzantine Empire (395–1204 and 1261–1453), the Latin Empire (1204–1261) and the Ottoman Empire (1453–1922), is an exceptional city of the Republic of Türkiye founded by Mustafa Kemal Atatürk.

Situated at a strategic location along the historic Silk Road, Istanbul is at the core of extending rail networks which span across Europe and West Asia along with the only sea route between the Black Sea and the Mediterranean.

The cultural, historical and economic pulses of the country are evident in Istanbul whose rooted origins have embraced varying beliefs, lifestyles and populace, which highlights the city's mosaic quality with blended fabric in a constant harmonious flow. This has enabled cultures to grow and be nurtured, which is profoundly rooted in its urban culture.

Computational Science constitutes the main pillar of most present research, industrial and commercial activities besides manifesting a unique role in exploiting and addressing innovative Information and Communication Technologies. Thus, the 25-year-old ICCSA conference series provides remarkable opportunities to get acquainted with leading researchers, scientists, scholars, practitioners and many more while exchanging innovative ideas and initiating new partnerships, associations and bonds.

With the hosting of Galatasaray University, I would personally and on behalf of the Local Organizing Committee, with the members Emre Alptekin, Gülfem Işıklar Alptekin, Cengiz Kahraman, Abdullah Çağrı Tolga and Ayberk Zeytin, like to convey our sincere gratitude and thanks to everyone who exerted their efforts in and contributed to the realization of ICCSA 2025. With these notes and remarks, welcome to Istanbul!

Cordially yours,

On behalf of the Local Organizing Committee.

June 2025   Yeliz Karaca

Organization

Honorary General Chairs

Bernady O. Apduhan	Kyushu Sangyo University, Japan
Kenneth C. J. Tan	Sardina Systems, UK

General Chairs

Yeliz Karaca	University of Massachusetts, USA
Osvaldo Gervasi	University of Perugia, Italy
David Taniar	Monash University, Australia

Program Committee Chairs

Beniamino Murgante	University of Basilicata, Italy
Chiara Garau	University of Cagliari, Italy
Ana Maria A. C. Rocha	University of Minho, Portugal
A. Çağrı Tolga	Galatasaray University, Türkiye

International Advisory Committee

Jemal Abawajy	Deakin University, Australia
Dharma P. Agarwal	University of Cincinnati, USA
Rajkumar Buyya	Melbourne University, Australia
Claudia Bauzer Medeiros	University of Campinas, Brazil
Manfred M. Fisher	Vienna University of Economics and Business, Austria
Pierre Frankhauser	University of Franche-Comté/CNRS, France
Marina L. Gavrilova	University of Calgary, Canada
Sumi Helal	University of Florida, USA & Lancaster University, UK
Bin Jiang	University of Gävle, Sweden
Yee Leung	Chinese University of Hong Kong, China

International Liaison Chairs

Ivan Blečić	University of Cagliari, Italy
Giuseppe Borruso	University of Trieste, Italy
Elise De Donker	Western Michigan University, USA
Maria Noelia Faginas Lago	University of Perugia, Italy
Maria Irene Falcão	University of Minho, Portugal
Robert C. H. Hsu	Chung Hua University, Taiwan
Yeliz Karaca	University of Massachusetts Chan Medical School, USA
Tae-Hoon Kim	Zhejiang University of Science and Technology, China
Vladimir Korkhov	Saint Petersburg University, Russia
Takashi Naka	Kyushu Sangyo University, Japan
Rafael D. C. Santos	National Institute for Space Research, Brazil
Maribel Yasmina Santos	University of Minho, Portugal
Anastasia Stratigea	National Technical University of Athens, Greece

Workshop and Session Organizing Chairs

Beniamino Murgante	University of Basilicata, Italy
Chiara Garau	University of Cagliari, Italy

Award Chair

Wenny Rahayu	La Trobe University, Australia

Publicity Committee Chairs

Elmer Dadios	De La Salle University, Philippines
Nataliia Kulabukhova	Saint Petersburg University, Russia
Daisuke Takahashi	Tsukuba University, Japan
Shangwang Wang	Beijing University of Posts and Telecommunications, China

Local Organizing Committee Chairs

Emre Alptekin	Galatasaray University, Türkiye
Gülfem Işıklar Alptekin	Galatasaray University, Türkiye
Cengiz Kahraman	İstanbul Technical University, Türkiye
A. Çağrı Tolga	Galatasaray University, Türkiye
Ayberk Zeytin	Galatasaray University, Türkiye

Technology Chair

Damiano Perri	University of Perugia, Italy

Program Committee

Vera Afreixo	University of Aveiro, Portugal
Vladimir Alarcon	Northern Gulf Institute, USA
Filipe Alvelos	University of Minho, Portugal
Debora Anelli	Polytechnic University of Bari, Italy
Hartmut Asche	Hasso-Plattner-Institut für Digital Engineering Ggmbh, Germany
Nizamettin Aydın,	İstanbul Technical University, Türkiye
Ginevra Balletto	University of Cagliari, Italy
Nadia Balucani	University of Perugia, Italy
Socrates Basbas	Aristotle University of Thessaloniki, Greece
David Berti	ART SpA, Italy
Michela Bertolotto	University College Dublin, Ireland
Sandro Bimonte	CEMAGREF, TSCF, France
Ana Cristina Braga	University of Minho, Portugal
Tiziana Campisi	Kore University of Enna, Italy
Yves Caniou	Université Claude Bernard Lyon 1, France
Alessandra Capolupo	Polytechnic University of Bari, Italy
José A. Cardoso e Cunha	Universidade Nova de Lisboa, Portugal
Rui Cardoso	University of Beira Interior, Portugal
Leocadio G. Casado	University of Almería, Spain
Mete Celik	Erciyes University, Turkey
Maria Cerreta	University of Naples Federico II, Italy
Ta Quang Chieu	Thuyloi University, Vietnam
Rachel Chien-Sing Lee	Sunway University, Malaysia
Birol Ciloglugil	Ege University, Turkey
Mauro Coni	University of Cagliari, Italy

Florbela Maria da Cruz Domingues Correia	Polytechnic Institute of Viana do Castelo, Portugal
Alessandro Costantini	INFN, Italy
Roberto De Lotto	University of Pavia, Italy
Luiza De Macedo Mourelle	State University of Rio De Janeiro, Brazil
Marcelo De Paiva Guimaraes	Federal University of Sao Paulo, Brazil
Frank Devai	London South Bank University, UK
Joana Matos Dias	University of Coimbra, Portugal
Aziz Dursun	Virginia Tech University, USA
Laila El Ghandour	Heriot-Watt University, UK
Rafida M. Elobaid	Canadian University Dubai, United Arab Emirates
Maria Irene Falcao	University of Minho, Portugal
Florbela P. Fernandes	Polytechnic Institute of Bragança, Portugal
Paula Odete Fernandes	Polytechnic Institute of Bragança, Portugal
Adelaide de Fátima Baptista Valente Freitas	University of Aveiro, Portugal
Valentina Franzoni	University of Perugia, Italy
Andreas Fricke	University of Potsdam, Germany
Raffaele Garrisi	Centro Operativo per la Sicurezza Cibernetica, Italy
Ivan Gerace	University of Perugia, Italy
Maria Giaoutzi	National Technical University of Athens, Greece
Salvatore Giuffrida	University of Catania, Italy
Teresa Guarda	Universidad Estatal Peninsula de Santa Elena, Ecuador
Sevin Gümgüm	Izmir University of Economics, Turkey
Malgorzata Hanzl	Technical University of Lodz, Poland
Maulana Adhinugraha Kiki	Telkom University, Indonesia
Clement Ho Cheung Leung	Chinese University of Hong Kong, China
Andrea Lombardi	University of Perugia, Italy
Marcos Mandado Alonso	University of Vigo, Spain
Ernesto Marcheggiani	Katholieke Universiteit Leuven, Belgium
Antonino Marvuglia	Luxembourg Institute of Science and Technology, Luxembourg
Michele Mastroianni	University of Salerno, Italy
Hideo Matsufuru	High Energy Accelerator Research Organization, Japan
Fernando Miranda	Universidade do Minho, Portugal
Giuseppe Modica	University of Reggio Calabria, Italy
Majaz Moonis	University of Massachusetts, USA
Nadia Nedjah	State University of Rio de Janeiro, Brazil
Paolo Nesi	University of Florence, Italy

Suzan Obaiys	University of Malaya, Malaysia
Marcin Paprzycki	Polish Academy of Sciences, Poland
Eric Pardede	La Trobe University, Australia
Ana Isabel Pereira	Polytechnic Institute of Bragança, Portugal
Damiano Perri	University of Perugia, Italy
Massimiliano Petri	University of Pisa, Italy
Telmo Pinto	University of Coimbra, Portugal
Alessandro Plaisant	University of Sassari, Italy
Maurizio Pollino	ENEA, Italy
Alenka Poplin	Iowa State University, USA
Marcos Quiles	Federal University of São Paulo, Brazil
Nguyen Huu Quynh	Thuyloi University, Vietnam
Albert Rimola	Universitat Autònoma de Barcelona, Spain
Humberto Rocha	University of Coimbra, Portugal
Marzio Rosi	University of Perugia, Italy
Lucia Saganeiti	University of L'Aquila, Italy
Francesco Scorza	University of Basilicata, Italy
Marco Paulo Seabra dos Reis	University of Coimbra, Portugal
Jie Shen	University of Michigan, USA
Francesco Tajani	Sapienza University of Rome, Italy
Rodrigo Tapia Mcclung	Centro de Investigación en Ciencias de Información Geoespacial, Mexico
Eufemia Tarantino	Polytechnic University of Bari, Italy
Sergio Tasso	University of Perugia, Italy
Ana Paula Teixeira	Universidade do Minho, Portugal
Yiota Theodora	National Technical University of Athens, Greece
Giuseppe A. Trunfio	University of Sassari, Italy
Toshihiro Uchibayashi	Kyushu University, Japan
Marco Vizzari	University of Perugia, Italy
Frank Westad	Norwegian University of Science and Technology, Norway
Fukuko Yuasa	High Energy Accelerator Research Organization, Japan
Ljiljana Zivkovic	Republic Geodetic Authority, Serbia

General Tracks

1. Computational Methods, Algorithms and Scientific Applications

Computational Biology
Computational Combustion
Computational Chemistry

Computational Fluid Dynamics
Computational Physics
Computational Geometry
Computational Mathematics
Computational Mechanics
Computational Electro-magnetics
Numerical Methods and Algorithms

2. High Performance Computing and Networks

Parallel and Distributed Computing
Cluster Computing
Supercomputing
Cloud Computing
Autonomic Computing
P2P Computing
Mobile Computing
Edge Computing
Workflow Design and Practice
Computer and Network Architecture

3. Geometric Modeling, Graphics and Visualization

Scientific Visualization
Computer Graphics
Geometric Modeling
Pattern Recognition
Image Processing
CAD/CAM
Web3D, Virtual and Augmented Reality

4. Advanced and Emerging Applications

Biochemistry
Bioinformatics
Astrophysics
Biometric Modeling
Environmental, Climate and Weather Modeling
Geology and Geophysics
Nuclear Physics
Financial and Economical Modeling
Computational Journalism

5. Information Systems and Technologies

Information Retrieval
Scientific Databases
Security Engineering
Risk Analysis
Reliability Engineering

Software Engineering
Data Mining
Artificial Intelligence
Machine Learning
Learning Technologies
Web-Based Computing
Web 2.0
Blockchain

6. Urban and Regional Planning

Urban and Regional Growth
Sustainable Urban and Regional Development
Socio-ecological Systems
Open Data/Big Data
Cultural Heritage
Smart and Sustainable Cities
Mobility and Intelligent Transport Systems
Geographical Information Systems
Decision Support Systems
Complexity Assessment and Mapping
Logistics

Sponsoring Organizations

ICCSA 2025 would not have been possible without the tremendous support of many organizations and institutions, for which all organizers and participants of ICCSA 2025 express their sincere gratitude:

Galatasaray University, Istanbul, Türkiye
(https://gsu.edu.tr/en)

African Mathematical Union
(https://www.africanmathunion.org/)

Springer Nature Switzerland AG, Switzerland
(https://www.springer.com)

The University of Massachusetts, USA
(https://www.umass.edu/)

University of Perugia, Italy
(https://www.unipg.it)

University of Basilicata, Italy (http://www.unibas.it)

Monash University, Australia
(https://www.monash.edu/)

Kyushu Sangyo University, Japan
(https://www.kyusan-u.ac.jp/)

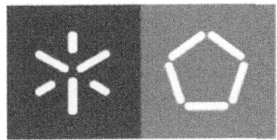

Universidade do Minho
Escola de Engenharia

University of Minho, Portugal
(https://www.uminho.pt/)
Venue
ICCSA 2025 took place in: **Galatasaray University, Istanbul, Türkiye**

Additional Reviewers

Reviewers
The review tasks for each workshop have been carried out by the workshop Organizers
and the members of the workshop Program Committee.

Plenary Lectures

Sky Safe with GAI and Post-quantum Computing

Elizabeth Chang

Professor of the Cyber Security and Head of Discipline, University of Sunshine Coast, Australia

Abstract. Professor Chang's talk in this presentation has two distinct parts. To start, she will introduce the landscape of cybersecurity development, attacks, threats, and vulnerabilities, as well as state-of-the-art cyber protection, cyber defence, and cyber incident prevention. This is followed by a discussion of the impact of Generative AI (GAI) and quantum-safe cryptographic computing, highlighting the major issues and challenges in research, education, and training. In conclusion, she will present a vision for Sky Safe solutions, aiming to achieve cyber resilience that supports business and economic stability, enhances human capabilities, and promotes environmental sustainability.

Disaster Preparedness and Risk Profiling in the Digital Era from Earth Observation Lens

Jagannath Aryal

Department of Infrastructure Engineering, University of Melbourne, Australia

Abstract. Natural hazards which turn into disasters result in severe losses of lives, infrastructure, and property. Disasters such as earthquakes and landslides and their impacts on transportation safety, infrastructure resilience, and displacement of people to new places are challenges. To address such challenges, earth observation data and intelligent methods can provide potential solutions in developing decision support systems. This talk will present the state of the in Earth observation for disaster resilience using intelligent methods. In the earth observation space, digitalisation has revolutionised the way we map, monitor, and develop decision support systems. Global case study examples covering earthquake-induced landslides from the Himalayan region will cover the digital capabilities. The digital capabilities will embrace object recognition, interpretation, and their accurate and precise capture to integrate into digital models. The developed digital models from representative case studies can be leveraged in other jurisdictions in profiling risks to protect lives and infrastructure and creating disaster preparedness in the era of digital age and digital economy.

Intelligent Image Enhancement for Real-World Applications in Adverse Atmospheric Conditions

Khan Muhammad

Department of Global Convergence, Sungkyunkwan University, South Korea

Abstract. The adverse impacts of atmospheric conditions such as haze, fog, and low-light environments pose significant challenges for real-world applications reliant on computer vision, including autonomous driving, surveillance, and remote sensing. This keynote explores cutting-edge advancements in intelligent image enhancement, drawing insights from two pivotal studies. The first introduces HazeSpace2M, a comprehensive dataset and novel classification-guided dehazing framework that improves image clarity across diverse atmospheric conditions, addressing the gap between synthetic and real-world dehazing performance. The second focuses on LoLI-Street, a benchmark for low-light image enhancement tailored to urban environments, extending beyond enhancement to enable robust object detection and scene understanding. Taken together, these contributions demonstrate how integrating domain-specific datasets, advanced algorithms, and performance benchmarks can significantly elevate the reliability of computer vision systems under challenging weather and lighting conditions. Attendees will gain valuable insights into the methodologies, datasets, and practical applications driving innovation in this field, with implications for research and industry alike.

In Memory of Carmelo Torre

Unfortunately, Professor Carmelo Torre, one of the cornerstones of the ICCSA Conference, passed away last December, leaving everyone stunned and deeply saddened. His loss has created a profound void within our academic community. Carmelo was not only a respected scholar and dedicated contributor to the success and growth of ICCSA, but also a generous colleague, mentor, and friend to many. His intellectual rigor, warm personality, and unwavering commitment to advancing research will be remembered with great admiration. As we continue the work he helped shape, we honor his legacy and the indelible mark he left on all of us. 'Carmelo Torre graduated in engineering at the Polytechnic of Bari with a thesis on urban planning under Dino Borri's guidance. He began his research career by collaborating with Franco Selicato. During his PhD at the University of Naples Federico II under Luigi Fusco Girard, he specialized in real estate market analysis and multi-criteria evaluation methods. He explored the social impacts of urban transformations with his lifelong friend Maria Cerreta. His first ICCSA participation was in Perugia in 2008, in the session Geographical Analysis, Urban Modeling, Spatial Statistics. Instantly captivated by the conference, his charisma enabled him to involve various Italian scientific communities, including those in real estate and statistics. ICCSA became a yearly commitment for him, where he valued the high editorial quality of the proceedings and the dynamic post-presentation discussions and debates he passionately and expertly enriched. In 2012, alongside Maria Cerreta and Paola Perchinunno, he organized the workshop Econometrics and Multidimensional Evaluation in the Urban Environment (EMEUE), fostering dialogue on critical topics. His influence steadily grew, drawing numerous research groups to ICCSA and establishing real estate and assessment as one of the conference's leading fields. A pillar of ICCSA, he was involved across all facets of the event. Torre's contributions to academic discourse were marked by intellectual rigor and innovative thinking. His conference interventions consistently challenged conventional wisdom, offering insights transcending disciplinary boundaries. Beyond the conference, he passionately advocated for equity and social justice. His left-leaning ideology, though firm, earned respect from those with differing views, thanks to his sincerity and loyalty. He was creative, generous, and always willing to help, even at a personal cost. Despite battling illness, he maintained his characteristic optimism, warmth, cheerfulness, and commitment, supported by his partner, Caterina Rinaldo. His legacy lives on in his ideas, dedication, and unmatched generosity.

Contents – Part III

Urban and Regional Planning

Information Systems and Technologies

Improving Anomaly Detection in Network Traffic Using Choquet-Based Feature Engineering for Random Forest and XGBoost Models

Abreu Quevedo[1], Denner Ayres[1], Gabriel Teixeira[1], Graçaliz Dimuro[1], Giancarlo Lucca[2] , and Bruno L. Dalmazo[1]($\boxtimes$)

[1] Federal University of Rio Grande, Rio Grand, Brazil
{abreu_rg,dennerayres,gabsi,gracaliz,dalmazo}@furg.br
[2] University Católica of Pelotas, Pelotas, Brazil
giancarlo.lucca@ucpel.edu.br

Abstract. Network traffic is essential for modern communication, ensuring the proper functioning of daily activities. In today's connected world, cybercriminals attempt to harm and extort users. To address this issue, various models have been proposed, yet they still underperform. This study proposes a new feature based on an aggregation method using the generalized Choquet integral, incorporating a parameter α. To validate its effectiveness, we perform anomaly detection with Random Forest and XGBoost models, assessing its impact on detecting Hulk DoS attacks. Experimental results showed that our proposal significantly improved accuracy. The Random Forest model increased from 93.53% to 97.82% (4.59% improvement), while XGBoost rose from 93.52% to 97.69% (4.46% increase). More importantly, recall for the minority class (attacks) improved substantially, from 0.68 to 0.93 (37% increase) with Random Forest and from 0.68 to 0.92 (35% increase) for XGBoost, reducing false negatives and enhancing intrusion detection. These findings highlight the potential of Choquet-based feature engineering in improving anomaly detection.

Keywords: Anomaly detection · Choquet Integral · Fuzzy · Random Forest · XGBoost

1 Introduction

Computer networks are an integral part of daily life worldwide, enabling global communication and supporting essential services such as banking, healthcare, education, and business operations. In today's interconnected society, the increasing reliance on network infrastructure highlights not only its importance but also its vulnerability [8].

Data network traffic has played numerous roles in the field of security; however, issues such as data leakage, user information exposure, and authentication

O. Gervasi et al. (Eds.): ICCSA 2025, LNCS 15650, pp. 3–16, 2025.
https://doi.org/10.1007/978-3-031-96962-1_1

remain significant challenges in the current network environment. Furthermore, the exponential growth of data volume intensifies the complexity of managing and analyzing network traffic, requiring efficient techniques to process and extract relevant information [5].

Among the most critical threats to network stability are Distributed Denial of Service (DDoS) attacks. Given the growing dependency on uninterrupted data services, malicious users may attempt to harm these services to disrupt access for individuals or organizations. In such attacks, multiple computers are hijacked and used to flood the target with excessive traffic, overwhelming the infrastructure and rendering it inaccessible.

These malicious activities often generate identifiable patterns or irregularities, known as anomalies. Detecting such anomalies is essential for mitigating attacks effectively. However, due to the high dimensionality and complexity of modern network data, it becomes necessary to reduce the dimensionality of the data extracted from the network and focus on the most relevant features. Concerned with current network security challenges, this study aims to detect anomalies [16] by implementing a feature engineering approach. The proposed method leverages techniques such as Feature Selection and the Generalized Choquet Integral to enhance the detection and mitigation of DDoS attacks.

In light of these challenges, the Choquet integral serves as a powerful tool for data aggregation, as the fuzzy measure allows for effectively modeling relationships within the given data [2,6]. Despite various methodologies in the literature aimed at enhancing existing algorithms such as Random Forest and XGBoost, no prior studies have applied the generalized Choquet integral to generate features for improving predictive performance. Addressing this gap, this paper introduces a novel feature engineering approach for network traffic analysis, leveraging the fuzzy Choquet integral framework. A key aspect of this method used in this work is the parameter α, which significantly impacts both the execution time and the accuracy of anomaly detection. The effectiveness of this approach is validated using real-world data from a reliable source, demonstrating its practical applicability in network management.

The remainder of the paper is organized as follows. Section 2 presents the related work. The proposal is presented in Sect. 3, and details of its evaluation in Sect. 4. Finally, in Sect. 5, some final remarks are made, and directions for future research are indicated.

2   Related Work

This section discusses research efforts related to the scope of this paper. Studies were gathered that made significant contributions in the areas of DDoS anomaly detection, fuzzy models, and network traffic management.

Wani *et al.* [16] present three well-known machine learning algorithms used in the field of network security, Random Forest, Naïve Bayes, and Support Vector Machine, to detect Distributed Denial of Service (DDoS) attacks. The study aims to contribute to the mitigation of DDoS attacks, which are classified as critical threats due to their potential to compromise network availability. In this study, the authors used a few tools to set up the testing environment and simulate the attacks. They used OwnCloud, an open-source cloud platform, as the target for the attacks, while the DDoS attacks were carried out using the Tor Hammer tool. Everything was run on the Kali Linux 2018.2 system (Kernel 4.15.0, GNOME 3.28.0). The paper also introduced a dataset with 9 features and 4 class labels, used to evaluate their algorithms. To measure performance, they used metrics like precision, recall, specificity, and F-measure. Overall, the SVM algorithm showed the best results across all metrics, followed by Random Forest.

In addition, Jiang et al. [10] proposed a model for detecting network intrusions using Particle Swarm Optimization (PSO) combined with eXtreme Gradient Boosting (XGBoost). Their goal was to improve accuracy, fine-tune parameters, and select the most relevant features to create a more effective anomaly detection model. Compared to other techniques, the PSO-XGBoost model showed a clear improvement in detecting anomalies. Even with the good results, the authors point out that achieving high precision in Network Intrusion Detection Systems (NIDS) remains a significant challenge, especially when dealing with anomaly detection.

Experimental results demonstrate that the PSO-XGBoost model usually outperforms traditional approaches such as Random Forest, Bagging, and AdaBoost, particularly in detecting minority-class attacks like U2R and R2L. However, the literature lacks studies that explore models for anomaly detection while maintaining low complexity, as fuzzy models do.

Aziz et al. [3] proposed a hybrid model to identify the core traffic of the network. First, a payload-based approach identifies most of the traffic. Any remaining unidentified traffic is then analyzed using a statistical unsupervised machine learning method, ensuring that no traffic is left unidentified. The main contributions include, capturing local IP traffic from a university network, identifying traffic using a payload-based method, labeling the unidentified traffic, and applying an unsupervised machine learning approach to classify the rest. In the proposed framework, DPI (Deep Packet Inspection) is employed as the first stage to classify application-layer traffic using predefined protocol signatures. Traffic flows that remain unidentified by DPI are then subjected to machine learning supervised or unsupervised methods. The authors developed and evaluated the framework using real traffic data, and the results demonstrate that the hybrid model effectively addresses the limitations of standalone DPI and machine learning methods. Although the study presents a hybrid system offering a solution for real-time traffic categorization, the proposal lacks a specialized solution for detecting anomalies in network traffic.

Following the networking traffic management field, Shetty et al. [15] presented a comprehensive study on the application of Artificial Intelligence (AI) and Machine Learning (ML) for intelligent network traffic control in modern communication systems. The primary objective is to address the limitations of traditional traffic management methods such as static routing, traffic shaping, and load balancing, which struggle to adapt to the dynamic and high-volume traffic of the today's networks. The authors propose the integration of AI/ML techniques to enhance traffic prediction, congestion control, bandwidth optimization, latency reduction, and Quality of Service (QoS) improvements. Supervised, unsupervised, reinforcement, and deep learning models are analyzed for their effectiveness in managing traffic flows. Real-world case studies from companies like Vodafone, Akamai, and Cloudflare demonstrate the practical value of AI/ML in telecom and content delivery networks.

Yao Hu and Bibo Tu [9] investigated an attack detection method based on the Fuzzy C-Means (FCM) clustering algorithm. Their approach focuses on identifying abnormal network behavior by enabling the system to autonomously learn both typical and atypical service patterns while effectively managing complex network interactions. Once malicious traffic is detected through FCM clustering, the system assesses the severity of the intrusion and initiates appropriate countermeasures. To evaluate the performance of the FCM algorithm, the author used two metrics: miss rate and bit error rate. These results were then compared to those from K-Means and DTSOM. The findings showed that FCM performed better, with lower error rates than the other methods.

As mentioned earlier, these popular machine learning algorithms tend to achieve high accuracy, but they often face challenges when adapting to network behavior, which can lead to false positives and limited generalization. Additionally, although hybrid models can improve accuracy in classifying anomalies, their main focus is usually on categorizing traffic rather than directly detecting anomalies. As a result, some vulnerabilities may remain in the network without being properly addressed.

To address these gaps in the literature, this paper proposes an anomaly detection method that leverages the Choquet integral to create a new feature and enhance detection performance. By incorporating fuzzy measures, the approach improves decision-making. Unlike traditional machine learning models [16], which rely heavily on accurate classifications, this method adaptively weighs traffic features, capturing complex dependencies and improving anomaly detection. As noted in the literature, two models commonly used in similar studies are XGBoost and Random Forest. Therefore, both models will be employed in this work to evaluate and compare the effectiveness of the proposed approach. This method offers a more flexible detection mechanism, capable of recognizing legitimate variations in network behavior and using them to improve detection accuracy.

3   Proposed Approach

This work proposes a novel approach to feature engineering, aiming to enhance anomaly detection regarding DDoS attacks. To achieve this, we first employ KBest [13] as a feature selection algorithm to identify the most relevant features for classification using Random Forest and XGBoost. Once the optimal set of features is determined, we further add a new variable derived from the prediction of network traffic using a Generalized Choquet Integral, with an adaptive α. This transformation allows the selected feature to be reformulated and reintegrated into the final set of chosen features. By incorporating this new refined feature, the study seeks to improve the model's accuracy, reliability, and efficiency in detecting anomalies.

3.1 Conceptual Model

Figure 1 provides the foundation of this work, detailing its stages and illustrating each step of the process along with its main components and interactions.

1. **Data**: A networking DDoS attack dataset is taken. (Step 1 in Fig. 1)
2. **Data preprocessing**: The data is processed to improve efficiency within the algorithms. (Step 2 in Fig. 1)
3. **Application of feature selection algorithm**: As the data have been processed, a feature selection algorithm is used to choose a range of the best features to use in the prediction algorithm. (Step 3 in Fig. 1)
4. **Application of Choquet integral to aggregation of data from one of the features**: Having selected the features, the first one is taken and the algorithm based on the generalizations of the Choquet integral with adaptive α is used, thus creating a new feature through aggregation and prediction of trends. (Step 4 in Fig. 1)
5. **Integrate the new feature with the selected ones**: This new feature is added along with the previously selected features. (Step 5 in Fig. 1)

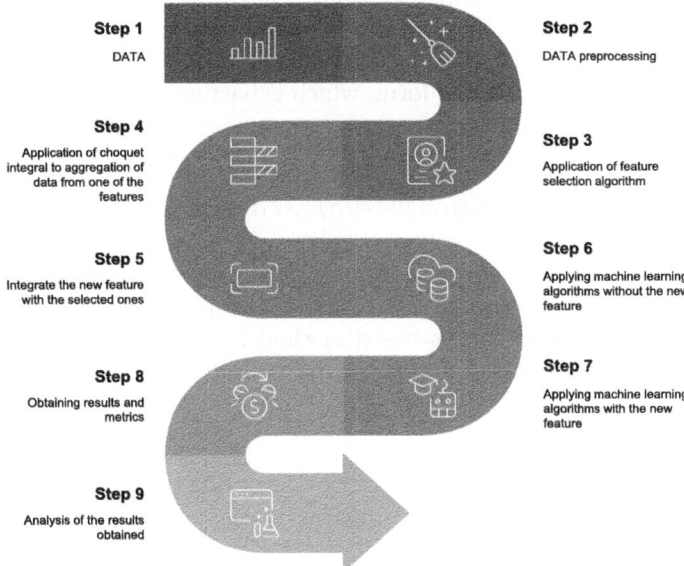

Fig. 1. Conceptual model.

6. **Applying machine learning algorithms without the new feature**: The algorithms used for prediction through machine learning are first applied to the data without the new feature. (Step 6 in Fig. 1)
7. **Applying machine learning algorithms with the new feature**: Then, the same algorithms are applied again, this time with the new feature included. (Step 7 in Fig. 1)
8. **Obtaining results and metrics**: Once the algorithms have been applied, results and performance metrics are obtained. (Step 8 in Fig. 1)
9. **Analysis of the results obtained**: Finally, the results and metrics are analyzed to evaluate the impact of the new feature. (Step 9 in Fig. 1)

3.2   Aggregation and Choquet Integral Functions

The Choquet integral [7] plays a fundamental role in data aggregation [4]. It is defined for a fuzzy measure $m : 2^N \rightarrow [0, 1]$, enabling a flexible way to combine inputs by considering the significance of each criterion.

$$\mathcal{C}_m(x) = \sum_{i=1}^{n} \left(x_{\sigma(i)} - x_{\sigma(i-1)} \right) m \left(A_{(i)} \right),$$

where $(x_{\sigma(1)}, \ldots, x_{\sigma(n)})$ represents a permutation of the input values arranged in ascending order, and $A_{(i)} = \{(i), \ldots, (n)\}$ is the subset of indices that correspond to the $n - i + 1$ highest elements of the input x.

Copulas [1] are mathematical functions, $C : [0, 1]^2 \rightarrow [0, 1]$, that establish relationships between two-dimensional probability distributions and their respective one-dimensional marginal distributions. They play a key role in the study of probabilistic metric spaces and have extensive applications in statistical analysis.

By leveraging the distributive property of the product, the Choquet integral can be expressed in an expanded form, which is particularly useful when dealing with α-parameterized copulas:

$$\mathcal{C}_m(x) = \sum_{i=1}^{n} \left(x_{(i)} \cdot m \left(A_{(i)} \right) - x_{(i-1)} \cdot m \left(A_{(i)} \right) \right),$$

In [11], this extended representation of the Choquet integral has been further generalized through copula functions, where both product operators are substituted by alternative copula-based methods.

In this work, the copula functions under consideration[1] are summarized in Table 1.

---

[1] Additional definitions, as well as their properties and mathematical formulations, can be found more deeply in [12].

Table 1. Table of Generalizations of the Choquet integral used to create a new feature.

Copula ID	Functions	α Properties
(A)	$C_\alpha(x,y) = xy[1 + \alpha(1-x)(1-y)]$	$-1 \leq \alpha \leq 1(\alpha \neq 0)$
(B)	$C_\alpha(x,y) = \frac{1}{1+\alpha} Max[x + y - 1 + \alpha - \alpha|x-y|, 0]$	$0 < \alpha < 1$
(C)	$C_\alpha = (1-\alpha)W + \alpha Min$	$0 < \alpha < 1$
(D)	$C_\alpha = \frac{\alpha^2(1-\alpha)}{2}W + (1-\alpha^2)P + \frac{\alpha^2(1+\alpha)}{2}Min$	$-1 < \alpha < 1(\alpha \neq 0)$

3.3   Dataset

The CIC-DDoS2019 [14] dataset is commonly used in machine learning research focused on network security, particularly for distinguishing between Distributed Denial of Service (DDoS) attacks and normal traffic. It was developed by the Canadian Institute for Cybersecurity (CIC) and the data was collected using CICFlowMeter-V3 that includes traffic from multiple devices, providing a scenario closer to a real network environment.

The dataset was compiled by CIC and is part of their CIC-DDoS2019 collection. It contains a mix of normal traffic and DDoS-related packet data. With over 200,000 rows, it provides data to train and evaluate machine learning models. The dataset includes a variety of traffic features, making it suitable for feature engineering and model optimization. The HULK attack, present in the CIC-DDoS2019 dataset, is a type of DoS attack that floods servers with a high volume of HTTP requests to make them unavailable. This attack was used to evaluate our approach in this work.

3.4   Implementation

For the implementation of this work, we used four algorithms: Random Forest, SelectKBest, XGBoost, and the Choquet Integral - the first three being well-known and widely used in the academic community.

It is worth noticing that SelectKBest is a machine learning technique used for feature selection, and it was applied in this work to identify and choose the most relevant variables from the dataset. This approach enhances model performance while reducing the risk of overfitting. SelectKBest is one of the most widely used methods within this technique and falls under the category of filter-based feature selection. It applies statistical tests such as Chi-Squared, ANOVA F-test, and Mutual Information Score to rank features based on their relationship with the target variable, selecting the top K features with the highest scores.

To predict DoS attacks, we employed two machine learning algorithms: Random Forest and XGBoost. Although both are based on decision trees, they utilize distinct techniques to enhance accuracy and robustness. Random Forest is an ensemble learning method that constructs multiple decision trees from different subsets of the training data. By selecting random features at each split, it reduces overfitting and improves generalization. The final prediction is determined by aggregating the outputs of all trees—typically through majority voting in classification tasks. This approach not only enhances robustness to noise but also provides valuable internal estimates for error monitoring. On the other hand, XGBoost (eXtreme Gradient Boosting) is a highly efficient and scalable gradient-boosting algorithm. Unlike Random Forest, it builds decision trees sequentially, with each new tree correcting the errors of the previous ones using gradient descent optimization. XGBoost is well known for its speed and ability to handle large datasets. We can have a look at how it behaves in the Algorithm 1.

Algorithm 1. Feature Selection and Model Evaluation

Input: Dataset D
Output: Model performance metrics

1: $D_{clean} \leftarrow$ Preprocess(D)   ▷ Data cleaning and preprocessing
2: $selectedFeatures \leftarrow$ KBest(D_{clean}, $k = 4$)   ▷ Select top 4 features using KBest
3: $choquetFeature \leftarrow$ ChoquetIntegral($selectedFeatures[0]$)   ▷ Generate additional feature
4: $finalFeatures \leftarrow selectedFeatures \cup \{choquetFeature\}$ ▷ Combine features
5: $D_{final} \leftarrow$ PrepareData(D_{clean}, $finalFeatures$)   ▷ Prepare dataset with selected features
6: $model1 \leftarrow$ Train(RandomForest, D_{final})   ▷ Train Random Forest
7: $model2 \leftarrow$ Train(XGBoost, D_{final})   ▷ Train XGBoost
8: $results1 \leftarrow$ Evaluate($model1$, D_{final})   ▷ Evaluate Random Forest
9: $results2 \leftarrow$ Evaluate($model2$, D_{final})   ▷ Evaluate XGBoost
10: $model1_{noFeature} \leftarrow$ Train(RandomForest, $D_{noFeature}$)   ▷ Train Random Forest without new feature
11: $model2_{noFeature} \leftarrow$ Train(XGBoost, $D_{noFeature}$)   ▷ Train XGBoost without new feature
12: $results1_{noFeature} \leftarrow$ Evaluate($model1_{noFeature}$, $D_{noFeature}$)   ▷ Evaluate Random Forest without new feature
13: $results2_{noFeature} \leftarrow$ Evaluate($model2_{noFeature}$, $D_{noFeature}$)   ▷ Evaluate XGBoost without new feature
14: **return** $results1$, $results2$, $results1_{noFeature}$, $results2_{noFeature}$ ▷ Return model performance metrics

---

The Choquet-based algorithm employed in this work was developed using copulas, as presented in Table 1, it is used for data aggregation and trend prediction. The algorithm takes a selected feature as input and processes it using specific techniques to compute the mean absolute error (MAE) associated with each of the four copulas and its α related to them. The copula and the α with the lowest MAE are then selected to produce the final output which will be used in the classification algorithms.

4   Evaluation

To prove the technical feasibility of the proposal, this section evaluates the influence of using the Generalization of the Choquet integral as a feature creator, and its results when used in algorithms to detect anomalies.

4.1   Generalization of the Choquet Integral

Was address the implementation of a prediction model using the Choquet Integral applied to a feature extracted from the dataset, where the mean absolute error (MAE) analysis is performed with different copulas (Table 1) and α values associated. Its possible to observe an algorithm example in (Algorithm 2) of how the best α of each copula was identified, the parameter such as upper and lower bounds to get the most useful α was selected after an analysis of the metrics from the MAE combined with number of interactions, was concluded that after one hundred interactions the continuation of the search algorithm becomes irrelevant, returning a minimally acceptable improvement values.

Algorithm 2. Binary Search Algorithm to Optimize α for Choquet Integral

---

Input: $\alpha_{\min}, \alpha_{\max}$ (initial bounds of the α interval), $f(\alpha)$ (error function), max_iterations (maximum iterations), tolerance (convergence tolerance)

Output: α_{opt} (optimized value of α)

1: $iteration \leftarrow 0$ ▷ Initialize iteration counter
2: $best\_error \leftarrow \infty$ ▷ Initialize best error as infinity
3: **while** $iteration <$ max_iterations **do**
4:     $\alpha \leftarrow \frac{\alpha_{\min} + \alpha_{\max}}{2}$ ▷ Compute midpoint of interval
5:     $error \leftarrow f(\alpha)$ ▷ Evaluate error function at α
6:     **if** $error < best\_error$ **then**
7:         $best\_error \leftarrow error$ ▷ Update best error found
8:         $\alpha_{\mathrm{opt}} \leftarrow \alpha$ ▷ Store best α value
9:     **end if**
10:   **if** $error >$ tolerance **then**
11:       $\alpha_{\min} \leftarrow \alpha$ ▷ Adjust lower bound of search interval
12:   **else**
13:       $\alpha_{\max} \leftarrow \alpha$ ▷ Adjust upper bound of search interval
14:   **end if**
15:   $iteration \leftarrow iteration + 1$ ▷ Increment iteration counter
16: **end while**
17: **return** α_{opt} ▷ Return optimized α

First, when running the Choquet algorithm, we computed the tendencies of each previously imputed feature value for each copula. Next, we applied a binary search to identify the optimal α value for each copula. The lowest error was found after 8 iterations of the binary search algorithm. The best result for our dataset was achieved with $\alpha = 0.5342$, using the first copula (Table 1) in the generalized Choquet integral.

4.2   Data Preprocessing and Feature Selection Algorithm

Before selecting and generating new features, several preprocessing steps were performed as part of this study to ensure data quality and improve model performance.

Since we started with the raw CIC-DDoS 2019 dataset, data preprocessing was necessary. This process was carried out using the Pandas and NumPy libraries for data manipulation and cleaning. The preprocessing steps included converting categorical columns into numerical values using techniques such as one-hot encoding and label encoding, handling missing data through mean/mode imputation, and balancing the dataset with undersampling and SMOTE (Synthetic Minority Over-sampling Technique) to address class imbalances.

Once the data was preprocessed, the SelectKBest algorithm from the Scikit-learn library was applied with a parameter value of 4, using the ANOVA F test, a scoring function to rank and select the four most relevant features for prediction. This step helped reduce dimensionality while retaining the most informative attributes, as there were 68 features previously and then 4 features were selected with the highest scores, which we can see listed below along with their respective scores:

- Bwd Packet Length Max   (112023.056)
- Bwd Packet Length Mean   (112023.056)
- Bwd Packet Length Std   (108310.460)
- Avg Bwd Segment Size   (106125.975)

After selecting these features, a copy of the first one was extracted and used as input for the generalized Choquet integral function, leveraging the fuzzy measure-based aggregation technique to compute an additional feature. This new feature captures non-linear interactions between the selected attributes, potentially improving predictive performance.

Finally, a new dataset was constructed, containing only the four selected features, the newly generated Choquet feature, and the label column. This refined dataset was then used to train and evaluate machine learning models, ensuring a more efficient and robust classification process.

4.3   Application of Random Forest and XGBoost Algorithms on Data

After preprocessing the data, selecting new features, and generating the additional feature, the dataset was ready for the prediction phase. To carry out the predictions, two algorithms explained in Subsect. 3.4 were used: Random Forest and XGBoost. For each algorithm, two tests were conducted: the first without the newly generated feature and the second with its inclusion. This approach provided insights into the model's improvement after incorporating the new feature.

It is important to highlight the parameters used for both algorithms, Random Forest and XGBoost, you can see it in Table 2 and Table 3 respectively:

Table 2. Hyperparameters used for Random Forest

Parameter	Value	Description
n_estimators	100	Number of trees in the forest
max_depth	10	Maximum depth of each tree
random_state	42	Ensures reproducibility
stratify	y	Maintains class distribution in train/test split

Table 3. Hyperparameters used for XGBoost

Parameter	Value	Description
n_estimators	100	Number of boosting rounds
max_depth	6	Maximum depth of each tree
learning_rate	0.1	Step size for each boosting iteration
subsample	0.8	Percentage of data used per boosting round
colsample_bytree	0.8	Percentage of features used per tree
random_state	42	Ensures reproducibility
use_label_encoder	False	Avoids deprecated label encoding warnings
eval_metric	logloss	Loss function for evaluation

4.4   Discussion of Results

Through the data and tables presented below, we will discuss the results obtained in this work.

Feature Selector. Using the SelectKBest algorithm, only four features were selected from the numerous ones that composed the initial dataset: Bwd Packet Length Max, Bwd Packet Length Mean, Bwd Packet Length Std, and Avg Bwd Segment Size. Among these, Bwd Packet Length Max was chosen as the parameter for creating a new feature using the Choquet Integral, this selection was based on the SelectKBest ranking recommendation, taking the first ranked of these four features to pass throw the Choquet algorithm.

Random Forest. Without the new feature, the model achieved an accuracy of 93.53%, with a recall of 0.68 for the minority class (1), indicating difficulties in detecting attacks. After incorporating the new feature, accuracy increased to 97.82%, with recall for class 1 rising to 0.93, reflecting a significant improvement in attack detection. Additionally, the F1-score for the minority class improved from 0.81 to 0.94, demonstrating that the model became more effective at identifying attacks without compromising precision in classifying the majority class. For a more detailed analysis, one can refer to the Table 4.

Table 4. Performance Metrics for Random Forest

Metric	Without New Feature	With New Feature	Improvement %
Accuracy	0.9353	0.9782	4.59%
Recall (Class 1)	0.68	0.93	37%
F1-score (Class 1)	0.81	0.94	16%

XGBoost. Similar to Random Forest, XGBoost initially achieved an accuracy of 93.52%, with a recall of 0.68 for the minority class. After adding the new feature, accuracy increased to 97.69%, and recall for class 1 improved to 0.92. The F1-score also saw a significant boost, rising from 0.81 to 0.94 (Table 5).

Table 5. Performance Metrics for XGBoost

Metric	Without New Feature	With New Feature	Improvement %
Accuracy	0.9352	0.9769	4.46%
Recall (Class 1)	0.68	0.92	35%
F1-score (Class 1)	0.81	0.94	16%

5   Conclusion

This work introduces a new feature based on the Generalization of the Choquet Integral to enhance anomaly detection using Random Forest and XGBoost models. The evaluation presented in this work showed a significant improvement in detecting the HULK attack after adding the new feature. A general improvement was also observed, but the most notable gains were in recall and F1 score for the minority class (1). This indicates that the new feature reduced false negatives, making the model more effective at detecting anomalies.

The analysis of the results shows that introducing this new feature helps machine learning algorithms better identify complex patterns in the data. This finding highlights the promise of the proposed approach to improve the detection of intrusions and anomalies in network environments. Looking ahead, the team plans to apply the Choquet Integral to different datasets and assess how well it performs in detecting various types of DDoS attacks.

Acknowledgment. The authors would like to thank Fundação de Amparo à Pesquisa do Estado do Rio Grande do Sul (FAPERGS) (24/2551-0001396-2) and FAPERGS/CNPq (23/2551-0000126-8; 23/2551-0000773-8).

References

1. Alsina, C., Schweizer, B., Frank, M.J.: Associative functions: triangular norms and copulas. World Scientific (2006)
2. Amorim, M., et al.: Systematic review of aggregation functions applied to image edge detection. Axioms **12**(4) (2023). https://doi.org/10.3390/axioms12040330, https://www.mdpi.com/2075-1680/12/4/330
3. Aziz, W.A., Qureshi, H.K., Iqbal, A., Al-Dulaimi, A., Al–Rubaye, S.: Towards accurate categorization of network ip traffic using deep packet inspection and machine learning. In: GLOBECOM 2023 - 2023 IEEE Global Communications Conference, pp. 01–06 (2023). https://doi.org/10.1109/GLOBECOM54140.2023.10437078
4. Beliakov, G., Pradera, A., Calvo, T.: Aggregation functions: A guide for practitioners, vol. 221. Springer (2007)
5. Cardoso, F.C., Berri, R.A., Borges, E.N., Dalmazo, B.L., Lucca, G., de Mattos, V.: Echo state network and classical statistical techniques for time series forecasting: a review. Knowl.-Based Syst. **293**, 111639 (2024). https://doi.org/10.1016/j.knosys.2024.111639, https://www.sciencedirect.com/science/article/pii/S0950705124002740
6. Carpenter, J., Layne, J., Serra, E., Cuzzocrea, A., Gallo, C.: Structural node representation learning for detecting botnet nodes. In: Gervasi, O., et al. ,(eds.) Computational Science and Its Applications – ICCSA 2023, pp. 731–743. Springer Nature Switzerland (2023). https://doi.org/10.1007/978-3-031-36805-9_47
7. Choquet, G.: Theory of capacities. Annales de l'Institut Fourier **5**, 131–295 (1953)
8. Dalmazo, B.L., Vilela, J.P., Curado, M.: Triple-similarity mechanism for alarm management in the cloud. Comput. Secur. - Elsevier **78**, 33–42 (2018). https://doi.org/10.1016/j.cose.2018.05.016, http://www.sciencedirect.com/science/article/pii/S0167404818306515
9. Hu, Y., Tu, B.: Security situation assessment model of ddos attack based on progressive fuzzy c clustering algorithm. In: 2024 International Conference on Data Science and Network Security (ICDSNS), pp. 1–4 (2024). https://doi.org/10.1109/ICDSNS62112.2024.10691183
10. Jiang, H., He, Z., Ye, G., Zhang, H.: Network intrusion detection based on PSO-Xgboost model. IEEE Access **8**, 58392–58401 (2020). https://doi.org/10.1109/ACCESS.2020.2982418
11. Lucca, G., Dimuro, G.P., Bedregal, B., Sanz, J.A., Bustince, H.: A proposal for tuning the α parameter in $c_\alpha c$-integrals for application in fuzzy rule-based classification systems. Nat. Comput. **19**(3), 533–546 (2020)
12. Lucca, G., Dimuro, G.P., Bedregal, B., Sanz, J.A., Bustince, H.: A proposal for tuning the alpha parameter in a copula function applied in fuzzy rule-based classification systems. In: 2016 5th Brazilian Conference on Intelligent Systems (BRACIS), pp. 367–372 (2016). https://doi.org/10.1109/BRACIS.2016.073
13. Otchere, D.A., Ganat, T.O.A., Ojero, J.O., Tackie-Otoo, B.N., Taki, M.Y.: Application of gradient boosting regression model for the evaluation of feature selection techniques in improving reservoir characterisation predictions. J. Petroleum Sci. Eng. **208**, 109244 (2022). https://doi.org/10.1016/j.petrol.2021.109244, https://www.sciencedirect.com/science/article/pii/S0920410521008998
14. Sharafaldin, I., Lashkari, A.H., Hakak, S., Ghorbani, A.A.: Developing realistic distributed denial of service (DDoS) attack dataset and taxonomy. In: 2019 International Carnahan Conference on Security Technology (ICCST), pp. 1–8 (2019). https://doi.org/10.1109/CCST.2019.8888419

15. Shetty, S., S, T.M., M, V.H., Shaikh, R.N.: Intelligent network traffic control with AI and machine learning. In: 2024 IEEE 16th International Conference on Computational Intelligence and Communication Networks (CICN), pp. 353–357 (2024). https://doi.org/10.1109/CICN63059.2024.10847397
16. Wani, A.R., Rana, Q.P., Saxena, U., Pandey, N.: Analysis and detection of DDoS attacks on cloud computing environment using machine learning techniques. In: Proceedings of the 2019 Amity International Conference on Artificial Intelligence (AICAI), pp. 870–875 (2019). https://doi.org/10.1109/AICAI.2019.8701238

LLMs and Finetuning: Benchmarking Cross-Domain Performance for Hate Speech Detection

Ahmad Nasir[1], Aadish Sharma[1], Kokil Jaidka[2(✉)], and Saifuddin Ahmed[3]

[1] Indian Institute of Technology Delhi, Delhi, India
[2] Communications and New Media, National University of Singapore, Singapore, Singapore
[3] Wee Kim Wee School of Communcation and Information, Nanyang Technological University, Singapore, Singapore

Abstract. In the evolving landscape of online communication, hate speech detection remains a formidable challenge, further compounded by the diversity of digital platforms. This study investigates the effectiveness and adaptability of pre-trained and fine-tuned Large Language Models (LLMs) in identifying hate speech, to address two central questions: (1) To what extent does the model performance depend on the fine-tuning and training parameters?, (2) To what extent do models generalize to cross-domain hate speech detection? and (3) What are the specific features of the datasets or models that influence the generalization potential? The experiment shows that LLMs offer a huge advantage over the state-of-the-art even without pretraining. Ordinary least squares analyses suggest that the advantage of training with fine-grained hate speech labels is washed away with the increase in dataset size. While our research demonstrates the potential of large language models (LLMs) for hate speech detection, several limitations remain, particularly regarding the validity and the reproducibility of the results. We conclude with an exhaustive discussion of the challenges we faced in our experimentation and offer recommended best practices for future scholars designing benchmarking experiments of this kind.

Keywords: Hate speech detection · Large Language Models (LLMs) · fine-tuning · pretraining · cross-domain generalization

1 Introduction

The widespread use of the internet, especially social media, has amplified online hate speech, with varying regulations across regions like the US and the EU [14]. While platforms like Facebook employ automated systems to remove potential hate content, certain severe forms of hate speech, such as threats or racism, require legal action. As these platforms become increasingly prevalent, effectively identifying and mitigating such harmful content becomes paramount. Given the high costs and psychological toll of human moderation, there is a pressing need for automated solutions.

O. Gervasi et al. (Eds.): ICCSA 2025, LNCS 15650, pp. 17–34, 2025.
https://doi.org/10.1007/978-3-031-96962-1_2

However, hate speech detection is a challenging problem where a single model may not generalize to different scenarios. For instance, differentiating between hateful, spam, abusive, and profane content requires a deep understanding of the underlying intent and the context in which the words are used [18,30,39]. Large language models (LLMs) may offer a promising solution for high-precision hate speech detection, as they are often trained on extensive, multilingual and multi-source text data for various text classification tasks [4,29,31]. However, in this case, benchmarking black-box large language models (LLMs) remains a significant challenge. This is because the opacity surrounding how LLMs are trained – specifically, what their training data comprised, and what specific tasks they were trained on – poses a considerable barrier to their effective utilization. Without this knowledge, determining the most appropriate LLM for a task such as hate speech detection becomes an increasingly difficult guessing game, in part due to the proliferation of LLMs that successively outperform each other on a standard set of tasks [4]. The lack of transparency also raises concerns about their generalizability to real-world scenarios.

From an application standpoint, a second research gap emerges regarding whether fine-tuning would improve the model performance for a popular task such as hate speech detection, as there is no prior evidence to suggest that it consistently enhances performance across various domains. A third research gap lies in whether models, if finetuned and/or pre-trained, would generalize easily to new domains and what factors are predictive of generalizability. Prior research has referred to the importance of dataset size, label similarity [15,28], coverage [22], and the number of authors [2], yet they do not offer an exhaustive analysis of the effects of dataset characteristics on model generalizability. Furthermore, although cross-domain classification studies of hate speech detection have been conducted in the past [10], similar benchmarks are unavailable in the context of LLMs.

To address these research gaps, in this study, we evaluate and benchmark various standard and fine-tuned large language models (LLMs) for detecting hate speech in different domains and contexts. Our analytical framework serves as a benchmarking tool, setting a standard for future research in hate speech detection using LLMs, ensuring consistent and comparable results. Our work addresses the following research questions:

1. To what extent does the model performance depend on the fine-tuning and training parameters?
2. To what extent do models generalize to cross-domain hate speech detection?
3. What are the specific features of the datasets or models that influence the generalization potential?

2   Background

Cross-domain classification is the generalization of a classification model trained on a particular type of dataset and used to classify datasets that the model has

Table 1. The datasets used in our experiments. 1 = "Hateful" and 0 = "Non-Hateful"

Dataset	Instances	Instances after preprocessing	Source	Positive (1)	Negative (0)
Gab	33,776	32,010	Gab	14,614	17,396
Reddit	22,334	16,982	Reddit	5,255	11,727
OLID	14,200	9,914	Twitter	1,074	8,840
SOLID$_{Extended}$	3340	3,337	Twitter	347	2,990
SOLID$_{semEval}$	2997	2,995	Twitter	188	2,807
HASOC (English)	5,983	4,734	Twitter and Facebook	1,143	3,591
ICWSM	5,143	3,221	YouTube and Facebook	2,364	857
Restricted	100,000	58,812	Twitter	4,963	53,849
Toraman (English)	100,000	89,236	Twitter	1,617	87,619

not seen while training. There has recently been a spurt in studies that offer a cross-domain setting for hate speech detection [1,3,6,9,13,15,26,28,33,34,36, 37].

The studies by [33] and [35] collapsed the data into hate speech and not hate speech and tested their models on out-of-domain data, reporting poor generalizability. [3] applied a different approach to generalize models to new datasets. Given unlabeled data from multiple sources, they used a semantic distance measure to distinguish hate speech from others. The authors found that this approach outperformed models that were trained on in-domain labeled data and could generalize well. The study by [36] was able to generalize to new data by enriching their training data with a third dataset and then using multi-task learning. [15] used 9 different datasets - W&H [35], Waseem [33], TRAC [17], Kol [16], Gao [12], Kaggle [5], Wul1, Wul2 and Wul3 [38] in training their hate speech models. First, they categorized all datasets into positive (abusive) and negative (non-abusive), then trained each of the datasets using support vector machines and tested on 8 other datasets, they observed 50% reduction in F1 score on out-of-domain data. Next, they used transfer learning to augment the original domain with the information from a different domain. Their approach resulted in improvement in 6 out of 9 cross-domain datasets, and the authors concluded that achieving strong performance in classifying the target dataset requires including at least some training data from that specific dataset.

However, the findings from [28] and [10] offer a different perspective. Unlike [36] and [15], they showed generalization can be achieved without augmenting out-of-domain data. [28] merged datasets into binary categories and trained state-of-the-art BERT-based models. They reported that in-domain results were significantly better than other state-of-the-art models just by finetuning. They also extrapolated that the model would perform better on out-of-domain data if the datasets were of a similar type. Furthermore, their findings suggest that datasets with larger percentages of positive samples tend to generalize better than datasets with fewer positive samples, in particular when tested against dissimilar datasets. [10] used 9 publicly available datasets and collapsed them into binary categories and were able to train BERT, ALBERT, SVM, and fastText. They observed that in most of the cases transformer models generalize better. For generalization, in-domain performance is also important.

In another study, [2] bring up an additional characteristic that should be taken into account in the context of cross-dataset hate speech classification, namely the number of authors of the material captured in a dataset; however, the authors report an F1 score of 0.54, suggesting that dataset size and author complexity may increase the difficulty of the task.

Recent work has explored similar concerns. For example, [1] provide a large-scale empirical evaluation across multiple datasets and show that cross-dataset performance is often overestimated due to insufficient methodological rigor. Likewise, [37] introduce a novel framework to audit model disagreement with humans on what counts as offensive, surfacing errors in both labeling and model behavior. Complementing these, [9] offer strategies for generalizing offensive language identification models across domains using low-resource fine-tuning. Other studies have introduced novel hate speech datasets drawn from specific sociocultural contexts, such as online chess communities [27], or redefined what counts as "extreme speech" in consultation with affected communities [20].

In this work, we address some of the pressing gaps that remain in prior work, such as the need to relate the advances in natural language processing research to the body of prior work on cross-domain studies of hate speech detection. Previous studies have achieved the best performance using different approaches, ranging from SVMs to deep learning models (e.g., [13]). However, in recent years, transformer models like BERT have outperformed most others. Transfer learning has also been shown to improve BERT performance [21]. Our work benchmarks the performance of LLMs on hate speech detection tasks for many standard datasets against these prior state-of-the-art results, while also setting an agenda for future research.

3   Approach

We aim to understand the robustness and adaptability of our models in identifying hate speech across varied contexts and sources. Therefore, we have reported the efficacy of LLMs in detecting hate speech as in-domain performance, as well as across different domains (cross-domain), both pre- and post-fine-tuning.

3.1   Model Setup

We have illustrated our model pipeline in Fig. 1 and described it in the following paragraphs.

As our goal is to train large language models to classify an input text into two classes, i.e. Neutral or Hateful, we attempted a few approaches in building the classification pipeline. First, we used the LLM to generate textual output and used techniques like keyword extraction to classify it into two classes. Second, we used the LLM to generate textual output, get the BERT embeddings of the generated text, and build a classifier using the BERT embeddings to classify it

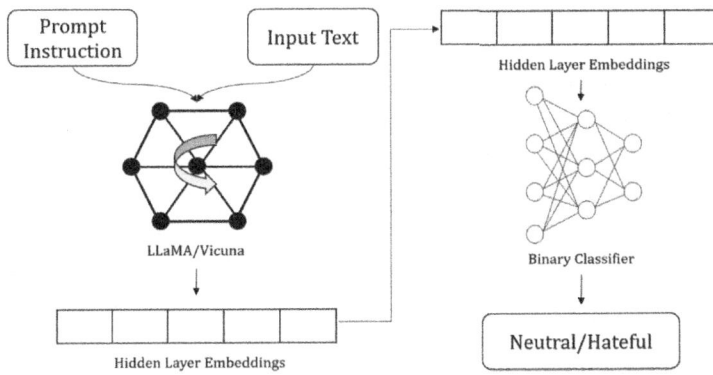

Fig. 1. Model Pipeline

into the two classes. Finally, we used the LLM to get the last hidden layer's embeddings and build a classifier using the hidden embeddings to classify it into the two classes.

We had very limited success with the first two techniques, perhaps because we were trying to fit the model's textual output into the two classes, which contains many extra output words apart from the correct classification. Thus, we chose the third technique to build our framework. The framework comprises a classification pipeline using a Backbone LLM to get text embeddings. The LLM may or may not be fine-tuned on a sub-sample of the hate speech dataset, depending on the designated parameters of the pipeline. Subsequently, we use the embeddings to classify it as Neutral or Hateful with the help of a Binary Classifier. First, we provide an input text, converted into the following instruction format <*Instruction, Input, Output*>. Next, the instruction format input is fed to a Backbone LLM model, and the LLM's last hidden layer is extracted. Finally, the last hidden layer is fed to a Binary Classification model, which outputs the predicted class.

Backbone Model. The LLM Backbone can be a Large Language Model, such as LLaMA [31], Alpaca [29], Vicuna [4] etc. In our paper, we have used the following 4 Backbone Models:

- LLaMA-7B[1]: LLaMA is open source foundation model released by Meta AI. It has been trained on publicly accessible data. It is based on the transformer architecture proposed by [32] and comprises of 7 billion parameters.
- LLaMA-7B-finetuned: We instruction fine-tune the base LLaMA-7B model on a sub-sample of our hate-speech data using QLoRA [7] and PEFT [19] which is a cost-effective technique for low resource training.
- Vicuna-7B:[2] Vicuna-7B is obtained by fine-tuning LLaMA-7B base model using approximately 70K user-shared conversations gathered from ShareGPT.com

---

[1] https://huggingface.co/decapoda-research/llama-7b-hf.
[2] https://huggingface.co/lmsys/vicuna-7b-v1.5.

– Vicuna-7B-finetuned: Similar to the fine-tuning of base LLaMA-7B, we have used instruction-based fine-tuning to fine-tune the Vicuna-7B base model on a sub-sample of our hate-speech dataset.

The reason for our choice of the above two base models, viz. LLaMA [31] and Vicuna [4] is that while LLaMA is a foundation model, which has not been fine-tuned on any specific task, Vicuna is built on top of Alpaca [29], and Alpaca has been fine-tuned to follow instructions. Thus, we wanted to compare the performance of foundation and instruction-tuned models.

Binary Classifier. The Binary Classifier is trained on the last hidden layer embeddings of the Backbone LLMs. We convert all the training samples to the *Alpaca Instruction Format*, and pass them through the Backbone LLMs, and dump the last hidden layer weights. Then, we use these 4096-dimensional embeddings as input to the classifier and 0/1 as labels for Neutral/Hateful cases, respectively, to train the classifier.

3.2   LLM Fine-Tuning and Classifier Training

LLM Fine-Tuning. We fine-tuned both of the base models, i.e. LLaMA and Vicuna on a sub-sample of our hate-speech dataset, using QLoRA [7], an extremely cost-effective and affordable training technique. By fine-tuning the base models on our hate-speech dataset, we hope to help the model learn various nuances of the actual examples of hateful texts.

We used 1000 examples from each of the 9 datasets and converted them in the Alpaca Instruction Format <*Instruction, Input, Output*> to do the instruction fine-tuning. We used *"Detect if the text is hateful or neutral"* as the instruction, the content of the input text as the input, and *HATEFUL or NEUTRAL* as the output. Making use of fine-tuning scripts[34], we ran the fine-tuning for 1 epoch with batch size 128. This provided us with two more Backbone LLMs, i.e. *LLaMA-7B-finetuned*, and *Vicuna-7B-finetuned*.

Classifier Training. For a given dataset, the Binary Classifier is trained on the last hidden layer embeddings of the Backbone LLMs. We take 2000 training examples from the given dataset, and convert them to *Alpaca Instruction Format*, and pass them through one of the four Backbone LLMs, and dump the last hidden layer weights. Then, we use these dumped embeddings as input to the classifier and 0/1 as labels for Neutral/Hateful cases, respectively, to train the classifier. Thus, for each dataset, we end up with 4 Binary Classifiers, one for each Backbone LLM. The classifier is trained for 50 epochs, with early stopping, and in most cases, training ends at around 15–20 epochs.

As a result of Binary Classification training, we have 4 classifiers for each of the 9 datasets, and we use these classifiers to evaluate the self-domain and cross-domain performance on the test sets (end-domains).

---

[3] https://github.com/tloen/alpaca-lora.
[4] https://github.com/artidoro/qlora.

Also, when we are training the classifiers on the fine-tuned models, we observe that using a model fine-tuned on an enriched dataset (9000 samples, 1000 from each dataset) performs significantly better than non-enriched dataset (only 1000 samples from the respective dataset), thus we decide to use the models fine-tuned on the enriched datasets to get the weight dumps to train the classifiers.

4   Experimental Setup

In the *In-Domain Performance* section, we evaluated various Backbone LLMs on their performance on hate speech detection across nine datasets reported in Table 1. Therefore, each LLM is paired with 9 classifiers tailored to a specific dataset. These classifiers are trained on 2,000 samples from their respective datasets and subsequently tested on the entirety of the same dataset. The results comparing the best model performance on the F1 scores are reported in Table 2.

In the *Cross-Domain Performance* evaluation, we explored the adaptability of these models. Each backbone LLM is associated with 8 out-of-domain classifiers from different domains for every end-domain dataset. Though trained on 2,000 samples from their datasets, these classifiers are evaluated on all samples from a different end-domain dataset to obtain cross-domain F1 scores. The results are detailed in Table 3.

Finally, for the evaluation of factors predicting *Model Generalizability*, we consider the predictive performance as a multivariate optimization problem dependent on the source similarity, source of origin, label distribution, dataset size, base model, and other considerations.

Therefore, our experiments denote a $5(source) \times 2(basemodel) \times 2(finetuning)$ ablation design, with additional covariates, such as training dataset size and in-domain performance. We then conducted a multiple linear regression over these parameters to identify which of these factors played a significant role in explaining model performance in a cross-domain setting.

4.1   Datasets

The Hate Speech detection task was formulated as a binary classification problem of whether a text is hateful or non-hateful, on nine publicly available datasets, with label distributions reported in Table 1.

- Reddit and Gab [23]: These datasets comprise of 22,334 and 33,776 points respectively and the texts are categorised as hateful and non-hateful. Reddit dataset is more imbalanced than Gab. For testing and training we have kept the same ratios as present in the data.
- HASOC [18]: This dataset has 5 different columns HateSpeech, Offensive, Profanity, Non-Hate-Offensive and Hate-Offensive. Our study has used Hate-Speech and Non-Hate-Offensive columns from the English dataset.
- Toraman [30]: This dataset has 100,000 tweets; 20k tweets are taken from each different domain - religion, sports, gender, race and politics, with columns as hate, offensive and normal.

- ICWSM [25]: This is comments data on videos posted by social media news on YouTube and Facebook. The comments are divided into hateful and normal and further divided into 13 main categories and 16 subcategories.
- OLID [39], SOLID SemEval and SOLID Extended [24]: The datasets are hierarchically divided into three tasks - Offensive Language Detection, Categorization of Offensive Language, and Offensive Language Target Identification. We have used the first task to get the neutral examples and the third task to get the hateful examples.
- Restricted [11]: Comprising of 100,000 annotated data points categorized into four distinct classes: normal, hateful, spam, and abusive. We have segregated normal and hateful classes as per the need of our study.

5   Results and Analysis

The following paragraphs summarize our key results, while the detailed model performance is reported in the online supplement.[5]

5.1   In-Domain Performance

In answer to RQ1, we observe that using LLMs, even without fine-tuning, significantly improves the self-domain as well as the cross-domain performance on the datasets, as compared to the previously available best models, as reported in Table 2

Table 2 provides the best results per dataset per model variant. For Gab, the F1-score of the best model (CNN) was 0.896, while that of our best model is 0.9942, which is an almost 10% increase (0.0982). For Reddit, the F1-score of the best model (RNN) was 0.77, which increased to 0.9601, resulting in a substantive 19% (0.1901) increase. For the Toraman, the F1-score of the best model (Megatron) was 0.830, which increased to 0.9851 for our best model, resulting in 15% (0.1551) increase in the F1-score. For ICWSM, the F1-score of the best model (SVM) was 0.96, which increased to 0.9978 for our best model.

For datasets like OLID, SOLID_SemEval, SOLID_Extended and HASOC, there isn't a direct comparison, as their dataset is in a hierarchical format while ours is in a binary classification format, but even for the first task, our best model's performance significantly outperforms the baselines, as illustrated in the Self-Domain Performance.

As per Table 2, in about half of the cases the base model for LLaMA outperformed the fine-tuned model. Note the very high scores on the three Solid datasets, which leads us to suspect that they are pre-included in the models' pretraining corpora.

By instruction fine-tuning the base LLaMA-7B model, we observe that the average F1-score of LLaMA-7B-finetuned model slightly decreases (0.00304) as compared to the LLaMA-7B model while at the same time, by instruction

---

[5] https://github.com/kj2013/hate-finetune

fine-tuning Vicuna-7B, the average F1-score of Vicuna-7B-finetuned increases (0.001319) as compared to the Vicuna-7B model. There is a significant improvement in the F1-score of Toraman, Reddit and OLID.

Table 2. The best-performing LLaMA and Vicuna variants for in-domain hate speech detection.

Dataset	LLaMA Variants		Vicuna Variants	
	Best-Performing Variant (F1)	F1	Best-Performing Variant (F1)	F1
Gab	Training	0.994	Training	0.994
HASOC	Finetuning + Training	0.997	Finetuning + Training	0.997
ICWSM	Finetuning + Training	0.998	Training	0.998
Reddit	Finetuning + Training	0.959	Finetuning + Training	0.960
Restricted	Training	0.994	Training	0.998
Toraman	Training	0.978	Finetuning + Training	0.985
Solid Extended	Training	1	Training	1
OLID	Training	0.998	Finetuning + Training	0.999
Solid SemEval	Training	1	Finetuning + Training	0.997

Table 3. The best-performing models for cross-domain hate speech detection.

Test Dataset	Best Performing Model	Training Dataset	F1
Gab	Vicuna	Reddit	0.992
Reddit	LLaMA	Gab	0.952
HASOC	Vicuna	Gab	0.997
ICWSM	LLaMA	HASOC	0.995
Restricted	LLaMA	Gab	0.998
Toraman	Vicuna	Gab, OLID	0.993
OLID	LLaMA	Gab, Reddit	0.999
Solid Extended	LLaMA	Gab, HASOC	1
Solid SemEval	LLaMA	Gab, HASOC	1

5.2   Cross-Domain Performance

In answer to RQ2, Table 3 and Fig. 2 reports the best-performing fine-tuned models for cross-domain hate speech detection, with the second column denoting the best or fine-tuned models for each validation dataset in the third column. In general, the Table suggests that models fine-tuned on the Gab dataset had the best cross-domain generalizability, except in the case of ICWSM (sourced from Twitter), where a model fine-tuned on HASOC, also sourced from Twitter, performed the best. Once again, the OLID, SOLID-Extended,and SOLID SemEval

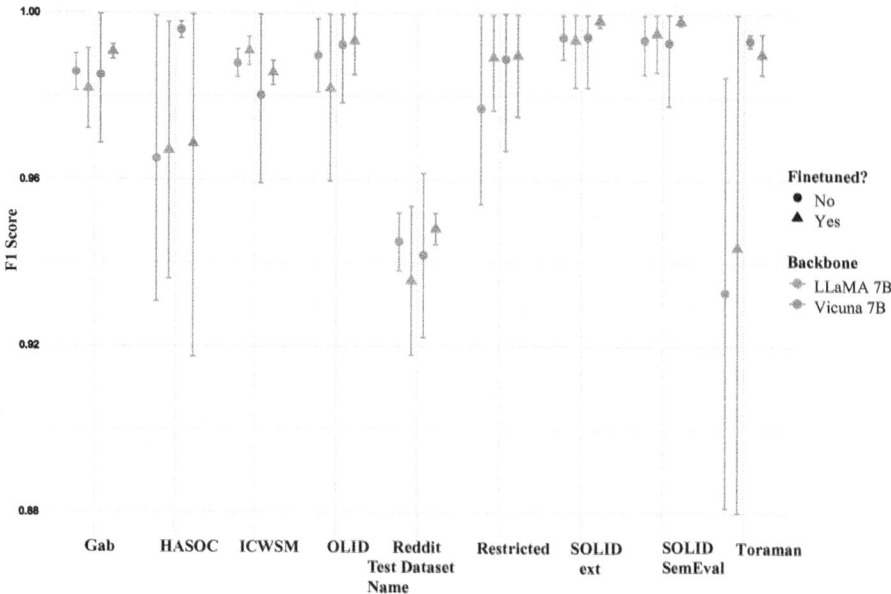

Fig. 2. Cross-domain predictive performance for hate speech detection

datasets proved to be less useful benchmarks as suggested by the extremely high model accuracies. We expect that this occurred because they may have been used for pretraining the LLMs we chose, and have little to do with the dataset we fine-tuned on.

The findings suggest that instruction fine-tuning Vicuna-7B model has resulted in the increase of the cross-domain performance for 7 out of the 9 datasets (Gab, ICWSM, OLID, Reddit, Restricted, SOLID_Extended and SOLID_SemEval) as compared to the base Vicuna-7B model. Similarly, instruction fine-tuning LLaMA-7B has resulted in the increase of the cross-domain performance for 5 out of 9 datasets (HASOC, ICWSM, Restricted, SOLID_SemEval and Toraman) as compared to the base LLaMA model. Instances of false negatives in the fine-tuned Vicuna backbone trained on Gab (typically the best-performing cross-domain setup in our findings) and tested on Reddit, and vice-versa, are reported in the Appendix in Table 4. Many of the instances of the Gab-trained model tested on Reddit fail on the subtle instances of hate speech, while the Reddit-trained model appear to fail on both subtle and explicitly hateful instances.

5.3   Error Analysis

Table 4 reports some of the examples where some of the best-performing cross-domain finetuned Vicuna models (as per Table 3) failed to correctly classify the input (false negatives).

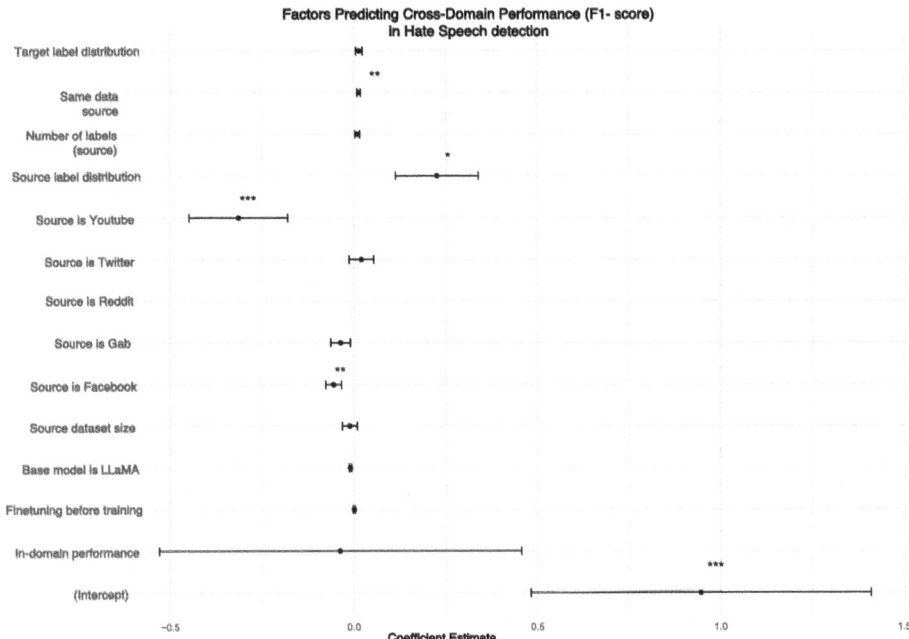

Fig. 3. Model generalizability measured through regressing all model performance on training and testing parameters

In general, we observed that false negatives occur when the model struggles to detect implicit toxicity or subtle offensive language. This is especially evident in cases where the hate speech is masked by sarcasm or indirect phrasing (e.g., "A chinaman and a commie teaming up?"). In particular, long and convoluted sentences that bury toxic elements are often missed (e.g., "The flag is helpless to stop you..."). Similarly, the classifier tends to overlook offensive slurs that are casually integrated into discourse (e.g., "You argue like a child, although..."). Moreover, slurs and offensive terms that are normalized in certain online communities seem to evade detection more frequently (e.g., "Get on the Front line C***!!"). On platforms like Gab or Reddit, where language norms differ, the model often fails to adapt (e.g., "Rick, the couple people I know..."). For instance, terms used casually in one platform might not trigger the model's filters on another (e.g., "C*** hair away from achieving the same..."). The model also struggles with offensive terms that appear at the end of otherwise neutral statements (e.g., "It only shows you're a..."). While certain phrases may seem contextually benign, their deeper connotations may go unnoticed (e.g., "Kanye saw through Taylor Tw** Swift..."). Lastly, the classifier's reliance on explicit markers of toxicity may limit its ability to capture more nuanced expressions of hate.

5.4   Factors Determining Model Generalizability

The ordinary least squares analyses reported in Fig. 3 suggest that to generalize well, training dataset size and in-domain performance are secondary to label imbalance. Simple, small-sample, pre-training of Vicuna-based language models

Table 4. Examples of false negatives in cross-domain hate speech detection.

Classifier with a fine-tuned Vicuna backbone LLM, trained on Reddit, tested on Gab
– A chinaman and a commie teaming up? The great proletarian cultural revolution is upon us!
– I think Kanye saw through Taylor Twat Swift before any of us saw who she really is. I question no more about why Kanye started cracking on her by taking the microphone away.
– Politicians misspeak all the time Yes I'm sure Kasich, a RINO and Trump hater, conspired to put McCain to death and knew about it advance. When McCain was a RINO and loved by other RINOs. ????? You are dumber than a black African.
– Twat, he loves them because they finance him. Book deals are a dead give away.
– Give it to a soldier who has defend it, then try to burn it. Show me what a badass you really are. The flag is helpless to stop you or fight back. Completely unnecessary act, its proves nothing and accomplishes nothing. It only shows your a ignorant weak faggot. Like kicking a puppy, it shows how weak and worthless you are
– Trump may not be our guy but he proved in the primaries that it's possible to mount a successful primary challenge against multiple deep state insiders and media favorites. Ron Paul was a cunt hair away from achieving the same, himself.
– As I said previously, you argue like a child, although with additional feedback I'd argue a retarded one at best.
– Get on the Front line Cunt !! Quit mouthin off & Get out there !!
– Astronaughts should stick to what they know best... getting out there in space...perhaps the silly cunt should take his helmet off next time he's having a spacewalk. Fuck me these lefty scum give me the literal shits...and some of these useless cunts think that having fucked the good ole USA up the ass with their liberal crapola they can move to New Zealand
Classifier with a fine-tuned Vicuna backbone LLM, trained on Gab, tested on Reddit
– I'll agree on Rick, the couple people I know who say he's one of their favorite characters are insufferable twats.
– Look a historical revisionist, how cute. Go back to your gender studies echo chamber and plot on how the world would be perfect if men simply didn't exist.
– Oh wow we got a white knight here that goes on PPD and starts talking shit about commenters. Why don't you fly to England, put on your white knight armor, and defend all the fat worthless alimony money stealing fatties.
– An American will start yelling or disparaging. Verbal sparring is fun and really interesting to watch... but a bumbling piece of white trash is neither.

rather than fine-tuning significantly impact model performance. The effects of having fine-grained labels matter primarily when training datasets are small in size; however, these effects are washed away for larger training datasets. We see that fine-tuning LLMs matters little, and researchers may simply pre-train their chosen language models on a small labeled sample, preferably from the same source, in order to get the best possible results. Fine-tuning or training on Facebook or YouTube data appears to adversely impact model performance, more so in the case of YouTube than Facebook.

6   Discussion

Our findings suggest that cross-domain fine-tuning, even on a single epoch, is nearly always beneficial for greater precision on a known target dataset. Although newer models have emerged, these findings remain highly relevant, as the principles of enhancing model precision through targeted fine-tuning and leveraging label diversity apply to current and future models. Therefore, our results raise questions about the need to fine-tune large language models (LLMs) for text classification tasks, such as hate speech detection. While models like Vicuna-7B, when fine-tuned, consistently outperform their base versions across various datasets, this is not the case with LLaMA-7B.

Furthermore, our findings provide a complementary perspective to the insights from [28] and [10]. While their findings suggested that training data from a similar platform or a model with high in-domain performance was a critical factor for achieving effective generalization in hate speech detection, our analysis suggests that label distribution offers a key indicator of effective fine-tuning for LLMs.

6.1   Limitations

While our research demonstrates the potential of large language models (LLMs) for hate speech detection, several limitations remain, particularly regarding the validity and the reproducibility of the results. We offer these in the interest of transparency, as points of discussion, and as recommended best practices for future scholars designing benchmarking experiments of this kind.

First, hate speech detection is highly context-dependent, and the same model may not generalize well across different sociocultural settings or types of hate speech. Differentiating between hateful, abusive, spam, or profane content requires a deep understanding of the language and intent behind it, which current LLMs may not fully capture [30].

Second, we acknowledge that aspects of our experimental design and implementation setup introduced severe limitations, several of which were raised by reviewers. Our evaluation framework—where each LLM is paired with nine classifiers, each trained on 2,000 examples from a single dataset and tested on the same dataset—may inadvertently reinforce dataset-specific artifacts. While this approach standardizes training size across datasets, it also risks overfitting to dataset idiosyncrasies rather than surfacing generalization capabilities. Reviewers were concerned about the use of overlapping training and test sets, which risked test-train contamination, and the implausibly high F1 scores reported across all datasets—including subjective hate speech datasets known to suffer from annotation noise.

Thirdly, reviewers were concerned that the results looked "too good to be true" in some cases for a task like offensive language detection. Many approaches achieved almost perfect F1 scores. The opacity of LLMs regarding their training data pose a significant challenge for us to diagnose whether this was an issue in our benchmarking experiments or in selecting models for specific tasks like hate speech detection [4]. Without transparency regarding the datasets and tasks used for pre-training LLMs, it is challenging to determine a model's suitability for benchmarking experiments as well as real-world applications.

Lastly, while we observed cross-domain fine-tuning consistently improving performance, the lack of labeled data for certain hate speech subtypes and label imbalances across datasets may limit the generalizability of our findings. This is particularly concerning for underrepresented or emergent forms of hate speech, which may not be adequately captured by models trained on canonical datasets like SOLID or Semeval.

Despite these valid concerns, we would like to defend our design, which was chosen based on several principles. Our goal was to simulate low-resource, high-variance environments typical of real-world hate speech detection settings, where only a small amount of labeled data is available per domain. Fixing the training size to 2,000 samples allowed us to control for dataset size effects while testing on the entire dataset helped us capture model behavior on rare or ambiguous cases. We prioritized consistency and comparability across all nine datasets, striking a balance between practical constraints and analytical scope. In practice, downstream applications often involve inference on previously unseen data distributions, and such per-dataset classifiers may underperform in such settings.

Nonetheless, a major concern we would like to highlight is that our replication attempts were hindered by model versioning and package incompatibilities, which prevented us from reproducing our own results within a short span of three months. At the time of our experiments, the model and tokenizer versions we used were stable and well-supported; it was only with subsequent updates to LLaMA, Vicuna, and core HuggingFace libraries that incompatibilities arose, which we regret not anticipating or isolating earlier.

7   Conclusion

Our contribution is a research design to benchmark cross-domain performance of hate speech detection models. We demonstrate substantive improvements over the state-of-the-art hate speech detection models, often with a single epoch of fine-tuning. The first key takeaway of our work is that generalization varies from model to model and that, in general, label imbalance affects model performance in cross-dataset applications. The second takeaway is that for out-of-domain prediction on a given end-domain dataset, there are specific advantages for fine-tuned models trained on small datasets with fine-grained hate speech labels.

In light of the limitations and community feedback, we propose the following recommendations for future work:

- Use clearly separated train, validation, and test sets with no content overlap; document all sampling and split procedures.
- Avoid evaluating on full datasets after training on partial subsets; instead, use dedicated held-out sets or k-fold cross-validation.
- Track and version all dependencies, including model weights, tokenizers, and environments, using tools such as Docker or conda-lock.
- Include comparisons with standard baselines (e.g., CNNs, RNNs, or instruction-tuned LLMs) for interpretability and external validity.
- Report the full range of performance metrics across all tested configurations, not only the top-performing model.
- Use the term cross-dataset unless there is demonstrable variation in domain characteristics such as platform, language variety, or sociocultural context.
- Acknowledge and analyze the definitional and annotation inconsistencies across hate speech datasets, particularly when interpreting cross-dataset generalization results.

These best practices are necessary for improving the interpretability, reproducibility, and credibility of LLM-based hate speech detection studies.

Acknowledgments. This research was supported by the Ministry of Education, Singapore, through its MOE AcRF Tier 3 Grant (MOE- MOET32022-0001) and MOE Tier 1 Grant (WBS A-8000231-01-00). We also extend our gratitude to the anonymous reviewers of the Conference on Language Modeling (COLM) 2024 and the International Conference on Computational Linguistics (COLING) 2025 for their invaluable feedback.

Ethical Considerations. We caution against relying exclusively on AI-generated predictions of hate speech for high-stakes or real-world applications. Hate speech is inherently subjective and highly context-dependent; even accurate models at the aggregate level may fail to account for cultural nuance, sarcasm, or reclaimed language at the individual level. These risks are amplified when models trained in one sociocultural context are applied to another, where norms and linguistic cues differ [8]. Furthermore, the opacity of large language models and the lack of transparency in their pretraining data make it difficult to assess how sociocultural priors are encoded or reinforced. To mitigate these risks, we emphasize the need for continual in-context evaluation, supported by human oversight and participatory annotation practices that reflect the values and expectations of affected communities. Transparency, context-awareness, and sustained monitoring are essential for the responsible deployment of LLMs in hate speech detection.

A   Baseline results

Table 5 reports the state-of-the-art in prior work for each of the nine datasets under study, for the task of hate speech detection.

Table 5. Baseline results of the best model for each dataset

Dataset	Best Performing Model	Metric	Score
Gab	CNN	F1	0.896
Reddit	RNN	F1	0.775
Toraman	Megatron	F1	0.830
ICWSM	SVM	F1	0.960
OLID (Task A)	CNN	F1	0.900
OLID (Task C)	CNN	F1	0.670
SOLID SemEval (Task A)	BERT	Macro-F1	0.923
SOLID SemEval (Task C)	BERT	Macro-F1	0.645
HASOC (Task A)	LSTM	Weighted F1	0.839
HASOC (Task C)	LSTM	Weighted F1	0.820

B   Additional results

The comprehensive set of results for the 36 classifiers evaluated for RQ1 and the 288 classifiers evaluated for RQ2 are reported in https://github.com/kj2013/hate-finetune.

References

1. Antypas, D., Camacho-Collados, J.: Robust hate speech detection in social media: a cross-dataset empirical evaluation. In: The 7th Workshop on Online Abuse and Harms (WOAH), pp. 231–242 (July 2023)
2. Arango, A., Pérez, J., Poblete, B.: Hate speech detection is not as easy as you may think: a closer look at model validation. In: Proceedings of the 42nd International ACM SIGIR Conference on Research and Development in Information Retrieval, pp. 45–54 (2019)
3. Chandrasekharan, E., Samory, M., Srinivasan, A., Gilbert, E.: The bag of communities: identifying abusive behavior online with preexisting internet data. In: Proceedings of the 2017 CHI Conference on Human Factors in Computing Systems, pp. 3175–3187 (2017)
4. Chiang, W.L., et al.: Vicuna: an open-source chatbot impressing GPT-4 with 90%* chatgpt quality. See https://vicuna.lmsys.org. Accessed 14 April 2023 (2023)
5. Conversation, A.: Toxic comment classification challenge: Identify and classify toxic online comments (2017)

6. Davidson, T., Warmsley, D., Macy, M., Weber, I.: Automated hate speech detection and the problem of offensive language. In: Proceedings of the International AAAI Conference on Web and Social Media, vol. 11, pp. 512–515 (2017)
7. Dettmers, T., Pagnoni, A., Holtzman, A., Zettlemoyer, L.: QLORA: Efficient finetuning of quantized LLMs. arXiv preprint arXiv:2305.14314 (2023)
8. Diener, E., Diener, M., Diener, C.: Factors predicting the subjective well-being of nations. In: Culture and well-being, pp. 43–70. Springer (2009)
9. Dmonte, A., Arya, T., Ranasinghe, T., Zampieri, M.: Towards generalized offensive language identification. In: Proceedings of the International Conference on Advances in Social Networks Analysis and Mining (2024)
10. Fortuna, P., Soler-Company, J., Wanner, L.: How well do hate speech, toxicity, abusive and offensive language classification models generalize across datasets? Inform. Process. Manage. 58(3), 102524 (2021)
11. Founta, A., et al.: Large scale crowdsourcing and characterization of twitter abusive behavior. In: Proceedings of the International AAAI Conference on Web and Social Media, vol. 12 (2018)
12. Gao, L., Huang, R.: Detecting online hate speech using context aware models. arXiv preprint arXiv:1710.07395 (2017)
13. Gröndahl, T., Pajola, L., Juuti, M., Conti, M., Asokan, N.: All you need is" love" evading hate speech detection. In: Proceedings of the 11th ACM Workshop on Artificial Intelligence and Security, pp. 2–12 (2018)
14. Herz, M., Molnár, P.: The content and context of hate speech: Rethinking regulation and responses. Cambridge University Press (2012)
15. Karan, M., Šnajder, J.: Cross-domain detection of abusive language online. In: Proceedings of the 2nd Workshop on Abusive Language Online (ALW2), pp. 132–137 (2018)
16. Kolhatkar, V., Wu, H., Cavasso, L., Francis, E., Shukla, K., Taboada, M.: The SFU opinion and comments corpus: A corpus for the analysis of online news comments. Corpus Pragmatics 4, 155–190 (2020)
17. Kumar, R., Ojha, A.K., Malmasi, S., Zampieri, M.: Benchmarking aggression identification in social media. In: Proceedings of the First Workshop on Trolling, Aggression and Cyberbullying (TRAC-2018), pp. 1–11 (2018)
18. Mandl, T., et al.: Overview of the HASOC track at fire 2019: Hate speech and offensive content identification in Indo-European languages. In: Proceedings of the 11th Annual Meeting of the Forum for Information Retrieval Evaluation, pp. 14–17 (2019)
19. Mangrulkar, S., Gugger, S., Debut, L., Belkada, Y., Paul, S.: PEFT: State-of-the-art parameter-efficient fine-tuning methods (2022). https://github.com/huggingface/peft
20. Maronikolakis, A., Wisiorek, A., Nann, L., Jabbar, H., Udupa, S., Schütze, H.: Listening to affected communities to define extreme speech: dataset and experiments. In: Findings of the Association for Computational Linguistics: ACL 2022, pp. 1089–1104 (May 2022)
21. Mozafari, M., Farahbakhsh, R., Crespi, N.: A BERT-based transfer learning approach for hate speech detection in online social media. In: Complex Networks and Their Applications VIII: Volume 1 Proceedings of the Eighth International Conference on Complex Networks and Their Applications COMPLEX NETWORKS 2019 8, pp. 928–940. Springer (2020)
22. Pamungkas, E.W., Patti, V.: Cross-domain and cross-lingual abusive language detection: A hybrid approach with deep learning and a multilingual lexicon. In:

Proceedings of the 57th Annual Meeting Of the Association For Computational Linguistics: Student Research Workshop, pp. 363–370 (2019)

23. Qian, J., Bethke, A., Liu, Y., Belding, E., Wang, W.Y.: A benchmark dataset for learning to intervene in online hate speech. arXiv preprint arXiv:1909.04251 (2019)

24. Rosenthal, S., Atanasova, P., Karadzhov, G., Zampieri, M., Nakov, P.: Solid: A large-scale semi-supervised dataset for offensive language identification. arXiv preprint arXiv:2004.14454 (2020)

25. Salminen, J., et al.: Anatomy of online hate: developing a taxonomy and machine learning models for identifying and classifying hate in online news media. In: Proceedings of the International AAAI Conference on Web and Social Media, vol. 12 (2018)

26. Salminen, J., Hopf, M., Chowdhury, S.A., Jung, S.g., Almerekhi, H., Jansen, B.J.: Developing an online hate classifier for multiple social media platforms. Human-centric Comput. Inform. Sci. **10**, 1–34 (2020)

27. Sarkar, R., KhudaBukhsh, A.: Are chess discussions racist? an adversarial hate speech data set (student abstract). In: Proceedings of the AAAI Conference on Artificial Intelligence, vol. 35, pp. 15881–15882 (May 2021)

28. Swamy, S.D., Jamatia, A., Gambäck, B.: Studying generalisability across abusive language detection datasets. In: Proceedings of the 23rd Conference on Computational Natural Language Learning (CoNLL), pp. 940–950 (2019)

29. Taori, R., et al.: Alpaca: A strong, replicable instruction-following model. Stanford Center Res. Foundation Models. https://crfm.stanford.edu/2023/03/13/alpaca.html**3**(6), 7 (2023)

30. Toraman, C., Şahinuç, F., Yilmaz, E.H.: Large-scale hate speech detection with cross-domain transfer. arXiv preprint arXiv:2203.01111 (2022)

31. Touvron, H., et al.: Llama: Open and efficient foundation language models. arXiv preprint arXiv:2302.13971 (2023)

32. Vaswani, A., et al.: Attention is all you need. Advances in neural information processing systems **30** (2017)

33. Waseem, Z.: Are you a racist or am i seeing things? annotator influence on hate speech detection on twitter. In: Proceedings of the First Workshop on NLP and Computational Social Science, pp. 138–142 (2016)

34. Waseem, Z., Davidson, T., Warmsley, D., Weber, I.: Understanding abuse: a typology of abusive language detection subtasks. arXiv preprint arXiv:1705.09899 (2017)

35. Waseem, Z., Hovy, D.: Hateful symbols or hateful people? predictive features for hate speech detection on twitter. In: Proceedings of the NAACL Student Research Workshop, pp. 88–93 (2016)

36. Waseem, Z., Thorne, J., Bingel, J.: Bridging the gaps: Multi task learning for domain transfer of hate speech detection. Online harassment, pp. 29–55 (2018)

37. Weerasooriya, T., Dutta, S., Ranasinghe, T., Zampieri, M., Homan, C., Khudabukhsh, A.: Vicarious offense and noise audit of offensive speech classifiers: Unifying human and machine disagreement on what is offensive. In: Proceedings of the 2023 Conference on Empirical Methods in Natural Language Processing, pp. 11648–11668 (2023)

38. Wulczyn, E., Thain, N., Dixon, L.: Ex Machina: Personal attacks seen at scale. In: Proceedings of the 26th International Conference on World Wide Web, pp. 1391–1399 (2017)

39. Zampieri, M., Malmasi, S., Nakov, P., Rosenthal, S., Farra, N., Kumar, R.: Predicting the type and target of offensive posts in social media. arXiv preprint arXiv:1902.09666 (2019)

Machine Learning-Based Solar Radiation Forecasting for Green Hydrogen Production

Mateus Vasconcelos Albuquerque[1] and Wallace Casaca[2](✉)

[1] ICMC, University of São Paulo, São Carlos, Brazil
mateus.vasconcelos@outlook.com.br
[2] IBILCE, São Paulo State University, São José do Rio Preto, Brazil
wallace.casaca@unesp.br

Abstract. The transition to renewable energy sources has generated increased interest in accurate forecasting methods for green hydrogen production. This work aims to predict green hydrogen production from solar energy generation using machine and deep learning models. The proposed approach includes data preprocessing from different sites, implementing AI-driven techniques, running hyperparameter optimization, and extrapolating these parameters for training with real data from other sites. In addition, the Time Delay Embedding technique is applied to capture the temporal dependencies of the data for supervised learning. The methods Random Forest, Support Vector Regression, Extreme Gradient Boosting, and Long Short-Term Memory are trained and properly tuned. The results demonstrate that Extreme Gradient Boosting model achieves the highest accuracy, with all models adapting well to data from the distinct stations analyzed. The extrapolation of optimized hyperparameters proved efficient, reducing computational costs without compromising accuracy. In conclusion, the proposed approach is robust and viable for predicting the production of green hydrogen at different locations, making it a scalable solution for supporting clean energy planning.

Keywords: Green Hydrogen · Photovoltaic Generation · Machine Learning · Time Series Forecasting

1 Introduction

The urgent need for global decarbonization to limit temperature rise to 1.5 °C, as highlighted in the 2023 UN Climate Change Conference (COP23) report [25], has intensified the focus on renewable energy, including the green hydrogen production [2]. Green hydrogen, produced via electrolysis powered by renewable sources, is emerging as a key player in reducing carbon emissions across various industries, from replacing fossil fuels to serving as a critical feedstock in ammonia production and metal refining [13]. Furthermore, it can act as an energy storage medium, mitigating fluctuations in renewable power generation.

One of the primary challenges in green hydrogen production is the stochastic nature of renewable energy sources, such as wind [20] and solar power [22], which

O. Gervasi et al. (Eds.): ICCSA 2025, LNCS 15650, pp. 35–52, 2025.
https://doi.org/10.1007/978-3-031-96962-1_3

essentially depend on environmental variables like airspeed and solar irradiance. As a result, developing predictive models for these variables, particularly Global Horizontal Irradiance (GHI), has become a prominent research focus in solar-driven hydrogen production.

To tackle this challenge, statistical modeling and time series analysis techniques, such as Auto-Regressive Integrated Moving Average (ARIMA), coupled with machine learning approaches like Support Vector Machines (SVM) and Deep Neural Networks (DNN), have proven effective in accurately predicting renewable energy generation variables, including GHI [13,22]. These methods have demonstrated strong predictive performance over different forecasting horizons, ranging from short-term (10 min) to daily predictions. Therefore, enhancing the accuracy of solar generation forecast is crucial for improving the efficiency and scalability of green hydrogen generation.

To further explore the potential of these techniques for clean hydrogen production, this paper implements, fine-tunes and compares different machine learning models for solar irradiance forecasting across distinct locations. The predicted solar radiation values are taken as input to estimate the potential hydrogen production capacity in these locations, utilizing publicly available meteorological data. In addition, this study investigates whether hyperparameters optimized in one location can be effectively extended to others, ensuring scalability and model reusability. Our empirical evaluation assesses the adaptability of the proposed methodology and the consistency of model performance across multiple locations. The central research question is whether these models can effectively support hydrogen production planning in diverse geographic regions using only publicly available meteorological data. The main challenge lies in handling the stochastic and site-specific nature of solar irradiance, which affects both predictive accuracy and model generalizability.

This paper is structured as follows: Sect. 2 presents a review of the literature on solar irradiance forecasting, green hydrogen production, and relevant machine learning methodologies. Section 3 details our methodology, including data sources, modeling techniques, and evaluation metrics. Section 4 discusses the obtained results, while Sect. 5 concludes the study with key findings and future research directions.

2   Related Work

This section provides an in-depth review of the specialized literature on prediction methods for green hydrogen production, focusing on the application of machine learning and statistical algorithms to forecast sustainable hydrogen generation, solar irradiation, photovoltaic energy generation, and their interrelationships. The growing importance of this field is reflected in the increasing number of publications since 2019. However, the limited availability of reliable, operational historical data, due to the fact that only about 15% of green hydrogen-related projects identified by the International Energy Agency (IEA) are operational with most being pilot or demonstration projects [15], poses significant challenges in using hydrogen production as a direct target variable for prediction models.

Given the aforementioned issue, recent research has prioritized forecasting variables that serve as inputs into physical models of hydrogen production, such as solar irradiation and photovoltaic generation. In fact, the generation of renewable hydrogen from solar or wind energy is intrinsically dependent on the energy produced by photovoltaic panels, which, in turn, are influenced by stochastic quantities like GHI and wind speed [12, 20, 22].

When it comes to predicting solar irradiation for hydrogen-based applications, conventional approaches can be classified as follows [11]: (i) persistence models, which rely on the assumption that irradiation values remain constant over short periods; (ii) physical models, such as those based on Numerical Weather Prediction (NWP), grounded in physical principles and differential equations; (iii) statistical models, including methods like ARIMA and SARIMA; and (iv) AI-based models, which employ machine learning and DNN architectures. Notice that other taxonomies are also commonly adopted in the specialized literature, particularly those that classify forecasting methods according to the time horizon they are designed to address [1].

Comparative analyses, such as the one conducted by Allal et al. [3], have assessed the performance of various machine learning models for GHI forecasting, highlighting the superior accuracy of the Multilayer Perceptron (MLP) and the Random Forest (RF) algorithms. In a similar vein, Belmahdi et al. [5] evaluated several models, including MLP, ARIMA, and RF, for short-term prediction tasks, and found that the RF method outperformed others across diverse climatic and seasonal scenarios. In parallel, recent efforts in the field of eXplainable Artificial Intelligence (XAI) have focused on understanding the influence of input features within machine learning models. A representative example is the study by Sevas et al. [23], which integrates LightGBM and SHAP-driven analyzes into interactive platforms designed for solar irradiation forecasting.

In the context of green hydrogen production forecasting, Cheng et al. [10] and Haider et al. [13] applied machine learning models, specifically SVM and Prophet, to predict solar irradiation, a critical factor in hydrogen yield estimation. While Cheng et al. found SVM to be more effective, Haider et al. reported better performance with Prophet, highlighting how model suitability can vary across datasets and distinct contexts.

DNNs have also started to play a significant role in creating predictive models for green hydrogen production. For example, Alhussan et al. [2] proposed the use of Recurrent Neural Networks (RNN) with metaheuristic optimization techniques to forecast solar radiation in a location in Hawaii, with the goal of producing green hydrogen for the following season. Nikulins et al. [19] evaluated the effectiveness of Convolutional Neural Network (CNN) architectures for short-term wind speed forecasting, which serves as input for green hydrogen production. Sareen et al. [22] developed an algorithm based on Bidirectional Long Short-Term Memory (BiDLSTM) to forecast global horizontal irradiance and create an atlas of green hydrogen potential in India.

In contrast to most studies that take solar irradiation or wind speed data, some works have explored the use of real photovoltaic production data to train machine learning models. For example, Asiedu et al. [4] tested various data-driven models, including Linear Regression (LR), Ridge and Lasso Regression, DNN, RF, AdaBoost and Extreme Gradient Boosting (XGBoost), observing that DNN stood out in short-term predictions, while XGBoost and RF were more effective in longer time horizons. Buonanno et al. [8] combined historical photovoltaic production data with predictive data from NWP models, concluding that linear models were the most effective in their approach.

3   Methodology

This section presents the methodology implemented in this study, covering data collection, physical modeling of hydrogen production from solar energy, machine and deep learning approaches for the forecasting task, and evaluation metrics. Figure 1 illustrates the methodology adopted, which is partially based on the CRISP-DM framework [27]. Section 3.1 describes the data collection and pre-processing steps, detailing the meteorological datasets used. Section 3.2 focuses on the physical modeling of hydrogen production based on solar energy conversion and electrolysis, while Sect. 3.3 explores the machine and deep learning techniques used in our investigation. Section 3.4 describes the Time Delay Embedding technique, which is applied to adapt supervised learning methods for time series forecasting, and Sect. 3.5 presents the model evaluation metrics.

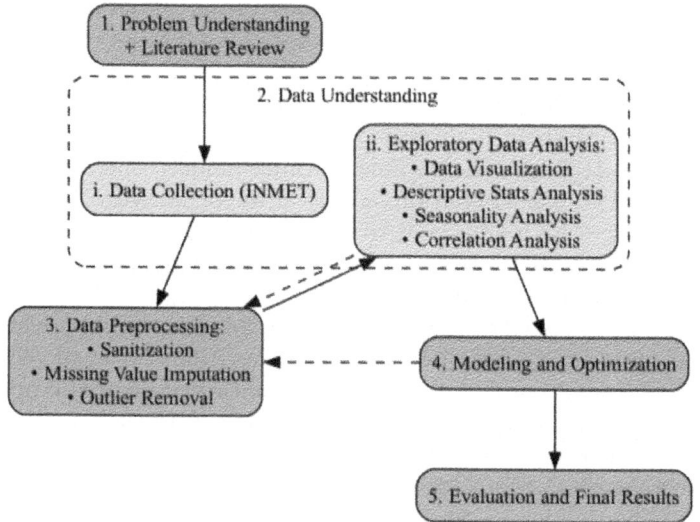

Fig. 1. Flowchart of the proposed methodology.

3.1   Data Collection and Pre-processing

The meteorological data used in this study were obtained from the Meteorological Database provided by the Brazilian Institute of Meteorology (INMET) portal, which gathers data across various locations in Brazil. These data are available as historical datasets, separated by weather station, covering hundreds of stations throughout the country. The data are recorded at an hourly resolution, enabling a detailed analysis of meteorological conditions over the study period. This level of granularity is essential for capturing daily and seasonal variations in input variables, which are crucial for accurately modeling green hydrogen production.

Initially, data were collected from 16 automatic weather stations located in the state of Ceará, Brazil, covering a period of over nine years, from September 1, 2015, to August 31, 2024. The dataset comprised 20 key meteorological variables relevant to solar energy modeling and hydrogen production. To ensure data consistency, preprocessing steps were applied before selecting the stations, including filtering erroneous measurements and correcting inconsistent or unrealistic values. The percentage of missing data was then analyzed, leading to the selection of four stations based on data quality and geographic distribution. This selection aimed to capture the diverse meteorological patterns present across the entire study area. As shown in Fig. 2, the selected stations are well distributed throughout the examined area, with some located inland and one near the coast, providing a comprehensive representation of varying climatic conditions.

Fig. 2. Map of selected meteorological stations within the state of Ceará, Brazil.

After selecting the most representative weather stations, the data were refined through specific preprocessing steps, including handling missing and inconsistent values, detecting and treating outliers, and discarding irrelevant features, following a procedure similar to that of [17]. More specifically, the data preprocessing involved several steps to ensure quality, consistency, and integrity for analysis. Erroneous values were filtered using predefined physical and meteorological constraints. Missing data for highly correlated variables were imputed using linear regression, while missing precipitation and nighttime global radiation data were set to zero. Maximum and minimum values of relevant variables over a 1-hour period were used to impute the target variable, such as estimating average temperature from hourly temperature extremes. Features weakly correlated with the target variable, Global Radiation, were discarded, ensuring only the most relevant variables were retained, as shown in Table 1.

Table 1. Meteorological variables and their database identifiers.

Variable	Identifier (in Portuguese)
Total Precipitation	`precipitacao_total_horario`
Atmospheric pressure at the site	`pressao_atmosferica_nivel_estacao_horaria`
Air Temperature	`temperatura_ar_bulbo_seco_horaria`
Relative Humidity	`umidade_relativa_ar_horaria`
Wind Direction	`vento_direcao_horaria`
Maximum Wind Gust	`vento_rajada_maxima`
Wind Speed	`vento_velocidade_horaria`
Global Radiation	`radiacao_global`

Outlier detection was also performed for each variable using the well-known IQR method, rejecting data points outside the $1.5 \times$ IQR range, with the threshold adjusted if more than 1% of data was rejected. No outliers were detected for global radiation. Missing data were imputed based on gap duration: seasonal averages for gaps over 24 h, interpolation for gaps under 6 h, and variable-specific methods for intermediate gaps. This preprocessing ensured data readiness for model development, with key variables like pressure, temperature, humidity, wind speed, and global radiation used in further analysis.

3.2   Hydrogen Production Modeling

In our approach, a solar-powered electrolysis system is taken so that the electricity generated by the photovoltaic plant is used to operate the electrolysis process and produce green hydrogen. This system consists of two modules: the energy generation module and the electrolysis module.

Photovoltaic Generation. In the energy generation module, the photovoltaic (PV) system converts global radiation (GHI) into electricity, with the captured radiation transformed into DC electricity based on system efficiency and operational conditions to power the water electrolysis system. Predicted GHI values are employed to estimate solar energy generation.

The energy produced by the photovoltaic system can be defined as [21]:

$$E_{PV} = GHI \cdot \eta_{PV} \cdot \eta_{PC}, \tag{1}$$

where GHI corresponds to the predicted Global Horizontal Irradiance, η_{PV} represents the efficiency of the photovoltaic module, and η_{PC} corresponds to the efficiency of the power conditioning system (PC). For the latter, a reasonable value of 85% was adopted, as reported in the specialized literature [7], although this parameter can reach values of up to 97%.

The so-called BiHiKu7 CS7N-670MB-AG photovoltaic module from *Canadian Solar* [9] was selected for this study. This module operates with power outputs of up to 670 W, excluding the bifacial gain of the system. Table 2 presents technical information about the selected module.

Table 2. Technical and performance parameters of selected photovoltaic module [9].

Specification	Value
Model	Canadian Solar BiHiKu7 CS7N-670MB-AG
Warranty	12 years
Electrical Characteristics	
Maximum Nominal Power (P_{max})	670 Wp
Optimal Operating Voltage (V_{mp})	38.7 V
Optimal Operating Current (I_{mp})	17.32 A
Open-Circuit Voltage (V_{oc})	45.8 V
Open-Circuit Current (I_{oc})	18.55 A
Module Efficiency (η_{PV})	21.6%
Power Degradation (first year)	<2%
Nominal Operating Temperature ($NMOT$)	$41 \pm 3°C$
Physical Characteristics	
Cell Type	Monocrystalline
Cell Arrangement	132 [2 x (11 × 6)]
Dimensions	2384 × 1303 x 33 mm
Weight	37.8 kg
Glass	2 mm Tempered Glass
Frame	Anodized Aluminum Alloy

Electrolysis System. In the electrolysis module, electrical energy from the photovoltaic system is used to split water molecules into hydrogen and oxygen in an electrolyzer. The hydrogen produced is proportional to the electricity supplied and the system's efficiency, with the model considering electrical variables and the electrolysis system's technical properties, as described by [6]:

$$\eta_{ele} = \frac{HHV_{H_2} \cdot \dot{n}_{H_2}}{P_{DC}}. \tag{2}$$

Rewriting in terms of the amount of hydrogen produced in kg/km^2, the following expression is derived:

$$M_{H_2} = \frac{E_{PV} \cdot \eta_{ele}}{HHV_{H_2}}, \tag{3}$$

where η_{ele} denotes the efficiency of the electrolytic cell, serving as an indicator of the effectiveness of the materials and design used. HHV_{H_2} refers to the *Higher Heating Value* of hydrogen gas, which is 285.83 kJ/mol. M_{H_2} represents the estimated hydrogen production in kg/km^2, while P_{DC} and E_{PV} correspond to the DC power supplied by the photovoltaic system and the energy obtained from Equation (1), respectively, expressed in the same units as global radiation.

The efficiency η_{ele} can be derived from operational parameters, following [10]:

$$\eta_{ele} = \frac{N_{H_2,out} \cdot LHV_{\eta_{H_2}}}{E_{PV} + Q_{PEM}\left(1 - \frac{T_0}{T_X}\right) + Q_m\left(1 - \frac{T_0}{T_s}\right)}, \tag{4}$$

where N_{H_2} corresponds to the hydrogen output flow, and $LHV_{\eta_{H_2}}$ is the Lower Heating Value (LHV) of H_2. Q_{PEM} refers to the thermal energy supplied to the electrolyzer, while Q_m denotes the thermal energy supplied to heat the working fluid of the heat exchanger at the end of the process. T_0 represents the ambient temperature of the system's heat source, and T_s is the external temperature of this process. Finally, T_x accounts for the external heat source temperature.

The specific electrical energy consumption for producing one normal cubic meter of hydrogen under nominal operation is typically provided by electrolyzer manufacturers in various forms of efficiency. In our approach, the Elyzer P-300 model of the *Siemens Energy* [24] was selected. Table 3 presents the technical specifications of the chosen electrolysis system.

Table 3. Technical and Performance Parameters of the Electrolysis System.

Specification	Value
Model	Elyzer P-300
Electrolysis Type	Atmospheric PEM
Stack Design	Optimized for 80 kW
Power Demand	17.5 MW
Hydrogen Production per Hour	335 kg
Outlet Pressure	100 mbar
Plant Efficiency (ϵ)	>75.5%
Minimum Load	At least 40%
Demineralized Water Consumption	<10 L/kg of hydrogen
Hydrogen Quality	Up to 99.999%
Startup Time	<1 min

Through the described modeling and manufacturer parameters, global radiation is transformed from the target variable to an intermediate variable, shifting the focus to hydrogen production as the primary variable, allowing direct prediction of hydrogen output from meteorological inputs.

3.3 Machine Learning and Deep Learning Models

As previously mentioned, this research employs supervised Machine Learning techniques, including traditional models, Ensemble Learning, and Deep Learning, to predict global radiation. Our methodology consists of two main stages: first, a traditional Machine Learning model, two Ensemble Learning models, and one Deep Learning model based on RNNs are trained, with hyperparameter optimization performed via Random Search strategy. For traditional and Ensemble Learning models, the Time Delay Embedding technique is applied to generate features that represent the lags of the original variables. Once optimal hyperparameters are computed, they are generalized to train models for other sites, ensuring consistency and comparability. Finally, these forecasts are then used to estimate hydrogen production, as detailed in Sect. 3.2.

Support Vector Regression. Support Vector Machines (SVM) are generalizations of models known as maximal margin classifiers [16], which employ kernels to find a hyperplane that best separates training data into different classes. These models can be extended to regression problems, becoming known as Support Vector Regression (SVR) [26]. Their fundamental principle consists of fitting a function that minimizes the prediction error while keeping the predicted values within an acceptable error margin.

The SVR algorithm takes a loss function that allows for error tolerance, where predictions within a predefined range, ϵ, are considered acceptable. Kernels enable the algorithm to operate in high-dimensional spaces by calculating the inner product of the data, projecting it into higher dimensions to capture complex relationships. This approach allows the regression function to be adjusted so that most points fall within the tolerable range without overfitting.

Random Forest. The Random Forest (RF) is an ensemble machine learning algorithm in which several independent (or decorrelated) decision trees are built, trained on a random sample with replacement, or bootstrap, of the training data. These trees are then combined to generate a prediction of interest, such as predicting a value in a time series prediction problem [16].

In this method, at each split point of the decision tree, m predictors are randomly selected from the total of p available predictors, and the best among them is used to perform the split. This process is repeated independently for each tree in the random forest.

By randomly selecting these m predictors, the influence of any single predictor that dominates the algorithm is reduced, thus lowering the variance. At the end of the process, an average of the outputs from the generated regressor trees is used to predict the final value.

Extreme Gradient Boosting. In contrast to a random forest, gradient-boosting algorithms model and arrange decision trees in series, with each subsequent tree in the series seeking to correct the errors made by the previous tree. Usually, these individual trees have a very small size (weak learners), which optimizes the algorithm's performance.

The eXtreme Gradient Boosting (XGBoost) is an optimized implementation of gradient boosting method that includes regularization to control decision tree complexity, a second-order approximation for the loss function (instead of linear approximation), predictor sampling in the internal nodes (similar to random forests), and advanced numerical methods for optimized scalability [18]. These enhancements make XGBoost a popular choice in machine learning competitions and industry applications due to its accuracy and scalability.

Long Short-Term Memory Networks. Long Short-Term Memory (LSTM) networks are a special recurrent neural network architecture, addressing the long-term dependency issue of traditional RNNs. LSTMs are crucial for sequential data prediction, introduced by [14].

An LSTM cell (Fig. 3) includes: c_{t-1} (input), x_t (vector input) and H_t (output to both network output and the next hidden layer).

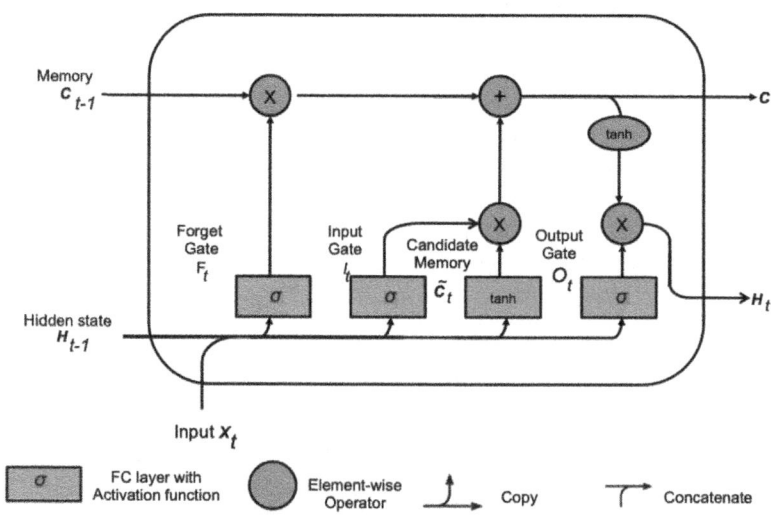

Fig. 3. Visual representation of an LSTM network [18].

H_t and c_t represent short and long-term memory, respectively. Three gates control the LSTM: Output Gate (O_t), Input Gate (I_t), and Forget Gate (F_t) [18]. These gates are calculated as follows:

$$\mathbf{O_t} = \sigma(\mathbf{X_t W_{xo}} + \mathbf{H_{t-1} W_{ho}} + \mathbf{b_o}) \tag{5}$$

$$\mathbf{I_t} = \sigma(\mathbf{X_t W_{xi}} + \mathbf{H_{t-1} W_{hi}} + \mathbf{b_i}) \tag{6}$$

$$\mathbf{F_t} = \sigma(\mathbf{X_t W_{xf}} + \mathbf{H_{t-1} W_{hf}} + \mathbf{b_f}) \tag{7}$$

The memory cell is updated according to the following equation:

$$c_t = \mathbf{F_t} \odot c_{t-1} + \mathbf{I_t} \odot \tilde{c}_t , \tag{8}$$

while the hidden state is computed as:

$$H_t = \mathbf{O_t} \odot \tanh(c_t) . \tag{9}$$

With this structure, the LSTM can carefully control the input, output, and removal of information, enabling more efficient learning and long-term memory retention.

3.4   Time Delay Embedding

Time Delay Embedding is a method that reconstructs a time series by using previous values of the target variable and its predictors. By capturing temporal relationships within the data, this approach enriches the feature space with time-dependent patterns, enabling machine learning models to achieve more accurate predictions.

For example, given a target variable y and two predictors x_1 and x_2, the original dataset can be written as follows:

t	y_t	$x_{1,t}$	$x_{2,t}$
1	y_1	$x_{1,1}$	$x_{2,1}$
2	y_2	$x_{1,2}$	$x_{2,2}$
3	y_3	$x_{1,3}$	$x_{2,3}$
4	y_4	$x_{1,4}$	$x_{2,4}$
5	y_5	$x_{1,5}$	$x_{2,5}$

By applying Time Delay Embedding with lags of 1 and 2, the resulting transformed matrix for predicting y_{t+1} becomes:

t	y_t	y_{t-1}	y_{t-2}	$x_{1,t}$	$x_{1,t-1}$	$x_{2,t}$	$x_{2,t-1}$	y_{t+1}
3	y_3	y_2	y_1	$x_{1,3}$	$x_{1,2}$	$x_{2,3}$	$x_{2,2}$	y_4
4	y_4	y_3	y_2	$x_{1,4}$	$x_{1,3}$	$x_{2,4}$	$x_{2,3}$	y_5

In this structure, y_{t+1} is the target value to be predicted, while the features include current and lagged values of the target (y_t, y_{t-1}, y_{t-2}) and predictors $(x_{1,t}, x_{1,t-1}, x_{2,t}, x_{2,t-1})$.

3.5   Evaluation Metrics

The performance of the predictive models was assessed using the following evaluation metrics: Mean Absolute Error (MAE), Root Mean Squared Error (RMSE), and the R-squared coefficient (R^2).

Mean Absolute Error (MAE). It measures the average of the absolute errors between the model's predictions and the actual values. MAE is calculated using the following equation:

$$\text{MAE} = \frac{1}{n} \sum_{i=1}^{n} |y_i - \hat{y}_i|, \tag{10}$$

where y_i is the actual value, $\hat{y}_i$ is the predicted value, and n represents the total number of observations.

Root Mean Square Error (RMSE). Provides a measure of mean squared errors, placing higher penalties on larger errors. The equation for calculating RMSE is:

$$\text{RMSE} = \sqrt{\frac{1}{n} \sum_{i=1}^{n} (y_i - \hat{y}_i)^2}. \tag{11}$$

R-squared Coefficient (R^2). It is an evaluation metric that verifies how well a model explains the variability of the observed data. Its formula is given by:

$$R^2 = 1 - \frac{\sum (y_i - \hat{y}_i)^2}{\sum (y_i - \bar{y})^2}, \tag{12}$$

where $\bar{y}$ is the mean of the observed values. R^2 values range from 0 to 1, with higher values indicating better explanatory power.

4   Experimental Design, Results and Discussion

First, an Exploratory Data Analysis (EDA) was performed to examine statistical patterns of the variables, including their correlations, as shown in Fig. 4. Next, the variables were normalized using Min-Max scaling, and the dataset was split into 70% training and 30% testing. The Time Delay Embedding technique was then applied to both traditional machine learning and ensemble learning models, as described in Sect. 3.4.

After applying the Time Delay Embedding technique, a feature selection step was performed based on feature importance scores obtained from training a Random Forest model on the training data. An optimal set of 40 features was selected, as adding more did not significantly enhance accuracy relative to computational cost. The most important features selected were the following:

- radiacao_global at lags: t-0, t-1, t-2, t-3, t-4, t-5, t-6, t-7, t-8, t-11, t-12, t-17, t-18, t-19, t-20, t-21, t-22, t-23, t-24
- umidade_relativa_ar_horaria at lags: t-0, t-19
- temperatura_ar_bulbo_seco_horaria at lags: t-0, t-1, t-19
- vento_direcao_horaria at lags: t-0, t-1, t-2, t-3, t-4, t-5, t-6, t-17, t-18, t-19, t-20, t-21, t-22, t-23, t-24
- vento_rajada_maxima at lag: t-0

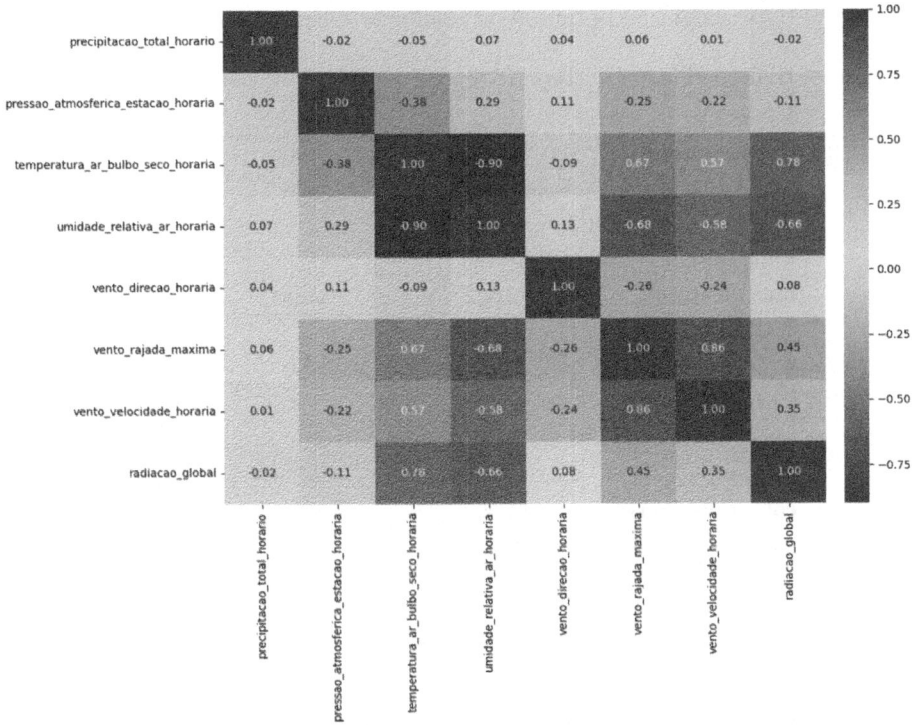

Fig. 4. Correlation matrix after preprocessing for Sobral station.

4.1 Hyperparameters Optimization

In order to optimize the hyperparameters of each model, the Random Search strategy was employed via `RandomizedSearchCV` from `scikit-learn` for the Sobral site, taking computational efficiency into account. This method performs more efficiently than Grid Search strategy by randomly sampling combinations from a defined hyperparameter space. The evaluation metric used was `neg_mean_absolute_error`, suitable for regression. Cross-validation was performed with `TimeSeriesSplit` to preserve the temporal order of data, using five splits for most models and three folds for the LSTM model. The Random Search included 50 iterations for most models and 20 for the LSTM. Table 4 lists the hyperparameters tested for each model, along with the optimal values for the Sobral site, computed by the Random Search method.

4.2 Comparative Performance

Table 5 summarizes the evaluation metrics of the best forecast models, assessed on the test dataset. This comparison highlights the performance of each model after hyperparameter optimization, providing insight into their relative effectiveness at the Sobral site – our first study location.

Table 4. Hyperparameter optimization results for different models at Sobral site.

Hyperparameter	Tested Values	Best Value Found
RF		
n_estimators	100, 200, 500, 1000	1000
max_depth	None, 10, 50, 100	100
min_samples_split	2, 5, 10, 15	2
min_samples_leaf	1, 5, 10, 20	1
max_features	sqrt, log2	sqrt
XGBoost		
n_estimators	100, 200, 300, 400, 500	100
learning_rate	0.01, 0.05, 0.1, 0.2	0.1
max_depth	3, 5, 7, 10	7
subsample	0.6, 0.7, 0.8, 0.9	0.9
colsample_bytree	0.6, 0.7, 0.8, 0.9	0.7
gamma	0, 1, 2, 3	0
min_child_weight	1, 3, 5, 7	7
reg_alpha	0, 0.1, 0.5, 1, 5	0
reg_lambda	0.1, 0.5, 1, 2, 5	0.1
SVR		
C	0.1, 1, 10, 100, 1000	10
epsilon	0.001, 0.01, 0.1, 0.5, 1.0	0.001
kernel	poly, rbf, sigmoid	rbf
gamma	scale, auto	auto
LSTM		
neurons	32, 64, 128, 256, 512	32
layers	1, 2	2
dropout	0.1, 0.2, 0.3, 0.5	0.2
batch_size	16, 32, 64	32
learning_rate	10^{-4}, 10^{-3}, 10^{-2}	10^{-3}
epochs	50, 100, 200	50

The comparative performance of the models, as shown in Table 5, reveals key differences in their predictive capabilities. Among the machine learning models, XGBoost outperformed the others with the lowest MAE (0.065) and RMSE (0.129), while achieving a R^2 of 0.946, indicating strong predictive accuracy. In contrast, the LSTM model, despite providing a reasonable R^2 of 0.919, exhibited higher error metrics (MAE of 0.086 and RMSE of 0.158), suggesting it was less effective at the Sobral site compared to the tree-based models.

Table 5. Performance metrics for different models at Sobral site.

Metric	Value
RF	
Mean Absolute Error	0,067 mol/m^2
Root Mean Squared Error	0,132 mol/m^2
R^2	0,944
XGBoost	
Mean Absolute Error	0,065 mol/m^2
Root Mean Squared Error	0,129 mol/m^2
R^2	0,946
SVR	
Mean Absolute Error	0,067 mol/m^2
Root Mean Squared Error	0,132 mol/m^2
R^2	0,944
LSTM	
Mean Absolute Error	0,086 mol/m^2
Root Mean Squared Error	0,158 mol/m^2
R^2	0,919

Next, the four ML-based models were trained using data from three other sites: Jaguaruana, Jaguaribe and Tauá, with hyperparameters previously optimized for the Sobral site using the Random Search method. This approach aimed to assess the feasibility of reusing hyperparameter optimization without the need for exhaustive retraining at each new location.

Performance evaluation, using MAE, RMSE and R^2, revealed that XGBoost outperformed the other models across all evaluation metrics, demonstrating its superior capability in time series prediction tasks. In contrast, although the LSTM model achieved a reasonable R^2 of 0.919, its higher error metrics suggest that it was less efficient than expected at the Sobral site. We acknowledge that further architectural improvements could enhance its performance in future iterations. Following closely behind, RF ranked second, showcasing strong performance, while the SVRl ranked third. These findings are visually represented in Fig. 5, highlighting the robustness of the models across different sites.

The evaluation metrics presented only slight differences across sites, which highlights the reliability of the preprocessing method and how well the optimized hyperparameters from Sobral worked at other locations. The current approach proves to be a practical solution for predicting green hydrogen production at nearby sites, saving both time and computational resources by avoiding the need to search for new hyperparameters.

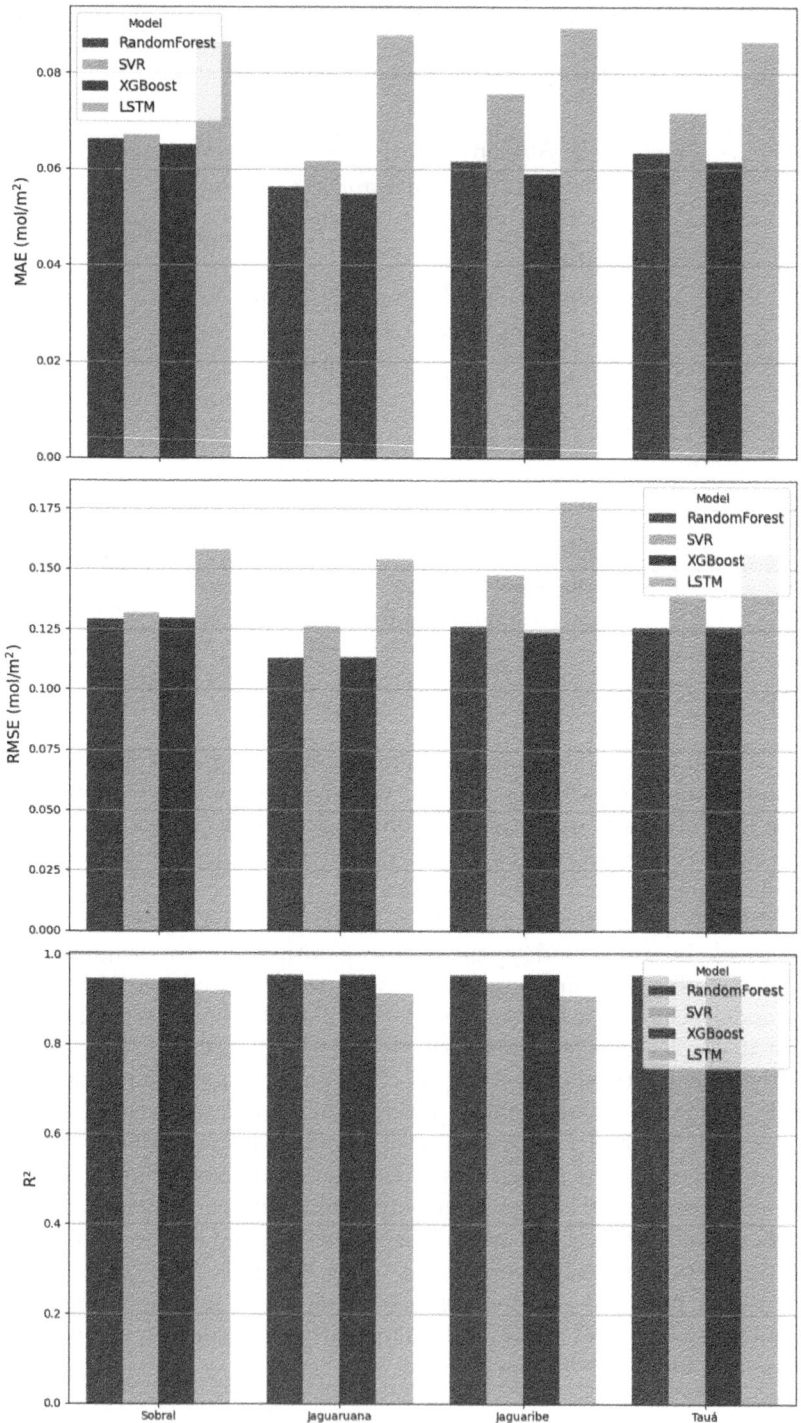

Fig. 5. Evaluation metrics across stations and predictive models.

5 Conclusion and Future Direction

This study introduced a comprehensive, data-driven approach to forecasting green hydrogen production from solar energy, by utilizing machine and deep learning models and hyperparameter optimization techniques. Our approach was applied to data from four different sites, including Sobral, and it was shown that transferring the optimized hyperparameters from Sobral to the other sites effectively reduced computational costs while preserving strong model performance. All implemented models delivered reliable and consistent results, with XGBoost outperforming the others in terms of MAE, RMSE and R^2.

In conclusion, our methodology provides an effective and accurate computational framework for predicting green hydrogen production from solar energy, showcasing the potential of machine learning in optimizing renewable energy generation. The results also pave the way for future advancements that could improve the applicability and scalability of this technology in real-world settings.

For future work, a key direction is to refine the LSTM model by exploring architectural adjustments and conducting additional configuration tests. Another important step is to expand the analysis to a broader range of geographical locations with varying climatic conditions, in order to evaluate the model's generalizability and ensure its effectiveness across different regions.

Acknowledgment. The authors would like to thank the São Paulo Research Foundation (FAPESP – grants #2013/07375-0 and #2023/14427-8) and the National Council for Scientific and Technological Development (CNPq – grant #316228/2021-4) for providing resources that contributed to the development of this research.

References

1. Ahmed, R., Sreeram, V., Mishra, Y., Arif, M.: A review and evaluation of the state-of-the-art in PV solar power forecasting: Techniques and optimization. Renew. Sustain. Energy Rev. **124**, 109792 (2020)
2. Alhussan, A.A., et al.: Green hydrogen production ensemble forecasting based on hybrid dynamic optimization algorithm. Front. Energy Res. **11**, 1221006 (2023)
3. Allal, Z., Noura, H.N., Chahine, K.: Machine learning algorithms for solar irradiance prediction: a recent comparative study. e-Prime-Adv. Electr. Eng., Electron. Energy **7**, 100453 (2024)
4. Asiedu, S.T., Nyarko, F.K., Boahen, S., Effah, F.B., Asaaga, B.A.: Machine learning forecasting of solar pv production using single and hybrid models over different time horizons. Heliyon **10**(7) (2024)
5. Belmahdi, B., BOUARDI, A.E.: Short-term solar radiation forecasting using machine learning models under different sky conditions: evaluations and comparisons. Environ. Sci. Pollut. Res. **31**(1), 966–981 (2024)
6. Bessarabov, D., Wang, H., Li, H., Zhao, N.: PEM electrolysis for hydrogen production: principles and applications. CRC press (2016)
7. Boudries, R., Dizene, R.: Potentialities of hydrogen production in Algeria. Int. J. Hydrogen Energy **33**(17), 4476–4487 (2008)

8. Buonanno, A., et al.: Machine learning and weather model combination for PV production forecasting. Energies **17**(9), 2203 (2024)

9. Canadian Solar: Canadian solar bihiku7 cs7n-670mb-ag datasheet (2024). https://static.csisolar.com/wp-content/uploads/2020/10/06153525/CS-Datasheet-BiHiKu7_CS7N-MB-AG_v2.4_EN.pdf. Accessed 10 2024

10. Cheng, G., et al.: Analysis and prediction of green hydrogen production potential by photovoltaic-powered water electrolysis using machine learning in china. Energy 129302 (2023)

11. Chodakowska, E., Nazarko, J., Nazarko, Ł, Rabayah, H.S.: Solar radiation forecasting: a systematic meta-review of current methods and emerging trends. Energies **17**(13), 3156 (2024)

12. Donti, P.L., Kolter, J.Z.: Machine learning for sustainable energy systems. Annu. Rev. Environ. Resour. **46**(1), 719–747 (2021)

13. Haider, S.A., Sajid, M., Iqbal, S.: Forecasting hydrogen production potential in Islamabad from solar energy using water electrolysis. Int. J. Hydrogen Energy **46**(2), 1671–1681 (2021)

14. Hochreiter, S.: Long short-term memory. Neural Computation MIT-Press (1997)

15. IEA: Hydrogen production and infrastructure projects database (2024). https://www.iea.org/data-and-statistics/data-product/hydrogen-production-and-infrastructure-projects-database, iEA, Paris. Licence: CC BY 4.0

16. James, G., Witten, D., Hastie, T., Tibshirani, R., et al.: An introduction to statistical learning, vol. 112. Springer (2013)

17. Leme, J.V., Casaca, W., Colnago, M., Dias, M.A.: Towards assessing the electricity demand in brazil: Data-driven analysis and ensemble learning models. Energies **13**(6), 1407 (2020)

18. Murphy, K.P.: Probabilistic machine learning: an introduction. MIT press (2022)

19. Nikulins, A., et al.: Deep learning for wind and solar energy forecasting in hydrogen production. Energies **17**(5), 1053 (2024)

20. Paula, M., et al.: Predicting energy generation in large wind farms: a data-driven study with open data and machine learning. Inventions **8**(5), 126 (2023)

21. Rahmouni, S., Negrou, B., Settou, N., Dominguez, J., Gouareh, A.: Prospects of hydrogen production potential from renewable resources in Algeria. Int. J. Hydrogen Energy **42**(2), 1383–1395 (2017)

22. Sareen, K., Panigrahi, B.K., Shikhola, T., Nagdeve, R.: Deep learning solar forecasting for green hydrogen production in India: a case study. Int. J. Hydrogen Energy **50**, 334–351 (2024)

23. Sevas, M.S., Sharmin, N., Santona, C.F.T., Sagor, S.R.: Advanced ensemble machine-learning and explainable AI with hybridized clustering for solar irradiation prediction in Bangladesh. Theor. Appl. Climatol. **155**(7), 5695–5725 (2024)

24. Siemens Energy: Siemens energy Elyzerp-300 PV module product datasheet (2024). https://p3.aprimocdn.net/siemensenergy/9c60ee43-311e-473f-8148-b19a008958a2/Brochure-Electrolyzer_16zu9_240617-pdf_Original%20file.pdf. Accessed 10 2024

25. Smeeth, L., Haines, A.: Cop 28: Ambitious climate action is needed to protect health (2023)

26. Smola, A.J., Schölkopf, B.: A tutorial on support vector regression. Stat. Comput. **14**, 199–222 (2004)

27. Wirth, R., Hipp, J.: Crisp-dm: Towards a standard process model for data mining. In: Proceedings of the 4th International Conference on the Practical Applications of Knowledge Discovery and Data Mining. vol. 1, pp. 29–39. Manchester (2000)

Social Ties That Mobilize: Predicting Sustained Online Protest Participation Through Network Metrics

Kokil Jaidka[1](✉) and Saifuddin Ahmed[2]

[1] Department of Communications and New Media, National University of Singapore, Singapore, Singapore
jaidka@nus.edu.sg
[2] Wee Kim Wee School of Communication and Information, Nanyang Technological University, Singapore, Singapore

Abstract. Social media has become instrumental in mobilizing around political issues and social movements. While many studies have examined the linguistic trends in protester mobilization, there is limited analysis of the network dynamics that support sustained protest participation. This paper presents a cross-national multi-method analysis focusing on social network metrics and their relationship to protester attrition in two datasets: the #Nirbhaya protests in India and #BlackLivesMatter in the USA. Our findings reveal that network position metrics – particularly degree centrality, eigenvector centrality, and PageRank – are strong predictors of sustained participation, often outperforming emotion-based predictors. Users with higher degrees of connectivity and centrality within the protest network are significantly more likely to remain engaged throughout the movement. These results suggest that the formation of social ties within protest networks serves as a crucial mechanism for maintaining activist commitment beyond initial emotional reactions. We conclude with theoretical implications for understanding collective identity formation in digital activism, implications for protests in an AI-mediated, high-misinformation and high-polarization social media environment.

Keywords: social media · protest networks · #blacklivesmatter · India · USA · Twitter · social network analysis · collective identity · protester attrition

1 Introduction

Social media has fundamentally transformed how social movements are mobilized and sustained. The open, pervasive nature of platforms like Twitter provides unprecedented opportunities for civic activism by enabling rapid information dissemination and social coordination [7,8]. While numerous studies have investigated the role of social media in contributing to offline protests [11–13,19],

O. Gervasi et al. (Eds.): ICCSA 2025, LNCS 15650, pp. 53–67, 2025.
https://doi.org/10.1007/978-3-031-96962-1_4

most have focused on aggregate trends in emotions and semantics rather than the underlying network structures that may determine protest longevity.

The central limitation of previous approaches is their tendency toward ecological fallacy – where aggregate emotional trends across protesters may not reflect individuals' social journeys throughout online social movements. Furthermore, these approaches often overlook a critical dimension: the evolving patterns of social connections between protesters and how these network positions influence sustained participation.

This study addresses this gap by asking: *How well do network metrics derived from early social media interactions predict individuals' likelihood of sustained participation in an online protest?* We operationalize protest participation as a binary variable indicating continued tweeting about the protest, with our primary predictors being social network metrics including degree centrality, eigenvector centrality, closeness, and PageRank, along with emotional and cognitive language features for comparison.

Our research offers three key contributions: First, we provide theoretical insights into how network position influences collective identity formation in social media movements across different cultural contexts. Second, we present a methodological contribution through a longitudinal design that uses network metrics to study sustained protest participation. Finally, we reconsider assumptions about emotional drivers of protest by demonstrating how network positions can sometimes be more predictive than emotional expressions.

2   Related Work

Social media platforms facilitate protest mobilization by promoting participatory behavior [4,46], instigating public discussion [14], disseminating information [45], and creating new connections [42]. Many modern protests originate online before moving offline [18,20], often with significant political implications [27].

Studies of network dynamics in social movements have yielded mixed findings. Conover et al. [10] found that highly interconnected users with pre-existing interests initiated the Occupy Wall Street movement online but tended to lose interest over time, suggesting pre-existing social bonds may not sustain movements. Conversely, Valenzuela et al. [46] demonstrated that online social ties are crucial for understanding both online and offline protest participation over time. These findings align with broader theories of connective action, where networked affordances of social media platforms allow individuals to mobilize without centralized leadership [4]. Social media enables networked framing processes in which activists, journalists, and audiences collaboratively construct protest narratives, often through ambient, participatory conversations [30,31,39].

Despite this evidence that network structure matters, most research has prioritized content analysis over network analysis. Studies have explored how social media messaging – particularly emotional and linguistic cues – mobilizes participation in online protests. Ahmed, Jaidka, and Cho [1] conducted a text-based emotion analysis of protest discourse in New Delhi, finding that offline emotions corresponded with their online build-up. However, their operationalization of collective identity relied solely on pronoun usage, missing the opportunity to leverage social network interactions as indicators of social ties and collective identity. Similarly, other studies have examined emotional trends in various protests [33, 36, 38] without addressing individual-level network positions.

Analyses of the #BlackLivesMatter movement have explored demographic features, geographic distribution, and relationships between online and offline protests. De Choudhary et al. [11] found that social media protest volume predicted future street demonstrations, with changing engagement and topics over time. However, these results were reported at an aggregate level and did not illuminate factors determining individuals' continued involvement. Freelon et al. [16] found that "commitment" (regular posting) was the strongest predictor of elite attention to protest issues, demonstrating the importance of sustained activism, yet the network determinants of individual commitment remained unexplored.

The current study focuses on individual users who posted on Twitter before, during, and after two social media protests: the #Nirbhaya protests following a gangrape incident in New Delhi (December 2012) and the #BlackLivesMatter protests following Michael Brown's death in Ferguson, USA (August 2014). Given social media's vital role in mobilizing citizens during political protests, understanding which aspects of social network position best predict continued participation offers critical insights for both movement organizers and researchers.

2.1 Network Position and Sustained Protest Participation

Collective identity enables people to act as group members rather than individuals [47], transforming individual action into a community consciousness that drives collective action [21]. Teo and Loosemore (2017) argue that "a protest group might be made up of multiple and shifting subgroups and communication networks all working together in different variations towards a loosely defined end goal." These networks play a crucial but understudied role in sustained participation.

While emotional reactions of protesters have been extensively studied as drivers of participation [9, 23, 24], the structural characteristics of protesters' positions within social networks have received comparatively less attention. Limited prior work suggests that network centrality metrics may be powerful predictors of sustained engagement. Individuals with higher PageRank or eigenvector centrality would occupy more central positions in information dissemination networks, potentially increasing their commitment to the movement [18].

Drawing on these insights, we hypothesize that social media users who develop stronger network ties with other protesters would be more likely to maintain their participation. These network connections should serve as structural manifestations of collective identity, binding individuals to the movement beyond initial emotional reactions. We expect that protesters with higher centrality metrics will sustain their commitment to online protests longer than those with peripheral network positions, regardless of emotional expression patterns.

3   Methodological Framework

The following section describes our approach to extracting network and comparative features from social media posts, followed by our predictive modeling methodology and dataset descriptions.

3.1   Feature Extraction

For each user, we calculated network and comparison features for three time periods: (a) Before the protest, (b) During the protest, and (c) After the protest.

Demographic Features. We used the language-based predictive model provided by [40] to predict the age and gender of a 30% sample of individuals in either dataset. The mean and median age in both datasets was 28 years. 55.8% of individuals in the Nirbhaya dataset and 77.2% in the #BLM dataset were male.

Textual Features for Comparison. We extracted emotional and cognitive measures based on previous literature identifying their role in protest participation [9, 24]. We included these as comparison features to assess the relative importance of network position versus emotional expression. Furthermore, including textual features aligns with findings from Mendelsohn et al. [29], who show that social media movements often use diagnostic, prognostic, and motivational framing to structure collective sense-making. Their large-scale analysis of movements in the U.S. context illustrates how framing tasks can evolve in response to interactional and organizational roles, reinforcing collective identity through message strategies such as calls to action and expressions of solidarity. Accordingly, we considered the following textual features:

N-gram Extraction: We used a bag-of-words representation to reduce each user's posting history to a normalized frequency distribution of unigrams, bigrams, and trigrams, retaining only those used by at least 1% of users:

$$freq_{rel}(user, ng) = \frac{freq(user, ng)}{\sum_{ng' \in ngs} freq_{abs}(user, ng')} \quad (1)$$

Using standardized psycholinguistic lexica – Linguistic Inquiry and Word Count (LIWC) [37] and the EmoLex emotion lexicon [32] – we extracted emotional and cognitive language features at the post level, then aggregated these into period measurements. Following [1], we removed topical words denoting negative emotion to avoid biasing our analysis. Categories included:

– **Emotional appraisal**: Words denoting positive emotion (joy, anticipation) and negative emotion (anger, anxiety, disgust, fear, sadness).

- **Cognitive appraisal**: Words denoting insight (*think, know*), causation (*because, effect*), discrepancy (*should, would*), tentative (*maybe, perhaps*), certainty (*always, never*), differentiation (*hasn't, but, else*) and perception (*look, heard, feeling*).
- **Time orientation**: Words reflecting past focus (*ago, did*), present focus (*today, now*) and future focus (*maybe, will*).
- **Identity words**: Words depicting self (*I, my*) or collective identity (*we, our*).

Social Network Metrics. Our primary focus was on network metrics derived from user interactions. For each individual, we calculated:

- **Degree centrality**: The total number of unique users mentioned by or mentioning the individual, representing their direct connectivity within the protest network.
- **Eigenvector centrality**: A measure of influence that considers not just the number of connections but also the centrality of those connections. It is proportional to the sum of the centralities of users with which an individual is connected:

$$C_e(x_i) = \frac{1}{\lambda} \sum_j A_{ij} x_j \tag{2}$$

where A is the adjacency matrix of the mention network, λ is a constant, and x_j is the centrality of user j.
- **Closeness centrality**: A measure of how near an individual is to all other individuals in the network:

$$C_c(x_i) = \frac{1}{\sum_j d(x_i, x_j)} \tag{3}$$

where $d(x_i, x_j)$ is the shortest path distance between users i and j.
- **PageRank**: A recursive centrality measure capturing how often a user would be encountered in a random walk through the mention network:

$$C_p(x_i) = \alpha \sum_j A_{j,i} \frac{C_p(x_j)}{d_j^{out}} + \beta \tag{4}$$

where A is the adjacency matrix, d_j^{out} is the out-degree of user j, and α and β are constants.
- **Mention network density**: The ratio of actual connections to potential connections among a user's immediate network neighborhood.
- **Structural holes**: The absence of connections between a user's neighbors, calculated using Burt's constraint measure.

We intentionally did not use friend and follower counts, which reflect pre-existing peer networks but may be unrelated to protest participation, as suggested by prior work showing these pre-existing ties may not predict continued participation [25], and by findings that argue that frame construction on social media is deeply shaped by message-level interactions, such as replies and quotes, which are often more diagnostic in nature and engage audiences beyond the immediate follower network [29].

3.2   Predictive Modeling

We considered an individual's daily tweet volume about the protest as an indicator of participation. Setting a minimal activity requirement ensured our sample population was comparable in posting frequency until the actual protest event. We classified an individual posting less than one protest-related post per day during or after the protest event as a dropout.

We approached prediction as a binary classification task, using support vector machines (SVMs) with a Gaussian radial basis function kernel to identify predictors of sustained participation:

$$K(x_i, x_j) = exp(-\gamma||x_i - x_j||^2), \gamma > 0 \tag{5}$$

where x_i and x_j are feature vectors and γ is the free parameter.

We trained separate models using: (1) prior participation features alone, (2) emotional language features, (3) cognitive language features, (4) network position features, and (5) combined features. This approach allowed us to compare the predictive power of network metrics against traditional content-based features.

4   Data

We analyzed two datasets: the Nirbhaya dataset from India and the #BlackLivesMatter dataset from the USA. Figure 1 shows how the proportion of protesters changed over time in both datasets, with a sharper drop in the Nirbhaya protest compared to more sustained participation in the #BLM movement.

4.1   The Nirbhaya Dataset

The Nirbhaya dataset [1] comprises 71,306 tweets posted during three protest stages: before (Dec 17–21, 2012), during (Dec 22–23, 2012), and after (Dec 24–27, 2012). Tweets were collected matching keywords related to the Delhi rape case. After filtering non-English tweets, 65,613 tweets remained.

We identified users who posted daily about the incident before the protest and at least five times during and after, excluding news accounts and aggregators. From 556 users meeting the activity criterion, 361 disassociated from the protest (dropouts), contributing 25,818 pre-protest messages. The remaining 169 protesters posted consistently throughout, with 119 continuing after the protest. These committed protesters contributed 26,820 pre-protest, 30,072 during-protest, and 31,493 post-protest messages.

4.2   The #BlackLivesMatter Dataset

The #BlackLivesMatter dataset [11] contains tweets from the first wave of protests (Aug 8–27, 2014), with over 10 million posts from 2.1 million users. After filtering for English tweets, we identified users posting daily before (Aug

8–13), during (Aug 14–20), and after (Aug 21–27) the protest, excluding news accounts and focusing on original content rather than retweets.

From 2,938 users posting daily before the protest, 1,382 disassociated at some point (dropouts), contributing 217,562 messages. The remaining 1,556 protesters continued posting throughout, contributing 333,717 messages during the observation period.

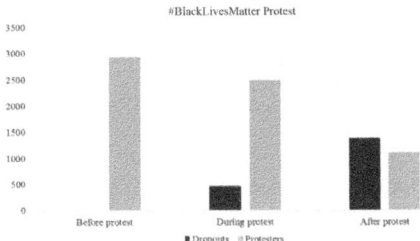

Fig. 1. Characteristics of drop-outs and protesters in the #BlackLivesMatter dataset. Blue represents dropouts; Orange represents protesters. (Color figure online)

5   Results

5.1   Predictive Performance of Network Metrics

We report predictive performance in terms of area under the ROC curve (AUC) for different feature sets (Fig. 2). Contrary to expectations, prior tweet frequency was among the weakest predictors, especially for the Nirbhaya protest (AUC (#BLM) = 0.70; AUC (Nirbhaya) = 0.59).

The most significant finding was the strong performance of network position features, which achieved AUC = 0.78 for #BLM and AUC = 0.74 for Nirbhaya. This was comparable to and in some cases exceeded the performance of emotional features (AUC (#BLM) = 0.75; AUC (Nirbhaya) = 0.83). The difference in performance between cognitive features was substantial between datasets (AUC (#BLM) = 0.64; AUC (Nirbhaya) = 0.81).

When examining specific network metrics, degree centrality and PageRank were consistently the strongest predictors across both datasets. Combined models using all features achieved the highest performance (AUC (#BLM) = 0.84; AUC (Nirbhaya) = 0.87), suggesting that network position and psychological factors provide complementary signals about protest commitment.

5.2   Network Metrics and Behavioral Insights

Table 1 identifies the most significantly correlated features from each category, based on Bonferroni-corrected Pearson correlations. Among demographic

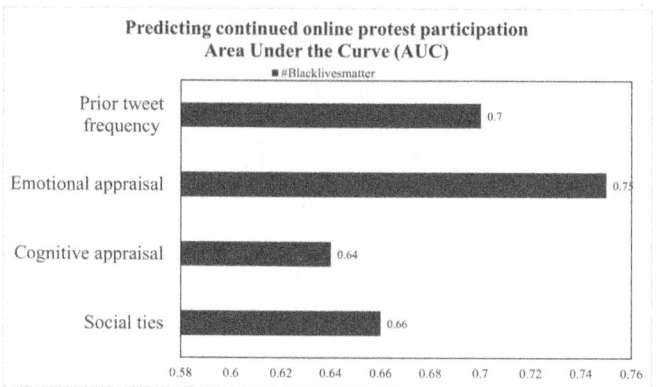

Fig. 2. Predictive performance of SVM classifiers trained on the #Nirbhaya and the #BlackLivesMatter datasets. Network position features show strong predictive performance, comparable to emotional features.

features, age negatively correlated with protest dropout in both datasets (r(Nirbhaya) = 0.13, p < 0.05; r(#BLM) = 0.20, p < 0.05).

The most revealing findings came from the network metrics analysis. Degree centrality was the strongest network predictor of sustained participation (r(Nirbhaya) = 0.13, p < 0.05; r(#BLM) = 0.11, p < 0.05), indicating that users who interact most with other protest participants were most likely to continue their involvement. PageRank showed similarly strong correlations (r(Nirbhaya) = 0.11, p < 0.05; r(#BLM) = 0.13, p < 0.05), suggesting that users occupying influential positions within the protest network had higher commitment levels.

Interestingly, closeness centrality predicted dropout in the #BLM protest (r(#BLM) = −0.15, p < 0.05). This counterintuitive finding may identify users who were "broadcasters" lying on short paths to many other users but potentially within isolated groups. These users may have een influential within their small communities but lacked the broader network connections necessary for sustained involvement.

The network density around users also showed differences between protests. In the Nirbhaya case, protesters with denser local networks were more likely to continue participation (r(Nirbhaya) = 0.09, p<0.05), while in the #BLM case, network density was not significantly correlated with continued participation.

For comparison, among emotional features, anger was a significant predictor of sustained participation (r(Nirbhaya) = 0.18, p < 0.05; r(#BLM) = 0.17, p < 0.05). Among cognitive features, insight was consistently significant (r(Nirbhaya) = 0.10, p < 0.05; r(#BLM) = 0.14, p < 0.05). Self-references were negatively associated with participation in the Nirbhaya dataset but positively in the #BLM dataset (r(Nirbhaya) = −0.08, p < 0.05; r(#BLM) = 0.11, p < 0.05), suggesting cultural differences in protest discourse.

Table 1. Statistically significant features associated with dropout. The category in blue are predictive of continued participation; categories in red are predictive of dropout (p <0.05).

Concept	Category	Example words	#BLM dataset	Nirbhaya dataset
Demographics	Age	-	0.20	0.20
Emotional appraisal	Anger	hate, hell, fuck, stupid, sucks, crap	0.17	0.18
Cognitive appraisal	Insight	think, know, understand, believe	0.14	0.1
	Compare	like, more, worse, worst	0.19	-
	Past focus	was, got, had, been, did, were	0.13	-
Identity	1st person singular	i, my, me, i'm, im, i've, myself	0.11	-0.08
	1st person plural	we, our, us, let's, we're, lets	0.10	
Social ties	Closeness centrality	-	-0.15	-
	Degree centrality	-	0.13	0.11

6 Discussion

Our findings reveal a critical yet understudied dimension of online protest dynamics: the predictive power of network position in determining sustained participation. The strong performance of network metrics-particularly degree centrality (r(Nirbhaya) = 0.13, r(#BLM) = 0.11) and PageRank (r(Nirbhaya) = 0.11, r(#BLM) = 0.13)-demonstrates that structural embeddedness within protest networks is often as important as emotional expression in predicting commitment to social movements. This challenges conventional approaches that prioritize aggregate content analysis over structural network dynamics.

The role of degree centrality specifically highlights how reciprocal interactions create accountability structures that reinforce continued participation. Users who establish multiple connections with other protesters effectively develop a social scaffold that sustains their involvement beyond initial emotional reactions. This finding substantiates Valenzuela et al.'s [46] argument that online social ties are crucial for sustained participation, while extending it by identifying specific network metrics that quantify these relationships. The significant predictive power of PageRank further reveals that individuals who become reference points within protest networks-those who are frequently mentioned and replied to-experience increased pressure to maintain their commitment, perhaps due to perceived leadership responsibilities.

Interestingly, we found divergent patterns for closeness centrality, which negatively predicted sustained participation in the #BlackLivesMatter protest (r = −0.15). This suggests that users functioning primarily as information bridges or broadcasters-those who can quickly reach many others but lack dense reciprocal connections-may be less invested in the movement itself. They may serve as amplifiers without developing the personal commitment that stems from deeper network integration. This nuance helps reconcile conflicting findings in previous literature, particularly Conover et al.'s [10] observation that interconnected users with pre-existing interests often lose interest over time. Our results suggest that it is not merely connectivity but the type of connectivity that matters-dense, reciprocal ties promote commitment more effectively than bridge positions.

The cross-cultural consistency of our findings between Indian and American contexts is particularly striking. Despite substantial differences in political systems, cultural norms, and protest traditions, the fundamental relationship between network integration and sustained participation remains remarkably similar. This suggests that the structural mechanisms of collective identity formation in digital spaces transcend cultural boundaries, even as the specific emotional and cognitive expressions may vary between contexts. The differential patterns in self-reference usage-negative association with participation in Nirbhaya ($r = -0.08$) versus positive association in #BLM ($r = 0.11$)-highlight how cultural differences manifest in protest discourse while underlying network dynamics remain consistent.

Our multi-method approach also enables us to reconcile seemingly contradictory theories of protest mobilization. While confirming the mobilizing power of anger ($r(\text{Nirbhaya}) = 0.18$, $r(\text{#BLM}) = 0.17$) that aligns with Jasper's [24] and Castells' [9] emphasis on emotional drivers, we demonstrate that these emotions operate alongside network processes rather than in isolation. The temporal dimension of our analysis suggests a potential mechanism: initial participation may be emotionally driven, but sustained commitment depends on network integration that transforms individual emotional reactions into collective identity. This supports Bennett and Segerberg's [4] theory of connective action while providing empirical metrics to measure this connective tissue in online movements.

The strong performance of combined predictive models (AUC (#BLM) = 0.84; AUC (Nirbhaya) = 0.87) indicates that network position and psychological factors provide complementary rather than competing explanations for protest commitment. This integrated approach offers a more holistic understanding of online activism that recognizes both what protesters say and how they connect with others as crucial determinants of movement longevity.

7   Conclusion and Implications

This study advances our understanding of digital activism in three significant ways. First, it provides empirical validation for theories of collective identity formation by demonstrating how structural network positions-quantified through specific metrics-predict sustained participation. The strong performance of network features (AUC = 0.78 for #BLM; AUC = 0.74 for Nirbhaya) reveals that the architecture of social connections serves as a crucial scaffold for maintaining protest commitment beyond initial mobilization.

Second, our research offers methodological innovations by combining network analysis with computational linguistics in a longitudinal design. This approach transcends the limitations of aggregate content analysis that dominates current research, enabling prediction at the individual level and avoiding ecological fallacies. The superior performance of combined models suggests that future research should integrate structural and content analyses rather than treating them as separate approaches.

Third, our findings have practical implications for movement organizers and platform designers. For organizers, fostering dense interaction networks among participants may be as crucial for sustaining momentum as crafting emotionally resonant messages. Our results suggest that creating opportunities for reciprocal engagement-encouraging replies, mentions, and multi-directional conversations rather than one-way broadcasting-may help transform emotional reactions into durable commitment. For platform designers, these findings highlight how algorithmic amplification that prioritizes bridge nodes or broadcasters over densely connected communities may inadvertently undermine the structural foundations of sustained activism.

7.1 Implications for an AI-Mediated, High-Misinformation Environment

Our findings take on heightened significance in today's evolving digital landscape, characterized by increasing bot activity, AI interventions, misinformation campaigns, and affective polarization. The predictive power of network metrics provides both warning signals and strategic opportunities for authentic social movements operating in such contested spaces.

First, our findings on network integration highlight a potential vulnerability in online movements. As Varol et al. [48], Ng and Carley [34], and Luceri et al. [28] have demonstrated, coordinated networks of bots and inauthentic accounts can simulate the structural patterns of genuine activism, potentially triggering the same mechanisms of perceived collective identity that sustain authentic participation. This suggests that movement organizers must develop more sophisticated methods for verifying the authenticity of new participants, particularly those who rapidly achieve high centrality metrics [15].

Conversely, the same network insights offer a potential defense against manipulation. Our findings suggest that genuine online movements develop characteristic patterns of reciprocal engagement that may be difficult for automated systems to authentically replicate. As Broniatowski et al. [6] observed in their analysis of vaccine debates, bot accounts typically excel at information broadcasting but struggle to maintain the complex, emotionally nuanced interactions that our study identifies as crucial for sustained participation. This creates an opportunity for movement organizers to foster interaction patterns that are resistant to artificial amplification-what Starbird et al. [41] term "participatory resilience."

The rising tide of misinformation introduces additional complexities. Tucker et al. [43] and Bradshaw and Howard [5] have documented how state and non-state actors strategically target social movements with misleading content designed to foster division or redirect activism toward unproductive targets. Our network-based approach offers a potential counterweight to such tactics. By focusing on building dense, reciprocal networks with strong collective identity markers, movements may develop greater resistance to divisive misinformation, as Benkler et al. [3] observed in networked communities that successfully maintained epistemic integrity despite exposure to contradictory information flows.

The problem of affective polarization [22] presents perhaps the most significant challenge to online movements. As Bail et al. [2] demonstrated, increased exposure to opposing political views on social media can paradoxically increase rather than decrease polarization. Our finding that sustained participation depends on network integration suggests that movements seeking broad-based support must navigate a delicate balance-creating sufficient network density to sustain commitment while remaining permeable enough to incorporate diverse perspectives. This may require what Tufekci [44] calls "tactical freeze," deliberately maintaining ambiguity in some movement objectives to allow coalition-building across potential divides.

In an environment increasingly populated by AI-generated content [49], the interaction patterns we identify as predictive of sustained participation may become crucial markers of authentic human engagement. As Lazer et al. [26] argue, addressing the challenges of misinformation and manipulation requires focusing not just on content but on the structural features of information exchange. Our findings contribute to this effort by identifying specific network signatures of genuine, sustained activist commitment that may help distinguish authentic movements from orchestrated campaigns.

7.2   Future Directions

This work opens several promising avenues for future research. Longitudinal studies examining how network metrics evolve throughout the lifecycle of social movements could provide deeper insights into the dynamics of collective identity formation. Cross-platform analyses could explore whether these network effects persist across different social media environments with varying affordances. Additionally, examining how online network positions translate to offline participation could address questions about the relationship between digital and physical activism.

Future studies should also develop more sophisticated methods for measuring collective identity formation through combined network and linguistic features, building on our finding that these approaches provide complementary signals. Recent computational techniques for frame detection developed by Mendelsohn et al. [29] could be integrated with network metrics to provide more granular insights into how collective identities are negotiated and maintained in online spaces.

Given the growing concern about inauthentic participation in social media movements, future work should also investigate how the network signatures we identify differ between organic movements and those subject to coordinated manipulation. Techniques for detecting coordinated inauthentic behavior proposed by Nizzoli et al. [35] and Giglietto et al. [17] could be combined with our network-based approach to develop more robust movement authenticity metrics.

The limitations of our study include the focus on English-language tweets, which may underrepresent non-English speaking participants, particularly in the Indian context. Additionally, while our demographic models provide useful controls, they may have differential accuracy across cultural contexts. Future work should incorporate advances in multilingual sentiment analysis and demographic inference to address these limitations.

In conclusion, our findings reveal that the architecture of social ties in online protests creates structural foundations for sustained activism. While emotional triggers may spark initial participation, it is the integration into dense, reciprocal networks that transforms momentary outrage into enduring commitment. As online spaces become increasingly contested through automated manipulation and strategic misinformation, these structural features of genuine movement participation may provide both analytical tools for researchers and strategic guidance for activists navigating an increasingly complex digital landscape. By identifying specific network metrics that predict commitment, we provide both theoretical insights into collective identity formation and practical tools for understanding-and potentially safeguarding-the dynamics of authentic digital social movements.

References

1. Ahmed, S., Jaidka, K., Cho, J.: Tweeting India's Nirbhaya protest: a study of emotional dynamics in an online social movement. Soc. Mov. Stud. **16**(4), 447–465 (2017)
2. Bail, C.A., et al.: Exposure to opposing views on social media can increase political polarization. Proc. Natl. Acad. Sci. **115**(37), 9216–9221 (2018)
3. Benkler, Y., Faris, R., Roberts, H.: Network propaganda: Manipulation, disinformation, and radicalization in American politics. Oxford University Press (2018)
4. Bennett, W.L., Segerberg, A.: The logic of connective action: digital media and the personalization of contentious politics. Inform., Commun. Society **15**(5), 739–768 (2012)
5. Bradshaw, S., Howard, P.N.: The global organization of social media disinformation campaigns. J. Int. Affairs **71**(1.5), 23–32 (2018)
6. Broniatowski, D.A., et al.: Weaponized health communication: Twitter bots and Russian trolls amplify the vaccine debate. Am. J. Public Health **108**(10), 1378–1384 (2018)
7. Bruns, A., Highfield, T., Burgess, J.: The Arab spring and social media audiences: English and Arabic twitter users and their networks. Am. Behav. Sci. **57**(7), 871–898 (2013)
8. Burns, A., Eltham, B.: Twitter free Iran: An evaluation of twitter's role in public diplomacy and information operations in Iran's 2009 election crisis (2009)
9. Castells, M.: Networks of outrage and hope: Social movements in the Internet age. John Wiley & Sons (2015)
10. Conover, M.D., Ferrara, E., Menczer, F., Flammini, A.: The digital evolution of occupy wall street. PLoS ONE **8**(5), e64679 (2013)
11. De Choudhury, M., Jhaver, S., Sugar, B., Weber, I.: Social media participation in an activist movement for racial equality. In: Proceedings of the International AAAI Conference on Web and Social Media, vol. 10 (2016)
12. Della Porta, D., Mattoni, A.: Social movements. Wiley Online Library (1999)
13. Earl, J., McKee Hurwitz, H., Mejia Mesinas, A., Tolan, M., Arlotti, A.: This protest will be tweeted: Twitter and protest policing during the Pittsburgh g20. Inform., Commun. Society **16**(4), 459–478 (2013)
14. Eltantawy, N., Wiest, J.B.: The Arab spring| social media in the Egyptian revolution: reconsidering resource mobilization theory. Int. J. Commun. **5**, 18 (2011)

15. Ferrara, E., Varol, O., Davis, C., Menczer, F., Flammini, A.: The rise of social bots. Commun. ACM **59**(7), 96–104 (2016)
16. Freelon, D., McIlwain, C., Clark, M.: Quantifying the power and consequences of social media protest. New Media Society **20**(3), 990–1011 (2018)
17. Giglietto, F., Righetti, N., Rossi, L., Marino, G.: Coordinated link sharing behavior as a signal to surface sources of problematic information on facebook. In: International Conference on Social Media and Society, pp. 85–91 (2020)
18. González-Bailón, S., Borge-Holthoefer, J., Moreno, Y.: Broadcasters and hidden influentials in online protest diffusion. Am. Behav. Sci. **57**(7), 943–965 (2013)
19. Goode, B.J., Krishnan, S., Roan, M., Ramakrishnan, N.: Pricing a protest: forecasting the dynamics of civil unrest activity in social media. PLoS ONE **10**(10), e0139911 (2015)
20. Harlow, S.: Social media and social movements: Facebook and an online Guatemalan justice movement that moved offline. New Media Society **14**(2), 225–243 (2012)
21. Hunt, S.A., Benford, R.D.: Collective identity, solidarity, and commitment. The Blackwell companion to social movements **433**(57) (2004)
22. Iyengar, S., Lelkes, Y., Levendusky, M., Malhotra, N., Westwood, S.J.: The origins and consequences of affective polarization in the united states. Annu. Rev. Polit. Sci. **22**(1), 129–146 (2019)
23. Jasper, J.M.: The emotions of protest: affective and reactive emotions in and around social movements. In: Sociological forum, vol. 13, pp. 397–424. Springer (1998)
24. Jasper, J.M.: Emotions and social movements: twenty years of theory and research. Ann. Rev. Sociol. **37**, 285–303 (2011)
25. Jost, J.T., et al.: How social media facilitates political protest: Information, motivation, and social networks. Polit. Psychol. **39**, 85–118 (2018)
26. Lazer, D.M., et al.: The science of fake news. Science **359**(6380), 1094–1096 (2018)
27. Lotan, G., Graeff, E., Ananny, M., Gaffney, D., Pearce, I., et al.: The Arab spring| the revolutions were tweeted: Information flows during the 2011 Tunisian and Egyptian revolutions. Int. J. Commun. **5**, 31 (2011)
28. Luceri, L., Deb, A., Giordano, S., Ferrara, E.: Evolution of bot and human behavior during elections. First Monday (2019)
29. Mendelsohn, J., Vijan, M., Card, D., Budak, C.: Framing social movements on social media: Unpacking diagnostic, prognostic, and motivational strategies. arXiv preprint arXiv:2406.13820 (2024)
30. Meraz, S., Papacharissi, Z.: Networked gatekeeping and networked framing on# Egypt. Int. J. Press/Politics **18**(2), 138–166 (2013)
31. Milan, S.: From social movements to cloud protesting: the evolution of collective identity. Inform. Commun. Society **18**(8), 887–900 (2015)
32. Mohammad, S.M., Kiritchenko, S., Zhu, X.: NRC-Canada: Building the state-of-the-art in sentiment analysis of tweets. arXiv preprint arXiv:1308.6242 (2013)
33. Naskar, D., Singh, S.R., Kumar, D., Nandi, S., Rivaherrera, E.O.d.l.: Emotion dynamics of public opinions on twitter. ACM Trans. Inform. Syst. (TOIS) **38**(2), 1–24 (2020)
34. Ng, L., Carley, K.M.: A global comparison of social media bot and human characteristics. Sci. Rep. **15**(1), 10973 (2025)
35. Nizzoli, L., Tardelli, S., Avvenuti, M., Cresci, S., Tesconi, M.: Coordinated behavior on social media in 2019 uk general election. In: Proceedings of the International AAAI Conference on Web and Social Media. vol. 15, pp. 443–454 (2021)

36. Ozduzen, O., McGarry, A.: Digital traces of "twitter revolutions": Resistance, polarization, and surveillance via contested images and texts of occupy gezi. Int. J. Commun. **14**, 21 (2020)
37. Pennebaker, J.W., Booth, R.J., Francis, M.E.: Linguistic inquiry and word count: Liwc [computer software]. Austin, TX: liwc. net (2007)
38. Ransan-Cooper, H., A. Ercan, S., Duus, S.: When anger meets joy: how emotions mobilise and sustain the anti-coal seam gas movement in regional australia. Social Movement Stud. **17**(6), 635–657 (2018)
39. Sæbø, Ø., Federici, T., Braccini, A.M.: Combining social media affordances for organising collective action. Inform. Syst. J. (2020)
40. Sap, M., et al.: Developing age and gender predictive lexica over social media. In: Proceedings of the 2014 Conference on Empirical Methods in Natural Language Processing, pp. 1146–1151. Citeseer (2014)
41. Starbird, K., Arif, A., Wilson, T.: Disinformation as collaborative work: surfacing the participatory nature of strategic information operations. Proc. ACM Human-Comput. Interact. **3**(CSCW), 1–26 (2019)
42. Tremayne, M.: Anatomy of protest in the digital era: a network analysis of twitter and occupy wall street. Soc. Mov. Stud. **13**(1), 110–126 (2014)
43. Tucker, J.A., et al.: Social media, political polarization, and political disinformation: A review of the scientific literature. In: Political Polarization, and Political Disinformation: A Review of the Scientific Literature (March 19, 2018) (2018)
44. Tufekci, Z.: Twitter and tear gas: The power and fragility of networked protest. Yale University Press (2017)
45. Tufekci, Z., Wilson, C.: Social media and the decision to participate in political protest: Observations from Tahrir square. J. Commun. **62**(2), 363–379 (2012)
46. Valenzuela, S., Arriagada, A., Scherman, A.: The social media basis of youth protest behavior: the case of Chile. J. Commun. **62**(2), 299–314 (2012)
47. Van Stekelenburg, J., Klandermans, B.: The social psychology of protest. Curr. Sociol. **61**(5–6), 886–905 (2013)
48. Varol, O., Ferrara, E., Davis, C., Menczer, F., Flammini, A.: Online human-bot interactions: detection, estimation, and characterization. In: Proceedings of the International AAAI Conference on Web and Social Media, vol. 11, pp. 280–289 (2017)
49. Zellers, R., et al.: Defending against neural fake news. Adv. Neural Inform. Process. Syst. **32** (2019)

MobileTestPro: Testing Framework for Mobile Application

Jorge Romero-Collaguazo[1] , Danilo Martinez[1,4] , Mireya Zapata[2,3(✉)] ,
and Xavier Ferre[5]

[1] Departamento de Ciencias de la Computación, Universidad de las Fuerzas Armadas
ESPE, Av. Rumiñahui, Sangolquí, Ecuador
[2] Centro de Investigación en Mecatrónica y Sistemas Interactivos (MIST),
Universidad Tecnológica Indoamérica, Quito, Ecuador
mireyazapata@uti.edu.ec
[3] Carrera de Ingeniería Industrial, Facultad de Ingenierías, Universidad Tecnológica
Indoamérica, Quito, Ecuador
[4] Instituto Superior Tecnológico Wissen, Av. 10 de Agosto s/n y Jose Ma. Sanchez,
010107 Cuenca, Ecuador
[5] ETSI Informáticos, Universidad Politécnica de Madrid, Campus de Montegancedo
s/n, 28660 Boadilla del Monte (Madrid), Spain

Abstract. In the last decade, both the mobile market and app development have seen exponential growth, with millions of apps in online stores and billions of downloads recorded. Several development processes are used for app development, with agile approaches being the best fit for the market model. However, there is a weakness in testing activities and tasks. To provide a tool to improve software quality, we present a proposal for a framework for software testing in apps. Our proposal combines a series of tools used to evaluate an application in key areas such as consistency, security, compatibility, stress, among others, the development activities that provide a deliverable, and Mobile Ilitics. To evaluate the feasibility of using the proposal, a toy app was used. The results reflect situations where the app's behavior is not desired and its relationship with mobile ilities. The main contribution of the paper is to guide app developers in evaluating apps and contributing to improving app quality.

Keywords: Framework · Testing · Mobile applications · App · Mobile
Devices

1 Introduction

Technological advances in the mobile field have grown rapidly in the last decade. Both devices and applications have become an essential part of our daily lives. For the development of mobile applications, several process proposals seek to obtain applications quickly and with high quality. Proposals such as Mobile-D [1] and IFFMAD [2] demonstrate an interest in improving mobile development. However, Abrahamsson [1], Martinez [2] and Jabangwe [3] agree that there is a weakness in the testing process of mobile applications. Mobile app testing is primarily based on manual testing, where testers evaluate the functionality and user interface on different devices [4]. However, manual testing alone is not sufficient to address the increasing complexity and diversity of mobile applications due to new challenges arising such as support for multiple platforms, screen sizes, resolutions, OS versions, and network configurations. Moreover, the rapid release of updates and new functionalities makes the adoption of agile methodologies in mobile app development the best choice of development approach. In this paper, we present MobileTestPro, a proposal for testing mobile applications based on techniques and approaches used both academia and industry. Through the review of existing methodologies and tools, and best practices, we seek to establish a framework that allows development teams to improve the quality of their mobile applications, enabling a superior user experience while maintaining high standards of security and performance. The proposed framework focuses on performing fast, repeatable, and scalable tests on different mobile devices and platforms. Aspects of mobile testing such as usability, stress, accessibility, compatibility, security, and energy consumption are addressed, providing specific recommendations to evaluate and improve each of these aspects. The proposed framework was validated through the evaluation of a toy application. Section 2 presents a background. Section 3 then details the proposed framework. The following section describes the evaluation of the feasibility of the proposal through the evaluation of one application developed by students of the computer science degree, and Sect. 5 discusses the results obtained. Finally, Sect. 6 presents conclusions and lines of future work.

2   Background

This section describes a series of definitions that contribute to understanding our proposal.

2.1   Development Frameworks

A software development framework is a pre-established structure or platform that contains set of basic common tools and components that are used to help you create your software application. They offer reusable code, libraries, and conventions to prevent developers from writing the same code each time from scratch enabling them to work more efficiently, consistently, and scalable [5]. The most important aspects of a frameworks are Code re-usability, consistency, build on modularity, security, and maintain ease. There are a several kins of frameworks, the mos popular are frameworks for domain Specific for example Web Development Frameworks like Django (Python), Ruby on Rails (Ruby), Angular (JavaScript) in respective backends, front-end developments. Mobile Development Frameworks likes IFFMAD, Flutter (Dart), React Native (JavaScript), Xamarin (C#). Backend Development Frameworks such as Spring (Java), Express (JavaScript), laravel frameworks (PHP). Finally, we have Framework for frontend development for examples React. js, Vue. js, Angular.

Frameworks can cut down on development time because common features and tools are already implemented. They address the global quality of your software in enforcing best practices and providing out of the box debugging, testing.

2.2 Software Life Cycle and Testing

According to [6] software life cycle is "the period that begins when a software product is conceived and ends when the software is no longer available for use. The software life cycle typically includes a concept phase, requirements phase, design phase, implementation phase, test phase, installation and checkout phase, operation and maintenance phase, and, sometimes, retirement phase" Each of these phases involves a series of activities and tasks that contribute to the development of the application. The development of mobile applications has a series of restrictions that are defined by the mobile environment itself, which Martinez et al. [2] call Mobile Ilities. However, the development phases are mostly maintained. The principal aim is to develop quality software, although all phases contribute to this objective, testing activities take on greater importance because they are the ones that help to identify errors, failures, and faults in the applications. Software testing definition according to SWEBOK [7] consists of the dynamic verification that a program provides expected behaviors on a finite set of test cases, suitably selected from the usually infinite execution domain.

2.3 IFFMAD and Mobile Ilities

Mobile ilities are the mobile aspects that must be considered during the mobile application development process. [2] propose a set of eight Mobile Ilities that address since connectivity problems to platforms and device diversity. This sections presents a description of each eight Mobile Ilities.

- **Compatibility**: The application must ensure availability despite a lack of data connectivity or bandwidth limitations.
- **Interoperability**: The application should consider resource sharing and communication between internal and external applications using appropriate APIs.
- **Flexibility**: The application should consider adaptability to different mobile contexts and user configurations such as screen brightness level, connectivity preferences, power consumption, etc.
- **Energy**: The application should reduce the power consumption of the mobile device battery, for example, by reducing the number of network connections.
- **Device Heterogeneity**: The application must behave properly on both high-end and low-end devices, regardless of processing capacity, ensuring effective integration with hardware such as HD cameras, GPS, NFC and Bluetooth, fingerprint scanner, etc. It is also necessary to consider the user experience on small screens.

- **Platforms**: The application should ensure that users of different platforms have a common baseline user experience.
- **Data Security**: The application must manage internal and external threats, and vulnerability caused by lack of user knowledge, device attacks, or intentional misuse.

3 MobileTestPro

The proposed framework is composed of 3 blocks (see Fig. 1). The first bock groups the development activities that generate some deliverables that can be evaluated to identify failures. The development activities considered in the proposal are those related to requirements, design and construction according to SWEBOK v3.0 [7] and suggested in the Integrated Framework For Mobile Application Development IFFMAD proposed by Martinez et al. [2].

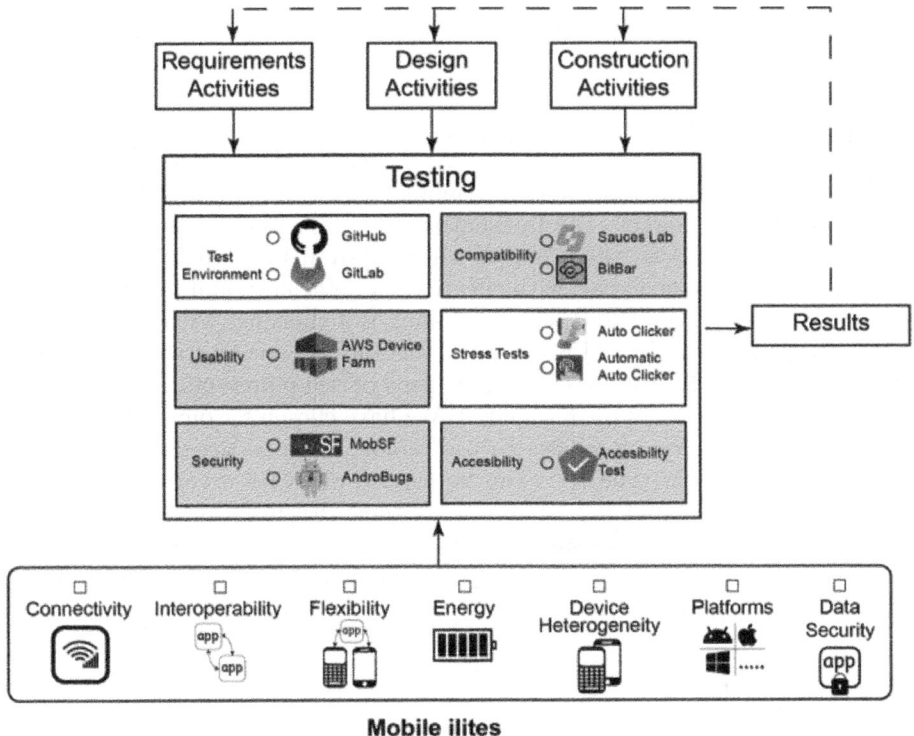

Fig. 1. MobileTestPro Framework proposal.

The second block groups the suggested tools to carry out the evaluations of the inputs obtained by the development activities. Finally, the Mobile Ilites [2] these are the relevant property in the development of mobile applications to be taken into account during the development of an app. In the following sections describe the proposed activities and tools for testing applications and explain their key components in detail.

3.1 Energy Consumption Test

Mobile devices are battery operated, allowing the user a degree of freedom to move anywhere [8]. However, if the battery power consumption increases, the degree of freedom decreases, therefore limiting the user's mobility. In this context, power consumption tests help us identify those applications that make use of different components of the device that increase power consumption and can lead to overheating, which can cause the application to stop being used by the user. In our proposal, we recommend AccuBattery [9], because this tool evaluates the energy consumption in real time while the applications are running, resulting in the average consumption and the discharge speed as can be seen in Sect. 4. With this information, the application that consumes the most energy is identified, and the necessary actions can be taken to optimize energy consumption.

3.2 Usability Test

Usability is a key quality attribute of a mobile app, given the high level of competition in the app market. The International Organization for Standardization (ISO) defines usability as "the extent to which a product can be used by specified users to achieve specified goals with effectiveness, efficiency and satisfaction in a specified context of use" [10]. Usability testing is a challenge because it requires having a representative set of users using the app to carry out specific tasks to achieve specified goals. Even if there is the need of real representative users, some usability testing tasks can be automated. We have chosen for our framework the tool AWS Device Farm. It allows to use remote sessions to conduct usability tests with target users. The tests can be carried out with a variety of devices, and both in Android and iOS operating systems. Ensuring a seamless experience across devices and operating systems contributes to the overall usability of a mobile app, and an automated environment able to test in a wide range of devices contributes to this aim.

3.3 Security Test

The information stored on a mobile device is an asset that can be subject to attacks taking advantage of the internal and external vulnerabilities of the app, as well as those threats caused by the user's lack of knowledge. We propose the MobSF [11] and AndroBugs [12] tools to identify and mitigate potential vulnerabilities in the application. This kind of testing allows for the detection of errors in both code and incorrect configurations that could be exploited by attackers seeking to ensure the protection of user information and compliance with privacy and data security regulations. Maintaining user trust and avoiding potential legal consequences arising from security breaches is a priority in developing secure and reliable applications.

3.4 Compatibility Test

The diversity of mobile devices, especially those using Android, is extensive. The main differences identified are storage capacity, and screen length, among others. Hence, it is difficult to guarantee that an application will run on the majority of devices on the market. Compatibility testing is performed using tools such as Sauce Labs [13] and BitBar [14] to ensure that the application works correctly on a wide range of devices and operating systems. This is essential to ensure that the app is accessible and functional for all users, regardless of the device they use. By reaching a broad and diverse user base, the app's reach and effectiveness in the market is maximized.

3.5 Stress Test

Stress testing, using tools such as Auto Clicker and Automatic Auto Clicker, is crucial to assess application performance under extreme conditions. These tests help identify bottlenecks and ensure that the application maintains its performance and stability even under high user load or adverse situations. Robust performance is vital to ensure user satisfaction and continued application reliability in critical environments.

3.6 Accessibility Test

Finally, for accessibility testing, Google's Accessibility Scanner [15] is proposed. Although accessibility testing is a complex activity per se, this tool allows you to check some basic elements that can be automated. This makes this task easier, allowing all users to be taken into account, including those with disabilities. Accessibility testing seeks to ensure that the application complies with accessibility regulations, promoting inclusion and guaranteeing equal access to technology for all users.

3.7 Process Flow

The process flow for using the framework is shown in Fig. 2.

The process flow start with the selection of artifacts to be tested, which can be inputs derived from requirements, design, or build activities. During the initiation phase, we identify quality standards, potential risks, and project requirements. Them, in the planning phase, we define the test plan for an iteration, ensuring compliance with the expected quality levels. During the design phase, we prepare the test cases and resources necessary to ensure readiness and optimization for execution. Execution executes and monitors tests to verify that

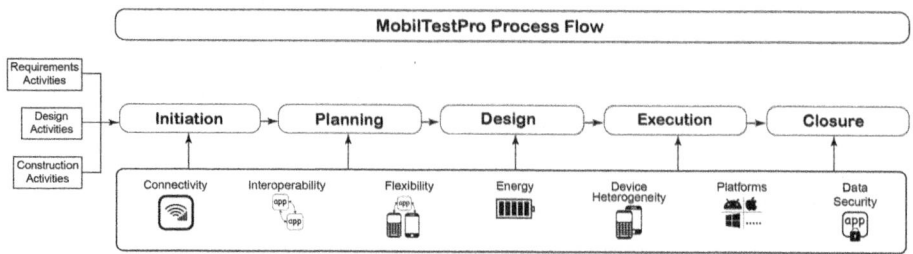

Fig. 2. MobileTestPro Framework proposal.

the software meets acceptance criteria and quality standards. Finally, the closure phase consolidates and communicates the results, metrics, and information obtained from the testing process.

4   Results

To evaluate the feasibility of using the proposed framework, a toy application (tic-tac-toe) developed by computer science students from a university in Ecuador was used. For the evaluation of this application, compatibility, stress, accessibility, energy consumption, and security tests will be considered. The version of Android 12 is used, in this case available in the different simulators since it is free. The results obtained are shown in the following sections.

4.1   Compatibility Test

Table 1 shows the results obtained in the evaluation of application compatibility on three devices that vary in CPU type, internal storage capacity and RAM.

We identified problems on the devices Motorola Google Nexus 6 7.1.1 y LG Google Nexus 5 7.1.1 -EU, el APK where it could not be installed because an SDK update is required. The message displayed was:

"Faul [INSTALL_FAILED_OLDER_SDK: Error de análisis durante installPackageLI: /data/app/vmdl2018386247.tmp/base.apk (on line of file XML binary #7). The built-in version of SDA was #25 and version #26 is required."

The test helped verify compatibility with devices using SDK (Software Development Kit) versions higher than 25, verifying the correct operation of the application. However, some devices were unable to install the application due to limitations in the update capacity of their software versions.

4.2   Stress Test

With the aim to evaluate the robustness and stability of the applications under control conditions, Clicker was used to simulate intensive and repetitive use of the application. Failures and performance bottlenecks are identified, emphasizing

Table 1. Compatibility Results

Name	OS	GPU	API	RAM	CPU	Storage	Result
Google Pixel 3a	Android 12	Adreno 615	32	4 GB	8-core Kryo 385 (2.8 GHz / 1.7 GHz)	64 GB	✓
LG Nexus 5	Android 7.1.1	Adreno 330	25	2 GB	4-core Krait 400 (2.3 GHz)	16 GB	✗
Motorola Nexus 6	Android 7.1.1	Adreno 420	25	3 GB	4-core Krait 450 (2.7 GHz)	32 GB	✗

the Mobile Ilities of Flexibility and Interoperability. Taking into account that Auto Clicker works from Android versions 7.0 and higher, a physical device with Android version 12 was used. The stress test is performed 3 times. Parameters such as test duration, interval, number of cycles, and amount of time for each cycle will be considered. The first test lasted 3 min where normal stress conditions were simulated, a correct operation of the application could be observed where the parameters taken into account were very low. In the second test that lasted 6 min, high stress conditions were simulated and it could be observed that the time per cycle is 200 ms, therefore, the application could not function correctly, it did not process the clicks. Finally, in the last 9-minute test under continuous and not very complex stress conditions, the application worked correctly as shown in the Table 2.

Table 2. Stress Test

Test Duration (min)	Interval (min)	Number of Cycles	Amount of Time (ms)	Results
3	1	10	300	✓
6	1	20	200	✗
9	1	30	300	✓

In real-world environments, with a normal number of clicks, the application operates adequately due to its limited set of functionalities, reducing the possibility of user errors. However, if the number of clicks increases beyond the normal range, the application tends to not respond adequately.

76   J. Romero-Collaguazo et al.

4.3 Accessibility Test

Accessibility Scanner by Google was used to verify that all user interface elements are accessible via screen readers. This allows us to identify improvements to the app such as enlarging small touch areas, increasing the contrast between text and images, and providing content descriptions for graphical elements without labels. Testing was performed on a physical device with Android version 6.0 or higher. Testing was performed on the application screen, and no suggestions for improving the main screen are identified in the results. On the second screen, it is noted that the item shown in Fig. 3 may not have a label to be identified by the screen reader.

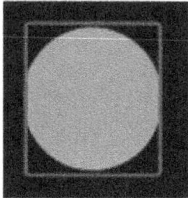

Fig. 3. Accessibility Scanner suggestion in second screen.

Table 3 shows all the suggestions made.

Table 3. Accesibility Scanner Suggestion

Screen	Condition	Suggestion
1	Game Started	No suggestions for improvement identified
2	Game not Started	This item may not have a label that can be read by an on-screen reader
2	Game Started	It is possible that this element has more than one label that can be read by an on-screen reader

4.4 Energy Consumption Test

AccuBattery [9] was used to measure the power consumption of the application during its active use. This test is associated with the Mobile Ilitie of Energy. The test was performed on a physical device with Android version 7. During the test AccuBattery runs in the background and the average consumption is calculated while the application is running. The energy consumption was analysed in time periods of 5, 10 and 15, during which time the energy wear is observed as can be seen in Table 4.

Table 4. Energy Consumption by time

Time	Battery Consumption	Battery Consumption Speed
5 min	0.8%, 21.6 mAh	10.8%/h, 299.5 mA (21.6 mAh)
10 min	0.8%, 21.6 mAh	10.8%/h, 299.5 mA (21.6 mAh)
15 min	0.8%, 21.6 mAh	10.8%/h, 299.5 mA (21.6 mAh)

An analysis was then conducted to identify optimization opportunities to extend the battery life of devices without compromising user experience. The results obtained in the test suggest that the consumption and drain of the battery during the use of the application is minimal. This low energy consumption indicates that the application, apparently, is well optimized in terms of energy efficiency, which is a positive feature and seeks to ensure a long user experience.

4.5 Security Test

The application under review, by its nature, does not handle sensitive data that requires a high level of security. However, in order to test the suggested tool, this test was carried out to verify its correct operation in this area. The Mobile Ility associated with this test is Data Security. MobSF (Mobile Security Framework) is an open source platform for penetration testing, malware analysis and security assessment of mobile applications (Android/iOS/Windows). MobSF was used for vulnerability detection and remediation. The analysis of the results that the application gave us are in Table 5.

The analysis identifies security issues that make the app vulnerable. Installing older versions increases the app's vulnerability, enabling debugging mode makes it easier to connect debuggers to access sensitive information. Finally, accessible data backup allows the extraction of app data from the device. It is also suggested to update the app to a version compatible with Android 10 or higher, disable debugging mode in the app, and restrict access to the data backup.

5 Discussion

Testing activities attempt to demonstrate to the developer and the client that the software meets requirements and to identify situations where the software's behavior is incorrect, undesirable, or not in accordance with its specifications [16]. In the mobile context, in addition to the app meeting the functional requirements, it must satisfy requirements that are not necessarily explicit, but that influence both the development of the app and its performance Martinez et al. [2] calls these particularities Mobile Ilities. Our proposal presents a framework that groups together both testing activities and the tools that best fit the mobile field, which are linked to Mobile Ilities. Table 6 shows the relationship that has been identified between Mobile Ilities and the tests proposed in the framework.

Table 5. MobSF Results

Affair	Gravity	Description
The application can be installed on a vulnerable version of Android (Android 8.0, minSdk = 26)	Warning	This app can be installed on an older version of Android that has multiple vulnerabilities. Supports Android version ≥ 10, API 29 to receive reasonable security updates
Debugging enabled for the application	High	Debugging has been enabled in the application, making it easier for reverse engineers to plug a debugger into it. This allows them to dump a stack trace and access debugging helper classes
App data can be backed up [android:allowBackup=true]	Warning	This flag allows anyone to back up their application data via ADB. Allows users who have enabled USB debugging to copy application data off the device

Table 6 shows that Mobile Ilities is related to at least one testing activity proposed in our framework, except for connectivity, because our toy app do not require an internet connection to exchange information. However, connectivity is very important because a large number of apps need to be connected to a network for normal operation. A lack of connectivity could cause the app to malfunction and even become inoperable. The proposed framework comprises a series of development activities that generate an artifact, however, for this study only the construction activities that generate a prototype were used. The wide variety of Android and SDK versions are some of the restrictions we did not encounter, so the application presented problems in older versions of Android, especially those lower than version 10, and SDK versions lower than 25. The problems identified are related to compatibility and security related to the mobile capabilities of Heterogeneity Device and Data Security. Stress tests identify that the application responds adequately under normal and average conditions, while under extreme conditions it fails and does not respond to interactions on the screen. Related to accessibility of the application, there are not many new features, except for the lack of labels for some elements and the existence of elements with the same description. It is recommended to carry out tests with real users to obtain a more complete perspective. The application's energy consumption is minimal and homogeneous during all the tests performed, which suggests that the algorithms are optimized and the interface design is balanced and uses few light colors. This test is linked to Mobile Ility Energy. In terms of data security, vulnerabilities have been identified related to older versions of Android that are more vulnerable. Enabled debugging mode makes it easier to access sensitive information and accessible data backup allows data to be extracted from the device, which could lead to the theft of sensitive user information.

Table 6. Relationship beetwen Mobile Ilities and Test activities proposal

Mobile Ilities	Test					
	Compatibility	Stress	Accessibility	Energy Consumption	Security	Usability
Connectivity						
Flexibility		✗	✗			✗
Interoperability		✗				✗
Energy				✗		
Device Heterogeneity	✗		✗			✗
Platforms	✗		✗			
Data Security					✗	

6   Conclussion and Future Works

We have proposed a framework for app evaluation, which suggests the different tests that should be performed on apps related to Mobile Ilities. The feasibility of the proposal is assessed by applying it to the development of a toy app by students of the software engineering degree. Following the recommendations of the framework, 5 tests were carried out using various testing tools that allowed us to identify certain deficiencies in the application. The main contribution of the paper is to guide app developers in evaluating apps and contributing to improving app quality. Furthermore, the relationship between Mobile Ilities and app testing activities is presented. As future work, more complex tests such as partition equivalence, decision tables, mutations and checking whether the application works correctly with any type of technology used for test development if required can be increased. In addition, it is suggested to implement automated usability tests using tools such as Espresso and Appium to detect possible problems in the user flow. To optimize accessibility tests, specialized tools such as Ax for Android could be incorporated. In addition, strengthening security assessments by integrating static and dynamic analysis with tools such as SonarQube and OWASP ZAP would allow vulnerabilities to be identified more thoroughly. Device connectivity tests should also be implemented. The proposal must be evaluated using a real-world application, which requires defining efficiency, effectiveness, and user satisfaction metrics to compare with other app evaluation approaches and contribute to software product improvement.

References

1. Abrahamsson, P., Hanhineva, A., Hulkko, H.: Mobile-d: An agile approach for mobile application development. In: Companion to the 19th Annual ACM SIG-PLAN Conference on Object-Oriented Programming, Systems, Languages, and Applications, pp. 174–175 (2004). http://dl.acm.org/citation.cfm?id=1028736
2. Martinez, D., Ferre, X., Guerrero, G., Juristo, N.: An agile-based integrated framework for mobile application development considering ilities. IEEE Access **8**, 72461–72470 (2020). https://doi.org/10.1109/ACCESS.2020.2987882

3. Jabangwe, R., Edison, H., Duc, A.N.: Software engineering process models for mobile app development: a systematic literature review. J. Syst. Softw. **145**, 98–111 (2018). https://doi.org/10.1016/j.jss.2018.08.028
4. Zhan, W., Yan, G.: Testing of mobile applications: a review of industry practices. https://www.bth.se, retrieved September 4, (2024)
5. Villalobos, G.M., Darío, G., Sánchez, C., Alberto, D., Gutiérrez, B.: Diseño de framework web para el desarrollo dinámico de aplicaciones. Scientia et Technica **16**(44) (2010). http://www.pdf4free.com
6. IEEE: 610.12-1990 IEEE standard glossary of software engineering terminology (1990). https://doi.org/10.1109/IEEESTD.1990.101064
7. IEEE Computer Society: Guide to the Software Engineering Body of Knowledge (SWEBOK Version 3.0). IEEE (2014)
8. Perrucci, G.P., Fitzek, F.H.P., Widmer, J.: Survey on energy consumption entities on the smartphone platform. In: IEEE Vehicular Technology Conference, pp. 1–6 (2011). https://doi.org/10.1109/VETECS.2011.5956528
9. AccuBattery: User manual – accubattery help center, https://accubattery.zendesk.com/hc/en-us/sections/202339749-User-manual. retrieved September 4, 2024
10. International Organization for Standardization: Ergonomics of human-system interaction—part 210: Human-centred design for interactive systems (2019)
11. Abraham, A.: Mobile security framework. https://mobsf.live/about, retrieved September 4, 2024
12. AndroBugs: Androbugs framework. https://www.androbugs.com/, retrieved September 4, 2024
13. Sauce Labs: Sauce labs: Cross browser testing, selenium testing & mobile testing (2024). https://saucelabs.com/
14. SmartBear: Bitbar dashboard (2024). https://cloud.bitbar.com/#testing/dashboard
15. Google: Accessibility scanner - apps on google play (2024). https://play.google.com/store/apps/details?id=com.google.android.apps.accessibility.auditor
16. Sommerville, I.: Software Engineering. Pearson, 7th edn. (2003)

Small-to-Large: Proportional Uniform Distribution Weights Transferring to Reduce Energy Consumption of Training the Models with Fully Connected Layers

Farzad Vazinram$^{(\boxtimes)}$ (iD)

Department of Computer Science, University of Twente, Enschede, The Netherlands
`f.vazinram@utwente.nl`

Abstract. Providing sufficient and sustainable energy for users has always been a concern for all related stakeholders. The development of Deep Learning (DL) models with various applications has increased the need for their training, consequently raising their energy consumption drastically. This work has concentrated on reducing energy consumption of training the models with Fully Connected (FC) layers. So, the energy consumption of Multilayer Perceptron (MLP) models with FC layers has been investigated first to come up with a proper solution. The idea is based on the concept that the energy consumption of DL models exponentially rises by increasing their size. So, a small model with much lower energy consumption has been used for good initialization of the large model. As a result, there would be fewer number of epochs and less energy needed to reach a specific accuracy in comparison to randomly initialization of the model. The transferring of weights from the small model to the large model has been carried out by proposing a method called Proportional Uniform Distribution (PUD). The proposed method has been examined in various cases. The results show that training the models using the proposed method has lower energy consumption. Moreover, it can be applied easily to any library. Keras library has been selected in this work as a case.

Keywords: Energy Consumption Reduction · Fully Connected
Layers · MLP · Proportional Uniform Distribution (PUD) · Training ·
Weight Transferring

1 Introduction

By developing the Deep Learning (DL) models and consequently increasing their complexity [1], the required energy for their training and usage is rapidly increasing [2]. So, any effort to reduce their energy consumption would have benefits for all related stakeholders and help to reduce carbon emissions.

Various efforts have been made to reduce the complexity of models and consequently make their training faster and with lower required computation.

© The Author(s), under exclusive license to Springer Nature Switzerland AG 2025
O. Gervasi et al. (Eds.): ICCSA 2025, LNCS 15650, pp. 81–97, 2025.
https://doi.org/10.1007/978-3-031-96962-1_6

Any effort to reduce the energy consumption of model training per se consumes energy. The key point is that this consumed energy must always be lower than the final energy consumption reduction (Fig. 1). This case would be critical for Fully Connected (FC) layers in comparison to the convolutional (CONV) layers. The reason is that the energy consumption of CONV layers is much more than FC layers due to the much higher amount of data movement in comparison to pure computation [3,4]. This is the main reason that in the AlexNet model [5] 96% of the total weights belong to the FC layers but they only consume 28% of the total energy consumption [3]. So, in CONV layers by consuming energy to limit the data movement, we will achieve a lot. However, this range of energy consumption in FC layers is so limited. As a result, only considering the removed weights may not be enough to say that the energy consumption of training the models has been reduced [3] and the energy consumption as an independent criterion needs to be considered.

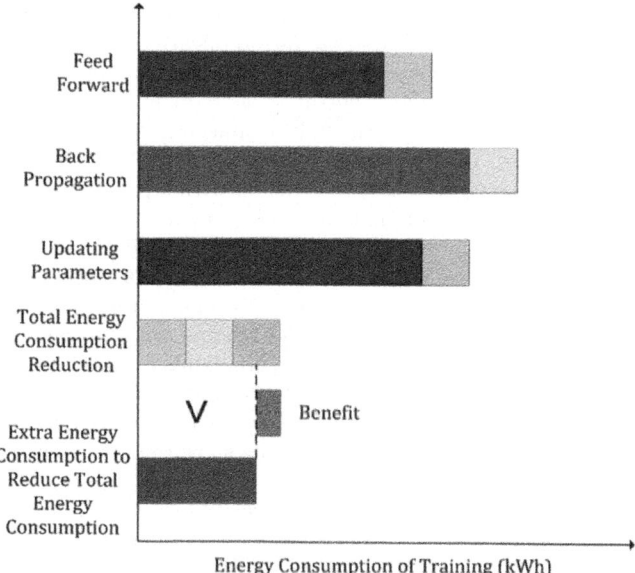

Fig. 1. Comparing the extra energy consumed to reduce the energy consumption of the model and the total energy consumption reduction of the model.

This work has been concentrated on energy consumption reduction of training Multilayer Perceptron (MLP) models with FC layers. The contributions of this work can be summarized as follows:

– Energy-based investigation of MLP models training with FC layers.
– Energy-based investigation of sparsifying technique in training of MLP models.

- A novel method to exploit the lower energy consumption of smaller models for better initialization of larger models to achieve the desired accuracy faster and reduce the energy consumption of MLP model training.

2 Related Works

There are so many attempts to make the training of DL models efficient with low or no effect on their accuracy. Most of the methods consider the training time, model parameters, Floating Point (FLOPs) Operations, Multiply-Accumulate (MACs) Operations, or a combination of them as criteria of efficiency. These methods are included but not limited to pruning, sparse training, model compression [6], quantization [7], efficient architecture design [8], and optimally set hyper-parameters [9]. However, as discussed in the introduction section, they may not be enough from viewpoint of energy consumption. In this work, the CodeCarbon package [10] has been used to measure the energy consumption of the training part of the models. This package is a project designed to measure the emission approximation and energy consumption of running codes.

Among the various methods, pruning and sparse training have been extensively studied in recent years. [11] has been provided with a good survey of various pruning methods. Various methods have been proposed to make models sparse. [12] covers the most recent works in this area. However, exploiting sparsity needs extra effort which has been an incentive for other researchers to concentrate on exploiting sparsity in the level of matrix multiplication. [13] focused on parallel multiplication of sparse and dense matrices. [14] mentioned a method for masked matrix multiplication by avoiding unnecessary computations. On the other side, some research avoids using masks and disregards all zero elements during training using sparse techniques with some overheads [15]. So, sparsity will be discussed shortly from the viewpoint of energy consumption in the next section.

Some other approaches include increasing the accuracy of the model which makes it faster to reach a specific accuracy and some of them can be similar to the mentioned directions. In [16], a new optimization model based on the Genetic Algorithm has been used for tuning the hyper-parameters of the MLP model with the aim of accuracy improvement. Averaging the prediction of various models trained in one dataset is another method used for increasing the performance of models [17]. In the same research path, [18] proposed a compression technique to distill the knowledge with the aim of computation reduction. In [19] the MLP projector has been used to better transfer the learning of unsupervised pretrained models. There are various other methods available for learning to transfer; however, they used another dataset or model type for transferring. Moreover, the author could not find any similar work carried out on FC layers specifically.

3   Methodology

The main- and sub-research questions have been defined as follows to systematically analyze the problem and their optimum possible solutions.

- **Main_Q**: How to reduce the energy consumption of MLP networks with FC layers with less impact on their accuracy?
- *Sub_Q1:* What are the energy consumption of different parts of the MLP models training with FC layers and what factors affect them?
- *Sub_Q2:* What are the energy consumption of different layers of the MLP model training?
- *Sub_Q3:* What is the relation among sparsity, its difficulty to be exploited, and final energy consumption of training MLP models with FC layers?

3.1   Sub_Q1: Discussion on Energy Consumption of MLP Models

This part aims to analyze the energy consumption of different parts of the training MLP model. So, the energy consumption of the different parts of an MLP model including Feed Forward, Back Propagation, and updating the parameters during training through the MNIST dataset with 784 input features and 10 different output classes was measured (Fig. 2). The input and output sizes are 784 and 10, respectively. The batch size of all training was chosen as 128. The hidden layer sizes are (128×200), (1280×2000), and (12800×20000) for small, medium and large models, respectively. The energy consumption of the model is divided into different parts of the training phase including Feed Forward, Back Propagation, and updating the parameters. The range of energy consumptions in small and medium models are close to each other but the differences are prominent in a large model. It is observed that the most energy-consuming part of the MLP model is Back Propagation and the updating the parameters part is in the second rank. These findings show that there is more potential to reduce the energy consumption of training MLP models rather than only focusing on weight pruning. The general solutions can be reducing the models' dimension or reducing the total number of required iterations by keeping the accuracy in an acceptable range.

Although the Feed Forward part had the lowest energy consumption in our case, increasing the batch size can increase considerably the energy consumption and has also effect on the Back Propagation part of the MLP model during the training but it does not have too much effect on update parameters part (Fig. 3). Increasing the batch size will reduce our required iterations and total energy consumption but with the cost of losing our accuracy. So, choosing the appropriate batch size has a direct effect on the time and energy consumption of the MLP model during training. In Fig. 3, the total energy and accuracy reduced from 0.002 kWh and 0.95 to 0.0009 kWh and 0.85, respectively when batch size increased from 128 to 1280.

It is also observed that (Fig. 2) the energy consumption of MLP model training will increase exponentially by increasing the neurons in their hidden layers

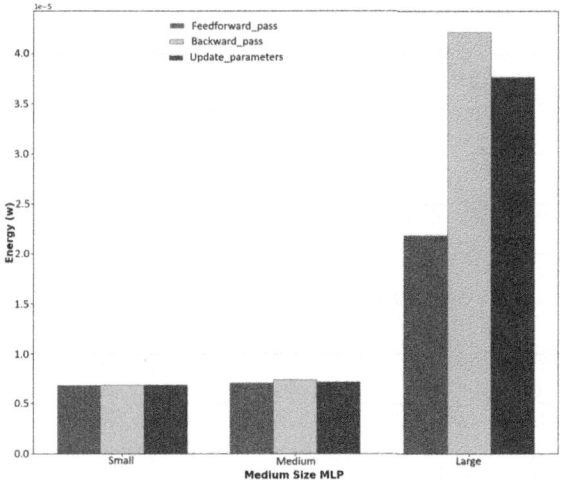

Fig. 2. The energy consumption of a model with two hidden layers with three different sizes.

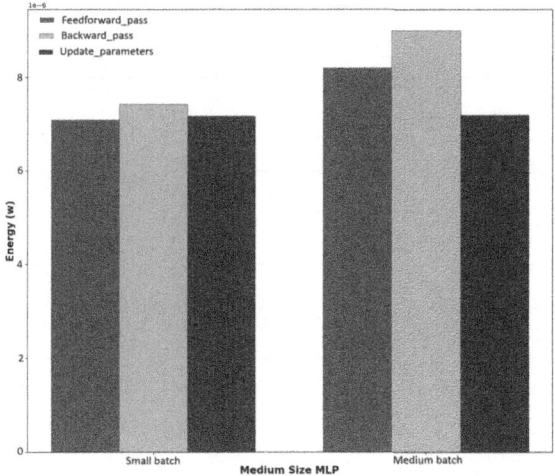

Fig. 3. Comparison of average energy consumption of different parts of an MLP model including two hidden layers with 1280 and 2000 neurons during training by MNIST dataset with 784 input features and 10 different output classes and two batch sizes of 128 and 1280.

which is compatible with the findings of [3]. So, the large models are more attractive to reduce their energy consumption and obviously choosing the appropriate size for the model is important from the viewpoint of energy consumption. Moreover, it is a great incentive for this paper to use small models for large model initialization.

3.2   Sub_Q2: Energy Consumption of Different Layers of the MLP Model

One idea to reduce the total energy consumption of models is to start reducing the layers that have the highest energy consumption. Because in FC layers, computation is a considerable portion of energy consumption unlike CONV layers which data movement is the key factor [3,4], it was observed that the energy consumption of FC layers is approximately related to the required computation. In other words, in FC layers, the energy consumption is related to the layer sizes that make our matrices. The results of observations are presented in Table 1. The energy consumption of each layer is measured after 10 iterations and the average is calculated.

Table 1. The energy consumption of different layers of MLP models with different sizes.

Model	Layer1_2 (kWh)	Layer2_3 (kWh)	Layer3_4 (kWh)
input_size = 784 hidden_size1 = 2000 hidden_size2 = 2000 output_size = 10	6.9495e-06	7.1233e-06	6.9043e-06
input_size = 784 hidden_size1 = 200 hidden_size2 = 200 output_size = 10	6.9298e-06	6.9151e-06	6.8985e-06
input_size = 784 hidden_size1 = 1280 hidden_size2 = 2000 output_size = 10	6.9396e-06	7.0510e-06	6.9002e-06

3.3   Sub_Q3: Discussion About Exploiting Sparsity to Reduce Energy Consumption and Speed of Training MLP Models with FC Layers

To reduce training model computation, there are various methods available that revolve around sparsity (zero parameters). However, the currently available hardware is fully optimized for dense computations [14]. Hence, using suitable hardware to exploit sparsity, e.g., Sputnik [20] and NVIDIA cuSPARSE [21] is one solution. The more common solution is using standard hardware along with some software techniques. The main idea is to only save the non-zero elements and disregard the zero elements from computations to save memory and computation. To do so, there are some libraries available e.g. SciPy [22], TensorFlow [23], etc.

Exploiting sparsity rooted in matrix multiplication which depends on the utilized method can be normal or element-wise. Sometimes, depending on the used method, the overhead of using sparse techniques is higher than we can achieve in the end. So, the multiplication of two matrices with various sizes, sparsity levels, values, distribution of non-zero elements, and data type of elements are examined using the Compressed Sparse Row (CSR) method of SciPy library [22]. The results show that having a dispersed pattern of non-zero elements, different values, and low sparsity levels in a sparse matrix can increase the energy consumption of matrix multiplication. The data type (e.g. float or integer) and matrix size have a direct effect on the energy consumption of matrix multiplication but cannot make a general rule for it. For example, by using the sparse technique and sparsity level of 99%, the energy consumption of multiplication of sparse and dense matrices (both sizes 5000×5000) was reduced from 0.08 kWh to 0.00002 kWh. However, by changing the matrix dimension, using the sparse technique increases the energy consumption in comparison to the normal multiplication.

All in all, lots of methods have been proposed to have sparse matrices. However, exploiting sparsity needs extra effort which makes these methods challenging and sometimes containing high overhead.

3.4 Main_Q: How to Reduce the Energy Consumption of MLP Networks

According to the discussion over research sub-questions, the proposed method to reduce the energy consumption of training the FC layers is increasing the model accuracy, with low overhead, to reduce the total number of iterations and consequently energy consumption. To do so, a small model with low energy consumption would be used to train over the same data and transfer its weights to the larger model with high energy consumption with the aim of good initialization. In this method, we will not lose any information or accuracy; however, the model would only be efficient for the training phase and not the inference phase. Based on the author's knowledge, there is no similar method with the aim of energy consumption reduction of training FC layers.

With consideration of having an MLP network with FC layers and two hidden layers as follows:

$$X_{(\text{input})} \times W^{(1)} + b^{(1)} = a^{(1)}$$
$$Z^{(1)} = \text{Relu}(a^{(1)})$$
$$Z^{(1)} \times W^{(2)} + b^{(2)} = a^{(2)}$$
$$Z^{(2)} = \text{Relu}(a^{(2)})$$
$$Z^{(2)} \times W^{(3)} + b^{(3)} = a^{(3)}$$
$$Y_{(\text{output})} = \text{Relu}(a^{(3)})$$

(1)

that the equations can be summarized as:

$$z_j = f(XW^{(L)} + b^{(L)})$$

where $X \in \mathbb{R}^{n \times x}$ is input features for the batch of n samples, $W^{(L)} \in \mathbb{R}^{m \times n}$ is weights of hidden layer L, and $b^{(L)} \in \mathbb{R}^{1 \times n}$ is biases of layer L, this method can be interpreted as:

$$\mathbf{W}^{(L)}_{j \times i} \& \mathbf{b}^{(L)}_{1 \times j} \mapsto \mathbf{W}'^{(L)}_{m \times n} \& \mathbf{b}'^{(L)}_{1 \times m} \text{ where } \begin{cases} m > j \\ n > i \end{cases} \quad m, n \in \mathbb{N} \qquad (2)$$

where $W^{(L)} \in \mathbb{R}^{m \times n}$ is weights of hidden layer L, and $b^{(L)} \in \mathbb{R}^{1 \times n}$ is biases of layer L. (W', b') and (W, b) are weights and biases of large and small models, respectively.

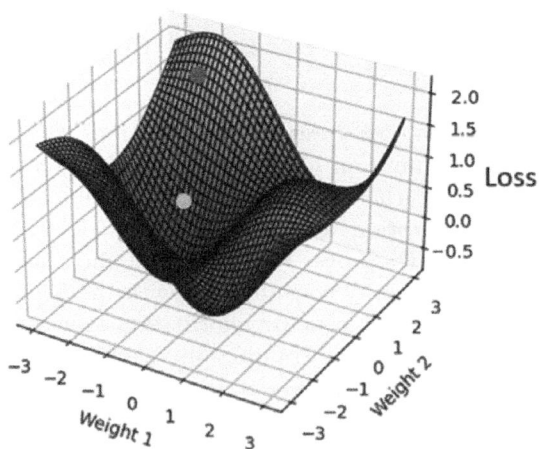

Fig. 4. The solution domain of weights and corresponding loss. Random initialization of the model (red dot). The transferred weights initialization (blue dot). (Color figure online)

The goal is to transfer the weights of a small model to the desired large model to have a good initialization instead of random initialization. As illustrated in

Fig. 4, the aim is starting optimization from blue point instead of red point with random initialization. This initialization is based on the input dataset and desired outputs. The random initialization of the model (red dot) will start from high loss (low accuracy) and need more iterations to reach the optimum point. The transferred weights initialization (blue dot) will start with better loss (accuracy) and need fewer iterations and energy consumption. To transfer weights to a larger model various methods have been tried. For example, transferring the weights of the smaller model and keeping the remaining weights zero or using various types of data distribution. The best method was using proportional uniform distribution (PUD) which the large model at initialization had close results to the small model after training.

The procedure of transferring weights from a small model to a large model $W \mapsto \mathbb{W}$ can be implemented by mapping each element of the small matrix to the corresponding segment of the large matrix as follows:

$$\mathbf{W}_{i \times j} \mapsto \mathbb{W}_{i' \times j'}^{(i,j)}, \text{where} \begin{cases} i' : row\_scale \\ j' : col\_scale \end{cases} \tag{3}$$

where $\mathbf{W}_{i \times j}$ is the element of the small matrix (Fig. 5 dark blue) and $\mathbb{W}_{i' \times j'}^{(i,j)}$ is the corresponding segment of the large matrix (Fig. 5 Light blue) with the size of $i' \times j'$, i' and j' are row and column scaled-up sizes based on the ratio of large to small models. So, each element of the corresponding segment in the large matrix is defined as follows:

$$\mathbb{W}_{i,j}^{(i,j)} = \frac{\mathbf{W}_{i,j}}{i' \times j'} \times \alpha \tag{4}$$

where $\mathbb{W}_{i,j}^{(i,j)}$ is the i, j element of the segment in the large matrix corresponding to the (i, j) element in the small matrix and α is a hyper-parameter that would apply to the transferred values with the aim of better efficiency.

So, all elements will be changed during the transferring procedure. It should be noted that this method is entirely different from what we call Progressive Training (or Progressive Growth) like the research carried out in [24] and our focus is on FC layers during training. Moreover, the training data are used for initialization not using general pretrained models which are trained with other data.

This method starts with training a small model size for a few epochs. Due to the small size, it consumes less energy and time for training. No need to have a large amount of epochs in this phase because the accuracy of the model will exponentially increase. Moreover, we are not interested in very high accuracy in this phase because we will lose some accuracy due to transferring our learning to the larger model in the next phase. Moreover, we are not willing to consume too much extra energy in this phase because it is an extra effort than just training a normal large model. The general concept of this method has been presented in Fig. 6 and the corresponding Pseudocode has been presented in Algorithm 1.

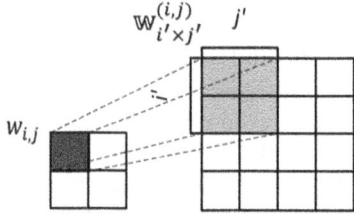

Fig. 5. Transferring weights from small matrix (left) to large matrix (right) corresponding to small and large models, respectively. The element of the small matrix (dark blue) will transfer to the larger matrix as a corresponding segment (light blue) with a size equal to the ratio of large to small matrix (model). (Color figure online)

Algorithm 1. Small-to-large: Weight Transfer

%Random initialization
Initialize the small MLP model
Set hyper-parameters
%Training
Initialize the large MLP model
Set hyper-parameters
%Transferlearning
    Transfer weight and bias values of small model to large
    matrices of large model with proportional distribution
%Training
    Training the large model
end

---

4   Experiments

The results of the proposed method have been presented in this section. All experiments have been executed using a standard laptop with the Hardware configuration: CPU Intel Core i7-13700H, 2.40 GHz, RAM 32 GB, Hard disk 1 TB. The MLP model was used for all experiments and MNIST [26] and CIFAR10 [25] datasets for training the models. To have a fair comparison among different cases, the same random initialization is used with the same base code, hyper-parameters, hardware, and no accelerator. The other random initializations were also tested to make sure the results were not an exception.

4.1   Small-to-Large: Initialization Using Transferring Weights with Proportional Uniform Distribution

The aim is to reach the same accuracy as a normal large model using the proposed method with less energy consumption. So, the simulations will be stopped once reach the same training energy and, approximately, time. At first, the small model with two hidden layers with a size of $(128, 200)$ was randomly initialized and trained using the MNIST dataset for only two epochs. Then, the weights

Small-to-Large: Weight Transfer with Proportional Distribution

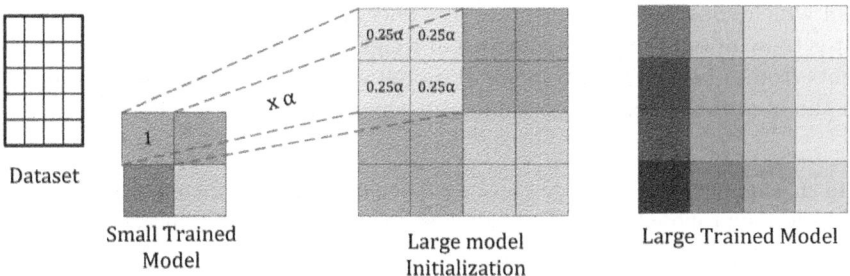

Dataset

Small Trained Model

Large model Initialization

Large Trained Model

Fig. 6. The general concepts of energy consumption reduction of training MLP model: training a small model and transferring the weights to the larger model using a proportional uniform distribution with the aim of good initialization of large model and reach to the desired accuracy in less time and with less energy consumption.

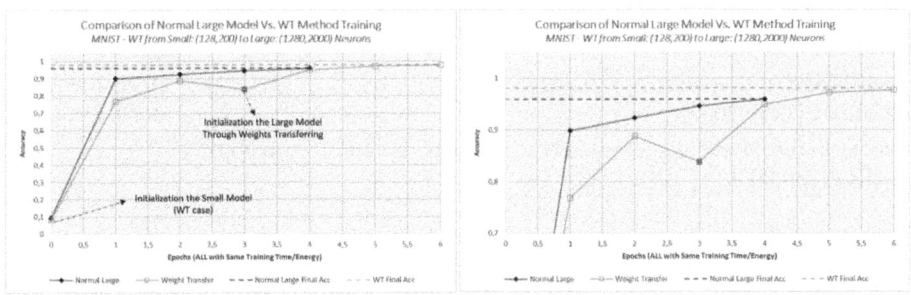

Fig. 7. Comparison of training results using MNIST dataset for normal large model and weights transferring methods with hidden layer sizes (1280,2000). The small model size used to initialize the large model is (128,200). All simulations stopped after the same amount of energy consumption (approximately the same time). The proposed method has better results.

are transferred to the large model using the proposed PUD method. The results have been illustrated in Fig. 7 and Table 2. It is obvious that the weight transfer has been carried out efficiently (accuracy drop from 0.88 to only 0.83) and that the accuracy of the large model at initialization is close to the accuracy of the small-size model at the final training epoch.

The large initialized model in Fig. 7 (orange line) has reached a higher efficiency than the normal large model (blue line) which means we can reach the same accuracy with less energy consumption. The proposed method reached the same accuracy as the normal large model after some iterations followed by the first epoch only with, approximately, 0.6 of energy consumption of training the normal large model (Table 2). It is to be noted that the initialization of the normal large model and proposed method are 0.09 and 0.83, respectively. The total epochs of the normal large model have been 4 and the large model after initialization reached better results only after a few iterations followed by the first epoch. However, we should consider the energy consumed to train the small model which considerably consumes less energy than the larger model.

It is to be noted that the same idea of weight transferring was tried to transfer weights from a large model to a small model with the reverse way of using PUD with the aim of matrix compression. But the results were not desirable.

Table 2. Comparison of energy consumption and time of training the normal large model and the proposed method including training the small and initialized large models.

MNIST Dataset	Energy RAM (Wh)	Energy CPU (Wh)	Time (s)	Final Accuracy	Accuracy of Weight Transferring
Small Model 2 epochs (128,200)	0.022	0.099	12	0.8883	-
Large Model < 4 epochs Initialized (1280,2000)	0.404	1.582	127	0.9808	0.8883 to 0.8384
Large Model < 2 epochs Initialized (1280,2000)	0.242	0.8914	85	0.9590	0.8883 to 0.8384
Normal Large Model 4 epochs (1280,2000)	0.421	1.669	140	0.9591	-

To observe the effect of different model sizes on the proposed method, both utilized small and large model sizes have been changed and the results have been presented in Fig. 8. In this experiment, the training of the proposed method has been stopped in the 10th epoch but without full iterations. The result of the proposed method is better than the normally trained model. The reason for different initialization accuracies is also different model sizes. In this case, the proposed method had also better results than the normally trained model.

To see the effect of the proposed method in different model structures, one hidden layer was added to the model. The proposed method has slightly better results in comparison to training the normal large model (Fig. 9). As is obvious, the trend of the accuracy of the proposed method (orange line) has a little fluctuation. Changing the learning rate can help to have a better final accuracy. The other point is that the advantage of the proposed method over the normal training of the model reduces in large epochs. Moreover, the small model is still too large which consumes lots of energy. So, reducing the hidden layer sizes can help to reduce the required energy consumption for the initialization of the large model while maintaining the quality of transferred weights.

In all previous cases, the small model had better results than the large model. So, that was the reason that the small model with few epochs reached a good accuracy which has a direct effect on the good initialization of the large model. In this case, as it is obvious in Fig. 10, the small model (blue line) has worse efficiency in comparison to the large model (orange line). This is the reason

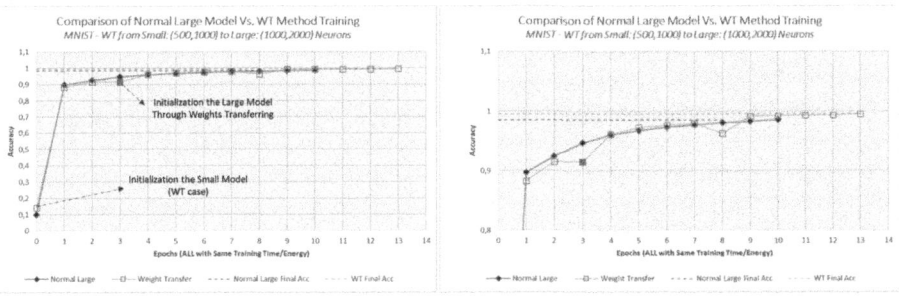

Fig. 8. Comparison of training results using MNIST dataset for normal large model and weights transferring methods with hidden layer sizes (1000,2000). The small model size used to initialize the large model is (500,1000). All simulations stopped after the same amount of energy consumption (approximately the same time). The proposed method has better results.

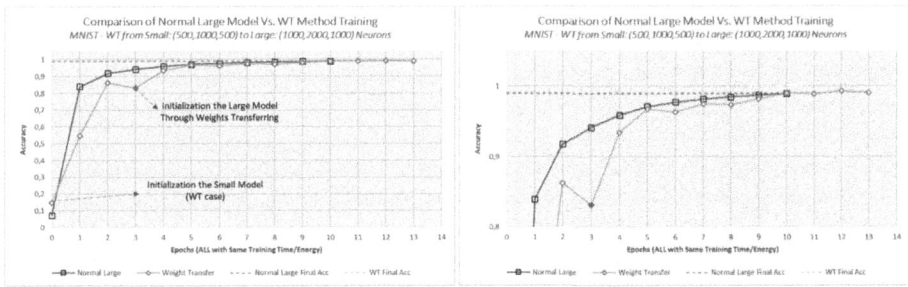

Fig. 9. Comparison of training results using MNIST dataset for normal large model and weights transferring methods with hidden layer sizes (1000,2000,1000). The small model size used to initialize the large model is (500,1000,500). All simulations stopped after the same amount of energy consumption (approximately the same time). The proposed method has slightly better results.

that the initialization of a large model has less accuracy in comparison to the previous cases. However, the final accuracy of the proposed method (gray line) is slightly better than the large model and much better than the small model. In this case, both small and large models are small and consume less amount of energy. So, training the smaller model does not have a prominent advantage from the viewpoint of energy consumption (Fig. 11 left oval).

The proposed method can be applied to any library. In this case, the method is applied to the Keras library [27] and the results are illustrated in Fig. 12. The energy consumption of model training using Keras is less than the code written by the author which makes it possible to train the small model with higher epochs. However, the effect of using the method has similar results in both codes.

To see the effectiveness of the proposed method on different datasets, the CIFAR-10 dataset has been selected to train the model with many more epochs.

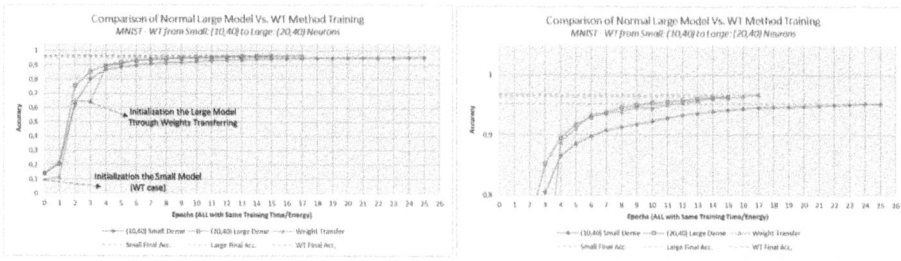

Fig. 10. Comparison of training results using MNIST dataset for normal large model, normal small model, and weights transferring methods with hidden layer sizes (20,40). The small model size used to initialize the large model is (10,40) and it has worse efficiency in comparison to the large model. All simulations stopped after the same amount of energy consumption (approximately the same time). The proposed method has better results.

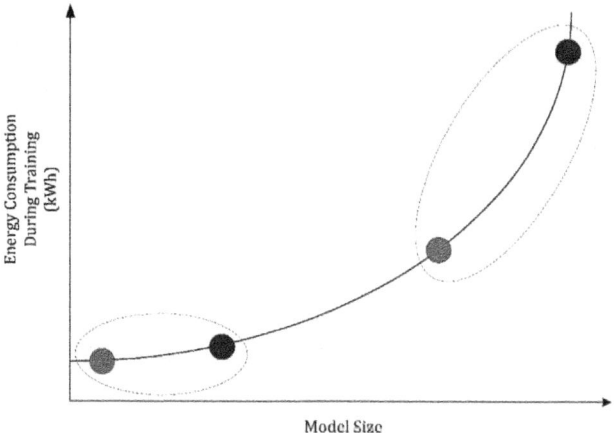

Fig. 11. The difference in energy consumption of small (blue circle) and larger (red circle) models when their sizes are both small (left oval). By increasing the model size, the difference in energy consumption of small and large models will be high due to the energy consumption increase of both models exponentially (right oval). (Color figure online)

The efficiency of the proposed method is obvious in Fig. 13. The proposed method (orange lines) has better results than the normal large model (blue line) during the whole training period. It should be noted that the small model trained over 100 epochs to be able to initialize the large model efficiently. It can be implied that the proposed method has better results when dealing with large datasets and models. The main reason has roots in increasing the energy consumption of model training exponentially. So, through training the small model, which consumes much less energy, with the aim of initialization of the large model, we can save lots of energy.

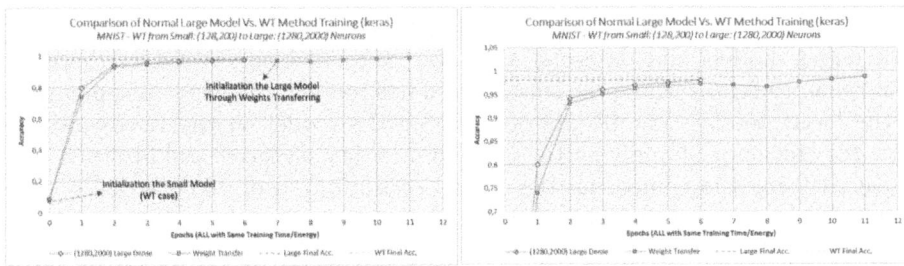

Fig. 12. Comparison of training results using MNIST dataset for normal large model and weights transferring methods with hidden layer sizes (1280,2000) using Keras library. The small model size used to initialize the large model is (128,200). All simulations stopped after the same amount of energy consumption (approximately the same time). The proposed method has better results.

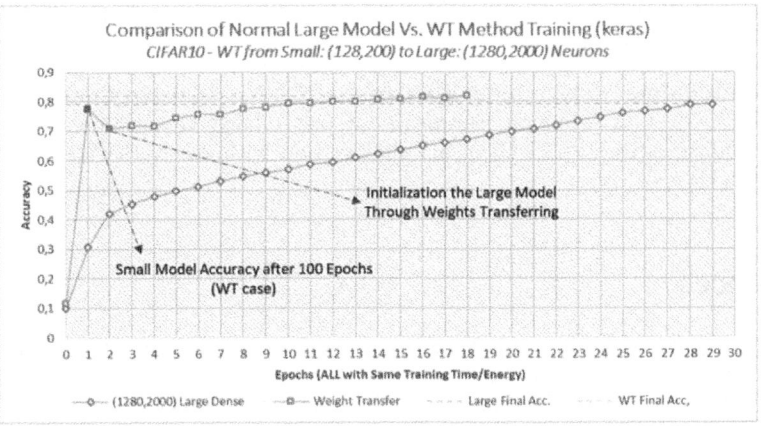

Fig. 13. Comparison of training results using MNIST dataset for normal large model and weights transferring methods with hidden layer sizes (1280,2000) using Keras library. The small model size used to initialize the large model is (128,200). All simulations stopped after the same amount of energy consumption (approximately the same time). The proposed method has better results.

5 Conclusion and Future Work

In this work, training the MLP model with FC layers has been investigated from the viewpoint of energy consumption. The exponential energy consumption increasing of training the DL models was the main incentive to propose the method. Based on that, the small model with low energy consumption is trained, and using the proposed PUD method its weights will be transferred to the larger model with the aim of better initialization. So, the larger model will need fewer epochs, and consequently, less energy consumption, to reach the same accuracy as the larger model. The method has been tested in various cases. It was observed that the proposed method has better efficiency in dealing with larger models and datasets. Moreover, the efficiency of the method will decrease in the cases where the small model has too low efficiency in comparison to the larger model. The results of applying the model on the Keras package show the efficiency of applying the method on other packages and libraries. One of the challenges in comparing the energy consumption of different methods is having a fair comparison. This includes the same base code of the model, the same hardware, using the same backend and accelerator, having the same data, model structure, random parameters, etc. So, comparing the results of different methods of the same group will be easier than comparing the results of various methods. This can be a good incentive for future work to have a fair comparison among all well-known available methods. Moreover, in some cases, the convergence of the proposed method accuracy during training had fluctuation which can be mitigated by modifying the hyper-parameters like learning rate. Finding a method to define optimally the hyper-parameters or a better optimization method can improve the method's efficiency.

Acknowledgments. This project has received funding from the European Union's Important Project of Common European Interest - Next Generation Cloud Infrastructure and Services (IPCEI CIS), in collaboration with the Netherlands Enterprise Agency (RVO).

References

1. Fedus, W., Zoph, B., Shazeer, N.: Switch transformers: scaling to trillion parameter models with simple and efficient sparsity. J. Mach. Learn. Res. **23**, 1–39 (2022)
2. Desislavov, R., Martínez-Plumed, F., Hernández-Orallo, J.: Compute and energy consumption trends in deep learning inference, arXiv [cs.LG], 12-Sep-2021
3. Yang, T.-J. ., Chen, Y.-H., Sze, V.: Designing energy-efficient convolutional neural networks using energy-aware pruning, arXiv [cs.CV], 15-Nov-2016
4. Yang, T.-J., Chen, Y.-H., Emer, J., Sze, V.: A method to estimate the energy consumption of deep neural networks," 2017 51st Asilomar Conference on Signals, Systems, and Computers, Pacific Grove, CA, USA, 2017, pp. 1916–1920. https://doi.org/10.1109/ACSSC.2017.8335698.
5. Krizhevsky, A., Sutskever, I., Hinton, G.E.: ImageNet classification with deep convolutional neural networks. Commun. ACM **60**(6), 84–90 (2017)
6. Dai, B., Zhu, C., Wipf, D.: Compressing neural networks using the variational information bottleneck. In: International Conference on Machine Learning (2018)
7. Courbariaux, M., Bengio, Y., David, J.P.: BinaryConnect: training deep neural networks with binary weights during propagations. In: Proceedings of the 29th International Conference on Neural Information Processing Systems - Volume 2, Montreal, Canada, 2015, pp. 3123–3131 (2015)
8. Velez, D., Santa, S., Patino, G.: MLP neural network based on PCA and K-means clustering for PM2.5 forecasting. In: Computing, Internet of Things and Data Analytics, 2024, pp. 202–212 (2024)
9. Spurlock, K., Elgazzar, H.: A genetic mixed-integer optimization of neural network hyper-parameters. J. Supercomput. **78**(12), 14680–14702 (2022)

10. Courty, B., et al., 'mlco2/codecarbon: v2.4.1'. Zenodo (May 2024)
11. He, Y., Xiao, L.: Structured pruning for deep convolutional neural networks: a survey. IEEE Trans. Pattern Anal. Mach. Intell. **46**(5), 2900–2919 (2024). https://doi.org/10.1109/TPAMI.2023.3334614
12. Mocanu, D.C., et al.: Sparse Training Theory for Scalable and Efficient Agents, arXiv [cs.AI], 02-Mar-2021
13. Koanantakool, P., et al.: Communication-avoiding parallel sparse-dense matrix-matrix multiplication. In: 2016 IEEE International Parallel and Distributed Processing Symposium (IPDPS) (2016)
14. Wheatman, B., Madhyastha, M., Burns, R.: Masked matrix multiplication for emergent sparsity. ArXiv:abs/2402.14118 (2024)
15. Wesselink, W., Grooten, B., Xiao, Q., de Campos, C., Pechenizkiy, M.: Nerva: a truly sparse implementation of neural networks, arXiv [cs.LG]. (2024)
16. El-Hassani, F.Z., Amri, M., Joudar, N.-E., Haddouch, K.: A new optimization model for mlp hyperparameter tuning: modeling and resolution by real-coded genetic algorithm. Neural Process. Lett. **56**(2), 105 (2024)
17. Dietterich, T.G.: Ensemble methods in machine learning. In: multiple classifier systems, 2000, pp. 1–15 (2000)
18. Hinton, G., Vinyals, O., Dean, J.: Distilling the knowledge in a neural network. In: NIPS 2014 Deep Learning Workshop, arXiv [stat.ML] (2015)
19. Wang, Y., et al.: 'Revisiting the transferability of supervised pretraining: an MLP perspective. In: IEEE/CVF Conference on Computer Vision and Pattern Recognition (CVPR) **2022**, pp. 9173–9183 (2022)
20. Gale, T., Zaharia, M., Young, C., Elsen, E.: Sparse GPU kernels for deep learning. In: Proceedings of the International Conference for High Performance Computing, Networking, Storage and Analysis (2020)
21. Nvidia, 'CuSPARSE'. https://docs.nvidia.com/cuda/cusparse/. Accessed 12 Jan 2025
22. Virtanen, P., et al.: SciPy 1.0: fundamental algorithms for scientific computing in Python. Nat. Methods **17**(3), 261–272 (2020)
23. Abadi, M., et al.:'TensorFlow: a system for large-scale machine learning'. In: 12th $USENIX Symposium on Operating Systems Design and Implementation (OSDI$ 16), pp. 265–283 (2016)
24. Gu, X., Liu, L., Yu, H., Li, J., Chen, C., Han, J.: On the Transformer growth for progressive BERT training, arXiv [cs.CL], 23-Oct-2020
25. Krizhevsky, A.: Learning Multiple Layers of Features from Tiny Images, University of Toronto (05 2012)
26. Deng, L.: The MNIST database of handwritten digit images for machine learning research. IEEE Signal Process. Mag. **29**(6), 141–142 (2012)
27. Chollet, F., et al.:'Keras' (2015). https://github.com/fchollet/keras

A Review of Comparative Studies on Performance Evaluation of Communication Mechanisms for Microservices

Berkcan Çiftçi[1]([✉])[ID] and Birol Çiloğlugil[2][ID]

[1] Institute of Natural Sciences, Department of Computer Engineering, Ege University, 35100 Bornova, Izmir, Turkey
berkcanciftci35@gmail.com
[2] Faculty of Engineering, Department of Computer Engineering, Ege University, 35100 Bornova, Izmir, Turkey
birol.ciloglugil@ege.edu.tr

Abstract. As organizations increasingly adopt microservices to improve agility and scalability, selecting the right communication mechanisms becomes critical for system efficiency and fault tolerance. Therefore, a variety of communication technologies, including but not limited to HTTP REST, HTTP/2, gRPC, GraphQL, MQTT, AMQP, Apache Kafka, RabbitMQ, NATS Streaming, RocketMQ, Apache Pulsar, Redis, ActiveMQ, ActiveMQ Artemis, and WebSocket, are employed in a wide range of applications. Benchmarking frameworks such as Apache JMeter and the OpenMessaging Benchmark Framework are utilized to evaluate performances of different communication technologies in a variety of environments. For this purpose, performance evaluation metrics such as throughput, latency and response time are assessed to compare the performances of inter-process communication (IPC) technologies. Hence, this paper presents a review of studies that provide a comparative analysis of communication mechanisms employed in microservice architectures, focusing on the communication technologies, benchmarking frameworks, and performance evaluation metrics utilized for IPC. The findings indicate that HTTP REST and gRPC are the most frequently evaluated synchronous communication technologies because of their simplicity and compatibility. Besides, Kafka and RabbitMQ, which enhance scalability and fault tolerance, are identified as the most widely assessed asynchronous communication technologies. In addition, Apache JMeter is determined as the most popular benchmarking framework to conduct comparative performance evaluations. Finally, the most commonly employed performance evaluation metrics are detected as throughput and latency.

Keywords: Microservice Architecture · Inter-process Communication · Inter-service Communication · Benchmark Framework · Performance Evaluation Metrics

O. Gervasi et al. (Eds.): ICCSA 2025, LNCS 15650, pp. 98–113, 2025.
https://doi.org/10.1007/978-3-031-96962-1_7

1   Introduction

Microservice architectures have received significant attention in recent years, as a result of the need for improved agility, scalability, and fault tolerance in modern software systems. As organizations transition from monolithic to microservice-based architectures, the selection of appropriate inter-process communication (IPC) mechanisms has emerged as a critical factor influencing system performance and reliability [1].

Microservice communication mechanisms can be categorized as synchronous and asynchronous communication technologies, with HTTP REST, HTTP/2, gRPC, and GraphQL being examples of synchronous blocking communication technologies, whereas Kafka, RabbitMQ, MQTT, AMQP, NATS Streaming, RocketMQ, Apache Pulsar, Redis, ActiveMQ, ActiveMQ Artemis and Web-Socket representing asynchronous non-blocking communication technologies [2].

The choice between synchronous and asynchronous communication mechanisms is crucial to increase system performance and enhance scalability and reliability [1]. Synchronous communication, exemplified by HTTP REST and gRPC, is widely adopted for its simplicity and compatibility, but may introduce inefficiencies in high-load scenarios [30]. Asynchronous communication, facilitated by message brokers like RabbitMQ and Kafka, supports decoupled, event-driven interactions, enhancing throughput and fault tolerance [31].

Apache JMeter [3] and the OpenMessaging Benchmark Framework [4], are utilized as benchmarking frameworks to evaluate IPC technologies by using various performance evaluation metrics. Throughput, latency, response time, availability, and scalability, are the most frequently assessed performance evaluation metrics to analyze efficiency and reliability of IPC technologies ([25, 26, 29]).

This paper aims to explore the communication technologies, benchmarking frameworks, and performance evaluation metrics utilized for IPC to provide a structured understanding of the studies presenting a comparative performance evaluation to optimize communication in microservice architecture. Hence, the research questions (RQs) of this study can be stated as given below:

- **RQ1.** Which technologies are utilized for inter-process communication in microservice architectures?
- **RQ2.** Which benchmarking frameworks are employed for evaluation of inter-process communication technologies?
- **RQ3.** Which performance evaluation metrics are leveraged for comparison of inter-process communication technologies?

2   Microservice Communication Technologies

Communication technologies can be categorized according to communication and collaboration styles such as syncronous blocking, asyncronous non-blocking, request-response and event-driven communication [2]. There are different technology choices that are used for implementation such as remote procedure call

(SOAP and gRPC), HTTP REST, GraphQL and message brokers. In addition, there are also protocols designed for specific environments (MQTT and AMQP). The most widely used inter-process communication technologies are briefly introduced below.

HTTP REST is a stateless architectural style for designing web services that use standard HTTP methods such as GET, POST, PUT, and DELETE. RESTful APIs are widely adopted due to their simplicity, scalability, and ease of integration with various platforms [5]. However, HTTP REST relies on polling mechanisms for real-time updates, which can introduce inefficiencies in high-frequency communication scenarios [6].

HTTP/2 is a major revision of the HTTP protocol, designed to improve web performance by reducing latency and optimizing resource usage. It introduces features like multiplexing, header compression, and server push, enabling faster and more efficient communication between clients and servers [7]. As HTTP/2 supports backward compatibility with HTTP/1.1 and provides high performance and scalability, it is widely adopted in modern web applications and APIs.

gRPC is an RPC framework developed by Google that uses HTTP/2 for data transfer and Protocol Buffers (protobuf) for interface definition. Because of its high performance and cross-language support, gRPC is widely used in microservices architectures, especially for real-time communication, and low-latency applications. It also supports bidirectional streaming, flow control, and authentication to develop more efficient systems with high interoperability [8].

GraphQL, developed by Facebook, is a query language for APIs that is widely used in modern web and mobile applications with complex data requirements and rapid iterations. HTTP REST relies on fixed endpoints while GraphQL makes it possible for clients to request exactly the data they need to reduce overfetching and underfetching of information [9]. GraphQL enables clients to define the structure of the response to support writing more efficient and flexible queries.

Message Queuing Telemetry Transport (MQTT) protocol is a lightweight messaging standard developed for low-bandwidth and high-latency networks that supports publish/subscribe (pub/sub) model. In the pub/sub model, which increases scalability and resilience, the producers send messages to topics, and consumers process them asynchronously. As it supports pub/sub messaging and provides low level of overhead and high quality of service, MQTT is highly adopted in constrained devices and Internet of Things (IoT) applications [10]. However, MQTT lacks built-in security mechanisms and requires additional layers for encryption and authentication [11].

Advanced Message Queuing Protocol (AMQP) is an open standard that provides reliable and interoperable messaging for message-oriented middleware. While protocols like MQTT focus on lightweight communication, AMQP is designed for robust transactional messaging with high reliability [12]. Due to its support of message queuing, routing, and security, AMQP is widely used in financial services and enterprise messaging systems [13].

Kafka is a distributed event streaming platform that is based on a pub/sub model to provide high-throughput and fault-tolerant data processing [14]. The partitioned architecture of Kafka enables efficient parallel processing as it is ideal for event-driven architectures and real-time analytics [15].

RabbitMQ is a message broker that facilitates reliability by using the AMQP protocol. RabbitMQ is highly adopted in distributed systems and microservices as it supports flexible routing, message durability and acknowledgment mechanisms in an effective way [16].

NATS Streaming is a lightweight and easy to deploy messaging platform developed based on the NATS platform. NATS Streaming is ideal for use cases like event sourcing and real-time data processing as a result of its support of features like message persistence, at-least-once delivery, and durable subscriptions [17]. Therefore, NATS Streaming provides a robust and scalable solution for distributed systems and microservices that require high-performance, fault tolerance, and guaranteed and low-latency message delivery.

RocketMQ is a distributed messaging and streaming platform developed by Alibaba which enables high availability, high throughput, low latency, high scalability, and fault tolerance, and widely used in large-scale, mission-critical applications. Due to its support for pub/sub messaging, message tracing and transactional messaging, it is generally employed in financial transactions, log aggregation, and real-time analytics [18].

Apache Pulsar combines the advantages of traditional messaging systems with the flexibility of streaming platforms to provide features like multi-tenancy, geo-replication, and tiered storage [19]. It is designed as a pub/sub messaging platform that offers low-latency message delivery, high performance, scalability, and durability which makes it useful for real-time analytics, event-driven architectures, and IoT applications.

Redis (Remote Dictionary Server) is an open-source, in-memory data storage technology that supports various data structures such as strings, hashes, lists, and sets. Thus, it is widely employed as a database and cache memory because of its speed and versatility. However, due to its pub/sub messaging capabilities, Redis can also be used as a message broker for lightweight, real-time communication in distributed systems that require high-performance operations with low latency [20].

ActiveMQ is an open-source message broker that implements the Java Message Service (JMS) API and supports message protocols like MQTT and AMQP to provide flexible and reliable communication of distributed systems [21]. ActiveMQ offers features such as message persistence, clustering and failover for developing enterprise applications.

ActiveMQ Artemis is successor of the ActiveMQ message broker and supports message protocols such as MQTT and AMQP. It provides a robust architecture to enable message persistence, clustering, and high availability [22] and offer high-performance, reliability, scalability and flexibility.

WebSocket is a full-duplex communication protocol that enables persistent, low-latency connections between clients and servers. While HTTP REST is a synchronous request-response driven protocol, WebSocket facilitates real-time communication with minimal overhead to develop interactive applications such as online gaming and financial trading [23]. However, WebSocket's persistent connections can increase server resource consumption, requiring careful management in large-scale deployments [24].

3   Related Work

The studies presented in Table 1 offer a comprehensive overview of research focused on the evaluation and optimization of communication protocols in microservice architectures. The studies are listed in ascending order by year, with four studies being conducted in the years 2020 and 2023; and two studies each in 2022 and 2024, reflecting the growing interest in this area. The studies in Table 1 are discussed below based on the IPC technologies used, benchmarking frameworks, and performance evaluation metrics as defined by the research questions.

Table 1. Primary Studies on Evaluation of Microservices Communication Mechanisms

ID	Year	Title	Ref
S1	2020	A study on Modern Messaging Systems- Kafka, RabbitMQ and NATS Streaming	[25]
S2	2020	Low Latency Message Brokers	[26]
S3	2020	Evaluating the Impact of Inter-Process Communication in Microservice Architectures	[27]
S4	2020	A Fair Comparison of Message Queuing Systems	[28]
S5	2022	Evaluating the Inter-Service Communication on Microservice Architecture	[29]
S6	2022	Microservice Communication For IoT-based Systems. Architecture Review and Performance Test	[30]
S7	2023	Benchmarking Message Queues	[31]
S8	2023	Comparative Evaluation of Java Virtual Machine-Based Message Queue Services: A Study on Kafka, Artemis, Pulsar, and RocketMQ	[32]
S9	2023	Optimized Strategy for Inter-Service Communication in Microservices	[33]
S10	2023	Evaluation of microservice communication while decomposing monoliths	[34]
S11	2024	Performance evaluation of microservices communication with REST, GraphQL, and gRPC	[35]
S12	2024	Performance Analysis of RESTFUL Web Services and RABBITMQ for Microservices based Systems on Cloud Environment	[36]

Sharvari and Sowmya Nag [25] compared the performance, features, and use cases of three message brokers which includes Kafka, RabbitMQ, and NATS Streaming. No experimental comparison was made. It was determined that Kafka is well-suited for high-throughput and low-latency applications, such as real-time analytics, due to its distributed commit log and partition-based architecture. RabbitMQ was identified as ideal for complex routing and critical systems requiring message persistence and guaranteed delivery, particularly in IoT scenarios. NATS Streaming was found to be lightweight and capable of rapid message delivery with at-least-once guarantees but exhibited higher latency compared to Kafka and RabbitMQ.

Hegde and Nagaraja [26] evaluated the performance, features, and use cases of three low-latency message brokers that Redis, Kafka, and RabbitMQ. No experimental comparison was made. It was observed that Redis demonstrated the highest throughput and lowest latency due to its in-memory architecture, making it suitable for scenarios prioritizing speed over guaranteed delivery. It was also stated that by providing robust scalability and flexible message delivery guarantees, Kafka is appropriate for big data streaming and real-time analytics. RabbitMQ was identified as offering advanced routing and message persistence, making it reliable for critical applications requiring guaranteed delivery.

Shafabakhsh et al. [27] evaluated the performance efficiency and availability of IPC methods in microservice architectures, comparing HTTP REST, gRPC and RabbitMQ. Through experimental load testing using Apache JMeter, it was highlighted that synchronous methods, particularly gRPC, perform better under low load conditions, demonstrated higher throughput and lower latency. However, under high-load scenarios, RabbitMQ outperforms synchronous methods, offering better throughput, scalability, and system resilience. It was also concluded that the choice of IPC mechanism should align with system requirements: synchronous communication is ideal for immediate response scenarios, while asynchronous communication is better suited for high-load, fault-tolerant systems.

Fu et al. [28] conducted a comparative analysis of five message queueing systems: Kafka, RabbitMQ, RocketMQ, ActiveMQ, and Pulsar, evaluated by a custom benchmarking framework. Kafka excels in high-throughput scenarios like log processing due to batch processing and partition-based storage. RocketMQ, optimized for low latency, is ideal for real-time applications. RabbitMQ supports advanced features like priority and delay queues, making it suitable for multi-functional messaging. ActiveMQ has limited scalability and is best for lightweight applications. Pulsar offers robust scalability and global ordering but incurs network overhead.

Weerasinghe and Perera [29] conducted an experiment in which the performance of HTTP REST, gRPC, and WebSocket technologies was compared in the context of inter-process communication in microservice architectures. Significant improvements were observed in response time, latency and throughput, with gRPC outperforming HTTP REST and WebSocket.

Zakutynskyi and Rabodzey [30] conducted evaluation of various communication protocols within IoT-based microservice systems. The technologies evaluated included HTTP REST, MQTT, AMQP, and gRPC. Performance metrics such as throughput, concurrency, scalability, and connection establishment time were analyzed using Apache JMeter. The study revealed that MQTT and AMQP demonstrated superior performance in high-load scenarios such as HTTP REST and gRPC, exhibited greater efficiency for large file transfers.

Md. Showkat Hossain Chy et al. [31] presented a comparative evaluation of four popular Java Virtual Machine (JVM) based message queue (MQ) services: ActiveMQ Artemis, Kafka, RabbitMQ and Redis. The evaluation is based on performance metrics like CPU utilization, memory usage, garbage collection, latency, and throughput using the OpenMessaging Benchmark Framework. Redis is optimal for low-latency use cases, Kafka for high-throughput scenarios, and ActiveMQ Artemis and RabbitMQ for balanced performance in moderate workloads.

Chy et al. [32] aimed to provide a comprehensive comparative evaluation of four prominent JVM-based MQ services—Kafka, Pulsar, Artemis, and RocketMQ—focusing on performance evaluation metrics such as latency, throughput, CPU utilization, memory usage, and garbage collection efficiency. Using the OpenMessaging Benchmark Framework, the study evaluates these MQ services. Kafka is optimal for high-throughput systems, Artemis excels in low-latency scenarios, and Pulsar offers a balanced approach with moderate resource usage. RocketMQ, while efficient for smaller messages, faces challenges with larger payloads.

Weerasinghe and Perera [33] proposed a solution to reduce the inter-process communication latency in microservices by using an asynchronous communication pattern with the Redis Stream data structure. Apache JMeter was used to benchmark the performance of the Redis-based solution against HTTP REST. Experimental results show that Redis outperforms HTTP REST in terms of response time and throughput.

Kazanavičius and Mažeika [34] conducted a comprehensive evaluation of communication technologies, focusing on the transition from monolithic architectures to cloud-native, microservices-based systems. Five communication technologies were compared: HTTP REST, RabbitMQ, Kafka, gRPC, and GraphQL, analyzing their performance, scalability, and suitability. The experimental setup was designed with microservices implemented in C#, and performance metrics such as latency, throughput, and memory consumption were evaluated. Different topologies, including linear, tree, and star, were also examined to understand how communication technologies perform in diverse architectural setups. The results revealed that the lowest latency for small messages was achieved by RabbitMQ, which was identified as being ideal for high-throughput, low-latency scenarios. GraphQL was recognized as flexible and efficient for querying structured data, but it was observed to incur higher CPU usage and was identified as being best suited for star topologies, where a central service functions as a query engine. Kafka, though effective for event-driven architectures, struggled with high-throughput scenarios. HTTP REST was acknowledged for its simplicity and widespread adoption, but limitations in throughput were observed under heavy loads. It was identified that gRPC is considered superior for low-latency and high-throughput applications.

Niswar et al. [35] conducted a comparative performance analysis of HTTP REST, GraphQL, and gRPC within a microservices architecture. Given the critical importance of selecting the appropriate communication protocol for optimal system performance in microservices, two distinct data retrieval methods, flat data fetching and nested data fetching, were focused on. Through experiments using Redis and MySQL databases, it was found that gRPC exhibited the fastest response times, while HTTP REST demonstrated the lowest CPU utilization. gRPC's utilization of HTTP/2, with its multiplexing feature allowing multiple requests over a single connection, makes it highly efficient for concurrent remote procedure calls. The simplicity and low resource consumption of HTTP REST are considered to offer distinct advantages. GraphQL, despite its flexibility, is less suitable for high-concurrency environments due to its higher CPU demands and slower response times.

Bux and Shenoy [36] investigated synchronous and asynchronous inter-process communication in microservices-based systems by comparing RESTful web services and RabbitMQ on Amazon Web Services (AWS) cloud environment. They found significant performance improvements, demonstrating that RabbitMQ outperforms HTTP REST in terms of throughput, average request processing time, and scalability, especially under high concurrent user loads.

4 Findings

The findings for each research questions are discussed below based on the primary studies listed in Table 1.

RQ1. Which technologies are utilized for inter-process communication in microservice architectures?

The communication technologies used in the primary studies listed in Table 1 are systematically summarized in Table 2. When the number of communication technologies compared in the primary studies was analyzed, [28,30,34] were the studies that evaluated the highest number of different technologies, with five technologies analyzed in each study. In these three studies, no common technologies were observed; however, HTTP REST and gRPC were evaluated in [30,34], whereas Kafka and RabbitMQ were examined in [28,34]. Furthermore, the performance of four technologies was compared in [31,32], with Kafka and ActiveMQ Artemis being the common technologies in both studies. Besides, three different technologies were evaluated in [25–27,29,35], while [32,36] compared the performance of two different technologies.

Figure 1 illustrated the frequency of IPC technologies compared in the primary studies based on Table 2, with a focus on the most widely used technologies

Table 2. Overview of Communication Technologies Utilized in Primary Studies

ID	HTTP REST	HTTP2	gRPC	Graph QL	MQTT	AMQP	Kafka	Rabbit MQ	NATS Stream-ing	Rocket MQ	Pulsar	Redis	Active MQ	Active MQ Artemis	Web Socket
S1							✓	✓	✓						
S2							✓	✓				✓			
S3	✓		✓					✓							
S4							✓	✓		✓	✓		✓		
S5	✓		✓												✓
S6	✓	✓	✓		✓	✓									
S7							✓	✓				✓		✓	
S8							✓			✓	✓			✓	
S9	✓											✓			
S10	✓		✓	✓			✓	✓							
S11	✓		✓	✓											
S12	✓							✓							

and listing the technologies utilized in three or more studies. RabbitMQ ([25–28,31,34,36]) and HTTP REST ([27,29,30,33–36]) were the technologies most frequently evaluated in primary studies, with seven different studies examining each technology, whereas three studies ([27,34,36]) utilized both technologies. Moreover, Kafka is also a widely used technology, with its performance being evaluated in six studies ([25,26,28,31,32,34]). Besides, gRPC is used in five studies ([27,29,30,34,35]), followed by Redis with three studies ([26,31,33]).

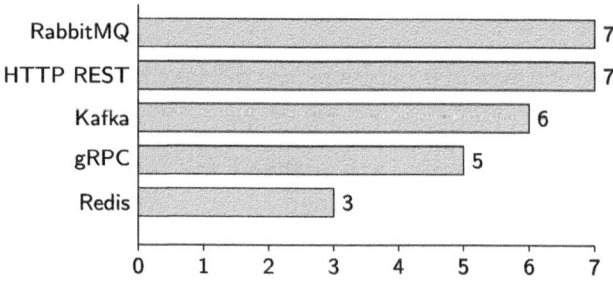

Fig. 1. Usage Statistics of Communication Technologies

As emerging technologies not listed in Fig. 1 for simplicity purposes, the performances of ActiveMQ Artemis ([31] [32]), RocketMQ ([28] [32]), Apache Pulsar ([28] [32]) and GraphQL ([34] [35]) were examined in two studies each. In addition, technologies such as HTTP/2 [30], NATS Streaming [25], ActiveMQ [28], WebSocket [29], and protocols like MQTT [30] and AMQP [30], were each investigated in one study.

RQ2. Which benchmarking frameworks are employed for evaluation of inter-process communication technologies?

Table 3. Benchmark Frameworks and Evaulation Metrics utilized in Primary Studies

ID	Benchmark Framework	Performance Evaulation Metrics
S1	No Benchmark	Message Delivery Guarantee, Message Persistence, Message Ordering, Latency, Throughput, Availability, Scalability
S2	No Benchmark	Message Delivery Guarantee, Message Persistence, Message Ordering, Latency, Throughput, Availability, Scalability
S3	Apache JMeter	Throughput, Availability
S4	Custom B. Tool	Latency, Throughput
S5	Apache JMeter	Response Time, Throughput, Latency, Payload Size Effect
S6	Custom B. Tool	Init connection time, Messages / Requests per second, Time to send 1M messages/requests, Throughput, Data transferring performance
S7	OpenMessaging B.F.	Latency, Throughput
S8	OpenMessaging B.F.	Latency, Throughput, CPU Utilization, Memory Usage, Garbage Collection
S9	Apache JMeter	Transaction Per Second (TPS), Response Time, Turnaround Time
S10	Custom B. Tool	Latency, Throughput, Request / Response Size, Microservice Application Size, Memory Usage Size, Boot Time, Architecture, Topology Libraries
S11	Apache JMeter	Response Time, CPU Utilization
S12	Apache JMeter	Total Number Of Request Processed, Throughput, Average Request Processing Time

The benchmarking frameworks utilized for evaluation of IPC technologies in primary studies listed in Table 1 are presented in Table 3 with the performance evaluation metrics used in each study, which will be discussed for RQ3. Figure 2 illustrated the frequency of the benchmarking frameworks used for comparison of IPC technologies based on Table 3. Apache JMeter is observed as the most widely used benchmarking framework, with a usage count of five ([27,29,33,35,36]), reflecting its popularity for performance testing in IPC evaluations. As the second popular approach, three studies([28,30,34]) developed their own custom benchmarking tool. The OpenMessaging Benchmark Framework is utilized in two studies ([31,32]), highlighting its role in standardized performance evaluations of messaging systems. Furthermore, two studies ([25,26]) conducted theoretical comparisons without using any benchmarking tools.

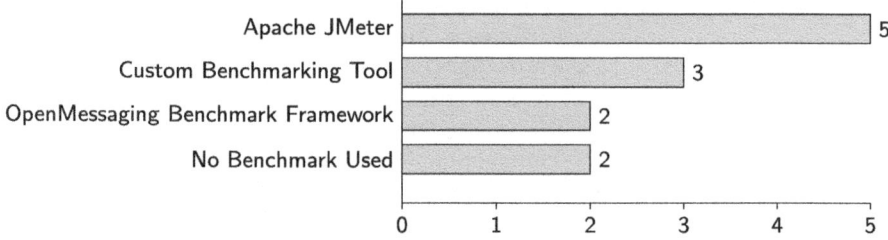

Fig. 2. Usage Statistics of Benchmarking Frameworks

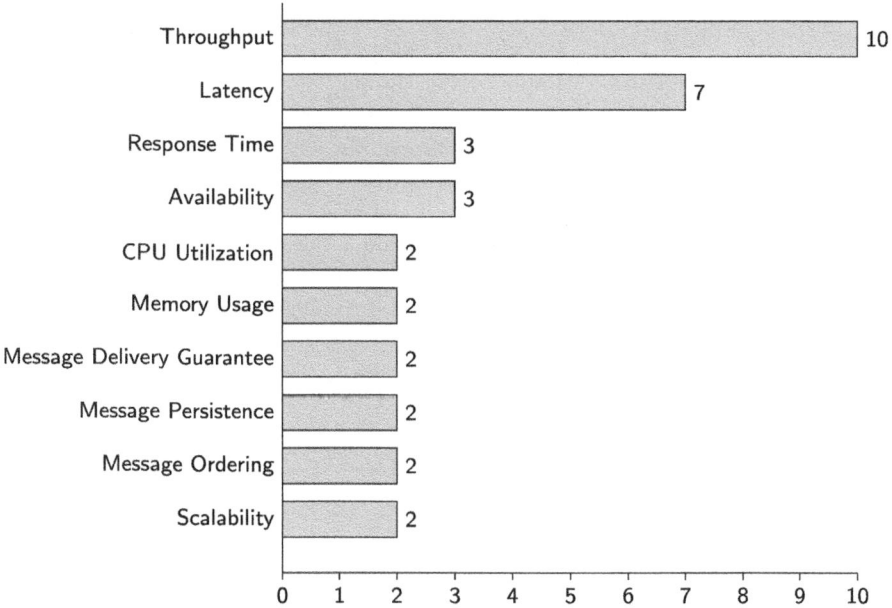

Fig. 3. Evaluation Metric-wise Distribution of Primary Studies.

Developing a custom benchmarking tool is a challenging task that requires a lot of effort; however, a new tool may need to be developed based on some specific requirements affecting the evaluation. A new custom benchmarking tool is developed by [28], because the evaluation parameters of ready-to-use tools can be set differently for each tool, so the parameters cannot be arbitrarily set as needed. On the other hand, each tool supports testing different number of metrics and measures them in different ways, thus new custom benchmarking tools utilizing new metrics were proposed by [30,34].

RQ3. Which performance evaluation metrics are leveraged for comparison of inter-process communication technologies?

The performance evaluation metrics used for comparing performance of IPC technologies in primary studies listed in Table 1 were presented in Table 3. To increase understandability, Table 4 presents a detailed representation of the metrics utilized by each primary study. Furthermore, Fig. 3 illustrated the frequency of the metrics used for comparison of IPC technologies.

Table 4. Overview of Performance Evaluation Metrics Utilized in Primary Studies

ID	Msg. Del.	Msg. Per.	Msg. Ord.	Latency	Through-put	Avail.	Scale.	Resp. Time	CPU Util.	Mem. Usage	Other Metrics
S1	✓	✓	✓	✓	✓	✓	✓				
S2	✓	✓	✓	✓	✓	✓	✓				
S3					✓	✓					
S4				✓	✓						
S5				✓	✓			✓			Payload Size Effect
S6					✓						Init, Msg/s, 1M Msg, Data
S7				✓	✓						
S8				✓	✓				✓	✓	Garbage Col.
S9								✓			TPS, Turn. Time
S10				✓	✓					✓	Req/Res, App Size, Boot, Arch, Topo
S11								✓	✓		
S12					✓						Req. Count, Avg. Time

Throughput is identified as the most frequently evaluated metric, appearing in ten studies ([25–32, 34, 36]), followed by latency, which is evaluated in seven studies ([25, 26, 28, 29, 31, 32, 34]). Besides, response time ([29, 33, 35]) and availability ([25–27]) were each utilized by three studies. Six metrics were used by two studies each, with four of them (Message Delivery Guarantee, Message Persistence, Message Ordering and Scalability) being used by the same non-experimental studies ([25, 26]). The other two metrics utilized in two studies are CPU utilization ([32, 35]) and Memory Usage ([32, 34]).

In addition, there are evaluation metrics used by only a single study, including Payload Size Effect [29], Init Connection Time [30], Messages/Request Per Second [30], Time to Send 1M Messages/Requests [30], Data Transferring Performance [30], Garbage Collection [32], Transaction Per Second (TPS) [33], Turnaround Time [33], Request/Response size [34], Microservice Application Size [34], Boot Time [34], Architecture [34], Topology [34], Total Number Of Request Processed [36], Average Request Processing Time [36].

5   Discussion and Conclusion

In this paper, a detailed analysis of comparative studies employing various communication technologies, benchmarking frameworks, and performance evaluation metrics to evaluate IPC technologies is provided. The findings are presented based on the utilized communication technologies, the benchmarking frameworks and the performance evaluation metrics, with each of them being investigated by a corresponding research question.

As the most dominant category among the primary studies represented in Table 1, [27, 29, 30, 33, 34, 36] explore the impact of inter-process communication in microservices in a broader way by comparing performances of synchronous and asynchronous communication technologies. As another dominant category, [25, 26, 28, 31, 32] focus on performance evaluation of modern message brokers like Kafka, RabbitMQ, while [35] is the only study conducting experiments with only synchronous communication technologies. In addition, some of these studies focused on evaluating the performance of communication protocols with specific deployment purposes such as IoT [30] and cloud environments [36].

The studies in Table 1 can be categorized into three according to the case studies employed; [25, 26] did not perform any experiments, [27–30] performed hypothetical experiments, and [31–35], and [36] conducted experiments in real-world scenarios.

HTTP REST, Kafka and RabbitMQ emerge as the most frequently studied technologies, HTTP REST is widely used due to its simplicity and compatibility features [30], while Kafka excels in high-throughput scenarios [31] and RabbitMQ performs well in environments requiring complex routing and fault tolerance [27]. The findings indicate that synchronous methods like HTTP REST and gRPC are ideal for low-load, immediate-response scenarios [30], while asynchronous methods such as RabbitMQ and Kafka are better suited for high-load, fault-tolerant systems [31].

Among benchmarking frameworks, Apache JMeter is pivotal for evaluating IPC performance, as it is the most frequently employed one ([27, 29, 33, 35, 36]). Besides, some custom benchmarking tools have been developed ([28, 30, 34]) based on specific requirements, and the OpenMessaging Benchmark Framework is also utilized in some studies ([31,32]).

Performance evaluation metrics, including throughput, latency, response time, CPU utilization, availability, memory usage, message delivery guarantee, message persistence, message ordering, and scalability, are frequently assessed to compare the efficiency of communication methods ([25,26,29]). Among these metrics, throughput and latency are the most commonly employed ones as illustrated in Fig. 3.

Future research could focus on hybrid communication architectures that combine synchronous and asynchronous methods, leveraging their respective strengths to address specific system requirements. Another promising avenue involves integrating machine learning techniques to dynamically optimize communication frameworks based on workload patterns, enhancing adaptability and performance. Finally, expanding the scope of case studies to include edge computing and 5G-enabled IoT environments could provide valuable insights into the scalability and reliability of IPC mechanisms in next-generation systems.

References

1. Karabey Aksakalli, I., Çelik, T., Can, A.B., Tekinerdogan, B.: Deployment and communication patterns in microservice architectures: a systematic literature review. J. Syst. Softw. **180**, 111014 (2021). https://doi.org/10.1016/j.jss.2021.111014
2. Newman, S.: (2021). Building Microservices: Designing fine-grained systems (2nd ed.). O'Reilly Media. ISBN 9781492034025
3. Apache Software Foundation (2025). Apache JMeter. Retrieved from https://jmeter.apache.org/
4. OpenMessaging Project (2025). OpenMessaging Benchmark Framework. Retrieved from https://openmessaging.cloud/benchmark/
5. Fielding, R.T.: Architectural styles and the design of network-based software architectures (Doctoral dissertation, University of California, Irvine) (2000)
6. Richardson, L., Amundsen, M.: RESTful Web APIs. O'Reilly Media (2013)
7. IETF. (2015). HTTP/2: Hypertext Transfer Protocol Version 2. RFC 7540. Retrieved from https://httpwg.org/specs/rfc7540.html
8. Google (2023). gRPC: A high-performance, open-source universal RPC framework. Retrieved from https://grpc.io
9. GraphQL Foundation (2023). GraphQL: A query language for your API. Retrieved from https://graphql.org/
10. Banks, A., Gupta, R.: MQTT version 3.1.1. OASIS Standard (2014)
11. Singh, K., Kim, T.: Security analysis of MQTT protocol in IoT applications. IEEE Internet Things J. **5**(6), 4680–4690 (2018)
12. Vinoski, S.: Advanced message queuing protocol. IEEE Internet Comput. **10**(6), 87–89 (2006)
13. Dobbelaere, P., Esmaili, K.: Kafka versus RabbitMQ: a comparative study of two distributed messaging frameworks. In: Proceedings of the International Conference on Cloud Engineering, pp. 35–42 (2017)
14. Kreps, J., Narkhede, N., Rao, J.: Kafka: a distributed messaging system for log processing. Proc. NetDB **11**(1), 1–7 (2011)

15. Narkhede, N., Shapira, G., Palino, T.: Kafka: The definitive guide. O'Reilly Media (2017)
16. Videla, A., Williams, J.: RabbitMQ in action. Manning Publications (2012)
17. NATS.io. NATS Streaming: A high-performance messaging system (2023). Retrieved from https://nats.io
18. Apache RocketMQ (2023). RocketMQ: Distributed messaging and streaming platform. Retrieved from https://rocketmq.apache.org/
19. Apache Pulsar (2023). Apache Pulsar: Distributed pub/sub messaging system. Retrieved from https://pulsar.apache.org/
20. Redis Labs (2023). Redis: The open-source, in-memory data store. Retrieved from https://redis.io
21. Apache ActiveMQ (2023). ActiveMQ: Open-source message broker. Retrieved from https://activemq.apache.org/
22. Apache ActiveMQ Artemis (2023). ActiveMQ Artemis: High-performance messaging broker. Retrieved from https://activemq.apache.org/components/artemis/
23. Fette, I., Melnikov, A.: The WebSocket Protocol. RFC 6455. Retrieved from https://www.rfc-editor.org/rfc/rfc6455 (2011)
24. Lubbers, P., Albers, B.: Pro HTML5 Programming: Powerful APIs for Richer Internet Application Development. Apress (2010). Retrieved from https://link.springer.com/book/10.1007/978-1-4302-2791-5
25. Sharvari, T., Sowmya Nag, K.: A study on modern messaging systems: Kafka, RabbitMQ, and NATS Streaming. J. Distrib. Syst. **15**(3), 123–145 (2020). https://doi.org/10.48550/arXiv.1912.03715
26. Hegde, R.G., Nagaraja, G.S.: Low latency message brokers. Int. Res. J. Eng. Technol. (IRJET), **7**(5), 2731–2738 (2020). https://www.irjet.net/archives/V7/i5/IRJET-V7I5523.pdf
27. Shafabakhsh, B., Lagerström, R., Hacks, S.: Evaluating the impact of inter-process communication in microservice architectures. In: 8th International Workshop on Quantitative Approaches to Software Quality (QuASoQ 2020). CEUR Workshop Proceedings (2020). http://ceur-ws.org/ISSN/1613-0073
28. Fu, G., Zhang, Y., Yu, G.: A fair comparison of message queuing systems. IEEE Access **8**, 220081–220093 (2020). https://doi.org/10.1109/ACCESS.2020.3046503
29. Weerasinghe, L.D.S.B., Perera, I.: Evaluating the inter-service communication on microservice architecture. In: 2022 IEEE International Conference on Innovations in Technology (INOCON), (pp. 1–6). IEEE (2022). https://doi.org/10.1109/INOCON60754.2024.10511747
30. Zakutynskyi, I.V., Rabodzey, I.E.: Performance characteristics of communication protocols in IoT-based microservice systems. Telecommun. Radio Eng. **4**(74), 73–78 (2022). https://doi.org/10.18372/1990-5548.74.17311
31. Maharjan, R., Chy, M.S.H., Arju, M.A., Cerny, T.: Benchmarking message queues. Telecom. **4**(2), 298–312 (2023). https://doi.org/10.3390/telecom4020018
32. Chy, M.S.H., Arju, M.A.R., Tella, S.M., Cerny, T.: Comparative evaluation of java virtual machine-based message queue services: a study on Kafka, Artemis, Pulsar, and RocketMQ. 1 Electronics **12**(23), 4792 (2023). https://doi.org/10.3390/electronics12234792
33. Weerasinghe, S., Perera, I.: Optimized strategy for inter-service communication in microservices. Int. J. Adv. Comput. Sci. Appl. **14** (2023). https://doi.org/10.14569/IJACSA.2023.0140233
34. Kazanavičius, J., Mažeika, D.: Evaluation of microservice communication while decomposing monoliths. Comput. Inform. **42**(1), 1–36 (2023). @split

35. Niswar, M., Safruddin, R.A., Bustamin, A., Aswad, I.: Performance evaluation of microservices communication with REST, GraphQL, and gRPC. Int. J. Electron. Telecommun. **70**(2), 429–436 (2024)
36. Bux, R., Shenoy, G.S.: Performance analysis of RESTful web services and RabbitMQ for microservices-based systems on cloud environment. In: 2024 3rd International Conference on Innovations in Technology (INOCON), (pp. 1–6). IEEE (2024). https://doi.org/10.1109/INOCON60754.2024.10511747

A Review on Computer Vision-Based Object and Safe Navigation Zone Identification for Autonomous Vehicles and Advanced Driver Assistance Systems (ADAS)

Vitor Augusto da Rosa Pereira[1]([⊠])(ID), Rafael Alceste Berri[2](ID),
and Fernando Santos Osório[1](ID)

[1] University of São Paulo, São Carlos, São Paulo 13566-590, Brazil
{vitor.arp,fosorio}@usp.br
[2] Federal University of Rio Grande, Rio Grande, Rio Grande do Sul 96203-900, Brazil
rafaelberri@furg.br

Abstract. Road safety is a global challenge, with most traffic accidents being attributed to human errors and recklessness, such as distractions and bad decision-making. ADAS play a crucial role in reducing traffic accidents caused by these mistakes, improving road safety. Computer Vision and Artificial Intelligence are essential for perception in mobile robots and autonomous vehicles, enabling them to analyze and interpret their surroundings. This paper presents a systematic review of Computer Vision and Artificial Intelligence techniques for object detection and safe navigation zone identification in Autonomous Vehicles and ADAS. The analysis compares the selected state-of-the-art works, highlighting their methods, accuracy, strengths, and limitations. In addition, the review compares multiple benchmark datasets employed across the studies, analyzing their characteristics and application scope in perception tasks. The results show advancements and considerable accuracy in object detection and safe navigation zone identification using semantic segmentation and bounding box methods, together with monocular depth estimation and multitask models that increase 3D perception and efficiency. Some approaches are able to run on embedded devices and achieve considerable FPS rate, allowing soft real-time performance. However, challenges like high computational costs and adverse weather conditions remain, showing that sensor fusion along with future research is necessary to improve robustness.

Keywords: Traffic objects · Safe navigation zone · Computer vision · Artificial intelligence · Autonomous vehicles · ADAS

1 Introduction

Driving, although a routine activity, carries several risks that can result in serious and even fatal accidents. A study conducted in the United States, using data

O. Gervasi et al. (Eds.): ICCSA 2025, LNCS 15650, pp. 114–131, 2025.
https://doi.org/10.1007/978-3-031-96962-1_8

from the period between 2005 and 2007 by the National Motor Vehicle Crash Causation Survey (NMVCCS), aimed to identify the main factors causing traffic accidents. Approximately 94% of accidents were attributed to human errors, including distractions, poor decision-making, and physiological factors such as drowsiness [29].

In this context, Autonomous Vehicles (AVs) and Advanced Driver Assistance Systems (ADAS) play a crucial role and have great potential in reducing traffic accidents, which are mainly caused by human errors, thus aiming to improve road safety [1]. Over the years, these systems have evolved significantly, driven by the continuous advancement of the technologies that compose them [32]. Moreover, their development has also driven the need for robust techniques to perceive and interpret the environment around the vehicle. Object detection and safe navigation zone identification are key for the safety of autonomous and assisted driving systems.

In mobile robots and AVs, Computer Vision and Artificial Intelligence are fundamental for robot perception, enabling them to analyze images and videos to interpret information about the objects on their surroundings [30]. This capability is directly linked to scene understanding, which involves identifying, locating, and describing elements in the environment, as well as their characteristics and dynamics. Research on new techniques has grown exponentially over the past decade due to its potential impact on various applications. Advances in Deep Learning, the availability of open-source datasets, and the increasing capacity of computational resources have driven the rapid evolution of scene understanding techniques [11].

The objective of this research is to review and analyze state-of-the-art Computer Vision and Artificial Intelligence techniques, mainly focused on RGB cameras for object detection and safe navigation zone identification in Autonomous Vehicles and ADAS.

In the planning phase of the systematic literature review [25], two research questions were defined:

1. Which Artificial Intelligence and Computer Vision techniques have been investigated for developing ADAS and autonomous vehicle systems focused on object and navigable area detection?
2. What types of objects are detected (e.g., vehicles, pedestrians)? Which sensors are utilized? What techniques are employed to complement detection? What actions do the proposed systems take? What limitations do the studies identify?

The literature searches were conducted using IEEE Xplore[1], Scopus[2], and Google Scholar[3], through the keywords "Traffic Object Detection", "Road Obstacle Detection", "Drivable Area Detection", "Computer Vision", "Artificial Intelligence", "ADAS", and "Autonomous Vehicles".

---

[1] Access the IEEE Xplore website at https://ieeexplore.ieee.org/Xplore/home.jsp.

[2] Access the Scopus website at https://www.scopus.com/home.uri.

[3] Access the Google Scholar website at https://scholar.google.com/.

The papers were first filtered by language, including only those written in English, and by publication year, considering only studies published since 2019. The articles were then selected based on predefined inclusion and exclusion criteria. To be included, a study had to be a primary research article focused on computer vision applications for object and navigation zone detection in vehicles. Exclusion criteria consisted of duplicate studies, studies not utilizing computer vision methods, research not involving land vehicles, extended abstracts, and articles that did not address the use of computer vision for traffic object detection in vehicles, as these were considered out of scope.

An initial set of 516 articles was identified and evaluated according to the defined criteria. Articles were first selected by title, limiting the set to 255. Next, abstracts were reviewed, reducing the number to 153 studies. Subsequently, the introductions and conclusions were read, reducing the selection to 55 articles. The full texts of these articles were then reviewed, leading to 19 studies being selected for inclusion in the review. Parsifal[4] was used to organize, select, and analyze studies in the systematic literature review.

This paper is organized as follows. Section 2 provides an overview of the state-of-the-art techniques in object detection and safe navigation zone identification using computer vision. Section 3 discusses the methods and techniques utilized in the reviewed studies. Finally, Sect. 4 summarizes the conclusions and future works from this research.

2   Object and Safe Navigation Zone Detection

This section presents studies from the past six years, identified through a systematic literature review.

2.1   Unknown Obstacle Detection

The detection of unknown obstacles and anomalies (Fig. 1) refers to the identification of objects on the track that are outside the training set of classification networks, also known as out-of-distribution (OoD) objects.

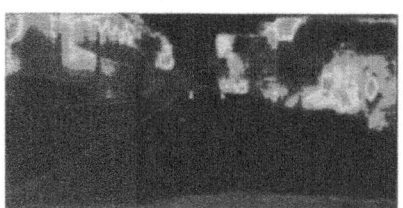 

Fig. 1. Unknown/anomalous obstacle detection [7].

---

[4] Avaliable at https://parsif.al/.

Ohgushi, Horiguchi, and Yamanaka [21] propose a method to detect unknown or complex objects (such as debris, boxes, tires, among others) that are not present in the training set. To achieve this, the authors use two datasets: the Lost and Found Dataset and their own dataset, the Highway Anomaly Dataset. The Lost and Found Dataset is designed for anomaly detection in urban scenarios, containing street images with unexpected objects such as cones and small obstacles. Its labels include pixel-wise segmentation masks for anomalous objects and semantic annotations inherited from the Cityscapes Dataset, covering categories such as "road" and "vehicle". On the other hand, the Highway Anomaly Dataset focuses on videos and images of highways with atypical events, such as stopped vehicles, pedestrians, or animals on the road. The labels are mostly binary ("normal" or "anomalous"), with some being categorized by type of anomaly, including annotations in bounding boxes or timestamps for precise localization of events. The authors use an unsupervised semantic segmentation technique through the ICNet network. Based on the semantic map generated by the network, entropy and perceptual loss are calculated, which, when combined, result in an anomaly map. The approach achieved an accuracy of 0.96 AUC-ROC on the Lost and Found Dataset and an F-measure of 0.452 on the Highway Anomaly Dataset.

In the work of Ci et al. [7], the detection of anomalous objects is performed using RGB images from two datasets: the Lost and Found Dataset and Road-Obstacle21. The latter is a dataset focused on images of segmented obstacles, with the road defined as the region of interest. The method combines various techniques, such as semantic segmentation, image resynthesis, monocular depth estimation, and dissimilarity networks, to detect anomalies and unknown obstacles. Anomaly detection achieved an average precision (AP) of 80.04% on the Lost and Found Dataset, with a false positive rate (FPR) of 5.31%. On the RoadObstacle21 dataset, the precision was 70.93%, with an FPR of 4.16%.

The approach proposed by Shoeb et al. [27] presents a modular method for the detection, tracking, and text-based retrieval of out-of-distribution (OoD) objects in videos of road scenarios. The system uses Mask2Former, trained on the Cityscapes dataset, to perform semantic segmentation. Objects are tracked across consecutive frames based on IoU and geometric centers. Additionally, the CLIP model enables textual queries, such as "dog", to retrieve relevant sequences. Tested on three distinct datasets—SOS (Street Obstacle Sequences), WOS (Wuppertal Obstacle Sequences), and CWL (Carla-WildLife)—the method achieved an AUPRC (Area Under the Precision-Recall Curve) above 75% in test cases, reaching 81% on the SOS dataset. Furthermore, the false positive rate (FPR95) was reduced to less than 1%, demonstrating the feasibility of detecting out-of-distribution objects.

In the study conducted by Vojir et al. [36], the JSR-Net was proposed, a network that combines partial image reconstruction and semantic segmentation for anomaly and unknown obstacle detection on roads. The model achieved an AP of 94.4% on the Road Anomaly dataset, as well as 79.4% on Lost and Found, 84.0% on Road Obstacles, and 85.5% on FishyScapes. Additionally, it recorded the lowest false positive rate (FPR95 = 4.4% on average). The approach enables the detection of out-of-distribution objects without requiring a complete retraining process, enhancing generalization. Nonetheless, the solution faces challenges in detecting fine structures and image artifacts.

2.2 Traffic Object Detection

The detection of elements in traffic scenarios, as illustrated in Figs. 2 and 3, consists of identifying and locating key objects for autonomous driving, such as vehicles, pedestrians, road signs, navigable zones, and obstacles.

Fig. 2. Lane segmentation and vehicle detection [14].

Fig. 3. (a) Instance segmentation for vehicle detection, (b) Lane segmentation and closest object detection [20], (c) Segmentation and width estimation of unmarked roads [22].

In an article by Ljepić et al. [18], a low-cost algorithm was proposed for obstacle detection on the roadway and automatic speed adjustment using only

RGB cameras. The method combines traditional computer vision algorithms, such as Canny and RANSAC, with simulations conducted in Carla. In tests with 152 images, the misclassification rate of vehicles as pedestrians was 6.58%, while the error rate in pedestrian detection was 5.26%. Speed adjustment showed limitations, with successful stops only at 10 km/h due to the low frame processing rate.

Ezzat et al. [10] present a forward collision warning system that combines computer vision and ultrasonic sensors. The method uses YOLOv3 Tiny for real-time vehicle detection, estimating depth through multivariate regression based on the area of bounding boxes and assigning vehicles to specific road lanes using a geometric analysis of the lower corners of the boxes. This technique divides the road into sections (right, left, and emergency). The system achieved 93% accuracy in vehicle detection and 80% in depth estimation, with a performance of up to 23 FPS on the NVIDIA Jetson TX2. Ultrasonic sensors complemented the detection in blind spots, dividing them into safe, warning, and critical zones.

The study by Shyam, Yoon, and Kim [28] presents a weakly supervised approach for object detection and lane marking recognition. The method uses pre-trained networks on the NuScenes and BDD100K datasets to generate pseudo labels for obstacles, integrating this data with lane detection datasets (CULanes, TUSimple, and CurveLanes) for training multi-task models. Two architectures were proposed: one based on CNNs and the other on Transformers. The CNN-based approach uses pixel classification to detect and group lane lines while employing an object detector, both sharing the same encoding backbone. Meanwhile, the Transformer-based approach uses dual decoders, one estimating object bounding boxes and the other calculating polynomial coefficients for lane lines. The Transformer-based approach achieved overall better performance, with an mAP of 81.2% for object detection and an IoU of 87.1% for lane segmentation, whereas the CNN-based approach achieved an mAP of 78.5% and an IoU of 85.4%. Computational efficiency was also analyzed, highlighting the advantage of the CNN architecture, which consumed 112 GFLOPs, compared to the Transformer-based architecture, which consumed 135 GFLOPs.

Usman et al. [35] propose combining instance segmentation and semantic segmentation techniques to improve object detection in autonomous vehicles and create a robust representation of the vehicle's surroundings. The approach integrates the Xception semantic segmentation model, trained on the ADE20K dataset, with the Mask R-CNN model, trained on the COCO dataset, for instance segmentation. The object classification network achieved 92% accuracy and a processing speed of 30 frames per second.

Chen [6] developed a multi-task model based on YOLOv5, integrating object detection and road segmentation. The network utilizes a multi-task branch, with one instance for classification using bounding boxes and another instance for semantic segmentation through a UNet decoder. Training utilized weighted loss strategies (cross-entropy loss) to balance the detection and segmentation tasks. The model achieved 98.5% mean average precision (mAP) for classification, 65.96% mean intersection over union (mIoU) for segmentation, operating at a rate of 57 FPS.

In the article by Thombre et al. [33], two methods were proposed to estimate the distance of vehicles and obstacles using a monocular camera, aiming to develop solutions for ADAS. The first method, based on the camera's optical principles, uses parameters such as focal length and the width of object bounding boxes to estimate depth. The second method, Depth Anything, employs deep learning to generate depth maps, and it was integrated into a regression model to enhance the results, using data from a LiDAR sensor as ground truth. The models Focal Length, Depth Anything (raw), and Depth Anything (with regression) were compared. The Depth Anything with regression method achieved the best performance, obtaining an RMSE of 1.542, while the Depth Anything (raw) and Focal Length methods obtained RMSE values of 2.857 and 2.947, respectively.

The work by Kenk et al. [12] aims to investigate the limitations of deep learning models based on the YOLO architecture in detecting road lanes and objects under adverse conditions (such as sharp curves, dense fog, sandstorms, heavy rain, and snowfall), seeking to provide guidance for developing more robust solutions. The YOLO algorithm was adapted for real-time lane segmentation and vehicle detection using an approach that divides the image into grids with fixed anchors to predict lane positions. The solution was evaluated using the DAWN dataset, which contains images and traffic data under various weather conditions. The study found that lane detection performance was impaired in sharp curves due to the difficulty of representing curved lanes with bounding boxes. In heavy rain conditions, reflections and distortions on the asphalt caused false positives. The evaluation metrics for detection included mean Average Precision (mAP), Recall, Precision, and False Positive Rate (FPR). Under challenging conditions, such as a rainy scenario, the method achieved 26.06% Precision, 31.38% Recall, 26.06% detection rate, and an FPR of 68.61%.

The method by Megalingam et al. [20] performs dynamic lane segmentation for autonomous vehicles by combining the Hough transform, FCN-8, and R-CNN. The Hough transform detects lanes in straight road segments, while FCN-8 segments the drivable area. R-CNN performs instance segmentation, identifying and locating obstacles in the scene. The model achieved 97% accuracy in lane segmentation, even on curves and under low lighting conditions, and 94% accuracy in detecting small or partially occluded obstacles. Distance estimates were derived from the area of bounding boxes, while vehicle speed adjustments were determined based on the computed distances. Despite the results, limitations were noted in scenarios with low visibility.

In the proposal by Bruno and Osório [3], a pedestrian detection and tracking system for autonomous vehicles and ADAS was developed, combining YOLOv7-DeepSORT and Kalman Filter on embedded hardware (Jetson Nano). After 20,000 training epochs, the model stabilized, achieving 91.85% mAP and 78.2% IoU in detection using bounding boxes. The frame rate during inference ranged between 5 and 10 FPS, allowing real-time operation but with limitations at higher speeds. The approach demonstrated effectiveness in urban scenarios but faces challenges under adverse conditions and in the absence of additional depth sensors.

In the system proposed by Li et al. [14], a multitask model integrating CNNs and Transformers for visual perception in autonomous vehicles simultaneously performs object detection, lane segmentation, and drivable area segmentation. The model was evaluated on the BDD100K dataset and achieved an mAP50 of 84.6% for object detection, an mIoU of 91.6% for drivable area segmentation, and an IoU of 32.3% for lane segmentation, outperforming networks like YOLOP and HybridNets. Additionally, it operated at 50 FPS, enabling real-time inference. However, the model has a higher computational cost due to the CNN-Transformer fusion and requires validation in extreme scenarios such as fog and heavy rain.

In the research by Sousa et al. [31], a Deep Learning-based ADAS system was developed for lane segmentation, object detection, and traffic sign classification, optimized for embedded devices NVIDIA Jetson Nano and TX2 NX. The datasets used included TuSimple and CULane, focused on lane segmentation, as well as a custom dataset created by the authors for traffic sign classification. The lane segmentation model, using U-Net and ResNet18, achieved 66.02% accuracy and an IoU of 0.6363, operating at 17.34 FPS on the Jetson Nano and 30.59 FPS on the TX2 NX. Object detection using TrafficCamNet obtained an IoU of 0.7997 at 640×480 resolution. Overall, the TX2 NX outperformed the Nano, achieving 27 FPS compared to the Nano's 15 FPS, making it a more suitable option for real-time applications. However, factors such as adverse lighting conditions and occlusions impacted the accuracy of the system.

As presented by Schieber et al. [26], a Pyramid Fusion Network was proposed, a multimodal and multi-scale fusion approach for 3D semantic segmentation in autonomous vehicles, combining data from RGB cameras and LiDAR. The architecture incorporates a Pyramid Fusion Backbone for hierarchical feature fusion and a Pyramid Fusion Head for final segmentation refinement. Tested on the SemanticKITTI and PandaSet datasets, the solution achieved an mIoU of 61.9%, outperforming previous methods such as Fusion3DSeg (61.8%) and LaserNet++ (56.2%). Additionally, adopting EfficientPS as the camera backbone increased the mIoU to 67.8%. The proposed method faces challenges such as high computational cost and reliance on sensor overlap. Future optimizations are suggested, including radar data integration to enhance perception in adverse conditions.

According to Tran et al. [34], a modular ADAS system based on a monocular camera and Jetson devices was developed to detect vehicles, pedestrians, traffic signs, and perform lane segmentation in real time. The model utilized Scaled-YOLOv4 for object detection and Ultra-Fast Deep Lane Detection for lane segmentation. Tested on the KATECH Dataset (Korea Automotive Technology Institute), the system achieved an mAP of 84.6%, surpassing previous methods such as YOLOP (76.5%) and DLT-Net (68.4%). Execution on the Jetson AGX Xavier reached 50 FPS, while on the Jetson Nano, it operated at 15 FPS.

In the investigation by Zhao et al. [41], a method for nighttime pedestrian detection was proposed, combining infrared images and millimeter-wave radar. The multimodal fusion approach utilizes an enhanced YOLOv5 (integrating GhostNet, SE, and SPPF) for visual detection, while an Extended Kalman Filter tracks pedestrians using radar data. A coordinate conversion process aligns the sensors, enabling decision-level fusion. Tested on the CVC-09 Infrared Dataset, the proposed method achieved 93.9% accuracy and 90% mAP.

In the work conducted by Palafox et al. [22], the SemanticDepth model was proposed, combining semantic segmentation and monocular depth estimation to enable autonomous vehicle navigation on roads without lane markings. The method generates a semantic 3D point cloud to measure road width and fence-to-fence distance, a term that, in this context, refers to walls or barriers. This is achieved by identifying the extreme points of the segmented road and projecting them into 3D based on the Monodepth disparity map. Measurements are obtained by converting disparities into absolute depths, considering known camera parameters such as focal length and virtual baseline. Tested on the Munich Test Set, Cityscapes, and Roborace datasets, the model achieved a mean absolute error of 0.48 m for road width and 0.91 m for fence-to-fence width. The solution has a high computational cost (approx. 0.64 s inference time per image) and depends on segmentation quality. Additionally, the Monodepth model requires manual scale adjustments, affecting the accuracy of 3D reconstruction.

3   Discussion

Based on the analysis of the selected articles, the distribution of corresponding authors by country is as follows: Germany (3 articles), China (3), India (3), Brazil (2), Egypt (2), South Korea (2), Croatia (1), the Czech Republic (1), Japan (1), and Taiwan (1). Figure 4 illustrates this distribution on a world map. Asia appears with the highest number of articles (10), followed by Europe (4), with Africa and South America each contributing with 2 publications.

Figure 5 displays the number of articles published per year over the past six years, with notable growth observed in 2021 and 2023.

In Sect. 2, state-of-the-art research related to autonomous vehicle perception and navigation was introduced, focusing on the detection of objects in traffic scenes and unknown obstacles. Table 1 presents a summary of the related works, detailing the type of detection, the sensors used, the approaches applied, the complementary methods, and the system's actuation, when available. Additionally, the limitations identified in each study are also highlighted.

From the review, it was observed that all works used RGB cameras as the primary sensor, except for one, which combined an infrared camera with radar [41]. This is due to the richness of information that cameras can capture (e.g., colors, textures, shapes), making them essential for visual perception tasks such as object detection, pattern recognition, and scene interpretation. Additionally, RGB cameras have a relatively low cost and enable the execution of various computer vision algorithms, making them a favorable option for autonomous

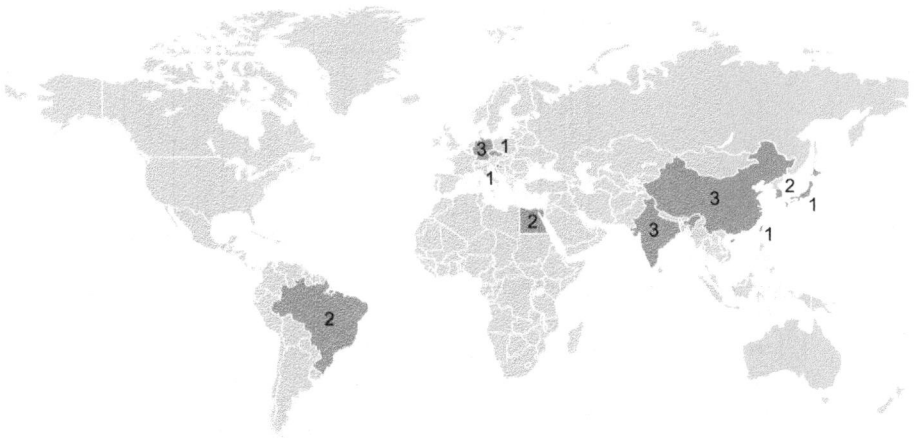

Fig. 4. Countries of the Corresponding Authors.

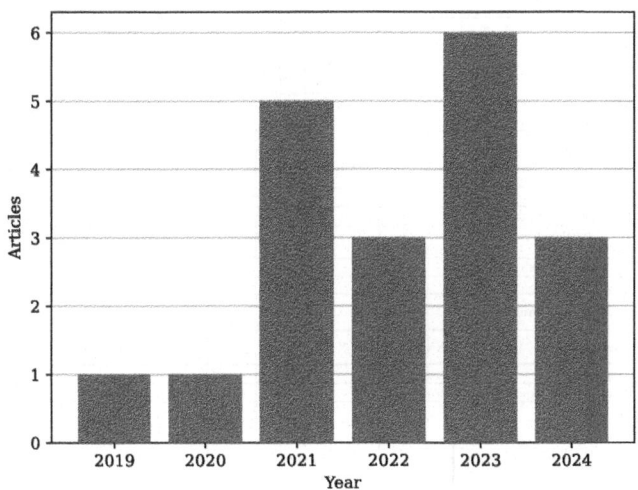

Fig. 5. Number of articles published by year.

vehicle and ADAS systems. Some approaches employ additional sensors through sensor fusion, such as ultrasonic, radar, and LiDAR [10,26,33], to enhance depth perception. 3D perception, mainly provided by sensors like LiDAR and radar, allows for spatial understanding of the environment, enabling the generation of 3D maps and point clouds. The integration of these 3D data with the visual information from RGB cameras enriches the environmental representation.

Most studies focus on identifying the navigable zone, pedestrians, and vehicles, as these are considered the most critical tasks for the safe navigation of autonomous vehicles. However, the detection of unknown obstacles and traffic

Table 1. Comparative table of selected articles.

Category	Item	Ohgushi, Horiguchi and Yamanaka [21]	Ci et al. [7]	Ljepic et al. [18]	Ezzat et al. [10]	Shyam, Yoon and Kim [28]	Shoeb et al. [27]	Usman et al. [35]	Chen [6]	Thombre et al. [33]	Kenk et al. [12]	Megalingam et al. [20]	Bruno and Osório [3]	Li et al. [14]	Vojir et al. [36]	Sousa et al. [31]	Schieber et al. [26]	Tran et al. [34]	Zhao et al. [41]	Palafox et al. [22]
Detection	Unknown or anomalous obstacles	X	X			X									X					
Detection	Traffic signs and road safety components					X										X	X	X		
Detection	Safe navigation zone	X	X	X	X	X	X		X		X	X		X	X	X	X	X		X
Detection	Pedestrians		X			X		X	X	X	X	X	X	X		X	X	X	X	
Detection	Vehicles			X	X	X		X	X	X	X	X		X		X	X	X		
Approach	Semantic segmentation	X	X				X	X							X		X			X
Approach	Monocular depth estimation		X							X										X
Approach	Digital image processing			X							X									
Approach	Bounding boxes				X	X				X	X		X					X	X	
Approach	Instance segmentation					X						X								
Approach	Row-wise classification for lane marker detection					X												X		
Approach	Polynomial coefficients for lane detection					X														
Complementary methods	Anomaly maps	X	X												X					
Complementary methods	Image reconstruction	X													X					
Complementary methods	Point cloud 3D reconstruction																			X
Complementary methods	Geometric analysis			X		X				X										
Complementary methods	Multitask models			X						X	X				X					
Complementary methods	Pyramid fusion networks																X			
Complementary methods	Hough transform											X								
Complementary methods	Object tracking															X			X	
Complementary methods	Kalman filter															X			X	
Complementary methods	Decision-level sensor fusion																		X	
Complementary methods	Regression with depth data									X										
Complementary methods	Depth estimation using bounding boxes					X				X		X				X				
Complementary methods	Statistical road width estimation																			X
Complementary methods	Not applicable			X				X	X							X		X		
Actuation	Speed/braking control			X	X							X								
Actuation	Not applicable	X	X			X	X	X	X	X	X		X	X	X	X	X	X	X	X
Limitations	Occlusions	X														X				
Limitations	Computationally expensive	X	X	X				X	X	X				X	X		X	X		X
Limitations	Image quality			X												X				
Limitations	Shadows					X														
Limitations	Lack of lane markers					X														
Limitations	Objects out of the road (false positives)						X													
Limitations	Low-visibility conditions										X	X				X				
Limitations	Adverse weather conditions							X			X	X							X	
Limitations	Uncommon or out-of-distribution objects									X										
Limitations	Curves					X						X								
Sensors	RGB camera	X	X	X	X	X	X	X	X	X	X	X	X	X	X	X	X	X		X
Sensors	Infrared camera																		X	
Sensors	Ultrasonic sensor			X																
Sensors	Radar																		X	
Sensors	LiDAR									X							X			

signs is also addressed, as they play a crucial role in ensuring safety and supporting the vehicle's decision-making in dynamic scenarios.

Regarding the approaches, semantic segmentation [7, 21, 22, 26, 27, 35, 36] and detection through bounding boxes [3, 10, 12, 28, 33, 34, 41] techniques stood out.

Semantic segmentation plays a key role in scene interpretation and the identification of complex elements, such as lanes, navigable zones, buildings, and walls, as well as the detection of anomalous obstacles. On the other hand, bounding boxes are essential for recognizing and tracking well-defined traffic objects, such as vehicles, pedestrians, cyclists, motorcyclists, and road signs. Some authors explore the integration of semantic segmentation and bounding box detection within the same system [6,14,20,31], either by combining different models or through multitask approaches. This fusion of techniques enables a more robust perception of the environment, leveraging semantic segmentation to identify surfaces and navigable regions, while bounding boxes detect specific objects.

The use of techniques such as instance segmentation [20,35] is also notable, as it not only identifies and segments different objects in a scene but also distinguishes them individually, providing more detailed segmentation. Additionally, the application of monocular depth estimation techniques using RGB cameras [6,7,22] has been observed. This approach allows for the inference of three-dimensional information from a single image. Given the high cost of depth sensors like LiDAR, AI algorithms for monocular depth estimation emerge as a viable alternative for inferring relative distances in a scene and enabling 3D reconstructions. Other techniques specifically used for lane and road marking detection include digital image processing [18,20] and line-based classification models [28,33].

Some of the developed systems employ complementary methods to refine analysis and interpret the data generated by the primary approaches. Among them is the use of distance estimation via bounding boxes [10,20,31,33], a technique that correlates the size of bounding boxes with the distance of vehicles relative to the camera. Complementary geometric analysis techniques were applied to enhance object tracking, lane detection, and distance estimation using the camera's intrinsic parameters [10,27,33]. Many approaches utilized multitask models [6,12,14,28], capable of simultaneously performing lane segmentation or detection and identifying traffic objects. This optimizes computational resources by using a single model instead of multiple distinct models, each dedicated to a specific function. Finally, anomaly maps were developed to detect unknown or out-of-distribution objects. An anomaly map highlights unexpected regions in a scene by comparing the original image with a version reconstructed by neural networks. Differences measured using metrics such as perceptual loss and entropy indicate potential anomalies. After refinements, this map is used to detect obstacles [7,21,36].

Only a small number of the studied systems proposed any type of action, such as longitudinal speed control or braking [7,10,20]. On the other hand, most approaches focused exclusively on developing perception techniques without implementing control mechanisms.

Among the identified limitations, high computational cost stood out, reflecting the complexity of perception tasks in autonomous vehicles. This limitation was mainly observed in approaches that employed semantic and instance segmentation, monocular depth estimation, and multitask models due to their processing demands. Similarly, extreme weather conditions and low-visibility scenarios were also recurring challenges, affecting the performance of solutions primarily based on RGB cameras, which rely heavily on lighting quality and environmental visibility. However, in such scenarios, the fusion of infrared cameras with radar helps mitigate these limitations by combining thermal data with depth information and object detection, providing a complementary perception to traditional RGB cameras [41].

3.1   Datasets

Diverse datasets were studied to implement and evaluate the system. This section provides a brief analysis of these databases. Table 2 summarizes the datasets, including their names, publication years, sensors used for data collection, dataset tasks based on annotations, and access links. The datasets were either publicly available or made public by their authors.

Most datasets employ monocular or stereo cameras, with only a few incorporating LiDAR. SemanticKITTI [2] provides LiDAR data exclusively, while PandaSet [37] and nuScenes [4] combine LiDAR with Inertial Measurement Unit (IMU) and GPS data. CARLA-WildLife [19] is a synthetic video dataset created using CARLA driving simulator [9], so it does not rely on any physical sensors.

Regarding the tasks provided, some focus on segmenting unknown obstacles (also known as anomalous or out-of-distribution obstacles) and the safe Navigation Zone (NZ) [5, 19, 24]. In these datasets, pixel-level classes typically include "obstacle" and "region of interest" The "region of interest" class represents the road or drivable area.

Object detection tasks in both 2D and 3D use bounding box (bbox) annotations: 2D bboxes for images and 3D bboxes for spatial data. For segmentation tasks, 2D data employs pixel-wise masks, while 3D data uses point cloud segmentation. The nuScenes dataset [4] stands out as one of the most comprehensive benchmarks, supporting tasks such as 2D/3D object detection, segmentation, tracking, and lane detection, though it does not include unknown obstacle detection. The dataset incorporates LiDAR data (enabling 3D detection and segmentation) along with IMU and GPS measurements for odometry tracking. As well as BDD100K [40], that similarly supports multiple perception tasks including 2D object detection, segmentation, tracking, and lane detection, while using only camera data.

The authors evaluated three lane detection specific datasets: CULanes [23], TUSimple [39], and CurveLanes [38]. Additionally, they incorporated general purpose 2D segmentation datasets including COCO [15] and ADE20K [42], aiming to create a unified framework for multi-task integration. Also, the DAWN dataset [13], focused in 2D bbox vehicle detection under adverse weather conditions.

For a comprehensive survey of autonomous driving datasets covering perception, planning, and control, see [17].

Table 2. Vision-based datasets.

Dataset	Year	Sensors	Tasks	Website
Lost and Found [24]	2016	Stereo camera	UO Seg, NZ Seg	Link
RoadObstacle21 [5]	2021	Camera	UO Seg, NZ Seg	Link
Road Anomaly [16]	2019	Camera	UO Seg	Link
Cityscapes [8]	2016	Stereo camera	2D Det, 3D Det, 2D Seg	Link
Obstacle Sequences [19]	2022	Camera	UO Seg, NZ Seg	Link
CARLA-WildLife [19]	2022	-	UO Seg, NZ Seg, T	Link
nuScenes [4]	2019	LiDAR, Radar, Camera, IMU, GPS	2D Det, 3D Det, 2D Seg, 3D Seg, T, LD	Link
BDD100K [40]	2020	Camera	2D Det, 2D Seg, T, LD	Link
CULanes [23]	2018	Camera	LD	Link
TUSimple [39]	2020	Camera	LD	Link
CurveLanes [38]	2020	Camera	LD	Link
COCO [15]	2015	Camera	2D Seg	Link
ADE20K [42]	2017	Camera	2D Seg	Link
DAWN [13]	2020	Camera	2D Det	Link
SemanticKITTI [2]	2019	LiDAR	3D Seg	Link
PandaSet [37]	2021	LiDAR, Camera, IMU, GPS	3D Det, 3D Seg, T	Link

[1] Det: Detection
[2] Seg: Segmentation
[3] T: Tracking
[4] LD: Lane Detection
[5] UO: Unknown Obstacle
[6] NZ: Navigation Zone

4 Conclusions and Future Work

This paper presents a literature review on object and navigation area detection using Computer Vision and Artificial Intelligence, focusing on applications for Autonomous Vehicles and ADAS. The study of state-of-the-art approaches showed important advancements in perception techniques, including object detection, segmentation, and distance estimation. These methodologies have demonstrated great accuracy on detecting and tracking navigable zones, pedestrians, vehicles, and road obstacles, which contributes to the improvement of safety in autonomous navigation.

Deep Learning and Vision Transformer-based methods, like semantic segmentation, play a crucial role in scene understanding. These models can detect and interpret complex elements and shapes, such as lanes, walls, and navigable or non-navigable areas, as well as objects that cannot be effectively represented using bounding boxes. Another important AI technique is monocular depth estimation, which provides a relative sense of depth in a scene using just a single image. Moreover, multitask models have shown to achieve efficiency by combining multiple perception tasks into a single framework. It is also noticed the use of more traditional techniques like image processing to detect lanes and geometric and statistical analysis to estimate objects distance.

Despite these advancements, some challenges remain. Many of the reviewed methods are computationally expensive, making them difficult to implement in real-time on embedded systems like intelligent vehicles or mobile robots. However, some approaches have demonstrated potential by running on embedded devices and achieving a considerable FPS rate, enabling soft real-time performance. Additionally, camera based systems are affordable and can capture detailed scene information, but they face difficulties in extreme weather and low light conditions. To overcome these limitations, combining data from LiDAR, radar, or infrared sensors has shown positive results.

In future research we propose the development of a computer vision system based on Deep Learning and Vision Transformers (ViTs), seeking to fuse semantic segmentation (2D data) and monocular depth estimation (3D data) to improve the detection of navigation zones, objects, and obstacles on roadways. The goal is to advance environmental perception and scene understanding, thus increasing the safety and reliability of autonomous vehicles and ADAS.

Acknowledgement. We thank PPG-CCMC[5](PPG-CCMC is the acronym for *Programa de Pós-Graduação em Ciências de Computação e Matemática Computacional* in Portuguese.), University of São Paulo and Federal University of Rio Grande, which made this work possible. This study was financed in part by the *Coordenação de Aperfeiçoamento de Pessoal de Nível Superior - Brasil* (CAPES) - Finance Code 001.

References

1. Aleksa, M., Schaub, A., Erdelean, I., Wittmann, S., Soteropoulos, A., Fürdös, A.: Impact analysis of advanced driver assistance systems (ADAS) regarding road safety-computing reduction potentials. Eur. Transp. Res. Rev. **16**(1), 39 (2024)
2. Behley, J., et al.: Semantickitti: a dataset for semantic scene understanding of lidar sequences. In: Proceedings of the IEEE/CVF International Conference on Computer Vision, pp. 9297–9307 (2019)
3. Bruno, D.R., Osório, F.S.: Real-time pedestrian detection and tracking system using deep learning and kalman filter: Applications on embedded systems in advanced driver assistance systems. In: 2023 Latin American Robotics Symposium (LARS), 2023 Brazilian Symposium on Robotics (SBR), and 2023 Workshop on Robotics in Education (WRE), pp. 549–554 (2023). https://doi.org/10.1109/LARS/SBR/WRE59448.2023.10333032
4. Caesar, H., et al.: nuscenes: A multimodal dataset for autonomous driving. arXiv preprint arXiv:1903.11027 (2019)
5. Chan, R., et al.: Segmentmeifyoucan: a benchmark for anomaly segmentation. In: Thirty-fifth Conference on Neural Information Processing Systems Datasets and Benchmarks Track (2021). https://doi.org/10.48550/arXiv.2104.14812

6. Chen, H.M.: Multitask yolo: Versatile perception network for autonomous driving. In: 2023 IEEE International Conference on Multimedia and Expo Workshops (ICMEW), pp. 46–51 (2023). https://doi.org/10.1109/ICMEW59549.2023.00014
7. Ci, W., Xuan, J., Lin, R., Lu, S.: A novel method for road anomaly objects detection in the traffic environment with multi-mechanism fusion. IEEE Access **12**, 28369–28381 (2024). https://doi.org/10.1109/ACCESS.2024.3359695
8. Cordts, M., et al.: The cityscapes dataset for semantic urban scene understanding. In: Proceedings of the IEEE Conference on Computer Vision and Pattern Recognition (CVPR) (2016)
9. Dosovitskiy, A., Ros, G., Codevilla, F., Lopez, A., Koltun, V.: CARLA: An open urban driving simulator. In: Proceedings of the 1st Annual Conference on Robot Learning, pp. 1–16 (2017)
10. Ezzat, A., Ibrahim, A.M., Younis, M., Hassan, R.M., Darweesh, M.S.: Demonstration of forward collision warning system based on real-time computer vision. In: 2020 16th International Computer Engineering Conference (ICENCO), pp. 47–50 (2020). https://doi.org/10.1109/ICENCO49778.2020.9357374
11. Iosifidis, A., Tefas, A.: Deep learning for robot perception and cognition. Academic Press (2022). https://doi.org/10.1016/C2020-0-02902-6
12. Kenk, M.A., Elsaidy, M., Hassaballah, M., Mansour, M.B.A.: Driving perception in challenging road scenarios: an empirical study. In: 2023 20th ACS/IEEE International Conference on Computer Systems and Applications (AICCSA), pp. 1–6 (2023). https://doi.org/10.1109/AICCSA59173.2023.10479343
13. Kenk, M.A., Hassaballah, M.: Dawn: vehicle detection in adverse weather nature dataset. arXiv preprint arXiv:2008.05402 (2020)
14. Li, J., Ke, X., Wang, Z., Wan, J., Tan, G.: Cutransnet: transformers to make strong encoders for multi-task vision perception of autonomous driving. In: ICASSP 2024 - 2024 IEEE International Conference on Acoustics, Speech and Signal Processing (ICASSP), pp. 7385–7389 (2024). https://doi.org/10.1109/ICASSP48485.2024.10445836
15. Lin, T.Y., et al.: Microsoft coco: Common objects in context (2015). https://arxiv.org/abs/1405.0312
16. Lis, K., Nakka, K., Fua, P., Salzmann, M.: Detecting the unexpected via image resynthesis (2019). https://arxiv.org/abs/1904.07595
17. Liu, M., et al.: A survey on autonomous driving datasets: Statistics, annotation quality, and a future outlook. IEEE Transactions on Intelligent Vehicles (2024)
18. Ljepić, S., Grbić, R., Kovačević, J., Krunić, M.: Detecting obstacles within the driving lane and vehicle speed adjustment. In: 2021 Zooming Innovation in Consumer Technologies Conference (ZINC), pp. 225–230 (2021). https://doi.org/10.1109/ZINC52049.2021.9499311
19. Maag, K., Chan, R., Uhlemeyer, S., Kowol, K., Gottschalk, H.: Two video data sets for tracking and retrieval of out of distribution objects. In: Proceedings of the Asian Conference on Computer Vision (ACCV), pp. 3776–3794 (December 2022)
20. Megalingam, R.K., Rudravaram, G., Kumar, D.V., Deepika, A.S., Smaran, K.S.: Dynamic lane segmentation for autonomous vehicles using neural networks. In: 2022 5th International Conference on Advances in Science and Technology (ICAST), pp. 444–449 (2022). https://doi.org/10.1109/ICAST55766.2022.10039575
21. Ohgushi, T., Horiguchi, K., Yamanaka, M.: Road obstacle detection method based on an autoencoder with semantic segmentation. In: Ishikawa, H., Liu, C.-L., Pajdla, T., Shi, J. (eds.) ACCV 2020. LNCS, vol. 12627, pp. 223–238. Springer, Cham (2021). https://doi.org/10.1007/978-3-030-69544-6_14

22. Palafox, P.R., Betz, J., Nobis, F., Riedl, K., Lienkamp, M.: Semanticdepth: fusing semantic segmentation and monocular depth estimation for enabling autonomous driving in roads without lane lines. Sensors **19**(14), 3224 (2019). https://doi.org/10.3390/s19143224
23. Pan, X., Shi, J., Luo, P., Wang, X., , Tang, X.: Spatial as deep: Spatial CNN for traffic scene understanding. In: AAAI Conference on Artificial Intelligence (AAAI) (February 2018)
24. Pinggera, P., Ramos, S., Gehrig, S., Franke, U., Rother, C., Mester, R.: Lost and found: detecting small road hazards for self-driving vehicles (2016). https://arxiv.org/abs/1609.04653
25. Scannavino, K.R.F., Nakagawa, E.Y., Fabbri, S.C.P.F., Ferrari, F.C.: Revisão sistemática da literatura em engenharia de software: teoria e prática (2017)
26. Schieber, H., Duerr, F., Schoen, T., Beyerer, J.: Deep sensor fusion with pyramid fusion networks for 3d semantic segmentation. In: 2022 IEEE Intelligent Vehicles Symposium (IV), pp. 375–381 (2022). https://doi.org/10.1109/IV51971.2022.9827113,
27. Shoeb, Y., Chan, R., Schwalbe, G., Nowzard, A., Güney, F., Gottschalk, H.: Have we ever encountered this before? retrieving out-of-distribution road obstacles from driving scenes (2023). https://arxiv.org/abs/2309.04302
28. Shyam, P., Yoon, K.J., Kim, K.S.: Weakly supervised approach for joint object and lane marking detection. In: 2021 IEEE/CVF International Conference on Computer Vision Workshops (ICCVW), pp. 2885–2895 (2021). https://doi.org/10.1109/ICCVW54120.2021.00323
29. Singh, S.: Critical reasons for crashes investigated in the national motor vehicle crash causation survey. Traffic Safety Facts (2018). https://crashstats.nhtsa.dot.gov/Api/Public/Publication/812506
30. Soori, M., Arezoo, B., Dastres, R.: Artificial intelligence, machine learning and deep learning in advanced robotics, a review. Cogn. Robot. **3**, 54–70 (2023)
31. Sousa, F.L.M.d., Silva, M.J.d., Santos, R.C.C.d.M., Silva, M.C., Oliveira, R.A.R.: Deep-learning-based embedded adas system. In: 2021 XI Brazilian Symposium on Computing Systems Engineering (SBESC), pp. 1–8 (2021). https://doi.org/10.1109/SBESC53686.2021.9628316
32. StraitsResearch: ADAS and autonomous driving component market segmentation, demand, growth, forecast to 2030 (2022). https://straitsresearch.com/report/adas-and-autonomous-driving-component-market
33. Thombre, A., Rai, A.K., Dumka, L., Agarwal, A.: Object distance estimation from a single moving camera for advanced driver assistance system. In: 2024 IEEE International Conference on Electronics, Computing and Communication Technologies (CONECCT), pp. 1–6 (2024). https://doi.org/10.1109/CONECCT62155.2024.10677218
34. Tran, D., Pham, L.H., Nguyen, H.H., Tran, T., Jeon, H.J., Jeon, J.W.: Universal detection-based driving assistance using a mono camera with jetson devices. IEEE Access **10**, 59400–59412 (2022). https://doi.org/10.1109/ACCESS.2022.3179999
35. Usman, M., K, T.A., Ahmed, M.R., Gudodagi, R., T, N.K.: Exploiting the joint potential of instance segmentation and semantic segmentation in autonomous driving. In: 2023 International Conference for Advancement in Technology (ICONAT), pp. 1–7 (2023). https://doi.org/10.1109/ICONAT57137.2023.10080167
36. Vojir, T., Šipka, T., Aljundi, R., Chumerin, N., Reino, D.O., Matas, J.: Road anomaly detection by partial image reconstruction with segmentation coupling. In: 2021 IEEE/CVF International Conference on Computer Vision (ICCV), pp. 15631–15640 (2021). https://doi.org/10.1109/ICCV48922.2021.01536

37. Xiao, P., et al.: Pandaset: Advanced sensor suite dataset for autonomous driving (2021). https://arxiv.org/abs/2112.12610
38. Xu, H., Wang, S., Cai, X., Zhang, W., Liang, X., Li, Z.: Curvelane-nas: Unifying lane-sensitive architecture search and adaptive point blending. In: ECCV (2020)
39. Yoo, S., et al.: End-to-end lane marker detection via row-wise classification (2020). https://arxiv.org/abs/2005.08630
40. Yu, F., et al.: Bdd100k: A diverse driving dataset for heterogeneous multitask learning (2020). https://arxiv.org/abs/1805.04687
41. Zhao, W., Wang, T., Tan, A., Ren, C.: Nighttime pedestrian detection based on a fusion of visual information and millimeter-wave radar. IEEE Access **11**, 68439–68451 (2023). https://doi.org/10.1109/ACCESS.2023.3291398
42. Zhou, B., Zhao, H., Puig, X., Fidler, S., Barriuso, A., Torralba, A.: Scene parsing through ade20k dataset. In: Proceedings of the IEEE Conference on Computer Vision and Pattern Recognition, pp. 633–641 (2017)

Assessing the Relationship Between DevOps Practices and Customer Satisfaction: A Preliminary Analysis

Sophia L. H. Franklin de Abreu and Fábio Fagundes Silveira$^{(\boxtimes)}$ (iD)

Federal University of São Paulo – UNIFESP, São José dos Campos, Brazil
{sophia.lapadula,fsilveira}@unifesp.br

Abstract. The advent of digitalization in the 21st century has significantly transformed how businesses develop and implement strategies. In this evolving context, DevOps practices have emerged as essential methodologies to improve the efficiency and effectiveness of software delivery and operations. Despite recognizing the benefits of DevOps, a significant research deficiency exists regarding the relationship between DevOps maturity and customer satisfaction. To address this gap, this study analyzes the relationship between DevOps maturity and business customer satisfaction. The methodology involved surveying IT professionals from several Brazilian companies to assess the implementation and maturity of their DevOps practices. Concurrently, customer satisfaction data were extracted from the Brazilian consumer feedback platform Reclame Aqui to establish an external metric for analysis. The preliminary analysis results revealed a moderate negative correlation between the change failure rate (CFR) and customer satisfaction, indicating that organizations that experience fewer deployment failures tend to achieve higher customer satisfaction levels. In contrast, no statistically significant relationships were observed between customer satisfaction and other performance indicators typically associated with DevOps, including deployment frequency, mean recovery time (MTTR), and change lead time. In conclusion, effective DevOps practices may improve customer satisfaction by reducing deployment failures. However, it emphasizes the need for more research involving larger datasets and a more comprehensive analysis to validate and extend these initial findings. Organizations are encouraged to improve deployment reliability and foster an organizational culture supportive of DevOps practices to realize more significant customer satisfaction benefits.

Keywords: Software Engineering · DevOps Practices · Customer Satisfaction · Continuous Improvement

1 Introduction

Ensuring robust and resilient software delivery requires safety nets that protect the customer experience from degradation as changes are introduced. As declared

O. Gervasi et al. (Eds.): ICCSA 2025, LNCS 15650, pp. 132–149, 2025.
https://doi.org/10.1007/978-3-031-96962-1_9

by Forsgren et al. [6], DevOps is not merely a set of tools or isolated practices; it is an integrated approach that demands attention to both technological processes and the underlying culture that supports them. Moreover, it emphasizes that while the rapid deployment of new features is crucial, these changes must not compromise the external quality experienced by customers, but rather refine internal operations.

When implementing DevOps practices, organizations often rely on continuous integration and automated testing as safety nets to preserve service quality. However, if these underlying processes are not robust, the benefits of rapid delivery can be negated by increased service disruptions or degraded performance [3]. Some researchers have suggested employing detailed performance monitoring and incident analysis to safeguard against such degradation [6]. Specifically, evaluating key performance indicators, such as deployment frequency, change failure rates, and recovery times, provides insight into how well the organization maintains service stability despite frequent changes. Forsgren et al. [6] demonstrate that comparing these metrics before and after the adoption of DevOps practices can reveal both improvements and potential shortcomings.

In this paper, we propose a study to assess the relationship between the maturity of DevOps practices and customer satisfaction. Unlike previous work that has focused solely on technical metrics, this study integrates quantitative customer satisfaction data with internal performance indicators to provide a comprehensive view of the impact of DevOps on business outcomes. Our research makes three main contributions: 1) extends established models by incorporating customer satisfaction as a key performance indicator; 2) proposes an integrated methodology to map DevOps maturity to customer experience; and 3) presents a preliminary analysis that explores the potential relationship between these dimensions.

The remainder of this paper is organized as follows: Sect. 2 provides the theoretical background necessary to understand the research question and the proposed approach. Section 3 reviews the related literature on DevOps and customer satisfaction. In Sect. 5, we detail our methodology for data collection and analysis. Section 4 presents the results of our study and discusses the findings. Finally, Sect. 6 concludes the paper and offers perspectives for future work and some recommendations.

2   Background

2.1   DevOps Principles and Performance Metrics

DevOps is a comprehensive approach that integrates software development with IT operations to accelerate delivery and improve product quality [7,12]. Central to this paradigm are practices such as continuous integration, continuous delivery, and continuous deployment, which enable teams to release updates frequently and reliably [1,8]. Fundamental principles include automation, measurement, and sharing, all supported by a culture of continuous improvement [7,15]. Key performance indicators – often referred to as the DORA metrics –

quantify DevOps maturity through measures such as deployment frequency, lead time for changes, mean time to recovery (MTTR), and change failure rate (CFR) [7,13,15]. Research has shown that companies with advanced DevOps practices experience fewer failures and faster recovery times, which streamline internal operations and contribute to superior business outcomes [1,8].

In addition to technical metrics, cultural factors play a crucial role. A robust DevOps culture – characterized by collaborative communication, shared responsibility, and a generative work environment, as defined by Westrum [16] – encourages teams to view failures as learning opportunities, thereby enhancing overall resilience [7,12]. Furthermore, lean methodologies that promote working in small batches enable early and iterative feedback, ensuring continuous refinement of both code and process [7,13]. In essence, standardized metrics provide a framework for organizations to benchmark their performance and drive targeted improvements, aligning operational excellence with strategic objectives [8,15].

2.2   Customer Satisfaction

Customer satisfaction is a critical indicator of an organization's success, reflecting the extent to which its products and services meet or exceed customer expectations [11,14]. It encompasses every touchpoint of the customer journey, from initial engagement to post-purchase support [2,5]. Widely adopted metrics, such as the Net Promoter Score (NPS) introduced by Reichheld et al. [14], classify customers as promoters, passives, or detractors based on their likelihood of recommending a brand [2,14]. In the Brazilian context, platforms like Reclame Aqui[1] (RA) aggregate consumer feedback and complaint resolution data to generate comprehensive reputation scores, serving as proxies for customer satisfaction [5,11]. High customer satisfaction is closely linked to customer retention, positive word-of-mouth, and improved financial performance [2,14]. Moreover, understanding customer satisfaction enables organizations to identify areas for product and service enhancement [5,13]. Researchers such as Becker [2] and Kucukosmanoglu [10] emphasize that the customer experience is multidimensional, encompassing cognitive, emotional, and behavioral responses throughout the entire journey. When companies integrate these external satisfaction metrics with internal performance data, like those obtained from DevOps practices, they achieve clarity on the efficacy of the internal processes concerning customer outcomes [7,14]. This integration is critical when developing strategies that enhance operational efficiency and competitiveness in the market [8,13].

3   Related Work

The past decade has witnessed both academic and rigorous industry approaches toward the advancement of software delivery processes and operations management. Within the scope of these works, it is hard to miss the book published

---

[1] http://www.reclameaqui.com.br.

by Forsgren et al. [7]. In their work, *Accelerate*, the authors claimed that after conducting a qualitative study for more than four years collecting evidence and technical practices along with cultural components of software organizations, their driving business value is the result of organizational engineering toward measurable results. Extracted from their work, there is much emphasis on critical value drivers —now popularized as DORA metrics: deployment frequency, lead time for changes, mean time to recovery, and change failure rate —also referred to as the maturity index of DevOps practices. This framework highlights the importance of technical automation and process integration and values a high-performance, supportive organizational culture.

Oriented by the principles of *Accelerate*, later studies aim to broaden and deepen the understanding of DevOps. For example, Bertolino et al. [3] proposed integrating reliability testing within the DevOps cycle, presenting the DevOpRET methodology. DevOpRET leverages operational profile-based testing, which uses real-world data to simulate user interactions and continuously refine reliability estimates. Their work demonstrates that by embedding reliability assessments into the acceptance testing phase, organizations can achieve more consistent and robust software performance, even as the frequency of deployments increases. This study, which emphasizes the integration of testing with deployment practices, complements the DORA metrics by providing an in-depth look at how software reliability can be systematically improved.

In their paper, Leite et al. [12] provide a detailed survey of DevOps concepts, tools, and challenges. It is especially commendable for attempting to organize the myriad practices and terms developed in DevOps. Leite et al. [12] divides DevOps into several dimensions such as automation, continuous integration, delivery, collaboration, and monitoring, giving organizations a self-contained framework to use to assess their practices. This survey also confirms many of the findings of *Accelerate* but additionally pointed out some other issues like cultural resistance, toolchain complexity, and lack of meaningful metrics. Their analysis illustrates that some level of technical capability is required, but more often than not, the difficulty lies in the people and structure of the organization.

Offerman et al. [13] conducted a worldwide survey to analyze the scope and effect of DevOps practices in the organization. Their research outlines 14 automated subsystem monitoring configuration management practices and subpractices. A significant takeaway from Offerman et al. [13] is the excellent degree of relations between the level of automation and the operational failure rate of a system. This adds to the argument that some level of automation, complemented by a good culture, significantly improves the reliability of services and business outcomes. In addition, the study underscores that companies with a developed DevOps culture dominated peers not only on internal performance measures but also on externally visible ones [13].

Agile practices, which have long been associated with rapid and flexible software development, are also central to the literature on DevOps. Ghimire and Charters [8] investigate the impact of Agile methodologies on project outcomes, focusing on the synergy between agile and DevOps practices. Their work reveals that the adoption of agile practices, such as stand-ups, user stories, and retrospectives, improves communication and alignment within teams, leading to clearer project requirements and better customer interactions. This is particularly important because agile methodologies emphasize iterative development and continuous feedback, principles that are fundamental to both DevOps and customer satisfaction. The integration of agile with DevOps creates a virtuous cycle: agile methods drive rapid iteration, while DevOps ensures that these iterations are delivered reliably, resulting in a smoother customer experience.

One of the many things discussed as part of DevOps in existing literature is the concept of organizational culture. The Westrum typology [16] defines three types of organizational culture: pathological, bureaucratic, and generative. Software delivery has been shown repeatedly to be better when there is a generative culture in place, which is marked by high cooperation, free flow of information, and collective accountability. Many of these studies, such as those conducted by Forsgren et al. [7] and Leite et al. [12], emphasize that culture is just as important as technical practices. Research evidence also supports that trying to understand why highly cross-functionally collaborative teams with a no-blame culture tend to make changes with greater speed, a lower failure rate, and faster recovery [8,13]. It is evident that technology and people need to be systematically integrated to attain excellent efficiency in DevOps.

Another important line of research examines the interplay between technical practices and customer satisfaction. Customer satisfaction is increasingly recognized as a critical metric for business success. Reichheld et al. [14] introduced the Net Promoter Score (NPS), which categorizes customers based on their likelihood of recommending a product or service. This metric has been widely adopted in various industries to assess customer loyalty and predict business growth. In Brazil, platforms such as Reclame Aqui offer an alternative perspective by aggregating consumer feedback and complaint resolution data to generate comprehensive reputation scores. Studies by Kucukosmanoglu [11] and Chrysochou [5] have explored the nuances of customer satisfaction and brand loyalty, illustrating how these metrics not only reflect product quality, but also capture the overall customer experience. The relationship between internal operational metrics, such as those provided by DevOps practices, and external customer satisfaction has become an area of intense study. By linking internal performance data (such as deployment frequency, lead time, and failure rates) with customer-centric metrics (such as NPS and Reclame Aqui scores), researchers are beginning to uncover how improvements in software delivery can translate into enhanced customer experiences.

The literature presents a comprehensive perspective on DevOps by emphasizing its technical and cultural dimensions. These dimensions, thoroughly articulated by Forsgren et al. [7], constitute the foundation of high-performing software organizations. This foundation is expanded by studies that integrate reliability testing [3], systematize the various DevOps practices [12], and quantify the impact of these practices on both internal performance and customer results [8,13]. Furthermore, the discussion of organizational culture [16] and customer satisfaction [5, 11, 14] highlights the interdependencies between how companies operate internally and how they are perceived externally.

In summary, the collective body of research indicates that while technical prowess in software deployment is necessary, the synergy between robust technical practices, a supportive organizational culture, and the continuous pursuit of improvement ultimately drives business success. This integrated approach lays the foundation for future studies and serves as the impetus for our research. By investigating the correlation between DevOps maturity and customer satisfaction, our work aims to extend these insights and provide actionable recommendations to organizations seeking to optimize both their internal processes and their external service quality.

4   Research Design and Data Collection

To examine the connection between customer satisfaction and DevOps practices, a mixed-method approach was used, combining qualitative insights with quantitative data collection and statistical analysis. The primary data collection method was a survey, and secondary data was collected from public customer feedback websites.

The survey was designed following established guidelines in the literature [9] and based on the foundational framework presented by Forsgren et al. [7]. It comprised closed-ended questions, including multiple-choice items and Likert scale questions, aimed at capturing a wide array of DevOps dimensions. The survey questions were systematically categorized into respondent profile questions (Table 1), technical metrics aligned with the DevOps Research and Assessment (DORA) framework (Table 2), and cultural dimensions encompassing organizational culture (Table 3), team burnout (Table 4), testing and deployment practices (Table 5), lean product development practices (Table 6), organizational identity and culture (Table 7), and leadership perception (Table 8).

The key metrics quantitatively assessed through the survey included deployment frequency, lead time for changes, mean time to recovery (MTTR), and change failure rate (CFR). Furthermore, cultural elements such as shared accountability, cross-team collaboration, and team maturity were qualitatively assessed to provide additional context on how these factors affect organizational performance in DevOps. Such a thorough categorization required advanced statistical analysis to identify the relationship between customer satisfaction and the factors considered.

The study population comprised Brazilian citizens working in large enterprises as Software Developers, DevOps Engineers, System Administrators, and IT Managers. The survey was sent out through emails and LinkedIn, which helped achieve representation in various roles. The responses were collected and presented at the corporate level to maintain anonymity and reduce bias toward individual respondents, as all identifying details were removed.

Concurrently, external data on customer satisfaction were obtained from the Reclame Aqui platform, a widely recognized platform in Brazil that aggregates consumer complaints and feedback to generate a comprehensive reputation score: the RA metric. This metric is calculated based on four weighted components: (i) the **response rate (RR)** – the percentage of complaints answered by the company (weight: 2); (ii) the **average evaluation (AE)** – the average customer rating on a scale from 0 to 10 (weight: 3); (iii) the **solution rate (SR)** – the percentage of complaints successfully resolved (weight: 3); and (iv) the **return business rate (RBR)** – the percentage of customers who would do business with the company again (weight: 2). The final RA score is computed using the following formula:

$$RA = \frac{(RR \times 2) + (AE \times 10 \times 3) + (SR \times 3) + (RBR \times 2)}{100}$$

Based on this score, companies are classified into five performance tiers: *Excellent* (8.0–10), *Good* (7.0–7.9), *Regular* (6.0–6.9), *Poor* (5.0–5.9), and *Not Recommended* (below 5.0). For the RA score to be considered valid, companies must have a response rate above 50% and at least 10 customer evaluations in the past six months. Moreover, companies that meet higher thresholds—such as RR and SR above 90%, AE above 7, RBR above 70%, and a minimum of 50 evaluations— may be awarded the prestigious *RA1000 Seal*, a distinction that signals consistent excellence in customer service.

Table 1. Respondent roles and DevOps involvement.

Question	Type
What is your position?	Open
In which company do you work?	Open
At what stage in your career are you?	Selection
Do you know what DevOps is?	Yes/No
Are you responsible for applying DevOps in your organization or do you participate in the application?	Yes/No
On a scale of 0 to 10, would you recommend the company you work for to a friend or family member?	Numerical
Employees agree to participate in the survey.	Likert

Table 2. Questions on DORA performance metrics.

Question	Type
In how many days does your company usually solve a critical problem like a bug? (MTTR)	Open
How long does it usually take from the moment a new idea or need for change is suggested until it is officially accepted for development? (Lead time for changes)	Open
When new updates or changes are made, what percentage of the time do you encounter problems or errors that require additional corrections or reversions to a previous version? (Change failure rate)	Open
How many times does your company deploy per month?	Open

Table 3. Items on organizational culture traits.

Question	Type
Information is actively sought	Likert
Messengers are not punished when delivering news of failures or other bad news	Likert
Responsibilities are shared	Likert
Collaboration between areas is encouraged and rewarded	Likert
Failures cause investigation	Likert
New ideas are welcome	Likert
Failures are primarily treated as opportunities to improve the system	Likert

Table 4. Questions measuring team burnout.

Question	Type
If they felt burnt out or exhausted	Likert
If they felt indifferent or cynical about work or felt ineffective	Likert
If their work was having a negative effect on their lives	Likert

Table 5. Testing and deployment practices questions.

Question	Type
We can do most of our tests without requiring an integrated environment	Likert
We can and do deploy or launch our application independently of other applications/services it depends on	Likert

Table 6. Questions on lean development behaviors.

Question	Type
My product team breaks products and features into small batches that can be completed in less than a week and released frequently, including the use of MVPs	Likert
Teams have a good understanding of the business workflow to customers and have visibility of this flow, including the status of products and features	Likert
Organizations actively and regularly seek customer feedback and incorporate this feedback into the design of their products	Likert
If development teams have authority to create and change specifications as part of the development process without needing approval	Likert

Table 7. Items on identity and organizational alignment.

Question	Type
I am satisfied to have chosen to work in this organization instead of another company	Likert
I talk about this organization to my friends as a great company to work for	Likert
I am willing to put in a lot of effort beyond what is normally expected to help my organization succeed	Likert
I think my values and the values of my organization are very similar	Likert
In general, people employed by my organization are working towards the same goal	Likert
I feel that my organization cares about me	Likert

Table 8. Leadership perception questions.

Question	Type
About my leadership [I am satisfied to have chosen to work in this organization instead of another company]	Likert
About my leadership [I talk about this organization to my friends as a great company to work for]	Likert
About my leadership [I am willing to put in a lot of effort beyond what is normally expected to help my organization succeed]	Likert
About my leadership [I think my values and the values of my organization are very similar]	Likert
About my leadership [In general, people employed by my organization are working towards the same goal]	Likert
About my leadership [I feel that my organization cares about me]	Likert

Data analysis incorporated both descriptive and inferential statistical techniques. The descriptive statistics summarized the central tendencies and dispersion of the survey responses, providing an initial overview of the current state of DevOps practices across the sample. For exploratory analysis, Pearson and Spearman correlation coefficients [17] were calculated to assess the relationships between the individual DevOps metrics and the RA metric. Pearson's correlation was employed to examine linear relationships, while Spearman's correlation was used to capture potential monotonic relationships, particularly given that some variables were measured on ordinal Likert scales.

Although this integrated methodology provides a robust framework for analysis, limitations such as sample size, reliance on self-reported data, and potential selection bias are acknowledged. These issues are carefully addressed through statistical confidence testing and are discussed in detail in subsequent sections. Overall, the methodological approach was intended to ensure that the study findings are valid and reliable, offering meaningful insights into how efficient DevOps practices can enhance customer satisfaction.

4.1   Survey Implementation and Sampling

According to Kasunic [9], identifying the target audience is essential when designing a survey. In this study, the target audience comprised managers, site reliability engineers, system administrators, software developers, agilists, and other IT professionals familiar with DevOps practices.

After gathering data, 62 responses were collected, allowing a comparative analysis of 23 different companies. The results were consolidated into Table 9 and Fig. 1. Table 9 provides a summary of the survey findings, presenting the minimum, maximum, and average values obtained for each question, effectively demonstrating the range and central tendency of the responses.

Table 9. Summary statistics of key survey responses.

Questions	Min	Max	Mean	Median
MTTR	0.05	7.00	2.15	1.00
Lead time for change in months	0.10	15.00	2.62	1.00
Change failure rate	0.01	1.00	0.21	0.10
Number of deployments per month	1.00	70.00	20.74	8.0
Information is actively sought	1.00	5.00	4.27	4.20
Messengers are not punished for reporting failures.	1.00	5.00	3.60	3.60
Responsibilities are shared	3.00	5.00	4.38	4.30
Collaboration across areas is encouraged	2.00	5.00	4.10	4.00
Failures lead to investigations	2.00	5.00	4.12	4.10
New ideas are welcome	1.00	5.00	4.45	4.40
Failures are treated as improvement opportunities	1.00	5.00	3.98	3.90
Employees feeling burned out	1.00	5.00	3.02	3.00
Employees feeling indifferent or ineffective	1.00	4.00	2.70	2.60
Employees feeling work negatively affects life	1.00	4.00	2.32	2.30
Most testing can be done without an integrated environment	1.00	5.00	3.06	3.00
Deployment can be independent of other services	1.00	5.00	3.40	3.40
Teams break features into small batches and use MVPs	1.00	5.00	4.09	4.00
Teams understand and have visibility of business flow	1.00	5.00	3.79	3.70
Organizations actively seek and incorporate customer feedback	1.00	5.00	4.11	4.10
Teams can change specifications without approval	2.00	5.00	3.63	3.60
Employees are happy they chose this company	1.00	5.00	4.29	4.20
Employees recommend the company to friends	1.00	5.00	4.15	4.10
Employees are willing to put in extra effort	1.00	5.00	4.33	4.30
Employees' values align with company values	1.00	5.00	3.90	3.90
Employees feel the company works towards the same goal	1.00	5.00	3.92	3.90
Employees feel the company cares about them	1.00	5.00	3.84	3.80
Employees agree to participate in the survey	4.00	4.00	4.00	4.00

To facilitate better visualization and understanding of the correlations among variables, Fig. 1 presents a detailed correlation analysis using both Pearson and Spearman correlation coefficients. This figure clearly illustrates the strength and direction of the correlations, helping to identify meaningful relationships and trends among the different variables measured in the survey. The visual representation improves readability and quickly conveys insights regarding the relationships between DevOps practices and customer satisfaction.

All data used in this research can be obtained through the replication package available at the Zenodo.org[2] repository.

5   Results and Analysis

The data collected from 62 questionnaires in 23 companies also indicate substantial variability in the implementation of DevOps practices, reflecting different levels of organizational maturity. As presented in Table 9, the mean time to recovery (MTTR) ranged from 0.05 to 7.00 d, with an average of 2.15 and a median of 1.00. Meanwhile, the lead time for changes fluctuated between 0.10 and 15.00 months, with an average of 2.62 and a median of 1.00. The change failure rate ranged from 0.01 to 1.00, with an average of 0.21 and a median of 0.10, while the frequency of monthly deployments varied from 1 to 70 (with an average of 20.74 and a median of 8). These indicators underscore both the agility of some continuous delivery processes and the challenges related to release quality, reflecting the heterogeneity of practices adopted by organizations.

The correlation analysis between these technical indicators and the RA index, which represents the customer satisfaction factor, in Fig. 2, reinforced the moderate negative relationship already mentioned between CFR and customer satisfaction. This finding suggests that lower change failure rates are associated with improved customer satisfaction, reinforcing the assertion by Forsgren et al. [7] that deployment reliability is a key driver of positive business outcomes.

In contrast, as noted by MTTR in Fig. 3, the lead time for changes in Fig. 4 and the deployment frequency in Fig. 5 did not exhibit statistically significant correlations with customer satisfaction, indicating that, on their own, these operational aspects may not directly reflect external perceptions of service quality. However, these findings go beyond the study by Forsgren et al. [6], which highlights deployment frequency and lead time for changes as a critical metric for elite performers, linking frequent deployments to faster feedback cycles and improved customer satisfaction. The absence of a similar correlation in this study may be attributed to differences in sample characteristics or methodological limitations, pointing to the need for more experiments in this research area.

In parallel, data on organizational culture, including shared responsibilities, collaboration between departments, failure investigation, and encouragement of innovation, showed weak to moderate positive correlations with customer satisfaction, as shown in 1. These findings support the idea that the consolidation of

---

[2] https://zenodo.org/records/15098963.

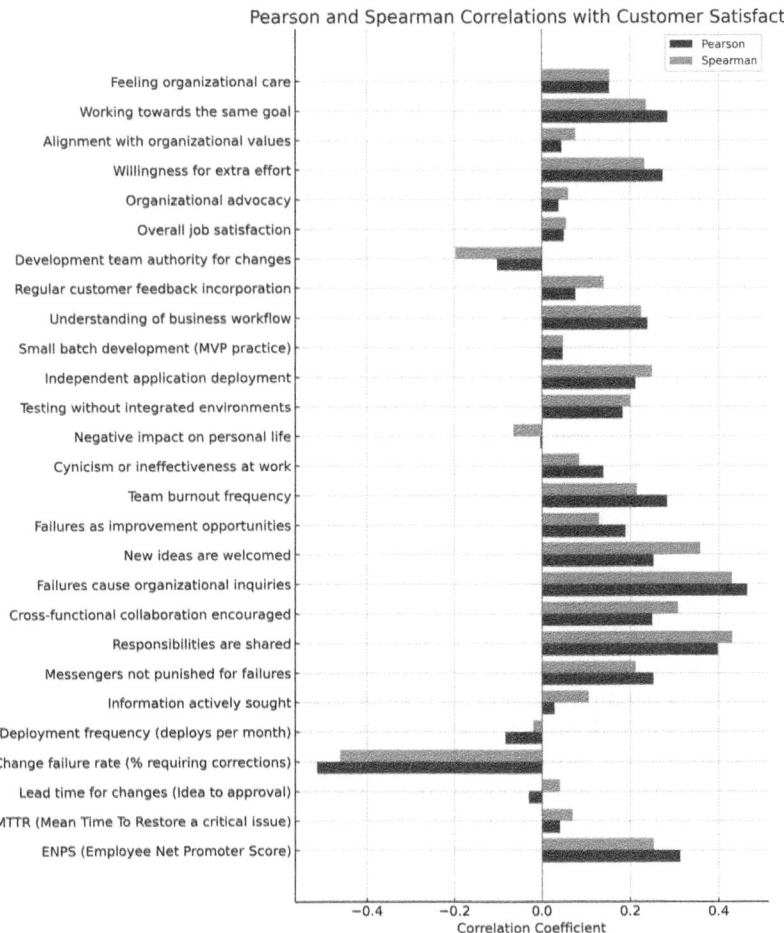

Fig. 1. Pearson and Spearman correlations between survey variables and customer satisfaction.

a collaborative and learning-oriented culture is key to positive client outcomes. Another key point from Fig. 1 reveals that organizational culture and employee well-being appear to have more consistently positive relationships with customer satisfaction than some of the classic DevOps indicators. Fostering an environment in which employees feel safe to report failures, actively seek information, and share responsibilities is positively correlated with external satisfaction metrics. It is worth noting that differences between Pearson and Spearman coefficients in several variables indicate that some relationships may be monotonic rather than strictly linear, suggesting potential threshold effects (for example, a "tipping point" in collaboration, after which satisfaction improves more sharply).

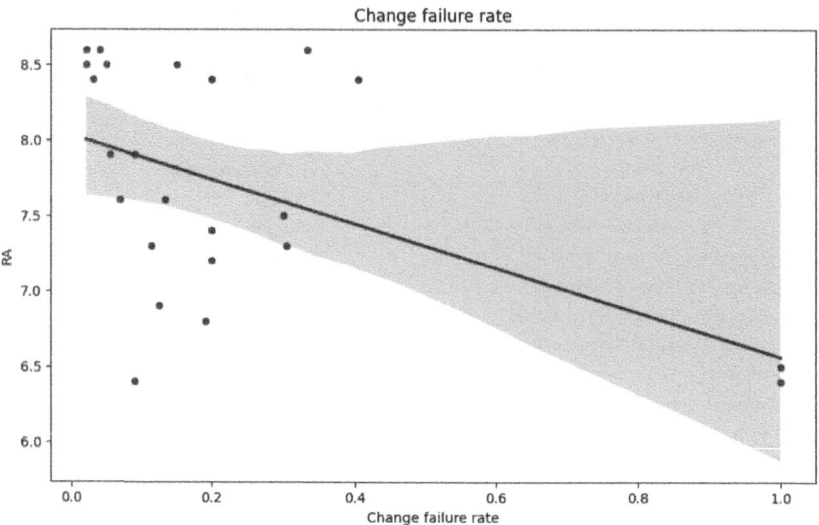

Fig. 2. Pearson and Spearman correlations between RA Metric and mapped companies change failure rates.

Continuing the examination of Fig. 1, although small-batch (MVP) development and independent deployments demonstrated mild to moderate correlations, they underscore the proposition that incremental, decoupled releases have the potential to enhance the user experience, particularly when integrated with com-

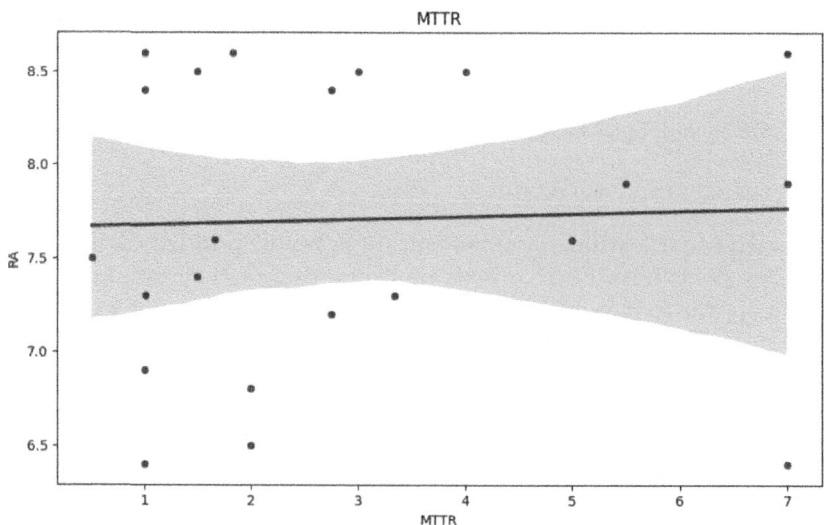

Fig. 3. Pearson and Spearman correlations between RA Metric and mapped companie's MTTR rates.

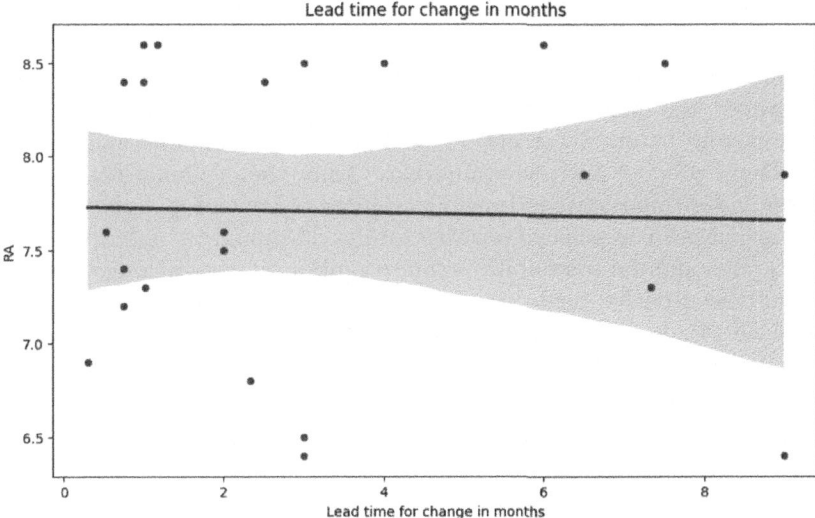

Fig. 4. Pearson and Spearman correlations between RA Metric and mapped companie's lead time for changes rates.

prehensive change management practices. In contrast, near-zero correlations for lead time and deployment frequency suggest that reliability, reflected by a lower CFR, may be more relevant to customers than speed or the sheer volume of releases.

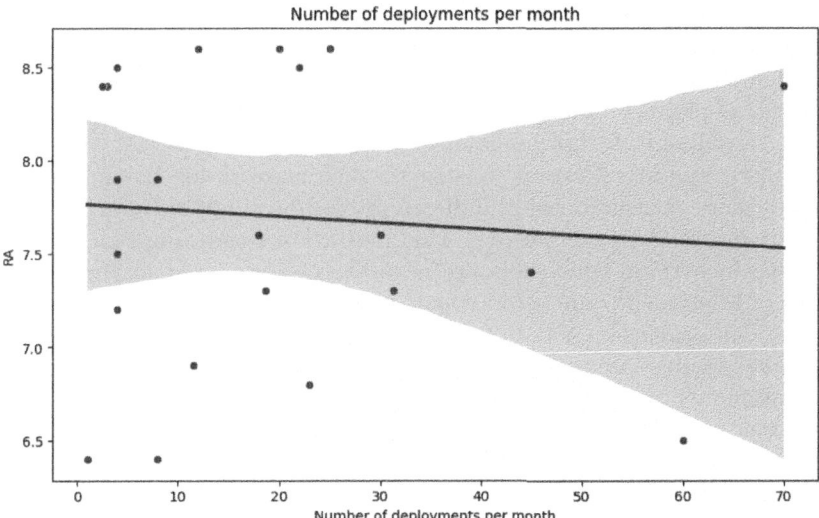

Fig. 5. Pearson and Spearman correlations between RA Metric and mapped companie's number of deployments rates.

In summary, these findings underscore the strategic relevance of reducing the change failure rate to improve customer satisfaction, aligning with continuous integration and continuous delivery practices to minimize implementation failures. However, the fact that other technical indicators do not show significant correlations with external perception suggests that operational efficiency alone is not enough to boost positive evaluations. Thus, the combination of technical excellence and a collaborative, learning-oriented organizational culture emerges as a promising path to achieve positive results. It should be noted that sample size limitations and data variability require caution in generalizing the findings, reinforcing the need for future research with larger samples and more refined methodologies to deepen the understanding of the relationship between DevOps practices and customer satisfaction.

5.1   Threats to Validity

Although this study provides valuable information on the relationship between DevOps practices and customer satisfaction, some limitations must be acknowledged. These limitations pertain to various threats to the validity of the findings, including the validity of internal, external, construct, and statistical conclusions.

Internal Validity: The study relied on survey data and public metrics, which may introduce biases such as self-reporting and selective sampling. Respondents' interpretations of the survey questions could vary, potentially affecting the consistency of the data. Furthermore, external factors influencing customer satisfaction, such as market dynamics or product quality, were not controlled, which confounds the observed relationships.

External Validity: The generalizability of the findings is constrained by the sample of 62 responses regarding DevOps parameters. Twenty-three companies had their RA metric listed, which focused on specific organizations and industries within the Brazilian region. The applicability of these results to other contexts or global organizations remains uncertain, highlighting the need for a more extensive sampling in future research.

Construct Validity: Certain constructs, such as work-life balance and team autonomy, were measured using indirect proxies or single metrics, which may not fully capture their complexity. This limitation raises questions about the degree to which these constructs are accurately represented in the study and their direct relationship to customer satisfaction.

Statistical Conclusion Validity: The statistical power of the study is limited by the small sample size and the variability of the data, even though it reached the minimum mentioned in Carpita and Manisera [4]. The wide confidence intervals observed in several correlations indicate uncertainty in the findings, emphasizing the importance of larger datasets to improve precision and reliability.

Although there are limitations, this study establishes a foundation for understanding the connections between DevOps practices and customer satisfaction. Addressing these validity threats in future research through improved data collection, broader sampling, and refined measurement techniques will enhance the robustness of subsequent findings and strengthen their implications for organizations.

6   Conclusion and Future Directions

In this study, the importance of developing solutions that integrate and streamline DevOps practices to improve customer satisfaction was highlighted.

The investigation made initial progress toward its objectives, as reflected in the preliminary results. First, a slight positive correlation was observed between metrics related to employee well-being and customer satisfaction, although with wide confidence intervals, indicating substantial uncertainty in estimates. Second, a moderate negative correlation was identified between the change failure rate (CFR) and the Reclame Aqui (RA) metric, suggesting that lower CFRs are associated with higher customer satisfaction. Third, exploratory analysis revealed that while variables such as mean time to recovery (MTTR), lead time for changes, and deployment frequency did not exhibit significant correlations with the RA score, cultural factors – including shared responsibilities, cross-functional collaboration, failure investigation, and the encouragement of new ideas – demonstrated weak to moderate positive correlations.

The investigation focused on addressing the critical challenges associated with linking internal DevOps practices to external customer satisfaction. The results partially resonate with the findings reported by Forsgren et al. [7], although limitations in sample size and data variability call for further research. In this study, the analysis has advanced the understanding of the interplay between technical performance and organizational culture in influencing customer satisfaction. These findings suggest that improvements in continuous delivery practices and the cultivation of a collaborative, learning-focused environment can drive enhanced customer outcomes.

In the future, providing more comprehensive studies that use larger and more diverse datasets will be crucial to improve generalizability and statistical power. Future research should also explore the indirect effects of DevOps practices by examining mediating variables such as employee productivity, team dynamics, and organizational culture. Longitudinal studies are recommended to capture how changes in DevOps maturity influence customer satisfaction over time, while mixed methods, combining quantitative surveys with qualitative interviews, can yield richer insights into the underlying mechanisms.

6.1   Practical Recommendations for Practitioners

Based on the findings of this study, organizations are encouraged to implement targeted actions that align with the strongest observed relationships between DevOps practices and customer satisfaction. These include the following:

1. **Reducing Change Failure Rates (CFRs):** Prioritize lowering CFRs by adopting robust continuous delivery practices. Investments in automated

testing, comprehensive configuration management, and efficient integration pipelines are essential to minimize deployment failures and improve operational reliability.
2. **Fostering Cross-Functional Collaboration:** Enhance interdepartmental collaboration by establishing clear communication channels, shared objectives, and accountability mechanisms. This kind of collaboration has been shown to contribute positively to customer satisfaction.
3. **Encouraging Shared Responsibilities:** Promote an equitable distribution of responsibilities within teams to strengthen accountability and improve overall performance.
4. **Investigating and Learning from Failures:** Cultivate a culture of continuous improvement by treating failures as opportunities for learning. Implement systems to analyze root causes and apply these insights to refine processes, ultimately leading to better customer experiences.

By acting on these recommendations, organizations may be better positioned to leverage DevOps practices to achieve tangible improvements in customer satisfaction and overall operational performance. Future research will aim to extend the integrated approach, expand the dataset, and refine the methodological instruments to further validate these preliminary findings.

Acknowledgments. The authors thank the São Paulo Research Foundation (FAPESP) – grant 2023/14646-1 – for partial financial support.

References

1. Beck, K., et al.: Manifesto for agile software development (2001). http://agilemanifesto.org
2. Becker, S.: Understanding customer experience: a multidimensional approach. Int. J. Customer Relation. Manage. **12**(3), 220–235 (2020)
3. Bertolino, A., et al.: Devopret: continuous reliability testing in devops. J. Softw.: Evol. Process (July 2020), published on: 20 July 2020
4. Carpita, M., Manisera, M.: On the imputation of missing data in surveys with likert-type scales. J. Classification **28**(1), 93–112 (Jan 2011), published on: 21 Jan 2011
5. Chrysochou, P.: Does brand loyalty decline? investigating brand loyalty evolution and the role of product category characteristics. J. Consumer Res. **52**(1), 1–20 (2025)
6. Forsgren, N., Humble, J., Kim, G.: Accelerate : the science behind DevOps : building and scaling high performing technology organizations. It Revolution (2018)
7. Forsgren, N., Humble, J., Kim, G.: Accelerate: The Science of Lean Software and DevOps. IT Revolution Press, Burlington, MA (2018)
8. Ghimire, S., Charters, A.: Impact of DevOps adoption on software delivery performance. J. Softw. Eng. **15**(2), 110–125 (2022)
9. Kasunic, M.: Designing an effective survey (09 2005). https://resources.sei.cmu.edu/library/asset-view.cfm?assetid=7277

10. Kucukosmanoglu, A.N.: Customer satisfaction: A central phenomenon in marketing. Academia.edu (2019). disponível em: https://www.academia.edu/1977823/CUSTOMER_SATISFACTION_A_CENTRAL_PHENOMENON_IN_MARKETING. Acesso em: 18 Nov. 2019
11. Kucukosmanoglu, H.: Customer satisfaction in the digital age: metrics and methods. J. Market. Anal. **7**(4), 250–265 (2019)
12. Leite, L., de Assis, A., de Souza, F., et al.: DevOps: concepts, practices, challenges and implications. IEEE Access **8**, 123456–123467 (2020)
13. Offerman, J., et al.: Adoption and impact of DevOps practices on organizational performance. IEEE Trans. Software Eng. **49**(5), 1342–1355 (2023)
14. Reichheld, F., Darnell, B., Burns, M.: Winning on Purpose: The Unbeatable Strategy of Loving Customers. Harvard Business Review Press, Boston, MA (2021)
15. Srivastava, R., et al.: Developer velocity: How Software Excellence Fuels Business Performance. McKinsey & Company, Report (2020)
16. Westrum, R.: A typology of organisational cultures. Quality & Safety in Health Care 13(suppl 2), ii22–ii27 (2004)
17. Wohlin, C., Runeson, P., Höst, M., Ohlsson, M.C., Regnell, B., Wesslén, A.: Experimentation in Software Engineering. Springer (2012)

Enhancing Money Laundering Detection: A Comparative Study of Machine Learning Techniques and Sampling Methods

Vinh Dinh Nguyen$^{(\boxtimes)}$ and Kha Hoang Nguyen

Department of Information Technology, FPT University, Can Tho Campus, Can Tho City, Vietnam

vinhnd29@fe.edu.vn, khanhce171115@fpt.edu.vn

Abstract. Money laundering poses a significant threat to global financial systems, enabling illicit activities such as drug trafficking and terrorism. Traditional anti-money laundering methods often fail to detect complex and evolving patterns in financial transactions. This paper explores advanced machine learning techniques to enhance the detection of suspicious activities. We evaluated the performance of six classifiers—RandomForest, LogisticRegression, KNeighbors, GradientBoosting, LightGBM, and XGBoost—on an imbalanced dataset for laundering transaction classification. Four sampling methods were employed: Without Sampling, SMOTE, RandomUnderSampler, and ADASYN. The results indicate that RandomForest, particularly when combined with SMOTE and ADASYN, consistently outperformed other classifiers. Without sampling, RandomForest achieved an F1 Score of 0.37 for the minority class (Class 1), which improved to 0.41 with SMOTE and 0.40 with ADASYN. These findings underscore the robustness of RandomForest in managing imbalanced datasets and emphasize the critical role of effective sampling techniques. This study offers valuable insights for enhancing predictive models in financial fraud detection.

Keywords: Money laundering detection · machine learning · imbalanced datasets · sampling techniques · fraud detection

1 Introduction

Money laundering is a major threat to global financial systems, facilitating illicit activities like drug trafficking and terrorism [1]. Traditional anti-money laundering (AML) methods often struggle to detect the evolving complexities of financial transactions, necessitating more sophisticated approaches [2]. This process allows criminals to disguise illicit funds as legitimate, significantly impacting society by enabling crimes such as human trafficking and terrorism, particularly in developing countries [3, 4]. Techniques like smurfing—breaking large sums into smaller transactions to evade detection—make tracing these funds difficult [1]. Detecting money laundering is challenging due to its secretive nature and multi-stage process, including placement, layering, and integration [5, 6]. The Financial Action Task Force (FATF) emphasizes the complexity

© The Author(s), under exclusive license to Springer Nature Switzerland AG 2025
O. Gervasi et al. (Eds.): ICCSA 2025, LNCS 15650, pp. 150–161, 2025.
https://doi.org/10.1007/978-3-031-96962-1_10

of laundering networks and the necessity of advanced detection systems [7]. Traditional rule-based AML approaches lack the flexibility to adapt to these challenges [8]. Recently, machine learning (ML) models have shown promise in improving detection by identifying hidden patterns in complex transactions [9]. However, applying ML to AML remains difficult due to the inherent class imbalance in the data—most transactions are legitimate, with only a small fraction being illicit [9]. This imbalance hinders the performance of ML algorithms, which often misclassify the minority class (illicit transactions) [10]. Researchers have developed various techniques to address this, including resampling methods like SMOTE, RandomUnderSampler, and ADASYN, which improve the representation of minority classes without modifying the predictive models [11]. The terms "imbalance learning technique" and "resampling technique" are used interchangeably in this study, as the focus is on enhancing the dataset rather than modifying the predictive model.

This study evaluates the performance of these resampling methods in combination with six popular ML models—RandomForest, LogisticRegression, KNeighbors, GradientBoosting, LightGBM, and XGBoost—using the IBM "Transactions for Anti-Money Laundering" dataset from Kaggle, which includes over 5 million records. The objective is to enhance AML detection by addressing class imbalance and leveraging advanced ML techniques.

2 Related Work

2.1 Supervised Algorithms-Based Methods for Fraud Detection

ML algorithm-based methods are divided into two categories: supervised and unsupervised algorithms [12]. Supervised ML algorithms are widely used in fraud detection due to their ability to learn from labeled datasets, which contain known instances of fraudulent and non-fraudulent activities [13]. These algorithms build models that can predict the likelihood of future transactions being fraudulent based on historical data, thereby supporting and improving the decision-making process in financial institutions [9]. It has been suggested to integrate SMOTE with various supervised ML techniques such as logistic regression (LR), decision trees (DT), neural networks (NN), and random forests (RF) to handle class imbalance effectively [14, 15]. This integration helps create a more balanced training set, enabling the algorithms to better identify and predict fraudulent transactions.

Nguyen et al. (2023) compared several supervised algorithms including DT, RF, Support Vector Machine (SVM), Artificial Neural Network (ANN), and Bayesian Logistic Regression (BLR). They found that ANN outperformed other algorithms in rare event classification, which is crucial in fraud detection where fraudulent transactions are significantly fewer than legitimate ones. Moreover, combining resampling techniques like SMOTE with algorithms such as SVM and RF yielded competitive results, demonstrating the importance of addressing class imbalance in improving model performance [15].

Khalid et al. (2024) demonstrated that XGBoost effectively addresses suboptimal outcomes in fraud detection classification tasks. XGBoost treats non-reported and normal alerts equally, allowing for the development of a robust detection algorithm that predicts the likelihood of fraudulent transactions [14]. This approach considers various factors, including transaction history and patterns, which enhances the accuracy and reliability of fraud detection systems.

Supervised algorithms leverage historical data to adapt to new fraud patterns, enhancing their ability to distinguish between legitimate and fraudulent activities, making them essential tools in combating financial fraud.

2.2 Class Imbalance in Fraud Detection and Anti-Money Laundering

Class imbalance is a critical issue in machine learning (ML), especially in fraud detection and AML, where most instances belong to the majority class, while the minority class represents rare but crucial events like fraudulent transactions or money laundering [16, 17]. In these domains, detecting the minority class is essential to prevent financial losses and protect system integrity [18]. However, ML models trained on imbalanced datasets often misclassify these minority instances due to their bias towards the majority class, achieving high accuracy at the expense of critical misclassifications [19].

This not only skews prediction results but also erodes public confidence, as failure to detect fraud accurately can result in significant financial losses and reduced trust in institutions [20, 21].

2.3 Addressing Class Imbalance with SMOTE, RandomUnderSampler, and ADASYN

To address the class imbalance problem, various resampling techniques have been developed to reduce the bias towards the majority class and enhance sensitivity towards the minority class [10]. These techniques can be categorized into three main approaches: data-level approaches (resampling techniques), algorithm-level approaches (modifying classification algorithms), and hybrid approaches (combining data and algorithm-level methods) [22].

This study focuses on comparing data-level approaches due to their widespread use and effectiveness in handling imbalanced datasets. Specifically, we examine RandomUnder-Sampler, SMOTE, and ADASYN (Adaptive Synthetic Sampling). By comparing these techniques, we aim to identify the most effective method for improving classification performance on imbalanced datasets [23].

RandomUnderSampler
Random undersampling reduces the number of majority class samples to balance the dataset. While straightforward, this method can lead to the loss of valuable information from the majority class [20]. Jones et al. (2017) proposed an undersampling technique leveraging the Naïve Bayes classifier. This method selects the most informational samples from the training dataset through random primary selection. The model is initially trained on a small set, followed by iterative teaching over the current samples, demonstrating that this undersampling technique is comparable to other resampling methods [20, 23]. Xie et al. (2021) introduced an innovative undersampling technique that utilizes consecutive density peaks to methodically remove samples from the majority class [24]. This approach evaluates two key factors to ascertain the importance of each sample,

creating an optimized sequence for training classifiers. The proposed algorithm demonstrated superior performance compared to six established undersampling methods across 40 public benchmark datasets. Undersampling can be seen as a "lower" computational burden compared to oversampling because it simplifies the dataset rather than expanding it. While oversampling aims to augment the minority class to match the majority class's size, undersampling reduces the majority class's size to achieve balance, often resulting in quicker processing times and lower storage requirements. Both techniques have their pros and cons, and the choice between them often depends on the specific characteristics of the dataset and the goals of the analysis [22].

SMOTE

SMOTE is a widely-used oversampling technique introduced by Chawla et al. [25]. It generates synthetic samples for the minority class by interpolating between existing minority class instances, thus increasing the number of minority class samples. SMOTE has been shown to improve the classification performance of ML models on imbalanced datasets [15, 25]. Several advanced versions of SMOTE have been proposed to further enhance its effectiveness. Dablain et al. (2022) introduced DeepSMOTE, an advanced version of SMOTE that combines an encoder/decoder structure, SMOTE-based properties, and an improved loss function. This method has demonstrated efficiency and power, particularly in GAN-based oversampling cases, enhancing model performance on imbalanced datasets [26]. Moreover, Maulidevi and Surendro (2022) proposed SMOTE-LOF, an enhancement of SMOTE that incorporates the Local Outlier Factor (LOF) to identify and handle noise in imbalanced datasets [27]. The results indicated that SMOTE and its variants outperformed traditional methods, particularly for large-scale datasets with small imbalance ratios, demonstrating their effectiveness in addressing imbalanced datasets [23].

ADASYN (Adaptive Synthetic Sampling)

ADASYN, introduced by He et al. (2008), operates similarly to SMOTE by generating synthetic samples for the minority class [28]. However, ADASYN focuses on creating more synthetic data for instances that are harder for the model to learn. Like SMOTE, it generates synthetic samples along a straight line between a minority class instance and its k-nearest minority class neighbors, typically set to 5. The key difference lies in how ADASYN prioritizes which instances to synthesize. It creates more synthetic samples for minority class instances that have a higher number of majority class neighbors within the k-nearest neighbors' region. Conversely, if a minority class instance has no majority class neighbors within this range, no synthetic samples are generated for that instance. This approach targets the more challenging instances for learning, enhancing the model's ability to handle imbalanced datasets effectively [29]. Thejas et al. (2022) proposed Kalman-SMOTE (KSMOTE), a development of SMOTE integrated with the Kalman filter, which shares similarities with ADASYN in terms of focusing on difficult-to-learn samples [11]. KSMOTE excludes noisy samples from the dataset, including both initial data and synthetically added samples, showing improved performance over existing methods.

3   Methodology

3.1   Dataset and Data Preprocessing

The dataset used is the "IBM Transactions for Anti-Money Laundering" from Kaggle, containing 5,078,345 transaction records with attributes such as timestamps, amounts, and currencies. Each transaction record includes 11 attributes (details see Table 1). Preprocessing steps involved handling missing values, encoding categorical features, and extracting useful features from timestamps [30, 31]. The Fig. 1 show the study framework. All experiments were conducted using Google Colab Pro, a cloud-based platform that provides enhanced computational resources for machine learning development. The models were implemented using Python 3.10 with libraries including pandas, scikit-learn, seaborn, etc. [32, 33] for data processing, machine learning algorithms and imbalanced-learn (Lemaître et al. 2017) for handling class imbalance with sampling techniques such as SMOTE and ADASYN.

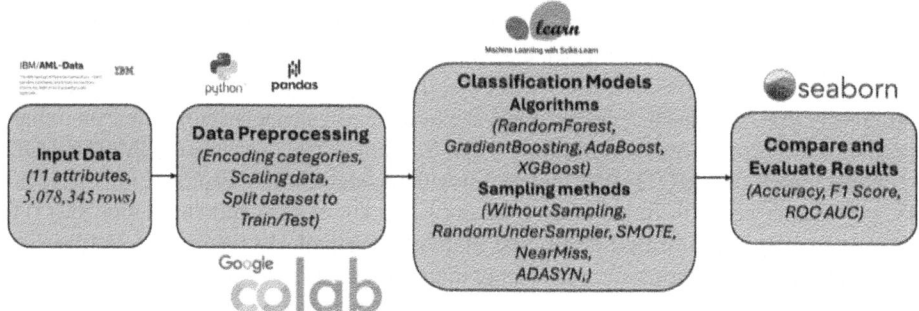

Fig. 1. Experimental workflow

The dataset exhibits a significant imbalance between the classes, with a disproportionately high number of normal transactions compared to laundering transactions. Specifically, there are 5,073,168 instances of non-laundering transactions, whereas laundering transactions account for only 5,177 instances. This pronounced disparity highlights the rarity of laundering transactions within the dataset, posing potential challenges for predictive modeling and necessitating the consideration of appropriate techniques to address class imbalance.

3.2   Imbalance Learning Techniques

To address the class imbalance in the dataset, three sampling methods were used:

- Random Undersampling [20]: Reduces the number of samples in the majority class.
- SMOTE [25]: Balances the dataset by oversampling the minority class.
- ADASYN [28]: Similar to SMOTE but focuses on harder-to-learn examples.Classification Models Training and Evaluation
- The study implements six ML models RandomForest, LogisticRegression, KNeighbors, GradientBoosting, LightGBM and XGBoost.

Table 1. Summary attributes of dataset

No.	Attribute	Data Type	Description
1	Timestamp	DateTime	The date and time when the transaction occurred
2	From Bank	String	Identifier of the originating bank
3	Account	String	Account number or identifier from which the funds were sent
4	To Bank	String	Identifier of the receiving bank
5	Account.1	String	Account number or identifier to which the funds were sent
6	Amount Received	Float	The amount credited to the recipient's account
7	Receiving Currency	Category	Currency in which the recipient received the funds (e.g., USD, EUR)
8	Amount Paid	Float	The amount debited from the sender's account
9	Payment Currency	Category	Currency in which the sender made the payment
10	Payment Format	Category	Method of payment (e.g., wire transfer, credit card, cash)
11	Is Laundering	Binary	Binary label indicating whether the transaction is identified as money laundering (1) or not (0)

3.3 Classification Models Training and Evaluation

The study implements five ML models to evaluate their effectiveness in detecting money laundering activities:

- RandomForest [34]: An ensemble learning method that constructs multiple decision trees during training and outputs the mode of the classes (classification) of the individual trees. It is robust to overfitting and can handle large datasets with high dimensionality.
- LogisticRegression [35]: A linear model used for binary classification tasks. It estimates the probability of a binary response based on one or more predictor variables and is effective for simple and linearly separable datasets.

$$J(\varphi) = -\frac{1}{m}\left[\sum_{i=1}^{m} y^{(i)} log h^{\varphi}\left(x^{(i)}\right) + \left(1 - y^{(i)}\right)\log(1 - h^{\varphi}\left(x^{(i)}\right))\right] \quad (1)$$

- KNeighbors (K-Nearest Neighbors) [36]: A non-parametric method used for classification by comparing the distance between different instances. It is simple to implement and understand but can be computationally intensive with large datasets. To measure the classification cost, we used the Minknowski distance as follows:

$$\Delta(x, y) = \left(\sum_{j=0}^{n=-1} |x_i - y_i|^p\right)^{1/p} \quad (2)$$

GradientBoosting [37]: An ensemble technique that builds models sequentially, each correcting the errors of its predecessor. It is highly effective for a variety of classification tasks but requires careful tuning to avoid overfitting. The loss function was calculated by using the log-likelyhood function as follows

$$\Upsilon = - \sum_{j=1}^{n} y_i \log(p) + (1-p)\log(1-p) \tag{3}$$

:

- LightGBM (Light Gradient Boosting Machine) [38]: A gradient boosting framework that uses tree-based learning algorithms. It is designed for speed and efficiency, capable of handling large datasets with low memory usage.
- XGBoost (Extreme Gradient Boosting) [39]: An efficient and powerful gradient boosting algorithm widely used for its high accuracy and performance. It features regularization to prevent overfitting, handles missing data well, and supports parallel processing. Its flexibility and scalability make it ideal for various ML tasks, including classification and regression. The loss function of XGBoost is depicted as follows:

$$\mathcal{H}^t = \sum_{j=1}^{n} \Upsilon\left(y_i, \widehat{y}_i^{t-1} + f_t(x_i)\right) + \Psi(f_t) \tag{4}$$

where $\Psi(f_t)$ is a regularization term.

The models were evaluated using precision (ζ), recall (∇), F1-score ($\mathcal{F}1$), and confusion matrices as follows:

$$\zeta = \frac{\rho}{\psi + \rho} \tag{5}$$

$$\nabla = \frac{\rho}{\rho + \alpha} \tag{6}$$

$$\mathcal{F}1 = 2 * \frac{\zeta * \nabla}{\zeta \mid \nabla} \tag{7}$$

where ρ, ψ, and α are the number true positives, number of false positives, and number of false negatives, respectively.

To evaluate the models, this study employs the confusion matrix, which systematically summarizes the number of correct and incorrect predictions in terms of true positives, false positives, true negatives, and false negatives [40]. This framework supports the calculation of key performance metrics, including precision, recall, and F1-score. In addition, metrics such as accuracy, ROC AUC, and F1-score are utilized to provide a comprehensive assessment of each model's effectiveness, particularly in handling class imbalance.

4 Experimental Results

4.1 Data Exploration

It is the process of discovering data insights via the use of various visualization approaches. It is the initial phase in the data analysis process. Pre-processing stage is a crucial stage in ML since it enhances the quality of the data, allowing us to extract relevant knowledge from big data with greater ease. Additionally, data becomes enough for modelling purposes. In this study, we evaluated the performance of six different classifiers: RandomForest, LogisticRegression, KNeighbors, GradientBoosting, Light-GBM, and XGBoost. Each classifier was tested using four different sampling methods: Without Sampling, SMOTE, RandomUnderSampler, and ADASYN. The performance metrics used for evaluation were Accuracy, F1 Score for Class 0 and Class 1, and ROC AUC. Given the imbalanced nature of the dataset, we will focus our discussion on the F1 scores, particularly for Class 1 (the minority class). Table 2 shows detailed metrics of the models.

Table 2. Summary results of ML models with sampling methods

Models	Sampling Methods	Accuracy	F1 Score (Class 0)	**F1 Score (Class 1)**	ROC AUC
Random Forest	*Without Sampling*	1	1	0.37	0.86
	SMOTE	**1**	**1**	**0.41**	**0.89**
	RandomUnderSampler	0.87	0.93	0.01	0.96
	ADASYN	**1**	**1**	**0.4**	**0.9**
Logistic Regression	*Without Sampling*	1	1	0	0.57
	SMOTE	0.62	0.76	0	0.75
	RandomUnderSampler	0.86	0.93	0.01	0.89
	ADASYN	0.86	0.92	0.01	0.89
KNeighbors	*Without Sampling*	1	1	0.1	0.56
	SMOTE	0.97	0.98	0.02	0.67
	RandomUnderSampler	0.67	0.8	0	0.74
	ADASYN	0.97	0.98	0.02	0.66
Gradient Boosting	*Without Sampling*	1	1	0.21	0.96
	SMOTE	0.96	0.98	0.04	0.96
	RandomUnderSampler	0.81	0.9	0.01	0.96
	ADASYN	0.96	0.98	0.04	0.96
LightGBM	*Without Sampling*	1	1	0.3	0.9
	SMOTE	0.99	1	0.13	0.96
	RandomUnderSampler	0.86	0.92	0.01	0.97
	ADASYN	0.99	1	0.12	0.96
XGBoost	***Without Sampling***	**1**	**1**	**0.41**	**0.97**
	SMOTE	0.99	0.99	0.08	0.96
	RandomUnderSampler	0.87	0.93	0.01	0.97
	ADASYN	0.99	0.99	0.1	0.96

4.2 Results Without Sampling

Without applying any sampling method, the classifiers exhibited high F1 scores for Class 0, indicating their effectiveness at identifying the majority class. However, the F1 scores for Class 1 were significantly lower across all classifiers, highlighting the difficulty in correctly identifying the minority class in an imbalanced dataset. For example, Random-Forest achieved an F1 Score of 1.00 for Class 0 and 0.37 for Class 1. LogisticRegression performed poorly for Class 1 with an F1 Score of 0.00 while maintaining an F1 Score of 1.00 for Class 0. KNeighbors had an F1 Score of 1.00 for Class 0 and 0.10 for Class 1. GradientBoosting, LightGBM, and XGBoost also showed similar trends, with high F1 Scores for Class 0 (around 1.00) and much lower scores for Class 1 (ranging from 0.21 to 0.41). For detailed values, see Table 2.

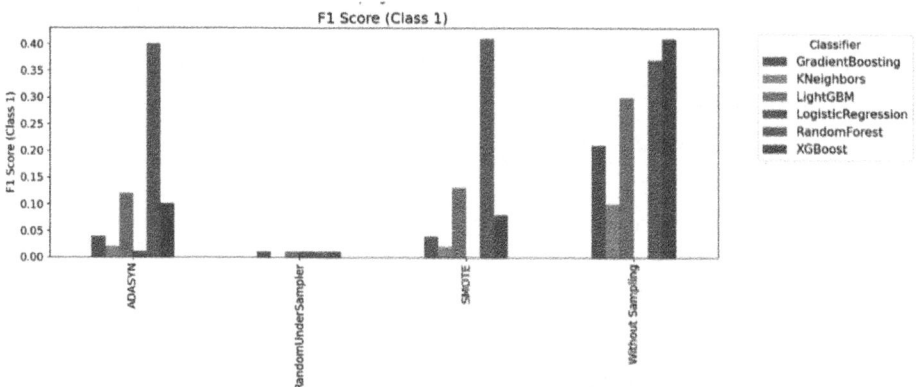

Fig. 2. The comparison F1 Scores of models and sampling methods

4.3 Results with Sampling Methods

Sampling methods were applied to address data imbalance, with notable improvements seen in F1 scores for Class 1 (minority class). Key findings are summarized below, with detailed values available in Table 2:

RandomUnderSampler: This method showed limited improvements for Class 1, with many classifiers exhibiting significant drops in F1 scores for Class 0. For example, RandomForest's F1 score for Class 1 remained at 0.01, with Class 0 slightly reduced to 0.93. Other classifiers, such as LogisticRegression and KNeighbors, also showed low improvements for Class 1.

SMOTE: This method generally boosted F1 scores for Class 1 across most classifiers. RandomForest saw a notable increase in its Class 1 F1 score to 0.41 while maintaining 1.00 for Class 0. LightGBM and XGBoost also saw moderate improvements for Class 1, with F1 scores improving to 0.13 and 0.08, respectively.

ADASYN: ADASYN provided results similar to SMOTE, with RandomForest's F1 score for Class 1 rising to 0.40. Other classifiers like GradientBoosting and Light-GBM also showed modest gains for Class 1, though LogisticRegression and KNeighbors showed little improvement. For further details, see Table 2 and Fig. 2.

5 Conclusion

In this study, we evaluated the performance of six classifiers—RandomForest, LogisticRegression, KNeighbors, GradientBoosting, LightGBM, and XGBoost—on an imbalanced dataset for laundering transaction classification. We employed four sampling methods: Without Sampling, SMOTE, RandomUnderSampler, and ADASYN, and assessed their impact on classifier performance, focusing on the F1 scores for the minority class (Class 1).

Our findings indicate that RandomForest, particularly when combined with SMOTE and ADASYN, consistently outperformed other classifiers. Without any sampling, RandomForest achieved an impressive F1 Score of 0.37 for Class 1, which improved to 0.41 with SMOTE and 0.40 with ADASYN. These results demonstrate the robustness of RandomForest in handling imbalanced datasets, particularly when augmented with effective sampling techniques (see Table 2).

Other classifiers, such as LogisticRegression and KNeighbors, struggled to achieve comparable performance, especially in identifying the minority class. Despite various sampling methods, these classifiers maintained low F1 scores for Class 1, indicating limited effectiveness in this context. Ensemble methods like GradientBoosting, Light-GBM, and XGBoost showed moderate improvements with sampling methods but did not reach the performance levels of RandomForest.

The application of sampling methods proved crucial in improving the classifiers' ability to detect minority class instances. SMOTE and ADASYN, in particular, were effective in enhancing the F1 scores for Class 1 across most classifiers, with RandomForest benefiting the most. RandomUnderSampler, on the other hand, yielded mixed results, often leading to a decrease in F1 scores for the majority class without significant gains for the minority class.

In conclusion, while techniques such as Random Forest and Logistic Regression are well-established, this study highlights their effectiveness in addressing class imbalance in AML detection—a context that remains underexplored. The findings underscore the critical importance of selecting appropriate combinations of classifiers and sampling methods to improve classification performance in imbalanced datasets [40]. Future research should focus on further model tuning, the development of advanced imbalance handling strategies, and the exploration of additional algorithms to enhance detection performance. These insights contribute to the development of more robust predictive models for financial fraud detection.

Acknowledgements. The authors would like to thank FPT University, CanTho Campus for funding this research.

Disclosure of Interests. . The authors declare no competing interests relevant to the content of this article.

References

1. Levi, M., Reuter, P.: Money laundering. Crime Justice **34**(1), 289–375 (2006)
2. Sobh, T.S.: An intelligent and secure framework for anti-money laundering. J. Appl. Secur. Res. **15**(4), 517–546 (2020)
3. Omar, N., Johari, Z.A.: An international analysis of FATF recommendations and compliance by DNFBPS. Procedia Econ. Financ. **28**, 14–23 (2015)
4. Remeikienė, R., Gaspareniene, L., Schneider, F.G.: The definition of digital shadow economy. Technol. Econ. Dev. Econ. Vilnius: Technika **24**(2) (2018)
5. Vogel, B.: Potentials and limits of public-private partnerships against money laundering and terrorism financing. In: Eucrim-the European Criminal Law Associations' Forum, no. 01, pp. 52–60 (2022)
6. Berg, S., McCarthy, K.J.: An introduction to the Challenges of Money Laundering. The Money Laundering Market, pp. 3–32 (2018)
7. Nance, M.T.: The regime that FATF built: an introduction to the financial action task force. Crime Law Soc. Chang. **69**, 109–129 (2018)
8. Bamberger, K.A.: Technologies of compliance: risk and regulation in a digital age. Tex. L. Rev. **88**, 669 (2009)
9. Bakhshinejad, N., Soltani, R., Nguyen, U., Messina, P.: A survey of machine learning based anti-money laundering solutions. Researchgate preprint. Accessed, vol. 5 (2023)
10. Johnson, J.M., Khoshgoftaar, T.M.: Survey on deep learning with class imbalance. J. Big Data **6**(1), 1–54 (2019)
11. Thejas, G., Hariprasad, Y., Iyengar, S., Sunitha, N., Badrinath, P., Chennupati, S.: An extension of synthetic minority oversampling technique based on kalman filter for imbalanced datasets. Mach. Learn. Appl. **8**, 100267 (2022)
12. Naeem, S., Ali, A., Anam, S., Ahmed, M.M.: An unsupervised machine learning algorithms: comprehensive review. Int. J. Comput. Digit. Syst. (2023)
13. Dhankhad, S., Mohammed, E., Far, B.: Supervised machine learning algorithms for credit card fraudulent transaction detection: a comparative study. In: 2018 IEEE International Conference on Information Reuse and Integration (IRI), pp. 122–125. IEEE (2018)
14. Khalid, A.R., Owoh, N., Uthmani, O., Ashawa, M., Osamor, J., Adejoh, J.: Enhancing credit card fraud detection: an ensemble machine learning approach. Big Data Cogn. Comput. **8**(1), 6 (2024)
15. Almhaithawi, D., Jafar, A., Aljnidi, M.: Example-dependent cost-sensitive credit cards fraud detection using SMOTE and Bayes minimum risk. SN Appl. Sci. **2**, 1–12 (2020)
16. Kute, D.V., Pradhan, B., Shukla, N., Alamri, A.: Deep learning and explainable artificial intelligence techniques applied for detecting money laundering–a critical review. IEEE Access **9**, 82300–82317 (2021)
17. Segovia-Vargas, M.-J.: Money laundering and terrorism financing detection using neural networks and an abnormality indicator. Expert Syst. Appl. **169**, 114470 (2021)
18. Priscilla, C.V., Prabha, D.P.: Influence of optimizing XGBoost to handle class imbalance in credit card fraud detection. In: 2020 Third International Conference on Smart Systems and Inventive Technology (ICSSIT), pp. 1309–1315. IEEE (2020)
19. Ramyachitra, D., Manikandan, P.: Imbalanced dataset classification and solutions: a review. Int. J. Comput. Bus. Res. (IJCBR) **5**(4), 1–29 (2014)
20. LemaÃŽtre, G., Nogueira, F., Aridas, C.K.: Imbalanced-learn: a python toolbox to tackle the curse of imbalanced datasets in machine learning. J. Mach. Learn. Res. **18**(17), 1–5 (2017)

21. Makki, S., Assaghir, Z., Taher, Y., Haque, R., Hacid, M.-S., Zeineddine, H.: An experimental study with imbalanced classification approaches for credit card fraud detection. IEEE Access **7**, 93010–93022 (2019)

22. Gong, P., Gao, J., Wang, L.: A hybrid evolutionary under-sampling method for handling the class imbalance problem with overlap in credit classification. J. Syst. Sci. Syst. Eng. **31**(6), 728–752 (2022)

23. Mohammed, R., Rawashdeh, J., Abdullah, M.: Machine learning with oversampling and undersampling techniques: overview study and experimental results. In: 2020 11th International Conference on Information and Communication Systems (ICICS), , pp. 243–248. IEEE (2020)

24. Xie, X., Liu, H., Zeng, S., Lin, L., Li, W.: A novel progressively undersampling method based on the density peaks sequence for imbalanced data. Knowl.-Based Syst. **213**, 106689 (2021)

25. Chawla, N.V., Bowyer, K.W., Hall, L.O., Kegelmeyer, W.P.: SMOTE: synthetic minority over-sampling technique. J. Artif. Intell. Res. **16**, 321–357 (2002)

26. Dablain, D., Krawczyk, B., Chawla, N.V.: DeepSMOTE: fusing deep learning and SMOTE for imbalanced data. IEEE Trans. Neural Netw. Learn. Systems **34**(9), 6390–6404 (2022)

27. Maulidevi, N.U., Surendro, K.: SMOTE-LOF for noise identification in imbalanced data classification. J. King Saud Univ. Comput. Inf. Sci. **34**(6), 3413–3423 (2022)

28. He, H., Bai, Y., Garcia, E.A., Li, S.: ADASYN: Adaptive synthetic sampling approach for imbalanced learning. In: 2008 IEEE International Joint Conference on Neural Networks (IEEE World Congress on Computational Intelligence), pp. 1322–1328. IEEE (2008)

29. Brandt, J., Lanzén, E.: A comparative review of SMOTE and ADASYN in imbalanced data classification (2021)

30. Ngai, E.W., Hu, Y., Wong, Y.H., Chen, Y., Sun, X.: The application of data mining techniques in financial fraud detection: a classification framework and an academic review of literature. Decis. Support. Syst. **50**(3), 559–569 (2011)

31. Jullum, M., Løland, A., Huseby, R.B., Ånonsen, G., Lorentzen, J.: Detecting money laundering transactions with machine learning. J. Money Laundering Control **23**(1), 173–186 (2020)

32. Pedregosa, F., et al.: Scikit-learn: machine learning in Python. J. Mach. Learn. Res. **12**, 2825–2830 (2011)

33. Molin, S.: Hands-On Data Analysis with Pandas: Efficiently perform data collection, wrangling, analysis, and visualization using Python. Packt Publishing Ltd (2019)

34. Breiman, L.: Random forests. Mach. Learn. **45**, 5–32 (2001)

35. Cox, D.R.: The regression analysis of binary sequences. J. R. Stat. Soc. Ser. B Stat Methodol. **20**(2), 215–232 (1958)

36. Fix, E., Hodges, J.L.: Discriminatory Analysis. Nonparametric Discrimination: Small Sample Performance. Report A, vol. 193008 (1951)

37. Friedman, J.H.: Greedy function approximation: a gradient boosting machine. Ann. Stat. 1189–1232 (2001)

38. Ke, G., et al.: Lightgbm: a highly efficient gradient boosting decision tree. Adv. Neural Inf. Process. Syst. **30** (2017)

39. Chen, T., Guestrin, C.: Xgboost: a scalable tree boosting system. In: Proceedings of the 22nd ACM SIGKDD International Conference on Knowledge Discovery and Data Mining, pp. 785–794 (2016)

40. Saito, T., Rehmsmeier, M.: The precision-recall plot is more informative than the ROC plot when evaluating binary classifiers on imbalanced datasets. Plos One **10**(3), e0118432 (2015)

Beyond the Like Button: Predicting How Risks Impact Trust on Instagram S-Commerce

Ahmed Shuhaiber(✉)

Zayed University, Abu Dhabi 144534, UAE
ahmed.shuhaiber@zu.ac.ae

Abstract. Social commerce (s-commerce) integrates social media with e-commerce, creating new opportunities for consumers and businesses. However, the success of s-commerce depends heavily on perceived risks and trust, which influence consumer decisions. Despite growing research, the interaction between different types of risks: financial, security, and time risks and various trust dimensions, such as merchant competence and merchant integrity, remains underexplored. This study addresses this gap by proposing a predictive model to examine these relationships, focusing on Instagram-based shopping. A quantitative approach was used, with an online survey administered to 267 university students across three UAE universities, analyzed using Structural Equation Modeling (SEM-PLS). The findings show that all three perceived risks significantly impact both merchant competence and merchant integrity, with security risks having the strongest effect on competence. The study underscores the importance of addressing these risks to build trust in s-commerce platforms. However, the sample's limitation to Generation Z students in the UAE suggests the need for broader research.

Keywords: S-commerce · Trust · Perceived Risk · Merchant Competence · Merchant Integrity · SEM-PLS · Instagram Shopping

1 Introduction

Social commerce (s-commerce) has emerged as a transformative approach to online shopping, where consumers engage in transactions on social media platforms or other online communities that incorporate social interactions. This rapidly growing field combines the social interaction aspect of social media with e-commerce, creating new opportunities for both businesses and consumers. However, as with traditional e-commerce, the success of s-commerce platforms is significantly influenced by two critical factors: perceived risks and trust [1]. These factors are crucial for consumer decision-making processes, as the digital nature of s-commerce introduces a unique set of risks that could potentially deter users from engaging with these platforms.

Perceived risks in s-commerce encompass various concerns that consumers have when transacting online, including privacy risks, financial risks, performance risks, and social risks. As noted by Torki Biucky et al. [2], these risks arise from the uncertainty

O. Gervasi et al. (Eds.): ICCSA 2025, LNCS 15650, pp. 162–172, 2025.
https://doi.org/10.1007/978-3-031-96962-1_11

associated with sharing personal information, making payments, and relying on the online platform to deliver the promised goods or services. These risks, if not adequately managed, can result in a lack of consumer confidence, reducing the likelihood of adoption and continued use of s-commerce platforms.

On the other hand, trust plays a critical role in mitigating these risks. Consumers' trust in s-commerce platforms influences their willingness to share personal information, make payments, and engage in social interactions on the platform. Tseng [5] emphasizes that trust can be broken down into several dimensions, such as system trust (trust in the technological infrastructure), institutional trust (trust in the platform or company behind the transactions), and interpersonal trust (trust in other users or community members). Effective trust-building mechanisms are essential for reducing perceived risks and promoting positive consumer behavior in s-commerce settings.

Previous studies have established that perceived risks and trust are central to the adoption and use of s-commerce platforms, but the relationship between these two constructs remains underexplored. While much research has incorporated perceived risks and trust into broader models of technology acceptance and s-commerce adoption, few studies have investigated the complex relationship between these factors. As pointed out by Farivar et al. [3] and Al-Kfairy et al. [4], understanding how different types of perceived risks (e.g., financial, privacy, performance) affect various dimensions of trust (e.g., system trust, institutional trust, interpersonal trust) is a critical gap in the literature. This paper proposes a predictive model to explore and analyze the relationship between perceived risks and trust in the context of s-commerce, aiming to provide deeper insights into how these constructs interact and influence consumer behavior. Through the development of this model, we aim to enhance understanding of trust-building strategies and risk mitigation in s-commerce environments. Accordingly, the research question of this study:

what perceived risks significantly impact user trust in Instagram shopping?

The remainder of this paper is structured as follows: Sect. 2 presents the literature review, offering an overview of existing studies on perceived risks and trust in the context of social commerce. Section 3 outlines the research methodology, including the design of the survey instrument, sampling procedures, and measurement approach. Section 4 provides the data analysis and findings using Structural Equation Modeling with Partial Least Squares (SEM-PLS). Section 5 discusses the results in light of prior research. Section 6 presents the theoretical and practical implications of the study, while Sect. 7 concludes the paper by outlining its limitations and suggesting directions for future research.

2 Literature Review

The relationship between perceived risks and trust has been a central theme in social commerce (s-commerce) research. While many studies have incorporated these constructs in models of s-commerce adoption and technology acceptance, few have explored the complex relationships between them. Additionally, research has largely ignored how different types of perceived risks (e.g., privacy risks, financial risks, performance risks) interact with different trust dimensions (e.g., institutional trust, system trust, interpersonal trust) in the s-commerce context. This literature review summarizes current research, identifies gaps in the literature, and points out the need for further exploration into how these constructs relate to one another in s-commerce environments.

Numerous studies have incorporated perceived risks and trust within technology acceptance models, especially in the context of s-commerce adoption. Indeed, previous research highlights how trust shapes s-commerce experiences. For example, Esmaeili's team [1] showed that privacy and financial risks make customers wary of social commerce platforms. Meanwhile, Torki Biucky's studies [2] used the Technology Acceptance Model (TAM) model to prove trust can ease these concerns. But while these studies confirm trust helps overcome risks, they oversimplify trust as one big concept - missing how different risks might affect specific aspects of trust.

Trust is the hub that holds social commerce together; it helps users feel safe enough to participate. For instance, Tseng's research [5] shows that when people worry about privacy, they rely heavily on system trust. However, the study doesn't explore how financial concerns might shake institutional trust, or if product risks damage buyer-seller trust. Farivar's team [3] agrees trust softens risk's impact, but like others, they lump all 'trust' together instead of pinpointing which risks threaten which specific trust layers.

In addition, Al-Kfairy's work [4] examines usability, risks, and trust in social commerce, but it lacks an important detail, which is about how certain concerns (such as privacy issues) undermine system trust or how financial considerations could erode platform trust. Although Soleimani's research [10] likewise emphasizes the impact of risk on s-commerce, it approaches trust as a single concept rather than dissecting the ways in which various risks affect distinct forms of trust. This leaves a critical gap in understanding how risk types can shape various trust factors.

The complexity of the relationship between perceived risks and trust in s-commerce is also highlighted by studies like Mendoza-Tello et al. [13], which examined cryptocurrencies within s-commerce platforms. The study shows that trust plays a critical role in influencing user intention and adoption, especially when risks, such as security concerns, are prevalent. However, the study did not explore how these risks affect different trust dimensions (e.g., institutional trust vs. system trust), which is a significant limitation.

Finally, Sharma et al. [18] apply the concept of trust to s-commerce but do not specify how perceived risks affect specific dimensions of trust. The literature often lacks depth in examining how trust interacts with various types of perceived risks in the context of s-commerce, leaving an important gap in understanding how to design effective strategies for trust-building and risk mitigation in these platforms.

In conclusion, while substantial research has been conducted on the roles of perceived risks and trust in s-commerce, the complex relationships between these constructs remain underexplored. Most studies treat perceived risks and trust as broad, unidimensional factors, without addressing how different types of perceived risks (e.g., privacy, financial, performance) affect specific dimensions of trust (e.g., system trust, institutional trust, interpersonal trust). This gap in the literature highlights the need for further research into the nuanced interactions between perceived risks and trust dimensions in the s-commerce environment, offering insights that could lead to more effective strategies for reducing risks and building trust.

3   Methodology

This study adopts a post-positivist philosophical paradigm to investigate the proposed research hypotheses, through a quantitative approach. This approach acknowledges the strengths and limitations of existing theories, recognizing that scholars' contributions are influenced by both their insights and potential biases. To measure users' trust in s-commerce, specifically on the Instagram platform, we developed an online survey. The survey was hosted on Google Forms, a platform chosen for its convenience, speed, and ability to easily import data for analysis.

The survey instrument was designed based on relevant literature in the field. We adapted existing trust-related constructs from e-commerce theories and customized them to suit the context of Insta-shopping. The survey included demographic questions such as gender, age, education, and occupation, providing a detailed breakdown of the respondent characteristics. The research questions, aligned with the research model, were organized into blocks that included the following variables and their associated items:

- Financial Risk (4 items)
- Security Risks (4 items)
- Time Risks (4 items)
- Merchant Competence (4 items)
- Merchant Integrity (3 items)

A five-point Likert scale was used to measure responses, with values ranging from 1 (Strongly disagree) to 5 (Strongly agree), where a score of 3 indicated a neutral stance. To target a relevant sample, we employed convenience sampling, focusing on Generation Z due to their high engagement with technology and social media. The respondents were university students from three institutions across different emirates of the UAE. Participants were recruited through e-learning platforms, social media groups, LinkedIn profiles, and email invitations.

To enhance the response rate and sample size, the snowball sampling technique was also used. Inclusion criteria for participants were as follows: (a) familiarity with Insta-shopping, either as buyers or sellers in the UAE; (b) being over the age of 18; and (c) willingness to provide feedback on their experiences and perceptions of Insta-shopping. A total of 267 valid responses were collected over a period of two months. After data collection, the responses were manually reviewed to ensure there were no biases or incomplete entries, and all responses were found to be complete and suitable for analysis. The research model that shows the research variable and the associated relationships is shown in Fig. 1.

In addition, the hypotheses associated with the research model are stated below:

- H1: Financial Risk has a significant effect on perceived Merchant Competence in Instagram-based social commerce.
- H2: Financial Risk has a significant effect on perceived Merchant Integrity in Instagram-based social commerce.
- H3: Security Risks have a significant effect on perceived Merchant Competence in Instagram-based social commerce.
- H4: Security Risks have a significant effect on perceived Merchant Integrity in Instagram-based social commerce.

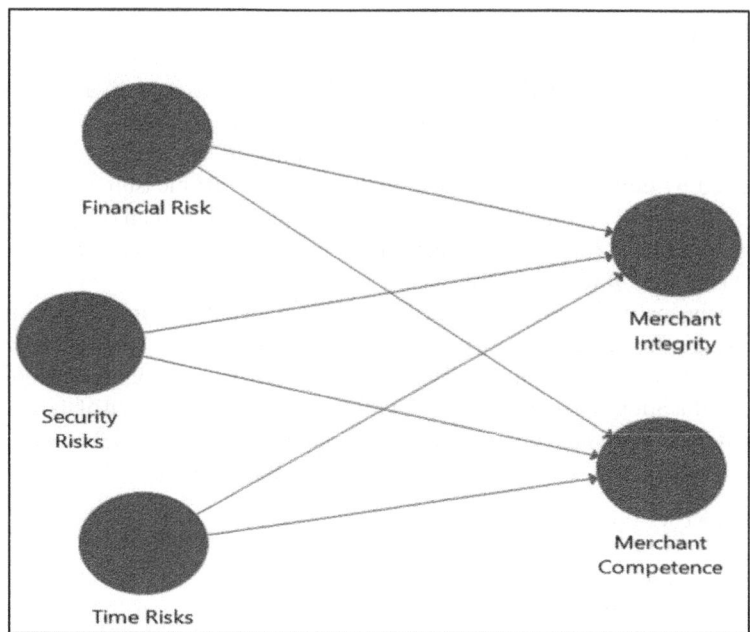

Fig. 1. Proposed Research Model

- H5: Time Risks have a significant effect on perceived Merchant Competence in Instagram-based social commerce.
- H6: Time Risks have a significant effect on perceived Merchant Integrity in Instagram-based social commerce.

4   Data Analysis and Findings

To examine the research model and related assumptions, the researcher used the SEM-PLS technique. A powerful statistical method for analyzing complex relationships between latent variables is structural equation modeling using partial least squares (SEM-PLS). Since SEM-PLS is a variance-based method that does not depend on big sample sizes or the presumption of a normal data distribution, it is especially useful when working with relatively small sample sizes [24]. This approach is ideal for application in social science and marketing research since it enables researchers to estimate several relationships inside a model at once. The outer model and the inner model are two crucial steps in SEM-PLS [24]. The measurement of latent variables and the evaluation of the correlation between the constructs and the observed indicators (items) are the focus of the outer model. In order to verify that the constructs are appropriately represented by the indicators, this step entails assessing the validity and reliability of the measurement model, usually using factor loadings, composite reliability, and average variance extracted (AVE).

Conversely, the inner model concentrates on the structural connections between latent variables. It evaluates the model's path linkages, enabling researchers to gauge the importance and potency of both direct and indirect impacts between constructs. Path coefficients, R-squared values, and the significance of these coefficients are commonly used to assess the inner model in SEM-PLS. Using SEM-PLS is appropriate given the study's small sample size. This method is appropriate for studying complex models with little data because it employs a bootstrapping strategy to determine the significance of path coefficients, which makes it robust to small sample sizes. The flexibility of SEM-PLS in handling both measurement and structural models, combined with its suitability for small sample sizes, makes it an ideal choice for this study.

Firstly, and starting with the item loadings, the results show that all items are valid, by scoring an item loading greater than the threshold of 0.6 [24]. This suggests that the survey items demonstrate validity, and ready for further tests. Secondly, the reliability and validity of the constructs are assessed. Table 1 presents the reliability and validity metrics for various constructs related to perceived risks and trust in the context of s-commerce. Cronbach's Alpha values indicate good internal consistency for all constructs, with Financial Risk (0.886) and Time Risks (0.876) showing particularly high reliability, while Security Risks (0.783) and Merchant Integrity (0.784) still maintain acceptable values. The Average Variance Extracted (AVE) values, ranging from 0.475 to 0.573, indicate that while some constructs meet the minimum threshold of 0.50 for convergent validity (e.g., Merchant Competence at 0.573), others, such as Security Risks (0.475), are slightly below the desired threshold. This suggests that while the constructs generally show strong internal consistency, some may need further refinement to improve their convergent validity and overall measurement quality.

Table 1. Constructs' Reliability and Convergent Validity.

Component	Cronbach's Alpha	AVE
Financial Risk	0.886	0.544
Security Risks	0.783	0.475
Time Risks	0.876	0.544
Merchant Competence	0.885	0.573
Merchant Integrity	0.784	0.531

Thirdly, the researcher assessed the discriminant validity of the research constructs. Table 2 presents the discriminant validity of various constructs, evaluated using the Fornell and Larcker (1981) criterion [24]. According to this criterion, discriminant validity is established if the square root of the Average Variance Extracted (AVE) for each construct is greater than its correlations with other constructs. The square root of AVE values for each construct (shown on the diagonal) are compared to the correlations between constructs. For example, the square root of the AVE for Financial Risk is 0.737, which is higher than its correlations with other constructs, such as Security Risks (0.627), Time Risks (0.654), Merchant Competence (0.393), and Merchant Integrity (0.356), indicating good discriminant validity. Similarly, Security Risks shows a square root of

AVE value of 0.689, which is greater than its correlations with other constructs, confirming its discriminant validity. Time Risks with an AVE square root of 0.738 also demonstrates distinctiveness from the other constructs, as its correlations are lower. For Merchant Competence and Merchant Integrity, the diagonal values of 0.757 and 0.730, respectively, are higher than their correlations with other constructs, indicating that both have adequate discriminant validity as well. Overall, the results meet the Fornell and Larcker (1981) criterion, as the square root of AVE for each construct is higher than the correlations with other constructs, confirming strong discriminant validity across all constructs.

Table 2. Constructs' Discriminant Validity

Construct	Financial Risk	Security Risks	Time Risks	Merchant Competence	Merchant Integrity
Financial Risk	0.737	0.627	0.654	0.393	0.356
Security Risks	0.627	0.689	0.674	0.535	0.495
Time Risks	0.654	0.674	0.738	0.507	0.477
Merchant Competence	0.393	0.535	0.507	0.757	0.412
Merchant Integrity	0.356	0.495	0.477	0.412	0.730

Table 3 presents the results of the path testing for various predictors and their influence on the criterion variables, Merchant Competence and Merchant Integrity. The table shows the Beta values, t-statistics, p-values, and whether the hypotheses were supported. The Beta values indicate the strength and direction of the relationships, with all relationships showing positive effects, suggesting that as Financial Risk, Security Risks, and Time Risks increase, both Merchant Competence and Merchant Integrity are positively influenced. The t-statistics for all paths are well above the threshold of 1.96, indicating that the relationships are statistically significant. The p-values for all paths are 0.000, confirming that these relationships are highly significant and not due to chance. As a result, all hypotheses are supported, demonstrating that each type of risk has a significant positive impact on the respective merchant attributes, indicating strong empirical support for the proposed relationships in the model.

5   Discussion

The hypothesis that Financial Risk significantly influences Merchant Competence is supported in this study with a beta of 0.393, a t-statistic of 9.654, and a p-value of 0.000. This result aligns with findings from Farivar et al. [3], where financial risks were found to influence consumer perceptions of merchant capabilities. Consumers tend to link the

Table 3. Path Testing (Beta, t-statistics, p-value, and hypothesis supported)

Predictor	Criterion	Beta	t-statistic	p-value	Hypothesis Supported?
Financial Risk	Merchant Competence	0.393	9.654	0.000	Yes
Financial Risk	Merchant Integrity	0.356	7.599	0.000	Yes
Security Risks	Merchant Competence	0.535	13.863	0.000	Yes
Security Risks	Merchant Integrity	0.495	10.969	0.000	Yes
Time Risks	Merchant Competence	0.507	13.078	0.000	Yes
Time Risks	Merchant Integrity	0.477	10.571	0.000	Yes

financial stability of a platform with the competence of the merchants using it. This suggests that when consumers perceive high financial risk, they question the ability of merchants to deliver reliable services, thus affecting their overall perception of merchant competence.

Similarly, the hypothesis that Financial Risk impacts Merchant Integrity is supported with a beta of 0.356 and a significant t-statistic (7.599). These findings are consistent with Torki Biucky et al. [2], where financial risks led to reduced trust in the integrity of e-commerce platforms. In s-commerce, financial risks such as payment security concerns can undermine trust in the platform's ethical practices and fairness. This result is in line with the assertion that consumers need assurances that their financial transactions are handled securely to trust the integrity of merchants.

The relationship between Security Risks and Merchant Competence was found to be highly significant (beta = 0.535, t-statistic = 13.863). This is supported by studies such as Tseng [5], who emphasized that perceived security risks can severely impact consumer trust in the competence of merchants, as these risks are directly associated with the platform's security measures. When consumers fear breaches or lack of proper security protocols, they are more likely to doubt the platform's ability to manage transactions effectively and efficiently, which reflects on their perception of merchant competence.

As predicted, Security Risks also affect Merchant Integrity significantly (beta = 0.495, t-statistic = 10.969). This finding is consistent with Farivar et al. [3], where security issues were seen as a critical determinant of merchant integrity. Concerns over security breaches or fraudulent activities naturally raise questions about the trustworthiness of merchants. If consumers perceive that a merchant's platform is vulnerable to security issues, their perception of that merchant's integrity becomes compromised, even if the merchant acts ethically.

The hypothesis that Time Risks affect Merchant Competence is supported by a significant beta of 0.507 and a high t-statistic of 13.078. This result resonates with Sharma et al. [18], who found that time-related concerns, such as delays in service delivery or inefficiencies lead to diminished trust in a merchant's competence. Perceived delays or inefficiencies can seriously harm a merchant's ability to execute on promises, which in turn affects their perceived competence in a time when customers expect rapid service.

Lastly, there is support for the hypothesis that Time Risks affect Merchant Integrity (beta $= 0.477$, t-statistic $= 10.571$). This outcome is consistent with Hsu et al. [19], who emphasized that delays in product delivery or transaction processing can cause customers to doubt the dependability and moral character of retailers. Customers may perceive the merchant's integrity as compromised if time risks indicate inefficiency. This finding underscores the importance of timely and efficient service in maintaining trust.

6 Conclusion and Implications

This study contributes to the growing discourse on the behavioral dynamics of s-commerce by focusing on one of its most critical yet underexplored relationships; the interplay between perceived risks and trust. Drawing on empirical data from Instagram-based shopping experiences, the findings offer a deeper understanding of how consumers form trust judgments based on different types of perceived risks: financial, security, and time. The results reveal that all three types significantly influence both merchant competence and integrity, with particularly strong associations found between security risks and competence, and between financial/time risks and integrity. What emerges is a clearer picture of how digital consumers, especially Gen Z, mentally navigate uncertainty while shopping on socially interactive platforms. These insights bring theoretical clarity to a subject that has largely been treated in a fragmented manner. This research not only affirms the essential role of trust in s-commerce but also reveals the nuanced pathways through which risks shape trust formation, offering a more predictive and contextual understanding of online consumer behavior.

Theoretically, this study introduces a novel predictive model that distinguishes between types of perceived risks and maps their influence on specific dimensions of trust within the s-commerce context; an approach not yet addressed in existing literature. While many previous studies have examined perceived risks and trust independently, or as part of broader acceptance frameworks, very few have attempted to isolate and empirically test the causal pathways between them. By doing so, this research adds to the conceptual foundations of s-commerce by validating the differential impact of risk dimensions on distinct forms of trust, namely merchant competence and integrity. This contribution is especially important for scholars aiming to refine or extend trust-based models in online environments, as it bridges the gap between general risk/trust frameworks and context-specific consumer behavior. As such, the proposed model is both a theoretical innovation and a practical diagnostic tool that can inform future scholarly investigations into risk perception, trust formation, and behavioral intention in digital commerce environments.

From a practical standpoint, this study carries several implications for stakeholders, including decision-makers, marketers, platform developers, and end users. For businesses operating in the s-commerce ecosystem, particularly on Instagram, the findings offer guidance on how to tailor risk-reduction strategies to the specific trust dimensions that influence customer loyalty and engagement. For example, addressing security risks through visible privacy policies and secure payment mechanisms may enhance perceptions of merchant competence, while ensuring transparent pricing and responsive customer service may foster trust in merchant integrity. Platform developers at Instagram can also leverage these insights to refine algorithms and features that amplify trustworthy sellers and flag those that exhibit risk signals. Moreover, policymakers and regulators concerned with digital commerce can use this model to craft more targeted consumer protection policies, especially for younger generations who are increasingly active in s-commerce. Ultimately, this research empowers users by demystifying the underlying psychological mechanisms that govern their online decisions, helping them become more informed and confident participants in the digital economy.

7 Limitations and Future Work

While this study provides valuable insights into the role of perceived risks and trust in s-commerce, several limitations must be acknowledged. First, the sample was restricted to Generation Z university students in the UAE, which limits the generalizability of the findings to other demographic groups or geographic regions. Future research could extend this study by including diverse demographic groups to understand the broader applicability of the model. Additionally, while the study used SEM-PLS to test the hypotheses, it would be beneficial to incorporate other advanced techniques, such as latent growth modeling or multigroup analysis, to examine the dynamic nature of risk perceptions over time or across different consumer segments.

Another limitation is the focus on Instagram as a single s-commerce platform. Future studies could compare various social media platforms to identify platform-specific risk and trust dynamics. Additionally, exploring other types of perceived risks, such as social risks, could offer a more holistic view of how risks impact consumer behavior in the broader s-commerce landscape. Finally, the current research could be expanded by integrating consumer behavioral intentions and post-purchase behavior, including customer loyalty and satisfaction.

References

1. Esmaeili, L., Mutallebi, M., Mardani, S., Golpayegani, S.A.H.: Studying the affecting factors on trust in social commerce. arXiv preprint arXiv:1508.04048 (2015)
2. Torki Biucky, S., Abdolvand, N., Rajaee Harandi, S.: The effects of perceived risk on social commerce adoption based on TAM model. Int. J. Electr. Commer. Stud. (2017)
3. Farivar, S., Yuan, Y., Turel, O.: Understanding social commerce acceptance: the role of trust, perceived risk, and benefit (2016)
4. Al-Kfairy, M., Shuhaiber, A., Al-Khatib, A.W., Alrabaee, S.: Social commerce adoption model based on usability, perceived risks, and institutional trust. IEEE Trans. Eng. Manag. **71**, 3599–3612 (2023)
5. Tseng, H.T.: Shaping path of trust: the role of information credibility, social support, information sharing and perceived privacy risk in social commerce. Inf. Technol. People **36**(2), 683–700 (2023)
6. Sun, X., Pelet, J.É., Dai, S., Ma, Y.: The effects of trust, perceived risk, innovativeness, and deal proneness on consumers' purchasing behavior in the livestreaming social commerce context. Sustainability **15**(23), 16320 (2023)
7. Farivar, S., Turel, O., Yuan, Y.: A trust-risk perspective on social commerce use: an examination of the biasing role of habit. Internet Res. **27**(3), 586–607 (2017)

8. Rouibah, K., Al-Qirim, N., Hwang, Y., Pouri, S.G.: The determinants of eWoM in social commerce: The role of perceived value, perceived enjoyment, trust, risks, and satisfaction. J. Glob. Inf. Manag. **29**(3), 75–102 (2021)

9. Salam, A.F., Rao, H.R., Pegels, C.C.: Consumer-perceived risk in e-commerce transactions. Commun. ACM **46**(12), 325–331 (2003)

10. Soleimani, M., Danaei, H., Jowkar, A., Parhizgar, M.M.: Factors affecting social commerce and exploring the mediating role of perceived risk. Interdiscip. J. Manag. Stud. **10**(1), 63–90 (2017)

11. Mahmoodi, I., Mojaddam, K.: Assessing the effect of social commerce structures, trust and perceived risk on the attitude and buying intention of customers. Bus. Manag. Explor. Q. **15**(31) (2023)

12. Ashoer, M., Said, S.: The impact of perceived risk on consumer purchase intention in Indonesia; a social commerce study. In: Proc. Int. Conf. Account. Manag. Econ. Soc. Sci. pp. 1–13 (2016)

13. Mendoza-Tello, J.C., Mora, H., Pujol-López, F.A., Lytras, M.D.: Social commerce as a driver to enhance trust and intention to use cryptocurrencies. IEEE Access **6**, 50737–50751 (2018)

14. Kim, S., Park, H.: Effects of various characteristics of social commerce on consumers' trust and trust performance. Int. J. Inf. Manag. **33**(2), 318–332 (2013)

15. PhamThi, V.: A game of perceived risk in social commerce transactions. Mark. Menedzsment **56**(1), 29–41 (2022)

16. Glover, S., Benbasat, I.: A comprehensive model of perceived risk of e-commerce transactions. Int. J. Electron. Commer. **15**(2), 47–78 (2010)

17. Kim, H., Chung, M.: The effects of clothes shopping orientation and perceived risk on purchase intention in social commerce. Res. J. Costume Cult. **23**(3), 384–399 (2015)

18. Sharma, S., Menard, P., Mutchler, L.A.: Who to trust? applying trust to social commerce. J. Comput. Inf. Syst. **59**(1), 32–42 (2019)

19. Hsu, J.S.C., Hung, Y.W., Chiu, C.M.: Cross-border social commerce: from a trust transfer perspective. J. Electron. Commer. Res. **23**(2), 115–137 (2022)

20. Hansen, J.M., Saridakis, G., Benson, V.: Risk, trust, and the interaction of perceived ease of use and behavioral control. Comput. Hum. Behav. **80**, 197–206 (2018)

21. Phamthi, V.A., Nagy, Á., Ngo, T.M.: The influence of perceived risk on purchase intention in e-commerce-systematic review. Int. J. Consum. Stud. **48**(4), e13067 (2024)

22. Al-Kfairy, M., Shuhaiber, A., Al-Khatib, A.W., Alrabaee, S., Khaddaj, S.: Understanding trust drivers of S-commerce. Heliyon **10**(1), eXXXXX (2024)

23. Ventre, I., Kolbe, D.: The impact of perceived usefulness of online reviews, trust and perceived risk on online purchase intention. J. Int. Consum. Mark. **32**(4), 287–299 (2020)

24. Hair, J.F., Hult, G.T.M., Ringle, C.M., Sarstedt, M.: A Primer on Partial Least Squares Structural Equation Modeling (PLS-SEM), 2nd edn. Sage Publications (2017)

STEAMigPOWER: Empowering Migrants Through Inclusive STEAM Education Introduction: Education as a Lifeline in the Migration Crisis

Andrea Lombardi[1,2,3]([✉]) [iD], Sofia Barbosa Pereira[4] [iD], Anna Dalosi[5],
Ozgur Erdur-Baker[6], Noelia Faginas-Lago[1,2,3] [iD], Yannis Kontos[7] [iD],
Luca Mancini[1] [iD], Catalina Jerez[8], Marzio Rosi[3,9] [iD], and Nicolaos Theodossiou[7] [iD]

[1] Dipartimento di Chimica, Biologia e Biotecnologie, Università Degli Studi di Perugia, Via Elce di Sotto 8, 06123 Perugia, Italy
andrea.lombardi@unipg.it
[2] Master-Tec srl, Via Sicilia 41, 06128 Perugia, Italy
[3] Istituto CNR di Scienze e Tecnologie Chimiche "Giulio Natta" (CNR-SCITEC), Via Elce di Sotto 8, 06123 Perugia, Italy
[4] ALGORITMI Research Center, University of Minho, Campus de Azurém, 4800-058 Guimarães, Portugal
[5] Cyprus Organization for Sustainable Education and Active Learning (S.E.A.L. CYPRUS), Foti Pitta 4, 2015 Strovolos, Nicosia, Cyprus
[6] Faculty of Education, Middle East Technical University, Dumlupinar Bulvary n.1, Ankara 06800, Turkey
[7] Department of Civil Engineering, Aristotle University of Thessaloniki, 54124 Thessaloniki, Greece
[8] Fundació Solidaritat UB (FSUB), Barcelona, Spain
[9] Dipartimento di Ingegneria Civile e Ambientale (DICA), Università Degli Studi di Perugia, Via G. Duranti, 06125 Perugia, Italy

Abstract. This paper presents the development of a web-based Virtual Learning Environment (VLE) designed to provide migrants, refugees, and asylum seekers—particularly women and upper secondary school students (aged 15–18)—with access to STEAM education. These groups are underrepresented in STEM fields due to widespread educational inequalities, limiting opportunities for marginalized populations. The initiative aims to address gender disparities in STEM education and empower women with the skills necessary for academic and professional growth. The five core STEAM courses, delivered both online and in person, will exploit the versatility of the VLE, and will cover Climate Change, Sustainable Development, Eco-Building Construction, the 5Rs (Reduce, Reuse, Recycle, Refuse, and Rot), and Sustainable and Renewable Energy. These thematic areas have been chosen according to the European educational priorities, addressing critical skill gaps in the home countries of the participants. The curriculum is designed in order to facilitate the student integration into the European workforce, at the same time equipping them with the knowledge and tools necessary to contribute to the sustainable reconstruction of their home nations. The VLE fosters inclusivity and accessibility, ensuring that displaced learners can acquire essential STEAM competencies regardless of geographical or socio-economic barriers. This initiative aspires to become a transformative force in migrant education, bridging skill gaps, promoting gender equality in STEM, and empowering learners to actively participate in shaping a sustainable future.

Keywords: STEM/STEAM education · web learning · inclusion and diversity · climate change

1   Introduction: Education as a Cornerstone in the Global Migration Era

The concerning list of global challenges of the 21st century include migrations as one of the main issues, arising as a consequence of wars, recurrent economic crises, political instability, and climate change. The United Nations High Commissioner for Refugees (UNHCR) in facts reports that over 26 million refugees and 4.2 million asylum seekers were displaced worldwide until 2020. Particularly, the Mediterranean region is a critical gateway for those seeking safety and opportunity in Europe [1]. The International Organization for Migration [2] estimates that 281 million people—amounting to 3.6% of the global population—lived outside their country of origin in 2020, giving an estimate of the scale of human mobility (IOM, 2021). For these individuals, education is not just an academic endeavor; it is a lifeline that offers pathways to rebuild lives, gain skills for self-sufficiency, and integrate into new societies. However, migrants face significant educational barriers, including disrupted schooling, lack of credential recognition, gender disparities, and limited access to technology. The UNHCR's Stepping Up report (2019) reveals that only 3% of refugees access higher education, compared to a global average of 37%. This gap represents a profound loss of potential, with the World Bank [3] estimating that excluding migrants from education costs economies billions in untapped human capital, hindering innovation and growth. In Europe, where the Mediterranean migration crisis has brought over 1 million arrivals since 2015 (Frontex, 2020), the need for inclusive education is acute. Southern European nations like Greece, Italy, and Spain have become frontline states, grappling with the dual challenge of humanitarian response and long-term integration (see Fig. 1).

The digital divide further exacerbates these challenges, and almost 3.7 billion people, half of the world's population, remain offline, particularly in regions where many migrants originate [4]. The COVID-19 pandemic highlighted this divide, as online education became the norm, leaving many migrants unable to participate [1]. STEAMigPOWER, an innovative initiative funded by the European Union's Erasmus + program, addresses these challenges by leveraging web-based learning to provide Science, Technology, Engineering, Arts, and Mathematics (STEAM) education to migrants, particularly women and youth aged (15–18 years old). By focusing on STEAM fields—critical for addressing global challenges like climate change, urbanization, and renewable energy—STEAMigPOWER empowers migrants to become contributors rather than burdens, aligning with the United Nations' Sustainable Development Goals (SDGs), notably SDG 4 (Quality Education) and SDG 10 (Reduced Inequalities) (United Nations, 2015).

Total number of international immigrants, 1990 to 2020

An immigrant[1] is someone moving to a country that they were not born in.

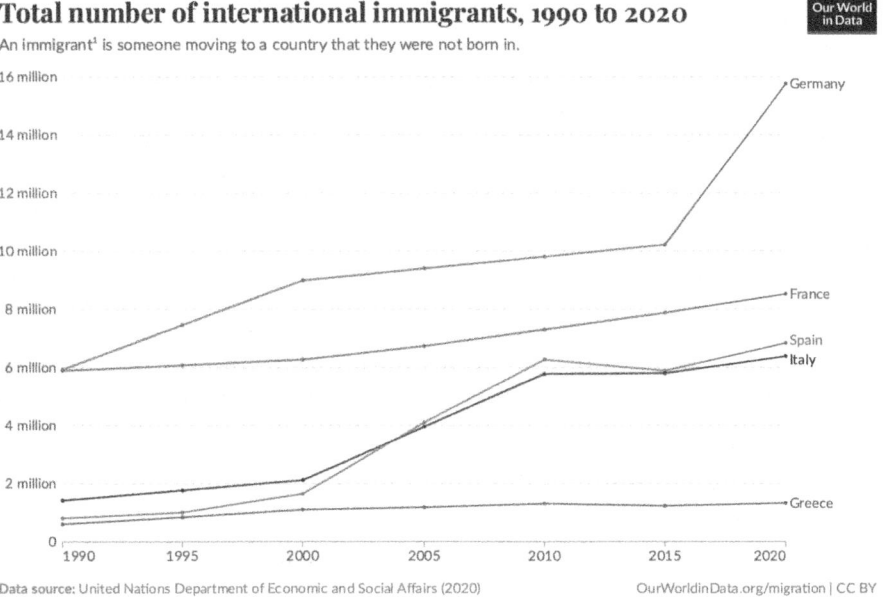

Data source: United Nations Department of Economic and Social Affairs (2020)   OurWorldinData.org/migration | CC BY

1. Migrant: Migrants have both an origin and a destination, meaning that international migrants can be viewed from two directions: - An emigrant is someone leaving their country of birth (origin). - An immigrant is someone moving to a country that they were not born in (destination).

Fig. 1. The trend of total immigrants in the main EU countries in the last 30 years (source: Our World in Data).

One of the main pillars of the present initiative is the Virtual Learning Environment (VLE), a web-based platform designed to allow access to STEAM education for migrants worldwide. Built on the Open edX platform, the VLE crosses geographical, linguistic, and socioeconomic barriers, leveraging the flexibility, scalability, and interactivity of online learning to provide education to those who need it most. This attempt relies on the role of web learning and the VLE in transforming migrant education, emphasizing its design, functionality, and impact.

2 The Context: Migration, Education and Opportunity in Europe

The Mediterranean basin has historically been the intersection area of migration fluxes, where waves of human movement sparkled by wars, extreme poverty, and environmental crises, were heading north. For example, since the Syrian conflict erupted in 2011, over 6.6 million Syrians have fled abroad, with Turkey hosting 3.6 million—by far the largest refugee population globally [1]. Greece and Italy have seen the arrival of hundreds of thousands of migrants, after crossing unsafe sea routes. Spain, too, has seen a surge in crossings from North Africa, with over 40,000 arrivals in 2020 alone [5]. These migrants bring, in principle, a wealth of potential—engineers, teachers, entrepreneurs—that has to be unlocked:

- Educational Disruption: Conflict and displacement shatter schooling. UNICEF [6] reports that in Syria, over 2 million children remain out of school, their foundational education fractured by years of war. For youth arriving in Europe, this gap often persists due to language barriers and resource shortages.
- Credential Recognition: Highly skilled migrants struggle to get their qualifications recognized. The Organization for Economic Cooperation and Development (OECD) [7] found that 60% of tertiary educated migrants in Europe work in low-skill jobs, a phenomenon called "brain waste".
- Gender Disparities: Migrant women face compounded challenges. Cultural expectations, caregiving responsibilities, and discrimination restrict their access to education and employment. The European Institute for Gender Equality (2020) notes that migrant women are twice as likely as men to be unemployed, even with comparable qualifications (see the report "Gender Equality Index 2020: Digitalization and Future of Work").
- Digital Divide: Technology access remains uneven. The International Telecommunication Union, (ITU) in his report *"Measuring Digital Development: Facts and Figs. 2021"* shows that only 47% of households in developing countries have internet, a disparity that follows migrants to Europe, limiting their participation in digital learning.

These barriers have far-reaching consequences. Europe faces a growing STEAM skills shortage: the European Centre for the Development of Vocational Training, see [8], projects a need for 1.2 million additional researchers and engineers by 2030. Migrants, if empowered, could fill this gap—a fact demonstrated by countries like Germany and Sweden. Germany's vocational training programs for refugees have boosted employment rates, with 54% of participants finding work within two years (OECD, [7]). Sweden's Komvux system, offering adult education to migrants, has similarly enhanced integration, reducing welfare dependency (Swedish National Agency for Education). STEAMigPOWER builds on these successes, tailoring its approach to Mediterranean realities and targeting underrepresented groups—women and youth—to maximize both individual and societal impact.

3 STEAMigPOWER Unveiled: A Collaborative Vision Across Borders

STEAMigPOWER is a testament to the power of collaboration, uniting five Mediterranean Higher Education Institutions (HEIs) with complementary strengths:

- University of Minho (UMinho), Portugal: A leading institution in sustainable development, UMinho plays a key role in the project's focus on eco-building, contributing across all designated areas. Its team comprises members from four distinct research centres and multiple fields of expertise, including Environmental Biology, Civil Engineering, Electronics, Molecular Biotechnology, Materials Science, Physics, and Mathematics. The university conducts cutting-edge fundamental and applied research to advance sustainable development (UMinho, 2021).

- University of Perugia (UniPG), Italy: The main expertise of the Perugia unit is in the field of computational chemistry (see e.g. [9–14]). Known for its digital humanities expertise, UniPG anchors the digital storytelling component. Its Digital Humanities Lab has produced award-winning multimedia projects, blending narrative with technology (UniPG, 2021).
- Aristotle University of Thessaloniki (AUTh), Greece: AUTh's climate science programs inform the curriculum's environmental focus. Its researchers have contributed to the Intergovernmental Panel on Climate Change (IPCC, [15]) reports, grounding STEAMigPOWER in cutting-edge science.
- Middle East Technical University (METU), Turkey: METU's top-ranked engineering faculty shapes the STEAM intensive, emphasizing practical applications like robotics and renewable energy systems (METU, 2021).
- University of Barcelona School of Formative Sciences (UBSF), Spain: UBSF's pedagogical expertise ensures the project's teaching methods are innovative and inclusive, drawing on decades of teacher training experience (UBSF, 2021).
- S.E.A.L CYPRUS (Cyprus Organization for Sustainable Development and Active Learning), Cyprus, Turkey.

These HEIs partner with NGOs like Greece's SolidarityNow, Portuguese Refugee Support Platform and Red Cross, which support migrant communities with legal aid and vocational training, ensuring the project remains responsive to real-world needs.

A concise prospect of the key expertise of the participant HEIs is shown in Table 1.

Table 1. Summary of the main expertise of the STEAMigPOWER participant HEIs

HEI	Key Expertise
UMinho	Sustainable Development
UniPG	Digital Humanities,
AUTh	Computational Chemistry
METU	Climate Science
S.E.A.L CYPRUS	Renewable Energy Systems Sustainable Development, Active Learning

4 The Educational Framework: Blending In-Person and Online Learning

4.1 STEAMigPOWER's Goals

The name "STEAMigPOWER" encapsulates its dual mission: empowering (POWER) migrants through STEAM education while harnessing their potential to enrich societies (Migration).

The main objectives of the project are centered around in person intensive programs and online learning. Two in person event have been programmed.

A 2-Day Blended Intensive Program: combines social inclusion workshops with digital storytelling training.

A 5-Day On-Site STEAM Intensive Program: covers five thematic areas through hands-on learning.

The online learning is based on the Virtual Learning Environment (VLE), an open-access platform targeting 500,000 learners worldwide. The online modules adapt in-person content for global scalability.

The Educational Framework has been designed to blend in-person and online learning, the STEAMigPOWER's dual delivery model, integrating in-person and online education, so to ensure flexibility, accessibility, and impact. Details of the in person and online education activities are outlined in the following.

4.2   2-Day Introductory Program

EU Social Inclusion: Participants explore legal rights (e.g., asylum processes), cultural norms (e.g., workplace etiquette), and civic duties (e.g., voting). Drawing on Sara Goodman's [16] framework of immigrant membership, the module emphasizes active citizenship as a pathway to belonging. Digital Storytelling:

Guided by Joe Lambert's methodology [17], learners create multimedia narratives. Imagine a Syrian teenager crafting a short film about her family's escape, linking it to sustainable energy solutions she designs in class. This fusion of personal and technical storytelling builds both skills and confidence.

4.3   5-Day STEAM Intensive Program

Rooted in constructivist learning theory (Piaget, 1950), where knowledge is constructed through experience, the curriculum uses project-based learning (PBL) to engage students actively:

- Climate Change: Learners analyze local climate data—say, rainfall patterns in Thessaloniki—and propose adaptation strategies, mirroring IPCC methodologies [15].
- Sustainable Development: Inspired by Copenhagen's bike-friendly urban design, participants draft sustainable community plans, integrating social and environmental goals (UN Habitat, 2020).
- Eco-Building Construction: Hands-on workshops integrating sustainability principles with hands-on engineering challenges, focusing on sustainable construction practices. These workshops encourage participants to consider environmental impacts in construction activities (Eurostat, [17]).
- The 5Rs (Reduce, Reuse, Recycle, Recover, Redesign): Upcycling projects turn plastic waste into functional items, embodying circular economy principles (Ellen MacArthur Foundation, [18]).
- Renewable Energy: Participants build small-scale solar panels or wind turbines, gaining practical insights into clean energy transitions (IRENA, [19]). These activities cultivate critical thinking, creativity, and collaboration—cornerstones of STEAM success (National Academy of Sciences, 2011).

4.4   The Virtual Learning Environment (VLE): Education Without Borders

Built on the Open edX platform (Open edX, 2021), the VLE expands the reach of STEAMigPOWER to a global audience. Its design prioritizes culturally responsive teaching (Gay, 2018), tailoring content to diverse learners:

- Microlearning Modules: Short, focused lessons (e.g., a 10-min video on solar panel basics) accommodate disrupted schedules or limited internet access.
- Multilingual Support: Courses launch in six languages (English, Portuguese, Italian, Greek, Turkish, Spanish), with plans for Arabic and French to reflect migrant demographics.
- Interactive Features: Discussion forums, virtual labs, and group projects foster a global learning community.
- Accessibility Standards: Compliance with WCAG 2.1 ensures usability for learners with disabilities (W3C, [21]).

The VLE also serves as a digital archive, hosting participant stories that blend personal narratives with STEAM innovations.

5   Digital Storytelling: Amplifying Marginalized Voice

One of the communication approaches adopted by STEAMigPOWER is Digital Storytelling, with the aim of stimulating participants to share their experiences through multimedia. Imagine a young woman from Eritrea producing a podcast about designing a low-cost irrigation system, weaving in her journey across the Sahara. This method can produce multiple benefits:

- Technical skills: learners master proper tools like Adobe Premiere or Audacity, boosting digital literacy (Robin, 2008).
- Emotional Resilience: crafting narratives fosters identity and action, as Nick Couldry argues [16], giving voice to those often silenced.
- Cultural Bridge: Published stories - shared through the VLE – challenge stereotypes, fostering empathy among host communities (UNHCR, [1]).

Globally, digital storytelling has proven capable to promote transformations. UNICEF's Voices of Youth platform amplifies adolescent perspectives on issues like climate change, while Canada's Digital Storytelling Project with Indigenous communities has preserved cultural heritage (see UNICEF, [6]; Lambert, [17]). STEAMigPOWER adapts this model, merging narrative with STEAM to create a powerful tool for inclusion. Social Integration: From Skills to Belonging. The civic integration module equips participants to navigate their new societies:

- Legal Knowledge: Covers EU asylum laws, labor rights, and access to health-care and education (European Commission, 2016).
- Cultural Competence: Explores social norms—e.g., punctuality in professional settings or community traditions—easing everyday interactions.
- Civic Engagement: Encourages volunteering or local advocacy, fostering a sense of ownership (see Bilgili et al., [23]).

The benefits extend beyond individuals. Research shows that integrated migrants enhance social cohesion and economic productivity—integrated refugees in Germany contribute € 1.5 billion annually in taxes (OECD, [7]). By pairing civic education with STEAM training, STEAMigPOWER creates well-rounded contributors who enrich their communities.

6 Empowering Women and Youth: Addressing Inequity at Its Roots

STEAMigPOWER targets two groups facing systemic barriers:

– Women:

The Challenge: Globally, women hold just 28% of STEM jobs (UNESCO, [24]). Migrant women face additional hurdles—gender-based violence, early marriage, and educational exclusion (OECD, 2018). The Strategy: Mentorship from female STEAM leaders provides role models. Dr. Ellen Stofan, former NASA Chief Scientist, famously said, "You can't be what you can't see" (Stofan, [25], a principle STEAMigPOWER embodies through workshops and networking.

– Youth (15–18):

The Challenge is to attract the interest in STEAM, that often declines in adolescence, especially among girls (Microsoft, 2018). Migrant youth face added disruptions from trauma or language barriers (Dryden-Peterson, [26]). The Strategy is based upon PBL, that ignites curiosity—building a wind turbine, for instance, could spark a lifelong passion for engineering. Early intervention ensures these learners enter adulthood equipped for STEAM careers. Diversity in STEAM drives innovation. McKinsey (2020, [27]) found that companies with diverse teams are 35% more likely to outperform peers, a lesson STEAMigPOWER applies to education.

7 Implementation: Turning Vision into Reality

The success of the Virtual Learning Environment (VLE) depends on a thoughtful and well-executed implementation strategy that prioritizes accessibility, usability, and engagement. At its core, the platform is designed with a user-centered approach, ensuring that every aspect—navigation, interface design, and content presentation—is intuitive and welcoming. A clean, visually guided layout makes learning straightforward, while beta testing with migrant communities allows developers to refine the platform based on real user feedback.

One of the technical challenges to learning is linguistic diversity, for this reason the VLE incorporates a robust multilingual support system. Whether through a live agent chat, email, or an extensive helpdesk, learners will easily access assistance for both technical issues and content-related queries. This ensures that no user is left alone in practicing with the platform, producing an inclusive digital space where education remains the primary focus.

Being not only a mere repository of knowledge, the VLE fosters a sense of community, which is critical for sustained engagement. Interactive elements such as virtual meetups, webinars, and Q&A sessions with experts in STEAM fields create an environment of collaboration and encouragement. These features transform the platform from a passive learning tool into an active, dynamic network where learners feel a sense of belonging and motivation to progress.

8 Outcomes and Impact: A Catalyst for Change in Web-Based Learning

The accessibility of the VLE is granted by the web-based nature of the interface. The quality STEAM education can be accessed by migrants and refugees from across the globe. From refugee camps in Jordan to urban centers in Germany, learners can access structured educational resources that fill gaps in traditional learning opportunities.

The state of the platform is also continuously evolving, leveraging integrated data tracking and analytics, to improve its approach based on user performance and engagement. By monitoring progress, educators and developers can identify areas that require additional support, tending to ensure a tailored experience to every learner. This data-driven methodology allows the VLE to evolve organically, adapting to the unique needs of its diverse user base.

Scalability is a cornerstone of the platform's design. Built on an open-source foundation, the VLE can expand with ease, accommodating new languages, subjects, and strategic partnerships. This adaptability allows for future growth, potentially turning the platform from an educational tool into a global hub for migrant education. In the long run, it could provide recognized certifications, career pathways, and micro-credentials, empowering learners with qualifications that hold real-world value in the job market.

9 Challenges and Innovations: Adapting Web Learning for the Future

Despite its many advantages and versatility, web-based learning is not without its difficulties. A common issue is many migrant learners may have little or no experience with online platforms, facing an initial barrier to engagement. To address this risk, the VLE integrates various introductory tutorials that are intended to drive the users into the digital learning experience. These initiatives create a supportive learning environment, ensuring that technical inexperience does not become an obstacle.

Furthermore, the engagement in an online setting presents itself also potential challenges, think about the digital fatigue and to keep alive the student interest. In this respect VLE incorporates interactive features such as virtual laboratories, immersive simulations, and feedback mechanisms. These elements are designed to create a dynamic learning experience that goes beyond passive content consumption, making education not only more effective but also more enjoyable. Thanks to its adaptability to the emerging technologies and to the evolution of the learner needs, the VLE remains at the forefront of innovative education. Through a combination of strategic planning, community-driven design, and forward-thinking solutions, it has the potential to redefine how migrant communities access and benefit from STEAM education.

10 Conclusions

The result of the project and of the VLE is a Model for a "Connected World Through Web Learning". STEAMigPOWER's Virtual Learning Environment transcends traditional education, offering a scalable, inclusive model for empowering migrants through web-based STEAM learning. By leveraging the flexibility, reach, and interactivity of online platforms, it transforms lives and communities, proving that investment in digital education yields progress for all. As global migration and education policies evolve, the VLE stands as a beacon, illuminating a path toward equitable, sustainable futures.

Acknowledgments. The authors acknowledge the Project STEAMigPOWER: STEAM approaches at higher education for mIGrants, refugees and asylum seekers' emPOWERment under the ERASMUS+ Program key action 2: Cooperation partnership in higher education – Agreement n. 2022–1-PT01-KA220-HED-000088221.

Disclosure of Interests. The authors have no competing interests to declare that are relevant to the content of this article.

References

1. UNHCR: Global Trends: Forced Displacement in 2019 (2020)
2. IOM: World Migration Report 2022. International Organization for Migration (2021)
3. Bank, W.: The Economic Cost of Educational Exclusion (2018)
4. ITU: Digital Trends in Europe 2021. International Telecommunication Union (2021)
5. Frontex: Risk Analysis for 2020 (2020)
6. UNICEF: Voices of Youth. (2021)
7. OECD: Settling In 2018: Indicators of Immigrant Integration (2018)
8. Cedefop: Skills Forecast: Trends and Challenges to 2030. European Centre for the Development of Vocational Training (2020)
9. Pannacci, G., et al.: A combined crossed molecular beam and theorerical study of the O (3 P, 1 D)+ acrylonitrile (CH 2 CHCN) reactions and implications for combustion and extraterrestrial environments. Phys. Chem. Chem. Phys. **25**(30), 20194–20211 (2023)
10. Giani, L., et al.: Revised gas-phase formation network of methyl cyanide: the origin of methyl cyanide and methanol abundance correlation in hot corinos. Mon. Not. R. Astron. Soc. **526**(3), 4535–4556 (2023)
11. Rosi, M. et al.: Electronic structure and kinetics calculations for the Si+SH reaction, a possible route of SiS formation in star-forming regions. In: Misra, S., et al. Computational Science and Its Applications – ICCSA 2019. ICCSA 2019. Lecture Notes in Computer Science(), vol. 11621, pp. 306–315. Springer, Cham (2019). https://doi.org/10.1007/978-3-030-24302-9_22
12. Liang, P., et al.: OH (2Π)+ C2H4 reaction: a combined crossed molecular beam and theoretical study. J. Phys. Chem. A **127**(21), 4609–4623 (2023)
13. Richardson, V., et al.: Fragmentation of interstellar methanol by collisions with He˙+: an experimental and computational study. Phys. Chem. Chem. Phys. **24**(37), 22437–22452 (2022)
14. Vanuzzo, G., et al.: Reaction N (2D)+ CH2CCH2 (Allene): an experimental and theoretical investigation and implications for the photochemical models of titan. ACS Earth Space Chem. **6**(10), 2305–2321 (2022)

15. IPCC: Climate Change 2021: The Physical Science Basis. Intergovernmental Panel on Climate Change (2021)
16. Goodman, S.W.: Immigration and Membership Politics in Western Europe. Cambridge University Press (2019)
17. Lambert, J.: Digital Storytelling: Capturing Lives, Creating Community. Rout-ledge (2013)
18. Eurostat: Employment in Construction (2021)
19. Foundation, E.M.: Circular Economy in Practice (2019)
20. IRENA: Renewable Energy and Jobs – Annual Review 2021. International Renewable Energy Agency (2021)
21. W3C: Web Content Accessibility Guidelines (WCAG) 2.1. (2018)
22. Couldry, N.: Mediatization or mediation? New Media Soc. **10**(3), 373–391 (2008)
23. Bilgili, et al.: The Impact of Civic Integration Policies on Immigrant Integration. Migration Policy Institute (2015)
24. UNESCO: Cracking the Code: Girls' and Women's Education in STEM (2019)
25. Stofan, E.: Quoted in Women in STEM. Smithsonian Institution (2018)
26. Dryden-Peterson, S.: Refugee education: the crossroads of globalization. Educ. Res. **46**(9), 473–482 (2017)
27. Company, M.: Diversity Wins: How Inclusion Matters (2020)

Urban and Regional Planning

SUPERTRENTO: A Practice-Led Design Process for Urban Transformation

Teresa Pedretti⬤ and Letizia Bollini(✉)⬤

Free University of Bolzano-Bozen, Bolzano, Italy
`letizia.bollini@unibz.it`

Abstract. The end of the Modern era represents the beginning of a new phase for city development that requires urban planners, policy makers and civil servants to experiment with open decision-making processes, contributions from disciplines beyond urbanism to face the increasing complexity of society. Although in recent years many Western cities become laboratories open to innovation and contamination, very few studies focus on analyzing participatory processes in large urban transformation and the management of their legacy. The contribution presents a detailed and reflective account of *SUPERTRENTO – Participatory Urban Scenarios for Ecology and Regeneration*, an experimental participatory urban planning process initiated by the Municipality of Trento in collaboration with the collective Campomarzio. The focus lies on describing the practice-led, research-through-design methodology developed to engage citizens in the urban transformation of a major railway area slated for undergrounding. Combining results with existing literature, it draws conclusions on how participatory urban planning becomes spaces to learn and exercise democracy and concludes on the relevance of research through design ways to institutionalize the legacy of these practices to serve as mines of knowledge on the city and places to improve urban policy design.

Keywords: participatory planning · urban transformation · research through design

1 Introduction: Urban Transformation as a Lab in Complex Contexts

The end of the Modern era represents, for most of the cities around the world, a variety of challenges that must be addressed. Between many other changes, digitalization and the transition from an economy based on industrial production to one centered on service production began to challenge the twentieth-century city model.

Until the late 1970s of the past centuries, cities had developed productive sites, railway areas essential for transport and trade, and zones designated for storage, production, and commerce in strategic locations. The centrality of industry, craftsmanship, and commerce made these areas not only crucial for the urban economy but also for the daily lives of its inhabitants. In Italy, due to the socio-economic condition of the south, a large migratory process affected northern cities' development [1] and their enlargement. Since

© The Author(s), under exclusive license to Springer Nature Switzerland AG 2025
O. Gervasi et al. (Eds.): ICCSA 2025, LNCS 15650, pp. 187–203, 2025.
https://doi.org/10.1007/978-3-031-96962-1_13

industrialization then, urban issues have always been related to expansion, and it is only starting from the late Sixties that things began to change. The crisis of the economic model on which Western societies were based forced to change, and the face of cities started to transform. Since then, urban issues have come to be related to the new demands of the contemporary city that shift from the culture of urban expansion to the culture of transformation [2].

Starting from this awareness, new sensibilities arose where the knowledge of the urbs and its physical characteristics has decisively taken on a guiding role for understanding and controlling the structuring aspects of the city [3]. "Transformation and requalification" took place before being occupied by "expansion and development", leading cities to ask for regeneration processes [4].

Alongside the need to rethink vast urban areas left vacant by industrial complexes following delocalization, city governance must also address the demands of an urban population that is growing numerically and becoming increasingly complex. Different social classes, diverse cultural backgrounds, and highly varied living needs coexist with competing forces: on one hand, movements advocating for development models that minimize environmental and social impact, and on the other, actors promoting speculative approaches that cater exclusively to certain social groups. This challenging new era leads research in urban planning to an experimental phase in which the definition of new strategies and the search for new tools, make public spaces as the fundamental of society again at the core of the debate [5].

Addressing these challenges effectively requires municipal administrations to experiment with new decision-making processes, to open themselves to contributions from disciplines beyond urban planning, and to seek support in understanding and managing the very complexity that these changes are bringing to the forefront.

To develop new models of collaborative governance in which public and private actors work collectively in distinctive ways, using particular processes, to establish laws and rules [6] for the provision of urban transformations, cities worldwide have become potential laboratories [7].

These laboratories promote collaboration between municipal administrations and university researchers, as seen in some North American cities like Chicago, Detroit, and Atlanta. In Europe, hybrid initiatives in cities such as Barcelona and Zurich contribute to a growing field of research and experimentation. The goal is twofold: to bring human needs back to the center of political and administrative decisions [7] and to innovate strategic urban planning models.

Alongside major urban conglomerates, small and medium-sized Italian cities are also facing these challenges. Among them, in addition to the well-known Bologna and Torino, the city of Trento stands out as an interesting context for innovation (Fig. 1).

1.1   SUPERTRENTO: A Laboratory for Practice-Led Innovation

Although Trento, since the early 2000s, had planned several major transformations, it is starting from the end of 2022 that the city has begun to shape new approaches in response to the need to address significant urban challenges.

The Variant to the General Regulatory Plan, drafted by the Catalan urbanist Joan Busquets and approved by the Council of Municipality of Trento in 2001, with his

Fig. 1. Former Scalo Filzi and northern part of the Area to be undergrounded. Ph. Nicola Cagol

envisioning about the undergrounding of the railway within the urban area, initiated a phase of reflection and debate. However, by the late 2010s, the construction of the freight railway bypass—an ancillary project for the southern access routes to the Brenner Base Tunnel—provided new momentum and concrete implementation opportunities for the undergrounding plan, which had remained purely conceptual until that point. Thus, in 2022, a new phase of experimentation began. Unlike the early 2000s, this process was not led by a single urban planner but instead aligned with the approach taken by major European cities: placing people at the centre of administrative policies and, consequently, at the core of decisions concerning large-scale urban transformations. As in other medium-sized cities, Trento also faces an urban transformation concerning its railway area, which has the potential to impact the entire city. When an urban master plan involves a district of a large city like Milan or Barcelona, its effects reverberate through the surrounding areas but rarely have a direct impact on the entire city. However, when a city with a population of one hundred thousand, such as Trento, decides to intervene and transform an area of 16 hectares, the changes in terms of functions, mobility, and new attraction hubs influence the dynamics of the entire city. For this reason, the experiments currently taking place in large cities to engage citizens in urban planning are interesting, but even more so, due to the effects they generate, are those initiated in medium-sized and small cities, where transforming an area means reflecting on the entire city.

SUPERTRENTO – Participatory Urban Scenarios for Ecology and Regeneration, a participatory process aimed at defining the guidelines for future design competitions for the railway area, fits within this framework.

The initiative was promoted by the municipal administration in collaboration with the multidisciplinary collective Campomarzio. The process involved a cross-sectoral engagement of the Mobility and Urban Regeneration Project, the Urban Planning Department, the Department of Culture, Tourism and Youth Policies, as well as the Cabinet and Public Relations Office, alongside two engineers, three architects, and me from the collective. The final goal of the process, launched in December 2022 and concluded in March 2024, was to produce a new kind of policy design-based document (referred to as the Guidelines) to consolidate the expectations, visions, concerns, and recommendations expressed by the participants throughout the process.

2   SUPETRENTO, a Practice-Led Design Process

Limited availability, alongside the diversity and disparities among existing similar practices on the involvement of citizens in addressing urban transformation, represents one of the first issues for Practitioners-Researchers [8] that lead the process. The research on similar cases to refer to has yielded fragmented results, whose analysis has proven to be more relevant for defining the reference framework in urban planning terms rather than for developing a working methodology. For this reason, what ultimately guided the phase-by-phase work was the definition of clear objectives to be achieved. These objectives, in turn, shaped not only the design of content but also the methodologies that gave form to the overall process.

Considering SUPERTRENTO as a process aimed at building a community willing to engage in the co-design of a major urban transformation, we first focused on identifying the key steps and dynamics that would support its creation. Participating in the co-design of an urban area's future requires an understanding of the ongoing transformation, the ability to reflect on the city's identity, and a willingness to learn from other contexts to envision better solutions to the challenges faced by contemporary cities. Population aging, gentrification, and the need to mitigate the effects of climate change are just some of the critical issues shaping today's urban discourse. Understanding, reflection, and learning were, therefore, essential steps in building the community needed to collectively shape the guidelines for the future of the underground area. The starting point was indeed a well-documented phenomenon in literature: the recognition that Trento inhabitants couldn't address or clearly define aspirations, needs, or concerns [9] about the undergrounding of the railway or the development of the newly liberated space, and after a couple of meetings, we understood the point.

Urban transformations affecting large areas are often challenging for citizens to fully grasp. The use of technical language by professionals and public administrators, combined with the difficulty of navigating and making sense of the urban fabric, creates significant barriers to public engagement in co-designing the future. To challenge this situation, one of our first objectives as a working group was to design a communication ecosystem capable of clearly conveying both the fundamental concepts of urban transformation and the explanation of ongoing developments.

In essence, we aimed to develop a process structured around the following key phases: first, fostering awareness and informed engagement through clear and compelling communication; second, identifying, during this informational stage, the issues that resonated most and the audiences they attracted; and finally, mobilizing these groups—formed around shared interests—in the concluding phase of the process, the co-design of the guidelines.

The need to involve all stakeholders and not limit the discourse to technicians and politicians was clear to us when we designed the route therefore creating a community of citizens capable of exchanging knowledge and reflecting together on emerging problems has proven to be necessary.

Addressing this challenge, then, required to entangle with the definition of *publics* as groups of people concerned about an issue organizing themselves to address it [10] and, therefore, build upon the awareness that there must be no one community or single public but multiplicity of publics, which probably will be often controversial but, at the same time, aware and interested in the participatory process. It also requires drawing upon Binders et al. notion of *democratic design experiments* in which designers define and experiment with citizens, policymakers, and grassroots organizations on the issues with which they are concerned [11].

The work undertaken to achieve this objective has been presented in Pedretti [16]. This contribution focuses instead on analyzing the role of the dedicated Instagram channel in supporting the informational process, as well as the unexpected outcomes related to the emergence of a new and unanticipated audience for SUPERTRENTO.

2.1 Methodology: Drawing the Method of an Experimental Process: *Get Inform, Imagine, Engage*

SUPERTRENTO has been designed to achieve the aim of drawing a new kind of document. What we decided to call "Guidelines for the future of the area freed by the railways" is, indeed, a core of 68 pages designed to orient planning strategies and urban-related policies for the next twenty years[1]. The document, therefore, is not a strategic plan, nor a master plan or an institutional program; it is a curated summary of all the issues, visions, decisions, and open questions that arose throughout meetings, workshops, and labs.

The methodological approach adopted to develop the guideline definition process was structured into three distinct phases. These three phases were also used to compose the payoff of the branding: *Phase 1: Get informed, Phase 2: Imagine, Phase 3: Engage* (Fig. 2).

The method chosen for the first phase of the process was based mainly on qualitative tools such as in-depth interviews. Design-oriented instruments such as informal meetings to discuss ideas and prototype solutions using different scales architectural models were also planned to make themes such as public place design or new mobility strategies easier to understand for different target groups of people.

Over the initial four months, the working team planned to be flexible enough to be able to organize the correct amount of meetings necessary to engage as many people as possible. Besides the importance of this phase in making people informed about SUPERTRENTO, it also was designed to allow the designers discover the relevant issues and concerns about urban transformations as well as support them in *framing* or

---

[1] Final document is downloadable following the link https://www.supertrento.it/#linee-guida (Italian language only)

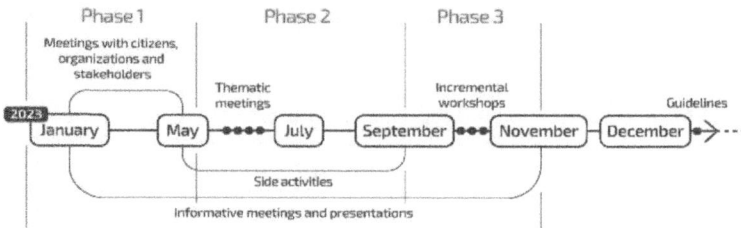

Fig. 2. The process SUPERTRENTO translated from the Italian version. Courtesy of Municipality of Trento and Campomarzio

in selecting the more salient aspects of the perceived reality and better define problems, causal interpretations, recommendations [12]. The methodological assumption was that this initial phase of the process, could have been the foundation upon which the following activities, contents, tools, and approaches for the second and third phase were designed and implemented.

The second part of the process was then designed to follow up on the first phase with more specific information about the relevant issues that emerged: to pursue the aim of supporting people in empowering their imagination and ideas about the future of the area freed by the railways. Drawing upon Appadurai, we decided to design the contents of the second phase (both for what concerns thematic meetings and @super_trento account) to foster imagination as a staging ground for action [13].

The four thematic meetings' objectives were initially designed to allow participants to understand how the same issues highlighted in Trento were addressed in different contexts; to dialogue with experiences from other contexts; and to co-create a shared map of expectations, ideas, and concerns. The goal of the second phase was, therefore, to initiate a process of ideation and imagination—not just to generate ideas and propose new functions. At the same time, while the first phase was valuable for engaging individuals, the purpose of this second phase was to build a community capable of raising complex questions and issues emerged from the first phase related to mobility, housing, employment, entrepreneurship, well-being, and the accessibility and production of cultural and creative activities.

The third phase of the process, consisting of three incremental workshops, was initially conceived as a series of design-based workshops centered at addressing the findings from the previous stages. These workshops, in the general overview of the one-year process, had the final scope to mediate discussions that arose between differing expectations, facilitate the negotiation of scenarios, and co-design the final structure and content of guidelines that were expected to lead the urban transformation of the 16-hectare area freed by the railways. They chose to adopt an incremental approach leading workshop by workshop, ensuring that at each meeting, the scenario developed in the previous session was refined by integrating new perspectives able to enhance step by step until the final version.

Together with the definition of the method, the steps, and the targets, the working team designed and defined the communication strategy. To support *in situ* activities, it was decided to focus primarily on two tools: a website for disseminating general information about the process and a new Instagram account (Fig. 3).

Fig. 3. Screenshot of the Instagram account @super_trento (March 2025)

The website's objective was mainly to inform about meetings, workshops, and urban explorations and to keep the archive of the entire process. As for what concerned the social media instead, the team decided to focus only on opening and creating graphic content and video reels for an Instagram account.

Social media allows individuals and organizations to connect with each other, upload photos and documents, and post, share, and forward messages. The wide user base, real-time, and open characteristics make it possible to engage many participants in planning processes. They have four types of support functions for collaborative planning, including information sharing, social networking, citizen participation, and communication [14].

The Instagram account @super_trento was conceived to provide information, additional content, and photos and videos of the urban transformations and of the process itself with the intent to involve a different target: people under 50 not previously interested in issues connected to urban planning.

The same content shared through @super_trento was also disseminated via the official Facebook page of the Municipality of Trento. A dedicated Facebook page for the project was not created because the main objective of the social media plan was to reach the specific target audience of Instagram. Conversely, in the case of Instagram, the choice not to use the institutional pages of municipal departments was based on insights from scholars on the role of media in fostering new forms of participation [15–17].

The social media management plan for the channel maintained an average of two posts per week over a span of more than 52 weeks. The shared content was structured according to the logic of the process itself: *get informed, imagine, participate.*

2.2 Leading the Experimental Process into Reality

The SUPERTRENTO process started with a press conference and a public event led by the Major of Trento on December 6th, 2023.

The process was designed to last one year, but the concomitance of the President and Council of the Province of Trento elections with the third phase led to postponing the incremental workshop and wrapping up the process by March 2024, with a three-month delay on the theoretical plan.

First Part: Get Informed. Beginning in January 2023, this phase engaged with 764 individuals, including citizens concerned with the city's future, third-sector entities, committees, professional associations, and businesses.

During this phase, meetings were conducted in small, homogeneous groups, primarily in person. Various approaches were used to engage interested participants, including organizing meetings in venues provided by the municipal administration; attending invited sessions at assemblies, meetings, and events organized by local entities and organizations; and offering the possibility of informal meetings for all those interested.

The general aim of the Instagram account @super_trento was also, in this first phase, to inform. Information on Instagram, however, focused on two main topics: urban planning and urban trends, using clear and simple language that foster the rise of a new public. All posts published between November 27, 2022, and April 14, 2023 were then conceived to provide additional information on the history of Trento, the ongoing transformations, and the areas involved in the changes. More specifically, two different spotlight series were created: 1. The #supercartolina to share highlights and tips on specific places by using vintage images and historical photography and 2. The #superglossario to explain key technical terms to citizens, facilitating a better understanding of the debate and encouraging participation without feelings of exclusion[2].

The dissemination of such content sought to lower the barriers to entry for public engagement in the ongoing discourse. The first category, indeed, included posts that explain definitions that may be self-evident to experts but that are not necessarily familiar to a broader audience, such as undergrounding, hypogeum, and bypass. These words have been made clear and understandable in relation to the city of Trento and its context.

The second category encompassed terms and expressions related to contemporary urban dynamics, such as social housing, community garden, tactical urbanism, and mixité. This second series of posts is intended to make people understand clearly the significance of words that scholars, designers, and policy makers use in common language that probably not have a unique and clear meaning for all citizens (Fig. 4).

As is often the case, the SUPERTRENTO process always risked being confined to a traditional audience—composed of the usual individuals in Trento who typically engage with topics related to urban planning, development, and infrastructure. This risk was mitigated not only by the post and the contents themselves but also through the diversification of language and tools employed.

The creation of short reels to show the less well-known urban areas employing a popular, engaging language, carefully designed visuals, and editing techniques reminiscent of action cinema attract audiences even without any paid sponsorship.

---

[2] #supercartolina and #superglossario mean #superpostcard and #superglossary where super is used to refer to super Trento

Fig. 4. Example of post edited and published to make citizens familiar with trends in urban transformation

Once the goal to inform people was achieved, at least for some citizens, it was crucial to support participants in imaginative processes that would help shape and make the key issues rise and tackle them.

Second Part: Imagine. The second part of SUPERTRENTO begins in May 2023 and lasts until the end of October of the same year. The core activities of this phase were centered on thematic workshops designed to inspire imaginative thinking about potential functions for the area liberated from the railway tracks. Thematic workshops lasted one day from 9,30 in the Morning until 17,30. They were held on the 6th and 20th of May and on the 10th and 24th of June in the Sala Carrozzeria at ex Atesina, a former bus depot specifically set up to host SUPERTRENTO.

If in the planning phase of the process we thought to limit these workshop only to the aims of envision new functions to address emerging urban challenges, inspire and mobilize individuals, as soon as we dealt with the wrap up of the first phase, we realized that we must focus also on the current situation of the city.

What emerged from the analysis of the more than 70 meetings of the first phase was general ignorance about strategies already implemented by the Municipality to deal with main urban issues and, more generally, a lack of knowledge on what already exists in terms of innovative goods and services. For these reasons, we settled on an agenda whose scope was double: to engage in imagining futures and to inform on what exists (Fig. 5).

During the workshops, a range of projects was presented, including urban landscapes thoughtfully designed to integrate corridors for sustainable mobility with recreational and sports facilities, as well as innovative residential solutions aimed at addressing the challenges of an aging population and the increasing issue of social isolation.

Projects, experiences, and practices presented were selected based on two criteria. To avoid feelings of impossibility, every case study was selected to show how, in other contexts, similar issues were faced. Indeed, the presentation of concrete solutions helps in attracting people interested in the issue and encourage them to contribute in order to assure that the process prioritizes this concern and the city can aspire in make those decisions reality [18].

Fig. 5. Advertising of the process SUPERTRENTO. Ph. Pietro V. Ambrosini

The second criterion was related to the ability of the cases to act strategically and address different issues. The request arose in the first phase of the process about new public spaces were collected and found a possible inspiring resolution in case studies like the Superkilen[3] in Nørrebro, Copenhagen where culture, sports, relax and entertainment areas are melted in a 30.000 square meters area designed by a multidisciplinary group of artist, architects and landscape designers.

Testimonials invited to show practices were invited to give a lecture during the morning and to take part in the discussion in the afternoon. These after-lunch round table, which kept citizens and experts, revealed their importance in supporting people interested in the comparison between different contexts, needs, and visions. 305 people took part in the four thematic workshops where 8 Municipality managers and 16 experts presented more than 100 projects.

This phase, along with the other, was also supported by communication efforts carried out through @super_trento. The contents of the posts published between April 28th and October 10th, 2023, can be divided into three main categories: 1. Reels summarizing the content of the thematic meetings through brief interviews with speakers and key interventions (Fig. 10) 2. Visually curated carousels that synthesize key emerging concepts, situating them within a broader analytical framework (Fig. 11) 3. Posts designed to inform about the final phase of the process, outlining its objectives and methodological approach.

The reels created to disseminate the key topics discussed during the thematic meetings were designed with a more journalistic approach compared to those produced in the first phase. They feature interviews with guest speakers from different contexts, along with video footage captured throughout the day. The graphic carousels, though

---

[3] Superkilen is a public space in Copenhagen divided into three main areas: The Red Square, The Black Square and The Green Park. The Red Square represents modern urban life with a café, music and sports, while The Black Square is a classic square with fountains and benches and The Green Park is a park for picnics, sports and walking the dog. Superkilen was designed by Superflex with BIG and Topotek1. Commissioned by the City of CCopenhagen and Realdania, Denmark.

receiving less visibility than video content—likely due to Instagram's own algorithmic mechanisms—were designed to explore specific topics in greater depth (Fig. 6).

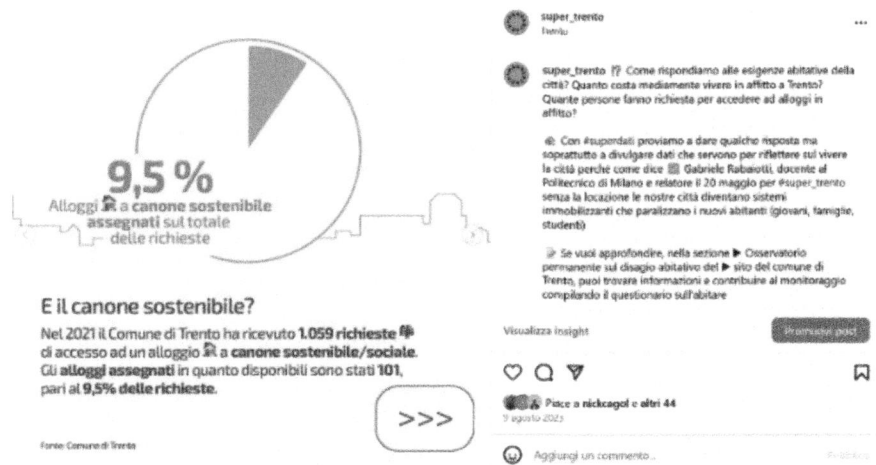

Fig. 6. Example of post published to introduce and wrap up discussion and themes

Following the thematic meetings, certain issues and interests emerged more prominently than others. During the summer, the carousels expanded and contextualized these key themes, aligning with the interests that resonated most with participants in the second phase. The aim was to solidify an engaged community around these topics while attracting new potential participants.

Third Part: Engage. The final phase of the process, dedicated to co-design and the definition of the Guidelines for the Future of the railway area freed from the tracks, consisted of three incremental workshops held one week apart. Hosted once again at the Sala Carrozzeria of the ex Atesina, on the afternoons of October 28th, November 4th, and November 11th, the community built over ten months of work came together to decide which of the emerging issues, proposed ideas, and possible directions should be selected to shape the guiding document. 170 people engage in this final phase of the process, with an average of 60 participants per workshop.

The scenarios and guidelines were developed incrementally, with the different areas integrated only after the process. The co-design site was divided into three distinct areas, allowing participants to either engage in a single working group or move between discussions running in parallel across the different areas. Each group crafted an initial scenario during the first workshop session, which was then presented in a plenary discussion at the end of the day. Over the following week, these preliminary scenarios were refined in the back office, incorporating feedback and insights. The second and third co-design sessions further built upon this foundation, adding or adjusting elements based on the work carried out by participants in the previous meetings. This incremental approach ensured that the final scenario emerged as a carefully developed synthesis, shaped progressively through successive refinements.

During this phase, the Instagram account played a key role in bridging the week-long intervals between workshops. It provided updates on the emerging scenario, offered previews, and highlighted unresolved themes that would be addressed in the following Saturday's session (Fig. 7).

Fig. 7. Photo of the area used to draft and share visions during the incremental workshops. Ph. Nicola Cagol

3   Results: SUPERTRENTO and Its Publics

Number of the Process. As previously described, the difficulties in identifying similar participatory processes to draw up led to SUPERTRENTO being carried out using an experimental method.

The initiative achieved results that not only the awards won and the national recognition gained but also researchers and policymakers have deemed highly significant. However, a comprehensive evaluation based on qualitative and quantitative reflection—assessing the process based on participation numbers, interactions, and its effectiveness in engaging citizens—remains challenging due to the absence of benchmarks for comparison.

Since this contribution aims to foster a discussion that may open new perspectives, the following section presents the quantitative analysis to ground reflections inspired by the design, experimentation, and overall management of the process and further considerations for future exploration (Fig. 8).

After the conclusion of the process, the Instagram account was used only to announce the date of the final presentation of the guidelines. Today, despite recent changes to

www.supertrento.it
24.186 visite
9.949 visitatori unici
149.538 pagine visualizzate totali

@super_trento
1.766 follower

Incontri informativi
764 persone incontrate
60+ riunioni

Esplorazioni urbane
200 partecipanti

Super Sondaggio
364 partecipanti

Incontri tematici
16 relator* nazionali
12 relator* locali
12 Isole tematiche con cittadin* ed espert*
305 partecipanti / sulle 4 giornate

Laboratori incrementali
9 Isole tematiche
170 partecipanti / sulle 3 giornate

Fig. 8. Results in terms of website visitors, Instagram followers, people involved in the first phase of the process (Incontri informative), Survey (Supersondaggio), the second phase of the process (Incontri tematici), and the final phase (Laboratori incrementali)

Instagram's post layout—causing some content to appear misaligned, the page remains an archive of the entire project. On March 25th, 2024, the day of the public presentation of the participatory guidelines for the future of the railway area, the account had 1,766 followers. By February 2025, nearly a year later, that number had grown to 1,866.

Results of Using Simple Language to Talk About Urban Planning. The primary challenge faced by the working group was not merely the management of the initiative, but first and foremost the design of a process that would enable effective participation in the production of this strategic document.

Research on previous processes highlighted the lack of existing practices to draw inspiration from. For this reason, the decision was to adopt a practice-based design approach to develop the process through concepts and scenarios [19].

The team working on SUPERTRENTO established to see participation as a process of making public marginalized aspirations and needs, and not a chance to ask citizens for ideas or advice. Therefore, the process was designed to be horizontal. No specific role was assigned to technicians or professionals, and we, as the working group, conceived our role as designers capable of facilitating the circulation of information and experimenting with feedback rather than as technicians seeking ideas. This approach, in a context where participation in urban planning is not yet a widespread or well-established practice, led technicians—such as architects and engineers—to refuse to take part in the process (as we later discover, in many other cities technicians refuse to engage in participatory planning without being firstly recognized as a professional with a clear role in the process). These phenomena allow us to assert that from the perspective of technical professions, what emerges with SUPERTRENTO is that, to support urban transformations and empower innovation in the discipline of urban planning, technicians must become a practitioner–researcher [8].

From the perspective of the outcomes generated using simple language to discuss urban transformations, in addition to effectively engaging diverse audiences, it allowed the public to form different issues to emerge. Beyond these ideas—promoted by citizen groups that either emerged to voice specific demands or were already active and participated in the process to see their concerns reflected in the planning guidelines—a series of other issues also surfaced.

Although not directly related to the railway undergrounding and the reclaimed area, these issues were nonetheless significant and capable of generating meaningful impacts. These include, for example, reflections on the societal shift from viewing sports primarily as a competitive, team-based activity to seeing it as an individual practice focused on personal well-being. This transformation has important implications for the design and management of sports infrastructure in a city like Trento. Or, likewise, the declining amount of time people can dedicate to volunteer activities and its impact on the third sector and the spaces designated for community gatherings and associations.

3.1 Discussion

Results presented as well as reflections emerged thanks to the broad engagement of the population are not strictly related to the core topic of the SUPERTRENTO participatory process. Nevertheless, they could represent a valuable body of knowledge for the design of participatory urban policies and for these reasons are discussed below.

One of the main issues that emerges at the end of a participatory process on urban transformation is about the lack of quantitative benchmarks. It means that there are no possibilities to assess not only the overall result of the project (that can be done using even just qualitative tools) but also to reflect on the experimental method used, on the communication plan designed for the different targets included or not.

While fully aware that numerical data on participation do not inherently indicate a positive or negative outcome, we believe that tracking the number of attendees at various events, as well as the individuals, institutions, associations, and organizations involved—using common categories and a standardized classification across participatory processes—could provide a comparative basis for integrating qualitative assessments of these initiatives and a referee for scholars, practitioners and civil servants working. In other words, while numerical data do not hold intrinsic value on their own, their collection within the multitude of participatory processes in different contexts could serve as a starting point for guiding discussions toward meaningful insights. Comparing raw participation figures from a participatory process in a small town with those from a large urban redevelopment initiative may not be appropriate. However, analyzing participation rates in relation to the local population, understanding the demographic composition of these groups, and representing them statistically could provide a valuable foundation for reflection. This, in turn, could help address a common challenge across all participatory processes: the need to engage and activate underrepresented groups.

Another reflection is on the importance of understanding the impact that social media can have not only on participation as a way to be active citizens, but more precisely on the methodology drafted and on the contents presented in a particular place and time of a specific city. Beyond the verification about the effective involvement of under 50 people made possible thanks to the realization of a survey, one thing had become evident: a significant number of people were interested in the themes of the project, actively engaging with online content, and willing to dedicate time sharing their ideas. However, these individuals were not the same as those who had participated in the in-person meetings. What, then, should be done with the ideas and opinions emerging from social network-based participation?

We reflected extensively on this issue but in the end decided not to incorporate feed-back, ideas, and opinion gathered through social network into the incremental workshops but instead to make them public through graphical storytelling posts on the Instagram page. This choice was driven by the awareness that our role—and, more broadly, the role of design in the participatory process—should enhance transparency and provide feedback to support advocacy practices. By making these responses visible, we aimed to empower different groups who identified with the expressed concerns, enabling them to mobilize and act [15].

3.2   Conclusion: The Legacy of SUPERTRENTO

SUPERTRENTO has been a successful process. The recent approvement by the City Council of Trento of the Variante al Piano Regolatore to integrate the SUPERTRENTO guidelines represent the highest achievable result. Furthermore, the review of the Cultural Strategic Plan of the City to insert the principles emerged from the participatory process represent another important – although not foreseen – result.

Drawing on Binder et al. we look at the SUPERTRENTO process as a twelve-month democratic design experiment in which designers rehearse with diverse citizens, organizations, and policymakers on how to organize themselves around issues with which they are concerned, in other words, as exercises in the craft of participation [11]. As experiments, these scenarios and their narrative joints articulate varied constellations of identities and practices that, from their side, would entail eliciting, articulating, and sharing pluralistic subjectivities as a mode of democratic inquiry into how we might differently conceive our civic conditions and experiences [20].

Even though it may seem that everything went well, today, the process is over, and the community involved, as well as all the issues mapped and made public, have been dispersed.

New participatory processes on the same issues emerged during SUPERTRENTO (housing needs, public place requirements,…) and have been started, irretrievably, from zero. Projects, suggestions, discussions, maps, and data graphics are preserved in a well-designed book that, in a short period, no one would read anymore. Losing public knowl-edge created and, above all, the community and pluralistic subjectivities composed, or, in other words, not having strategies or tools to empower the legacy of the participatory process for urban transformation, represents a failure not only for SUPERTRENTO, but common to many different processes carried out in urban contexts.

Research on design-based solutions to make the legacy of participatory processes long-lasting and permanently available for citizens and policy makers would therefore enable a more convincing participation. Furthermore, it would also be a mine of well-structured and thoroughly investigated issues to address, knowledge, visions, and skills to activate.

Research on this issue would even allow a different way for urban policy making and planning to develop and address the challenges of today's complex city. Partici-patory process in urban planning could indeed become a space for learning, dialogue, contribution to problem definition, and, not least, exercise democratic practices. Institu-tionalizing these spaces for participation could, at the same time, address the demand for engagement that has emerged in SUPERTRENTO, as well as in other processes, and, again, assure the citizens spaces where they can actively contribute to foster democratic processes and shape policies to improve city life.

In the same years that state-centered democracy is increasingly questionable and people start not going anymore to vote, diverse claims to democracy and a diffuse willingness to participate in collective decisions about the future seem to be increasing in urban areas [21]. The high number of people engaged, whether in the workshops or online, certainly highlights that the city of Trento claims open democratic processes to define its future and also that a productive relation between urbanization and democracy [22] is present and vivid.

References

1. Ianni, P.A.: Il valore della città storica in Italia: mutamenti culturali e politiche urbane attraverso le ricostruzioni post-sisma negli ultimi cinquant'anni. Ciudades **19**, 143–161 (2016)
2. Campos Venuti, G., Oliva, F.: L'urbanistica riformista. Etaslibri, Milano (1991)
3. Gasparrini, C.: L'attualità dell'urbanistica: dal piano al progetto dal progetto al piano. Etaslibri, Milano (1994)
4. Bevilacqua, G.: La città storica e la nuova questione urbana, Aracne, Roma (2020)
5. Borja, J., Muxi, Z.: El espacio publico: ciudad y ciudadanìa. Random House, Barcelona (2003)
6. Ansell, C., Gash, A.: Collaborative governance in theory and practice. J. Public Adm. Res. Theory **18**, 543–571 (2008). https://doi.org/10.1093/jopart/mum032
7. Dioguardi, G.: Prefazione. In: Il fenomeno urbano e la complessità. Bollati Borighieri, Torino (2019)
8. Jarvis, P.: The Practitioner-Researcher: Developing Theory from Practice. Jossey-Bass Publishers, San Francisco (1999)
9. Callon, M., Lascoumes, P., Barthe, Y.: Acting in an uncertain world: an essay on technical democracy. MIT press, Cambridge (2009)
10. Dewey, J., Rogers, M.L.: The public and its problems: An essay in political inquiry. Penn State Press, University Park PA (2012)
11. Binder, T., Brandt, E., Ehn, P., Halse, J.: Democratic design experiments: between parliament and laboratory. CoDesign **11**, 152–165 (2015). https://doi.org/10.1080/15710882.2015.108 1248
12. Entman, R.M.: Framing: toward clarification of a fractured paradigm. J. Commun.Commun. **43**, 51–58 (1993). https://doi.org/10.1111/j.1460-2466.1993.tb01304.x
13. Appadurai, A.: The Scarcity of Social Futures in the Digital Era. In: Kemp, S., Andersson, J.: Futures, 1st ed. Oxford University Press (2021)
14. Lin, Y.: Social media for collaborative planning: a typology of support functions and challenges. Cities **125**, 103641 (2022). https://doi.org/10.1016/j.cities.2022.103641
15. Asad, M., Le Dantec, C.A., Nielsen, B., Diedrick, K.: Creating a sociotechnical API: designing city-scale community engagement. In: Proceedings of the 2017 CHI Conference on Human Factors in Computing Systems. ACM, Denver Colorado USA, pp 2295–2306 (2017)
16. Pedretti, T.: SUPERTRENTO. The role of participatory processes as spaces for urban planning and exercise of democracy. In: Selected Article from the International Conference on Designing in Disorder: Urbanpromo 2024, 5-8 November, Florence, Italy. Springer Nature (2025). (in print)
17. Corbett, E., Le Dantec. C.A.: The problem of community engagement: disentangling the practices of municipal government. In: Proceedings of the 2018 CHI Conference on Human Factors in Computing Systems (2018) https://doi.org/10.1145/3173574.3174148

18. Appadurai, A.: Le aspirazioni nutrono la democrazia, Et al., Milano (2011)
19. Koskinen, I., Zimmerman, J., Binder, T., et al: Field. In: Design Research Through Practice. Elsevier, pp 69–87 (2012)
20. DiSalvo, C.: Design as democratic inquiry: putting experimental civics into practice. The MIT Press, Cambridge, Massachusetts (2022)
21. Beissinger, M. R.: The individual and collective action in urban civic revolution. In: The Revolutionary City. Princeton University Press, pp 271–318 (2022)
22. Beveridge, R., Koch, P.: Seeing democracy like a city. Dialogues Urban Res. **2**, 145–163 (2024). https://doi.org/10.1177/27541258231203999

Dynamic Parking Space Allocation for Real-Time Urban Management

Dariush Ebrahimi[1]($\boxtimes$), Darpan Rathwa[1], Ishan Shah[1], Rushil Shah[1], Krish Gohil[1], and Fadi Alzhouri[2]

[1] Department of Physics and Computer Science, Wilfrid Laurier University, 75 University Ave W, Waterloo, ON N2L 3C5, Canada
debrahimi@wlu.ca, {rath9450,shah8443,shah3670,gohi9630}@mylaurier.ca
[2] Department of Electrical and Computer Engineering, Gulf University for Science and Technology (GUST), Mishref, Kuwait
alzhouri.f@gust.edu.kw

Abstract. Urbanization and rising vehicle ownership have intensified the challenge of finding parking in metropolitan areas. This research presents the Dynamic Parking Space Allocation System (DPSAS), an advanced framework for real-time parking management optimization. The system models the urban environment as a weighted graph, where intersections and parking zones are nodes, and roads, affected by dynamic traffic conditions, form the edges. A key innovation is the use of hexagonal grid partitioning, which efficiently segments the urban space, reducing the search area and accelerating computational processes for real-time applications. Additionally, DPSAS features dynamic adaptation mechanisms that continuously recalibrate routes and parking availability in response to evolving traffic conditions. The system adapts to dynamic factors such as travel time, cost, and parking availability, ensuring user-centric optimization and adaptability in fluctuating urban settings. Extensive simulations demonstrate that DPSAS significantly reduces parking search times, optimizes traffic flow, and improves resource utilization. The results highlight the system's robustness and scalability, positioning DPSAS as a transformative solution to urban parking challenges, bridging gaps in existing systems, and enhancing urban mobility.

Keywords: Time-Dependent Shortest Path · Vehicle Routing with Time Windows · Dynamic Parking Allocation · Urban Mobility Optimization

1 Introduction

In recent years, urbanization and the increasing number of vehicles per household have led to a growing demand for parking in metropolitan areas [1]. As urban spaces expand, the challenge of finding reasonable parking increases due to limited parking supply and heightened traffic congestion. Traditional parking systems, which are typically static, fail to offer flexible, dynamic solutions

O. Gervasi et al. (Eds.): ICCSA 2025, LNCS 15650, pp. 204–220, 2025.
https://doi.org/10.1007/978-3-031-96962-1_14

that can adapt to changing traffic conditions and user requirements [2]. This not only results in long search times, high costs for private drivers, and worsening congestion, but also contributes to pollution and inefficiencies in urban mobility. Dynamic pricing has emerged as a key strategy for managing parking demand and availability [3,4].

The primary goal of this research is to develop smarter and more interactive parking solutions capable of handling new challenges such as real-time traffic fluctuations, current parking infrastructure status, and growing user demands. Recent studies highlight the difficulties faced by existing systems in real-time parking allocation, particularly due to the lack of seamless integration of traffic, location, and cost data in a scalable, user-friendly manner. Works such as [5] on parking optimization and [6] on traffic-aware navigation expose the limitations of current methods, which often fail to consider both traffic-induced delays and user preferences in real-time. While IoT-based parking systems and GPS navigation technology have seen improvements, a gap remains in their integration to provide more optimized and cost-effective solutions [6,7].

This paper proposes a dynamic parking allocation system that utilizes a greedy algorithm to assign parking spots based on real-time traffic conditions, proximity to destinations, travel time, and parking costs. The system models each parking zone as a node in a weighted graph, where intersections are also nodes representing potential delays due to congestion. It calculates the best parking spot within a 1–2 km radius of the user's destination, using a weighted formula that incorporates travel time, distance, and parking charges. The inclusion of traffic data at intersection nodes provides more accurate estimates of travel times to parking zones, enabling better decision-making.

The proposed system introduces several innovations that set it apart from existing solutions. Unlike traditional systems, it divides urban areas into hexagonal grids, allowing for more efficient spatial queries and reducing computational complexity [8–10]. The system combines traffic analytics with dynamic parking management in a unique way, enabling seamless updates and recalculations based on changing conditions. This offers superior adaptability compared to previous approaches. Additionally, the integration of hexagonal grids and dynamic graph updates reduces computational overhead, making the system scalable and capable of handling larger metropolitan networks—something that static or heuristic-based methods often fail to do [11].

This work contributes to the advancement of real-time parking systems by addressing both travel time and cost while incorporating traffic-induced delays. The remainder of this paper is organized as follows: Sect. 2 reviews related work in dynamic parking and traffic-aware navigation systems. Section 3 describes the setup of the proposed system, including the design of the data structure, algorithm, and infrastructure. Section 4 delves into the algorithm design and analysis, detailing the optimization techniques used. Section 5 presents the experimental setup and performance analysis, demonstrating the system's effectiveness under simulated conditions. Finally, Sect. 6 concludes the paper.

2   Literature Review

As urbanization continues and vehicle ownership rises globally, parking allocation systems have become a critical concern [1]. Modern parking systems often
suffer from long search times for available parking spaces, excessive traffic, environmental harm, and inefficient use of resources [7]. Researchers have explored
various approaches, including graph-based optimization, constraint modeling,
dynamic pricing, and machine learning, to address these issues, but a unified,
comprehensive framework remains elusive [2,8].

Dynamic parking allocation frameworks have emerged as one of the most
promising solutions to address the inefficiencies of static systems. For example,
[1] introduced a scalable framework that adjusts parking allocations dynamically using 0–1 programming models. This system relies on real-time GPS data
to assign parking spaces to vehicles, helping reduce congestion and maximize
resource utilization. However, it lacks dynamic pricing and fails to incorporate
user-specific preferences, such as proximity to destinations or priority access.

In contrast, [2] proposed a constraint optimization model that considers user
schedules, organizational constraints, and shifting priorities. The system reallo-
cates unused parking spaces dynamically to ensure flexible utilization. Despite
its benefits, this approach does not integrate real-time traffic data or include
adaptive mechanisms to handle fluctuating demand, limiting its scalability and
effectiveness in complex urban environments.

Dynamic pricing has become a vital mechanism for balancing parking
demand and availability. In [7], the authors developed a game-theoretic model
that uses machine learning to predict parking occupancy and adjust pricing
dynamically. Their approach optimizes revenue for parking authorities while
enhancing user satisfaction by considering the interaction between restricted
parking users and parking pricing.

While the above approaches offer valuable insights, they tend to address individual aspects of the parking allocation problem rather than providing a unified
solution [4]. Most systems focus either on allocation efficiency or revenue optimization, neglecting user-centric features like dynamic prioritization, real-time
traffic adjustments, and equitable resource distribution. Furthermore, reliance
on static datasets or predefined parameters often hinders the scalability and
adaptability of these systems in real-world conditions.

Our research builds upon the strengths and addresses the limitations of previous work by proposing a unified framework for dynamic parking allocation
[8,9]. By leveraging real-time traffic data and occupancy predictions, parking
allocations are adjusted dynamically, along with pricing adjustments according
to current demand. We employ graph-based models to treat parking zones and
intersections as nodes, facilitating efficient route and slot optimization while
accounting for congestion and travel costs. Additionally, our framework incorporates user-specific dynamics, such as high-priority access for frequent users or
proximity to destinations. Furthermore, adaptive revenue optimization ensures
balanced revenue generation while providing value to users, promoting long-term
sustainability. Together, these components form a flexible, scalable framework

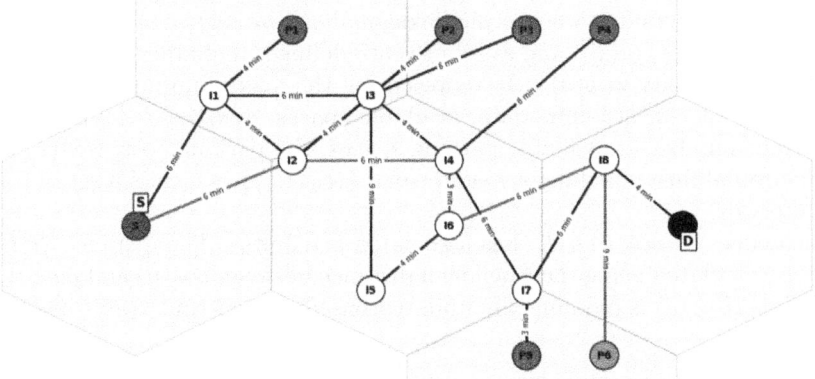

Fig. 1. Graphical representation of the urban road network, where nodes denote intersections, parking lots, the source (*S*), and the destination (*D*). Edges represent roads with dynamic travel times. Hexagonal cells enable efficient spatial queries.

capable of solving long-standing problems and responding to the changing needs of modern urban parking systems.

This work's primary innovation lies in its holistic framework, combining real-time traffic analytics, dynamic pricing, and user-centric prioritization [10, 11]. By integrating these elements, our system optimizes parking allocation, reduces search times, enhances user satisfaction, and maintains scalability to accommodate diverse urban environments. This unified approach marks a significant advancement in the field of parking allocation systems.

3   System Model and Problem Description

In this section, we present the system model for Dynamic Parking Space Allocation (DPSAS) and Route Planning in an urban environment and formally define the problem addressed. The system aims to guide users from a source location to an available parking slot near their destination while accounting for dynamic traffic conditions and parking availability.

3.1   System Model

The urban environment, as illustrated in Fig. 1, is modeled as an undirected graph $G = (V, E)$, where V is the set of nodes, $V = \{v_1, v_2, \ldots, v_n\}$, representing intersections, parking lots, the source, and the destination, and E is the set of edges, $E = \{e_1, e_2, \ldots, e_m\}$, representing roads connecting the nodes. Each node $v \in V$ has associated attributes. The position of a node is given as $pos(v) = (x_v, y_v)$, representing its coordinates in a 2D plane. Each node is assigned a type, $type(v) \in \{\text{source}, \text{destination}, \text{intersection}, \text{parking\_lot}\}$. Additionally, nodes are mapped to hexagonal cells using the function AssignHexCell($pos(v)$), which assigns the node to a specific hexagonal cell $hex(v) = (q_v, r_v)$. For nodes of type parking lot, additional attributes are defined, including the parking slot ID, $id(v)$, a capacity, $cap(v) \in \mathbb{N}$, representing the maximum number of vehicles the parking lot can accommodate, available spaces, $avail(v) \in \mathbb{N}$, representing the current number of available parking spaces, the parking cost, $cost(v) \in \mathbb{R}^+$, and the availability schedule, $schedule(v) = \{(t_{s_i}, t_{e_i})\}$, which is a set of booked time intervals.

Each edge, $e = (u, v) \in E$, has associated attributes. The distance $dist(e) = d(u, v)$ is calculated using the Euclidean distance between $pos(u)$ and $pos(v)$. The travel time $time(e)$ is dynamically updated based on real-time traffic conditions.

Dynamic Traffic Model: The travel time on each edge is affected by dynamic traffic conditions [12]. At any time t, the travel time $time_t(e)$ is calculated as:

$$time_t(e) = \left(\frac{dist(e)}{v_{\text{adjusted}}(e, t)} \right) \times 60, \tag{1}$$

where $v_{\text{adjusted}}(e, t)$ is the adjusted speed on edge e at time t, computed as:

$$v_{\text{adjusted}}(e, t) = \max(v_{\text{base}} \times tf(e, t), \epsilon), \tag{2}$$

with v_{base} being the base speed (e.g., 60 km/h), $tf(e, t) \in [0.3, 1]$ being a traffic factor simulating congestion, and ϵ being a small constant to avoid division by zero.

Hexagonal Cell Partitioning: The area is partitioned into hexagonal cells to optimize spatial queries [10]. The function AssignHexCell($pos(v)$) maps the position of a node v to a hexagonal cell (q_v, r_v). The set of hexagonal cells within a certain radius R of a node v is denoted as $\mathcal{H}_v(R)$.

3.2   Problem Explanation

The core problem is to find an optimal path from the source node S to an available parking slot p^* near the destination D, considering dynamic traffic conditions and parking slot availability, and to book the parking slot for a desired time duration Δt.

Objectives: The objectives of the problem include minimizing the total travel time, selecting the optimal parking slot, and ensuring dynamic adaptation. The total travel time is minimized by finding a path $P = \{v_0, v_1, \ldots, v_k\}$ from S to p^* that minimizes the total travel time:

$$T_{\text{total}} = \sum_{i=0}^{k-1} time_t(e_i), \tag{3}$$

where $e_i = (v_i, v_{i+1})$. The parking slot p^* should balance proximity to the destination and parking cost. Additionally, the path and parking slot selection must adapt dynamically in response to real-time changes in traffic and parking availability [11].

Constraints: The problem is subject to several constraints. The parking slot p^* must be available for booking during the desired time interval $[t_{start}, t_{end}]$, where t_{start} is the estimated arrival time at p^*, and $t_{end} = t_{start} + \Delta t$. The path from S to p^* must traverse nodes within the relevant hexagonal cells $\mathcal{H}$ to limit the search space and improve computational efficiency [8,13]. Additionally, the travel times on edges are subject to dynamic updates due to traffic conditions, which may impact the optimality of the path over time.

Problem Definition: Given a graph $G = (V, E)$ with dynamic edge weights $time_t(e)$, a source node S, a destination node D, a desired parking duration Δt, and the current time $t_{current}$, the objective is to find a parking slot $p^* \in V$ with $type(p^*) = $ parking_lot that is available for booking during $[t_{start}, t_{end}]$. Additionally, a path $P = \{v_0, v_1, \ldots, v_k\}$ must be identified, starting at $v_0 = S$ and ending at $v_k = p^*$, such that T_{total} is minimized. If traffic conditions or parking availability change, the path and p^* must be dynamically updated.

The problem is further constrained by parking slot capacity, which requires:

$$\left| \left\{ (s_i, e_i) \in \text{schedule}(p^*) \mid [t_{start}, t_{end}] \cap [s_i, e_i] \neq \emptyset \right\} \right| < \text{cap}(p^*). \tag{4}$$

Nodes in the path P must be within the hexagonal cells $\mathcal{H}$ relevant to S, D, and p^*. Additionally, real-time updates to $time_t(e)$ and $avail(p)$ for $e \in E$ and $p \in V$ must be considered.

Challenges and Complexity: The problem presents several challenges. The dynamic nature of the environment requires the algorithm to adapt in real-time to changes in both traffic conditions and parking availability. The combinatorial nature of the problem, with numerous possible paths and parking slot combinations, adds to its complexity, especially in densely connected urban graphs. Furthermore, the multi-objective optimization aspect, which involves balancing travel time, parking cost, and proximity to the destination, introduces trade-offs that complicate the optimization process. This problem can be classified as a variant of the *Time-Dependent Shortest Path Problem* (TDSPP) with additional constraints, which is known to be NP-hard [13].

3.3   Example Scenario

This example illustrates how the system guides a user from a source location to an available parking lot near their destination.

The urban road network consists of a start point (S), a destination (D), intersections $(I_1, I_2, ..., I_8)$, and parking lots $(P_1, P_2, ..., P_6)$. Intersections allow movement in different directions, while parking lots, connected to certain intersections, may change availability dynamically due to new bookings or cancellations. Roads (edges) link these points and have travel times that update in real-time based on traffic conditions, allowing the system to adjust the optimal route as the user progresses. The network is divided into hexagonal cells, enabling efficient spatial queries and faster route calculations [8]. The system continuously recalculates the best route to direct the user through intersections to an available parking lot near D, adapting dynamically to traffic and parking changes.

As shown in Fig. 1, the system computes an initial optimal route from S to a selected parking lot (P_6) near D, highlighted in red. Nodes are organized within hexagonal partitions, ensuring focused spatial processing. Intersections serve as key junctions, while parking lots are color-coded based on availability. Edge travel times are dynamically updated based on current traffic conditions.

Upon reaching intersection I_2, the system reevaluates travel times due to traffic changes, potentially altering the planned path. Similarly, at intersection I_4, fresh traffic data is incorporated, refining the route to P_6. The figure illustrates this adaptive process, demonstrating how real-time updates influence navigation decisions. The use of hexagonal spatial partitioning localizes computations, ensuring an efficient and responsive navigation approach.

3.4   Key Considerations in Solving the Problem

To effectively address the problem, the solution must:

– Dynamically manage parking slot availability and bookings.
– Identify the shortest path from S to an available parking slot p^* within relevant hexagonal cells, considering real-time traffic conditions.
– Adapt to changing conditions by rebooking parking slots and recalculating routes when necessary.
– Reduce computational complexity by constraining the search space using hexagonal cell partitioning.

These considerations guide the development of our approach. In the next section, we propose an algorithm that incorporates these principles to optimize parking and routing decisions in dynamic urban environments.

4   Algorithm Design

To propose the *MainTraversalAndBooking* solution for the Dynamic Parking Space Allocation (DPSAS) problem, we first define three key functions: *ManageParkingSlots*, *GetHexCellsBetweenNodes*, and *FindShortestPathWithHexGrid*. Afterward, we present the main algorithm.

4.1   ManageParkingSlots

The *ManageParkingSlots* algorithm dynamically updates and queries the availability of parking lots to secure a suitable booking time window. Initially, it attempts to identify any available parking slots within a set of hex cells $\mathcal{H}$ near the destination. If no such slots are found, the algorithm broadens its search, considering all available parking lots in the network as a fallback.

Each slot is then prioritized according to its proximity to the destination and its associated cost. These metrics are inserted into a priority queue, ensuring that the most desirable options (i.e., closest and least expensive) are evaluated first. The algorithm then checks whether the slot can accommodate the desired booking interval $[t_{\text{start}}, t_{\text{end}}]$ given its capacity and existing reservations. If it can, the interval is added to the slot's schedule, and this slot is immediately returned as the chosen option. If no candidate slot can fulfill the requirements, the algorithm returns None, indicating that a suitable parking opportunity was not found. The time complexity of this process is $O(|P| + |P_{\text{available}}| \log |P_{\text{available}}|)$, where $|P|$ is the total number of parking slots and $|P_{\text{available}}|$ is the subset currently available for consideration. This reflects the complexity of first identifying suitable candidates and then efficiently extracting and validating them via the priority queue.

4.2   GetHexCellsBetweenNodes

The *GetHexCellsBetweenNodes* function identifies all hexagonal cells that lie between two nodes in the graph. It retrieves the hex cell assignments for the start node S and the end node D, calculates the minimum and maximum indices along the hexagonal grid axes (q and r), and slightly expands this range to account for potential deviations.

4.3   FindShortestPathWithHexGrid

The *FindShortestPathWithHexGrid* algorithm, illustrated in Algorithm 1, computes the shortest path between two nodes u and v, considering only nodes within specified hex cells $\mathcal{H}$. This modification of Dijkstra's algorithm enhances efficiency by reducing the search space to relevant areas [10]. The algorithm initializes a priority queue Q and maintains distance estimates $d[n]$ and predecessor links $\pi[n]$. Select the node with the smallest tentative distance and explore its neighbors, considering only those within $\mathcal{H}$. Once the destination node v is reached, the algorithm reconstructs the shortest path using the predecessor links. The total travel time T is obtained from the final distance estimate $d[v]$.

The time complexity is $O(|E'| + |V'| \log |V'|)$, where $|V'|$ and $|E'|$ are the number of nodes and edges within the hex cells $\mathcal{H}$. Since $|V'| \ll |V|$ and $|E'| \ll |E|$ as the search is restricted to nodes within a specific subset of hexagonal cells $\mathcal{H}$, rather than considering the entire graph. These hex cells are chosen based on proximity to the source and destination, significantly reducing the number of nodes evaluated. This algorithm is more efficient than standard Dijkstra's algorithm on the full graph.

Algorithm 1. FindShortestPathWithHexGrid

Require: Graph G, Start node u, End node v, Hex cells $\mathcal{H}$
Ensure: Shortest path P, Total travel time T
 1: Initialize priority queue $Q \leftarrow [(0, u)]$
 2: Set distances $d[n] \leftarrow \infty$ for all $n \in G$
 3: Set predecessors $\pi[n] \leftarrow$ None for all $n \in G$
 4: Set $d[u] \leftarrow 0$
 5: **while** Q is not empty **do**
 6:     Extract node with smallest distance: $(d_{\text{current}}, n_{\text{current}}) \leftarrow Q.\text{pop}$
 7:     **if** $n_{\text{current}} = v$ **then**
 8:         **break**
 9:     **end if**
10:     **for** each neighbor m of n_{current} **do**
11:         **if** $m.\text{hex\_cell} \notin \mathcal{H}$ **then**
12:             **continue**
13:         **end if**
14:         Calculate tentative distance: $d_{\text{tentative}} \leftarrow d_{\text{current}} + G[n_{\text{current}}][m].\text{time}$
15:         **if** $d_{\text{tentative}} < d[m]$ **then**
16:             Update distance: $d[m] \leftarrow d_{\text{tentative}}$
17:             Update predecessor: $\pi[m] \leftarrow n_{\text{current}}$
18:             Add $(d[m], m)$ to Q
19:         **end if**
20:     **end for**
21: **end while**
22: Reconstruct path P using predecessors π
23: **return** $P, d[v]$

4.4 MainTraversalAndBooking

The *MainTraversalAndBooking* algorithm, detailed in Algorithm 2, orchestrates the process of navigating from the source node S to a parking slot near the destination D, while dynamically managing traffic and parking conditions. It begins by attempting to book a parking slot p^* close to the destination within the desired time frame. The algorithm divides the road network into hexagonal cells and identifies relevant hex cells near the destination for the search and management of parking.

The algorithm enters a loop where it continually updates traffic conditions and parking availability to reflect real-time changes. If the previously booked parking slot p^* becomes unavailable, it attempts to rebook another slot. The parking slot selection is stabilized once the user enters a hex cell adjacent to the destination D's hex cell [9] because it provides a seamless experience by locking in the parking choice when the user is close to their destination, avoiding unnecessary detours or last-minute changes that could cause inconvenience.

At this point, the algorithm finalizes the selected parking slot, stops further availability updates, and prevents rebooking to ensure a seamless experience as the user approaches their final destination.

Algorithm 2. MainTraversalAndBooking

Require: Graph G, Source node S, Destination node D, Desired parking duration Δt
Ensure: Final path P_{final}, Total travel time T_{total}
1: Initialize $u \leftarrow S$, $T_{\text{total}} \leftarrow 0$, $P_{\text{final}} \leftarrow [u]$
2: $\mathcal{H} \leftarrow$ GetHexCellsNearDestination(D)
3: $p^* \leftarrow$ ManageParkingSlots$(G, t_{\text{current}}, [t_{\text{current}}, t_{\text{current}} + \Delta t], \mathcal{H})$
4: **if** $p^* = $ **None then**
5:     **return** Failure
6: **end if**
7: $\mathcal{H} \leftarrow \mathcal{H} \cup$ GetHexCellsBetweenNodes(S, p^*)
8: $\mathcal{H}_{\text{adjacent}} \leftarrow$ GetAdjacentHexCells(D), $adjacentZoneReached \leftarrow$ **False**
9: **while** $u \neq p^*$ **do**
10:     **Update:** Traffic, t_{current}, and parking availability
11:     **if** p^*.availability $=$ False **and not** $adjacentZoneReached$ **then**
12:         $p^* \leftarrow$ ManageParkingSlots$(G, t_{\text{current}}, [t_{\text{current}}, t_{\text{current}} + \Delta t], $None$)$
13:         **if** $p^* = $ **None then**
14:             **return** Failure
15:         **end if**
16:         $\mathcal{H} \leftarrow \mathcal{H} \cup$ GetHexCellsBetweenNodes(u, p^*)
17:     **end if**
18:     $(P_{\text{temp}}, T_{\text{temp}}) \leftarrow$
            FindShortestPathWithHexGrid$(G, u, p^*, \mathcal{H})$
19:     Move to next node: $u \leftarrow$ next node in P_{temp}, $P_{\text{final}} \leftarrow P_{\text{final}} + [u]$, $T_{\text{total}} \leftarrow T_{\text{total}} + T_{\text{temp}}$
20:     **if** $u \in \mathcal{H}_{\text{adjacent}}$ **and not** $adjacentZoneReached$ **then**
21:         $adjacentZoneReached \leftarrow$ **True**; Stop updates and finalize p^*
22:     **end if**
23: **end while**
24: **return** $P_{\text{final}}, T_{\text{total}}$

At each iteration, the algorithm computes the shortest path from the current node u to the parking slot p^* using the *FindShortestPathWithHexGrid* algorithm. It then moves to the next node along this path, updating the final path P_{final} and the total travel time T_{total}.

The algorithm ensures correctness by dynamically adapting to changing traffic and parking conditions while locking the parking selection when the user approaches the destination. Assuming the number of iterations is k, the overall time complexity is approximately $O(k \cdot |V'| \log |V'|)$, since the dominant operations involve the computation of the shortest path within the hex cells. The use of hex grids and the adjacent hex cell stabilization mechanism helps to limit the size of $|V'|$ and $|E'|$ considered in each iteration, keeping the algorithm efficient for real-time applications.

Although this complexity may seem high, in practice, the number of iterations k is bounded by the distance to the parking slot and the frequency of traffic updates. By dynamically updating only a subset of the graph and focusing computations within relevant hex cells, the algorithm maintains scalability even in large urban networks.

4.5   Correctness Proof

We will prove that the *MainTraversalAndBooking* algorithm correctly finds a feasible path from the source to an available parking slot near the destination, while dynamically adapting to traffic and parking availability updates.

Initialization: The algorithm begins by initializing the graph and trying to book a parking space near the destination. If a parking slot is successfully booked, it proceeds to find a path to that slot.

Dynamic Updates: During traversal, the algorithm updates traffic conditions and parking availability at each time step. If the parking slot becomes unavailable, it attempts to rebook another slot and recalculates the path.

Termination: The algorithm terminates when the user reaches the parking slot. Since the algorithm always attempts to find an available parking slot and computes the shortest path to it, it ensures that the user can reach a parking slot if one is available.

Correctness of Sub-algorithms

– *ManageParkingSlots*: Correctly maintains parking slot availability and selects an optimal parking slot based on proximity and cost.
– *FindShortestPathWithHexGrid*: Correctly computes the shortest path within the specified hex grid cells using a modified Dijkstra's algorithm.

By ensuring that each component of the algorithm functions correctly and handles dynamic updates appropriately [4], the *MainTraversalAndBooking* algorithm achieves its intended goal of guiding the user to an available parking slot near the destination while adapting to real-time conditions.

5   Performance Evaluation

For evaluation, we generated a geometric structure similar to [11] and integrated a dynamic, stochastic traffic model. A traffic factor tf $\in [0.3, 1]$ is sampled to modify the base speed v_{base}, yielding an edge-specific adjusted speed v_{uv}. To maintain realism, v_{uv} never approaches zero, ensuring that traffic may slow but rarely comes to a complete stop. The adjusted speed, combined with the computed distance, determines the travel time t_{uv} for each edge, which is then stored as a graph attribute.

We tracked key performance metrics to evaluate our system's effectiveness, focusing on execution time, travel time to destinations, scalability, and robustness. Execution time measures responsiveness, crucial for real-time applications, while travel time indicates routing efficiency. Scalability assesses the system's ability to handle increasing complexity, and robustness reflects its adaptability to dynamic conditions. Together, these metrics ensure the system meets its objectives of minimizing travel time and maintaining efficiency.

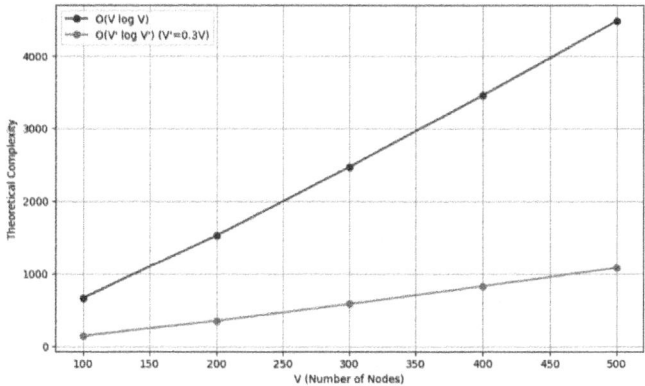

Fig. 2. Theoretical Complexity: Normal vs. Hex-grid Approach

To thoroughly test the system's performance, we vary several parameters. The number of users, or simultaneous queries, is increased from 10 to 50 to test how well the system handles multiple concurrent route requests. This parameter directly influences execution time and tests scalability under high demand. The traffic factor, ranging from 0.3 to 1.0, simulates congestion levels. A low traffic factor, around 0.3, represents heavy congestion, while a factor close to 1.0 indicates near-free-flow conditions. Varying the traffic factor tests the algorithm's ability to adapt to changing road speeds and conditions. The number of nodes, which ranges from 100 to 500, scales the size of the graph to test how well the approach handles increasing problem complexity. By comparing various algorithms at different network sizes, we assess which methods are more scalable. Furthermore, algorithmic approaches are compared by evaluating the proposed Hex grid Dijkstra approach against the Normal Dijkstra and the heuristic-based A* method. Including A* provides a benchmark from the literature, helping us identify where our spatial filtering method stands relative to established shortest path algorithms [9, 11, 12]. We evaluated the proposed solution against a variety of parameters to showcase its behavior and performance.

Figure 2 illustrates the theoretical complexity $O(|V| \log |V|)$ of Normal Dijkstra and $O(|V'| \log |V'|)$ for the hex-grid approach, where $|V'| \ll |V|$. The complexity curve for the hex-grid approach consistently remains lower, as it effectively reduces the problem size by only considering relevant hexagonal cells. This theoretical insight aligns quite well with the empirical results, confirming that spatial filtering diminishes computational overhead and improves scalability.

Figure 3 shows execution time scaling for Normal Dijkstra, Hex-grid Dijkstra, and A* as the graph size increases from 100 to 500 nodes. Normal Dijkstra experiences rapid growth, reaching approximately 0.0175 s at 500 nodes. Hex-grid Dijkstra, however, remains under 0.003 s at the same scale, significantly narrowing the gap. A* outperforms both, barely exceeding 0.001 s at 500 nodes. Although A* is known for its heuristic efficiency, the hex-grid approach provides a substantial advantage over plain Dijkstra, moving closer to A* performance.

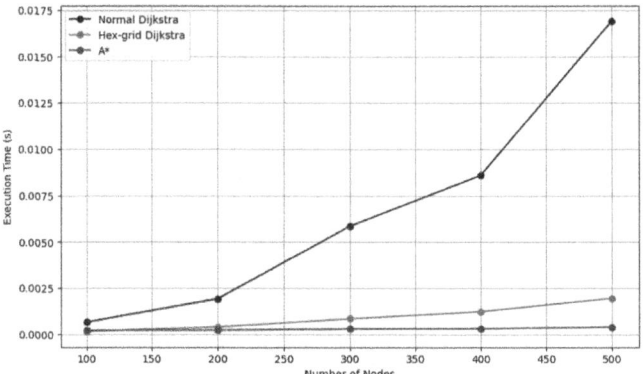

Fig. 3. Execution Time vs Number of Nodes

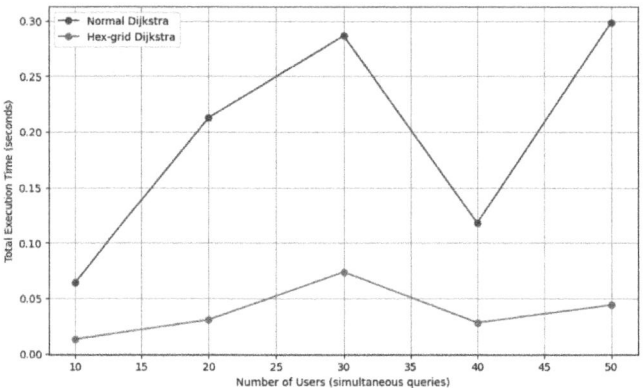

Fig. 4. Number of Users vs. Execution Time

Figure 4 compares the execution times of Normal Dijkstra and Hex-grid Dijkstra as the number of users increases from 10 to 50. Normal Dijkstra's execution time rises substantially, peaking around 0.30 s at heavy loads. In contrast, Hex grid Dijkstra remains under 0.10 s, demonstrating improved scalability and quicker response under higher user loads. The spatial filtering reduces the search space, resulting in more stable and efficient computations.

In Fig. 5, the allocation success rate decreases as the number of users increases from 10 to 50. Hex-grid Dijkstra maintains a success rate above 88% under high user loads, closely following A*'s performance. Normal Dijkstra shows a sharper decline, dropping to 82%. These results demonstrate Hex-grid Dijkstra's robust handling of multiple users, outperforming Normal Dijkstra while staying competitive with A*. The use of spatial filtering in Hex-grid Dijkstra ensures better resource utilization, reducing computational overhead as user demand increases. This highlights its potential to scale effectively in dense urban scenarios.

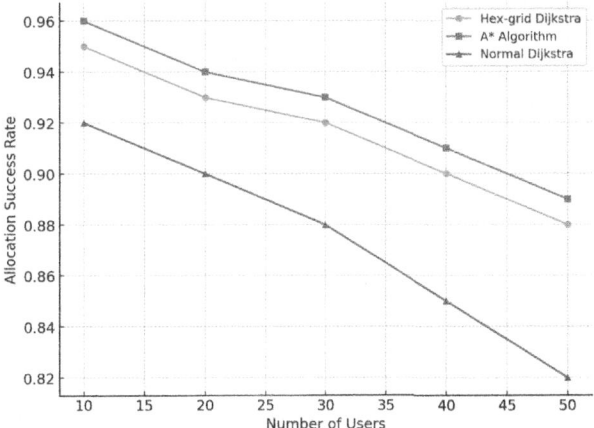

Fig. 5. Allocation Success Rate vs. Number of Users

In Fig. 6, travel time decreases as the traffic factor increases from 0.3 (heavy congestion) to 1.0 (free-flow). Hex-grid Dijkstra demonstrates consistent adaptability, reducing travel times from over 16 min to below 6 min. A* performs slightly better, while Normal Dijkstra exhibits the longest travel times across all traffic conditions. The results highlight Hex-grid Dijkstra's ability to dynamically adjust to traffic variations, approaching A* performance.

5.1 Comparisons with Other Techniques

A* serves as a well-regarded benchmark in shortest path literature [12]. While the hex-grid approach does not surpass A*, it significantly outperforms Normal Dijkstra and edges closer to A*'s execution times by restricting the search space. This result confirms that spatial partitioning can partially emulate the benefits of heuristic-driven search.

A naïve approach that ignores traffic dynamics or simply selects the closest parking lot by Euclidean distance would fail to adapt to real-world complexity [2], resulting in longer and less reliable travel times. By contrast, our dynamic approach, continuously updating edge weights and re-evaluating parking availability, delivers more accurate route and parking recommendations.

While no direct comparisons are shown, genetic algorithms or ML-based approaches often require extensive training or tuning. Our method yields consistent and predictable results with straightforward graph-based techniques.

The implementation handles dynamic changes in parking availability, allowing re-booking when a previously chosen parking slot becomes unavailable. Despite these fluctuations, the hex-grid approach and the A* method maintain low execution times and stable travel times. In practice, this robustness ensures that users receive timely updates and reliable guidance, even in evolving and unpredictable traffic and parking scenarios.

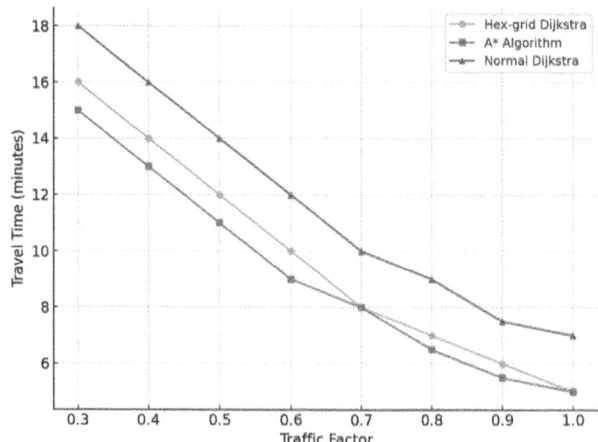

Fig. 6. Travel Time vs Traffic Factor

Overall, the performance evaluation confirms that the proposed hex-grid Dijkstra approach provides a substantial improvement over Normal Dijkstra, especially under heavy user load and large network sizes. It narrows the performance gap with A*, demonstrating that spatial constraints can serve as a powerful means of optimization. The combination of dynamic hex-grid partitioning and continuous adaptation to traffic conditions yields a practical, efficient, and robust solution for dynamic parking space allocation systems.

We summarize the key observations. First, it offers improved scalability as hex-grid Dijkstra remains efficient even as the number of users and nodes increases. This scalability enables the system to significantly outperform Normal Dijkstra in handling large-scale urban networks. Additionally, the system exhibits adaptability to traffic conditions, with travel times predictably decreasing as traffic improves. This behavior indicates the correct and responsive updating of route calculations, ensuring the system remains effective under dynamic conditions.

Furthermore, the comparative efficiency of the approach is evident. While hex-grid filtering may not match the speed of A*, it effectively reduces complexity and execution time. This brings its performance closer to heuristic methods, such as A*, without relying on custom heuristics and hence enhancing its generalizability. Finally, the system's robustness is underscored by its ability to handle dynamic parking availability and changing traffic conditions without significant performance loss. This resilience highlights its practicality and applicability in real-world scenarios.

The combination of dynamic hex-grid partitioning and continuous adaptation to traffic conditions yields a practical, efficient, and robust solution for dynamic parking space allocation systems.

6   Conclusion

The Dynamic Parking Space Allocation System (DPSAS) presents a novel, user-centric approach to urban parking management by integrating real-time data with hexagonal grid-based spatial partitioning. This design enhances computational efficiency while ensuring responsive and adaptive decision-making. At its core, DPSAS leverages a modified Dijkstra's algorithm to dynamically recommend optimal parking slots, continuously adjusting to traffic conditions and availability changes. The hexagonal partitioning framework not only improves route computation efficiency but also ensures temporal scalability by distributing the computational load effectively. As a result, users experience more efficient travel with minimal delays caused by congestion and parking uncertainties. Comparative analysis shows that DPSAS outperforms traditional and heuristic-based methods by bridging the gap between computational simplicity and state-of-the-art performance. By seamlessly integrating real-time analytics, adaptive optimization, and scalable processing, DPSAS offers a practical and intelligent solution for smart cities. Its contributions establish a transformative model for addressing the evolving challenges of urban mobility, paving the way for future advancements in intelligent transportation systems.

References

1. Mladenović, M.N., Nourinejad, M., Foreman, K., Kouvelas, C.: A framework for dynamic reallocation of parking spaces in parking facilities. Transport. Res. Part C: Emerg. Technol. **123**, 102990 (2021)
2. Elfaki, A.O., Messoudi, W., Bushnag, A., Abuzneid, S., Alhmiedat, T.: Constraint optimization model for dynamic parking space allocation. Sensors **24**, 3988 (2024)
3. Wang, T., Chen, Y., Yu, J., Xie, S.: Formation mechanisms and clustering differences in risky riding behaviors of electric bike riders. IEEE Access **9**, 119 712–119 721 (2021)
4. Wang, T., Chen, Y., Yan, X., Li, W., Shi, D.: Traffic risk assessment based on warning data. J. Adv. Transp. **2022**, 1 (2022)
5. Liu, Y., Wang, C., Xu, S., Zhou, W., Chen, Y.: Multi-weighted graph 3D convolution network for traffic prediction. Neural Comput. Appl. **35**(20), 15 221–15 237 (2023)
6. Shi, D., Wang, T., Chen, Y., Liu, C.: Exploring the effects of request time, secondary task, and take-over mode on take-over performance. In: International Conference on Intelligent Transportation Engineering. Springer Nature Singapore, pp. 1001–1014 (2021)
7. Saharan, S., Kumar, N., Bawa, S.: An efficient smart parking system based on deep learning and IoT technologies. IEEE Trans. Intell. Transp. Syst. **24**(2), 1–12 (2023)
8. Chen, Y., Wang, T., Yan, X., Wang, C.: An ensemble optimization strategy for dynamic parking-space allocation. IEEE Intell. Transp. Syst. Mag. **15**(1), 347–362 (2023)
9. An, Z., Rui, X., Gao, C.: Improved a* navigation path-planning algorithm based on hexagonal grid. ISPRS Int. J. Geo Inf. **13**(5), 166 (2024)

10. Sahr, K.: Hexagonal discrete global grid systems for geospatial computing, ResearchGate (2011)
11. Li, D., Shi, X., Dai, M.: An improved path planning algorithm based on a* algorithm. In: Proceedings of the 13th International Conference on Computer Engineering and Networks, pp. 187–196 (2024)
12. Ou, Y., Fan, Y., Zhang, X., Lin, Y., Yang, W.: Improved a* path planning method based on the grid map. Sensors **22**(16), 6198 (2022)
13. Wang, Y., Yu, X., Liang, X.: Design and implementation of global path planning system for unmanned surface vehicle among multiple task points, arXiv preprint arXiv:1807.08106 (2018)

Well-Being in Italy: A Comprehensive Statistical Analysis Beyond GDP

Najada Firza[✉][iD] and Dante Mazzitelli[iD]

Department of Economics and Finance, University of Bari "Aldo Moro", Largo Abbazia Santa
Scolastica, Bari, Italy
najada.firza@uniba.it

Abstract. The aim of this work is to analyze the variables responsible for long
stays in patients with cardiovascular diseases to monitor the health of patients and
better manage the financial resources of health facilities in relation to this problem. The United Nations 2030 Agenda for Sustainable Development indicators
were developed to address the global economic, social and environmental crisis.
These measures of sustainability aim to go beyond the traditional reliance on Gross
Domestic Product as the only measure of prosperity. The Italian National Institute
of Statistics collects indicators of societal well-being first using the Equitable and
Sustainable Well-Being indicators and later adapting the system developed by the
United Nations known as the Sustainable Development Goals. While the Equitable
and Sustainable Well-Being System is specific to the Italian territory, the Sustainable Development Goals System is suitable for measuring and comparing sustainability at international level. We considered Environment, Economic well-being
and Society of the Equitable and Sustainable Well-Being domains according to a
three-way holistic framework. In this contest we put all Sustainable Development
Goals indicators on this specific Equitable and Sustainable Well-Being domains
to analyze Italy at regional level. Specifically, we used two independent methodologies: Fuzzy c-medoids clustering algorithm and Principal Component Analysis
to investigate and to ranking each Italian Region in selected Equitable and Sustainable Well-Being domains. Our research provides a comprehensive overview
of Italy's status in these Equitable and Sustainable Well-Being dimensions and
provides valuable insights for local and national stakeholders, researchers and
policy makers to identify regional challenges and formulate targeted intervention
measures. The regional ranking resulting from our analyses for the Equitable and
Sustainable Well-Being/Sustainable Development Goals areas is a valuable tool
for measuring and monitoring progress towards these goals, facilitating ongoing
monitoring and evaluation of progress, highlighting areas for improvement and
guiding targeted interventions.

Keywords: SDGs · BES · Composite Indicators · PCA · Factor analysis · KPI

1 Introduction

Gross Domestic Product (GDP) is a useful measure for tracking a country's economic
growth and comparing it with other countries over time. However, GDP presents some
limitations that need to be emphasized (Bleys 2012). One key limitation is that GDP

© The Author(s), under exclusive license to Springer Nature Switzerland AG 2025
O. Gervasi et al. (Eds.): ICCSA 2025, LNCS 15650, pp. 221–236, 2025.
https://doi.org/10.1007/978-3-031-96962-1_15

fails to consider critical factors such as environmental, social, human, and health aspects, which are integral components of economic activities (Costanza et al. 2009). Furthermore, several studies have demonstrated that relying solely on GDP as a measure of well-being has its drawbacks. For example, Talberth et al., argue that there is a threshold point beyond which increasing GDP (Talberth, Cobb et al. 2007) no longer results in higher levels of well-being. In fact, there are some factors not accounted by GDP (Max-Neef 1995) such as depletion of natural resources, growing income inequality and lack of quality leisure time.

There is a need to adopt alternative metrics to assess the overall well-being of society that extends beyond GDP.

Therefore, evaluating well-being has gained worldwide meaning, prompting the establishment of a global movement to proceed beyond GDP (Giovannini et al. 2018).

Moreover, going beyond GDP also means dealing sustainably with all areas of human development (Neumayer 2012).

To overcome the limitations of GDP, United Nations (UN) created the Sustainable Development Goals (SDGs) system. The 2030 Agenda of UN, consisting of the 17 SDGs, was developed to address global crises in the economic, social and environmental sectors. These goals comprise 169 specific targets aimed at ensuring a better future for current and new generations. The program underlines the need to address sustainability issues by going beyond the current model. Challenges such as inequality, climate change, and job automation are interconnected and require a committed global effort from the 192 signatory countries of the 2030 Agenda. The overarching aim of the SDGs is to track and promote progress toward achieving these goals. In Italy, the National Institute of Statistics (ISTAT) collects and publishes data on the Sustainable Development Goals (SDGs) every six months, as requested by the UN Statistical Commission (ASVIS Report 2022).

Prior to this activity, however, building on the observations of the CMEPSP[1] (Stiglitz et al. 2009), the EU Commission (2009) and OECD (Hall et al. 2010) developed guidelines to move beyond the GDP development model. ISTAT in Italy created a system of indicators for equitable and sustainable well-being (BES, that is 'Benessere Equo & Sostenibile') at the regional or provincial level. This system was inspired also by numerous studies on quality-of-life indicators (e.g. Maggino & Zumbo 2012) and integrates economic indicators with additional factors that highlight the multidimensional nature of well-being (Morrone 2013).

Since 2015, ISTAT has provided a composite index for each domain, producing an annual report on the well-being situation in Italy. This report aids the government's economic planning for public policies of well-being and sustainability.

The BES system is divided into 12 domains, which are further grouped into 130 indicators (D'Urso et al. 2022). It measures the well-being of a territory by integrating and complementing the GDP, providing an overview of the territory's health. (Alaimo 2018). As a result of those developments, the meaning of the SDGs and BES are closely linked to

---

[1] The *Commission on the Measurement of Economic Performance and Social Progress*, commonly known as the Stiglitz-Sen-Fitoussi Commission, was established by the French Government in 2008 to investigate alternative methods of measuring a nation's wealth and social progress beyond the limits of the one-dimensional GDP.

providing a reliable foundation for measuring sustainable development and well-being. The two sets of indicators are complementary, although only partially overlapping. It is worth noting that several BES indicators are directly included in the SDGs framework. The reason for choosing the BES system over the SDGs system is that the former is tailored to the specific situation of the Italian territory, while the latter, being an internationally approved system, omits many important local indicators. We believe that the SDGs system is flexible enough to allow the use of certain subsets that are just as useful as the pre-existing BES, and possibly other indicator systems that have not been considered here.

This work examines the relationship between BES and SDGs by analyzing the indicators shared by both domains at the regional level in Italy. The data used in this study was provided by ISTAT from 2004 to 2021. Specifically, we outlined at a regional scale the existence of general spatial patterns for different well-being factors. We divided the considered indicators into 4 macro-categories: economy, social, health and environment. By means of the fuzzy cluster c-medoids algorithm (FCMdd), we carried out a spatial analysis to group Italian regions in different clustering according to their common features for each considered macro-area. Then, through PCA and Factor Analysis, we built an index to rank the regions for each macro-category.

Finally, after the calculation of the composite indicator, we implemented a regional comparison. The article is organized as follows. In section "Materials and methods" we presented the dataset and the statistical techniques used in our research. In section "Results" we reported the main findings of our analysis. Finally, in section "Discussion" we argued our results.

2   Connection Between Well-Being and SDGs for a New Prospective of Development

The UN Agenda 2030 highlights the importance of a new development model compatible with the planet's resources that leverages an inclusive economic system in which levels of inequality are flattened. The availability of data beyond GDP measuring well-being and its sustainability is crucial for the development of new paradigms focused on well-being (Costanza et al. 2014). It is essential to improve the methodological harmonization of BES and SDGs data to create a more effective well-being assessment system at global level (Costanza et al. 2016).

According to Maggino (2017), a harmonization between the two systems is necessary because they have different purposes: BES serves as a system that portrays the well-being situation in various aspects within Italy and its regions, on the other hand, the SDG indicators have been specifically designed to set goals and targets, addressing a different purpose.

Furthermore, the harmonization of the two indicator systems will make data on sustainable development and well-being more accessible, underlining the importance of the information they provide. Consequently, this purpose will facilitate their use in policy planning as decision support for medium and long-term strategies promoting collective well-being.

It is important to note that while the SDGs act as simplified indicators applicable to all countries, the BES indicators follow an Italian approach and provide a wider range of measures for specific phenomena.

The matching between BES and SDGs, is also important to ensure uniform Italian policies at European level. This approach will allow for the creation of a global system that evaluates Italian well-being by considering different aspects and integrations.

3   Materials and Methods

In this publication we consider 4 of the 12 BES domains according to a conception of Gibson et al. (Gibson et al. 2005), which considers well-being as the intersection of the domains: Economy, Environment and Society. Our work considered the "Society" aspect, the *Health* domain which is one of the fundamental services in an advanced society and the *Quality of services* domain which is the emblem of services (Chalmin-Pui et al. 2021). To investigate how the two systems interact for the 4 BES domains, all the SDGs indicators that belong to these 4 domains were considered.

Specifically, the 25 indicators belonging to 8 SDGs (see Table 1) investigated the sustainable development of the Italian territory at a regional level, in a time window of 18 years (2004–2021). We carried out a spatial analysis considering the average of the BES indicators on the reference time interval because not all the considered variables have values on the reference time window analyzed. Our analysis includes 2 parts, one more qualitative and one more quantitative. Firstly, we applied the FCMdd algorithm to group the Italian regions with similar characteristics. In the second step, we built Key Performance Indicators (KPI), synthetic indicators based on PCA, factor analysis to assign a score to each region and rank them with respect to the 4 analyzed BES domain. The workflow of the implemented analysis is shown in Fig. 1.

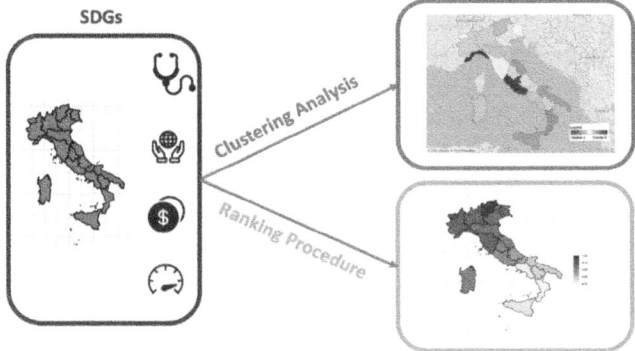

Fig. 1. The flowchart of the proposed methodology. We grouped all the SDGs of Italian Regions in 4 macro-areas: health, environment, economic well-being and quality of services. For each area we applied a clustering analysis based on the FCMdd algorithm and a ranking procedure exploiting factorial analysis, PCA (Key Performance Indicators).

3.1 Data Collection

The dataset for the SDGs at the regional level (2022 edition) used here was collected from the ISTAT public data warehouse (https://www.istat.it/en/well-being-and-sustainability/sustainable-development-goals/istat-indicators-for-sustainable-development). For additional information on the SDGs database, please refer to table S1 in the supplementary information section. The statistical measures of the SDGs exhibit synergies and interrelations with the BES indicators system. Specifically, 64 statistical measures from SDGs overlap with the BES system. We analyzed all SDGs indicators for 4 BES domains (SDGs ISTAT Report 2022). As Table 1 shows, the total number of SDGs indicators is 25 (there are 30 indicators in total but 5 of them do not have a time series and are not considered for the data analysis).

3.2 Exploratory Methods and Fuzzy c-Medoids

In the machine learning and data mining fields, data scaling and data normalization refer to the same preprocessing technique. Their purpose is to convert or transform the data into ranges and formats suitable for modeling and analysis. Models trained on scaled data typically exhibit much better performance than those trained on unscaled data, making data scaling a crucial step in data preprocessing. This process is especially important for methods that rely on distance measures, such as nearest neighbor classification and clustering (Cao, 2016). In methodology, two data scaling algorithms are extensively used: Z-score algorithm and Min-max algorithm. In this publication we used Min-max algorithm 0–1, instead of Z-score, because in the preliminary analyses our data (heterogeneous variables) revealed different discriminant power due to their different variance:

$$x' = \frac{x - \min(x)}{\max(x) - \min(x)}$$

Firstly, we used k-means with Euclidean distance as an exploratory analysis. As a confirmatory analysis to obtain more robust results we used fuzzy c-means (FCM) (Bezdek 1974, 1981). Fuzzy c-means is a generalization of the classical k-means method. Given an $(n \times p)$ matrix, X, where n and p are the number of units and variables, respectively, the aim is to partition the units into k groups, where each group is characterized by a prototype (centroid). Each row vector $x_i = [x_{i1}, x_{i2}, \ldots, x_{ip}]$ represents the i-th observation. The optimization problem of the FkM can be formalized by minimizing an objective function J as follows:

$$\min_{U, H} J_{FkM} = \sum_{1=1}^{n} \sum_{g=1}^{k} u_{ig}^m \|x_i - h_g\|^2$$

where the $(n \times k)$ matrix U denotes the membership degree matrix, where each element $u_{ig} \in [0, 1]$ represents the membership degree of unit i to cluster g. The row-wise sum of U is equal to 1. The $(k \times p)$ matrix H denotes the prototype (centroid) matrix, where each row $h_g = [h_{g1}, h_{g2}, \ldots, h_{gp}]$ $(g = 1, \ldots, k)$ is prototype of cluster g. Finally, parameter m > 1 is used to tune the fuzziness of the obtained partition. The greater the

Table 1. The total number of SDGs indicators is 25 for 4 BES domains.

H	Goal	Global indicator	Measured by	Years
E A	3	3.4.1 - Mortality rate attributed to cardiovascular disease, cancer, diabetes or chronic respiratory disease	Healthy life expectancy at birth	2009-2021
L T	3	3.4.1 - Mortality rate attributed to cardiovascular disease, cancer, diabetes or chronic respiratory disease	Excess weight (standardized rates)	2005-2021
H	3	3.a.1 - Age-standardized prevalence of current tobacco use among persons aged 15 years and older	Smoking (standardized rates)	2005-2021
	3	3.5.2 - Alcohol per capita consumption (aged 15 years and older) within a calendar year in litres of pure alcohol	Alcohol (standardized rates)	2007-2021

E	Goal	Global indicator	Measured by	Years
N V I	1	1.4.1 Proportion of population living in households with access to basic services	Submission of municipal waste to landfill	2004-2021
R O	11	11.6.2 Annual mean levels of fine particulate matter (e.g., PM2.5 and PM10) in cities (population weighted)	Air quality - PM2.5	2004-2021
N M E N	13	13.3.1 Extent to which (i) global citizenship education and (ii) education for sustainable development are mainstreamed in (a) national education policies; (b) curricula; (c) teacher education; and (d) student assessment	Concern about climate change	2004-2021
T	6	6.3.1 Proportion of domestic and industrial wastewater flows safely treated	Wastewater treatment	2004-2021
	15	15.1.2 Proportion of important sites for terrestrial and freshwater biodiversity that are covered by protected areas, by ecosystem type	Protected areas	2004-2021
	7	7.2.1 Renewable energy share in the total final energy consumption	Electricity from renewable sources	2004-2021
	15	15.3.1 Proportion of land that is degraded over total land area	Soil sealing from artificial cover	2004-2021

E	Goal	Global indicator	Measured by	Years
C O N	10	10.1.1 - Growth rates of household expenditure or income per capita among the bottom 40 per cent of the population and the total population	Gross disposable income per capita	2004-2020
O M I	10	10.1.1 - Growth rates of household expenditure or income per capita among the bottom 40 per cent of the population and the total population	Net income inequality (s80/s20)	2004-2020
C	1	1.2.2 - Proportion of men, women and children of all ages living in poverty in all its dimensions according to national definitions	Risk of poverty	2004-2021
W E L L	1	1.2.2 - Proportion of men, women and children of all ages living in poverty in all its dimensions according to national definitions	Severe material deprivation	2004-2021
B E I	1	1.2.2 - Proportion of men, women and children of all ages living in poverty in all its dimensions according to national definitions	Low labor intensity	2004-2021
N G	1	1.4.1 - Proportion of population living in households with access to basic services	Housing cost overcharge	2004-2021

Q	Goal	Global indicator	Measured by	Years
U A L I	3	3.8.1 - Coverage of essential health services	Beds in residential social-welfare and social-health facilities	2009-2019
T Y	16	16.6.2 - Proportion of population satisfied with their last experience of public services	Difficulties in accessing some services	2006-2020
O	1	1.4.1 - Proportion of population living in households with access to basic services	Irregularities in water distribution	2006-2021
F	11	11.2.1 - Proportion of population that has convenient access to public transport, by sex, age and persons with disabilities	Seat-km offered by the Tpl	2004-2020
	11	11.2.1 - Proportion of population that has convenient access to public transport, by sex, age and persons with disabilities	Frequent users of public transportation	2005-2021
S E R V I C	1	1.3.1 - Proportion of population covered by social protection floors/systems, by sex, distinguishing children, unemployed persons, older persons, persons with disabilities, pregnant women, newborns, work-injury victims and the poor and the vulnerable	Waiver of health care benefits	2017-2021
E S	3	3.c.1 - Health worker density and distribution	Doctors	2012-2021
	3	3.c.1 - Health worker density and distribution	Nurses and midwives	2013-2020

value of m, the further away from 1 and 0 the membership degrees are (Ferraro, 2021). For m → 1 FkM reduces to the k-means (kM) algorithm. Empirical results depend on the selection of this parameter, which is commonly chosen between 1.5 and 2 in practice (Pal and Bezdek, 1995). Among the various proposals for robust fuzzy clustering methods, we use the Fuzzy c-medoids (FCMdd). Its method consists in replacing the centroids with the medoids. The FCMdd, known as a partition clustering algorithm like the k-means algorithm is used for grouping the Italian regions. This algorithm partitions simultaneously object by considering multiple dissimilarity matrices. Its design aims to provide a fuzzy grouping and profile for each fuzzy cluster, as well as to learn the specific relevance weights for each dissimilarity matrix to optimize an objective function. Each element x_i, belonging to a cluster j, is assigned a random membership weight u_{ij}. Through an iterative process, the algorithm dynamically moves the cluster medoids z_j to minimize an objective function, which is defined as the sum of distances between each point and each cluster center:

$$\underset{U,H}{min}\, J_{FCMdd} = \sum_{i=1}^{M} \sum_{j=1}^{N} u_{ij}^m \|x_i - z_j\|^2$$

where the medoid of cluster j is represented by z_j, and M denotes the total number of instances in the dataset. N represents the desired number of clusters specified by the researcher. To calculate the distances between the cluster centers and each observation in the sample, we used the Euclidean distance metric. The FCMdd procedure was employed to assign membership to each Italian region within a specific cluster. Finally, we computed the silhouette coefficient to choose the optimal number of clusters within the dataset. This coefficient evaluates the quality of clustering by measuring the proximity of each point in a cluster to the points in neighboring clusters.

3.3 The Key Performance Indicators

For each analyzed macro-area, we built a synthetic indicator to rank the Italian regions. These indicators, called Key Performance Indicators (KPI), are based on both Principal Component Analysis (PCA) and Factor Analysis (FA). FA is a statistical method that identifies the underlying dimensions of a dataset. In its exploratory approach, PCA is commonly used (but not exclusively) to extract these dimensions. PCA is a multivariate analysis technique that can examine, summarize, and simplify a set of observed characteristics (see, e.g., Delvecchio 2010; Mulaik 2010). This simplification involves reducing the complexity of the data by using linear combinations. In our work we implemented the procedure named "backward elimination." This method involves selecting components with eigenvalues above a certain threshold and removing items with low communality. Communality represents the proportion of variance explained by the extracted solution. We set a threshold of 0.5 on the communality value. The elimination process begins with the items having the lowest values and proceeds until all variables present a communality value greater than the selected threshold. Under these conditions, for the 4 BES domain we chose a few components explaining over 70% of the total variance. We summarized our setups in Table 2.

Table 2. The number of principal components selected and corresponding percentage of cumulate variance.

Macro-area	Number of selected components	Cumulate % of variance
Health	1	77
Environment	3	78
Economics wellbeing	2	97
Quality of services	2	80

In general, the Key Performance Indicators (KPI) encompass a collection of metrics that gauge the efficiency, level, and quality of services. These indicators play a crucial role in determining the overall value of a service and aim to identify a comprehensive set of information that can effectively evaluate the performance and competitiveness of a particular service or process. The KPI is defined as:

$$KPI = \frac{\sum_{i=1}^{N} c_i v_i}{\sum_{i=1}^{n} c_i}$$

where c_i are the communality values of each original variable v_i multiplied by the sign of its main factorial weight. Furthermore, we normalized KPI values between 0 and 1.

4   Results and Discussion

In this work we developed an analysis framework to study all 25 indicators belonging at 8 SDGs Goals and 4 BES domain (see table 1 for further details), at the Italian regional level for a time window of 18 years. We initially carried out a clustering analysis using the FCMdd which outlined, for the macro-areas Health, Environment and Economic Well-being, the existence of two distinct clusters (see the upper panel of Fig. 2). Notably, the Economic Well-being BES domain, our findings confirmed the existence of two blocks of regions: Northern and Southern ones. Italy is a country that has historically highlighted a multitude of territorial differences that find their origin in the so-called NORTH-SOUTH gap (Alaimo & Maggino 2020). We are obviously talking about social and economic inequalities which were further marked by the crisis resulting from the pandemic situation. Mapping the territory is the first step in monitoring it and can support and guide policies by giving them a factual basis, starting with the National Recovery and Resilience Plan (PNRR)[2]. Our analyses also confirmed the results of the ISTAT SDGs 2022 Report: the radar chart referring to Economic Wellbeing in Fig. 3 shows very different trends for the two clusters, underlining the deep economic gap between

---

[2] For more information: https://www.italiadomani.gov.it/content/sogei-ng/it/en/home.html.

Northern and Southern Italy. Among the 5 indicators examined within the Economic Well-being of BES domain, "*the risk of poverty*" emerges as the indicator that most prominently underscores the regional disparity between the North and South in our analyses. As highlighted in the methods section, our analysis proceeded through the construction of an index with the use of PCA to assign each region a ranking for 4 BES domains. This ranking confirms the findings obtained with FCMdd highlighting a North-South gradient for the Economic Wellbeing area. Our results are exactly in line with ISTAT SDGs 2022 Report: in the Autonomous Province of Bolzano, 10% of the resident population faced the risk of poverty or social exclusion, while in Campania, this indicator reached half of the population (50.2%). Similarly high percentages, exceeding 40%, were observed in other southern regions such as Calabria and Sicily. In contrast, some northern regions (Trentino Alto Adige, Valle d'Aosta, Emilia-Romagna, and Marche) displayed percentages below 15% (ISTAT SDGs 2022 Report). We can state that regional gaps have diminished in the last two years. Nevertheless, there is no evident trend of convergence in the last decade (ISTAT SDGs 2022 Report).

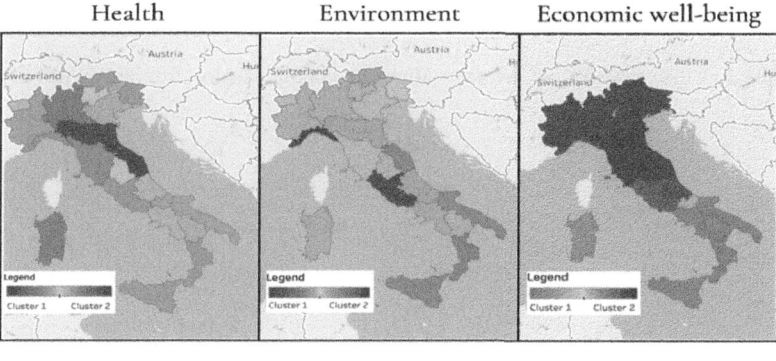

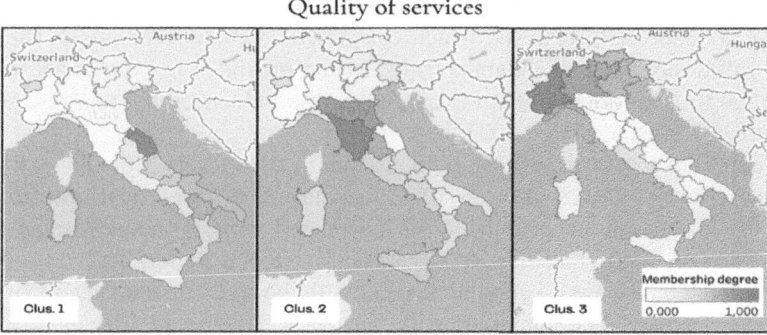

Fig. 2. (The upper panel) The clustering analysis using the FCMdd algorithm which confirmed, for the macro-areas Health and Economic Well-being, the existence of two distinct blocks: Northern regions and Southern ones. (The lower panel) The cluster analysis performed for the macro-area Quality of services suggested the existence of three clusters.

For the other two BES domains (Health and Environment) the FCMdd didn't find a clear geographic pattern.

First, we can say that the trend of the data for each region was strongly influenced by the pandemic, because the values in 2020 and 2021 never returned to the previous ones. This is one of the reasons why the analyses and the division of the regions into groups, especially in the other three BES areas considered, do not always follow a clearly defined criterion. FCMdd segmented the Health domain into two clusters, using the four common BES/SDGs variables.

Notably, two of these variables (*excess weight* and *smoking*) show similar values in both clusters. A paradox arises for the other two features of this domain: regions with *the highest life expectancy at birth* also demonstrate the highest recorded *alcohol consumption*. From a methodological perspective, it is noteworthy that the two independent analyses (FCMdd and KPI) do not align. As is known in the literature (Dubes, 1993), the results obtained with the cluster method are very sensitive to the number of variables used. Therefore, in our analysis the use of only 4 variables leads to a clustering not very robust (silhouette value < 0.5) as reported in Table 3. Additionally, the subjective nature of cluster selection is evident, given the close silhouette values for k = 2 and k = 3.

Table 3. Cluster validation: Average silhouette coefficients for different values of k.

Dimensions of well-being	$k = 2$	$k = 3$	$k = 4$
Health	0,43	0,40	0,28
Environmental	0,34	0,31	0,29
Economic	0,75	0,65	0,62
Quality of Services	0,57	0,58	0,50

Conversely, the KPI analysis, which categorizes regional rankings in the Health domain, yields more understandable results. Regarding the "life expectancy" variable, it's essential to acknowledge that the analyses were influenced by data regarding the Covid period (Eurostat, March 2023[3]).

Life expectancy at birth in 2021 did not return to 2019 levels, although in the North the indicator recovered 0.8 years in 2020, reaching 82.9 years. Instead in the South in 2021 the loss of life expectancy at birth appeared more pronounced than in 2020 (0.5 years less on 2020), reaching 81.3 years (ISTAT SDGs Report 2022).

Our ranking data shows a good agreement with the study of Eurostat about the life expectancies in Italy. The autonomous provinces of Trento and Bolzano are among the European areas with the highest life expectancies at birth (Eurostat, November 2023[4]). Conversely, Sicily and Campania have lower life expectancies, with averages of 83.3 years for women and 79.2 and 78.7 years for men, respectively. Nevertheless,

---

[3] https://ec.europa.eu/eurostat/en/web/products-eurostat-news/w/ddn-20230316-1.

[4] https://ec.europa.eu/eurostat/en/web/products-eurostat-news/w/ddn-20231106-1.

all Italian regions overcame the EU average, which stands at 82.9 years for women and 77.2 for men (Eurostat, November 2023[5]).

Both the clustering analysis and the KPI highlight a critical environmental situation in Italy. However, the results of the two independents analyze do not agree very much. The clustering results report a lack of statistical significance, given the low silhouette values (shown in Table 3), probably because the environmental variables used are uninformative and contradictory. In future analysis we will add other variables to improve the robustness of our results.

To add further considerations about the Environmental well-being indicator we can show the panel B of Fig. 3. It is evident that 5 northern regions (Piedmont, Lombardy, Veneto, Emilia Romagna and Friuli) present more critical situation related to environmental issues. These regions, show a worst air quality linked to the presence of high concentrations of particulate matter (in particular PM 2.5) with an average value of "Annual means level of particulate matters in cities" equal to 95.3 much higher than the average Italian value of 84.8.

Furthermore, these regions present a more critical hydrogeological situation. Instead, the 4 regions with the least environmental problems are equally distributed between the North (Valle d'Aosta and Trentino) and the South (Molise and Basilicata). These regions have a greater concentration of mountains and a higher average altitude (1164 m) than the national average value (293 m) [https://it-ch.topographic-map.com/map-lk69m/Ita lia/], moreover they are among the region with lower degree of urbanization [https://www.istat.it/it/archivio/137001].

Instead, the cluster analysis performed on the BES domain "Quality of services" suggested the existence of three clusters as shown in the lower panel of Fig. 2. Lighter shades of color in Fig. 2, indicate a higher fuzzy degree.

Compared to the other two groups, the first group has low scores for two variables related to public transport (seat/km, public transport users), higher scores for irregularity of water supply and Waiver's health services, while the difficulty of access to services is on par with the second group. The second group is characterized by the highest number of doctors in the region, the lowest number of nurses and the lowest number of beds compared to the other groups. The third group is characterized by the highest number of beds and nurses and the lowest number of doctors. In addition, it also has the lowest number of people abandoning healthcare, the lowest number of irregularities in water distribution and the lowest number of difficulties in accessing services.

All outcomes can be compared with the KPI results of the ranking created and with the ISTAT 2022 SDGs Report: The persistence of the pandemic has led to a homogenization of areas in terms of the extent to which health services are foregone, with a more significant increase in the northwest, northeast and center.

According to the ISTAT SDGs Report in 2021, 9.4% of families report that the water supply in their homes is irregular (8.9% in 2020). Irregularities affect all regions in a heterogeneous way, with higher intensity in the South, where they are perceived by 1.5 million families (63.9% of the total), and especially in Sicily (29.0%) and Calabria (28.8%). In the north-west and north-east, the figures are low (3.1% and 3.5% respectively), while in the center less than one in ten families report irregularities in service.

---

[5] https://ec.europa.eu/eurostat/en/web/products-eurostat-news/w/ddn-20231106-1.

In this regard, Italy is characterized by an accentuated fragmentation of management, especially in those areas of the country where integrated water supply has not been fully implemented (in particular Calabria, Molise, the autonomous provinces of Trento and Bolzano, Sicily and Valle d'Aosta), which may slow down the achievement of a wide coverage of the territory by water security plans (SDGs ISTAT Report 2022).

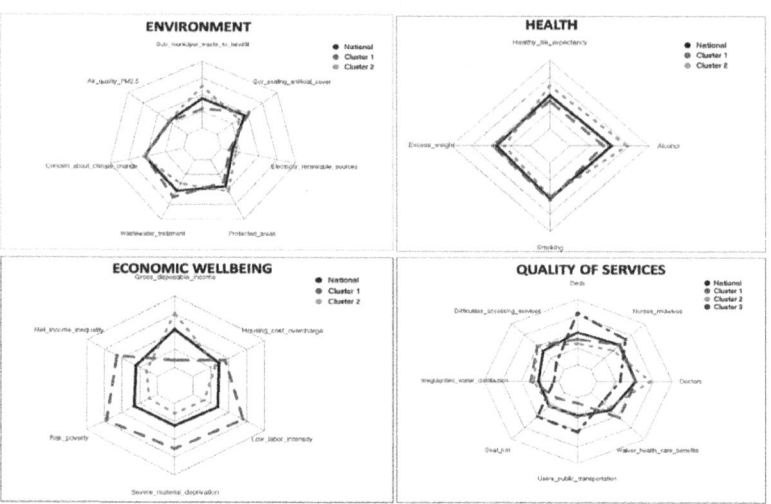

Fig. 3. Radar plot for each cluster of the four macro-categories analyzed. The black line indicates the national average.

Figure 3 displays radar charts for the 4 BES domains considered in which average values of the features of each cluster are compared with the national average value. The graph relating to the environment highlights how the trends of the variables of the two clusters are compatible except for 2 features: "Submission of municipal waste to landfill" where in cluster 2 there is a higher percentage of waste sent to landfill compared to cluster 1; "Wastewater treatment" where in cluster 1 there is on average a greater quantity of treated wastewater.

From the radar chart relating to the Health category, we can see that group 2 has an excess weight which is on average lower than the national average associated with a higher life expectancy despite a slightly higher alcohol consumption. The radar chart referring to Economic Wellbeing shows two very different trends for the two clusters, underlining the profound economic differences between Northern and Southern Italy. However, in the Quality of Services area we notice very different situations for the 3 clusters, for group 3 indicated by the dotted blue line where it is possible to notice the low presence of doctors in contrast with the wider availability of hospital beds.

As displayed the result of the index we calculate in Table 4, in the 4 considered macro-areas, the most virtuous regions in the Ranking of the Italian Regions are Valle d'Aosta and Trentino Alto Adige, while those with the greatest deficits in terms of Economy, Health and Quality of Services are Sicily, Calabria and Campania.

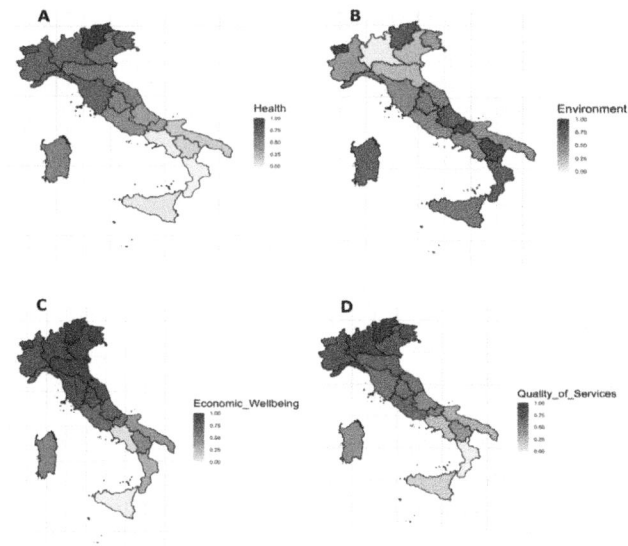

Fig. 4. Geographical distribution of KPI for the 4 considered BES domain.

Table 4. Ranking of the Italian Region in the 4 considered macro-areas.

Position	Health	Environment	Economic wellbeing	Quality of Services
1	Trentino A. A.	Aosta Valley	Trentino A. A.	Trentino A. A.
2	Aosta Valley	Basilicata	Friuli V. G.	Liguria
3	Liguria	Molise	Aosta Valley	Lombardy
4	Piedmont	Trentino A. A.	Emilia Rom	Friuli V. G.
5	Friuli V. G.	Calabria	Veneto	Piedmont
6	Tuscany	Sardinia	Lombardy	Veneto
7	Lombardy	Abruzzo	Tuscany	Aosta Valley
8	Veneto	Sicily	Marche	Emilia Rom
9	Emilia Rom	Umbria	Umbria	Lazio
10	Marche	Liguria	Piedmont	Tuscany
11	Sardinia	Marche	Liguria	Marche
12	Umbria	Lazio	Abruzzo	Umbria
13	Lazio	Tuscany	Lazio	Molise
14	Molise	Campania	Molise	Abruzzo
15	Abruzzo	Apulia	Sardinia	Sardinia

(continued)

Table 4. (*continued*)

Position	Health	Environment	Economic wellbeing	Quality of Services
16	Apulia	Friuli V. G.	Basilicata	Basilicata
17	Basilicata	Piedmont	Apulia	Apulia
18	Sicily	Veneto	Calabria	Campania
19	Campania	Emilia Rom	Campania	Calabria
20	Calabria	Lombardy	Sicily	Sicily

5   Conclusion

In this paper, we implemented two independent analyses to examine the Italian situation using BES and SDGs indicators. The two analyses show two different perspectives: the more qualitative clustering algorithm and the more quantitative composite indicators based on KPI (PCA and factor analysis).

Both methods underline the strong existence of the North-Sud gap for macro-area: Economic Well-being how widely reported in literature.

In the two other BES areas (Health, Quality of Services), there does not appear to be any agreement between the two methods considered. While the KPI still underlines a North-South divide, the results obtained with the FCMdd show a rather confusing situation. These differences can be attributed to the small number and low information content of the variables used for clustering, which is underlined by the silhouette values found.

A separate discussion must be held for the environment, where the KPI does not show a clear geographical trend indicating a critical situation in the northern regions due to environmental pollution.

The results of the KPI procedure confirm that 5 northern regions are at the bottom of the ranking. Indeed, the northern regions are on average more polluted than the southern ones and have a more critical hydrogeological situation.

The 4 least polluted regions are evenly distributed between the North (Valle d'Aosta and Trentino) and the south (Molise and Basilicata).

Our analyses show that the Italian framework is complex, multidimensional and contradictory.

The use of publicly available ISTAT data and widely recognized statistical techniques ensures a high degree of replicability, enabling future researchers or policymakers to apply the same framework to updated datasets or to different territorial contexts within or beyond Italy. However, several methodological limitations must be acknowledged. First, the limited number of indicators per BES domain, particularly in Health and Quality of Services, reduces the richness and discriminative power of the analyses, as reflected in the low silhouette values of the clustering. Second, discrepancies between the two analytical methods (e.g., conflicting patterns in regional classification) point to the sensitivity of results to methodological choices and the need for caution in interpretation. Lastly, the KPIs' reliance on aggregation may obscure localized nuances and heterogeneities. Future developments should aim at expanding the indicator set, integrating higher-frequency or disaggregated data, and testing advanced machine learning models for improved granularity and accuracy. Moreover, incorporating participatory or qualitative inputs could enrich the understanding of regional well-being and better align the analysis with the 2030 Agenda's ambition of "leaving no one behind."

References

Alaimo, L.S.: Sustainable development and national differences: An European cross-national analysis of economic sustainability. RIEDS-Rivista Italiana di Economia, Demografia e Statistica -The Italian Review of Economics, Demography and Statistics, **72**(3), 101–123 (2018)

Alaimo, L.S., Maggino, F.: Sustainable development goals indicators at territorial level: conceptual and methodological issues—the Italian perspective. Soc. Ind. Res. Int. Interdisc. J. Qual. Life Measur. Springer **147**(2), 383–419 (2020). https://doi.org/10.1007/s11205-019-02162-4

ASVIS Report, Italy and the Sustainable Development Goals (2022). ISBN 979-12-80634-18-4

Bezdek, J.C.: Cluster validity with fuzzy sets. J. Cybern. **3**(3), 58–73 (1974). https://doi.org/10.1080/01969727308546047

Bezdek, J.C.: Pattern Recognition with Fuzzy Objective Function Algorithms. Plenum Press, New York (1981)

Bleys, B.: Beyond GDP: classifying alternative measures for progress. Soc. Indic. Res. **109**(3), 355–376 (2012). https://doi.org/10.1007/s11205-011-9906-6

Cao, X.H., Stojkovic, I., Obradovic, Z.: A robust data scaling algorithm to improve classification accuracies in biomedical data. BMC Bioinform. **17**, 1–10 (2016)

Chalmin-Pui, L.S., et al.: It made me feel brighter in myself-the health and well-being impacts of a residential front garden horticultural intervention. Landsc. Urban Plan. **205**, 103958 (2021)

Costanza, R., Hart, M., Posner, S., Talberth, J.: Beyond GDP: The Need for New Measures of Progress. Pardee Paper No. 4, Boston: Pardee Center for the Study of the Longer-Range Future (2009)

Costanza, R., et al.: Development: time to leave GDP behind. Nature **505**(7483), 283–285 (2014). https://doi.org/10.1038/505283a

Costanza, R., et al.: Modelling and measuring sustainable wellbeing in connection with the UN sustainable development goals and the dynamics of well-being. Ecol. Econ. **130**, 350–355 (2016). https://doi.org/10.1016/j.ecolecon.2016.07.009

Delvecchio, F.: Statistica per l'analisi di dati multidimensionali, CLEUP, Padova (2010)

Dubes, R.C.: Cluster analysis and related issues. In: Chen, C.H., Pau, L.F., Wang, P.S.P. (eds.) Handbook of pattern recognition and computer vision, World Scientific Publishing Co, pp. 3–32. Inc, River Edge, NJ (1993)

D'Urso, P., Alaimo, L.S., De Giovanni, L., Massari, R.: Well-being in the Italian regions over time. Soc. Indic. Res. **161**, 599–627 (2022). https://doi.org/10.1007/s11205-020-02384-x

EU Commission. GDP and beyond: measuring progress in a changing world, Explanatory Memorandum to COM (2009) 433 (2009)

Ferraro M.B.: Fuzzy k -Means: history and applications. Econometrics Stat. (2021)

Gibson, B., Hassan, S., Tansey, J.: Sustainability assessment: criteria and processes. Routledge, London (2005). https://doi.org/10.4324/9781849772716

Hall, J., Giovannini, E., Morrone, A., Ranuzzi, G.: A Framework to Measure the Progress of Societies, OECD Statistics Working Papers, 210/5, OECD Publishing (2010)

Giovannini, E., Rondinella, T.: Going beyond GDP: theoretical approaches. In: D'Ambrosio C. (ed.), Handbook of Research on Economic and Social Well-Being. Edward Elgar Publishing Ltd (2018). https://doi.org/10.4337/9781781953716.00006

Maggino, F., Zumbo, B.D.: Measuring the quality of life and the construction of social indicators. In: Land, K., Michalos, A., Sirgy, M. (eds.) Handbook of Social Indicators and Quality of Life Research. Springer, Dordrecht (2012). https://doi.org/10.1007/978-94-007-2421-1_10

Maggino, F.: Developing indicators and managing the complexity. In: Maggino, F. (ed.) Complexity in Society: From Indicators Construction to their Synthesis. Social Indicators Research Series, vol. 70, pp. 87–114. Springer, Cham (2017). https://doi.org/10.1007/978-3-319-605 95-1_4

Max-Neef, M.: Economic growth and quality of life: a threshold hypothesis. Ecol. Econ. **15**(2), 115–118 (1995). https://doi.org/10.1016/0921-8009(95)00064-X

Morrone, A.: The role of subjective indicators in measuring the equitable and sustainable wellbeing in Italy. In: Proceedings of 59th ISI World Statistics Congress, 1924–29. Hong Kong: the International Statistical Institute (2013)

Mulaik, S.A.: Foundations of Factor Analysis. Chapman & Hall (2010)

Neumayer, E.: Human development and sustainability. J. Hum. Dev. Capabilities **13**(4), 561–579 (2012). https://doi.org/10.1080/19452829.2012.693067

Stiglitz, J., Sen, A., Fitoussi, J.: Report by the Commission on the Measurement of Economic Performance and Social Progress, Paris (2009)

Talberth, D.J., Cobb, C., Slattery, N.: The Genuine Progress Indicator 2006: A Tool for Sustainable Development. Oakland, California: Redefining Progress (2007)

https://www.istat.it/it/files//2023/05/2022-SDGS-Report_Inglese.pdf

https://www.governo.it/sites/governo.it/files/PNRR.pdf

https://www.italiadomani.gov.it/content/sogei-ng/it/en/home.html

https://ec.europa.eu/eurostat/en/web/products-eurostat-news/w/ddn-20230316-1

Composite Indicators for Performance Evaluation in Healthcare

Najada Firza$^{(\boxtimes)}$ ⓘ and Dante Mazzitelli ⓘ

Department of Economics and Finance, University of Bari "Aldo Moro", Largo Abbazia Santa Scolastica, Bari, Italy
najada.firza@uniba.it

Abstract. Key Performance Indicators (KPIs) are essential tools for assessing and ensuring high standards of quality and efficiency in the delivery of healthcare services within the National Health System. This study focuses on four critical dimensions of healthcare quality: Accessibility, Equity, Effectiveness and Efficiency each of which must be evaluated using composite KPIs that reflect their inherent complexity and interconnections.

Healthcare quality data includes a mix of quantitative and qualitative variables, often nominal or ordinal in nature, and typically involve large datasets. A major challenge is the dimensionality reduction of this complex data into a manageable set of indicators that retain meaningful insights. To address this, we employ Principal Component Analysis (PCA), a widely accepted statistical technique, alongside Exploratory and Confirmatory Factor Analysis, to identify and extract the most relevant components.

This research aims to develop a structured system of KPIs tailored to evaluate the quality and adequacy of primary care services provided by public health facilities in the Puglia Region. Through multivariate analysis specifically PCA we construct, aggregate, and weight KPIs to build a comprehensive performance evaluation model. This model is designed to highlight the relative importance of each indicator, thereby supporting evidence-based decision-making and continuous improvement in healthcare delivery.

Keywords: Composite Indicators · PCA · Factor analysis · KPI · Health Indicators · Performance Evaluation

1 Introduction

The importance of a system of indicators is given by the fact that the indicator allows us to describe and analyze complex phenomena through a synthetic evaluation of the phenomenon and to make decisions to obtain changes. Again, art. 1, paragraph 2 of the Ministerial Decree of Health of 24 July 1995 states: "the indicators represent information selected for the purpose of measuring the changes that occur in the observed phenomena and, consequently, to guide the decision-making processes of the various institutional levels". In fact, of each detected unit, they represent characteristics that can be measured

© The Author(s), under exclusive license to Springer Nature Switzerland AG 2025
O. Gervasi et al. (Eds.): ICCSA 2025, LNCS 15650, pp. 237–248, 2025.
https://doi.org/10.1007/978-3-031-96962-1_16

and that are closely associated with the phenomenon of interest that is not directly measurable. A measure or a set of measures constitute an indicator of a given phenomenon when it is able to change as the aspects of the phenomenon itself vary. As is known, the issue of health care provided to protect the health of the citizen is a complex phenomenon that involves various segments of care. It is necessary to define a system of indicators, capable of bringing a fragment of knowledge, such as to compose a synthetic picture of the level of health guaranteed throughout the national territory. The indicators must also reflect compliance with the criteria of equity in access to services, effectiveness and appropriateness of the health care provided. The methodological and applicative characteristics that the indicators must have been reported as follows: Methodological characteristics of the indicators:

- Reproducible
- Accurate
- Sensitive to change
- Specific to the phenomenon investigated.

  Applicative characteristics of the indicators:

1) Linked to the potential usefulness:

   - Relevant
   - Scientifically founded
   - Inserted in a decision-making model
   - Easily understandable
   - Simple, not unnecessarily complex.

2) Linked to the methods of detection:

   - Complete
   - Easily detectable
   - Inexpensive to detect and analyze
   - Timely

As for the data source, indicators can be built from current administrative or clinical data sources. While there are undoubted advantages, since the data are collected continuously, they are constantly updated, on the other hand there are some disadvantages such as relatively high costs and frequent need for sampling.

Characteristics of a Health Performance Indicator: Although a health performance indicator can often be expressed as a single numerical value, that figure encapsulates a range of specific characteristics that define its identity typically documented within a technical data sheet.

The technical sheet includes several key components, among which the most important are:

Name, Code, and Reference Year. These elements uniquely identify the indicator, ensuring it can be accurately referenced and tracked over time.

Rationale for Construction and Selection: This is a structured explanation of the reasons behind the indicator's development and the purpose it serves within the monitoring framework.

Numerator, Denominator, and Multiplication Factor: These define the formula used to calculate the indicator, clarifying its quantitative foundation.

Original Data Source: This provides transparency regarding the origin and reliability of the raw data used to derive the indicator.

Evaluation Criteria and Reference Values: These criteria enable interpretation of the indicator's value by comparing it to benchmarks or standardized thresholds, thus giving it meaningful context.

Indicators can be aggregated at various levels to reflect broader trends. Typically, these are composite indicators that synthesize several sub-indicators, allowing for comprehensive evaluations across different system dimensions such as departments, healthcare organizations, network pathways, or geographic areas (regional, national, or international). These aggregated indicators are often incorporated into structured evaluation systems and stored in dedicated reference databases for use by policymakers and decision-makers. However, a key limitation of such systems lies in their tendency to focus primarily on what is easily measurable, potentially neglecting critical aspects of management and service quality that are inherently more complex and less amenable to standardization through indicators.

2 Materials and Methods

2.1 Some Health Efficiency Indicators

The National Health Plan aims to optimize resources and improve the cost-efficiency ratio of health services. The model used to measure efficiency and assign a rate to remunerate the services provided by hospital facilities is the D.R.G. This rate reflects an estimate of the average cost of each hospitalization, based on which hospital activity is remunerated; see Annex 2 guidelines no. 1/1995 of the Ministerial Decree 14/12/1994. The D.R.G. is the acronym for Diagnosis Related Group and divides hospital admissions into homogeneous groups in which they present similar characteristics in terms of resource consumption and similar care loads. To measure the complexity of the caseload of each acute hospital facility in relation to a reference standard, the case-mix index is used, which can be expressed either in economic terms (following the directives of Annex 2 to the Guidelines no. 1/1995, issued in application of the Ministerial Decree 14/12/1994 and published in the Official Journal, general series, no. 150 of 29/06/1995), or in terms of hospital resources. The first formulation is therefore

$$ICM_{hr} = \frac{\sum_{d=1}^{D}(a_d \cdot N_{dh}) \bigg/ \sum_{d=1}^{D} N_{dh}}{\sum_{d=1}^{D}(a_d \cdot N_{dr}) \bigg/ \sum_{d=1}^{D} N_{dr}}$$

where:

D = total number of entries in the tables of the current D.R.G.;

ad = specific weight relative to each D.R.G.;

Ndh = discharged patients belonging to the d-th D.R.G. in the h-th healthcare institution; Ndr = discharged patients belonging to the d-th D.R.G. in the r-th region.

Each specific weight relative to ad indicates the care complexity in terms of consumption of resources associated with the D.R.G. and therefore can be used to indicate the complexity of the pathology in question.

In these terms, the D.R.G. with ad $< = 1$ are generally associated with pathologies of low care complexity. Taking into account that the specific weights of the D.R.G. are calculated on the basis of standardized cost parameters, therefore, the Case-Mix index is given by the quotient between a "cost-output" indicator relating to the healthcare institution under observation and the same "cost-output" indicator relating, however, to the entire territory in which the hospital service is institutionally required to operate. This is a relative index, with a range of variation [0,1], where the upper limit is reached if and only if the healthcare institution considered is the only one to provide the service to which the h.th D.R.G. refers.

The second formulation of the case-mix index is instead the following:

ICM = average weight of the single unit/standard average weight where: average weight of the single unit = sum of weights/total hospitalizations in the unit;

standard average weight = sum of weights/total hospitalizations in the context.

If the case-mix index is greater than 1, the hospital structure's caseload is more complex than the standard, while if the case-mix index is less than 1, it indicates that the caseload is less complex than the standard. In this research, reference will be made to the second formulation. As regards the classic indicators or flow indicators that express the efficiency of hospital structures, they originate from three basic phenomena:

- admissions in a given period
- the total number of days of hospitalization
- the number of beds.

The first four classic reference indicators are:

- the average hospital stay, which defines the days on which on average a patient is hospitalized in a given hospital structure, and is calculated by comparing the total days of hospitalization and the admissions in the same period (DM = GD / R);
- the bed occupancy rate, obtained as the ratio between actual hospital days and theoretical hospital days per period and is expressed as a percentage (TU = GD / GD* %); - the bed rotation index, which is calculated by the ratio between the total number of hospitalizations and the available beds (Ir = R / PL), and provides in detail the number of patients who have occupied a single bed;
- the turn-over interval, calculated by comparing the difference between theoretical and actual hospital days to the total number of hospitalizations:

$$IT = (GD* - GD) / R = (365 \cdot PL - GD) / R$$

These indicators are used to construct the Barber nomogram, a graphic analysis that allows the comparison between indicators, thus building a comparison metric between different facilities or services provided in the same hospital facility related to time. Specifically, Barber's nomogram is nothing more than a graphic representation using the Cartesian axes system, in which we will find the turnover index placed on the abscissa axis and the average hospital stay placed on the ordinate axis. In this graphic context, the occupancy index and the bed rotation index further divide the plan. In the plan thus divided, an acceptability area is identified depending on the objectives that the hospital unit sets itself.

2.2 Data Collection

The reference data set is characterized by 38 public hospitalization health facilities in the Puglia Region, within which 523 departments are distributed, classified according to the province they belong to, as can also be seen in table 1. From the data in the table, we note that there is a homogeneous distribution of health facilities in the territory with an average of approximately 5 facilities per province. The exception is the province of Bari with 12 facilities. Furthermore, as regards the departments, we note a greater concentration in the province of Bari with 31%, Lecce with 21% and Foggia with almost 20%. Finally, the province of Brindisi has the lowest number of departments (48) distributed in the territory. Classifying the departments according to the disciplines they deal with, we can state that there are 44, catalogued and distributed in the Region. The departments that we find most in the area are: General Surgery (36 units), Cardiology (34 units), General Medicine (34), Orthopedics and Traumatology (34), Obstetrics and Gynecology (34), Pediatrics (30) and finally Coronary Unit (30) (Table 2).

Table 1. Distribution of the hospitals in the territory, divided into Departments.

Province affiliation ASL	Hospitals	Departments	%
ASL BA	12	162	31
ASL BR	4	48	9,2
ASL BT	4	50	9,6
ASL FG	6	102	19,5
ASL LE	7	109	20,8
ASL TA	5	52	9,9
Total	38	523	100

Source: National Sanitary Informative system, 2019.

Another interesting piece of information that we can draw from a first descriptive analysis of the data is the singularity of some Departments which are located in a single point of the territory, this is the case of the following Departments: Pediatric Cardiac Surgery, Pediatric Nephrology, Pediatric Urology which are located only at the Policlinico of Bari, the Dentistry and Stomatology department is located only in Acquaviva delle Fonti (Bari), the Radiology department is located in San Giovanni Rotondo (Foggia) and finally the Spinal Unit is located in Cassano delle Murge (Bari).

Table 2. Distribution of the hospitals in the territory, divided into Departments.

| | PROVINCE | | | | | | |
DEPARTMENT	BR	TA	BT	BA	FG	LE	APULIA
Paediatric Cardiac Surgery	0	0	0	1	0	0	1
Cardiac Surgery	0	0	0	1	1	1	3
Cardiology	3	4	4	10	6	7	34
General Surgery	3	5	4	11	6	7	36
Maxillo-Facial Surgery	0	0	0	1	1	1	3
Paediatric Surgery	0	0	0	1	2	1	4
Plastic Surgery	1	0	1	2	1	1	6
Thoracic Surgery	0	0	0	2	2	1	5
Vascular Surgery	1	1	0	3	1	1	7
Haematology	1	1	1	2	2	2	9
Endocrine Diseases	1	1	0	2	2	1	7
Geriatrics	1	1	1	4	2	3	12
Infectious/ Tropical Diseases	1	1	1	2	1	2	8
General Medicine	3	5	4	9	6	7	34
Spinal Unit	0	0	0	1	0	0	1
Nephrology	2	3	2	6	4	4	21
Neurosurgery	1	1	1	2	2	1	8
Neurology	1	1	2	5	2	3	14
Child Neuropsychiatry	0	0	0	1	1	0	2
Ophthalmology	1	1	2	5	3	2	14
Dentistry and Stomatology	0	0	0	1	0	0	1
Orthopaedics and Traumatology	3	5	4	9	6	7	34
Obstetrics and Gynaecology	3	5	4	9	6	7	34
Otolaryngology	1	1	2	5	3	2	14
Paediatrics	3	4	4	7	5	7	30
Psychiatry	2	1	2	4	3	4	16
Urology	1	2	2	5	3	4	17
Large Burns	1	0	0	1	0	0	2
Intensive Care	1	1	3	7	4	4	20
Coronary Unit	2	3	3	9	6	7	30
Dermatology	1	0	0	2	2	1	6

(*continued*)

Table 2. (*continued*)

DEPARTMENT	PROVINCE						
	BR	TA	BT	BA	FG	LE	APULIA
Recovery and Rehabilitation	1	0	0	4	3	2	10
Gastroenterology	0	0	1	4	3	2	10
Long-Term Patients	2	2	1	5	2	5	17
Neonatology	1	1	0	3	2	2	9
Oncology	1	1	1	3	1	3	10
Paediatric Oncology	0	0	0	0	1	1	2
Pneumology	2	0	0	7	2	4	15
Radiotherapy	0	0	0	0	1	0	1
Rheumatology	0	0	0	1	1	0	2
Neonatal Intensive Care	1	1	0	3	2	2	9
Neurorehabilitation	2	0	0	0	1	0	3
Paediatric Nephrology	0	0	0	1	0	0	1
Paediatric Urology	0	0	0	1	0	0	1
TOTAL	48	52	50	162	102	109	523

2.3 Principal Component Analysis

Key Performance Indicators KPI are a set of indicators that measure the efficiency, level and quality of services in general. They are used to define the value of the service offered as a whole. With this method, a global set of information is identified, capable of optimally evaluating the performance and competitiveness of a given service or process under all characterizing aspects, maintaining a small number of components. In order to reflect the characteristics of the KPI, the Principal Component Analysis method is used [1, 2]. Principal Component Analysis (PCA) is an accredited methodology in multivariate analysis to study, summarize and simplify a set of observed features, reducing the complexity of the data through linear combinations of the same [3]. The two essential conditions for carrying out this operation are that:

– Each main component is attributed to the maximum overall variability of the system;
  - The main components created are independent of each other.

This work aims to create a definition of efficiency of the system subject to the data in our possession, for this reason we are going to calculate a synthetic indicator that provides the importance to the original indices and assigns them weights. Once we have divided the indicators and assigned them weights, we divided them by departments and hospital structures in order to carry out an analysis of the distribution of these indicators [4]. The starting indicators are seven:

– ICM

- Entropy Index
- Beds used/beds available
- Bed occupancy rate
- Turnover interval
- Department utilization rate
- Day hospital admissions/total admissions

We have opted for the normalization of the indicators so that they have the same range of oscillation and consequently assume equal weights within the construction of a synthetic index (Table 3).

Table 3. Total variance explained by the principal components analysis method and results of the subsequent Factor analysis.

Component	PCA: Extracted eigenvalues			Factor Analysis: Rotated eigenvalues		
	Total	% of variance	Cumulate % of variance	Total	% of variance	Cumulate % of variance
1	1.549	25.82	25.82	1.519	25.32	25.32
2	1.354	22.57	48.39	1.381	23.01	48.33
3	1.142	19.03	67.42	1.145	19.09	67.42
4	0.821	13.68	81.10			
5	0.703	11.71	92.81			
6	0.431	7.19	100.00			

Through the analysis of principal components, the 7 indices were examined. We proceeded to identify the indices with a commonality greater than or equal to 0.51 and consequently, using the backward stepwise method we eliminated the indices with poor commonality (<0.51).

In this way we have preserved a set of 4 indices connected to 2 principal components. The two principal components have eigenvalues greater than 1, therefore they are able to explain more variability than the indices that compose them. We also note that the two eigenvalues explain about 80% of the variance. To have better, more robust results and to obtain the solution that interprets the results in a better and simpler way, we started a factor analysis through Varimax orthogonal rotation of the identified principal components [5]. The rotated component matrix is almost identical to the non-rotated component matrix, the results obtained do not improve the model with the rotation. In this way, two distinct ACPs were identified and selected which allowed us to identify the importance of the indices observed within each correlation structure, to identify the existence of significant relationships between them and the latent variables that can best explain the observed phenomenon. We proceeded with the analysis because the Bartlett sphericity test is very significant (p < 0.0000002).

Table 4. Factor weights and commonality of the indicators that make up the synthetic performance indicator.

| Indicators | Factors | | | Communalities |
	Resources efficiency	Organizational efficiency	Internal effectiveness	
Average Length of Stay	−0.824			0.683
Rotation Index	0.769			0.597
Bed Occupancy Rate		0.827		0.713
Outpatient / Inpatient Rate		0.824		0.703
Entropy Index			0.733	0.674
Standardized HMQ			−0.744	0.676

The factorial weights resulting from the previous factorial analysis (Table 4) identify the nature of the three latent dimensions of the healthcare performance in Apulia:

- resources efficiency (explaining 25.3% of the total variance)
- organizational efficiency (23.0% of the total variance)
- internal effectiveness (19.1% of the total variance).

The last column of Table 6 shows the communalities of the selected variables, that is, the proportion of their variance explained by the factorial system. They are all sufficiently high to imply that the factorial solution is reliable.

2.4 Construction of Key Performance Indicators (KPI)

The Key Performance Indicators (KPI) are defined, in general, as a set of indicators measuring the efficiency, the level and the quality of services. Such indicators are used to define the value of the whole service or the success of an organization [6].

This method identifies a global set of information, able to assess optimally the performance and competitiveness of a specific service or process. The characterizing aspects are kept, but a lot of information in the data are excessive and should be removed.

The KPI is defined as a synthetic indicator with specific weights given to each index, computed as follows for each department of each health facility:

$$KPI = \frac{\sum_{i=1}^{N} w_i x_i}{\sum_{i=1}^{N} w_i}$$

where z_i: standardized value of the elementary index i;

w_i: weights attributed to each elementary indices.

Here the KPI (defined as a synthetic indicator with specific weights given to each index) is built by using the Factorial Analysis findings, giving w_i = communality of each original variable multiplied by the sign of its main factorial weight.

Therefore, the empirical formulation of KPI for the Apulian health facilities is:

$$KPI = \frac{-0,683z_1+0,597z_2+0,713z_3+0,703z_4+0,674z_5-0,676z_6}{-0,683 + 0,597 + 0,713 + 0,703 + 0,674 - 0,676}$$

This formula highlights those increments of Average Length of Stay, as well as increments of Standardized Hospital Mortality Quotient, cause the worsening of the healthcare department/facility performance. This is surely a correct outcome.

All things being equal, the KPI here computed can be used to assess also the performance of elementary units and any combination of them, in this case each hospital department, each healthcare facility or each territorial area.

Thus, aggregating the KPI of healthcare departments and hospitals according with the Apulian provinces[1], the Table 5 is obtained. The table highlights that healthcare facilities in the province of Brindisi have a minimum KPI, so here organizational changes are required urgently, while the best results are obtained by the structures of the provinces of Foggia and B.A.T.

Table 5. Final computing steps of provincial and regional KPI of Apulian healthcare facilities in 2019.

Provinces	Sum of		
	KPI_j*Admissions$_j$	Admission	KPI
Bari	42,041.71	143,039	0.294
Barletta-Andria-Trani	19,332.34	35,160	0.550
Brindisi	113.53	36,173	0.003
Foggia	55,738.53	99,467	0.560
Lecce	37,273.03	83,666	0.445
Taranto	13,555.39	37,836	0.358
Apulia	168,054.53	435,341	0.386

3   Conclusion

The construction of a composite Key Performance Indicator (KPI) for Apulian healthcare facilities has enabled a standardized, data-driven evaluation of departmental and territorial performance across the region. By applying Factorial Analysis to assign weights

---

[1] The KPI of each department of each structure is initially weighted for admissions recorded in itself, and then the sum of these values is divided, for each territorial area, the relative number of admissions.

based on the communalities and dominant factor loadings of original variables, the resulting KPI effectively captures the multidimensional nature of healthcare service quality.

The model's sensitivity to critical factors such as Average Length of Stay and Standardized Hospital Mortality Quotient reinforces its validity, as increases in these variables appropriately correspond to poorer performance outcomes. Furthermore, the KPI proves flexible and scalable, allowing performance assessment at multiple levels: from individual departments to entire facilities and provincial systems.

The application of this methodology in the Apulia Region reveals significant variability in healthcare performance. Notably, Brindisi shows the lowest KPI, indicating an urgent need for organizational intervention, while Foggia and B.A.T. provinces achieve the highest scores, suggesting more effective resource allocation and operational efficiency.

This KPI framework not only provides a robust tool for comparative analysis but also serves as a foundation for targeted improvements and strategic planning in regional healthcare systems.

The results of this work demonstrate the importance of statistical techniques in order to derive information from data of a different nature and optimize their use.

The Factor Analysis (by using PCA) allowed us to take off the less relevant indicators, leading to a division into three groups of performance indicators. The first group (dimension) is composed by resources efficiency indicators, while the second group is composed by organizational efficiency indicators, and the third one is composed by internal effectiveness indicators.

The construction of performance indicators, especially in health services, is a practice of significant utility, not only to use a strategy of spending review in the provision of specific services but mainly to rationalize working methods of projecting to the results. The synthetic index KPI was built weighting each relevant indicator according with specific weights that are obtained from the Factorial Analysis.

The proposed model can be used for the efficient and profitable management of health departments and whole hospitals, paying attention also to the wellbeing of admitted patients.

This scientific study, however, is still experimental, and it was applied to non-date data. In the further developments this method will be finalized based on the latest data, and then their dynamics over time will be verified, as part in designing of a more complete performance measurement system. Potential developments include the integration of clinical outcome and user satisfaction indicators and the use of the model as a support for regional decision-making.

References

1. Delvecchio, F.: Statistica per l'analisi di dati multidimensionali, CLEUP, Padova (2010)
2. Rench, A.C.: Methods of multivariate analysis, wiley-Interscience (2002)
3. Del Vecchio, F.: Analisi Statistica di dati multidimensionali, Cacucci, Bari (1992)
4. Franci, A., Bruscaglia, G., Belbusti, G.: Strumenti operativi per la gestione delle Unità Sanitarie Locali. Studi e ricerche, Montefeltro Edizioni, Urbino (1978)

5. Kaiser, H.F.: The varimax criterion for analytic rotation in factor analysis. Psychometrika **23**, 187–200 (1958)
6. Fitz-Gibbon, C.T.: Performance indicators, Multilingual Matters, BERA Dialogues (2) (1990)
7. Legge 15/2009 – Riforma
8. D.lgs 150/2009 – Misurazione e Valutazione delle performance
9. Delibera Civit 88/2010 – Linee guida per la definizione degli standard di qualità
10. Delibera Civit 89/2010 – Indirizzi in materia di parametri e modelli di riferimento del Sistema di Misurazione e Valutazione delle Performance
11. Delibera Civit 112/2010 – Struttura e modalità di redazione del piano della performance
12. Delibera Civit 113/2010 – Applicabilità agli enti del Servizio Sanitario Nazionale

Territorial Dynamics of Housing: Structural Patterns, Market Accessibility, and Public Policy Implications

João Lourenço Marques(✉) ⓘ, João Canas ⓘ, and Monique Borges ⓘ

Department of Social, Political and Territorial Sciences, GOVCOPP, University of Aveiro,
Campus Universitário de Santiago, Aveiro, Portugal
jjmarques@ua.pt

Abstract. This study presents a spatially disaggregated analysis of housing dynamics in Portugal. Using a quantitative and spatial approach, the research integrates census data, administrative records, and public policy documentation to examine key housing indicators across municipalities. Synthetic indicators were constructed to capture multidimensional aspects of housing supply and demand, affordability, and market dynamics to identify territorial patterns and disparities. The findings reveal marked spatial heterogeneity: beyond the expected pressures in metropolitan and coastal municipalities, certain inland district capitals display unexpectedly high levels of housing demand and affordability tensions, while some peripheral municipalities with limited market activity exhibit misalignments between income and housing costs. The findings underscore the coexistence of structural imbalances and socio-territorial inequalities, highlighting the need for geographically targeted housing policies and more effective implementation of public programs.

Keyword: Housing market dynamics · Housing affordability · Territorial inequalities · Spatial multivariate analysis

1 Introduction

The 2008 global financial crisis profoundly impacted housing provision and access, exposing structural supply, affordability, and planning weaknesses. In response, Portugal launched the National Housing Strategy (*Estratégia Nacional de Habitação*) in 2015, aiming to reorient housing policies through three foundational pillars: promoting urban rehabilitation by simplifying building restoration processes, revitalizing the rental market, and improving housing quality. This strategy also incorporated a strong social dimension, emphasizing the inclusion and protection of vulnerable groups while acknowledging emerging demographic and territorial challenges.

Building on this foundation, the government introduced the New Generation of Housing Policies (*Nova Geração de Políticas de Habitação* – NGPH) in 2018 [1]. This new framework emerged from the findings of the National Housing Needs Survey (*Levantamento Nacional das Necessidades de Realojamento Habitacional*) [2], which identified tens of thousands of families living in substandard conditions across the country, even though the recent strategic documents made by the municipalities – Municipal Housing Plans (*Cartas Municipais de Habitação*) – have identified a lot more families in need. The NGPH expanded the scope of housing policies, integrating and relating concepts of "housing" and "habitat", turning the focus from the "house" (object) to the "person" or the access to housing (objective), while extending support to a broader range of beneficiaries through programs such as First Right, a housing support program for vulnerable households (*1° Direito*), a rental subsidy specifically designed for people up to 35 years old (*Porta 65 Jovem*), and a building rehabilitation program to increase rental supply (*Reabilitar para Arrendar*).

In 2019, the Housing Framework Law (*Lei de Bases da Habitação*) was enacted, formally establishing housing as a fundamental right and defining the State's responsibilities in ensuring its provision. More recently, significant legislative developments—namely the More Housing (*Mais Habitação*)package (- measures aimed at improving housing affordability, increasing supply, and regulating the rental market in Portugal - Law No. 56/2023) and the National Housing Program 2022–2026 (Law No. 2/2024)—have outlined concrete policy instruments and objectives, from increasing affordable housing stock to implementing fiscal incentives for housing rehabilitation and access. The most recent policy initiative, Building Portugal: A New Housing Strategy (*Construir Portugal: Nova Estratégia para a Habitação*)— the most recent national housing policy framework introduced in 2024, aimed at expanding access, promoting affordability, and incentivizing homeownership among younger generations. It includes tax exemptions (IMT and IS) for home purchases by individuals under 35, aiming to improve access for younger generations.

While the constitutional right to housing has been recognized since 1976, the realization of this right has remained uneven. Despite the proliferation of programs and legal frameworks, various challenges persist: fragmentation across policy instruments, territorial implementation disparities, and persistent affordability and segregation issues. The coexistence of tax incentives for foreign investors, short-term rental legislation, and programs aimed at vulnerable populations have often produced contradictory outcomes, as well as housing speculation, over-reliance on tourism-driven demand, and a mismatch between public policy goals and market behavior have contributed to rising tensions in the housing sector [3–6].

The housing crisis in Portugal (as well as housing public policies) has been a matter of study throughout the years, especially after the subprime crisis and its repercussions. While some studies (for the Portuguese context) try to approach the problem more qualitatively by doing a critical analysis and exploring their contradictions to the various housing policies and programs [7–9], others try to measure housing needs and affordability issues using different quantitative methods and approaches. For instance, while some try to measure the reality of the problem using survey methods [10, 11], others have significantly different approaches, mainly to assess housing affordability [12], with some even using k-means clustering and linear regressions to find similar affordability patterns in mainland Portugal [13, 14].

This paper presents a comprehensive and spatially disaggregated analysis of the housing situation in Portugal. It seeks to characterize the structure and condition of the housing stock, evaluate the territorial distribution of housing needs, while trying to understand the influence of new housing demands. With this, we try to answer three research questions (RQ):

RQ1: How has the housing stock developed in the last decade throughout the territory concerning household variation?

RQ2: How does affordability change regarding the relation between housing prices and household income, as well as the Price Consumer Index?

RQ3: How do the "new demand patterns" influence (or are influenced by) the previous two questions?

Through this approach, the study contributes to a deeper understanding of the socio-territorial inequalities that shape the contemporary Portuguese housing landscape, using a differentiated approach in the Portuguese context. However, the approach used is being widely applied on other territorial contexts, especially related to housing markets, where Principal Component Factor Analysis (PCFA) is used as a pre-process for clustering [15–17].

2 Methodology

The study adopted a quantitative and spatial analysis approach, focusing on identifying territorial patterns through statistical analysis of housing stock characteristics, demographic and family structure trends, and key housing market indicators such as rental prices and ownership costs. The analysis relied primarily on official datasets and administrative records to ensure accuracy and consistency. The core sources included:

- National Census data from the National Statistics Institute (INE)
- Reports from the Institute for Housing and Urban Rehabilitation (IHRU) and the National Statistics Institute (INE)
- Policy documents and program data from the Housing Portal, Centre for Planning and Policy Evaluation (PlanAPP), and Tourism of Portugal

The methodological framework of this study involved integrating and harmonizing multiple datasets to enable a spatially detailed analysis of housing dynamics across Portuguese municipalities. The first phase of data processing focused on aggregating census data from 2011 and 2021, initially sourced at the sub-municipal level (BGRI). From the 2011 census, only variables directly relevant to the housing dimensions specifically the number of classic family dwellings and private households—were retained. The 2021 census dataset, comprising approximately 1.99 million entries, was fully incorporated. Following a process of variable selection, filtering, and spatial aggregation to the municipal scale (NUTS IV), a dataset of 1,848 valid spatial units was obtained. In parallel, a second dataset was constructed using 2021 housing market indicators published by the National Statistics Institute (INE), including variables such as rental prices, purchase prices, and income levels. This dataset covered 2,464 territorial units. Subsequently, both datasets were merged using a common geographical identifier. The resulting integrated dataset, comprising 5,236 aggregated records, provided the empirical foundation for developing composite indicators and spatial typologies explored in the subsequent analytical stages.

Two main quantitative methods were applied to achieve these territorial patterns: PCFA – used to develop synthetic indicators that try to demonstrate three different housing dynamics (Housing Supply vs. Demand; Affordability; New Demand Patterns) and K-Means Clustering, used to aggregate the results given by the first method (pre-process), thus representing municipalities with similar characteristics that can describe distinct territorial patterns.

Key variables analyzed included housing typologies, occupancy status, vacancy rates, age of the housing stock, rental regimes, and construction trends. Municipalities (NUTS IV) were selected as the territorial units of analysis, providing sufficient spatial detail to capture local housing dynamics while maintaining coherence with national-level patterns. In addition, synthetic indicators—such as affordability, market dynamics, and housing demand profiles—were developed to facilitate interpretation. Most of the data utilized in this study is publicly available in open-source formats such as.csv,.xlsx, and geopackage (.gpkg) files. Data processing and analysis were conducted using Python, employing libraries for data manipulation, visualization, and spatial analysis. Table 1 summarizes the merged dataset.

Table 1. Housing and socioeconomic variables.

Attribute	Data type	mean	max	min	std
Housing buying price (€/m²)	Float	822.2	3412.0	191.8	487.5
Municipal property tax (€)	Float	4876.0	124252.0	16.0	10147.9
Property tax associated with buying a house (€)	Float	4444.2	Float	0.0	17793.3
Average building age (years)	Float	46.7	67.2	33.0	6.1
Number of houses sold (units)	Integer	1423.2	23162.0	0.0	2724.6
Ratio between the number of families and the number of dwellings	Float	1.8	3.2	1.1	0.4
Ratio between empty/vacated dwellings and the total of existing dwellings	Float	0.1	0.3	0.1	0.0
Average dwelling size (m²) ,	Float	122.7	155.4	82.4	11.8
Housing rental price (€/m²)	Float	4.4	11.2	2.0	1.7
Average income post taxes and deductions (€)	Float	1166.8	1945.6	914.0	161.9
Consumer Price Index	Float	82.4	186.3	60.7	15.7
Number of rental contracts (units)	Integer	447.9	9548.0	33.0	898.8
Number of families (units)	Integer	13471.1	242571.0	155.0	23362.2
Number of classical (conventional) dwellings	Integer	19394.4	242571.0	205.0	29345.4
Dwelling variation between 2011 and 2021	Float	0.0	0.1	-0.1	0.0
Families variation between 2011 and 2021	Float	0.0	0.2	-0.3	0.1

3   Results

This section presents the main results, structured into four interconnected analytical components. The first component examines the relationship between housing supply and demand by quantitatively comparing housing stock availability with the number of resident families. The second component addresses overall housing affordability without distinguishing between tenure types (ownership or rental), thereby considering housing prices in aggregate terms. The third component explores emerging patterns of housing demand, emphasizing recent dynamics within the housing market that may signal shifts in demographic, economic, or spatial preferences.

To support the analytical framework, synthetic indicators (SIs) were developed by applying PCFA, a multivariate statistical technique designed to reduce dimensionality in complex datasets. The resulting indicators are statistically robust, providing a simplified yet comprehensive overview of complex housing dynamics without compromising the depth and relevance of the original information.

To perform this analysis, after value standardization (using the z-score method) for each one of the parameters, a correlation matrix was constructed for each of the cases to extract the eigenvalues, thus making it possible to develop the principal component score expression. This process is better detailed in the Appendix.

Finally, the fourth component of the analysis involves aggregating the three previously constructed synthetic indicators through a clustering procedure using the k-means algorithm. This step aims to generate a comprehensive typology that synthesizes the housing situation across Portugal, highlighting territorial patterns and spatial disparities. In addition, regression analyses were conducted to investigate the relationships and explanatory power of the synthetic indicators further.

The following table (Table 2) presents the attributes and variables selected for constructing each synthetic indicator.

Table 2. Selected variables for synthetic indicators on housing supply, affordability, and market dynamics.

Indicators	Variables/Attributes
3.1 Housing Supply vs. Demand	Average building age
	Percentage of Vacant Dwellings
	Household Variation (2011 – 2021)
	Variation in Classic Family Dwellings (2011 – 2021)
3.2 Affordability	Income
	Housing buying price
	Housing rental price
	Consumer Price Index (CPI)
3.3 New Demand Patterns	Percentage of Primary Residences
	Percentage of Rental Contracts
	Percentage of Completed Transactions

While the results derived from the synthetic indicators are both interpretable and informative, additional analyses were conducted to deepen the understanding of the categories associated with each indicator. Specifically, relationships between selected critical variables—identified as essential to characterizing each dimension—were further explored. It was established by the authors that, taking into account the min and max value for each SI and to better compare them, the number of five intervals was chosen.

K-means clustering was applied to group territorial units based on similarity, with the optimal number of clusters for each case determined through an elbow method analysis (see Appendix) [18–20]. Subsequently, additional linear regression models were employed within each cluster to examine the internal dynamics and strengthen the interpretative framework of the findings.

3.1 Housing Supply vs. Demand

This indicator enables a simultaneous analysis of the evolution in the number of dwellings and households alongside the average age of the building stock, thereby highlighting contrasts between more and less dynamic territories. The lowest and negative values (e.g., ranging from –2.42 to –0.45 standard deviations below the mean) are associated with municipalities characterized by an older housing stock and a higher proportion of vacant dwellings, a significant share of which are likely uninhabitable. In contrast, higher and positive values correspond to areas that experienced above-average growth in the number of dwellings and households between 2011 and 2021. These areas also align with the pattern identified in Indicator 3.3, which reflects the predominance of primary residences relative to other forms of occupancy, such as secondary residences and vacant units. The results are illustrated in Fig. 1.

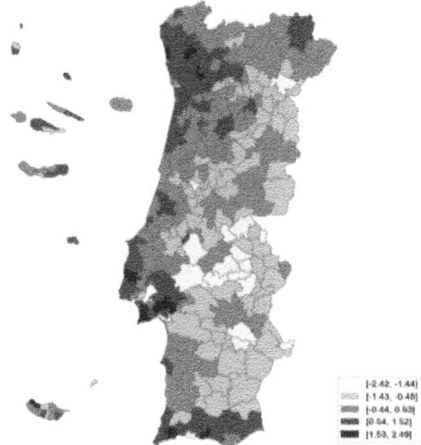

Fig. 1. Spatial dynamics of housing stock renewal and demographic growth (2011–2021).

3.2 Affordability

The affordability indicator enables the comparative analysis of housing market prices, household income, and purchasing power across municipalities. Higher indicator values correspond to territories where all variables exceed the national average. However, it is essential to note that elevated values do not inherently signify a balanced relationship between housing costs and income levels. A more detailed examination of this dimension is provided in Sect. 3.4, which identifies key scenarios, including (i) municipalities where housing prices exceed what would be expected based on income levels and (ii) municipalities where prices are relatively low in comparison to household incomes. These patterns are reflected in the present analysis, particularly in values ranging from 0.19 to 1.66 standard deviations above the mean.

It is not possible to directly infer economic accessibility levels or to unequivocally identify municipalities under the greatest housing pressure solely from this indicator. Nonetheless, intermediate and lower values are indicative of a greater misalignment between the analyzed variables. This may occur in contexts where both prices and incomes fall below the median or where prices are below the median while incomes remain comparatively higher (e.g., values between −1.28 and 0.19 standard deviations). These spatial dynamics are illustrated in Fig. 2.

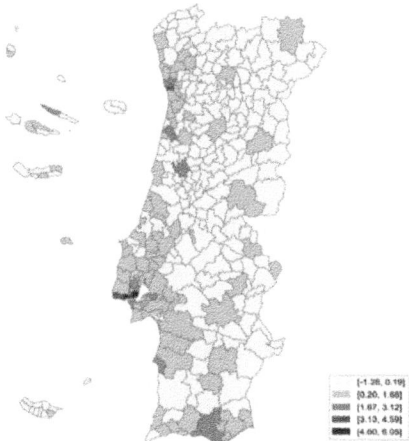

Fig. 2. Spatial distribution of housing affordability: the relationship between prices, income, and purchasing power.

3.3 New Demand Patterns

The housing market dynamics indicator, which integrates variables such as the number of rental contracts, the volume of residential property transactions (purchases/sales), and the proportion of owner-occupied primary residences, distinguishes municipalities exhibiting higher market activity and turnover levels. These spatial patterns of market dynamism are illustrated in Fig. 3.

3.4 Final Territorial Patterns

An integrated analysis of the three previously constructed composite indicators was conducted to identify and interpret distinct territorial patterns. Based on the results of the elbow method (see Annex I), the selection of three clusters was deemed methodologically appropriate, offering a meaningful balance between explanatory power and model parsimony.

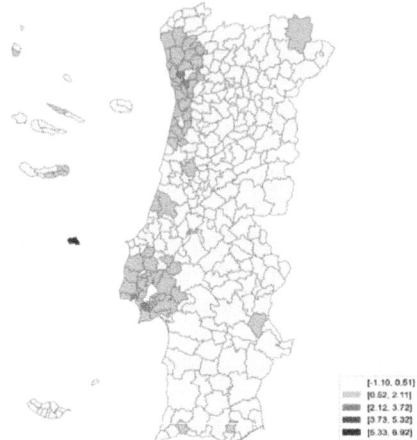

Fig. 3. Spatial patterns of housing market dynamism: transactions, rental activity, and owner-occupancy.

The resulting clusters allow for the differentiation of territorial profiles, as illustrated in Fig. 4.

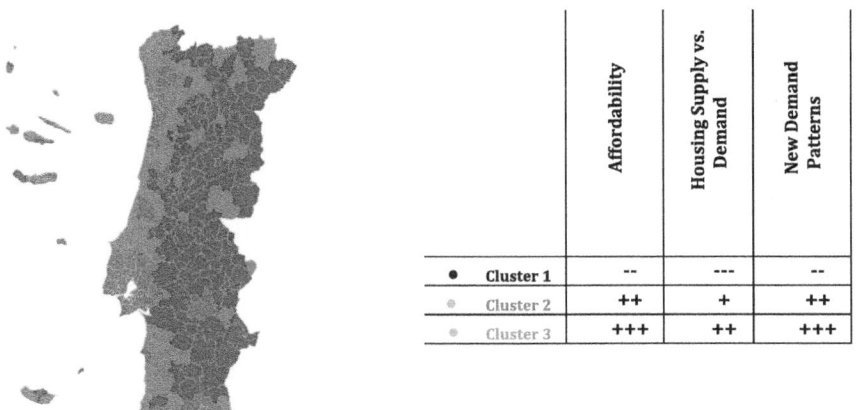

		Affordability	Housing Supply vs. Demand	New Demand Patterns
●	Cluster 1	--	---	--
●	Cluster 2	++	+	++
●	Cluster 3	+++	++	+++

Fig. 4. Spatial Clustering of municipal housing profiles according to composite housing indicators. (Color figure online)

Cluster 1 (blue): Mainly composed of municipalities commonly associated with the country's interior regions, with a few exceptions. This cluster is where all three composite indicators show the least significant values: the housing stock has evolved modestly, the housing market is less dynamic, and both prices and/or incomes are relatively low compared to the average.

Cluster 2 (orange): Associated with coastal municipalities (excluding the metropolitan areas) but also includes some inland municipalities such as district capitals (Viseu, Bragança, Guarda, Castelo Branco). In these municipalities, prices and incomes are particularly high, which is reflected in the intensity of the economic accessibility indicator. At the same time, the number of transactions and new rental contracts points to a more dynamic housing market. These municipalities also recorded positive changes in the number of dwellings and households between 2011 and 2021.

Cluster 3 (green): Associated with metropolitan areas and their surrounding municipalities, including some municipalities in the Algarve region and other district capitals such as Aveiro, Coimbra, and Évora. These municipalities stand out for having the highest values across all indicators, showing a significant disparity compared to other territories.

3.5   Complementary Cluster and Regression Analysis

A two-stage methodological approach and its resulting territorial typology, combining affordability analysis and housing supply-demand dynamics to produce a final clustering of Portuguese municipalities.

To assess housing affordability across municipalities, a bivariate typology was constructed using two key variables: total housing price (2021) (x-axis) and average household income (2021) (y-axis). Municipalities were classified into six distinct categories based on their relative position to the national medians (red and blue dashed lines) and the least squares regression line (green). This approach allows for a nuanced interpretation of affordability dynamics grounded in observable deviations from national averages and expected trends. This analysis is seen in Fig. 5.

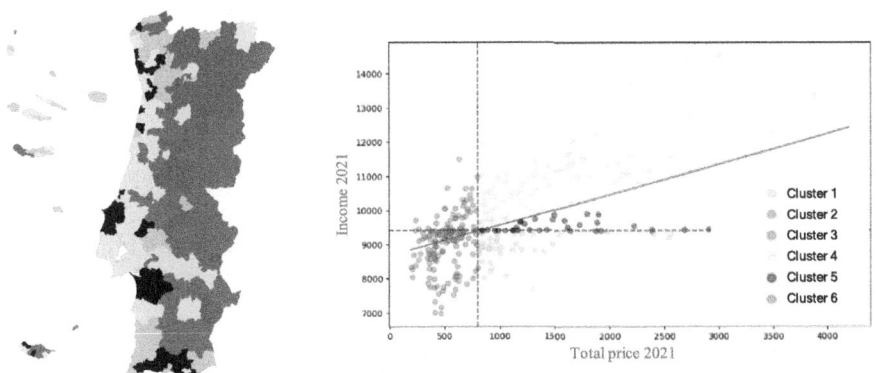

Fig. 5. Spatial clustering of municipal housing profiles according to total housing price (2021) and average household income (2021) (Color figure online)

The classification is as follows:

- Cluster 1 (light green): Territories positioned below the income median and above the price median, indicating critical affordability pressure.

- Cluster 2 (light blue): Cases above the regression line represent municipalities with income levels higher than expected given local housing prices, suggesting relatively favourable affordability ratios.
- Cluster 3 (blue): Municipalities above the income median and below the housing price median suggest areas with more favourable affordability conditions.
- Cluster 4 (yellow): Municipalities above both medians, corresponding to high-cost and higher-income environments, where market dynamics may remain relatively balanced.
- Cluster 5 (dark grey): Areas below both medians, typically associated with lower-cost but also lower-income contexts, where affordability issues may persist despite low prices.
- Cluster 6 (light grey): Municipalities below the regression line, where income is disproportionately low relative to housing prices, indicating worsened affordability conditions.

Following the previous analysis, the next Fig. 6 applies a similar methodological approach, using the same segmentation logic—based on medians and the regression line—to examine the relationship between the number of classic family dwellings and the number of private households. This allows for the identification of distinct territorial typologies regarding the balance (or imbalance) between housing supply and local household structure.

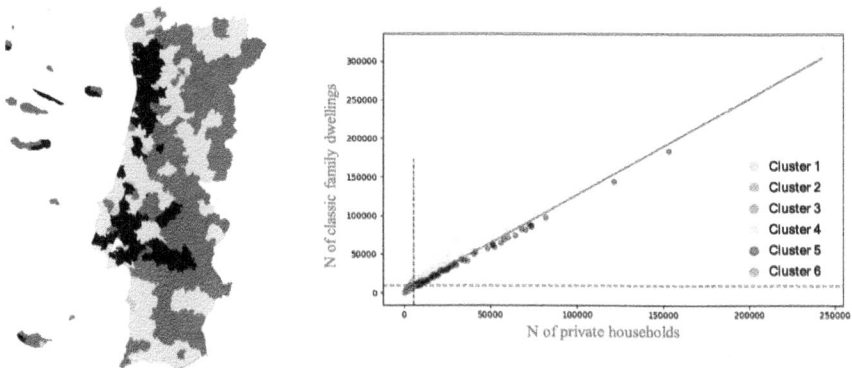

Fig. 6. Spatial clustering of municipal housing profiles according to the number of classic family dwellings (2021) and the number of private households (2021) (Color figure online)

The combination of the two previous analyses—focusing respectively on affordability dynamics and the balance between housing supply and household structure—resulted in the integrated analysis presented below. This synthesis enables a broader territorial classification, capturing areas with overlapping or divergent housing pressures and providing a more comprehensive view of the structural dynamics shaping housing accessibility in Portugal (Fig. 7).

The integrated analysis reveals four distinct territorial patterns across Portugal:

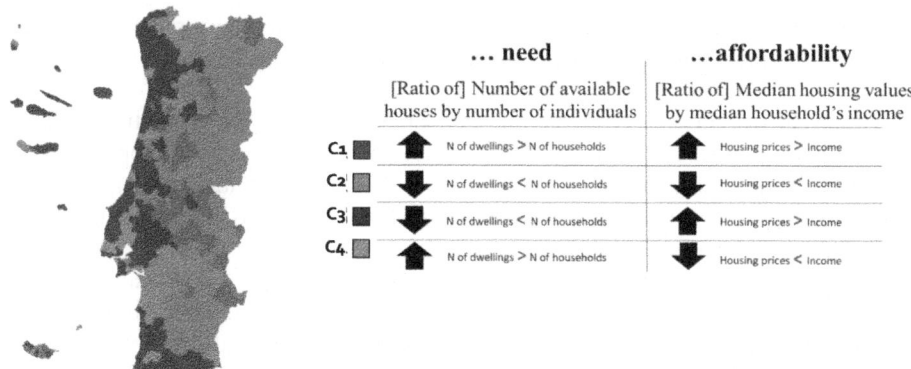

Fig. 7. Spatial clustering of municipal housing profiles according to the needs and affordability. (Color figure online)

- Cluster 1 (red) highlights municipalities under compounded housing pressure, with high affordability constraints and limited alignment between housing supply and demand. These are mainly concentrated along the southern coast and some inland southern regions.
- Cluster 2 (green) represents areas with more balanced conditions, where income and housing costs are relatively aligned, and the housing supply meets household needs. These are typically found in central and northern interior municipalities.
- Cluster 3 (blue) identifies territories where affordability appears favourable but may conceal mismatches in supply dynamics—suggesting potentially underutilized housing stock or stagnant markets.
- Cluster 4 (orange) includes municipalities where affordability issues are less pronounced but where housing stock evolution may not have kept pace with demographic shifts. These are often transitional or peri-urban areas.

This analysis gives a slightly different view from the one that uses the SI. With this, we tried to illustrate that some municipalities that, by comparison, don't seem too critical regarding affordability using the SI appear as critical in this last analysis.

4   Discussion

The analysis confirms the existence of significant spatial disparities in housing dynamics across Portugal, underscoring the complex interplay between structural housing characteristics, affordability, and emergent demand patterns. Despite a nominal surplus in housing stock, effective accessibility remains uneven, particularly for low-income and vulnerable groups, revealing a critical mismatch between housing availability and adequacy.

The findings reinforce that metropolitan and coastal municipalities—especially Lisbon, Porto, and the Algarve—continue to experience intense affordability pressures driven by tourism, short-term rentals, and foreign investment. These areas are characterized by high prices, increased market turnover, and demographic dynamism but also reveal growing exclusionary housing access trends. In contrast, interior and low-density municipalities face stagnation, high vacancy rates, and aging housing stock, further deepening socio-territorial inequalities.

A relevant insight emerges from the comparison between the synthetic indicator-based clustering and the bivariate typology combining affordability and supply-demand dynamics. While both approaches capture similar territorial divides, the latter proves more sensitive in highlighting affordability tensions in inland municipalities often overlooked in national-scale metrics.

This study emphasizes that a one-size-fits-all housing policy is inadequate for responding to Portugal's territorial contexts' diversity. Instead, tailored strategies that account for both market dynamics and socio-demographic realities are necessary. Addressing spatial inequalities in housing will require targeted investment and rehabilitation, particularly in underperforming regions, and stronger coordination across national and municipal scales, along with clear mechanisms to monitor, evaluate, and adjust policy implementation.

5   Conclusion

This study conducted a spatially disaggregated assessment of housing dynamics in Portugal, using multivariate and geospatial methodologies to uncover structural imbalances and territorial disparities. Through the integration of census data, market indicators, and socioeconomic variables, it was possible to construct synthetic indicators that revealed not only well-known affordability tensions in metropolitan and coastal areas, but also emerging pressures in inland and peri-urban municipalities.

The analysis demonstrated that nominal housing availability often fails to translate into real accessibility, especially where market prices exceed local purchasing power or housing supply lags behind demographic shifts. The complementary typology further revealed municipalities whose affordability challenges may be obscured by aggregated indicators, reinforcing the need for granular and multidimensional assessments.

Portugal's housing challenges are shaped by more than just supply —they reflect deep-rooted issues of affordability, inequality, and spatial mismatch [21]. Addressing these requires territorially differentiated policies that align with local needs, greater coordination between national and municipal interventions, and robust monitoring systems. As new market forces—such as tourism and foreign investment—continue to reshape demand, future housing strategies must emphasize rehabilitation, rental regulation, and the integration of housing into broader territorial cohesion frameworks, ensuring that the constitutional right to housing is realized across all regions.

Acknowledgments. The authors are grateful to the two reviewers for many helpful comments and suggestions, which helped us improve upon the paper. The usual disclaimer applies. This work has been supported by Portuguese national funds through the Foundation for Science and Technology, FCT, I.P., in the context of the JUST_PLAN project (PTDC/GES-OUT/2662/20); Research Unit on Governance, Competitiveness and Public Policy (GOVCOPP), Grant/Award Number: UID/CPO/04058/2019.

Appendix

1. PCFA results

The standardization method used was the z-score method. After this, the methodological approach is similar to the one used by Wiersma et. al [15]. The principal components (PC) extracted summarize the underlying structure of the dataset, which is then divided for each corresponding SI. The factor loading indicates the strength and direction of each attribute's contribution to the first component and so on. In the other hand, the communalities tell the proportion of each variable's variance that is explained by the respective component. Only the first factor appears because the Kaiser Criterion was used, and for all of the SIs, the first components turned out to be the most significant (eigenvalue > 1), which means that the first factor can explain most of the variance. The results are in Table 3.

Table 3. PCFA results

SI	Attribute	Loading	Communalities
Housing Supply vs. Demand	Average building age	−0.691292	0.477885
	Percentage of Vacant Dwellings	−0.552037	0.304744
	Household Variation (2011 – 2021)	0.803568	0.645722
	Classic Family Dwellings (2011– 2021)	0.595093	0.354136
Affordability	Income	0.720293	0.518822
	Housing buying price	0.823472	0.678107
	Housing rental price	0.728841	0.531209
	CPI	0.911034	0.829983
New Demand Patterns	Percentage of Primary Residences	0.688881	0.474557
	Percentage of Rental Contracts	0.658927	0.434185
	Percentage of Completed Transactions	0.876827	0.768825

2. The elbow method for K-Means Clustering

The elbow method is used to determine the ideal number of clusters in K-Means, since it helps to balance the trade-off between the variance within clusters and the number of clusters. It is often complemented with a visual support that consists of plotting a chosen range of cluster counts against the within-cluster sum of squares. The graphical result of this is a curve. At the point where the curve starts to "stabilize" is the ideal number of clusters to choose.

References

1. Author, F.: Article title. Journal **2**(5), 99–110 (2016)
2. República Portuguesa: Resolução do Conselho de Ministros n.º 50-A/2017 – Aprova a Nova Geração de Políticas de Habitação. In: Diário da República, 1.ª série, N.º 121, 26 de junho de, pp. 3222-(2)-3222-(9) (2017)
3. Instituto da Habitação e da Reabilitação Urbana, I.P.: Levantamento Nacional das Necessidades de Realojamento Habitacional. In: Fevereiro de (2018)
4. Barata-Salgueiro, T., Mendes, L., Guimarães, P.: Tourism and urban changes: lessons from Lisbon. In: Tourism and Gentrification in Contemporary Metropolises, pp. 255–275. Routledge, London (2017)
5. dos Santos, J.P., Strohmaier, K.: All that glitters? golden visas and real estate. In: PSE Working Papers (2024)
6. Franco, S.F., Santos, C.D.: The impact of Airbnb on residential property values and rents: evidence from Portugal. Regional Sci. Urban Econ. **88**, 103667. Elsevier, Amsterdam (2021). https://doi.org/10.1016/j.regsciurbeco.2021.103667
7. Branco, R., Alves, S.: Urban rehabilitation, governance, and housing affordability: lessons from Portugal. Urban Res. Pract. **13**(2), 157–179. Taylor & Francis, London (2020). https://doi.org/10.1080/17535069.2019.1578960
8. Allegra, M., Tulumello, S., Colombo, A., Ferrão, J.: The (hidden) role of the EU in housing policy: the Portuguese case in multi-scalar perspective. Eur. Plan. Stud. **28**(12), 2307–2329 (2020). https://doi.org/10.1080/09654313.2020.1719474
9. Mendes, L.: Nova Geração De Políticas De Habitação Em Portugal: Contradições Entre O Discurso e as Práticas No Direito À Habitação. Finisterra, **55**(114), 77–104 (2020). https://doi.org/10.18055/Finis19635
10. Azevedo, A.B., Santos dos, J.P.: Barómetro da Habitação (Versão 7). Fundação Francisco Manuel dos Santos (2024)
11. Ribeiro, R., Poeschl, G., Santos, A.C.: The different sides of the housing crisis in Portugal: a contribution to building inclusive, fair, and effective solutions. Polit. Psychol. (2025)
12. Fragoso Januário, J., Oliveira Cruz, C., Varum, H., Faria e Sousa, V.: Is housing be-coming less affordable? a study of affordability in the Portuguese housing market. Property Manage. **41**(5), 698-728 (2023)
13. Marques João, L., Batista, P., Borges, M., Gonçalves, C.: Spatial patterns of affordable housing needs in Portugal. J. Econ. Soc. Dev. **7**(2), 1–13. Journals Press, Zagreb (2020)
14. Batista, P., Marques, J.L., Castro, E.A.: Territorial patterns of housing affordability in Portugal. The real estate market in Portugal prices, rents, tourism and accessibility. Fundação Francisco Manuel dos Santos (2022)
15. Wiersma, S., Just, T., Heinrich, M.: Segmenting German housing markets using principal component and cluster analyses. Int. J. Housing Mark. Anal. **15**(3), 548–578 (2021)
16. Wu, C., Sharma, R.: Housing submarket classification: the role of spatial contiguity. Appl. Geogr. **32**(2), 746–756 (2012)
17. Owen, S.M., et al.: Urban land classification and its uncertainties using principal component and cluster analyses: a case study for the UK West Midlands. Landsc. Urban Plan. **78**(4), 311–321 (2006)

18. Syakur, M.A., Khotimah, B.K., Rochman, E.M.S., Satoto, B.D.: Integration k-means clustering method and elbow method for identification of the best customer profile cluster. In: IOP Conference Series: Materials Science and Engineering, vol. 336, p. 012017. IOP Publishing (2018)
19. Cui, M.: Introduction to the k-means clustering algorithm based on the elbow method. Acc. Auditing Finance 1(1), 5–8 (2020)
20. Humaira, H., Rasyidah, R.: Determining the appropriate cluster number using the elbow method for the k-means algorithm. In: Proceedings of the 2nd Workshop on Multidisciplinary and Applications (WMA), pp. 1–8 (2020)
21. Feitosa, F.O., Batista, P., Marques, J.L.: How to assess spatial injustice: distinguishing housing spatial inequalities through housing choice. Cities **140**, 104422 (2023)

Enhancing Malaria Control in Nigeria: A Data-Driven Approach to Prioritizing Insecticide-Treated Net Assessment

Abimbola H. Afolayan[1]([✉]), Gideon E. Igbo[2], and Oluwafemi A. Sarumi[3]

[1] Information Systems Department, Federal University of Technology, Akure, Nigeria
ahafolayan@futa.edu.ng
[2] Computer Science Department, Federal University of Technology, Akure, Nigeria
[3] Institute of Computer Science, Heinrich-Heine University Düsseldorf, Düsseldorf, Germany

Abstract. Malaria remains a major public health challenge in sub-Saharan Africa, with Nigeria accounting for 31.9% of global malaria deaths in 2020. Despite efforts to control malaria through World Health Organization (WHO)-recommended interventions such as insecticide-treated nets (ITNs) and indoor residual spraying, the disease persists. Effective malaria control requires informed decision-making at multiple levels, with community health workers (CHWs) playing a crucial role in implementing and assessing interventions at the grassroots level. This study applies the Analytic Hierarchy Process (AHP) to evaluate ITNs effectiveness from the perspective of CHWs. Eight key criteria were analyzed: affordability, availability, accessibility, acceptability, suitability, previous experience, beliefs, and malaria knowledge. Data was collected through structured questionnaires and analyzed using AHP. The results showed malaria knowledge as the top priority (24.8%), followed by previous experience with malaria (22.9%). These findings provide valuable insights for policymakers to enhance ITNs distribution and malaria prevention efforts. By incorporating CHWs' perspectives, resource allocation can be optimized, leading to more effective malaria control strategies.

Keywords: Malaria Epidemic · Insecticide Treated Nets · Decision Criteria · Analytic Hierarchy Process

1 Introduction

Malaria remains a critical public health challenge, particularly in sub-Saharan Africa, where it is a leading cause of morbidity and mortality. The disease, caused by Plasmodium parasites and transmitted through the bites of infected female Anopheles mosquitoes, disproportionately affects tropical and subtropical regions [1]. Among the five Plasmodium species known to cause malaria in humans, Plasmodium falciparum is the most virulent and is responsible for the majority of malaria-related deaths, particularly in Africa [2]. Despite decades

O. Gervasi et al. (Eds.): ICCSA 2025, LNCS 15650, pp. 264–276, 2025.
https://doi.org/10.1007/978-3-031-96962-1_18

of global and regional efforts to control malaria, the disease persists as a major burden, with Nigeria being the most affected country.

According to the World Health Organization [3], Nigeria accounted for 31.9% of global malaria deaths in 2021, translating to approximately 200,000 fatalities. The overall malaria incidence has increased, with cases rising from 227 million in 2019 to 241 million in 2020. Similarly, the number of deaths surged from 558,000 in 2019 to 627,000 in 2020, underscoring the urgency for more effective intervention strategies. Various control measures, such as long-lasting ITNs, indoor residual spraying, larval source management, and intermittent preventive treatment for pregnant women, have been implemented, but challenges persist in achieving sustained reductions in malaria prevalence and mortality [3].

Vector control remains the cornerstone of malaria prevention, with ITNs being one of the most effective strategies [4]. ITNs provide a physical barrier against mosquito bites while also delivering insecticidal effects, significantly reducing transmission rates when properly used. Since the WHO launched mass ITNs distribution campaigns in 2007, aiming for universal coverage (one net per two individuals), there has been a notable increase in ITNs usage in sub-Saharan Africa [5]. However, ensuring continued ITNs effectiveness requires sustained efforts, including replacing worn-out nets and addressing challenges related to accessibility, affordability, and acceptability. Studies indicate that many distributed ITNs deteriorate before their intended lifespan, reducing their efficacy in malaria control [6].

Effective malaria control depends on well-coordinated decision-making at multiple levels of governance, from national policymakers to local authorities and healthcare providers [7]. In Nigeria, the National Malaria Control Program formulates policies in collaboration with international organizations, while the State Malaria Elimination Programs adapt these strategies at the state level. At the grassroots level, CHWs serve as the link between public health initiatives and local populations, ensuring the effective distribution of ITNs and educating communities on malaria prevention. Despite their critical role, CHWs' perspectives on ITNs distribution and effectiveness are often overlooked in policy and resource allocation decisions. Engaging CHWs in decision-making can enhance the adoption and sustainability of ITNs interventions by addressing locally relevant barriers and community concerns.

Given the complexity of malaria control, Multi-Criteria Decision Analysis (MCDA) methodologies provide a systematic approach to evaluating and prioritizing intervention strategies. The AHP [8] is one of the most widely used MCDA techniques for structuring complex decision problems. AHP allows the integration of qualitative and quantitative factors through pairwise comparisons, ensuring a more objective and consistent prioritization process [9]. This method has been applied in various malaria-related studies, including identifying high-risk zones, evaluating intervention effectiveness, and optimizing resource allocation [10–12].

Although previous research has employed AHP to rank malaria control strategies, few studies have focused specifically on assessing ITNs from the perspective of CHWs. Given their frontline experience and direct engagement with at-risk populations, CHWs offer valuable insights into the real-world factors influencing ITNs effectiveness, including community preferences, behavioral patterns, and logistical challenges. Incorporating their perspectives into decision-making can lead to more effective and context-specific malaria control policies. This study aims to evaluate decision criteria for assessing ITNs using the AHP methodology, with a particular focus on the perspectives of CHWs. By systematically ranking key factors such as affordability, accessibility, acceptability, durability, and prior experience, this research provides a structured framework to guide policymakers in optimizing ITNs distribution and utilization. The findings will contribute to evidence-based decision-making, improve the efficiency of malaria intervention programs, and ultimately enhance malaria prevention and control efforts in Nigeria.

2   Materials and Methods

The research utilized both primary and secondary data sources. Primary data were collected through structured questionnaires distributed to 40 CHWs in Akure, the capital of Ondo State, located in southwestern Nigeria, with an estimated population of 803,062 based on recent projections from the World Population reviews. Akure serves as an ideal location for investigating the roles of CHWs in accessing the intervention of ITNs for malaria control, given its diverse population, active governmental health programs through community healthcare providers.

The CHWs were selected through purposive sampling. The questionnaire comprised two sections: one focused on demographic information and the other designed to capture respondents' insights. The demographic composition of respondents indicated a predominance of females (65%) over males (35%). Participants were categorized by age as follows: 62.5% were between 26 and 40 years old, 25% were between 41 and 55 years old, and the remaining 12.5% were between 56 and 70 years old. In terms of professional qualifications, 12.5% held the position of Junior Community Health Extension Workers, 37% were Community Health Extension Workers, and 5% were Senior Community Health Extension Workers. Additionally, 2.5% held Certificates in Community Health, 20% had Diplomas in Community Health, and 22.5% possessed Bachelor's degrees in Community or Public Health. The secondary data were obtained from literature and other relevant sources on malaria interventions.

In analyzing the effects of ITNs, we considered eight crucial decision criteria as shown in Table 1 based on previous studies [12,13], and guidelines from the Nigeria Federal Ministry of Health. The CHWs rated the importance of each criterion, comparing their efficacy in assessing ITNs. The questionnaire sought to transform responses into nine-point AHP scale numbers. These values were then used to calculate each decision criterion's relative weights and rank them using the AHP. The AHP technique's primary feature is pair-wise comparisons, enabling the evaluation of alternatives for different criteria and the estimation of criteria weights [14]. The AHP method organizes complex decision-making problems into hierarchies, defines criteria, evaluates their interactions, and synthesizes data to derive weights representing preferences [15]. The AHP approach adopted in this study comprises five steps, as illustrated in Fig. 1.

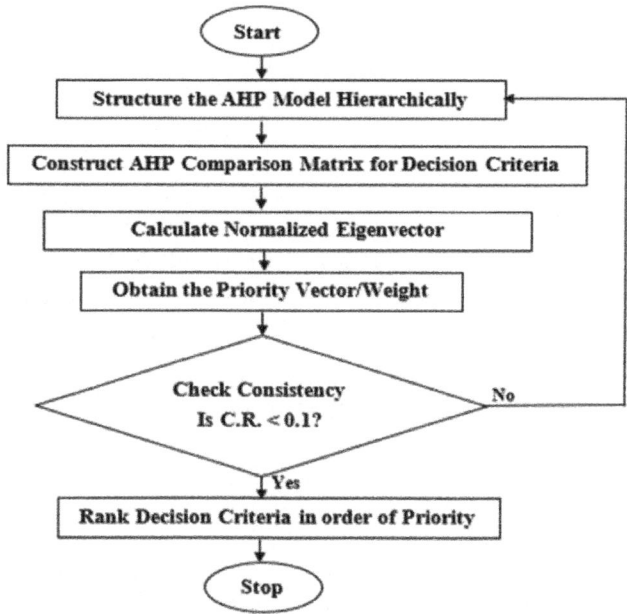

Fig. 1. Flowchart of AHP Process.

The hierarchical structure as shown in Fig. 2 consists of three levels. The first level (target level) describes the goal of the whole hierarchical structure, which is the ranking of decision criteria for assessing ITNs for malaria control. The second level contains the decision criteria to be evaluated and ranked. The third level contains the WHO-recommended malaria intervention strategy for ITNs.

This research considered eight decision criteria. Table 1 lists and briefly describes each of the decision criteria.

The CHWs were asked to rank the significance of decision criteria for evaluating ITNs for malaria control. The ratings were based on the 9-point Saaty AHP scale: (1) = Equally Important, (3) = Weakly Important, (5) = Fairly Important, (7) = Strongly Important, and (9) = Absolutely Important. The judgments from the respondents were entered using the Saaty AHP scale for pairwise comparisons. Based on the Saaty AHP scale, the expert's preferences were obtained, and Equation (1) was used to construct the AHP pairwise comparison matrix of the decision criteria. A matrix A is created to elicit pairwise comparisons performed at a given time. Matrix A in Eq. (1) shows the experts' judgment

Table 1. Evaluated decision criteria.

S/No	Criteria	Description
1	Affordability	Affordability of ITNs
2	Availability	Availability of ITNs to the population
3	Accessibility	Accessibility of ITNs
4	Acceptability	Acceptability of ITNs by the population
5	Suitability	Suitability of the use of ITNs
6	Previous Experience	Previous experience of the population with the use of insecticide-treated nets
7	Beliefs	Beliefs of the population
8	Malaria Knowledge	Malaria knowledge of the population

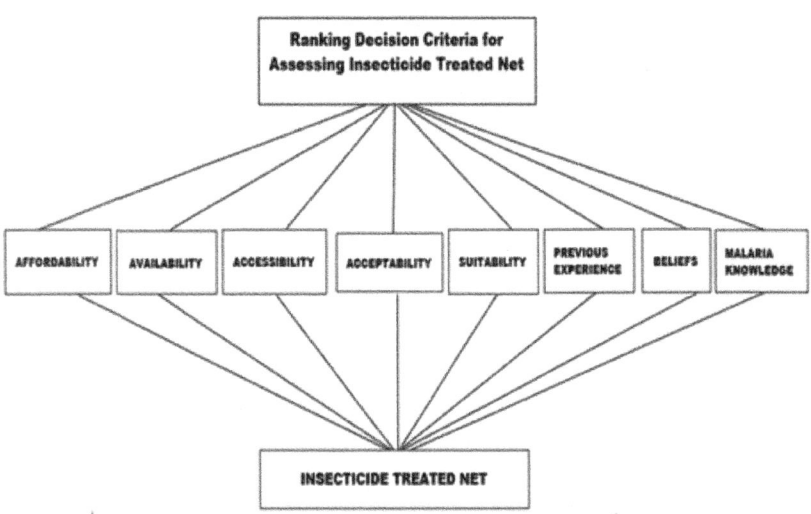

Fig. 2. Analytic Hierarchy Process Structure.

preference for the ith criterion over the jth criterion. The pairwise comparison for all respondents is shown in Fig. 3.

$$A = \begin{bmatrix} 1 & a_{12} & a_{13} & \cdots & a_{1n} \\ \frac{1}{a_{12}} & 1 & a_{23} & \cdots & a_{2n} \\ \frac{1}{a_{13}} & \frac{1}{a_{23}} & 1 & \cdots & a_{3n} \\ \vdots & \vdots & \vdots & \ddots & \vdots \\ \frac{1}{a_{1n}} & \frac{1}{a_{2n}} & \frac{1}{a_{3n}} & \cdots & 1 \end{bmatrix} \quad (1)$$

where A is the pairwise comparison matrix, and a_{ij} represents the relative importance of criterion i compared to criterion j.

Matrix		Affordability	Availability	Accessibility	Acceptability	Suitability	Previous Experience	Beliefs	Malaria Knowledge
		1	2	3	4	5	6	7	8
Affordability	1	1	1	1	7/8	3/7	1/3	1 1/2	1/4
Availability	2	1	1	1 1/2	1	1/2	2/5	1 2/3	1/3
Accessibility	3	1	2/3	1	1	3/8	1/4	1 1/2	2/7
Acceptability	4	1 1/7	1	1	1	1/2	2/7	1 2/3	2/7
Suitability	5	2 1/3	2 1/9	2 3/4	2	1	2/3	2 2/3	3/4
Previous Experience	6	3 2/7	2 1/2	3 4/5	3 1/3	1 4/9	1	3 5/6	4/5
Beliefs	7	2/3	3/5	2/3	3/5	3/8	1/4	1	2/7
Malaria Knowledge	8	3 4/5	3	3 1/3	3 5/8	1 1/3	1 1/4	3 3/5	1
Column Sum		14.28	11.85	14.99	13.51	5.948	4.46	17.37	3.99

Fig. 3. Pairwise comparison for all respondents.

To determine the normalized eigenvector, the element in each cell is divided by its corresponding column total, as shown in Eq. (2).

$$b_i = \frac{a_{ij}}{D} \tag{2}$$

where b_i is the normalized eigenvector and D is the column total of the decision criteria.

The Priority weight W_i is calculated by dividing the sum of all elements in each row of the normalized eigenvector by the number of elements in the row, as shown in Eq. (3).

$$W_i = \frac{\sum_{j=1}^{8} b_i}{n} \tag{3}$$

where W_i is the priority weight and b_i is the normalized eigenvector.

The priority vector/weights $W_1, W_2, W_3, W_4, W_5, W_6, W_7, W_8$ are then shown in a single matrix in Eq. (4).

$$\mathbf{W} = \begin{bmatrix} W_1 \\ W_2 \\ W_3 \\ W_4 \\ W_5 \\ W_6 \\ W_7 \\ W_8 \end{bmatrix} \tag{4}$$

Also, we verified the consistency of the expert judgments while doing the AHP analysis. We observed some inconsistency in the pairwise comparison because the numerical values were obtained from people's arbitrary preferences. Thus, we calculated the consistency ratio using the Saaty model [15] as shown in Eq. (5)

$$C.R = \frac{C.I}{R.I} \tag{5}$$

where $C.R$ is the consistency Ratio, $C.I$ is the consistency Index and $R.I$ is the Random Index

Based on the Saaty model, reasonable judgments are those with a consistency ratio of less than 0.1, and those with a consistency ratio of more than 0.1 are either corrected or dismissed. RI refers to random pairwise comparisons with judgments that have been input arbitrarily, which is affected by the size of matrix n. The consistency index can be defined as a deviation or degree of consistency as shown in Eq. (6)

$$C.I = \frac{\lambda_{\max} - n}{n - 1} \tag{6}$$

where n is the decision matrix's row count and $\lambda_{\max}$ is the comparison matrix's eigenvalue

To determine the comparison matrix's largest eigenvalue $\lambda_{\max}$ is calculated using Eq. (7).

$$\lambda_{\max} = \frac{S_i}{n} \tag{7}$$

where S_i is the sum total of all s_i as shown in Eq. (8).

$$S_i = \sum_{j=1}^{n} s_i \tag{8}$$

where s_i is the product of the priority weight and the column total of individual criteria as shown in Eq. (9).

$$s_i = \sum_{i=1}^{n} W_i * D \tag{9}$$

where W_i is the priority weight and D is the column total of the individual criteria.

Therefore, the decision criteria were ranked in order of priority after ascertaining that the consistency ratio was lower than 0.1.

3   Results

The priority determination for each criterion is derived from a questionnaire survey, with the first section gathering demographic information and the second section posing questions for respondent input. CHWs assess the importance of eight decision criteria for evaluating ITNs in malaria control, utilizing a 9-point Saaty AHP scale. The study evaluates eight decision criteria: affordability, availability, accessibility, acceptability, suitability, previous experience, beliefs, and malaria knowledge. The ranking of decision criteria employs the AHP package developed by [16], resulting in the synthesis of priorities and the subsequent identification of the most crucial decision criterion for ITNs assessment in malaria control, as presented in Table 2.

Table 2. Ranking of Priority Weights for All Respondents.

Criterion	Criteria	Weights	Rank
C_8	Malaria Knowledge	0.2475	1
C_6	Previous Experience	0.2294	2
C_5	Suitability	0.1665	3
C_2	Availability	0.0849	4
C_4	Acceptability	0.0768	5
C_1	Affordability	0.0716	6
C_3	Accessibility	0.0688	7
C_7	Beliefs	0.0545	8

Figure 4 indicates that malaria knowledge is the most crucial factor influencing the decision-making process for using ITNs in malaria prevention, given its highest priority weight of approximately 24.7%. Subsequently, Previous Experience holds significant importance with a priority weight of 22.9%, while Suitability, Availability, Acceptability, Affordability, and Accessibility follow in descending order of priority weights. Beliefs rank the lowest, with a priority weight of 5.5%. In practical terms, this implies that when decisions are made concerning adopting ITNs for malaria prevention, a focus on enhancing malaria knowledge is paramount.

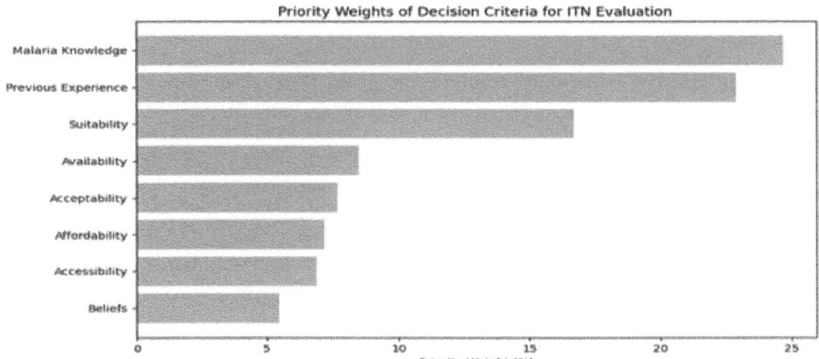

Fig. 4. Visualization of the ITNs decision criteria ranking highlights malaria knowledge as the most influential factor in the decision-making process.

3.1   Discussion

Despite numerous initiatives to curb malaria transmission in Nigeria, the prevalence of malaria cases has persistently risen. In the fight against malaria in Nigeria, [12,13] have recommended prioritizing ITNs. The selection of appropriate criteria for evaluating ITNs in malaria control is a critical decision for healthcare policymakers, particularly those in secondary and tertiary healthcare.

This research builds upon the work of [13] by incorporating a broader perspective from community health workers, strengthening the understanding of key factors in malaria prevention. Notably, malaria knowledge emerged as the most critical criterion, with a priority weight of 24.8%, underscoring its pivotal role in combating the disease. This finding aligns with studies [17] and [18], which highlight the ongoing challenge of low malaria awareness among vulnerable groups, including rural communities, mothers, pregnant women, and caregivers of young children. Furthermore, this study reinforces the findings of [19], which emphasize the effectiveness of health education interventions in promoting the use of ITNs among pregnant women. By demonstrating the crucial role of increased knowledge in ITNs ownership, usage, and awareness, our results highlight the urgent need for targeted educational initiatives to enhance malaria prevention efforts.

Moreover, this study identifies prior experience with ITNs as the second most influential factor in determining their usage, carrying a significant priority weight of 22.9%. This emphasizes the crucial role of familiarity and past exposure in promoting long-term adoption and effective utilization. Additionally, the study highlights a persistent issue: despite owning ITNs, many individuals continue to use them sub-optimally. This trend is consistent with findings from previous research [5,20–24], indicating ongoing challenges in achieving proper ITNs utilization. These insights underscore the pressing need for targeted awareness campaigns, behavioural interventions, and policy measures to bridge the gap between ITNs ownership and sustained use, ultimately enhancing malaria prevention efforts.

In this study, suitability ranked as the third most influential factor, with a priority rating of 16.7%. This underscores its crucial impact on user adherence, as discomfort and perceived warmth continue to deter consistent ITNs use, an issue echoed in previous research [25]. By drawing attention to this barrier, our study emphasizes the urgent need for innovative ITNs designs that improve breathability and comfort without compromising effectiveness. These findings advocate for targeted interventions, including educational initiatives to help users adapt to ITNs and policy-driven efforts to promote user-friendly net designs. Addressing these challenges is essential for closing the gap between ITNs ownership and regular use, ultimately enhancing malaria prevention efforts in vulnerable communities.

According to the Nigeria Malaria Indicator Survey 2015 [26], 69% of households in Nigeria owned at least one ITNs. However, despite this widespread ownership, actual utilization remained significantly low, with only 37% of households consistently using mosquito nets. In our study, availability emerged as the fourth most influential factor affecting ITNs usage, with a priority weight of 8.5%, highlighting ongoing disparities in access and distribution. This finding underscores the urgent need for targeted interventions to enhance awareness, improve accessibility, and promote behavioural adoption of ITNs, particularly among vulnerable populations at high risk of malaria.

In this study, acceptability ranks as the fifth most influential factor in ITNs utilization, with a priority weight of 7.7%. This finding aligns with previous research [5], which highlights the widespread misuse of ITNs for unintended purposes, such as bed covers, blankets, fishing nets, or window treatments. This misuse reduces their effectiveness in malaria prevention and reflects gaps in awareness and adherence. Addressing cultural and practical misconceptions through targeted educational campaigns is essential to improving ITNs acceptability. By understanding these behavioural patterns, policymakers and health workers can implement more effective interventions to enhance ITNs usage and strengthen malaria prevention efforts.

Affordability and accessibility ranked as the sixth and seventh most influential factors in ITNs utilization, emphasizing Nigeria's reliance on international donors like The Global Fund for malaria interventions [2]. Despite increased ITNs distribution, challenges persist in ensuring proper usage [27]. A major concern is the resale of freely distributed ITNs, driven by financial hardship and lack of awareness, which hinders accessibility for vulnerable groups [28]. Additionally, logistical barriers, including poor distribution networks, further limit access [29]. To address these issues, stronger monitoring, improved distribution strategies, and community engagement efforts are essential [2,30]. Strengthening these areas will help bridge the gap between ITNs ownership and effective utilization.

Beliefs ranked as the least influential factor in ITNs utilization (5.5%), as CHWs prioritize more pressing barriers like malaria knowledge, accessibility, affordability, and comfort [2,31]. Despite this low ranking, misconceptions about

ITNs rooted in distrust of Western interventions and a perceived low malaria risk still hinder their proper use [28,30]. However, CHWs view these beliefs as manageable through sustained education and community engagement. Strengthening culturally tailored health campaigns and involving trusted local leaders can help dispel myths and improve ITNs adoption [2].

4   Conclusion

Malaria stands as a critical global public health challenge, especially prevalent in Africa, with Nigeria reporting the highest incidence. Introducing ITNs is a pivotal malaria control strategy endorsed by the WHO. Involving CHWs in prioritizing decision criteria for assessing ITNs for malaria control in Nigeria helps provide valuable insights into the key criteria for assessing ITNs in malaria control at the community level. By leveraging this information, state and central-level policymakers can make informed decisions, optimize resource allocation, improve program effectiveness, and ultimately contribute to more successful malaria control efforts in Nigeria. The AHP assessed and prioritised eight decision criteria: affordability, availability, accessibility, acceptability, suitability, previous experience, beliefs, and malaria knowledge. The analysis reveals a high ranking of malaria knowledge by CHWs, underscoring its significance in decisions concerning ITNs for malaria control. This research aids healthcare providers in comprehending the importance of each decision criterion, facilitating improved decision-making. It is important to note that this study focuses solely on ranking decision criteria for ITNs. This study was conducted in Akure, Ondo State, Nigeria. In future research, we aim to expand the scope of data collection to include additional states and regions across the country, broaden the evaluation criteria and sub-criteria, and incorporate a wider range of malaria intervention strategies recommended by the WHO across multiple case studies.

Disclosure of Interests. The authors declare that there is no competing interest.

References

1. World Health Organization. World Malaria Report. WHO, Geneva (2015). https://www.who.int/. Accessed 05 Feb 2022
2. World Health Organization: World Malaria Report. WHO, Geneva (2021). https://www.who.int/teams/global-malaria-programme/reports/world-malaria-report-2021. Accessed 10 Feb 2022
3. Ahmad, R., et al.: Mapping of mosquito breeding sites in malaria-endemic areas in Pos Lenjang, Kuala Lipis, Pahang. Malaysia. Malaria J. **10**, 361 (2011)
4. Pryce, J., Richardson, M., Lengeler, C.: Insecticide-treated nets for preventing malaria. Cochrane Datab. Syst. Rev. **11**(11), CD000363 (2018)
5. Kilian, A., Boulay, M., Koenker, H., Lynch, M.: How many mosquito nets are needed to achieve universal coverage? Recommendations for the quantification and allocation of long-lasting insecticidal nets for mass campaigns. Malar. J. **9**, 1–9 (2010)

6. World Health Organization. Achieving and maintaining universal coverage with long-lasting insecticidal nets for malaria control. WHO, Geneva (2017). https://www.who.int/publications/i/item/WHO-HTM-GMP-2017.20. Accessed 11 Mar 2022

7. Ukoha, N.K., et al.: Influence of organizational structure and administrative processes on the performance of state-level malaria programs in Nigeria. Health Syst. Reform **2**(4), 331–356 (2016)

8. Saaty, T.L.: The Analytic Hierarchy Process. McGraw-Hill, New York (1980)

9. Canco, I., Kruja, D., Iancu, T.: AHP, a reliable method for quality decision making: a case study in business. Sustainability **13**(24), 13932 (2021)

10. Bhatt, B., Joshi, J.P.: Analytical hierarchy process modeling for malaria risk zone in Vadora District, Gujarat. Int. Arch. Photogram. Remote Sens. Spat. Inf. Sci. **9**(8), 171–176 (2014)

11. Lei, L., Jack, S.R., Zhi-Hong, L., Yan-Feng, G., Shao-Zai, Z., Ning, X.: A framework for assessing local transmission risk of imported malaria cases. Infect. Dis. Poverty **8**(43), 1–8 (2019)

12. Simon, J., Adamu, A., Abdulkadir, A., Henry, A.S.: Analytical Hierarchy Process (AHP) model for prioritizing alternative strategies for malaria control. Asian J. Probabil. Stat. **5**(1), 1–8 (2019)

13. Modibbo, U.M., Heman, E.D., Hafisu, R.: Multi-criteria decision analysis for malaria control strategies using analytic hierarchy process: a case of yola north local government area, Adamawa state Nigeria. Amity J. Comput. Sci. (AJCS) **3**(2), 1–15 (2019)

14. Cavallo, B., Ishizaka, A.: Evaluating scales for pairwise comparisons. Ann. Oper. Res. **325**, 951–965 (2023)

15. Saaty, T.L.: Decision Making for Leaders: The Analytic Hierarchy Process for Decisions in a Complex World, 5th edn. RWS, Pittsburgh (2012)

16. Goepel, K.D.: Implementation of an online software tool for the analytic hierarchy process (AHP-OS). In: Proceedings of the International Symposium on the Analytic Hierarchy Process, Hong Kong, China, pp. 13–15 (2018)

17. Adebayo, A.M., Akinyemi, O.O., Cadmus, E.O.: Knowledge of Malaria prevention among pregnant women and female caregivers of under-five children in rural Southwest Nigeria. PeerJ **3**, e792 (2015)

18. Idowu, O.A., Mafiana, C.F., Luwoye, I.J., Adehanloye, O.: Perceptions and home management practices of malaria in some rural communities in Abeokuta. Nigeria. Travel Med. Infect. Dis. **6**(4), 210–4 (2007)

19. Onyinyechi, C.A., Ismail, S., Nazan, A.: Prevention of malaria in pregnancy through health education intervention programs on insecticide-treated nets use: a systematic review. BMC Public Health **24**, 755 (2024)

20. Fana, S.A., Bunza, M.D., Anka, S.A., Imam, A.U., Nataala, S.U.: Prevalence and risk factors associated with malaria infection among pregnant women in a semi-urban community of North-Western Nigeria. Infect. Dis. Poverty **4**, 24 (2015)

21. Oyeyemi, A.O., Alawode, A., Sogunro, R.: Ownership and utilization of LLIN after LLIN distribution campaign in the South Western State of Nigeria. Malar. J. **9**(Suppl 2), P34 (2010)

22. Noland, G.S., Graves, P.M., Sallau, A., Eigege, A., Emukah, E., Patterson, A.E.: Malaria prevalence, anemia and baseline intervention coverage prior to mass net distributions in Abia and Plateau States, Nigeria. BMC Infect. Dis. **14**, 168 (2014)

23. Afolabi, B.M., Sofola, O.T., Fatunmbi, B.S., Komakech, W., Okoh, F., Saliu, O.: Household possession, use and non-use of treated or untreated mosquito nets in

two ecologically diverse regions of Nigeria-Niger Delta and Sahel Savannah. Malar. J. **8**, 30 (2009)

24. Eteng, M., Mitchell, S., Garba, L., Ana, O., Liman, M., Cockcroft, A.: Socioeconomic determinants of ownership and use of treated bed nets in Nigeria: results from a cross-sectional study in cross river and Bauchi States in 2011. Malar. J. **13**, 316 (2014)

25. Ekeleme, N.C., et al.: Attitudes and practices of insecticide treated bed nets usage among rural dwellers in Oyo State, Nigeria. Int. J. Tropical Dis. Health **44**(15), 43–58 (2023)

26. National Malaria Elimination Programme (NMEP), National Population Commission (NPopC), National Bureau of Statistics (NBS), and ICF International. Nigeria Malaria Indicator Survey 2015. Abuja, Nigeria, and Rockville, Maryland, USA: NMEP, NPopC, and ICF International (2016). https://www.dhsprogram.com/pubs/pdf/MIS20/MIS20.pdf. Accessed 16 June 2022

27. Solanke, B.L., Soladoye, D.A., Birsirka, I.A., Abduraraheem, A., Dalau, O.R.: Utilization of insecticide-treated nets and associated factors among childbearing women in Northern Nigeria. Malar. J. **22**, 184 (2023)

28. Onwujekwe, O., Hanson, K., Fox-Rushby, J.: Inequalities in purchase of mosquito nets and willingness to pay for insecticide-treated nets in Nigeria: challenges for malaria control interventions. Malar. J. **16**(3), 6 (2004)

29. Afolabi, B.M., et al.: Household possession, use and non-use of treated or untreated mosquito nets in two ecologically diverse regions of Nigeria-Niger Delta and Sahel Savannah. Malar. J. **8**, 30 (2009)

30. Roll Back Malaria. Strategies for Enhancing Malaria Prevention Programs (2019). https://endmalaria.org/sites/default/files/RBM%20Annual%20Report%202019.pdf. Accessed 18 May 2022

31. Adebayo, A.M., Akinyemi, O.O., Cadmus, E.O.: Ownership and utilisation of insecticide-treated mosquito nets among caregivers of under-five children and pregnant women in a rural community in southwest Nigeria. J. Prev. Med. Hyg. **55**(2), 58–64 (2014)

Governance Matters! Developing the Foundations for a Transnational Integrated Planning Network

Yannis Paraskevopoulos⬛, Stefanos Tsigdinos⁽✉⁾⬛, Ioannis Chatziioannou⬛, and Efthimios Bakogiannis⬛

National Technical University of Athens, 15780 Zographos, Attica, Greece
distlp@mail.ntua.gr

Abstract. Spatial planning is a dynamic process, continuously evolving throughout the years. As complexity increase and basic needs change, this requires new perspectives in planning considering diverse roles, disciplines, and methods to address spatial, environmental, and societal challenges. Hence, integrated approaches should be at the forefront, building new initiatives that bring all these actors together. This calls for the establishment of wide Network fostering systemic transnational collaboration, under a multi-stakeholder scheme, that considers planning-related HED institutions and relevant practice, policy, research actors, and the planning community in general. Moreover, this network should cultivate an inclusive and active participatory approach in all actions of the network and especially in the knowledge exchange/co-creation/sharing process.

Bearing upon this critical gap, this study will lay the Charter of this Transnational Network developed via a detailed scoping literature review on related endeavours. Thereupon, the organisational model (depicted in the charter) describes the scope, governance, principles, values and activities of the network, as well as the means and processes for systemic knowledge exchange, sharing, and co-creation among its members. This model also explains the procedures for joining the network and how this differs for individuals and organisations.

Establishing a Network for Integrated Planning is a challenging endeavour; however, it is essential for novel planning actions. There is an imperative need for truly realising integrated actions in planning practice and engaging different actors (academia, policymakers, practitioners and citizens). Subsequently, this study comprises an initial step for embracing integrated planning in various scales and dimensions.

Keywords: Integrated Planning · Urban governance · Cooperation · Policy · Network development

1 Introduction

Planning is an ongoing and dynamic process that continuously adapts and evolves over time [1]. With societal needs shifting and urban and environmental complexities intensifying, planning must embrace new perspectives that integrate multiple roles, disciplines, and methodologies [2]. These evolving challenges necessitate a more holistic and collaborative approach to spatial, environmental, and societal issues [3]. Therefore, it is important to prioritise integrated strategies that bring together diverse stakeholders, fostering cross-disciplinary dialogue and cooperation [4].

In response to these pressing demands, the establishment of a broad and inclusive network is essential; one community that promotes systemic, transnational collaboration under a multi-stakeholder framework (similar communities are the International Conference on Computational Science and Its Applications, ICCSA, Interdisciplinary Social Sciences Research Network, etc.). This network should actively engage higher education institutions (HEIs) focused on planning, alongside practitioners, policymakers, researchers, and the wider planning community [5]. By doing so, it can facilitate knowledge-sharing, innovation, and coordinated action across different sectors and geographical boundaries. Furthermore, an inclusive and participatory approach should be embedded in all aspects of the network's activities, particularly in the processes of knowledge exchange, co-creation, and dissemination [6].

Addressing this critical gap, the present study seeks to lay the groundwork for such a Transnational Network through a comprehensive scoping literature review of existing initiatives and related endeavours. More specifically, the objective of this paper is to articulate the conceptual and organisational model of a Transnational Integrated Planning network, reflecting its need and role both in the academic and policymaking realm. This entails a thorough assessment of the existing framework, policies, and operational guidelines governing relevant organisations/associations dealing with urban planning, transport, geography, environment, participatory and evidence-based planning. This review will reveal the key points of existing organisational models, providing a foundation for the development of a robust and comprehensive charter for an Integrated Planning Network.

This charter will function as a helpful tool in guiding the network's future activities. It will outline the vision, mission, and strategic objectives of a Transnational Network. What is more, it will show the structure, roles and responsibilities and define distinct protocols for decision-making. Moreover, it will explicitly underscore membership conditions and the merits of joining the network. Notably, the charter will align with international standards to ensure the network operates efficiently and sustainably. Last, this charter will also be a means for communicating the objectives of the network itself. By developing a coherent organisational framework, this paper aspires to improve stakeholder engagement and foster a collaborative environment that promotes clarity and collaboration.

The remainder of the paper is structured as follows. The second section build the theoretical background including the necessity for a charter in integrated planning. The third section briefly describes the methods followed, while the fourth presents the main results of this study and builds a solid charter for an Integrated Planning Network. Finally, the fifth section discusses the results and illustrates the concluding remarks of this research work.

2 Theoretical Background

Charters or statutes could be deemed as an indispensable element for associations and organisations, underlining the basic objectives and regulations [7]. A "charter" indicates the terms governing the operation of an organisation or association [8]. It is demonstrated that well-functioning governance enhances the trustworthiness of the organisation [9]. Every association requires a charter, which must be drawn up and agreed on common principles by the founding members of the association. In other words, one could stress that a charter is the equivalent of a constitution. Similarly to countries, organisations should adhere to specific regulations and ensure rights and duties to their members. Hereby, there are several key reasons why articulating a solid charter is meaningful for every association and organisation or network [9, 10].

- Clarity of purpose and vision: a charter should present the mission and objectives of the network in a distinct manner, preparing the ground for a common understanding among the members. Transparent procedures contribute to efficient operationalisation of efforts and resources
- Guidance for actions: a charter can formulate the organisational framework of a network including governance, decision-making process and proper procedures for memberships, meetings and activities. To this end, it prepares the appropriate standards.
- Member rights and duties: a charter should demonstrate the rights and obligations of members, ensuring fairness and protection within the network. It safeguards its members against arbitrary decision-making and provides recourse in case of disputes or conflicts.
- Transparency and accountability: By clearly displaying the member rights and duties, as well as the responsibilities of the administrative board, a charter ensures transparent procedures within the network. Based on a cohesive charter, the network can establish key monitoring processes for oversighting every action.
- Legal and formal recognition: a charter is a means for establishing legal recognition to the network, based on the official requirements. It formalises the entity's legal existence and is usually essential for obtaining funding, engaging into contracts, or in other legal transactions.
- Sustainability and continuity: a charter provides a stable framework for the network's operations, promoting continuity over time and achieving a sustainable profile. Through administering procedures that help adapt to different circumstances or needs, makes a charter a so-much needed document for every network.
- Credibility and trust: a well-articulated charter improves the credibility of the network, both internally (members) and externally (stakeholders, public). Credible network structure will ensure integrity and soundness.

To summarise, a charter is an essential document which not only describes the purpose and vision of a network or an organisation, but also articulates the governance structure, regulations, principles that dictate its operation and activities, thus stimulating transparency, continuity and clarity. Bearing upon the importance of delivering a coherent charter for the Transnational Integrated Planning network, this paper explored relevant charters.

3   Methods

This section demonstrates a comprehensive narrative review of charters or statutes established by similar organisations, networks or associations, aiming to illuminate their fundamental principles and elements. This descriptive technique offers a broad understanding of the topic, allowing for a flexible selection of core documents [11–13]. By delving into these documents, we seek to unveil the underlying frameworks governing their operations and endeavours. Through detailed examination, we will elucidate the key points encapsulated within these charters, offering insights into how we can develop a similar charter for our network. This qualitative analysis serves as a basis for understanding the organisational landscapes that steer the selected associations missions. The basic steps of the review process can be found in the next diagram (see Fig. 1).

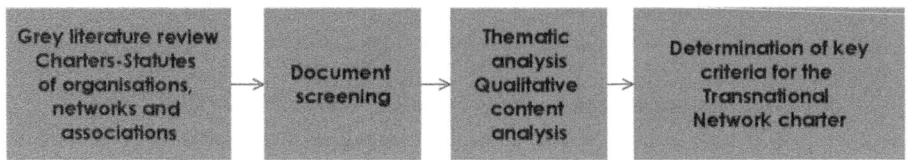

Fig. 1. Basic steps for reviewing relevant charter documents

It should be highlighted that the selected methodology adopts a comprehensive research design to ensure robust findings on relevant charters or statutes. Initially, an extensive review of grey literature meaning charters and statutes of planning related networks, associations and organisations takes place. This process ensures the formulation of a solid document pool that will undergo a detailed screening process, assessing their relevance based on specific fields, language and availability criteria to ensure consistency and applicability. All relevant and available documents will be subjected to a thematic analysis and particularly to a qualitative content analysis for determining key criteria and elements for the new charter.

3.1   Selected Associations and Organisations

In this stage, we selected the associations or organisations to be included in the sample for reviewing their charter documents. These entities should be related to urban, transport, spatial, environmental or participatory planning and they should operate under some basic regulations. The initial sample consisting of 25 documents is displayed in Table 1. Notably, Table 1 provides a comprehensive overview of the selected charters, detailing various aspects including the name, the type and the range of the authoring organisation or association, as well as the membership type, the availability of the document and some general comments on the document.

Concerning the potential values encountered in Table 1, the type of organisation could be professional/advocacy, academic or both. Next, the selected associations are categorised based on their focus or range of operation, i.e., international, national or regional level. The membership type could be individuals, organisations or both. Finally, the availability of the charter documents could be either full, partial or not applicable (in case the document is not found). This detailed breakdown briefly elucidates the structure and key characteristics of relevant charters, providing valuable insights into its operational structure and member engagement strategies.

Table 1. Reviewed charter documents

id	Name	Type	Focus/ range	Membership	Thematic focus	Availability
1	Association of European Schools of Planning AESOP [14]	Academic	European	Organisations Individuals	Planning	Full 10 article groups with 29 articles
2	Association of Geographic Information Laboratories in Europe AGILE	Academic	European	Organisations	Geography	N/A
3	Walk 21 Europe [15]	Professional	International	Individuals	Transport	Full 21 articles with 68 sub-articles
4	European Association of Geographers EUROGEO [16]	Academic Professional	European	Individuals	Geography	Full 11 main articles with 52 sub-articles
5	International Seminar on Urban Form ISUF [17]	Academic	International	Organisations Individuals	Architecture	Full 9 articles
6	Association for European Transport AET [18]	Academic Professional	European	Individuals	Transport	Partial A vision statement and a brief structure
7	Transportation Research Board TRB	Academic Professional	National	Individuals	Transport	N/A
8	International Sociological Association ISA [19]	Academic Professional	International	Organisations Individuals	Sociology	Full 15 articles with 8 bylaws
9	Regional Studies Association RSA [20]	Academic Professional	International	Individuals	Planning	Full 9 main articles with 15 sub-articles
10	International Society of City and Regional Planners ISOCARP [21]	Professional	International	Organisations Individuals	Planning	Full 15 articles

(*continued*)

Table 1. (*continued*)

id	Name	Type	Focus/range	Membership	Thematic focus	Availability
11	International Association of Public Transport UITP [22]	Professional	International	Organisations	Transport	Full 22 Titles with 73 articles
12	Association of African Planning Schools AAPS [23]	Academic	African	Organisations	Planning	Full 11 articles
13	European Platform of Transport Sciences EPTS [24]	Academic	European	Organisations Individuals	Transport	Full 17 articles
14	Institute of Transportation Engineers ITE [25]	Professional	National	Individuals	Transport	Full 11 articles with 62 sections
15	Hellenic Institution of Transportation Engineers SES [26]	Academic Professional	National	Individuals	Transport	Full 15 articles
16	Association of Greek Urban & Spatial Planners SEPOX [27]	Academic Professional	National	Individuals	Planning	Full 6 sections with 15 articles
17	Union of International Associations UIA [28]	Academic Professional	International	Organisations Individuals	Science	Full 5 sections with 15 articles
18	Transport Planning Society TPS [29]	Professional	National	Organisations Individuals	Transport	Full 32 articles
19	American Planning Association APA [30]	Professional	National	Individuals	Planning	Partial A vision statement and strategic goals
20	European Geography Association for students and young geographers EGEA [31]	Academic	European	Individuals	Geography	Full 18 articles
21	European Council of Spatial Planners ECTP-CEU [32]	Academic Professional	European	Organisations Individuals	Planning	Full 6 chapters with 30 articles
22	International Federation of Landscape Architects IFLA-Europe [33]	Academic Professional	European	Organisations Individuals	Architecture	Full 21 chapters with 52 articles

(*continued*)

Table 1. (*continued*)

id	Name	Type	Focus/ range	Membership	Thematic focus	Availability
23	International Council for Local Environmental Initiatives ICLEI [34]	Professional	International	Organisations	Policymakers	Full 8 articles with 37 charters
24	European Network of Living Labs EnoLL [35]	Academic Professional	European	Organisations	Policymakers	Full 4 Titles with 27 articles
25	C40-Cities	Professional	International	Organisations	Policymakers	N/A

Notably, the thematic focus of the examined charters varies greatly; seven different disciplines are represented, ensuring once more a broad range of perspectives and specialisations. The majority belongs to transport and planning (32% and 28% respectively), while science and technology are only 8% (4% each). Afterwards, we reviewed the documents that were fully available. Consequently, 20 documents were included in the final pool of reviewing (Table 1). Most of them (65%) have over 10 sections or main articles.

4   Results

4.1   Literature Review Findings

Hereupon, we proceed with the main findings related to the structural elements of the proposed Charter. In reviewing the relevant charters, we identified four core categories that encapsulate the foundational elements necessary for establishing a robust and effective network: a) Mission, b) Content, c) Governance, and d) Logistics, as depicted in the following conceptual diagram (Fig. 2). Each category comprises key structural elements that collectively ensure the network's comprehensive and efficient operation.

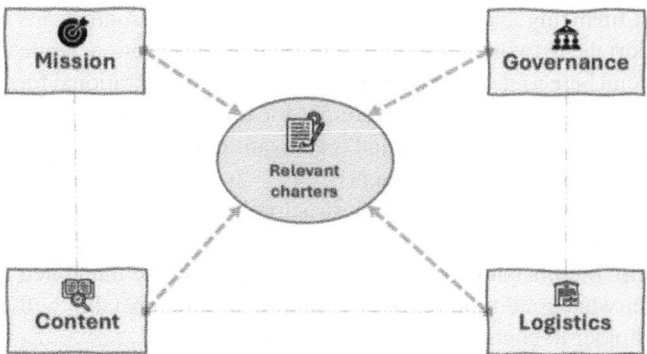

Fig. 2. Core categories for an Integrated Planning Network charter

Mission: The mission of any network is its driving force, providing a clear sense of purpose and direction. In the context of our study, the mission encompasses the network's vision, objectives, principles, and type of organisation. Vision portrays the strategic aspiration of the network, in other words what is the new ethos that the network tries to promote. Objectives detail the specific goals the network aims to achieve, guiding all activities and initiatives. Principles reflect the core values and ethical standards upheld by the network, ensuring consistency and integrity. The type of organisation defines the nature and scope of the network, outlining its structural and operational framework. Additionally, membership criteria fall under this category, specifying who can join the network and the terms of their participation, thus fostering the network's commitment to inclusivity and diversity.

Content: This category focuses on the substantive elements that define the network's operational framework. More specifically, it includes the rights and duties of members, providing clarity on the roles and responsibilities within the network. This category also outlines how committees are structured and operate, which is very pivotal for decision-making processes or monitoring. The advisory board, which is another crucial element, provides expert and strategic guidance, thus facilitating the network's effectiveness. Additionally, the procedures for modifying the charter are detailed in this category. Modifying a charter will increase the network's responsiveness to emerging needs and challenges.

Governance: Governing structures and the process of governing per se, are critical for maintaining credibility and transparent operations within the network. This category includes the assembly, which functions as the primary decision-making body, and the regulations that dictate the network's operations. The directorate of the network is responsible for implementing decisions and managing daily activities, properly ensuring alignment with the network's purpose and objectives. Plus, funding and financing mechanisms are integral to this category, since they provide the financial resources necessary not only for fostering, but also expanding the network's activities. This category also stresses the role of advisory boards and committees in supporting all types of governance actions, thereby supporting decision-making processes.

Logistics: This category addresses the practical and administrative aspects truly essential for the network's operation. It includes the name and address of the network, which are the most common identifiers. This category also entails the logistical aspects of funding and financing and has the potential ensure that resources are managed efficiently to support the network's activities. The type of organisation, while also a mission element, is crucial here as it defines the structural and administrative form required for logistic endeavours. Additionally, procedures for joining the network, detailed within this category, outline how individuals and organisations can become part of the network, thereby fostering growth and engagement.

What is more, we identified some key structural elements common in most relevant charters:

Membership: Membership criteria define who can join the Integrated Planning Network and under what conditions. Inclusive and diverse membership will enable a wide range of stakeholder to engage into the network's activities.

Objectives: The objectives present the specific goals that the network aims to achieve. They provide a clear direction for all the network's activities and initiatives, thus ensuring the purpose of the network.

Principles: Principles represent the core values and ethical standards adopted by the network. They guide decision-making processes and actions, ensuring integrity and consistency.

Rights and Duties: This element clarifies the roles and responsibilities of network members. Transparency and accountability can only be ensured, when a network defines clearly what is expected from and what is entitled to each member.

Committees: These are special groups destined to handle specific tasks or topics within the network. Committees facilitate effective decision-making, contributing to the efficient operation of the entire network.

Advisory Board: The advisory board provides expert guidance and oversight. Its role is to support the network's leadership with ideas, insights and recommendations. It could facilitate the network's efficiency.

Modification of Charter: Procedures for modifying the charter ensure that the network remains responsive to upcoming needs and challenges. This element allows for updates and (major or minor) changes to the document representing and governing the network.

Assembly: The assembly reflects the primary decision-making body within the network. It is responsible for major decisions and policies, safeguarding that the network's activities align with its objectives.

Regulations: Regulations are the rules that govern the network's operations. They provide consistency through a coherent but flexible framework for all activities and interactions within the network.

Directorate: The directorate is responsible for implementing decisions and managing daily activities of the network. This element ensures that the network's strategic objectives are translated into practical actions.

Funding-Financing: These elements involve the mechanisms for acquiring and managing financial resources necessary for sustaining the network's activities. Without proper funding the network might not experience growth or even stability.

Type of Organisation: This element defines the structural framework of the network. It outlines the nature and scope of the organisation, providing a clear understanding of its orientation, purpose and actions.

Name: The name is the main identifier of the network. It provides a unique identity, ensuring recognition and differentiation from other entities.

Address: The address serves as the physical or official location of the network. It is essential for administrative purposes and provides a point of contact for stakeholders.

The following table (Table 2) offers a detailed classification of these key structural elements across the four core categories. For instance, membership is crucial both for defining the network's mission and for ensuring a structured content framework. Similarly, funding and financing span governance and logistics, highlighting their dual role in strategic management and operational sustainability. This overlap manifests the interconnected nature of such categories, demonstrating how elements like advisory boards and committees are vital for various aspects of the network's structure.

Table 2. Reviewed charter documents

	Mission	Content	Governance	Logistics
Membership	✓	✓	✓	
Objectives	✓			
Principles	✓			
Vision	✓			
Rights and Duties		✓		
Committees (Thematic, Advisory board and Directorate)		✓	✓	
Modification of charter		✓	✓	
Assembly			✓	
Regulations			✓	
Funding - Financing			✓	✓
Type of Organisation	✓			✓
Name				✓
Address				✓

In case the Transnational Network of Integrated Planning Labs, addresses the afore-mentioned elements properly, then it can ensure a robust organisational and conceptual model. This model not only supports effective knowledge exchange and collaboration among members but also ensures the network's resilience and adaptability in a dynamic environment. The comprehensive framework provided by these categories facilitates a structured yet flexible approach to building and sustaining the network, aligning its strategic objectives with practical operational needs.

4.2 Building a Charter for a Transnational Integrated Planning Network

The proposed Transnational Network should foster innovation, collaboration, and knowl-edge exchange among professionals, academics, and organisations. This section demon-strates the development of a proper charter, which is a rather critical step to ensure a successful operation of a network. Apparently, this charter outlines the vision, mission, structure, and guiding principles of the network, providing a solid foundation for its operations and growth. Before concentrating on the charter itself, we should under-score the key terms and the operational framework that dictate the rationale of such a network focused on Integrated Planning. First and foremost, this Network endeavours to influence higher education ecosystem towards integrated planning by approaching integration under a comprehensive threefold framework:

- *Discipline-based integration*: Highlighting the complementary value of different dis-ciplines relevant to sustainable planning (urbanism, mobility, transport planning, participatory planning, evidence-based planning, urban analytics, social sciences etc.)

- *Method-based integration*: Initiating the dialogue among different approaches and schools of thought involved in planning (quantitative approaches, qualitative approaches, participatory approaches)
- *Role-based integration*: Including the different city-panning knowledge actors (urban education and research, urban practice, urban policy) and the different experiences they provide, as crucial input for creating knowledge towards integrated planning.

The key terms of this charter are: a) Integrated Planning and b) Network.

Integrated Planning reflects a holistic approach to spatial development, combining urban planning, mobility, and participatory processes to ensure sustainable and functional urban communities. Our focus extends beyond traditional rationales where planners acted independently, thus fostering multi-disciplinary collaboration to address the complex challenges of modern cities.

The Transnational Network is a gathering of professionals, academics, policymakers and community leaders connected across various places, but united by a common goal: to initiate the dialogue between the different city planning approaches in terms of disciplines, methods and roles. Through this network, members gain access to a rich reservoir of resources, data, expertise, and collaborative opportunities. The network facilitates active interaction and communication between each member and promotes Integrated Planning principles to the broader community.

The most essential parts (i.e., starters) are shown with red line colour, whereas parts that should be addressed in the future, following the establishment of the network, are illustrated in orange line colour (Fig. 3).

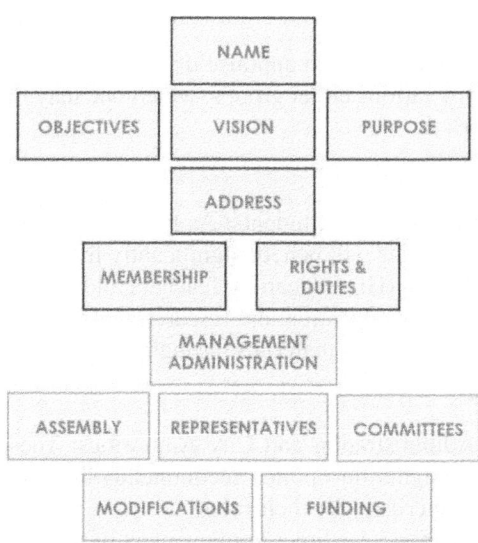

Fig. 3. Structure of the proposed Transnational Network Charter

Hereby, we present each article of the charter. First, we show the most essential parts (8 articles) that should be well-defined by the initiators.

1. Network Name: Transnational Network of Integrated Labs
2. Objectives: The multi-stakeholder network will aim at: a) Systemic transnational collaboration between different Labs, b) inclusive and participatory approach during the Network's activities, c) knowledge co-creation between various planning actors, d) upskilling planning actors on climate-resilient integrated planning, e) cultivating an integrated planning culture and f) a long-term hub bringing together different stakeholders.
3. Vision: The network envisions becoming a leading network of (diverse) labs that pioneers integrated urban planning methods and drives the global agenda for climate-resilient and vibrant cities. Plus, the network endeavours to advance HEd ecosystem knowledge for promoting truly integrated planning. Actually, this planning concept embraces integration based on combining disciplines, roles and approaches (qualitative, quantitative and participatory).
4. Purpose: The purpose of the Transnational Network of Integrated Labs is to facilitate knowledge exchange, research collaboration, and capacity-building activities among member institutions, promoting best practices and innovative solutions in spatial planning, urban planning, and transport planning.

4a. Principles

The network is firmly dedicated to core principles which are the following: Sustainability, Climate Justice, Spatial Justice and Equity, (Active) Participation, Democratic procedures, Knowledge exchange and Inclusiveness. These principles function as a strong guidance for the network's operations and underpin our commitment to an Integrated Planning rationale. The network stands for bringing different actors together under the common vision of making our cities better.

5. Target groups: The project aims to appraise diversity and cooperation; therefore, it addresses the needs of various target groups, which one may find below, categorised in primary and other:

Primary target groups

- City Planning Higher-Education Students: As future practitioners and academics in city planning, these students will benefit significantly from the network's initiatives.
- City Planning Academics (HE Education Teachers and Researchers): These essential actors in city planning education and research will be provided with innovative educational methods, tools, and materials through the network's database.

Other target groups

- Officers in Public Administration and City Authorities: These city planning policymakers will gain insights into policy recommendations and integrated planning applications, which are crucial for their roles.
- City Planning Practitioners: As direct implementers of urban and mobility projects, practitioners will benefit from improved insights into the needs for integrating comprehensive planning in practice.
- Community Members and Associations: Representing a broader group, community members and local associations interested in climate-resilient and integrated planning approaches receive fruitful support from the network. Plus, the network may provide

substantial basic knowledge on integrated planning to these groups and help them engage actively in planning processes.

6. Registered address:
    The administrative headquarters of the network shall be located at a designated office address, as determined by the initiators.
7. Membership: Membership is open to individuals, institutions, associations, organisations and civic society dealing with spatial, urban or transport planning. Our network aims to support diversity by bringing together members coming from different expertise and perspectives. These members could be supported by the network to co-create innovative planning solutions.
8. Rights and Duties:
8a. Rights:

- Participation in Activities: Members have the right to participate in all network activities like seminars or webinars, workshops, and conferences.
- Access to Resources: Members can access several data resources and information shared within the network.
- Collaboration and Synergies: Members can collaborate with other members to develop synergies and support the network's role.
- Plan Communication Events: Members can organise academic and professional events to share their knowledge and best practices.
- Receive Updates: Members will receive the latest news and publications from the network.

8b. Duties:

- Adherence to Policies: Members have to respect the network's principles and ethical guidelines. This will ensure that activities are carried out with integrity and professionalism.
- Contribution to Initiatives and Actions: Members should contribute to various initiatives, working groups, and committees in order to advance the network's objectives.

8c. Desirable contributions:

- Active Participation: Members are expected to actively engage in meetings, projects, initiatives and discussions, (especially) fostering collaboration actions.
- Data Contribution: Members are encouraged to contribute their own data to support the network's initiatives. All data contributions will be reviewed before being included in the Virtual Knowledge Hub by the Executive Committee.

By upholding these rights and duties, members help create a dynamic, inclusive, and effective network dedicated to innovative planning solutions.

Hereupon, we demonstrate the parts that should be decided in advance. We do not only briefly describe these parts, but in some of them we also provide initial thoughts.

9. Management-Administration: The network shall be managed and administered by an Executive Committee, composed of representatives from member institutions. The Executive Committee is responsible for strategic planning, resource allocation, and decision-making processes.
10. Assembly: An annual assembly of members (representatives) shall be convened addressing the following: a) to review the network's activities, b) to discuss key issues, and c) set priorities for the upcoming year or years. The assembly is the central platform for discussion, collaboration, and networking among the members of the network.
11. Representatives: In case of an institution, then a representative shall be appointed to serve as a liaison with the network and participate in meetings and other decision-making events on behalf of their respective institutions. The Members-Representatives are pivotal for the network with key responsibilities such as:

- Representation: Presenting the endeavours of their organisations and (preferably) echoing diverse perspectives in decision-making.
- Annual Meetings: Attending and (if possible) contributing to discussions on strategic decisions or local initiatives.
- Working Groups: Participating in committees dealing with research, policy, member engagement and specific projects.
- Voting Rights: Voting on key issues; for instance, elections of Executive Committee members and approval of projects/actions.

12. Committees: The Executive Committee will establish thematic committees or working groups to address specific topics, initiatives or projects, considering the network's activities and objectives. These committees shall mainly consist of members appointed by the Executive Committee. Nevertheless, they could also include external experts or stakeholders if needed.
12a. Executive Committee: This group is responsible for daily management and oversight of the network. Composed of elected and appointed members, their responsibilities include:

- Strategic Leadership: Setting the strategy, developing long-term plans and monitoring process.
- Policy Development: Formulating policies on membership, ethics, partnerships and financial management.
- Financial Monitoring: Managing financial conditions, preparing budgets and achieving sustainability through fundraising and grants.
- Operational Management: Steering initiatives, supporting the actions of working groups and managing the members of the network.
- Communication and Outreach: Setting communication strategies, managing the website, social media, newsletters and public relations.
- Evaluation and Improvement: Assessing network performance, collecting feedback and making necessary adjustments for improvement.

12b. Thematic committees: These groups focus on specific areas, supporting decision-making and the strategy of the network. Each committee will include diverse experts and stakeholders that will meet specific criteria and will have crystal-clear leadership roles. Their primary responsibilities shall be the following:

- Research and Events: Conducting research, organising events and developing policy recommendations.
- Trend Analysis: Identifying trends, challenges, and opportunities within their topic.
- Collaboration: Working with other committees and external partners to enrich insights and strategies.
- Regular Meetings and Reporting: Meeting regularly, submitting reports and adhering to the network's principles.
- Performance Evaluation: Carrying out regular evaluations and incorporating feedback for continuous improvement.

13. Modification of Articles: Any modification to this charter shall require approval by a two-thirds majority vote of the Executive Committee, followed by ratification by the general assembly of members. Amendments may be proposed by the Executive Committee or by member institutions in good standing, with due consideration given to the network's objectives and principles.
14. Funding-Financing: This is a forthcoming element. Specifically, funding and financing issues should be addressed in the future, following the establishment of the network. Initially, the network will not have the capacity to manage economic resources and funding.

5 Discussion and Conclusions

This deliverable has successfully established a preliminary charter for an Integrated Planning Network by incorporating a comprehensive narrative review of existing charter documents. As a foundational step in the creation of the Transnational Network, this charter is of preeminent importance, as it describes the scope, governance, principles, values, and activities of the network (in line with [7, 36]). However, it does not only outline the operational framework of the network but could also serve as a vital instrument for outreach and engagement, facilitating the dissemination of the Integrated Planning principles within the broader planning community. After all, dissemination is an integral part of any research initiative [37].

The developed charter underscores the democratic identity of the network, highlighting the necessity for integrated planning when it comes to contemporary urban, mobility and environmental challenges [4]. By adhering to the outlined methodology, we ensured that the development process was thorough and inclusive, reflecting a wide range of perspectives and best practices from existing charter documents. Notably, this study lays a solid foundation for future efforts, providing a clear and structured basis for potential members to join and actively participate in such a network. To this end, the authors developed two fundamental tools for accommodating potential members to join the network; a) an open leaflet outlining the key principles and actions of the network and b) a user friendly form enabling registration with the network. Furthermore, the cohesive and participatory structure of the charter ensures that it can effectively guide the network towards its goals of fostering collaborative and integrated planning solutions. Moving on to the target groups, it has been already underlined that this paper aims to foster diversity and cooperation. Consequently, the developed charter targets various groups that will benefit distinctly from the activities of the proposed network. Demarcating explicitly the target groups of planning processes will support the actions of the Integrated Planning Network through an inclusive manner.

The establishment of a Transnational Planning Network reveals significant implications for integrated spatial planning [38]. By fostering a transnational collaboration framework, the network can serve as a prototype for promoting interdisciplinary approaches and ensuring that planning processes consider diverse perspectives. The importance of such a network lies in its capacity to facilitate knowledge exchange and support innovative planning strategies tailored to contemporary urban, transport and environmental challenges. However, making this network a reality requires overcoming key obstacles, such as aligning different planning methodologies and governance structures. The development of the charter was a crucial step in this process, as it obtained insights from multiple existing charters. This process, while invaluable in ensuring solid findings, also presented a notable challenge in terms of interpreting diverse sets of information coming from different organisational frameworks.

Despite the preliminary formulation of the charter, several limitations and areas for future research remain. Additional charters from various associations could further refine the principles and operational mechanisms of the present network, thus, ensuring broader representation. Moreover, a participatory approach in co-creating or periodically updating the charter would enhance its responsiveness to evolving planning needs. Another critical take is the dissemination of the network; strategies should be developed to enhance its visibility and encourage active engagement from policymakers, practitioners, and researchers. Plus, further exploration is needed to clarify the specific benefits the network offers to its members, ranging from knowledge-sharing platforms to policy implications and collaborative projects. These considerations will be crucial for strengthening the network's long-term impact and ensuring its role as a vivid and inclusive space for integrated planning initiatives.

Acknowledgments. Research for this paper benefited from the "InPlaLabs: Transnational Network of Integrated Planning Labs" research project, co-founded by the European Union and the Greek State Scholarships Foundation under the grant agreement No. 2023–1-EL01-KA220-HED-000160477 Erasmus+. Views and opinions expressed, are , however those of the author(s) only and the European Commission's support for the production of this publication does not constitute an endorsement of the contents which reflects the views only of the authors, and the Commission or the Hellenic National Agency cannot be held responsible for any use, which may be made of the information contained therein. InPlaLabs project is implemented by a collaborative group of five partners: National Technical University of Athens, workers' cooperative Commonspace, University of Cyprus, the company Urban Calculator and the social cooperative Bond of Union.

Authors' Contributions. YP devised the main conceptual idea and approach while YP and ST designed the research for developing the InPlaLabs Charter. ST led the work for constructing the InPlaLabs charter and drafted the first version of this article with contributions of YP and IC. EB overviewed this research. All authors provided feedback and reviewed the final manuscript.

Disclosure of Interests. The authors have no competing interests to declare that are relevant to the content of this article.

References

1. Komninos, N., Kakderi, C., Panori, A., Tsarchopoulos, P.: Smart city planning from an evolutionary perspective. J. Urban Technol. **26**(2), 3–20 (2018)
2. Milojevic, B. Integrated planning as a mechanism for creating sustainable and resilient settlements. In: Anguillari, E, Dimitrijevic, B. Integrated urban planning directions, resources and territories, pp. 037–061. TU Delft Open (2018)
3. Sadeghi, A.R., Khakzand, M.: Environmental planning and management of urban natural landscapes. Int. J. Hum. Capital Urban Manage. **1**(3), 209–220 (2016)
4. Vigar, G.: Towards an integrated spatial planning? Eur. Plan. Stud. **17**(11), 1571–1590 (2009)
5. Anacker, K.B.: The evolution of the four eras of urban planning education in the United States. J. Plan. Educ. Res. **44**(4), 2294–2304 (2023)
6. Tiwari, P., Mathur, M.: Knowledge mapping on environmental health in context of city planning. J. Scientometric Res. **13**(2), 625–635 (2024)
7. Anwar-McHenry, J., Donovan, R.J.: The development of the perth charter for the promotion of mental health and wellbeing. Int. J. Ment. Health Promot. **15**(1), 58–64 (2013)
8. Institute, T.: Great Transition Initiative Visions and Pathways for a Hopeful Future. When the World Rules Corporations, Pathway to a Global Corporate Charter (2010)
9. Enjolras, B.: A governance-structure approach to voluntary organizations. Nonprofit Volunt. Sect. Q. **38**(5), 761–783 (2008)
10. von Schnurbein, G.: Patterns of governance structures in trade associations and unions. Nonprofit Manage. Leadersh. **20**(1), 97–115 (2009)
11. Baumeister, R.F.: Writing a literature review. In: Prinstein, M.J., Patterson, M.D., (eds.) The Portable Mentor: Expert Guide to a Successful Career in Psychology, pp. 119–132. Springer (2013)
12. Siddaway, A.P., Wood, A.M., Hedges, L.V.: How to do a systematic review: a best practice guide for conducting and reporting narrative reviews, meta-analyses, and meta-syntheses. Ann. Rev. Psychol. **70**, 747–770 (2019)
13. Ferrari, R.: Writing narrative style literature reviews. Med. Writing **24**(4), 230–235 (2015)
14. AESOP: Association of European Schools of Planning Charter (2019)
15. Walk21 Europe: Akte van oprichting stichting (2020)
16. EUROGEO: Statutes (2013)
17. ISUF Homepage. https://urbanform.org/isuf-constitution/. Accessed 19 Mar 2025
18. AET: 2020 Vision and Action Plan (2012)
19. ISA: Statutes of the International Sociological Association (2014)
20. RSA: Memorandum of Association of the Regional Studies Association (2006)
21. ISOCARP: Amendment to Articles of Association (2018)
22. UITP: Bylaws of International Association of Public Transport (2022)
23. AAPS: Constitution of the Association of African Planning Schools (2012)
24. EPTS: Statutes of the Association EPTS Foundation e.V. (2018)
25. ITE: Constitution (2017)
26. SES: Katastatikon Syllogou Ellinon Sygkoiniologon SES (1978)
27. SEPOX: Katastatiko Schedio (1998)
28. UIA: Structure and Statutes (2005)
29. TPS: Articles of Association of The Transport Planning Society Ltd (2006)
30. APA Homepage. https://www.planning.org/mission/. Accessed 19 Mar 2025
31. EGEA: Statutory Base (2009)
32. ECTP-CEU Homepage. https://ectp-ceu.eu/about-us/statutes-statuts/. Accessed 19 Mar 2025
33. IFLA-Europe: Statute (2022)
34. ICLEI: Charter (2011)

35. EnoLL: Memorandum of association-assignment (2010)
36. Meck, S.: Growing Smart Legislative Guidebook. Routledge, Model Statutes for Planning and the Management of Change (2020)
37. Marín-González, E., Malmusi, D., Camprubí, L., Borrell, C.: The role of dissemination as a fundamental part of a research project: lessons learned from SOPHIE. Int. J. Health Serv. **47**(2), 258–276 (2016)
38. Rode, P.: Urban planning and transport policy integration: the role of governance hierarchies and networks in London and Berlin. J. Urban Aff. **41**(1), 39–63 (2017)

Application of Machine-Learning Techniques for Water Quality Assessment in Coastal Environments: A Case Study of the Jacarepaguá Lagoon System at Rio de Janeiro/BR

Dannylo Cardoso Mauricio[1], Jader Lugon Jr[2], André Merlo[1],
Mayara Omai[1], Pedro Henrique González[3], Raphael Guerra[4],
Wagner Telles[4], and Diego Brandão[1(✉)]

[1] Federal Center for Technological Education of Rio de Janeiro, Rio de Janeiro, Brazil
{dannylo.mauricio,andre.merlo}@aluno.cefet-rj.br,
{mayara.omai,diego.brandao}@cefet-rj.br
[2] Federal Fluminense Institute, Niterói, Brazil
jaderlugon@iff.edu.br
[3] System Engineering and Computer Science Program, Federal University of Rio de Janeiro, Rio de Janeiro, Brazil
pegonzalez@cos.ufrj.br
[4] Federal Fluminense University, Niterói, Brazil
{rguerra,wrambaldi}@id.uff.br

Abstract. Coastal environments, such as beaches, canals, and estuaries, are ecologically vital, supporting diverse species and regulating the interface between continental and oceanic systems. Despite their importance, these ecosystems face growing threats from anthropogenic activities that compromise their environmental balance. In this context, data-driven approaches such as machine learning offer promising tools for monitoring and managing water quality. However, many existing studies focus on limited indicators and often overlook temporal and spatial dynamics. This study addresses these gaps by applying machine-learning models to assess water quality in the Jacarepaguá Lagoon System, a complex of four interconnected lagoons in Rio de Janeiro, Brazil. While the analysis centered on biochemical oxygen demand (BOD), future work will incorporate additional indicators such as turbidity and dissolved oxygen, and adopt temporal modeling strategies. The models developed achieved a mean squared error of $17(\text{mg/L})^2$, constrained by the sparsity of monitoring data. These findings underscore both the potential and limitations of current predictive approaches and highlight the need for more comprehensive and continuous data collection to support evidence-based environmental management.

Keywords: Estuaries · Water Quality · Machine learning · Computational Modeling

O. Gervasi et al. (Eds.): ICCSA 2025, LNCS 15650, pp. 295–306, 2025.
https://doi.org/10.1007/978-3-031-96962-1_20

1   Introduction

Coastal environments—such as beaches, estuaries, and lagoon systems—play a vital ecological and socio-environmental role by supporting diverse aquatic and terrestrial species and regulating hydrological dynamics between continental water bodies and the oceans [1–3]. These ecosystems are also crucial for human activities, including fisheries, tourism, and urban development. However, increasing anthropogenic pressures—such as industrial effluent discharge, untreated domestic sewage, and unplanned urban expansion—have resulted in severe environmental degradation [4,5]. Coastal water contamination reduces biodiversity, degrades water quality, and poses serious public health risks, undermining local communities and ecosystem resilience.

One of the most critical consequences of this degradation is eutrophication, driven by excessive nutrient inputs—particularly nitrogen and phosphorus—which can lead to harmful algal blooms (HABs), oxygen depletion, and the collapse of aquatic ecosystems [6]. This issue is especially prevalent in coastal lagoon systems, where rapid urbanization has intensified pollution in estuarine zones [7]. In this context, water quality monitoring is essential to assess pollution levels and guide mitigation strategies in alignment with the United Nations Sustainable Development Goals (SDGs)—notably Goal 6 (Clean Water and Sanitation), which promotes improved water quality and wastewater management, and Goal 14 (Life Below Water), which emphasizes the conservation and sustainable use of marine and coastal ecosystems [8].

Although accurate, conventional water quality assessment methods rely on periodic field sampling and laboratory analysis, which are resource-intensive, time-consuming, and often unable to provide real-time data [9]. Computational modeling has emerged as a complementary approach, enhancing environmental data analysis and enabling trend prediction [7,10–14]. In particular, machine learning (ML) techniques have demonstrated considerable potential in environmental applications by supporting data-driven decision-making and delivering more accurate forecasts [11,15].

This study evaluates and compares the performance of machine learning models for predicting water quality parameters in the Jacarepaguá Lagoon System (JLS)—a complex of interconnected lagoons located in Rio de Janeiro, Brazil. The methodology begins with an exploratory data analysis (EDA) to examine the distribution, trends, and interrelationships among key water quality variables. Subsequently, multiple ML models—including Artificial Neural Networks (ANN), Support Vector Regression (SVR), Decision Tree Regressor (DTR), and Random Forest Regressor (RFR)—are trained and evaluated using the Mean Squared Error (MSE) metric to quantify predictive accuracy. Results indicate that data scarcity substantially limits model performance, increasing error rates and reducing reliability. These findings highlight the critical importance of high-resolution, continuous environmental monitoring to support the development of accurate, ML-based predictive models for water quality management.

The remainder of this paper is structured as follows: Sect. 2 presents the theoretical framework, discussing water quality assessment methods and machine learning applications. Section 3 details the methodology, including data collection, preprocessing, and model selection. Section 4 reports the results of the ML model comparison and discusses the findings. Finally, Sect. 5 concludes with final remarks and recommendations for future research.

2   Theoretical Framework

Assessing water quality in coastal environments is a multidisciplinary challenge that combines conventional environmental monitoring with computational intelligence to enhance predictive capabilities and decision-making. This section reviews the foundational concepts of water quality assessment, focusing on applying machine learning (ML) techniques in recent studies.

2.1   Water Quality and Environmental Impact

Coastal lagoons and estuarine systems are key in maintaining biodiversity and regulating hydrological cycles. However, these environments are particularly susceptible to anthropogenic pressures, such as untreated domestic and industrial effluents, unregulated urbanization, and land-use changes [5]. One of the most severe consequences of water pollution in such systems is *eutrophication*—a process triggered by excessive nutrient loading (notably nitrogen and phosphorus), leading to algal blooms, oxygen depletion, and the degradation of aquatic ecosystems [6].

Water quality is typically assessed through parameters such as Dissolved Oxygen (DO), Biochemical Oxygen Demand (BOD), pH, turbidity, total phosphorus, and thermotolerant coliforms. These indicators provide critical insights into the level and sources of pollution and potential ecological risks [9].

The deterioration of coastal water bodies is a global concern addressed in the United Nations Sustainable Development Goals (SDGs). Specifically, **SDG 6 (Clean Water and Sanitation)** aims to improve water quality and expand access to wastewater treatment. In contrast, **SDG 14 (Life Below Water)** promotes the conservation and sustainable use of marine and coastal ecosystems [8].

2.2   Traditional Methods for Water Quality Monitoring

Traditional water quality monitoring relies on field sampling and laboratory analysis, often guided by environmental standards set by institutions such as the Instituto Estadual do Ambiente (INEA) and the National Environmental Council (CONAMA) [17–19]. Although these methods produce high-precision results, they are resource-intensive, limited in temporal resolution, and often unable to capture rapid changes in water conditions.

To address these limitations, computational models—particularly hydrodynamic models—have been employed to simulate physical, chemical, and biological processes in aquatic systems [20]. However, these models typically require large, high-quality datasets and substantial computational resources, limiting their real-time or large-scale monitoring applicability.

2.3   Machine Learning Techniques for Water Quality Prediction

Recent advances in Machine Learning have created new possibilities for improving water quality assessments' accuracy, scalability, and responsiveness. ML models can handle high-dimensional data, identify complex patterns, and provide robust predictions based on historical and real-time inputs [7]. Several ML techniques have been successfully applied to water quality modeling, including:

- **Artificial Neural Networks (ANNs)**: Inspired by biological neural systems, ANNs consist of interconnected neurons arranged in layers. These models are particularly effective in capturing non-linear relationships among variables and have been used for predicting BOD, DO, pH, and nutrient concentrations [9,16].
- **Support Vector Machines (SVMs)**: SVMs perform classification or regression tasks by finding optimal hyperplanes in feature space. Variants using kernel functions—such as linear, polynomial, and radial basis function (RBF)—can model non-linear interactions between environmental variables with high accuracy [7].
- **Decision Trees (DTs) and Random Forests (RFs)**: DTs are rule-based models that segment data into decision paths, making them intuitive and interpretable. RFs aggregate multiple DTs using bootstrap aggregation (bagging), improving robustness and reducing overfitting. These models are widely used in ecological modeling for predicting parameters such as turbidity and nutrient concentrations [7].
- **Gradient Boosting Machines (GBMs)**: GBMs are ensemble methods that build a sequence of weak learners (typically decision trees), where each new model attempts to correct the errors of the previous ones. Algorithms like XGBoost and LightGBM have shown excellent predictive accuracy in environmental modeling, especially in datasets with missing values and complex feature interactions.
- **k-Nearest Neighbors (k-NN)**: A non-parametric method based on proximity in feature space, k-NN has been applied in water quality classification tasks. While simple and interpretable, its performance can degrade in high-dimensional spaces or with noisy data.
- **Deep Learning Architectures**: Deep learning extends ANNs by introducing multiple hidden layers and non-linear activation functions. For example, convolutional Neural Networks (CNNs) and Recurrent Neural Networks (RNNs) have been used with satellite imagery and time series data to model spatiotemporal variations in water quality.
- **Hybrid and Ensemble Models**: Recent studies have explored hybrid architectures that combine ML models (e.g., ANN-SVR or RF-ANN), as well as ensemble techniques such as stacking and voting, to improve robustness and generalization in water quality forecasting tasks.

Integrating these machine learning models into water quality monitoring systems offers significant advantages, including real-time analysis, automated anomaly detection, and predictive modeling under data-scarce conditions. This research applies such approaches to the Jacarepaguá Lagoon System, aiming to support evidence-based management and align with global sustainability objectives using intelligent, data-driven methods.

2.4 Jacarepaguá Lagoon System

The region of Jacarepaguá Lagoon System (JLS) is located in the West Zone of Rio de Janeiro, Brazil, encompassing rapidly urbanizing neighborhoods such as Barra da Tijuca, Jacarepaguá, and Rio das Pedras. Since the 1970s, this region has undergone substantial demographic expansion, with its population nearly tripling over the past few decades. The JLS consists of a complex network of interconnected coastal lagoons—Lagoa da Tijuca, Lagoa de Jacarepaguá, Lagoa do Camorim, and Lagoa de Marapendi—which are hydrologically connected and influenced by both freshwater inputs (e.g., rivers and stormwater runoff) and tidal exchanges with the Atlantic Ocean via the Joatinga Canal, as presented in Fig. 1. As the primary drainage basin for several densely populated urban areas, the JLS plays a vital ecological and infrastructural role by supporting diverse aquatic biodiversity and mitigating flood risks. However, the system faces significant environmental pressures due to accelerated urbanization, unregulated land occupation, and insufficient wastewater management. These factors have intensified water quality degradation, underscoring the importance of continuous environmental monitoring and sustainable urban planning to conserve this sensitive coastal ecosystem.

3   Methodology

The first practical stage of the research was to collect historical data on water quality monitoring in the JLS (Fig. 1), taken from INEA's indoor monitoring raw data spreadsheet, available on the agency's website [17–19].

We checked which parameters had the lowest rate of temporal discontinuity, resulting in 10 potential variables as presented in Table 1. Of these, 9 were selected as predictive variables (features), and the remaining (BDO) was determined as a target variable. In addition to the water quality data, maximum rainfall data was collected in the lagoon system region at five different time intervals: 15 min, 1 h, 4 h, 24 h, and 96 h. This data was obtained from the Sistema Alerta Rio website for the Barrinha station closest to the ocean. The rainfall data was merged with the water quality data using a standardized reference time. As all the data collected by INEA occurred after 5 a.m., this was the time selected to extract the rainfall data and append it to the other data.

Next, an initial analysis of the data involved the Cluster Analysis (CA) process using the k-means method. The aim was to establish groups containing the collection points based on the similarity between each parameter. Outliers were

Source: INEA (2013).

Fig. 1. Lagoons and data collect point in JLS.

identified and removed using Tukey's method. The data preprocessing procedure is detailed in the flowchart shown in Fig. 2.

For the modeling stage, initial models were selected based on those most frequently used in recent studies on computational modeling applied to coastal water quality assessment, along with experimental models developed in the context of this research. The selected models included Artificial Neural Networks (ANN) [9], Support Vector Regressor (SVR) [7], Decision Tree Regressor (DTR), and Random Forest Regressor (RFR). Considering the diversity of ANN and SVM specializations, these were subdivided into two and three variations, respectively. For neural networks, both a simple linear regression model and a deep learning model with multiple layers were created. For the SVM-based models, three kernels were used: Linear, Polynomial, and Radial Basis Function (RBF). Table 2 presents the list of models and their corresponding training hyperparameters.

Before training, the data was normalized using min-max scaling to avoid bias among variables. After rescaling, the dataset was split into training and testing sets, with 90% of the data used for training and 10% reserved for testing the model predictions and evaluating their performance. The metric used to assess model performance was the Mean Squared Error (MSE), computed as the mean of the squared prediction errors.

The training focused on the data point with the highest parameter dynamics, aiming to evaluate the models under the most complex scenario. Thus, Point 1—near the Joatinga Canal—was selected for model training.

Table 1. List of Features

n	Parameter	Abbreviation	Unity	Source
1	Dissolved Oxygen	DO	mg/L	INEA
2	Total Phosphorus	TF	mg/L	INEA
3	Turbidity	–	UNT	INEA
4	Conductivity	CE	(µS/cm)	INEA
5	Ortho-Phosphate Dissolved	OPD	mg/L	INEA
6	Coliforms	CT	NMP/100 mL	INEA
7	pH	–	–	INEA
8	Water Temperature	T	Celsius	INEA
9	Maximum Precipitation in (time range)	PM	mm	AlertaRio
10	Biochemical Oxygen Demand	BOD	mg/L	INEA

Each was trained over 50 generations using randomly sampled data to establish a comparative criterion among models. The Mean Square Error (MSE) was used to evaluate the methods presented in Eq. 1, and central tendency statistics were calculated. At the end of each generation, the model with the lowest MSE was assigned a point. After all generations were completed, a final ranking was produced based on the accumulated scores, listing the models in descending order of performance.

$$\text{MSE} = \frac{1}{n} \sum_{i=1}^{n} (y_i - \hat{y}_i)^2 \tag{1}$$

where n is the size of the sample, in the units of observed (y_i) and predicted $(\hat{y}_i)$ values.

4   Numerical Results

The analyses performed during the research were carried out using the Python 3.12 programming language, equipped with libraries for carrying out the necessary operations: *NumPy* for algebraic operations, *Scipy* and *Statistics* for tests and statistical operations, *Scikitlearn* and *Keras by Tensorflow* for training the models and numerical analysis.

Three groups were defined for the cluster analysis based on the elbow method. After model fitting, the total variance among centroids was 1256.92. Figure 3 presents the 3D scatter plot of the principal components (PCs), with data points colored according to their respective clusters.

Once the data points were assigned to clusters, a percentage distribution table of the sampling points was generated, showing results consistent with their spatial distribution.

The dendrogram in Fig. 4 illustrates a well-defined cluster separation. Points 1 and 2 (orange), closest to the ocean, form a distinct group with high inter-cluster Euclidean distance relative to the other points (green) but low distance

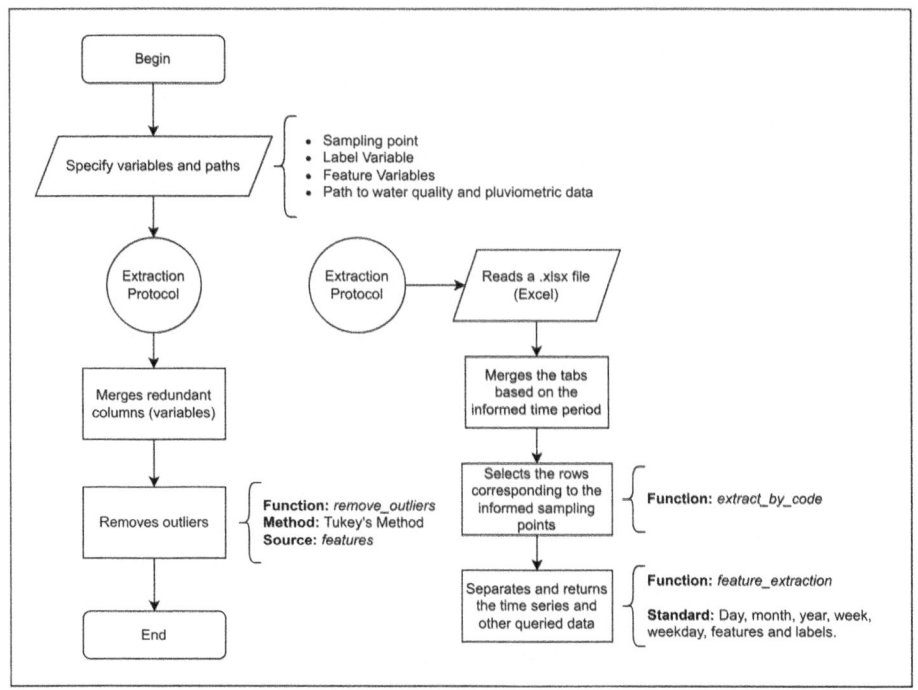

Fig. 2. Data preprocessing procedure.

between themselves. Points 6 and 3 were the most similar among the inland points, likely due to their proximity to river mouths and canals that discharge effluents into the system. Point 5, located in the Camorim Lagoon, showed moderate divergence from Points 6 and 3 in the same group, possibly explained by its morphology, which favors pollutant accumulation.

Point 4, in turn, formed an isolated third group due to its distinct behavior. Located in the central region of the lagoon system, it exhibited mixed characteristics—typical of ocean water and domestic sewage contamination—such as elevated conductivity. This singular combination of features led to its classification as an outlier in the clustering analysis.

Statistical validation through the Mann-Whitney U test for Points 1 and 2 yielded significant results, as did the Kruskal-Wallis test for Points 3, 5, and 6, showing p-values greater than 0.95, indicating strong internal consistency within these groups. No similarity test was applied to the third group, as it consisted solely of Point 4.

The seven models were trained over 50 generations using randomly sampled datasets. The performance analysis revealed clear trends, as summarized in Table 3.

SVR-based models showed consistent performance, particularly SVR-L ($\bar{x} \approx 17.2 \pm 11.4$) and SVR-P ($\bar{x} \approx 21.1 \pm 13.0$). In contrast, SVR-RBF underper-

Table 2. Models and training hyperparameters.

Name	Abv.	Architecture/Hyperparameters
Basic Neural Networks	BANN	Sequential model with 2 processing layers; Perceptrons: (16-1); Activations: (elu-selu); Optimizer: Adam
Deep Neural Networks	DANN	Sequential model with 2 processing layers; Perceptrons: (128-(Dropout 0.25)-64-16-1); Activations: (tanh-elu-selu-relu); Optimizer: Adam
Support Vector Regressor - Linear	SVR-L	Default configuration from the *sklearn* library
Support Vector Regressor - Polynomial	SVR-P	Default configuration from the *sklearn* library
Support Vector Regressor - RBF	SVR-RBF	Default configuration from the *sklearn* library
Decision Tree Regressor	DTR	Max Depth: Length of the training data vector; Min Samples Split: Total data vector length divided by 12
Random Forest Regressor	RFR	Number of Estimators: 64

Table 3. Model performance statistics over 50 iterations.

–	MSE			
Nome	Score	$\bar{x}$	std	Max	Min
DTR	15	17.0	12.6	54.6	3.6
SVR-L	14	17.2	11.4	54.9	1.8
RFR	7	29.0	23.2	92.3	1.6
SVR-P	7	21.1	13.0	55.2	1.7
DANN	4	29.0	18.2	90.0	0.8
SVR-RBF	3	42.9	32.7	196.9	7.6
BANN	0	70.3	38.4	168.8	7.8

formed, with the highest maximum MSE and the second largest standard deviation. The Decision Tree Regressor (DTR) achieved the best overall performance ($\bar{x} \approx 17.0 \pm 12.6$), with a score slightly higher than SVR-L. However, DTR also presented a higher minimum error, suggesting less consistency in lower-error scenarios.

Random Forest Regressor (RFR) ranked third ($\bar{x} \approx 29.0 \pm 23.2$), but its overall score was significantly lower than SVR-L. Neural network-based models exhibited suboptimal results. BANN performed the worst across all metrics and received no score. DANN matched RFR in mean MSE but demonstrated slightly lower variance ($\bar{x} \approx 29.0 \pm 18.2$). Figure 5 presents the MSE trajectory of each model across the 50 generations.

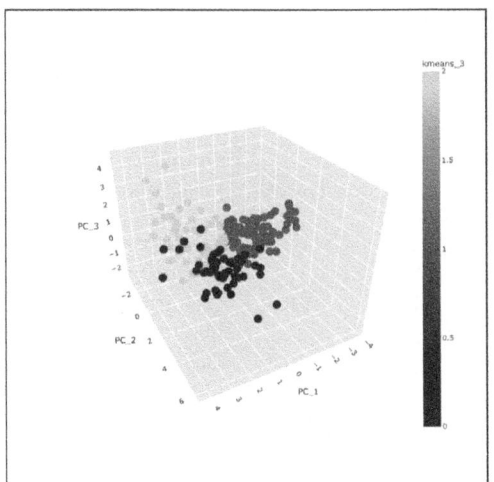

Fig. 3. 3D scatter plot of principal components and clusters.

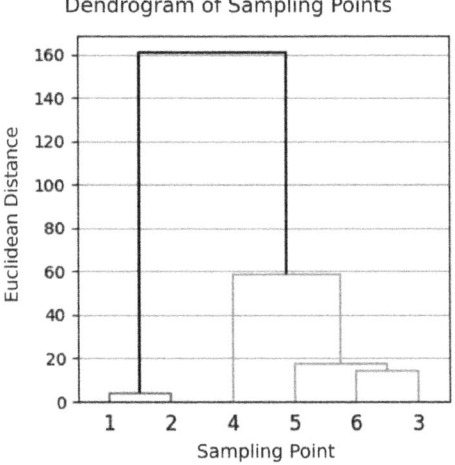

Fig. 4. Dendrogram of cluster group percentages.

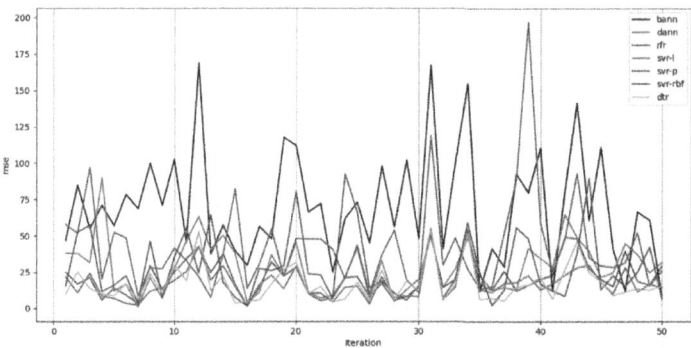

Fig. 5. Mean Squared Error (MSE) of models across 50 iterations.

5   Final Remarks

Monitoring water quality in estuarine environments is essential for sustainable urban development and aligns closely with the United Nations Sustainable Development Goals, particularly SDG 6 (Clean Water and Sanitation) and SDG 11 (Sustainable Cities and Communities). This study presented a preliminary approach to assessing water quality in the Jacarepaguá Lagoon System (JLS), using Biochemical Oxygen Demand (BOD) as the target variable.

Several machine learning models were evaluated, including Decision Tree Regressor (DTR), Random Forest Regressor (RFR), Support Vector Regressors with different kernels (SVR-L, SVR-P, SVR-RBF), and neural network-based models (DANN and BANN). Among them, the DTR model achieved the best performance, with a Mean Squared Error (MSE) of approximately $17\,(\text{mg/L})^2$.

While the initial results are encouraging, we acknowledge key limitations such as data scarcity, reliance on a single target variable, and the absence of spatial and temporal modeling. To address these issues, future work will incorporate remote sensing data, apply data augmentation techniques, and expand the analysis to include additional water quality indicators (e.g., turbidity and dissolved oxygen). We also plan to employ advanced models capable of capturing spatiotemporal dynamics, such as Long Short-Term Memory (LSTM) networks, and evaluate performance using more comprehensive metrics like F1-score and R^2.

These enhancements aim not only to improve predictive accuracy and model robustness but also to provide actionable insights that support evidence-based environmental management and policymaking.

Acknowledgement. The authors would like to thank the following Brazilian Agencies: CAPES and the National Council for Scientific and Technological Development - CNPq. DB thanks Fundação Carlos Chagas Filho de Amparo à Pesquisa do Estado do Rio de Janeiro (FAPERJ) for the financial support through grants E-26/210.798/2024. PHG thanks Federal University of Rio de Janeiro (23079.227622/2023-70), National Council for Scientific and Technological Development - CNPq (307663/2021-3) and

Fundação Carlos Chagas Filho de Amparo à Pesquisa do Estado do Rio de Janeiro - FAPERJ (E-26/201.341/2022) for the financial support.

References

1. Chacón Abarca, S., et al.: Understanding the dynamics of a coastal lagoon. Geosciences **11**(8), 301 (2021)
2. Silva, R., et al.: A framework to manage coastal squeeze. Sustainability **12**(24), 10610 (2020)
3. de Araújo, A., et al.: General system architecture and COTS prototyping of an AIoT-enabled sailboat. IEEE IoT J. **11**(3), 3801–3811 (2024)
4. Pinto, F.P., et al.: Seasonal assessment of water quality in Mirim Lagoon. Anais da ABC (2020)
5. Ferrão-Filho, A., Moscatelli, M.: Recreational risk associated with the presence of cyanobacteria (in Portuguese). SciELO Preprints (2020)
6. Preece, E.P., et al.: A review of microcystin detections. In: Harmful Algae, pp. 31–45 (2017)
7. Sun, Z., Fan, Y.: A combined water quality prediction model using Spark. In: Aqua (2022)
8. Carlsen, L., Bruggemann, R.: The 17 United Nations' sustainable development goals. Int. J. Sust. Dev. World Ecol. **29**(3), 219–229 (2022)
9. Zhou, J., et al.: Water quality prediction using IGRA and LSTM. Water **10**, 1148 (2018)
10. Telles, W.R., et al.: Modeling surface waterflood with MOHID. In: Mathematics, Computers and Environment, pp. 125–143 (2019)
11. de Andrade Costa, D., et al.: Water quality estimates using ML. J. Hydroinf. **26**(11), 2798–2814 (2024)
12. de Oliveira, M., et al.: Mathematical modelling in microplastic research. Environ. Rev. **33**, 1–18 (2025)
13. Asadollah, S., et al.: Dissolved organic carbon estimation in lakes. Water Res. **277**, 123350 (2025)
14. Banerjee, S., et al.: Sensitivity of parameters in modeling hydrological services. Model. Earth Syst. Environ. **11**(4), 1–16 (2025)
15. Costa, D., et al.: Water quality estimates using machine learning techniques in an experimental watershed. J. Hydroinf. **26**(11), 2798–2814 (2024). https://doi.org/10.2166/hydro.2024.132
16. Zhou, J., et al.: Water quality prediction method based on IGRA and LSTM. Water **10**(9) (2018)
17. Instituto Estadual do Ambiente (INEA): Consolidated Water Quality Report for the Jacarepaguá Lagoons (2022). (in Portuguese). https://www.inea.rj.gov.br/wpcontent/uploads/2022/05/Lagoas-JPA-Consolidado-2020-2021.pdf
18. Instituto Estadual do Ambiente (INEA): Bathing Water Quality Bulletin – RJ (2024). (in Portuguese). https://www.inea.rj.gov.br/wpcontent/uploads/2024/02/Zona-oeste-e-Zona-sul-15-02-24.pdf
19. Instituto Estadual do Ambiente (INEA): Monitoring of Inland Waters (2024). (in Portuguese). https://www.inea.rj.gov.br/ar-agua-e-solo/como-e-feito-o-monitoramento-das-aguas-interiores/
20. Lamparelli, M.C.:Lamparelli, M.C.: Trophic States in Water Bodies of the State of São Paulo (in Portuguese). Ph.D. thesis, University of São Paulo (2004). https://www.teses.usp.br/teses/disponiveis/41/41134/tde-20032006-075813/pt-br.php

PHD Showcase Papers

CFD Prediction of Slot Jet Impingement Heat Transfer

Rossella D'Addio$^{(\boxtimes)}$ (ID), Antonio Mezzacapo (ID), and Giuliano De Stefano (ID)

Engineering Department, University of Campania Luigi Vanvitelli, 81031 Aversa, Italy
rossella.daddio@unicampania.it

Abstract. This work numerically investigates the heat transfer characteristics of a wide-slot jet impinging orthogonally on an isothermal hot plate. The case study consists of an incompressible turbulent jet flow with a Reynolds number of 11000. Two-dimensional Reynolds-averaged Navier–Stokes (RANS) simulations are performed utilizing three different turbulence closures, namely, realizable k-ϵ, k-ω SST, and the recently developed generalized k-ω (GEKO) models. Diagnostics include air flow characteristics, as well as surface pressure and local Nusselt number distributions. The influence of using production limiters to mitigate the excessive generation of turbulent kinetic energy in the stagnation region is addressed by means of detailed comparisons against reference experimental findings. The various models capture the pressure distribution on the plate with good accuracy. As far as classical approaches are concerned, the realizable k-ϵ model significantly overestimates heat transfer due to excessive turbulent diffusion, whereas the k-ω SST model provides much better agreement with experiments. Moreover, the default GEKO parameters are found to inadequately represent the flow physics of the slot jet configuration. To address this limitation, two alternative sets of model coefficients are proposed, which provide better results.

Keywords: Computational fluid dynamics · slot jet impingement · RANS equations · Nusselt number · two-equation eddy-viscosity models · generalized turbulence modeling · production limiters

1 Introduction

Impinging jets are frequently employed in various industrial applications for the purpose of transferring energy and mass. Examples of such applications include the cooling of electronic devices, the utilization of thermal spray jets in manufacturing processes, the operation of launch platforms, the function of jet deflectors, as well as their use in extra-terrestrial landings and in the context of V/STOL (vertical and/or short take-off and landing) aircraft [1]. Nguyen et al. [2] noted that jet flow physics might be influenced by several geometric parameters, namely the diameter of the nozzle exit, the distance from the nozzle to the wall, and the angle of inclination of the plate [3].

© The Author(s), under exclusive license to Springer Nature Switzerland AG 2025
O. Gervasi et al. (Eds.): ICCSA 2025, LNCS 15650, pp. 309–324, 2025.
https://doi.org/10.1007/978-3-031-96962-1_21

On the one hand, the true reproduction of the jet flow physics in experimental studies is very demanding. To analyze the aerodynamic field, several experimental campaigns have been performed, for either supersonic or subsonic jets. For example, Nakai et al. [4] studied the jet flow structures by means of Schlieren images, while Senter and Solliec [5] used the particle image velocimetry (PIV) technique. In addition, experimental measurements of heat transfer have been largely addressed in subsonic jet impingement. For example, Gardon and Akfirat [6] used transducers with high spatial resolution to measure the jet heat transfer characteristics. On the other hand, with the increase of computational power, computational fluid dynamics (CFD) is being largely used to study the eddy structures in turbulent jet flows. For example, Tsubokura et al. [7] performed a numerical study to understand how inlet disturbances may affect the eddy structures, while Hattori and Nagano [8] numerically studied the effects of the impingement distance on the jet heat transfer using direct numerical simulation (DNS). Although DNS data have sometimes been used to evaluate the performance of lower-order turbulence models [9], however, the Reynolds-averaged Navier-Stokes (RANS) approach remains the most widely used to obtain rapid results of engineering interest, e.g. [10]. Several studies with different RANS turbulence models have been performed to assess their capability to reproduce the Nusselt number distribution on the plate. For example, Bovo et al. [11] performed steady-state and transient simulations with different turbulence models. According to their findings, the large-eddy simulation (LES) approach is able to reproduce the turbulent structures with a high degree of accuracy. As far as RANS models are concerned, the k-ϵ model is not sufficiently accurate in predicting heat transfer in the impingement zone, while the k-ω appears more accurate.

In this context, the primary objective of this work is to study the heat transfer characteristics of an impinging slot jet using modern turbulence models. Actually, as standard models have been widely validated, e.g. [12], and their limitations across various flow regimes are well documented, this study focuses on the recently developed generalized k-ω (GEKO) model, including a customized set of parameters. Recently, this model was demonstrated to provide acceptable predictive accuracy for circular jets [13]. Herein, in contrast to conventional circular jet configurations, the wide slot jet setup is chosen for its ability to promote a more uniform heat transfer distribution across the impingement surface, making it particularly suitable for applications requiring consistent thermal management, e.g. [14]. In addition, the influence of Kato-Launder and production limiters, which play a crucial role in predicting the Nusselt number distribution, is investigated. As highlighted by Gurgul et al. [15], RANS models often fail to accurately predict heat transfer due to excessive production of turbulent kinetic energy, especially in the near-wall region. These discrepancies are strongly affected by uncertainties in boundary conditions, turbulence modeling choices, and geometric configurations.

Assessing the ability of modern turbulence models to accurately predict jet impingement heat transfer is crucial for various engineering applications where stagnation flow regions influence pressure drag and aerodynamic efficiency, affecting fuel consumption and structural integrity. Additionally, in high-speed flows, such as in turbomachinery or spacecraft reentry applications, stagnation flow regions can lead to excessive thermal loads and material erosion. In this applied CFD work, numerical simulations are performed with fixed nozzle-to-plate distance and Reynolds number, and the obtained results are compared with the experimental data available in the literature. The effect of various turbulence models, with and without limiters, is investigated. As all models show good capabilities in predicting the Nusselt number peak and reproducing the experimental trend of velocity and pressure fields, the Nusselt number distribution is approximated with various degrees of accuracy by the different models.

The remainder of the paper is organized as follows. In Sect. 2, the physical model for the jet flow under investigation is introduced, including the mean flow governing equations and the turbulence closures. Section 3 provides the overall computational model, including the numerical settings and the boundary conditions. The main results of the simulations are given and discussed in Sect. 4, while some concluding remarks are offered in Sect. 5.

2 Physical Model

2.1 Case Study

The present applied CFD work investigates the steady incompressible jet flow issuing from a finitely long nozzle with constant section. The reference configuration can be found in the experimental works by either Gardon and Akfirat [6] or Senter and Solliec [5] that were performed with wide slot nozzles. Practically, the case study consists of a two-dimensional air jet impinging orthogonally on an isothermal plate at a fixed distance. Here, the nozzle-to-plate distance is set to $6D_j$, where D_j is the inlet duct diameter, according to reference experimental [6] and numerical [16] works.

The jet flow Reynolds and Mach numbers are defined as follows:

$$Re = \frac{\rho V_j D_j}{\mu}, \tag{1}$$

$$Ma = \frac{V_j}{\sqrt{\gamma R T_j}}, \tag{2}$$

where V_j is the inlet velocity, and T_j stands for the inlet temperature. Due to expected small temperature variations [17], the thermophysical properties of air are considered constant, with the prescribed values summarized in Table 1. Therefore, given and known the inlet conditions provided in Table 2, the above two flow parameters take the values $Re = 11000$ and $Ma = 0.044$, respectively.

The turbulent jet impingement heat transfer is analyzed in terms of local Nusselt number distribution along the cooled wall. This non-dimensional parameter is defined as follows:

$$Nu = \frac{\dot{q} D_j}{\lambda (T_w - T_j)}, \tag{3}$$

Table 1. Constant thermophysical properties of air.

Density ρ, kg/m³	Heat Capacity C_p, J/(kg·K)	Thermal Conductivity λ, W/(m·K)	Dynamic Viscosity μ, Pa·s
1.225	1006.43	0.0242	1.7894×10^{-5}

Table 2. Inlet boundary conditions.

Boundary type	Values
Velocity inlet	$V_j = 16.25\,\text{m/s}$; $T_j = 338\,\text{K}$; 9% turbulent intensity

where $\dot{q}$ is the heat transfer, with λ representing the thermal conductivity.

The pressure distribution on the plate and the heat transfer coefficient predicted by the present numerical calculations are compared against the experimental data in [6], obtained for the same nozzle-to-plate distance of $6D_j$ at the same Reynolds number. In addition, the mean velocity profiles are compared with the corresponding experimental findings in [5], which were observed for a nozzle-to-plate distance of $8D_j$ at a slightly different Reynolds number, namely $Re = 10600$.

2.2   Governing Equations

Due to the particular jet configuration under investigation, the mean turbulent flow can be assumed to be two-dimensional. In the steady RANS framework, the mathematical equations governing the mean incompressible jet flow can be written as follows:

$$\frac{\partial U_i}{\partial x_i} = 0, \tag{4}$$

$$\frac{\partial}{\partial x_j}(U_i U_j) = -\frac{1}{\rho}\frac{\partial P}{\partial x_i} + \frac{\partial}{\partial x_j}\left(2\nu S_{ij} - \overline{u_i' u_j'}\right), \tag{5}$$

$$\frac{\partial}{\partial x_i}(U_i \Theta) = \frac{\partial}{\partial x_i}\left(a\frac{\partial \Theta}{\partial x_i} - \overline{u_i' \Theta'}\right). \tag{6}$$

They represent the resolved transport equations for mass, momentum, and energy, respectively. In the above equations: U_i ($i = 1, 2$) correspond to (U,V) that are the mean velocity components; P is the mean pressure; Θ is the mean temperature. Moreover, ρ and ν are the constant density and kinematic viscosity of the fluid, while a stands for its thermal diffusivity. The mean strain rate tensor components are given by:

$$S_{ij} = \frac{1}{2}\left(\frac{\partial U_i}{\partial x_j} + \frac{\partial U_j}{\partial x_i}\right). \tag{7}$$

The RANS equations contain unknown terms that are expressed in terms of velocity fluctuations (u_1', u_2') and temperature fluctuations Θ', specifically

Reynolds stresses $\overline{u_i'u_j'}$ and turbulent heat flux components $\overline{u_i'\Theta'}$, which need to be modeled. As such, additional equations are necessary to model the turbulence closure in the mathematical model.

2.3   Turbulence Closure

In the present study, the performances of three different RANS turbulence models are evaluated, namely: realizable k-ϵ, k-ω SST (shear-stress transport) and generalized k- ω (GEKO) models. All these two-equation eddy-viscosity models use the following approximation for the Reynolds stresses:

$$\overline{u_i'u_j'} = -2\nu_t S_{ij}, \tag{8}$$

where ν_t represents the turbulent viscosity that is the model parameter. Two additional equations are solved to determine the eddy viscosity field, corresponding to the transport equations for turbulent kinetic energy (k) and dissipation (ϵ) or specific dissipation $(\omega = \epsilon/k)$. These equations, which are not reported here for brevity, can be found, for instance, in [18].

As far as the turbulent heat flux is concerned, the following approximation is used:

$$\overline{u_i'\Theta'} = -a_t \frac{\partial \Theta}{\partial x_i}, \tag{9}$$

where a_t represents the turbulent diffusivity. The latter parameter is determined by relying on the turbulent Prandtl number Pr_t, defined as:

$$Pr_t = \frac{\nu_t}{a_t}, \tag{10}$$

which is assumed constant.

The realizable k-ϵ represents an improved version of the original k-ϵ model, designed to enhance accuracy in flow cases involving strong streamline curvature, vortices and rotational effects. The adjective "realizable" refers to its ability to satisfy the positivity of normal stresses and Schwarz inequality for shear stresses. In particular, Shih et al. [19] improved the eddy viscosity formulation by using a revised dissipation equation, effectively addressing the round jet anomaly observed in the standard k-ϵ model [20]. The k-ω SST model was specifically designed to improve the prediction of flow separation under adverse pressure gradients by incorporating transport effects into the eddy-viscosity formulation.

The GEKO model represents a very recent version of the k-ω model [21]. It features six adjustable coefficients that allow users to fine-tune the modeling procedure without affecting the fundamentals calibrations for basic flows. Among these coefficients, two parameters are intended for wall-bounded flow, other two for free shear flow, one for corner flow simulation, and one for curvature correction, e.g. [22]. The various parameters of GEKO model are summarized in Table 3, together with the associated controlling function, recommended range of variation, and default value. Specifically, the parameters C_{sep} and C_{nw} are defined for wall-bounded flows, while C_{mix} is actually computed from C_{sep};

C_{corner} and C_{curv} are used for the corner flow correction and the curvature correction, respectively, while C_{jet} is a parameter which controls the accurate prediction of jet flows.

Table 3. GEKO model parameters.

Parameter	Controlling	Range	Default
C_{sep}	Separation behavior	0.7–2.5	1.75
C_{nw}	Near wall behavior	−2.0–2.0	0.5
C_{mix}	Spreading rate of free shear flows	0.5–1.0	C_{mix}^{opt}
C_{jet}	Free jet flows	0.0–1.0	0.9
C_{corner}	Corner flows	0.0–1.5	1.0
C_{curv}	Curvature correction	0.0–1.5	1.0

3 Applied CFD Model

3.1 Computational Domain

A schematic view of the two-dimensional computational domain is reported in Fig. 1, where $(x, y) \equiv (x_1, x_2)$ represent the wall-parallel and wall-normal directions, respectively. The spatial extents of the domain are explicitly indicated, with the impacted wall corresponding to $y = 0$, while $x = 0$ coincides with the duct axis. In particular, the rectangular domain extends up to $40D_j$ in the wall-parallel direction to avoid the influence of outlet boundary conditions on the core region of the impinging jet flow. The inlet duct has a length of $20D_j$, in order to ensure a fully developed velocity profile at the exit duct section.

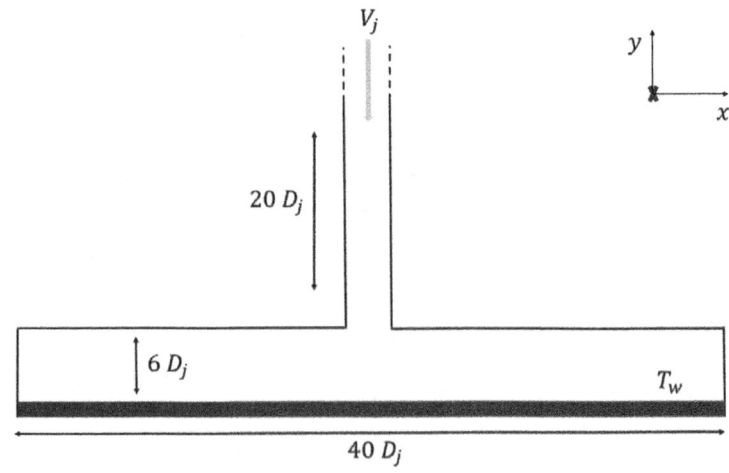

Fig. 1. Schematic view of the computational domain (not in scale).

3.2 CFD Solver

The present numerical simulations are performed by employing the commercial CFD software ANSYS Fluent 2022 R2, which is based on the Finite Volume (FV) approach for incompressible flow, e.g. [23]. The steady RANS governing equations are supplied with suitable boundary conditions. Specifically, the no-slip boundary condition is applied to the solid walls. At the nozzle inlet, a velocity-inlet boundary condition is imposed, while the pressure outlet condition is applied at the outlet boundaries. The outlet and wall boundary conditions are summarized in Table 4.

Due to the incompressible nature of the flow, the SIMPLE algorithm is selected for pressure-velocity coupling, while the gradients are determined using the least squares cell-based method. For the spatial discretization of pressure field, the second-order scheme is chosen. The first-order upwind scheme is used to calculate the momentum, turbulence variables, and energy equation terms. The solution is considered converged when the normalized residual of each variable became less than 10^{-6}.

Table 4. Outlet and wall boundary conditions.

Boundary	Type	Values
Outlet	Pressure outlet, fixed pressure	101325 Pa
Impingement wall	No-slip, fixed temperature	$T_w = 373$ K

3.3 Numerical Mesh

An overview of the numerical mesh is reported in Fig. 2, along with a close-up view in the proximity of the wall impingement zone. The production mesh consists of about forty-two thousand FV cells, with structured elements in the close proximity of the wall, and triangular elements away from the plate. The meshing strategy enables a gradual transition from structured to unstructured mesh elements, effectively reducing the overall computational complexity of the CFD model. Special attention is paid to the height of the first computational cell in the wall-normal direction, which is maintained at the order of $0.01D_j$, which ensures $y^+ \approx 1$.

To address the spatial grid dependence, a mesh convergence study was conducted using the GEKO model, without any limiters. Three different spatial resolutions were employed, namely using 30k (Grid I), 42k (Grid II), and 52k (Grid III) computational cells. The corresponding distributions of Nusselt number are shown in Fig. 3. The medium grid is considered suitable for this work, and was used to generate the results presented in Sect. 4.

4   Results and Discussion

The results of the present simulations allow to assess the capability of the novel GEKO model for incompressible impinging jet flow. Differently from both realizable k-ϵ and k-ω SST models, representing classical approaches to turbulent flow simulation, the modern GEKO model enables fine-tuning and optimal adjusting of the turbulence closure through free model coefficients, e.g. [22]. The default values of GEKO model coefficients, namely those reported on the last column of Table 3, are initially used for the current CFD analysis. Notably, the terms

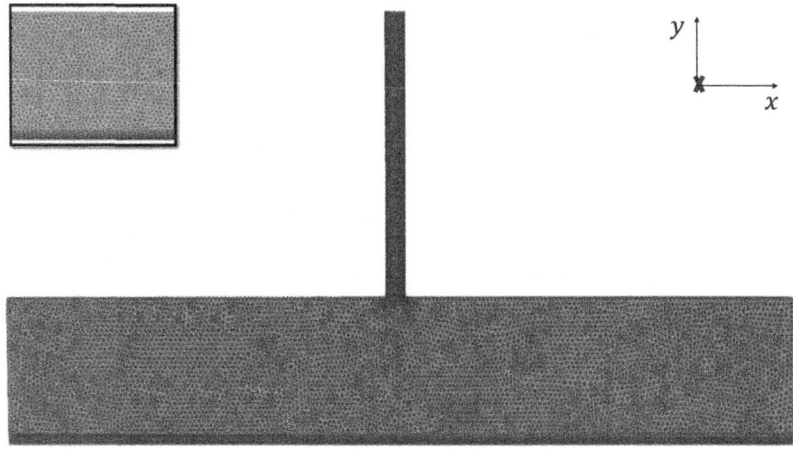

Fig. 2. Sketch of the computational grid, with zoomed-in picture of the wall region.

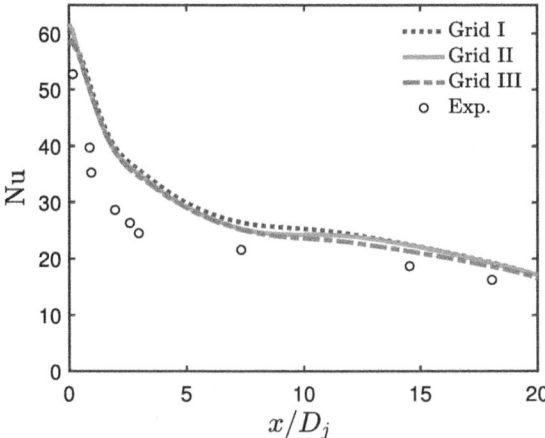

Fig. 3. Nusselt distribution for GEKO solution with varying numerical resolution, compared to experimental data [6].

involving the corner and curvature corrections are neglected. Regardless of tubulence modeling, the value of 0.85 is prescribed for the turbulent Prandtl number.

Table 5. Turbulence models and optional limiters.

Model	Options
Realizable k-ϵ	Production limiter, enhanced wall treatment
k-ω SST	Production Kato–Launder, production limiter
GEKO	Production Kato–Launder, production limiter

In RANS calculations, turbulence production limiters are often needed to prevent excessive turbulence generation in regions with strong streamline curvature, stagnation, or strong strain rates. As such, the influence of Kato-Launder and production limiters on the predicted Nusselt number is also investigated. The different modeling approaches are summarized in Table 5.

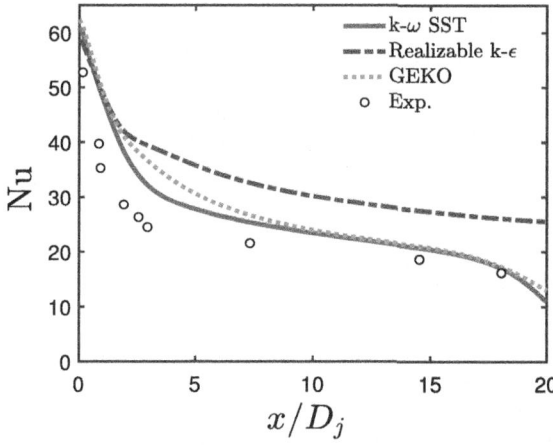

Fig. 4. Nusselt number distribution for different turbulence models without using any limiters, compared to experimental data [6].

Figure 4 shows the Nusselt number distribution along the impingement plate for the three different turbulence models, without using any limiters, compared against experimental measurements [6]. Figure 5 shows the same data obtained by activating both Kato-Launder and production limiters for k-ω SST and GEKO, whereas only the production limiter option is enabled for realizable k-ϵ. From inspection of these pictures, it is possible to observe that all the turbulence models tested follow the general trend of the experimental data, yet with varying degree of accuracy. The k-ω SST and GEKO models show a better

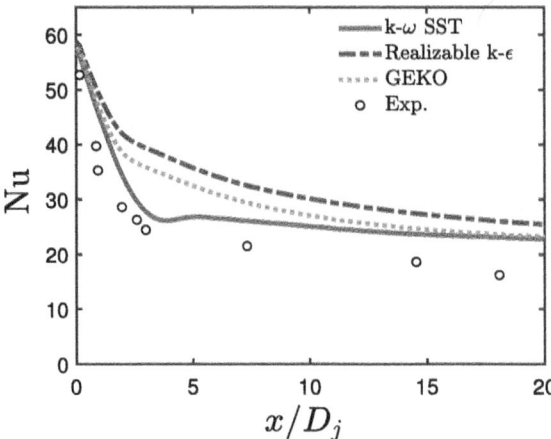

Fig. 5. Nusselt number distribution for different turbulence models with using limiters (see Table 3), compared to experimental data [6].

agreement with the experimental values, particularly in the region close to the stagnation point $(x/D_j < 5)$. However, further downstream, these models tend to overpredict heat transfer, especially the realizable k-ε model, which shows significant discrepancies throughout the plate surface. This model systematically overestimates the Nusselt number, being unable to correctly predict the turbulence structure and energy dissipation in the impinging jet configuration. When correction limiters are enabled, the agreement with experimental data improves significantly, particularly for the k-ω SST and GEKO models. Apparently, the k-ω SST procedure accurately captures the sharp drop in the Nusselt number in the downstream region, showing the best overall correlation with the experimental findings. However, the GEKO model still overpredicts the Nusselt number distribution along the plate, but shows an improved trend compared to the limiter-free case. Finally, the realizable k-ε model continues to struggle in matching the experimental data, indicating that even using limiters, this model does not represent the best choice for predicting heat transfer in impinging slot jets, confirming previous findings [15].

The current results show that the default GEKO parameters are not optimal for heat transfer jet applications. Recently, Yüksekdağ et al. [13] conducted a research on the variations of the GEKO parameters in incompressible round jet impingement. The best agreement with the experimental findings was obtained with the values reported in Table 6, where $C_{nw,sub}$ and $C_{bf,t}$ are two auxiliary parameters. Specifically, $C_{nw,sub}$ is used to modify the log-layer shift to either laminar or turbulent regime, while $C_{bf,t}$ is a parameter linked to the blending function (which is used to deactivate C_{mix} and C_{jet} inside the boundary layer).

The effect of using these additional coefficients is illustrated in Fig. 6, showing the Nusselt number distribution for the two different sets of parameters, with and without using limiters. In both cases, the results of the default GEKO parameters

Table 6. Values of GEKO parameters.

Parameter	Value
C_{sep}	1.1
C_{nw}	2
C_{mix}	−0.7 (constant value)
C_{jet}	0.9
C_{corner}	disabled
C_{curv}	disabled
$C_{nw,sub}$	2.25
$C_{bf,t}$	3.0

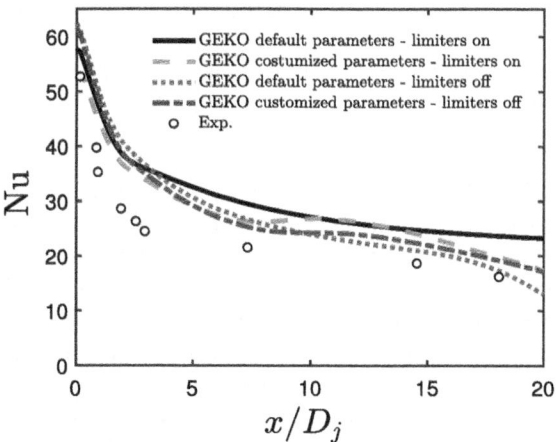

Fig. 6. Nusselt number distribution for different settings of GEKO model parameters with and without using limiters, compared to experimental data [6].

and the newly calibrated GEKO are plotted alongside the experimental values. When considering the Nusselt number peak in the stagnation flow region, the use of customized GEKO parameters and production limiters provides results more aligned with the experiments, suggesting improved predictive performance. However, despite this improvement, both sets of parameters overestimate the Nusselt number in regions further downstream. Basically, as the new GEKO parameters provide a better match to experimental results when limiters are applied, further refinements are however necessary to address overestimation in the outer flow regions.

The pressure distribution along the plate is presented in Fig. 7, normalized by P_0. Making a comparison against reference experimental data [6], the pressure distribution exhibits a maximum value at the stagnation point $(x/D_j = 0)$ due to the direct impact of the jet. This peak is followed by a nearly exponential decay as the flow spreads along the wall-parallel direction, aligning with the

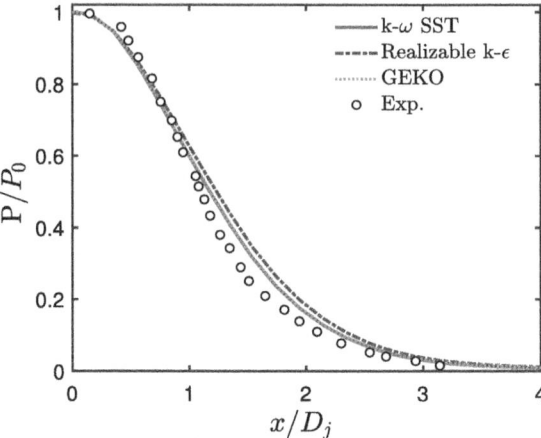

Fig. 7. Normalized pressure distribution over the plate for different turbulence models, compared to experimental data [6].

classical theory of impinging jets [20], as well as experimental findings [24]. This behavior highlights the strong normal pressure gradient in the stagnation region and the subsequent reduction in pressure as the jet transitions into a wall jet. Among the various turbulence models analyzed, the k-ω SST and GEKO models exhibit better agreement against experimental data, particularly near the stagnation point. However, beyond $x/D_j=1$, deviations from experimental values become more pronounced, particularly for the realizable k-ϵ model, which tends to slightly overestimate the pressure away from the impingement region, due to excessive turbulent diffusion. Minor discrepancies between numerical and experimental data might result from the inherent limitations of RANS turbulence models in accurately capturing unsteady vortical structures along the plate, as observed in [25, 26].

Furthermore, the profiles of wall-normal velocity component and velocity magnitude at different locations from the plate are presented in Fig. 8 and Fig. 9, respectively, compared to reference experimental data [5]. Both quantities are normalized using the inlet jet velocity V_j. Importantly, the ability of turbulence models to accurately capture velocity distribution plays a crucial role in predicting heat transfer behavior [27]. All turbulence models appear to provide reasonable predictions of the mean velocity field, particularly at $x/D_j=2$. However, the k-ω SST and GEKO models demonstrate better agreement with the experiment [5], which also leads to improved predictions of both pressure and Nusselt number. However, the realizable k-ϵ tends to underpredict velocity distributions, causing discrepancies in pressure decay and heat transfer predictions. This suggests that the model struggles to fully capture momentum transfer within the jet, likely due to its limitations in handling highly sheared and recirculating flows. Despite these differences, the overall agreement between numerical and experimental results remains acceptable, demonstrating that all the investigated

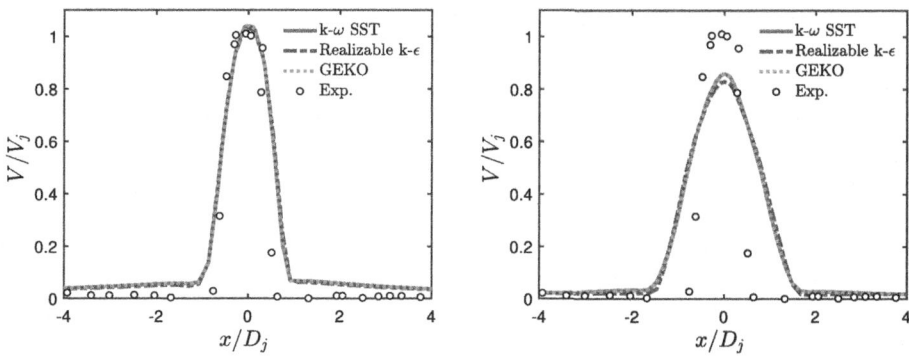

Fig. 8. Profiles of wall-normal velocity component at $y/D_j = 5$ (left) and 2 (right), for different turbulence models, compared against experimental data [5].

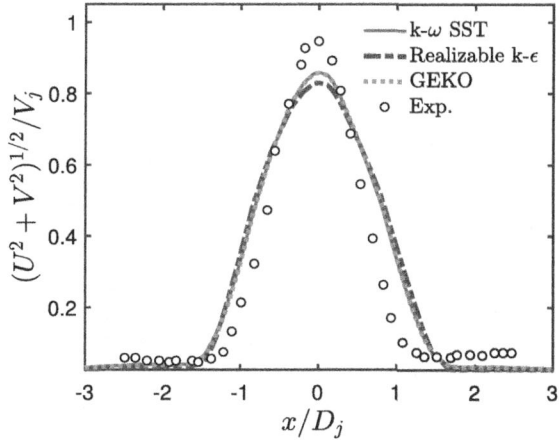

Fig. 9. Profiles of normalized velocity magnitude at $y/D_j = 2$, for different turbulence models, compared against experimental data [5].

turbulence models are generally quite effective in predicting the velocity distribution and spreading characteristics of the impinging jet.

5   Conclusions

This study presents a comparative numerical investigation of heat transfer in a wide slot jet impinging orthogonally on an isothermal flat plate under incompressible flow conditions. Various simulations of the jet cooling process were performed using three RANS-based turbulence models, namely realizable k-ϵ, k-ω SST and the generalized k-ω (GEKO) models. The numerical results were validated against experimental data in terms of Nusselt number distribution, surface pressure profile, and mean velocity fields.

All models accurately captured the pressure peak in the stagnation region, but notable differences emerged in their heat transfer predictions. The realizable k-ϵ model consistently overpredicted the Nusselt number due to excessive turbulent diffusion, making it unsuitable for this particular flow configuration. In contrast, the k-ω SST model showed strong agreement with the experimental data, particularly near the stagnation point. The GEKO model was evaluated either using the default coefficients or employing two alternative sets of parameters. In fact, the default coefficients were found to inadequately represent the physics of the impinging jet flow, leading to an overestimation of the Nusselt number. By modifying key model parameters, including a couple of auxiliary coefficients, which adjust the log-layer behavior and deactivate shear-related terms within the boundary layer, the generalized model achieved substantially better alignment with experimental observations.

Additionally, the implementation of production limiters was shown to improve the accuracy of numerical predictions, particularly in reducing the excessive turbulent kinetic energy generation at the stagnation region, which represents a common limitation in RANS simulations of impinging jets. In summary, while the k-ω SST model performs robustly without calibration, the GEKO model, when suitably tuned, offers enhanced flexibility and potential for accurate heat transfer prediction in jet impingement applications.

Future work will explore the influence of additional parameters on the Nusselt number distribution, assessing the performance of the generalized modeling procedure under diverse flow conditions. Specifically, further investigations will focus on testing the accuracy of the GEKO model in jet flow configurations involving a moving plate and different nozzle-to-plate distances, to evaluate the generalizability of the results and the robustness of the model under dynamic conditions. The analysis will be performed by also exploring more advanced turbulence models, such as detached-eddy simulation (DES), delayed detached-eddy simulation (DDES), and wall-modeled large-eddy simulation (WMLES), e.g. [28–30], where surface roughness effects could possibly be addressed [31].

Acknowledgments. The authors acknowledge financial support under the National Recovery and Resilience Plan (NRRP), Mission 4, Component 2, Investment 1.1, Call for tender No. 104 published on 2.2.2022 by the Italian Ministry of University and Research (MUR), funded by the European Union – NextGenerationEU – Project 2022B2X937 Title "Next Generation Space Propulsion Design Techniques" – CUP E53D23003080006 - Grant Assignment Decree No. 961 adopted on 30.6.2023 by MUR.

Disclosure of Interests. The authors have no competing interests to declare that are relevant to the content of this article.

References

1. Jiang, C., Han, T., Gao, Z., Lee, C.H.: A review of impinging jets during rocket launching. Prog. Aerosp. Sci. **109**, 100547 (2019)
2. Nguyen, T., Maher, B., Hassan, Y.: Flowfield characteristics of a supersonic jet impinging on an inclined surface. AIAA J. **58**, 1240–1254 (2020)

3. Mezzacapo, A., De Stefano, G.: Computational evaluation of turbulent supersonic jet impinging on inclined plate. Appl. Sci. **14**, 7910 (2024)
4. Nakai, Y., Fujimatsu, N., Fujii, K.: Experimental study of underexpanded supersonic jet impingement on an inclined flat plate. AIAA J. **44**, 2691–2699 (2006)
5. Senter, J., Solliec, C.: Flow field analysis of a turbulent slot air jet impinging on a moving flat surface. Int. J. Heat Fluid Flow **28**, 708–719 (2007)
6. Gardon, R., Akfirat, J.C.: The role of turbulence in determining the heat-transfer characteristics of impinging jets. Int. J. Heat Mass Transf. **8**, 1261–1272 (1965)
7. Tsubokura, M., Kobayashi, T., Taniguchi, N., Jones, W.P.: A numerical study on the eddy structures of impinging jets excited at the inlet. Int. J. Heat Fluid Flow **24**, 500–511 (2003)
8. Hattori, H., Nagano, Y.: Direct numerical simulation of turbulent heat transfer in plane impinging jet. Int. J. Heat Fluid Flow **25**, 749–758 (2004)
9. Jaramillo, J.E., Trias, F.X., Gorobets, A., Pérez-Segarra, C.D., Oliva, A.: DNS and RANS modelling of a turbulent plane impinging jet. Int. J. Heat Mass Transfer **55**, 789–801 (2012)
10. Uddin, N., Kee, P., Weigand, B.: Heat transfer by jet impingement: a review of heat transfer correlations and high-fidelity simulations. Appl. Therm. Eng. **257**, 124258 (2024)
11. Bovo, M., Davidson, L.: On the numerical modeling of impinging jets heat transfer - a practical approach. Numer. Heat Transf. A Appl. **64**, 290–316 (2013)
12. Dutta, R., Dewan, A., Srinivasan, B.: Comparison of various integration to wall (ITW) RANS models for predicting turbulent slot jet impingement heat transfer. Int. J. Heat Mass Transf. **65**, 750–764 (2013)
13. Yüksekdağ, R., Koçak, D., Şentürk, U.: Prediction of heat transfer for a single round jet impingement using the GEKO turbulence model. Int. J. Heat Fluid Flow **109**, 109538 (2024)
14. Cademartori, S., Cravero, C., Marini, M., Marsano, D.: CFD simulation of the slot jet impingement heat transfer process and application to a temperature control system for galvanizing line of metal band. Appl. Sci. **11**, 1149 (2021)
15. Gurgul, S., Fornalik-Wajs, E.: On the measure of the heat transfer performance of RANS turbulence models in single round jet impingement. Energies **16**, 7236 (2023)
16. Aghahani, M., Eslami, G., Hadidi, A.: Heat transfer in a turbulent jet impinging on a moving plate considering high plate-to-jet velocity ratios. J. Mech. Sci. Technol. **28**(11), 4509–4516 (2014). https://doi.org/10.1007/s12206-014-1018-1
17. Isman, M.K., Pulat, E., Etemoglu, A.B., Can, M.: Numerical investigation of turbulent impinging jet cooling of a constant heat flux surface. Numer. Heat Transf. A **53**, 1109–1132 (2008)
18. Wilcox, D.C.: Formulation of the k-ω turbulence model revisited. AIAA J. **46**, 2823–2838 (2008)
19. Shih, T.H., Liou, W.W., Shabbir, A., Yang, Z., Zhu, J.: A new k-ε eddy viscosity model for high Reynolds number turbulent flows. Comput. Fluids **24**, 227–238 (1995)
20. Pope, S.B.: Turbulent Flows. Cornell University, New York (2000)
21. Menter, F.R., Matyushenko, A., Lechner, R.: Development of a generalized k-ω two-equation turbulence model. Notes Numer. Fluid Mech. Multidisc. Des. **142**, 101–109 (2020)
22. Rossano, V., De Stefano, G.: Testing a generalized two-equation turbulence model for computational aerodynamics of a mid-range aircraft. Appl. Sci. **13**, 11243 (2023)

23. De Stefano, G., Denaro, F.M., Riccardi, G.: Analysis of 3D backward-facing step incompressible flows via a local average-based numerical procedure. Int. J. Numer. Meth. Fluids **28**, 1073–1091 (1998)
24. Li, X., Liu, X., Liu, Y., Peng, D.: Experimental study of near-wall underexpanded jet impingement on a flat plate using temperature-insensitive semi-transparent pressure-sensitive paint. Exp. Fluids **61**(11), 1–17 (2020). https://doi.org/10.1007/s00348-020-03068-5
25. Yadav, H., Agrawal, A.: Effect of vortical structures on velocity and turbulent fields in the near region of an impinging turbulent jet. Phys. Fluids **30**, 035107 (2018)
26. Hadžiabdić, M., Hanjalić, K.: Vortical structures and heat transfer in a round impinging jet. J. Fluid Mech. **596**, 221–260 (2008)
27. Liu, L., Ahmed, U., Chakraborty, N.: A comprehensive evaluation of turbulence models for predicting heat transfer in turbulent channel flow across various Prandtl number regimes. Fluids **9**, (2024)
28. De Stefano, G., Vasilyev, O.V.: Hierarchical adaptive eddy-capturing approach for modeling and simulation of turbulent flows. Fluids **6**, 83 (2021)
29. Ge, X., De Stefano, G., Hussaini, M.Y., Vasilyev, O.V.: Wavelet-based adaptive eddy-resolving methods for modeling and simulation of complex wall-bounded compressible turbulent flows. Fluids **6**, 331 (2021)
30. De Stefano, G., Vasilyev, O.V.: "Perfect" modeling framework for dynamic SGS model testing in large eddy simulation. Theor. Comput. Fluid Dyn. **18**, 27–41 (2004)
31. Salomone, T., Piomelli, U., De Stefano, G.: Wall-modeled and hybrid large-eddy simulations of the flow over roughness strips. Fluids **8**, 10 (2023)

Short Papers

Classification of Strawberry Maturity Level from Images Using Supervised Classifiers and Convolutional Neural Networks as Feature Extractors

Érika Kayoko Hamaguti and Fabricio Aparecido Breve$^{(\boxtimes)}$ (iD)

São Paulo State University, Rio Claro, SP 13506-900, Brazil
{erika.k.hamaguti,fabricio.breve}@unesp.br

Abstract. The appearance of strawberries is a crucial factor for both consumers and the fruit processing industry. The visual quality of strawberries is directly related to their degree of ripeness. With the advancement of deep learning, the analysis of strawberry appearance has become more accurate, though these methods still require significant time and computational power. In this article, we analyze the efficiency of hundreds of different combinations of convolutional neural network (CNN) models and supervised classifiers to evaluate the quality of strawberries. We utilized seventy-one CNN models to extract features from strawberry images and applied ten different classifiers to perform the classification. The best results were obtained with CNNs from the ConvNeXt family (ConvNeXtBase, ConvNeXtSmall, and ConvNeXtTiny) and VGG models (VGG16 and VGG19) in combination with Gradient Boosting, Histogram-Based Gradient Boosting, and SVM classifiers, achieving accuracies up to 78% and F1-scores up to 85%. The objective of our study is to help farmers accurately classify the appearance of strawberries in real-world situations. The methods used can facilitate the future development of intelligent strawberry classification systems.

Keywords: Convolutional Neural Network · Machine Learning · Strawberry Classification · Supervised Learning

1 Introduction

Strawberry is a perishable and non-climacteric fruit, meaning it does not ripen after being harvested. It is cultivated worldwide and is very popular for its sweet taste and nutrients. The strawberry growth cycle has three main phases: flowering, fruiting, and ripening. Currently, there is no single standard for determining the ripening stage of strawberries, so farmers still need to inspect them manually, which can be inefficient and time-consuming [21]. Therefore, it is important to develop an automatic system to classify the maturity of strawberries. In recent years, machine learning (ML) has been very successful in agriculture, helping to

O. Gervasi et al. (Eds.): ICCSA 2025, LNCS 15650, pp. 327–335, 2025.
https://doi.org/10.1007/978-3-031-96962-1_22

classify and detect different items by analyzing large volumes of data to identify complex features [34].

Several studies have explored the use of ML and convolutional neural networks (CNNs) for strawberry recognition. For example, Gao et al. [14] used hyperspectral imaging to extract information from strawberry images and Support Vector Machines (SVM) for maturity classification, achieving a ROC greater than 95%. Behera et al. [4] combined LBP, HOG, and GLCM features with K-Nearest Neighbors (KNN), SVM, and Naïve Bayes classifiers to compare the results obtained in papaya maturity classification. The best result found was KNN with HOG, achieving 100% accuracy and a training time of 0.0995 s. Benmouna et al. [6] used Visible/Near Infrared (Vis/NIR) to extract features from images and used artificial neural networks (ANN), SVM, and KNN to classify the maturity of Fuji apples, achieving correct classification rates (CCR) of 89.5%, 95.93%, and 91.68% for ANN, SVM, and KNN, respectively.

Despite various studies, there are still many combinations of CNN models and classifiers that have not been tested to find the best method for recognizing the quality of strawberries. In this article, we analyze seventy-one CNNs combined with ten classifiers to recognize strawberries. We extract deep features with different CNNs and use them in various classifiers to predict the maturity of strawberries.

The rest of the paper is structured as follows. In Sect. 2, we describe the datasets, CNN models, and classifiers used in this study. Section 3 presents the experimental results, including the combinations of CNNs and classifiers that achieved the best accuracy and F1-score. Section 4 discusses specific aspects of the results. Finally, Sect. 5 summarizes the conclusions.

2   Materials and Methods

In the following subsections, we present the datasets, CNN models, and classifiers used in this paper.

2.1   Dataset

The image datasets used in this work are Strawberry-DS[1] [10] and StrawDI_Db1[2] [25]. Strawberry-DS contains 247 RGB images of strawberry plantations with a resolution of 3840×2160 pixels. StrawDI_Db1 contains 3100 images of strawberry plantations with a resolution of 1008×756 pixels. In this work, the images were separated and labeled by an expert as "Harvest" and "Not_harvest", with "Harvest" being images that have at least one strawberry ready for harvesting, and "Not_harvest" being images without strawberries ready for harvesting. For Strawberry-DS, 170 images were labeled as "Harvest" and 77 images were labeled as "Not_harvest". For StrawDI_Db1, 1780 images were labeled as "Harvest" and 1320 images were labeled as "Not_Harvest".

Some examples of images are shown in Fig. 1.

---

[1] Available at https://data.mendeley.com/datasets/z6dtfdpzz8/1.
[2] Available at https://strawdi.github.io.

(a)

(b)

Fig. 1. Example of images from Strawberry-DS and StrawDI_Db1: (a) Images from Strawberry-DS; (b) Images from StrawDI_Db1.

2.2 Convolutional Neural Network (CNN)

Traditional CNN methods are often used to extract features from images [3]. These methods are usually pre-trained on large datasets, such as ImageNet [27], and then applied to other tasks. In our study, we used CNN models as feature extractors to obtain detailed information from strawberry images.

The 71 CNN models we used in this research are shown in Table 1.

2.3 Principle Components Analysis (PCA)

The output from the last convolutional layer of the CNN models is large, with thousands of elements. Therefore, after extracting features from the images with the CNN models, we use the PCA algorithm [23] to reduce its dimensionality. PCA is the most widely used linear dimensionality reduction algorithm. It is able to preserve the maximum variation in the data by performing a linear projection of these data, minimizing the reconstruction error.

In this paper, PCA is applied to preserve from 90% to 99% of variance, in steps of 1%, for all the combinations of the 71 CNN extractors and 10 classifiers, totaling 7100 different configurations used for the Strawberry-DS dataset. For StrawDI_Db1, some CNN models could not be applied

Table 1. CNN Models used as feature extractors in this paper.

Model	Reference
VGG16, VGG19	[29]
ResNet50, ResNet101, ResNet152	[16]
ResNet50V2, ResNet101V2, ResNet152V2	[17]
ResNetRS50, ResNetRS101, ResNetRS152, ResNetRS200, ResNetRS270, ResNetRS350, ResNetRS420	[5]
InceptionV3	[31]
InceptionResNetV2	[30]
DenseNet121, DenseNet169, DenseNet201	[20]
Xception	[9]
MobileNet	[19]
MobileNetV2	[28]
MobileNetV3Large, MobileNetV3Small	[18]
NASNetLarge, NASNetMobile	[35]
EfficientNetB0, EfficientNetB1, EfficientNetB2, EfficientNetB3, EfficientNetB4, EfficientNetB5, EfficientNetB6, EfficientNetB7	[32]
EfficientNetV2B0, EfficientNetV2B1, EfficientNetV2B2, EfficientNetV2B3, EfficientNetV2S, EfficientNetV2M, EfficientNetV2L	[33]
RegNetX002, RegNetX004, RegNetX006, RegNetX008, RegNetX016, RegNetX032, RegNetX040, RegNetX064, RegNetX080, RegNetX120, RegNetX160, RegNetX320, RegNetY002, RegNetY004, RegNetY006, RegNetY008, RegNetY016, RegNetY032, RegNetY040, RegNetY064, RegNetY080, RegNetY120, RegNetY160, RegNetY320	[26]
ConvNeXtTiny, ConvNeXtSmall, ConvNeXtBase, ConvNeXtLarge, ConvNeXtXLarge	[22]

due to insufficient RAM in the tested platform. These models are Xception, NASNetLarge, RegNetY160, RegNetY320, InceptionV3, DenseNet201, ResNetRS152, ResNetRS200, ResNetRS270, ResNetRS350, ResNetRS420, EfficientNetB0, EfficientNetB1, EfficientNetB2, EfficientNetB3, EfficientNetB4, EfficientNetB5, EfficientNetB6, EfficientNetB7, EfficientNetV2B0, EfficientNetV2B1, EfficientNetV2B2, EfficientNetV2B3, EfficientNetV2S, EfficientNetV2M, EfficientNetV2L, ConvNeXtLarge, and ConvNeXtXLarge. Therefore, for the StrawDI_Db1 dataset, 4300 different configurations were tested.

2.4   Classifiers

Choosing the classifier is an important step, as different techniques can produce varying results with the same data, and selecting the best classifier is essential for obtaining good results. In this study, we chose ten classifiers to predict the ripening stage of strawberries, which are show in Table 2.

Table 2. Classifiers used in this paper.

Classifier	Reference
Support Vector Machine (SVM)	[7]
Linear Support Vector Machine (LSVM)	[11]
Logistic Regression (LR)	[7]
K-Nearest Neighbors (KNN)	[7]
Gaussian Naïve Bayes (GNB)	[7]
Decision Tree (DT)	[7]
Gradient Boosting (GB)	[13]
Histogram-based Gradient Boosting (HGB)	[2]
Random Forest (RF)	[8]
Perceptron	[7]

2.5 Implementation

The free version of Google Colab [15] was used for programming the models. It uses Python version 3 [12] as the programming language and runs the code on Google's cloud infrastructure, meaning the platform provides the computational resources to execute the code without the need for powerful computational resources on the local machine. The RAM is fixed at 12.67GB, but the hardware configuration is defined each time the execution environment is connected. Since the environment can occasionally disconnect and reconnect, execution times were not included as results due to the significant imprecision in execution time. The CNN implementations used are from the TensorFlow package [1], and the classifier implementations are from the Scikit-learn package [24].

3 Results

For each combination of CNN extractor, PCA configuration, and classifier, the training is performed using Cross Validation with 5 folds. First, the models were trained without weight balancing, and then with weight balancing, except for KNN, NB, and GB classifiers because there is no parameter in Scikit-learn for these three classifiers to balance the weights. The performance of each model is evaluated by the averages of accuracy, F1-score, recall, and precision. These evaluation criteria play a critical role in assessing the results of this experiment.

The ten best results obtained for Strawberry-DS are shown in Table 3, and the ten best results obtained for StrawDI_Db1 are shown in Table 4[3]. Based

---

[3] The complete tables with all the results can be viewed at the following link https://bit.ly/3EGoYlB.

on tests conducted on the Strawberry-DS and StrawDI_Db1 datasets, the best combinations found were ConvNeXt family (ConvNeXtBase, ConvNeXtSmall, and ConvNeXtTiny) and VGG models (VGG16 and VGG19) in combination with Gradient Boosting, Histogram-Based Gradient Boosting, and SVM classifiers, achieving accuracy above 72% and F1-scores above 78%.

Table 3. Ten best results for Strawberry-DS. Best accuracy, F1-Score, Recall, and Precision are highlighted in bold.

Techniques	Balanced	PCA	Accuracy	F1-Score	Recall	Precision
VGG16 + GB	No	0.97	0.7796	**0.8512**	0.9118	0.7991
VGG19 + P	No	0.96	0.7592	0.8509	0.9824	0.7517
VGG19 + HGB	Yes	0.90	**0.7837**	0.8468	0.8456	**0.8293**
VGG19 + HGB	No	0.90	0.7796	0.8467	0.8882	0.8120
ConvNeXtTiny + LR	No	0.90	0.7796	0.8449	0.8706	0.8226
VGG19 + GB	No	0.91	0.7714	0.8448	0.9059	0.7932
VGG19 + LR	No	0.93	0.7592	0.8424	0.9294	0.7704
ConvNeXtBase + SVM	Yes	0.94	0.7388	0.8385	0.9706	0.7350
VGG19 + LR	Yes	0.95	0.7510	0.8367	0.9118	0.7697
VGG19 + RF	Yes	0.90	0.7265	0.8358	**1.0000**	0.7184

Table 4. Ten best results for StrawDI_Db1. Best accuracy, F1-Score, Recall, and Precision are highlighted in bold.

Techniques	Balanced	PCA	Accuracy	F1-Score	Recall	Precision
ConvNeXtBase + GB	No	0.91	**0.7694**	**0.8111**	0.8612	0.7666
ConvNeXtBase + HGB	No	0.93	0.7677	0.8105	0.8646	0.7630
ConvNeXtBase + HGB	Yes	0.91	0.7665	0.8067	0.8483	**0.7691**
ConvNeXtBase + SVM	No	0.90	0.7213	0.7965	**0.9494**	0.6861
ConvNeXtSmall + GB	No	0.95	0.7471	0.7921	0.8393	0.7501
ConvNeXtSmall + HGB	No	0.91	0.7442	0.7916	0.8455	0.7443
ConvNeXtSmall + SVM	No	0.90	0.7223	0.7878	0.8978	0.7019
ConvNeXtSmall + HGB	Yes	0.92	0.7458	0.7869	0.8169	0.7593
ConvNeXtTiny + HGB	No	0.91	0.7319	0.7847	0.8500	0.7291
ConvNeXtSmall + SVM	Yes	0.90	0.7326	0.7818	0.8337	0.7361

4   Discussion

Regarding the Strawberry-DS dataset, it is notable that two different families of CNNs, VGG and ConvNeXt, yielded the best results. While ConvNeXt represents the state of the art in CNNs, VGG, proposed over a decade ago, slightly outperformed ConvNeXt in this dataset. Interestingly, 6 of the 10 best results, including the highest F1-score, were obtained without addressing the dataset imbalance.

Conversely, for the StrawDI_Db1 dataset, the ConvNeXt family dominated, indicating that this newer architecture excels with this dataset. Similarly, 7 of the 10 best results, including the highest F1-score, were achieved without addressing the dataset imbalance. It is worth noting that the best accuracy and F1-score were obtained when PCA retained only 91% of the variance. All top results used 95% variance or less, suggesting significant redundancy in the CNN models' outputs.

5   Conclusions

Convolutional neural networks (CNNs) have proven effective in classifying strawberries due to their ability to extract detailed features from images. However, these methods can be influenced by data quality and may not always be robust. Currently, there are no official standards for classifying strawberry ripeness. While human experts can accurately label images, this process can be subjective and time-consuming. To address this issue, we tested various CNN methods as feature extractors alongside supervised classifiers to find the most suitable solution. Our ultimate goal is to assist farmers in accurately classifying strawberry ripeness in real-life situations. We envision developing a system for mobile applications to be used in plantations.

This study analyzed different methods for assessing strawberry appearance quality using neural networks and classifiers. Seventy-one CNNs were used to extract features from strawberry images, which were then analyzed by ten classifiers. The results indicated that the best performance was achieved with the ConvNeXt family (ConvNeXtBase, ConvNeXtSmall, and ConvNeXtTiny) and VGG models (VGG16 and VGG19) in combination with Gradient Boosting, Histogram-Based Gradient Boosting, and SVM classifiers, achieving accuracy above 72% and F1-scores above 78% in all the top ten scenarios for both evaluated datasets. In the best case, an accuracy of 78% and F1-Score of 85% were achieved.

References

1. Abadi, M., et al.: Tensorflow: Large-scale machine learning on heterogeneous systems. https://www.tensorflow.org/. software available from tensorflow.org (2015)
2. Al Adwan, J., Alzubi, Y., Alkhdour, A., Alqawasmeh, H.: Predicting compressive strength of concrete using histogram-based gradient boosting approach for rapid design of mixtures. Civil Eng. Infrastruct. J. **56**(1), 159–172 (2023)
3. Alzubaidi, L., et al.: Review of deep learning: concepts, CNN architectures, challenges, applications, future directions. J. Big Data **8**(1), 1–74 (2021). https://doi.org/10.1186/s40537-021-00444-8

4. Behera, S.K., Rath, A.K., Sethy, P.K.: Maturity status classification of papaya fruits based on machine learning and transfer learning approach. Inf. Process. Agric. **8**(2), 244–250 (2021)
5. Bello, I., et al.: Revisiting resnets: improved training and scaling strategies. Adv. Neural. Inf. Process. Syst. **34**, 22614–22627 (2021)
6. Benmouna, B., García-Mateos, G., Sabzi, S., Fernandez-Beltran, R., Parras-Burgos, D., Molina-Martínez, J.M.: Convolutional neural networks for estimating the ripening state of fuji apples using visible and near-infrared spectroscopy. Food Bioprocess Technol. **15**(10), 2226–2236 (2022)
7. Bishop, C.M., Nasrabadi, N.M.: Pattern Recognition and Machine Learning, vol. 4. Springer, Heidelberg (2006)
8. Breiman, L.: Random forests. Mach. Learn. **45**, 5–32 (2001)
9. Chollet, F.: Xception: deep learning with depthwise separable convolutions. In: Proceedings of the IEEE Conference on Computer Vision and Pattern Recognition, pp. 1251–1258 (2017)
10. Elhariri, E., El-Bendary, N., Saleh, S.M.: Strawberry-ds: dataset of annotated strawberry fruits images with various developmental stages. Data Brief **48**, 109165 (2023)
11. Fan, R.E., Chang, K.W., Hsieh, C.J., Wang, X.R., Lin, C.J.: Liblinear: a library for large linear classification. J. Mach. Learn. Res. **9**, 1871–1874 (2008)
12. Foundation, P.S.: Python language reference, version 3 (2024). https://www.python.org/
13. Friedman, J.H.: Stochastic gradient boosting. Comput. Stat. Data Anal. **38**(4), 367–378 (2002)
14. Gao, Z., Shao, Y., Xuan, G., Wang, Y., Liu, Y., Han, X.: Real-time hyperspectral imaging for the in-field estimation of strawberry ripeness with deep learning. Artif. Intell. Agric. **4**, 31–38 (2020)
15. Google: Google colaboratory (2024). https://colab.research.google.com
16. He, K., Zhang, X., Ren, S., Sun, J.: Deep residual learning for image recognition. In: Proceedings of the IEEE Conference on Computer Vision and Pattern Recognition, pp. 770–778 (2016)
17. He, K., Zhang, X., Ren, S., Sun, J.: Identity mappings in deep residual networks. In: Leibe, B., Matas, J., Sebe, N., Welling, M. (eds.) ECCV 2016. LNCS, vol. 9908, pp. 630–645. Springer, Cham (2016). https://doi.org/10.1007/978-3-319-46493-0_38
18. Howard, A., et al.: Searching for mobilenetv3. In: Proceedings of the IEEE/CVF International Conference on Computer Vision, pp. 1314–1324 (2019)
19. Howard, A.G., et al.: Mobilenets: efficient convolutional neural networks for mobile vision applications. arXiv preprint arXiv:1704.04861 (2017)
20. Huang, G., Liu, Z., Van Der Maaten, L., Weinberger, K.Q.: Densely connected convolutional networks. In: Proceedings of the IEEE Conference on Computer Vision and Pattern Recognition, pp. 4700–4708 (2017)
21. Ibba, P., et al.: Supervised binary classification methods for strawberry ripeness discrimination from bioimpedance data. Sci. Rep. **11**(1), 11202 (2021)
22. Liu, Z., Mao, H., Wu, C.Y., Feichtenhofer, C., Darrell, T., Xie, S.: A convnet for the 2020s. In: Proceedings of the IEEE/CVF Conference on Computer Vision and Pattern Recognition, pp. 11976–11986 (2022)
23. Pearson, K.: Liii. on lines and planes of closest fit to systems of points in space. Lond. Edinburgh Dublin Phil. Maga. J. Sci. **2**(11), 559–572 (1901)
24. Pedregosa, F., et al.: Scikit-learn: machine learning in python. J. Mach. Learn. Res. **12**, 2825–2830 (2011). https://scikit-learn.org/

25. Pérez-Borrero, I., Marín-Santos, D., Gegúndez-Arias, M.E., Cortés-Ancos, E.: A fast and accurate deep learning method for strawberry instance segmentation. Comput. Electron. Agric. **178**, 105736 (2020). https://doi.org/10.1016/j.compag.2020.105736.   http://www.sciencedirect.com/science/article/pii/S0168169920300624
26. Radosavovic, I., Kosaraju, R.P., Girshick, R., He, K., Dollár, P.: Designing network design spaces. In: Proceedings of the IEEE/CVF Conference on Computer Vision and Pattern Recognition, pp. 10428–10436 (2020)
27. Russakovsky, O., et al.: Imagenet large scale visual recognition challenge. Int. J. Comput. Vision **115**, 211–252 (2015)
28. Sandler, M., Howard, A., Zhu, M., Zhmoginov, A., Chen, L.C.: Mobilenetv2: inverted residuals and linear bottlenecks. In: Proceedings of the IEEE Conference on Computer Vision and Pattern Recognition, pp. 4510–4520 (2018)
29. Simonyan, K., Zisserman, A.: Very deep convolutional networks for large-scale image recognition. arXiv preprint arXiv:1409.1556 (2014)
30. Szegedy, C., Ioffe, S., Vanhoucke, V., Alemi, A.: Inception-v4, inception-resnet and the impact of residual connections on learning. In: Proceedings of the AAAI Conference on Artificial Intelligence, vol. 31 (2017)
31. Szegedy, C., Vanhoucke, V., Ioffe, S., Shlens, J., Wojna, Z.: Rethinking the inception architecture for computer vision. In: Proceedings of the IEEE Conference on Computer Vision and Pattern Recognition, pp. 2818–2826 (2016)
32. Tan, M., Le, Q.: Efficientnet: rethinking model scaling for convolutional neural networks. In: International Conference on Machine Learning, pp. 6105–6114. PMLR (2019)
33. Tan, M., Le, Q.: Efficientnetv2: smaller models and faster training. In: International Conference on Machine Learning, pp. 10096–10106. PMLR (2021)
34. Wei, M.C.F., Maldaner, L.F., Ottoni, P.M.N., Molin, J.P.: Carrot yield mapping: a precision agriculture approach based on machine learning. AI **1**(2), 229–241 (2020)
35. Zoph, B., Vasudevan, V., Shlens, J., Le, Q.V.: Learning transferable architectures for scalable image recognition. In: Proceedings of the IEEE Conference on Computer Vision and Pattern Recognition, pp. 8697–8710 (2018)

Software System for Intelligent Monitoring of Storage Systems Through Log Analysis

Eugeny Mytarin$^{(\boxtimes)}$, Vadim Moshkin , and Ilya Andreev

Ulyanovsk State Technical University, Severny Venets Street, 32, 432027 Ulyanovsk, Russia
eugenytornado9@yandex.ru

Abstract. The article presents a description of the developed software platform that provides automation of data storage server state monitoring using a hybrid algorithm. The developed algorithm combines an ontological approach and machine learning elements. A comparative assessment of various approaches was carried out: cluster analysis, autoencoders, LSTM, fuzzy ontologies and hybrid models - when analyzing methods for searching for anomalies in time series. The hybrid evaluation model showed the best results for all criteria. It was chosen to develop a prototype of the software platform. Experiments were conducted on hardware storage system data. The software platform proved its effectiveness in solving the problem.

Keywords: monitoring · anomalies · storage system · ontology · time series · software system

1 Introduction

Modern technical systems are highly complex and consist of many interacting components, which makes their monitoring and diagnostics a very difficult task. Traditional approaches to assessing the state of such systems often face problems of uncertainty, data inaccuracy and the need to process large amounts of information. In this regard, there is a need to search for new effective methods for analyzing and predicting the state of complex technical systems [1].

One of the promising areas is the integration of machine learning methods and fuzzy ontologies. Machine learning automates the process of extracting knowledge from large amounts of data and creates models that can adapt to changing operating conditions [2].

Fuzzy ontologies provide an opportunity to formalize expert knowledge and work with incomplete and inaccurate data. This is especially important when analyzing the states of complex technical systems [3].

Within the framework of this project, a software platform was implemented that automates the process of predictive diagnostics of a complex technical system (using a data storage server as an example) by integrating machine learning methods and subject ontology [4].

O. Gervasi et al. (Eds.): ICCSA 2025, LNCS 15650, pp. 336–345, 2025.
https://doi.org/10.1007/978-3-031-96962-1_23

2   Comparative Analysis of Technical Time Series Anomalies Detection Methods and Software

a. Software analogues

Currently, separate software tools are used to solve the problem of data storage system diagnostics. The most common and effective software systems are:

Papertrail is software that collects diagnostic data from text files, Apache, MySQL DBMS, Heroku applications, Windows event log, routers and other objects [5].

Loggly is a service for monitoring and analyzing event logs. It centralizes and analyzes logs from various devices and applications in real time. Loggly supports data collection via various protocols, including Syslog, HTTP/HTTPS, TCP and UDP [6].

Sumo Logic is a cloud platform for log management, monitoring and security. Sumo Logic supports data collection via various protocols, including Syslog, HTTP/HTTPS, TCP and UDP [7].

Splunk is a software platform for monitoring, analyzing and visualizing data that allows you to collect data from multiple sources: application logs, network equipment, databases and other devices, to analyze it in real time and draw conclusions based on the data obtained [8].

Each of these tools has its own unique features and advantages, which makes them suitable for different use cases in the field of assessing complex technical systems.

However, the main drawback of the presented systems is the lack of modules that provide forecasting of the system's behavior in the future based on the current values of the characteristics. These systems work only in real time.

b. Analysis methods

Let us present a comparative characteristic of the most popular approaches to detecting anomalies in technical time series.

The main parameters by which we will conduct the comparison are:

- accuracy: an assessment of how well the method correctly identifies anomalies in the data;
- speed: indicates the time required to process the data and obtain the results;
- interpretability: describes the ease of understanding the results of the method and the mechanisms of its operation;
- noise resistance: characterizes the ability of the method to maintain its effectiveness in the presence of random variations or errors in the data;
- memory consumption: indicates the amount of RAM required to execute the method [9, 10].

The comparative table of characteristics of time series anomaly detection methods is an important tool for systematizing and analyzing different approaches.

Table 1 helps researchers quickly evaluate the advantages and disadvantages of each method. This facilitates a more informed choice of algorithm depending on the specifics of the problem, available resources, and requirements for accuracy, speed, interpretability, and noise resistance.

In addition, this table helps identify the area where each method may be most effective or limited. This is essential for the successful application of the methods in real-world conditions.

Table 1. Comparative table of characteristics of methods for searching anomalies in time series

Method	Accuracy	Speed	Interpretability	Noise Resilience	Memory Consumption
Cluster Analysis	low (70 – 85%)	very high (1 – 10 s)	high (easy to visualize and explain clusters)	low (robust to some types of noise, but sensitive to outliers)	low (100 – 500 MB) [11, 12]
Autoencoders	High (80 – 95%)	medium (30 – 600 s)	low (lack of explicit rules makes it difficult to determine which features of the data influence their inferences)	High (able to deal effectively with noise due to its filtering ability)	high (1 – 10 GB) [13, 14]
LSTM	high (85 – 95%)	low (60 – 600 s)	low (it is difficult to understand the influence of individual time dependencies on the model's output)	High (good tolerance to noise, especially in time series)	high (1 – 8 GB) [15, 16]
Fuzzy ontologies	medium (75 – 85%)	high (5 – 60 s)	medium (rules can be understandable and accessible for analysis, their complexity and number can make it difficult to fully understand the results)	Medium (the ability to take into account uncertainties and noise, but the effectiveness depends on the quality of the rules and the structure of the ontology)	medium (200 – 800 MB) [17]
Hybrid model	very high (90 – 98%)	low (60 – 600 s)	high (the ability to explain the results through fuzzy rules, while LSTM processes time dependencies)	high (combination of the strengths of both methods)	very high (3 - 15 GB) [18, 19]

In this regard, the task of implementing a predictive diagnostics approach to technical systems using intelligent data analysis methods in the form of a software platform is relevant.

3 Software Platform Architecture

The software platform developed within the project is intended for two groups of users - the system user and the subject area expert:

- the subject area expert creates a fuzzy ontological model, fills in SWRL rules and sets fuzzy annotations [20];
- the system user loads the prepared CSV source data, selects the values by which the time series will be created, searches for anomalies using the selected intelligent model (using the LSTM model as an example), and obtains a semantic output for each metric using the fuzzy ontology [21].

The main use cases are shown in Fig. 1.

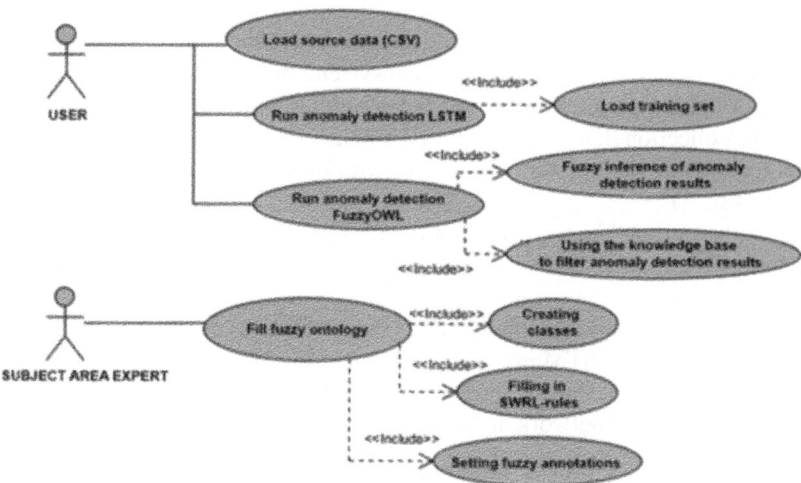

Fig. 1. Diagram of use cases for the developed software platform

The developed software platform consists of the following software modules:

- The preprocessing module loads the source data.
- The neural network module is the pytorch library, which allows training the LSTM model to work with the processed data.
- The module for working with fuzzy ontology is the owlready2 library, a file with fuzzy ontology in OWL format, SWRL rules in a text document, the FuzzyOwl plugin for working with fuzzy ontology and an API for working with SWRL rules [22, 23].

Figure 2 shows a diagram of the components of the developed software platform.

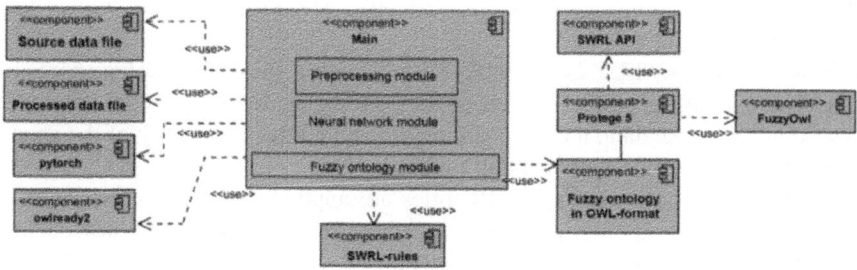

Fig. 2. Component diagram

4 Implementation of the Software Platform Prototype and Working Example

The software platform assumes the ability to load data in the form of time series, previously extracted from the logs of the technical system, pre-processed and presented as a CSV file. For operation, the source file must contain a "date" column, which stores the values of the collection date of all metrics (Table 2).

After loading the file, the user has the opportunity to select one of the columns from the dataset (Fig. 3).

The "Build a graph" button creates a time series, with the X axis showing the collection date of the metric selected by the column and the Y axis showing the values of this metric (Fig. 4).

The "LSTM anomaly search" button starts training the neural network. The architecture of the used LSTM network is shown in Fig. 5.

The autoencoder uses the backpropagation method.

The proposed neural network architecture includes the following layers:

– ConvLSTM1D is an LSTM layer. All input and output transformations within ConvLSTM1D are convolutional transformations.
– Conv1DTranspose is the transposed convolutional layer.
– Dropout is a layer that serves to prevent retraining of the neural network.

Once completed, the graph will highlight the expected anomalous metric values with red dots (Fig. 6).

When you click the "Load ontology" button, a dialog box appears for selecting a file in owl/rdf format to load the fuzzy ontology.

A fuzzy ontology file can contain various classes and properties. A file with SWRL rules can contain an unlimited number of rules. Each rule must start on a new line. The example of a SWRL rule for the data storage system condition assessment domain is shown below:

Metric(?m) ^ MetricHasName(?m, "totalNumberCreate") ^ hasValue(?m, ?value) ^ hasProbabilityOfAnomaly(?m, ?prob) ^ equal(?prob, 1) ^ greaterThanOrEqual(?value, 200) - > hasConclusion(?m, "Anomaly detected. Synchronization failure is highly probable.").

When you click the "FUZZY Anomaly Search" button, the fuzzy ontology processing begins. A new ontology object is created for each metric by the selected column, the values from the source data, the name are recorded, and the probability of the anomaly is set using the trapezoidal membership function.

After recording each metric, SWRL rules are applied. First, if the conditions are met, the has Anomaly properties are set, and then for all methods, the hasConclusion property is recorded with a fuzzy inference (Fig. 7).

The user can specify the upper bound of the trapezoidal membership function when the metric value with 100% probability will be anomalous (Fig. 8).

Table 2. Example of csv file for uploading to information system

lineNumber	date	time	countPers	countContracts	totalNumberCreate	totalNumberUpdate	createPers	createCitizenship	...	createInfo	createHistory
1	02.11.2024 0:00	126	5117	0	27	7	0	3	...	12	3
2	04.11.2024 0:00	173	5116	0	44	8	0	3	...	26	3
3	08.11.2024 0:00	138	5126	0	97	10	0	11	...	39	11
4	09.11.2024 0:00	139	5122	5079	24	2	2	2	...	10	2
5	11.11.2024 0:00	189	5138	5078	164	44	3	19	...	75	20
6	12.11.2024 0:00	217	5138	5080	458	8	24	24	...	106	24
7	14.11.2024 0:00	212	5139	5159	74	8	4	7	...	26	7
8	17.11.2024 0:00	174	5145	5166	90	12	7	9	...	35	9
...	...	...	...	...	...	...	...	...	...	...	...
n	29.11.2024 0:00	196	5135	5156	29	0	2	2	...	12	2

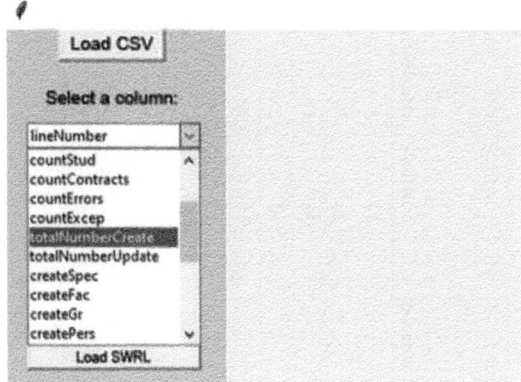

Fig. 3. Selecting a column

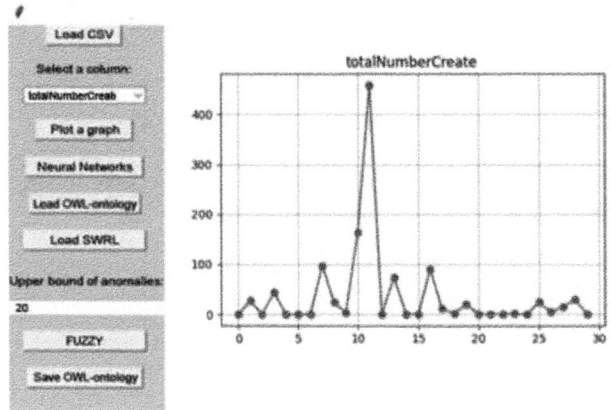

Fig. 4. Plotting a graph based on the original data

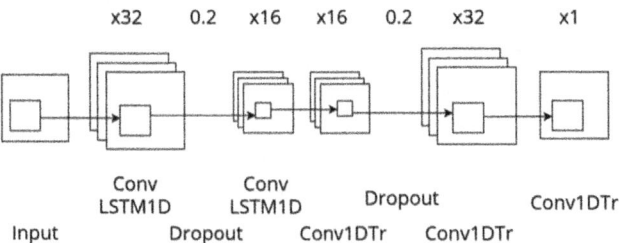

Fig. 5. Neural network structure

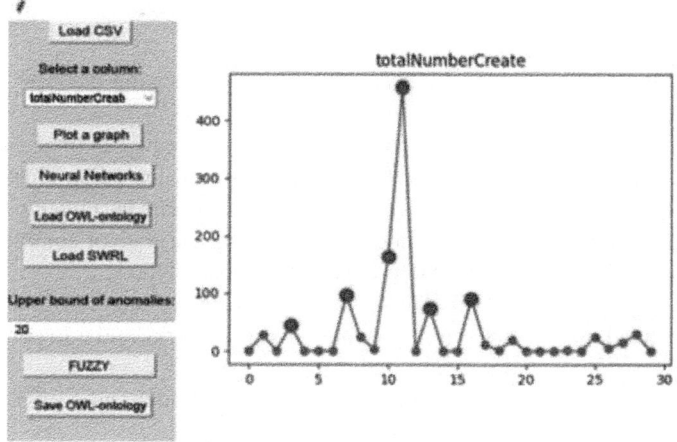

Fig. 6. Detected anomalies using LSTM

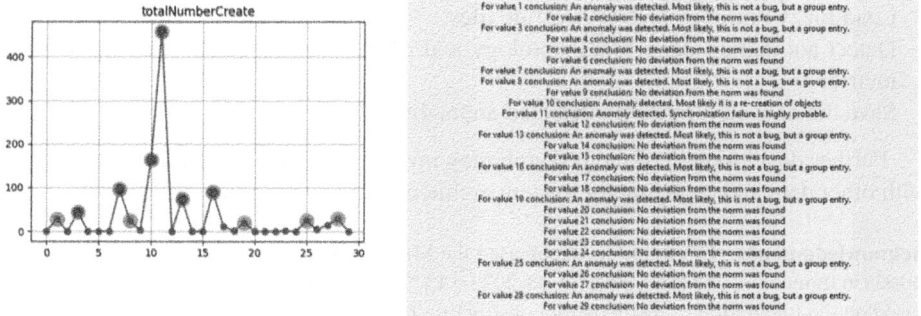

Fig. 7. Detected anomalies using fuzzy ontology and fuzzy inference

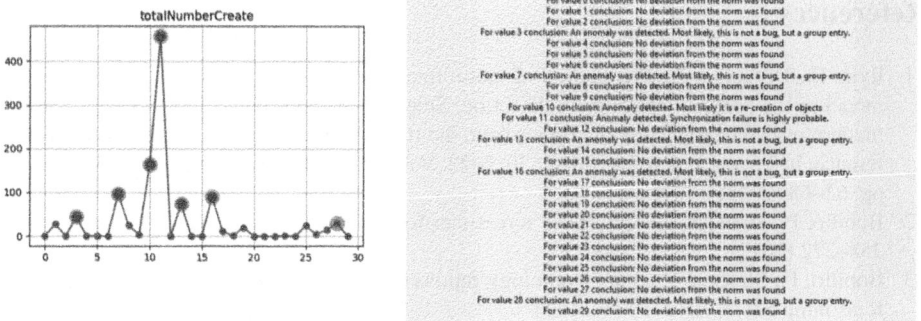

Fig. 8. Anomalies with a changed upper anomaly boundary

5 Conclusions

As a result of the project, the methods and services for assessing the state of complex technical systems were analyzed.

As part of the analysis of methods for searching for anomalies in time series, a comparative assessment of various approaches was carried out, including cluster analysis, autoencoders, LSTM, fuzzy ontologies and hybrid models. The best results for all criteria were demonstrated by the hybrid model for assessing the state of complex technical systems, which was selected for the development of a prototype.

To achieve the goal of the study, a software platform for searching for time series anomalies was designed and developed, using neural networks and a fuzzy ontological model.

The initial data were prepared, a fuzzy ontological model and SWRL rules were formed, and a prototype of the hybrid model was developed.

In general, the prototype allows you to:

- Load the initial data and select metrics for constructing a time series;
- Detect anomalies in a time series using LSTM and plot a graph;
- Load fuzzy ontology and SWRL rule files;
- Detect anomalies using fuzzy ontology and assign fuzzy logical inference to each metric;
- Save the new ontology with detected anomalies to a file.

Further development of the research may involve using the system in an enterprise with other data and changing the system architecture to work with real-time data.

Acknowledgments. This study was supported the Ministry of Science and Higher Education of Russia in framework of project No. 075-03-2023-143 "The study of intelligent predictive analytics based on the integration of methods for constructing features of heterogeneous dynamic data for machine learning and methods of predictive multimodal data analysis".

References

1. Ilyin, E., Dryuchin, E.: Preparation of multidimensional data for training a neural network model in the problem of anomaly detection. Science, students, education: current issues of modern research: collection of articles from the III International scientific and practical conference: in 2 parts, Penza, November 30, 2022. Volume Part 1, Penza: Science and Education, pp. 62–68 (2022)
2. Bobillo, F., Straccia, U.: DeLorean: a reasoner for fuzzy OWL 2. Expert Syst. Appl. **39**(1), 258–272 (2012)
3. Bobillo, F., Straccia, U.: Fuzzy ontology representation using OWL 2. Int. J. Approximate Reasoning **52**(7), 1073–1094 (2011)
4. Fang, X., Yuan, Z.: Performance enhancing techniques for deep learning models in time series forecasting. Eng. Appl. Artif. Intell. **85**, 533–542 (2019). https://doi.org/10.1016/j.engappai.2019.07.011
5. Papertrail. https://www.papertrail.com. Accessed 22 Feb 2025
6. Loggly. https://www.loggly.com. Accessed 22 Feb 2025

7. Sumo Logic. https://www.sumologic.com. Accessed 22 Feb 2025
8. Splunk. https://www.splunk.com. Accessed 22 Feb 2025
9. Hewamalage, H., Ackermann, K., Bergmeir, C.: Forecast evaluation for data scientists: common pitfalls and best practices Data Min. Knowl. Discov. **37**(2), 788–832 (2023). https://doi.org/10.1007/s10618-022-00894-5
10. Mosin, V.G., Kozlovsky, V.N., Pantyukhin, O.V.: Detection of information channel anomalies based on predictive models in solving content quality analysis problems. Bullet. Tula State Univ. Tech. Sci. **3**, 421–425 (2024)
11. Polezhaev, M.N., Finogeev, A.A.: Predictive analysis of critical event indicators using a recurrent neural network with a transformer. Modern Sci. Intensive Technol. **4**, 63–68 (2024)
12. Himeur, Y., et al.: Artificial intelligence based anomaly detection of energy consumption in buildings: a review, current trends and new perspectives Appl. Energy, **287**, 116601 (2021). https://doi.org/10.1016/j.apenergy.2021.116601
13. Dietterich, T.: Machine learning for sequential data: a review Struct. Syntactic Stat. Pattern Recogn. 15–30 (2002). https://doi.org/10.1007/3-540-70659-3_2
14. Hinton, G.E., Salakhutdinov, R.R.: Reducing the dimensionality of data with neural networks. Science **313**, 504–507 (2006)
15. Bohara, B., et al.: Short-term aggregated residential load forecasting using BiLSTM and CNN-BiLSTM. In: Proceedings of the International Conference on Innovation and Intelligence for Informatics, Computing, and Technologies (3ICT), pp. 37–43. IEEE
16. Elchenkov, R.A., Dunaev, M.E., Zaitsev, K.S.: Forecasting time series in real-time streaming data processing. Int. J. Open Inf. Technol. **10**(6), 62–69 (2022)
17. Fuzzy Ontology Representation using OWL 2. - http://www.umbertostraccia.it/cs/software/FuzzyOWL/index.html. Accessed 22 Feb 2025
18. Moshkin, V., Kurilo, D., Yarushkina, N.: Integration of fuzzy ontologies and neural networks in the detection of time series anomalies. Mathematics **11**(5), 1204 (2023)
19. Moshkin, V., Egov, E., Gavrilova, Y.: Development of a time series forecasting method based on entropy measures of diagnostic information. In: 2024 International Ural Conference on Electrical Power Engineering (UralCon), Magnitogorsk, Russian Federation, pp. 725–729 (2024). https://doi.org/10.1109/UralCon62137.2024.10718924
20. Protégé: ontology editor. - https://protege.stanford.edu. Accessed 22 Feb 2025
21. Trofimov, I.V.: Evolution of the expressive capabilities of the OWL language. Softw. Syst. Theory Appl. **2**, 4(8), 85–94 (2011)
22. Arkadov, G.V., Kotsoev, K.I., Trykova, I.V.: Detection of anomalous events of the detection system of free and loosely fixed objects using a convolutional autoencoder. questions of atomic science and technology. Series Nuclear Reactor Constants, 3, 245–253 (2023)
23. Moshkin, V.S., Kurilo, D.S., Andreev, I.A.: Hybridization of ontologies and neural networks in the problems of detecting anomalies of time series. Pattern Recognit Image Anal. Image Anal. **33**, 425–431 (2023). https://doi.org/10.1134/S105466182303032X

Unsupervised Learning for Calorimeter Response Correction: A WGAN-Based Method

Saraa Ali$^{(\boxtimes)}$ (ID), Artem Ryzhikov (ID), Denis Derkach (ID), Fedor Ratnikov (ID),
and Vladimir Bocharnikov (ID)

HSE University, Myasnitskaya Ulitsa 20, 101000 Moscow, Russia
{thraaali,aryzhikov,dderkach,fratnikov,vbocharnikov}@hse.ru

Abstract. The long-term stability of calorimeters is crucial in high-energy physics experiments, where precise energy measurements are essential for accurate particle reconstruction. This study introduces a Wasserstein GAN (WGAN)-based machine learning approach for calibrating calorimeter responses affected by aging and other systematic shifts. Our methodology is applied to realistic, high-granularity calorimeter data that more accurately mimic physical detector conditions. The dataset reflects energy deposition across all calorimeter cells, following an exponential energy spectrum and eliminating artificial peaks in the distribution. By leveraging Wasserstein distance minimization, our model estimates aging coefficients of cells, realigning degraded detector responses with their undamaged counterparts. The results highlight the potential of a data-driven approach for calorimeter calibration, demonstrating correcting energy measurement discrepancies with a reduced number of required events, making it a valuable tool for future detector calibration strategies.

Keywords: Calorimeter · Calibration · Generative Adversarial Networks · Wasserstein GAN

1 Introduction

1.1 Calorimeter

A calorimeter is an essential component in high-energy physics, designed to measure the energy of incoming particles by absorbing their energy and converting it into detectable signals [2,10,13]. These detectors play a crucial role in experiments conducted at facilities like the Large Hadron Collider (LHC) [2] and other major research infrastructures worldwide. By analyzing the energy deposited by particles, calorimeters provide critical insights into particle interactions and properties. Their applications extend beyond high-energy physics to fields such as nuclear reactor monitoring and medical imaging techniques, including radiation therapy [10,13]. Ensuring the accuracy and stability of calorimeter measurements over time is a significant challenge, as detector responses can degrade

O. Gervasi et al. (Eds.): ICCSA 2025, LNCS 15650, pp. 346–355, 2025.
https://doi.org/10.1007/978-3-031-96962-1_24

due to radiation exposure, material aging, and environmental effects. Calibration techniques are essential for maintaining precision in energy measurements, compensating for variations across different detector regions, and correcting shifts in response due to operational wear [2,10,13].

1.2 Machine Learning in High-Energy Physics

The integration of machine learning (ML) techniques into high-energy physics (HEP) has significantly advanced our ability to analyze complex particle interactions and fundamental processes [6]. With modern experiments, such as the Large Hadron Collider (LHC) and its upcoming high-luminosity upgrade (HL-LHC), generating vast amounts of data, traditional analysis methods are often insufficient for efficient processing. ML algorithms provide powerful tools for reducing data complexity, identifying patterns, and optimizing event reconstruction and particle classification [7].

Among the ML approaches that are used in HEP are Boosted Decision Trees (BDTs) [8] and Neural Networks (NNs), which have proven to be highly effective in classifying particles and distinguishing between different event types. These methods offer superior performance over conventional techniques by improving classification accuracy and increasing computational efficiency [12].

Another application of ML in HEP is realistic event simulation, which is essential for comparing experimental results with theoretical models. Deep learning architectures, such as Generative Adversarial Networks (GANs) [5] and Variational AutoEncoders (VAEs), have demonstrated their capabilities in generating synthetic particle interactions and modeling detector responses. These generative models not only enhance the precision of simulations but also significantly reduce the computational burden associated with Monte Carlo methods, making large-scale data processing more feasible.

Given the enormous data rates produced in modern experiments, real-time data processing is critical. HEP detectors operate at extreme acquisition speeds, often generating information that exceeds traditional storage capacities. To manage this, ML-powered techniques facilitate data compression, filtering, and zero suppression, allowing for more efficient processing at the hardware level. Integrating edge computing and ML-driven analytics into data center architectures ensures faster decision-making and improved storage efficiency [11].

Another challenge in particle physics is signal-background separation, particularly in environments with high event overlap, a phenomenon known as pile-up. Advanced ML algorithms, such as graph neural networks (GNNs) and adaptive filtering techniques, are now used for pile-up suppression, significantly improving signal clarity and background rejection [9]. These approaches enhance event reconstruction precision, enabling physicists to extract valuable insights from rare physical processes.

We want to expand the role of ML in HEP, by offering data-driven solutions for calorimeter calibration.

1.3 Calorimeter Calibration

Calibrating calorimeters is essential for ensuring the accuracy and reliability of energy measurements. Ideally, all sections of a calorimeter should respond identically when exposed to the same type and energy of particles. However, due to manufacturing differences, construction misalignments, and aging effects, detector responses can vary across different calorimeter cells [10,13]. Ensuring accurate energy measurements in calorimeters requires periodic calibration. Various calibration techniques exist to align responses across detector cells and compensate for systematic deviations. The main approaches include:

1. **Hardware-Based Calibration:** This includes methods like electronic pulse injection to verify response uniformity [10] or the use of radioactive sources and laser signals to establish reference energy levels [13].
2. **Test Beam Calibration:** Dedicated particle beams with known energy levels are directed at the calorimeter to measure and standardize responses [10, 13]
3. **In Situ Calibration:** During active experiments, well-characterized particle interactions, such as decays of W and Z bosons, are used to fine-tune calibration parameters [6,10,13].

Despite these calibration procedures, calorimeters degrade over time due to radiation exposure and other environmental factors. Periodic recalibration is necessary to counteract these effects and maintain accurate energy measurements [10]. The traditional approach to recalibration requires significant experimental resources and can be labor-intensive.

To address these challenges, we developed a machine learning technique that offers a promising alternative. By leveraging deep learning models, it is possible to automate the calibration process, reducing manual intervention and optimizing detector performance [6,12]. Specifically, generative models, such as Wasserstein GANs [3], learn to correct energy misalignment by predicting aging effects.

2 Experimental Data and Simulation Setup

In this study, we employ Monte Carlo simulations using the Geant4 framework [1] to model hadronic showers in a calorimeter. Specifically, we simulate 100,000 single-pion events, each with an energy of 10 GeV. The detector geometry follows a high-granularity configuration, representative of next-generation collider experiments [4]. The simulated calorimeter features a layered sampling structure, where the absorber consists of 20 mm-thick copper plates, while the active detection elements are polystyrene scintillator tiles. These tiles are organized in a 24×24 matrix with a thickness of 5 mm. This setup provides a high level of spatial resolution, allowing precise analysis of energy deposition patterns.

To investigate the impact of detector aging, we introduce synthetic degradation effects into the simulation. This degradation is modeled by assigning a cell-specific aging coefficient A_i, which depends on the cumulative energy absorbed by each readout channel over the entire dataset. This approach mimics real-world radiation damage, where prolonged exposure leads to a decline in detector sensitivity.

2.1 Defining the Aging Coefficients

The aging coefficient A_i quantifies the extent of response deterioration in each calorimeter cell over time. It represents the discrepancy between the original signal (before damage) and the altered signal (after exposure to aging effects). For a given calorimeter cell i, we define its coefficient as follows:

$$A_i = \frac{E_{\text{undamaged}_i}}{E_{\text{damaged}_i}} \tag{1}$$

where:

1. $E_{\text{undamaged}_i}$ is the reference energy measurement from an unaffected calorimeter.
2. E_{damaged_i} is the recorded energy from the same cell after simulated aging.

An ideal cell, unaffected by aging, will have $A_i = 1$, meaning its response remains unchanged. Conversely, values $A_i < 1$ indicate signal attenuation due to degradation, which necessitates corrective calibration. By estimating these coefficients across all readout channels, our methodology compensates for aging-induced distortions, thereby restoring the accuracy of energy measurements.

2.2 Dataset Structure and Unsupervised Learning Approach

The dataset consists of two distinct groups:

1. Undamaged dataset: Represents energy measurements from a pristine calorimeter.
2. Damaged dataset: Contains data from the same detector after simulated degradation effects have been applied.

Unlike traditional supervised learning tasks, where models learn from labeled inputs, our approach follows an unsupervised paradigm. Since the ground truth aging coefficients are not explicitly provided, the model must infer them directly from the data. This eliminates the need for separate training and testing subsets—both datasets are utilized in full to optimize calibration parameters.

The histograms in Fig. 1 illustrate the changes in energy sum distributions between the undamaged and aged calorimeters. A noticeable shift in these distributions confirms the impact of synthetic degradation effects, emphasizing the need for robust calibration techniques.

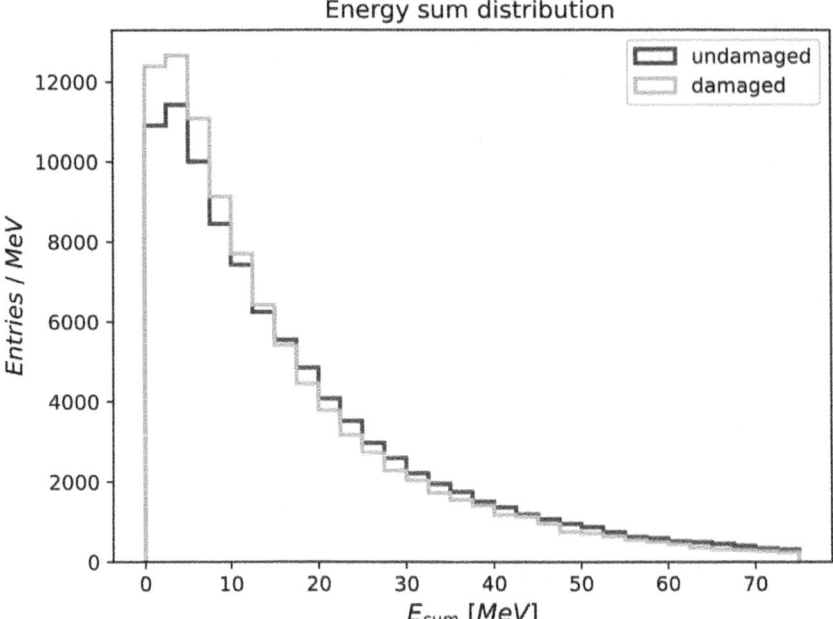

Fig. 1. Comparison of energy sum distributions for undamaged and degraded calorimeters.

2.3   Addressing Radiation Damage in Detector Performance

Over time, prolonged exposure to radiation gradually weakens the detector's response, reducing signal amplitudes in affected regions. This work focuses on correcting signal loss at the individual cell level by leveraging deep learning techniques. By developing a data-driven calibration framework, we aim to extend the operational lifespan of calorimeters, ensuring their long-term reliability in high-energy physics experiments.

3   Generative Adversarial Networks for Calorimeter Calibration

The Wasserstein GAN (WGAN) [3] framework is designed to minimize the Earth Mover's distance (Wasserstein distance) between two data distributions, ensuring a stable and effective learning process. Leveraging this principle, we developed a WGAN-inspired calibration model to predict aging-induced distortions in calorimeter measurements. Instead of generating new data, our approach focuses on distribution alignment, transforming degraded calorimeter readings to match their undamaged counterparts.

In this setup, the Generator learns a mapping function that predicts the aging coefficients for each calorimeter cell. These coefficients, once applied, adjust the damaged calorimeter's response to restore its original accuracy. The Critic, rather than performing binary classification as in traditional GANs, evaluates the Wasserstein distance between the corrected (synthetic) and undamaged (real) data distributions. The Generator iteratively refines its predictions by minimizing this distance, progressively improving the calibration process.

A detailed schematic of our WGAN-based calibration architecture, including the Generator and Critic components, is depicted in Fig. 2. This framework demonstrates how adversarial learning can be adapted to detector recalibration, improving long-term performance in high-energy physics experiments.

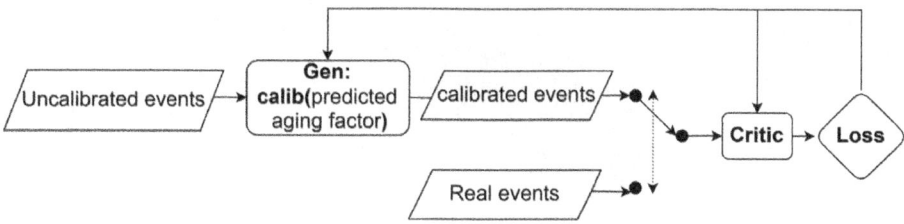

Fig. 2. Architecture of the WGAN-Based calibration model for correcting aging effects in calorimeter data.

4   Results and Discussion

The effectiveness of our WGAN-based calibration approach is demonstrated by the model's ability to estimate aging coefficients and align the damaged calorimeter's response with its undamaged counterpart. Figure 3 presents a scatter plot comparing the predicted and true aging coefficients. The strong correlation between the two, with data points clustering along the diagonal $y=x$ line, confirms the model's capability to learn and approximate the degradation patterns.The overall trend suggests that the model successfully captures the underlying distribution of energy shifts in the calorimeter. The Root Mean Squared Error (RMSE) trend through learning aging coefficients process, shown in Fig. 4, highlights the progressive improvement in prediction accuracy as training progresses. Initially, the RMSE starts above 0.08, but as the number of training epochs increases, the error steadily declines, stabilizing around 0.02 after approximately 60 epochs, with R^2 value of 0.88. This consistent reduction indicates that the model minimizes discrepancies between calibrated data and the undamaged data by tuning aging coefficients parameters that are getting closer to actual aging coefficients, reinforcing its ability to generalize well across different calorimeter regions.

The decreasing RMSE trend underscores the stability of the training process, demonstrating that the WGAN-inspired model refines its predictions. The smooth and monotonic decline in error suggests that the Wasserstein loss function provides reliable gradient updates, leading to aging coefficients estimations.

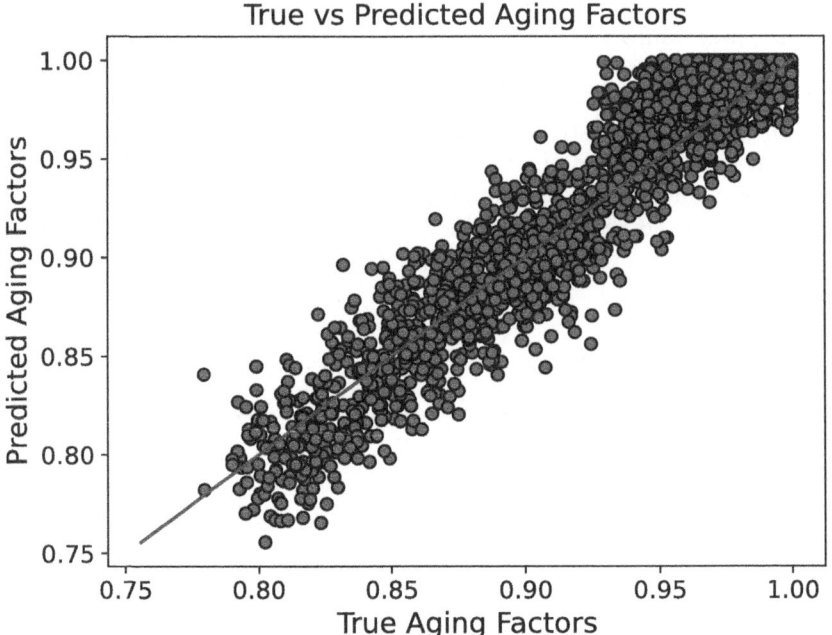

Fig. 3. Scatter plot of true vs. predicted aging coefficients, demonstrating the model's calibration ability.

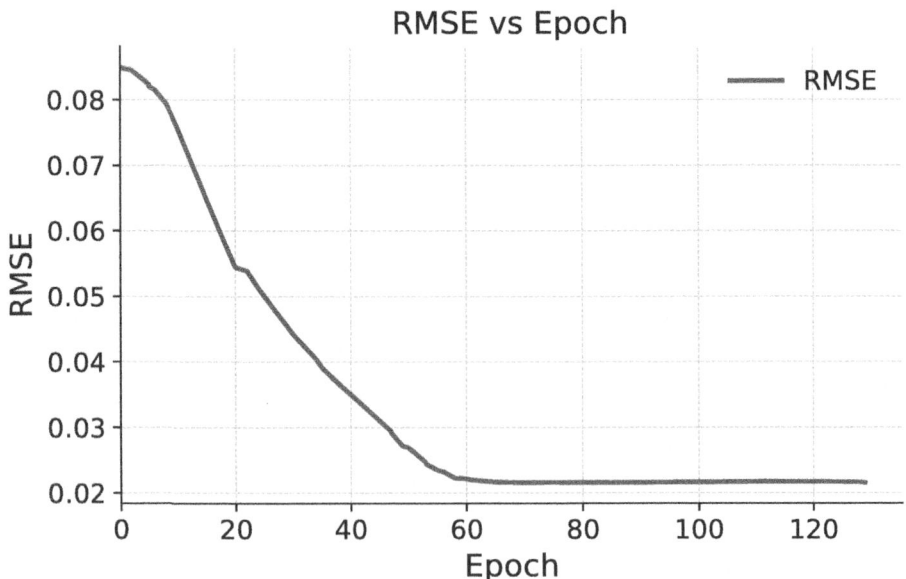

Fig. 4. RMSE versus epochs showing convergence of the model during aging coefficient estimation.

Figure 5 demonstrates the impact of Calibration on Energy Distributions By applying the predicted aging coefficients, the calibrated calorimeter data exhibits improved alignment with the undamaged dataset.

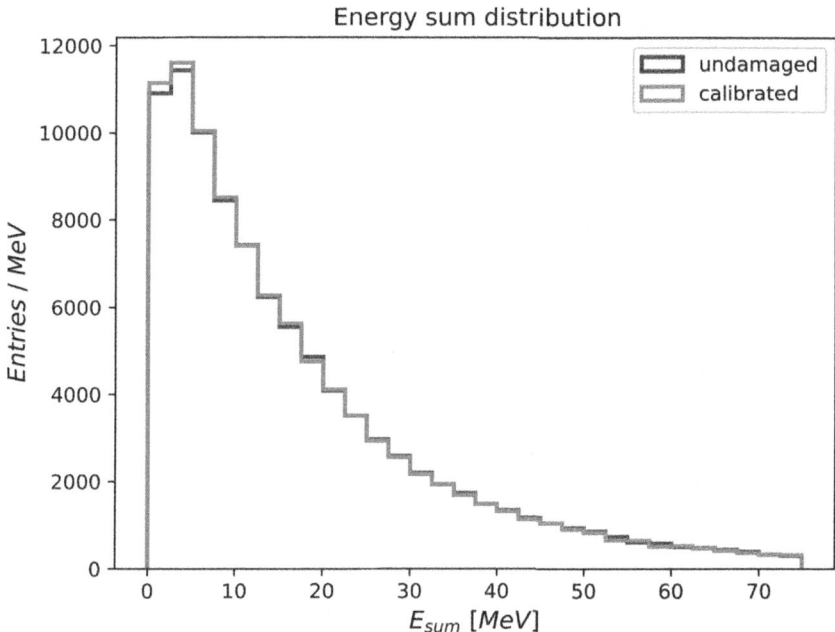

Fig. 5. Energy sum distribution before and after calibration, showing alignment with undamaged data.

5 Conclusion

In this work, we presented a Wasserstein GAN (WGAN)-based approach for calibrating calorimeter responses affected by aging effects. Traditional calibration methods, while effective, require significant manual intervention, computational resources, and repeated experimental procedures. By leveraging deep learning techniques, particularly generative models, we demonstrated a potential data-driven approach that can autonomously learn the aging coefficients to correct energy misalignment in calorimeters.

Our experimental results validate the potential of the proposed model in predicting aging coefficients and realigning energy distributions. The correlation between predicted and true aging factors, as shown in scatter plots Fig. 3, confirms that the model captures detector degradation patterns. Furthermore, the steady decline in Root Mean Squared Error (RMSE) during the learning process highlights the stability of the process. The improved alignment between calibrated and undamaged calorimeter data further reinforces the model's capability to restore detector accuracy.

This study showcases how machine learning can revolutionize detector calibration in high-energy physics (HEP), offering a scalable and automated alternative to conventional recalibration techniques. By integrating ML-driven solutions, we can enhance the longevity and precision of calorimeters, ensuring that future HEP experiments maintain high-quality data acquisition while minimizing the operational burden of detector maintenance.

Acknowledgments. This work is supported by HSE Basic research fund. The computation for this research was performed using the computational resources of HPC facilities at HSE University.

References

1. Agostinelli, S., Allison, J., Amako, K., et al.: Geant4–a simulation toolkit. Nucl. Instrum. Methods Phys. Res., Sect. A **506**, 250–303 (2003). https://doi.org/10.1016/S0168-9002(03)01368-8
2. Alves, A.A., Ben-Haim, E., Bettinardi, D., et al.: The lhcb detector at the lhc. J. Instrum. **3**, S08005 (2008). https://doi.org/10.1088/1748-0221/3/08/S08005
3. Arjovsky, M., Chintala, S., Bottou, L.: Wasserstein gan. arXiv (2017)
4. Arratia, M., Barish, K., Blanchard, L., et al.: A high-granularity calorimeter insert based on sipm-on-tile technology at the future electron-ion collider. Nucl. Instrum. Methods Phys. Res., Sect. A **1047**, 167866 (2023). https://doi.org/10.1016/j.nima.2022.167866
5. Butter, A., Plehn, T.: Generative networks for lhc events. In: Calafiura, P., Rousseau, D., Terao, K. (eds.) Artificial Intelligence for High Energy Physics, pp. 191–240. World Scientific Publishing Co. Pte. Ltd. (2022). https://doi.org/10.1142/9789811234033_0007
6. Calafiura, P., Rousseau, D., Terao, K. (eds.): Artificial Intelligence for High Energy Physics. World Scientific Publishing Co. Pte. Ltd. (2022). https://worldscientific.com/worldscibooks/10.1142/12200
7. Carleo, G., et al.: Machine learning in high energy physics community white paper. arXiv (2018)
8. Coadou, Y.: Boosted decision trees. In: Calafiura, P., Rousseau, D., Terao, K. (eds.) Artificial Intelligence for High Energy Physics, pp. 9–55. World Scientific Publishing Co. Pte. Ltd. (2022). https://doi.org/10.48550/arXiv.2206.09645
9. Duarte, J., Vlimant, J.R.: Graph neural networks for particle tracking and reconstruction. In: Calafiura, P., Rousseau, D., Terao, K. (eds.) Artificial Intelligence for High Energy Physics, pp. 387–436. World Scientific Publishing Co. Pte. Ltd. (2022). https://doi.org/10.1142/9789811234033_0012
10. Fabjan, C.W., Gianotti, F.: Calorimetry for particle physics. Rev. Mod. Phys. **75**, 1243–1286 (2003). https://doi.org/10.1103/RevModPhys.75.1243
11. Harris, P., Tran, N.: Fast ml for real-time readout and near-detector triggering. In: Calafiura, P., Rousseau, D., Terao, K. (eds.) Artificial Intelligence for High Energy Physics, pp. 265–309. World Scientific Publishing Co. Pte. Ltd. (2022). https://doi.org/10.1142/9789811234033_0009

12. Inter-experimental Machine Learning Working Group: Hep ml living review (2022). https://iml-wg.github.io/HEPML-LivingReview/. Accessed 8 Mar 2025
13. Korpachov, S.S., Chadeeva, M.V.: Study of the uniformity of the response of scintillation tiles for high-granularity calorimeters. Brief Commun. Phys. Lebedev Inst. (10), 52–56 (2018). https://cyberleninka.ru/article/n/izuchenie-odnorodnosti-otklika-stsintillyatsionnyh-taylov-dlya-vysokogranulyarnyh-kalorimetrov

A Data-Driven Approach
on Bioconvection Flow

Bengisen Pekmen$^{(\boxtimes)}$ and Merve Gurbuz-Caldag

Department of Mathematics, TED University, 06420 Ankara, Turkey
bengisenpekmen@gmail.com, merve.gurbuz@tedu.edu.tr

Abstract. In this study, machine learning modeling is utilized on a bio-convection flow problem. The two dimensional, time independent natural convection flow problem in the presence of oxytactic bacteria is considered inside a unit square cavity. The dimensionless governing equations in terms of stream function, temperature, oxygen concentration, bacteria density and vorticity are numerically solved by radial basis function collocation method. In variation of Rayleigh, bioconvection Rayleigh, Peclet, Lewis and buoyancy ratio parameter, average Nusselt, Sherwood and bacteria density along the heated wall as well as average bacteria density throughout the entire cavity are calculated, and organized into a matrix to form a dataset. This dataset is used for neural network modeling to model the outcomes as averages. The obtained mean squared error metric results show the good fit even by one layer neural network. A feature importance analysis also approves the importance of Rayleigh number on average Nusselt number, and Peclet number on all other averages.

Keywords: Oxytactic Bacteria · Bioconvection Flow · Neural
Network · Radial Basis Function · Feature Importance

1 Introduction

Bioconvection refers to the convective motion of a fluid induced by the directional swimming of microorganisms under the influence of gravity, a magnetic field, oxygen, or light. In the literature, various bioconvection problems have been examined in different channels, particularly involving gravitactic, oxytactic, or gyrotactic bacteria. Alloui et al. [1] investigated gravitactic bioconvection in a rectangular cavity, employing the control volume method to simulate contour plots of stream function, temperature, and concentration for various physical parameters. They also analyzed the bifurcation diagram of the stream function. Kuznetsov [8] applied the Galerkin finite element method to study bioconvection driven by gyrotactic microorganisms in a horizontal layer, concluding that the presence of these microorganisms has a destabilizing effect. Sheremet and Pop [10] examined heat and mass transfer in a nanofluid containing oxytactic bacteria within a square porous cavity. Using the finite difference method, they

O. Gervasi et al. (Eds.): ICCSA 2025, LNCS 15650, pp. 356–365, 2025.
https://doi.org/10.1007/978-3-031-96962-1_25

visualized streamlines, isotherms, and isoconcentrations of oxygen and bacteria for different values of Rayleigh, bioconvection Rayleigh, Peclet, and Lewis numbers. Their findings indicate that the average Nusselt number increases with higher Rayleigh numbers or lower Lewis numbers. Saini and Sharma [9] investigated thermo-bioconvection in porous media with gravitactic microorganisms, reporting that the Lewis number enhances bioconvection. Balla et al. [2] investigated the numerical solution of nanofluid flow in a porous square cavity with oxytactic bacteria by using weighted residual Galerkin finite element method. They showed that both the heat transfer and mass transfer increase with the augmentation of Lewis number and Brownian motion. Pekmen Geridonmez and Oztop [5] implemented radial basis function with finite difference (RBF-FD) to the bioconvection flow in a cavity with solid block field by SiO_2-water containing oxytactic bacteria subjected to the periodic magnetic field. They reported that mass transfer is a decreasing function of bioconvection Rayleigh number, but it is an increasing function of the other problem parameters. Habibishandiz et al. [6] studied the heat transfer characteristics of natural convection flow in a square porous cavity filled with a nanofluid containing oxytactic bacteria. They employed the finite element method to solve the nondimensional governing equations under constant and periodic temperature boundary conditions. Their results demonstrated that microorganisms enhance heat transfer, particularly under periodic temperature distributions. In [7], numerical and artificial neural network studies are investigated for the bioconvection flow in H-type cavity containing oxytactic bacteria and nano-enhanced phase change material. It is obtained that the rise in Hartmann number lessens the heat transfer, but improves the mass transfer. They also depicted that the artificial neural network (ANN) models are capable to predict each parameter with high accuracy.

In this study, a machine learning technique is integrated into the bioconvection flow in a square cavity including oxytactic bacteria. RBF is used to produce the dataset from the numerical results of the nondimensional governing equations. In neural network process, the inputs are Rayleigh, bioconvection Rayleigh, Peclet and Levis numbers, and the buoyancy ratio term. Outputs are the average Nusselt and Sherwood numbers, mean and average values of microorganism concentration. Feature importance analysis is also performed on the dataset.

2   Problem in Mathematical Terms

This study investigates a steady, two-dimensional natural convection flow inside a unit square cavity, influenced by oxytactic bacteria. The problem setup is depicted in Fig. 1. The left wall acts as a heated boundary, while the right wall is maintained at a lower temperature. In contrast, the top and bottom walls are thermally insulated.

The buoyancy effect is incorporated using the Boussinesq approximation due to both temperature and density differences. Viscous dissipation and radiation effects are disregarded.

The dimensional equations consist of continuity, momentum, energy, oxygen concentration, and microorganism density, are formulated as follows

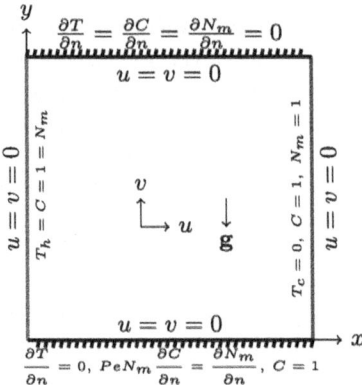

Fig. 1. Problem Setup and Boundary Conditions.

$$\frac{\partial u'}{\partial x'} + \frac{\partial v'}{\partial y'} = 0, \tag{1}$$

$$\nu \nabla^2 u' = u' \frac{\partial u'}{\partial x'} + v' \frac{\partial u'}{\partial y'} + \frac{1}{\rho} \frac{\partial p'}{\partial x'}, \tag{2}$$

$$\nu \nabla^2 v' = u' \frac{\partial v'}{\partial x'} + v' \frac{\partial v'}{\partial y'} + \frac{1}{\rho} \frac{\partial p'}{\partial y'}$$
$$+ \frac{g}{\rho} \left(\gamma \Delta \rho n' - \rho \beta (T' - T_c) + \rho_o \beta_o (C' - C^*) \right), \tag{3}$$

$$\nabla^2 T' = u' \frac{\partial T'}{\partial x'} + v' \frac{\partial T'}{\partial y'}, \tag{4}$$

$$D_c \nabla^2 C' = u' \frac{\partial C'}{\partial x'} + v' \frac{\partial C'}{\partial y'} + \delta n', \tag{5}$$

$$\frac{\partial}{\partial x'} \left(u'n' + \frac{bW_c}{\Delta C'} \frac{\partial C'}{\partial x'} n' - D_n \frac{\partial n'}{\partial x'} \right) + \frac{\partial}{\partial y'} \left(v'n' + \frac{bW_c}{\Delta C'} \frac{\partial C'}{\partial y'} n' - D_n \frac{\partial n'}{\partial y'} \right) = 0, \tag{6}$$

where ρ is the density of water, ρ_o is the density of oxygen, β is the thermal expansion coefficient of water, β_o is the thermal expansion coefficient of oxygen, α is the thermal diffusivity, ν is the kinematic viscosity, u', v' are velocity components, p' is the pressure, g is the gravitational acceleration, γ is the mean volume of microorganism, D_c is the diffusivity of oxygen concentration, n' is the density of bacteria, W_c is the maximum cell swimming speed, b is the chemotaxis constant, D_n is the diffusivity of microorganism, T' is the temperature, C' is the concentration, $\delta n'$ is the oxygen consumption by the bacteria, and $\Delta C' = C - C^*$ with $C^* = C_{\min}$.

The dimensionless transformation parameters are defined as follows

$$(x, y) = \frac{(x', y')}{L}, \quad (u, v) = \frac{L}{\alpha}(u', v'), \quad p = \frac{L^2}{\rho\alpha^2}p', \tag{7}$$

$$T = \frac{T' - T_c}{\Delta T}, \quad C = \frac{C' - C^*}{\Delta C}, \quad N_m = \frac{n'}{n_0}, \tag{8}$$

where L is the characteristic length, ΔT is the temperature difference, ΔC is the concentration difference, α is the thermal diffusivity and n_0 is the reference average density of bacteria.

Utilizing these transformation parameters, the dimensional equations are converted into the following non-dimensional form

$$\frac{\partial u}{\partial x} + \frac{\partial v}{\partial y} = 0, \tag{9}$$

$$Pr\nabla^2 u = u\frac{\partial u}{\partial x} + v\frac{\partial u}{\partial y} + \frac{\partial p}{\partial x}, \tag{10}$$

$$Pr\nabla^2 v = u\frac{\partial v}{\partial x} + v\frac{\partial v}{\partial y} + \frac{\partial p}{\partial y} - RaPr\left(T - R_b N_m - NrC\right), \tag{11}$$

$$\nabla^2 T = u\frac{\partial T}{\partial x} + v\frac{\partial T}{\partial y}, \tag{12}$$

$$\frac{1}{Le}\nabla^2 C = u\frac{\partial C}{\partial x} + v\frac{\partial C}{\partial y} + \frac{1}{Le}N_m, \tag{13}$$

$$\frac{1}{Le}\nabla^2 N_m = \chi\left(u\frac{\partial N_m}{\partial x} + v\frac{\partial N_m}{\partial y}\right) + \frac{Pe}{Le}\left(N_m\nabla^2 C + \frac{\partial C}{\partial x}\frac{\partial N_m}{\partial x} + \frac{\partial C}{\partial y}\frac{\partial N_m}{\partial y}\right), \tag{14}$$

where $\chi = \dfrac{D_c}{D_n}$, N_m is the number of microorganisms. Prandtl, Rayleigh, bioconvection Rayleigh, Peclet numbers, buoyancy ratio parameter and Lewis numbers are

$$Pr = \frac{\nu}{\alpha}, \quad Ra = \frac{g\beta\Delta T L^3}{\nu\alpha}, \quad R_b = \frac{\gamma n_0 \Delta\rho}{\rho\beta\Delta T}, \quad Pe = \frac{bW_c}{D_n},$$

$$Nr = \frac{(\rho_o - \rho)\beta_o\Delta C}{\rho\beta\Delta T}, \quad Le = \frac{\alpha}{D_c}.$$

By employing the stream function formulation, $(u, v) = \left(\dfrac{\partial\psi}{\partial y}, -\dfrac{\partial\psi}{\partial x}\right)$ and defining vorticity as $\omega = \dfrac{\partial v}{\partial x} - \dfrac{\partial u}{\partial y}$, the governing non-dimensional equations are expressed in terms of the stream function and vorticity as follows

$$\nabla^2 \psi = -\omega, \tag{15}$$

$$\nabla^2 T = u\frac{\partial T}{\partial x} + v\frac{\partial T}{\partial y}, \tag{16}$$

$$\frac{1}{Le}\nabla^2 C = u\frac{\partial C}{\partial x} + v\frac{\partial C}{\partial y} + \frac{1}{Le}N_m, \tag{17}$$

$$\frac{1}{Le}\nabla^2 N_m = \chi\left(u\frac{\partial N_m}{\partial x} + v\frac{\partial N_m}{\partial y}\right) + \frac{Pe}{Le}\left(N_m\nabla^2 C + \frac{\partial C}{\partial x}\frac{\partial N_m}{\partial x} + \frac{\partial C}{\partial y}\frac{\partial N_m}{\partial y}\right), \tag{18}$$

$$Pr\nabla^2\omega = u\frac{\partial \omega}{\partial x} + v\frac{\partial \omega}{\partial y} + RaPr\left(-\frac{\partial T}{\partial x} + R_b\frac{\partial N_m}{\partial x} + Nr\frac{\partial C}{\partial x}\right). \tag{19}$$

The boundary conditions are specified as follows

$$\text{on } x = 0 : u = v = \psi = 0, \, T = 1, \, C = N_m = 1, \tag{20}$$

$$\text{on } x = 1 : u = v = \psi = 0 = T, \, C = N_m = 1, \tag{21}$$

$$\text{on } y = 0 : u = v = \psi = 0, \, \frac{\partial T}{\partial y} = 0, \, C = 1, \, PeN_m\frac{\partial C}{\partial y} = \frac{\partial N_m}{\partial y}, \tag{22}$$

$$\text{on } y = 1 : u = v = \psi = 0, \, \frac{\partial T}{\partial y} = \frac{\partial C}{\partial y} = \frac{\partial N_m}{\partial y} = 0, \tag{23}$$

The following expressions are used to determine the average Nusselt number, Sherwood number, and the average bacterial density along the heated wall.

$$\overline{Nu} = -\int_0^1 \frac{\partial T}{\partial x}dy, \quad \overline{Sh} = -\int_0^1 \frac{\partial C}{\partial x}dy \quad \overline{N_m} = -\int_0^1 \frac{\partial N_m}{\partial x}dy \tag{24}$$

$\overline{Nu}$ represents the ratio of convective heat transfer to conductive heat transfer, while $\overline{Sh}$ denotes the ratio of convective mass transfer to conductive mass transfer. $\overline{N_m}$ along the heated wall represents the mean variation in bacterial density along the left heated boundary.

After establishing the governing equations and boundary conditions that describe the flow behavior, we next turn to the numerical strategy adopted to solve these equations. The radial basis function (RBF) collocation method is utilized due to its meshfree nature and flexibility in handling complex geometries.

3   Numerical Method

The Radial basis function (RBF) method [3,4] is a meshfree collocation technique, where the problem domain and its boundary are discretized using N_d number of interior and N_b number of boundary points. In this method, the unknown ζ is approximated using an RBF $g(r)$ as follows

$$\zeta(x, y) = \sum_{i=1}^{N_d+N_b} a_i g(||x - x_i||), \tag{25}$$

in which $r = ||x - x_i||$ represents the Euclidean norm between the field point x and collocation point x_i. The collocation form of (25) is expressed by $\zeta = Ga$, where the matrix G has dimensions $(N_d + N_b)^2$, while the vector a is of length $(N_d + N_b)$.

By treating the partial derivatives of the RBF $g(r)$ as the matrices G_x, G_y, G_{xx} and G_{yy}, the differentiation matrices are straightforwardly obtained as $P_x = G_x G^{-1}$, $P_y = G_y G^{-1}$, $P_L = (G_{xx} + G_{yy})G^{-1}$.

In the current study, polyharmonic spline RBF $g(r) = r^7$ is used to solve the equations (15)–(19). The equations in their discretized form can be written as follows

$$P_L \psi^{k+1} = -\omega^k, \tag{26}$$

$$(P_L - K) T^{k+1} = 0, \tag{27}$$

$$(P_L - LeK) C^{k+1} = N_m^k, \tag{28}$$

$$\left(P_L - Le\chi K - PeP_L[C^{k+1}]_d - Pe(P_x[C^{k+1}]_d P_x + [P_y C^{k+1}]_d P_y)\right) N_m^{k+1} = 0, \tag{29}$$

$$(PrP_L - K) \omega^{k+1} = RaPrP_x(-T^{k+1} + R_b N_m^{k+1} + NrC^{k+1}), \tag{30}$$

where $K = ([P_y \psi]_d P_x + [P_x \psi]_d P_y)$, $P_x = G_x G^{-1}$, $P_y = G_y G^{-1}$ and $P_L = (G_{xx} + G_{yy})G^{-1}$. $[.]_d$ represents the diagonal matrix, k denotes the iteration level. The iterative process proceeds until the stopping condition is met

$$\sum_{\Xi = \psi, T, C, N_m, \omega} \frac{||\Xi^{k+1} - \Xi^k||_\infty}{||\Xi^{k+1}||_\infty} < 10^{-5}, \tag{31}$$

During this iterative process, the vorticity boundary conditions are obtained from the definition of vorticity as follows

$$\omega^{k+1} = P_x v^{k+1} - P_y u^{k+1}, \tag{32}$$

and a relaxation parameter $\tilde{\gamma} \in (0, 1)$ is applied to the vorticity, as shown below

$$\omega^{k+1} = (1 - \tilde{\gamma})\omega^k + \tilde{\gamma}\omega^{k+1}, \tag{33}$$

where k is the iteration level. $\overline{Nu}$, $\overline{Sh}$ and $\overline{Nm}$ are evaluated using the Composite Simpson's 1/3 rule for numerical integration.

A bioconvection problem previously solved in [10] is revisited for validation of the method, and the obtained $\overline{Nu}$ and $\overline{Sh}$ along the heated left vertical wall are compared in Table 1. Our results demonstrate a strong agreement with those presented in the reference.

Once the numerical simulations are conducted across a broad parametric space, the results are structured into a dataset suitable for machine learning. To extract deeper insights and predict outcomes more efficiently, we employ neural network modeling as described below.

Table 1. Validation with Ref. [10]

Ra	R_b	Le	Pe	$\overline{Nu}$	$\overline{Sh}$	$\overline{Nu}$	$\overline{Sh}$
				Sheremet and Pop [10]		Current Study	
10	10	1	0.1	1.0775	0.3368	1.0772	0.3366
			1	1.0720	0.3296	1.0715	0.3293
		10	0.1	1.0771	0.2556	1.0769	0.2553
			1	1.0397	0.2298	1.0393	0.2295
	100	1	0.1	1.0717	0.3447	1.0711	0.3444
			1	1.1723	0.3650	1.1806	0.3675
100	10	1	0.1	3.0910	0.2506	3.1236	0.2494
			1	2.6560	0.2270	2.6563	0.2261

4   Modelling

In this part, investigation on neural network modeling is presented. The input features in the range of $Ra \in [100, 10^4]$, $Rb \in [10, 100]$, $Pe \in [0.1, 5]$, $Le \in [1, 10]$, $Nr \in [0, 1]$ are combined in a set. The target variables are considered as $\overline{Nu}$, $\overline{Sh}$, $\overline{Nm}$, $mean(Nm)$. By this means, a dataset of dimension 1895×9 with 5 input columns and 4 output columns is saved performing the numerical method in each input combination. The numerical results are obtained by setting $Pr = 6.8$, $\chi = 1$. Additionally, $mean(Nm)$ is the statistical mean of density of bacteria all around the cavity.

Neural network modeling by using 'fitrnet' in Matlab is utilized. The activation function is adopted as rectified linear unit (ReLU). The input data is standardized (z-score standardization).

The data is divided into train (70%), validation (15%) and test (15%) sets. The dimension of these sets is $1327, 284, 284$, respectively. Firstly, models are trained with train dataset, and tested with validation set in 10 runs. The best model inside these runs is saved. Then, the saved best model is used for prediction on test dataset. In order to assess the quality of the model, mean squared error (MSE/mse) metric is used. We used Mean Squared Error (MSE) to evaluate how well the model performed on both the training and test data, ensuring that the results reflect the model's accuracy and ability to generalize to new, unseen data. The obtained MSE metric results on both train and test datasets are compared in different number of hidden layers in Table 2. The column of layer info corresponds to the number of hidden layers as well as the size of the hidden layer. As is noted that the rise in the number of layers reduces both the train and test MSE metric results. However, one layer neural network is also enough to get satisfying MSE metric results.

Figure 2 illustrates NN modeling on test dataset with one layer of size 100. In the first column, black dots very close to the perfect prediction line show the good fit. Also, the residuals changing between small intervals verifies the fine

Table 2. MSE metric results in different layer sizes.

LayerInfo	MSE	$\overline{Nu}$	$\overline{Sh}$	$\overline{Nm}$	$mean(Nm)$
100	train	5.4e–4	8.4e–5	1.3e–4	1.3e–5
	test	6.8e–4	1.1e–4	2.2e–4	1.4e–5
100,100	train	1.8e-4	6.6e-5	1.1e–4	9.0e–6
	test	3.0e–4	8.2e–5	1.7e–4	1.0e–5
100,100,100	train	8.7e–5	5.8e–5	1.0e–4	6.6e-6
	test	1.9e–4	7.5e–5	1.7e–4	6.9e–6

modeling. MSE metric results on the test data for each output is also given on the residual plots, and these also confirm the good quality of fitting.

Holding layer size at 100 with one hidden layer, feature importance analysis is also addressed in the following steps:

* Our best model and MSE metric results on test data, say mse_test, are kept.
* An input column, say i, $i = 1, 2, 3, 4, 5$, both in train and test datasets, is shuffled.
* The shuffled form of dataset is predicted by the model.
* The result of the MSE metric as a result of model prediction on shuffled case, say $mse\_shuffled\_i$, are computed.
* The absolute difference between mse_test and $mse\_shuffled\_i$ is stored.
* Since shuffling is randomly done, the process is returned 50 times.
* The average of absolute differences are calculated for each i.
* The highest value of these mean results refers to the most important feature causing the target to be predicted in difficulty.

In view of these steps, the same importance order of parameters Ra, Rb, Pe, Le, Nr is found both in train and test datesets. Table 3 demonstrates the order of parameter importance on the corresponding target variable. As is expected that Ra is the most important parameter in $\overline{Nu}$ prediction. Peclet number is revealed the most important feature in all other target variables. In each cases, the least effect emerges in the presence of buoyancy ratio term Nr.

Table 3. Feature Importance Analysis

Output	Feature Order
$\overline{Nu}$	$Ra > Pe > Rb > Le > Nr$
$\overline{Sh}$	Pe, Ra, Rb, Le, Nr
$\overline{Nm}$	Pe, Rb, Ra, Le, Nr
$mean(Nm)$	Pe, Ra, Rb, Le, Nr

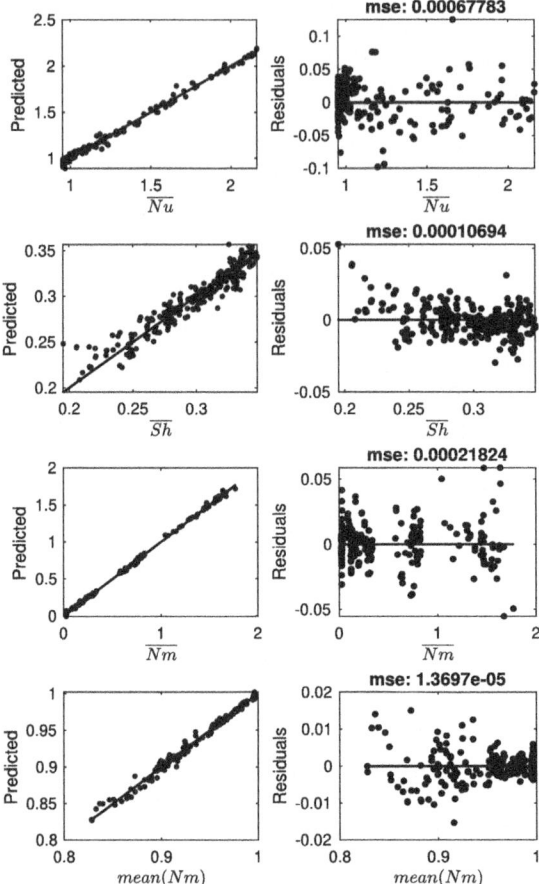

Fig. 2. One layer NN modeling.

5   Conclusion

This study successfully applies machine learning modeling to a bioconvection flow problem, demonstrating its effectiveness in capturing the complex behavior of natural convection in the presence of oxytactic bacteria. The two-dimensional, steady-state flow inside a unit square cavity is analyzed using the radial basis function collocation method to numerically solve the dimensionless governing equations for stream function, temperature, oxygen concentration, bacterial density, and vorticity.

A detailed dataset is generated by varying key dimensionless parameters, including the Rayleigh, bioconvection Rayleigh, Peclet, Lewis, and buoyancy ratio numbers. The corresponding average Nusselt number, Sherwood number, and bacterial density along the heated wall, as well as the average bacterial density throughout the entire cavity, are computed and structured into a matrix for neural network modeling.

The results indicate that even a single-layer neural network achieves a good fit, as reflected in the mean squared error metric. Furthermore, a feature importance analysis highlights the dominant influence of the Rayleigh number on the average Nusselt number and the Peclet number on all other computed averages. These findings underscore the potential of machine learning in modeling complex bioconvection phenomena, offering a data-driven approach for predicting flow characteristics with high accuracy.

References

1. Alloui, Z., Nguyen, T., Bilgen, E.: Numerical investigation of thermo-bioconvection in a suspension of gravitactic microorganisms. Int. J. Heat Mass Transf. **50**(7–8), 1435–1441 (2007)
2. Balla, C.S., Haritha, C., Naikoti, K., Rashad, A.: Bioconvection in nanofluid-saturated porous square cavity containing oxytactic microorganisms. Int. J. Numer. Methods Heat Fluid Flow **29**(4), 1448–1465 (2019)
3. Fasshauer, G.E.: Meshfree Approximation Methods with Matlab. World Scientific Publications, Singapore (2007)
4. Fasshauer, G.E., McCourt, M.: Kernel-based Approximation Methods using MATLAB. World Scientific Publications, Singapore (2015)
5. Pekmen Geridonmez, B., Oztop, H.: Conjugate natural convection flow of a nanofluid with oxytactic bacteria under the effect of a periodic magnetic field. J. Magn. Magn. Mater. **564**, 170135 (2022)
6. Habibishandiz, M., Saghir, Z., Zahmatkesh, I.: Thermo-bioconvection performance of nanofluid containing oxytactic microorganisms inside a square porous cavity under constant and periodic temperature boundary conditions. Int. J. Thermofluids **17**, 100269 (2023)
7. Hussain, S., Aly, A.M., Alsedias, N., Çolak, A.B.: Integrating artificial intelligence in investigating magneto-bioconvection flow of oxytactic microorganisms and nano-enhanced phase change material in h-type cavity. Thermal Sci. Eng. Prog. **49**, 102497 (2024)
8. Kuznetsov, A.V.: The onset of nanofluid bioconvection in a suspension containing both nanoparticles and gyrotactic microorganisms. Int. Commun. Heat Mass Transf. **37**(10), 1421–1425 (2010)
9. Saini, S., Sharma, Y.: Numerical study of nanofluid thermo-bioconvection containing gravitactic microorganisms in porous media: effect of vertical throughflow. Adv. Powder Technol. **29**(11), 2725–2732 (2018)
10. Sheremet, M.A., Pop, I.: Thermo-bioconvection in a square porous cavity filled by oxytactic microorganisms. Transp. Porous Media **103**, 191–205 (2014)

Finding Sustainable Clusters in Supply Chains Dynamics via Graph Partitioning

Raffaele D' Ambrosio, Stefano Di Giovacchino, and Carmela Scalone$^{(\boxtimes)}$

Department of Engineering and Computer Science and Mathematics,
University of L'Aquila, Via Vetoio, Loc. Coppito, 67100 L'Aquila, Italy
{raffaele.dambrosio,stefano.digiovacchino,carmela.scalone}@univaq.it

Abstract. This paper regards the clustering problem of supply chains. From a mathematical point of view, it is well-known that they may be modeled by connected graphs. Through this work, following the algorithm in [9], we address our attention on finding the smallest possible perturbation of the adjacency matrix of the graph associated to such supply chain, such that makes it disconnected. On a numerical analysis perspective, this problem consists in studying suitable approximations of a gradient system via spectral theory. Differently from standard methods like NMF or spectral clustering, the presented approach enables structured and interpretable perturbations, allowing for targeted policy analysis and scenario-based cluster exploration. Finally, selected numerical experiments on the special case of Japanese automotive industries will be reported.

Keywords: graph partitioning · differential equations · supply chain

1 Introduction

Nowadays, industrial and environmental sustainability is capturing a wider and wider attention among the scientific community and it represents an emergent real-world open issue. In particular, one of the most relevant addressed point is certainly the reduction of CO_2 emissions, that is one of the most effective responsible of climate warming. From a mathematical point of view, contributions concerning this topic are becoming increasingly common in the literature. In particular, we are interested in the possibility of studying the CO_2 emissions of supply chains of industries, through the clustering algorithms of graph theory. To a large extent, the interaction between industries may be studied by exploiting graphs and matrix theory; one of the main targets of such analysis has been oriented to the problem of finding appropriate algorithms for clustering nodes of the graphs. In a supply chain cluster, you group together actors (industries, sectors, or suppliers) that are closely interconnected and that contribute significantly to environmental impacts (e.g., CO_2 emissions) through energy and resources embedded in products. Members of a cluster share similar features, such as high levels of embodied energy or emissions, because their activities are

O. Gervasi et al. (Eds.): ICCSA 2025, LNCS 15650, pp. 366–374, 2025.
https://doi.org/10.1007/978-3-031-96962-1_26

closely related (e.g., steel production and automobile manufacturing). By identifying clusters, efforts to improve energy efficiency or reduce emissions can be focused on the supplier groups that have the greatest overall impact. Not a single isolated actor or product is analyzed, but the entire network of relationships in the supply chain, improving the effectiveness of environmental strategies. Knowing which clusters are most critical helps design policies that have a broader impact and focus investments on the most influential areas.

In the scientific literature, there are few interesting contribution on that direction [7,8,13]. They mainly apply numerical algorithms, such as Fiedler partitioning and nonnegative matrix factorizations, for graphs clustering. They are based on associating a weighted graph with the supply chain using Leontief's model and then partitioning it using the above algorithms to identify clusters. The analysis is carried out considering the case study of the Japanese automotive industry. In this paper, we are interested in the same analysis of the aforementioned supply chain of clusters through the use of an algorithm that is perturbative in its own nature. Such a method has been introduced in [9] and it relies on finding the smallest possible perturbation of the *adjacency matrix* such that the corresponding graphs becomes disconnected ($\lambda_2 = 0$, being λ_2 the second eigenvalue of the *Laplacian* matrix associated to the graph.). The main tool of such method is the numerical analysis of a suitable gradient system. In this paper, first, using recursively the aforementioned approach, we provide the clusters of the graph, based on similar CO_2 emissions and then we will detect those most impacting on that direction. The reason for proposing the use of this method lies in the fact that it is robust with respect to the phenomenon of ambiguity, see [10], which we will discuss briefly in the paper, and is very flexible for studying the graph with respect to structured perturbations. While traditional approaches such as NMF or Fiedler-based spectral clustering extract partitions without structural constraints, the method adopted here allows for the explicit modeling of emission-related constraints and the design of scenario-specific perturbations. This makes it possible to simulate, for instance, the effect of freezing emission exchanges of specific industries or grouping them for policy purposes, offering interpretability and practical relevance often missing in standard graph partitioning. This paper proceeds as follow. In Sect. 2, we recall the existent methods for clustering graphs and we highlight their strength points and drawbacks. In Sect. 3, we illustrate the application of the algorithm in [9] to graph clustering problems. Finally, selected numerical experiments will be provided in Sect. 4.

2   Graph Partitioning and Supply Chain

We here introduce the notation and the mathematical framework for modelling supply chains. We denote as $n \in \mathbb{N}$ the number of all the commodities. The matrix $A \in \mathbb{R}^{n \times n}$ stands for the *direct requirement matrix*, i.e., its (i, j)-th element, (a_{ij}), $i, j = 1, \ldots, n$, indicates the input of commodity i directly required for producing one input of the commodity j. The matrix $B = (I - A)^{-1}$, where

I is the identity matrix of dimension n, is the *total requirement matrix*, i.e., its (i,j)-th element, $(b_{ij}), i, j = 1, \ldots, n$, indicates the input of commodity i directly and indirectly required for producing one input of the commodity j.

Moreover, to the generic commodity k, we associate the *final demand vector* $f_k \in \mathbb{R}^n$ with all zero elements except the one in position k and the output vector $x_k \in \mathbb{R}^n$, containing the commodities output induced by the final demand on the commodity k.

Also, for a given integer $m > 0$, we denote by $E \in \mathbb{R}^{m \times n}$, with elements $(e_{ij}), i = 1, \ldots, m, \ j = 1, \ldots, n$, the *direct factor input intensity matrix*; e_{ij} contains the quantity of factor inputs i, such as energy, that need for production of one unit of input of the commodity j. The vector $\tilde{E} \in \mathbb{R}^n$ contains all the consumptions of factor inputs needed for one unit of input of the commodity j, for any $j = 1, \ldots, n$.

If we denote by q the vector whose element $(q_i), i = 1, \ldots, n$ contains the total input factor that has been required directly or indirectly to produce the commodity i associated to the final demand of the commodity k, then, it is well-known that q satisfies the following equation

$$q = \operatorname{diag}(\tilde{E})x_k = \operatorname{diag}(\tilde{E})(I - A)^{-1}f_k. \tag{1}$$

By exploiting Taylor series arguments, after direct manipulations, one gets

$$Q = \operatorname{diag}(\tilde{E})\operatorname{diag}(f_k) + \operatorname{diag}(\tilde{E})A\operatorname{diag}(B_k)f_k, \tag{2}$$

where B_k is the k-th column of the matrix B and the matrix $Q \in {}^{n \times n}$ can be regarded as a weighted direct graph, whose elements (Q_{ij}) stand for the total factor input of commodity i. purchased to produce one input of j, finally needed for the final demand of the commodity k.

From Q, we derive a graph $G = (V, E)$, with $V = \{1, 2, \ldots, n\}$ the set of nodes, $E = \{(i, j) : Q_{ij} > 0\}$ the set of edges and being Q_{ij} the weight to the edge connecting the nodes i and j.

From Q, we can construct the adjacency matrix Q^* as follows

$$Q_{ij}^* = \begin{cases} Q_{ij} + Q_{ji}, & i \neq j, \\ 0, & i = j. \end{cases}$$

Following [17], in [7] the authors makes use of Fiedler partition to cluster the graph in a manner that can be recalled as follows. Given two set C and D, the problem is to minimize the number of neglected edges and maximize the factor input intensity within each group. We may formulate this problem as follows.

$$\min \operatorname{Ncut}(C, D) = \frac{\operatorname{cut}(C, D)}{\sum_{u \in C} d_u} + \frac{\operatorname{cut}(D, C)}{\sum_{v \in D} d_v}, \tag{3}$$

with $C \cup D = V$ and $C \cap D = \emptyset$, where

$$\text{Cut}(C, D) = \|Q^*_{CD}\| = \sum_{u \in C} \sum_{v \in D} Q^*_{uv}, \quad \text{Cut}(D, C) = \|Q^*_{DC}\| = \sum_{u \in D} \sum_{v \in C} Q^*_{uv}$$

and

$$d_u = \sum_{v \in V} Q^*_{uv}, \qquad d_v = \sum_{u \in V} Q^*_{vu}.$$

The problem in (3) can be reformulated as follows [17]

$$\min \frac{y^T (D - Q^*) y}{y^T D y},$$

under the constraint $y^T D i = 0$, with $y_j \in \{1, -b\}$, $j = \{1, \ldots, n\}$, i is the vector of all ones and b is defined as

$$b = \frac{\displaystyle\sum_{i \in Y} d_i}{\displaystyle\sum_{i \in V \setminus Y} d_i}, \quad Y = \{i \in V | y_i = 1\}.$$

Here, the matrix D is a diagonal matrix whose diagonal elements are weighted degrees d_u. Also, the above problem can be reformulated in the following manner

$$\min \lambda = \frac{y^T (D - Q^*) y}{y^T D y}, \tag{4}$$

subject to $y^T D i = 0$, for any $y_i \in \mathbb{R}$, $i = 1, \ldots, n$. It is well-known that Equation (4) is solved by λ_2, were λ_2 is the second eigenvalue of the Laplacian matrix. Such eigenvalue is also denoted Friedler eigenvalue.

3   A Gradient System Method for Clustering

We refer to [9] to describe the numerical approach used in the present paper, see also [5,6]. Consider a graph $(\mathcal{V}, \mathcal{E})$, where $\mathcal{V} = \{1, \ldots, n\}$ is the vertex set and edge set $\mathcal{E} \subset \mathcal{V} \times \mathcal{V}$. We suppose that the graph is *undirected*: if $(i, j) \in \mathcal{E}$, then $(j, i) \in \mathcal{E}$. With the undirected graph we associate *weights* w_{ij} for $(i, j) \in \mathcal{E}$, such that $w_{ij} = w_{ji} \geq 0$ for all $(i, j) \in \mathcal{E}$. The graph is *connected* if for all $i, j \in \mathcal{V}$, there exists a path from i to j for arbitrary length. Setting $w_{ij} = 0$ for $(i, j) \notin \mathcal{E}$, we have the symmetric weight matrix

$$W = (w_{ij}) \in \mathbb{R}^{n \times n}.$$

The degrees $d_i = \sum_{j=1}^{n} w_{ij}$ are collected in the diagonal matrix

$$D = \text{diag}(d_i) = \text{diag}(W \mathbb{1}), \qquad \text{where } \mathbb{1} := (1, \ldots, 1)^T \in \mathbb{R}^n.$$

The *Laplacian matrix* $L = \mathrm{Lap}(W)$ is defined by

$$L = D - W, \quad \text{i.e.,} \quad \mathrm{Lap}(W) = \mathrm{diag}(W\mathbb{1}) - W.$$

All eigenvalues of L are nonnegative, and $L\mathbb{1} = 0$, so that $\lambda_1 = 0$ is the smallest eigenvalue of L. From Fiedler Theorem [11], we know that the connectivity of the graph is characterized by the second-smallest eigenvalue of L. In particular, the graph is disconnected if and only if $\lambda_2 = 0$. Moreover, if $0 = \lambda_2 < \lambda_3$, then the entries of the corresponding eigenvector orthogonal to $\mathbb{1}$ assume only two different values, of different sign, which mark the membership to the two connected components.

For this reason, the second smallest eigenvalue λ_2 of L is called *algebraic connectivity* of W. If λ_2 is simple, then the corresponding eigenvector is known as the *Fiedler vector*.

A typical strategy for partitioning a graph is to compute the Fiedler vector and to partition the graph according to the signs of the values of its components. This procedure becomes unreliable when a small perturbation of the weights yields a coalescence of the eigenvalues λ_2 and λ_3. In [9], the authors propose an approach based on finding the minimal norm perturbation of the weigth matrix W able to disconnect the graph, i.e. such that the second smallest eigenvalue of the corresponding perturbed Laplacian is zero.

The structure of the algorithm can be summarized as follows:

1. Given $\varepsilon > 0$, we search for a symmetric matrix $E = (e_{ij}) \in \mathbb{R}^{n \times n}$ with the same sparsity pattern as W (i.e., $e_{ij} = 0$ if $w_{ij} = 0$), of unit Frobenius norm, with $W + \varepsilon E \geq 0$ (with componentwise inequality) such that the second smallest eigenvalue of $\mathrm{Lap}(W + \varepsilon E)$ is minimal. The obtained minimizer is denoted by $E(\varepsilon)$.
2. We look for the smallest value of ε such that the second smallest eigenvalue of $\mathrm{Lap}(W + \varepsilon E(\varepsilon))$ equals 0.

For a given ε, the computation $E(\varepsilon)$ is performed using a suitable constrained gradient system for the functional

$$F_\varepsilon(E) = \lambda_2\big(\mathrm{Lap}(W + \varepsilon E)\big),$$

under the constraints of unit Frobenius norm and $W + \varepsilon E \geq 0$ and the symmetry and the sparsity pattern of E.

The optimal ε, denoted $\varepsilon^\star$, is computed by a Newton-bisection method.

The algorithm computes a partition of the graph as provided by the Fiedler vector corresponding to the weight matrix $W + \varepsilon^\star E(\varepsilon^\star)$.

4   Numerical Experiments

In this section we prove that partitioning problems associated to supply chains can be interesting applications of the perturbative method described in the previous section.

In particular, we refer to the data of the Japanese benchmark input-output table for the produced prices in 2000, see [12][1]. From the energy input-output database, the total energy consumption of each sector is calculated by summing the energy inputs for each sector. The total direct energy intensity of sector j, $\tilde{e}_j$, is then determined by dividing the total energy consumption by the sector's production output. Next, a diagonal matrix (393×393) containing the total energy intensities is created, and the adjacency matrix of energy consumption, Q, is constructed. This is done by substituting the energy intensity matrix $\text{diag}(\tilde{E})$, the input coefficient matrix A from the benchmark input-output table, and the diagonalized matrix for automobile domestic final demand (i.e., household consumption expenditure on automobiles, fixed capital formation in automobiles, and the increase in the stock of automobiles) $\text{diag}(F_{auto})$ into the right-hand side of Eq. 2. We observe that the graph contains several isolated nodes and a large connected component comprising 305 nodes. Naturally, we focus on this component to study its partitioning. Another important observation is the presence of many edges with very small weights, i.e., values close to zero. We proceed to remove these very weak connections (less than 10^{-3}) and truncate the decimal part of the remaining weights to improve the conditioning of the eigenvalue computations. Such techniques are commonly used to eliminate information that does not significantly influence the graph's structure, as discussed in [9]. We consider a partitioning of the graph, hierarchically applying the algorithm described in Sect. 2. We consider as parameters of the Newton-bisection method $\varepsilon_0 = 10^{-3}$ and the upper and lower bounds for the parameter ε, $\varepsilon_{lb} = 10^{-4}$ and $\varepsilon_{ub} = 10$. The tolerance parameter for accuracy is chosen as $tol = 10^{-6}$ and we consider a maximum number of nodes for each cluster equal to 40. Clearly, this choice is not unique. At the end we find 15 clusters. In Fig. 1, we report the structure of the fourth cluster obtained. In the following table, we report the results of the hierarchical partitioning:

For the correspondence between nodes and industries in the case studied we refer to the works [7,8]. Following [7,8],we measure the impact of industries in terms of CO_2 emissions in tons, considering the within-group sum estimates

$$\sum_{i \in C_k} \sum_{j \in C_k} Q^*.$$

In particular, after computing such quantity for all the obtained clusters in Table 1, we find that the most impactful are clusters number 9, 5 and 4, with sum estimates 2866, 985.74 and 409.54, respectively. The importance of using this algorithm compared to others used in the literature lies in the possibility of offering an interpretation of the results with respect to different scenarios. In fact, it is possible to study partitioning with respect to structured perturbations, for example, that have a certain sparsity pattern. The advantage is that this can be done with a simple projection onto the pattern considered in the method. This means that we are assuming that we are not perturbing certain weights

---

[1] The energy input data are from the website http://www.cger.nies.go.jp/publicatio ns/report/d031/eng/datafile/embodied/2000/401.htm.

Table 1. Distribution of the nodes in the graph clusters.

Cluster	Nodes
1	13, 23, 44, 47, 49, 50, 51, 52, 164, 179, 181, 185, 196, 216,
1	226, 227, 235, 271, 280, 303, 310
2	216, 226, 227, 235, 271, 280, 303, 310
3	151, 202, 203, 224, 273, 301, 307
4	15, 82, 89, 90, 91, 146, 149, 152, 153, 184, 190, 191, 194
4	199, 207, 219,220, 228, 237, 240, 241, 244, 257, 258, 262
5	4, 5, 6, 7, 10, 16, 17, 18, 19, 20, 25, 31, 32, 34, 37, 39, 45,
5	56, 58, 60, 62, 102, 120, 174, 176, 186, 236, 249, 252, 266,
5	267, 278, 279, 283, 293, 304, 311
6	11, 14, 24, 30, 72, 76, 77, 92, 96, 109, 110, 113, 117, 130,
6	160, 192, 195, 201, 208, 210, 225, 234, 247, 248, 251, 253,
6	255, 256, 269, 290, 296, 299, 305
7	217, 270
8	48, 57, 74, 88, 121, 122, 139, 144, 145, 159, 161, 162, 169,
8	218, 242, 261, 288, 289, 292, 294, 306
9	21, 29, 63, 69, 75, 101, 115, 119, 131, 133, 134, 135, 136,
9	141, 175, 182, 214, 215, 245, 246, 264, 265, 268, 287
10	9, 33, 36, 40
11	26, 55, 61, 66, 78, 84, 87, 94, 97, 98, 103, 105, 111,
11	114, 1, 16, 118, 127, 137, 138, 140, 143, 148, 150,
11	154, 170, 173, 187, 221, 230, 233, 238, 243, 263, 274,
11	275, 281, 300
12	67, 79, 80, 81, 85, 93, 95, 100, 112, 167, 177, 178,
12	180, 213, 232, 254, 260, 276, 282, 284, 285, 286, 298,
12	308, 309
13	59, 64, 65, 70, 73, 83, 147, 155, 166, 198, 206, 211,
13	212, 250, 259, 291, 297
14	22, 28, 68, 71, 123, 128, 156, 158, 163, 188, 193, 197,
14	200, 205, 229, 295
15	1, 2, 3, 8, 12, 27, 41, 42, 43, 53, 54, 86, 99, 104, 107,
15	108, 124, 125, 126, 129, 132, 157, 165, 168, 171, 172,
15	209, 222, 223, 231, 239, 277

(emissions) of certain nodes (industries). This makes it possible to provide an analysis of the clusters obtained for different configurations. The possibility of including membership constraints may also be of application interest, when one wants to constrain a group of industries in the same pattern for other environ-

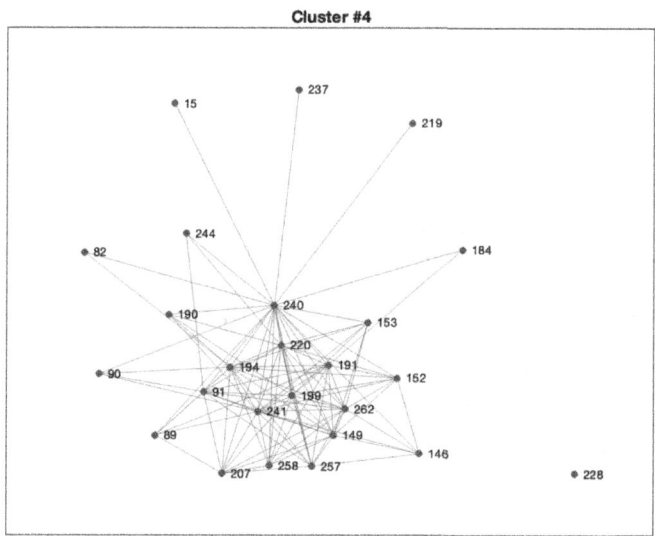

Fig. 1. Subgraph of the cluster 4.

mental impact reasons and then observe the repercussions in the hierarchical partitioning.

5   Conclusion

In this paper, we present a method suitable for partitioning a graph associated to a supply chain. This kind of analysis has provided a clustering useful to describe the impact of industrial groups in terms of CO_2 emissions. As also observed in [7], the direct effect of this analysis is meaningful in understanding how cluster-wide supply chain effort would contribute to saving energy and mitigating climate change. Future research perspectives could lead to the merging of clustering techniques in the supply chain domain with a machine learning context, see [1] and the extension of the theory presented in [3] to study the stability of stochastic networks associated with the presented model, as well as to establishing a formal paradigm of stochastic numerics (see [2, 4, 18]) for sustainability.

Acknowledgement. The work is supported by PRIN 2022 project "Stochastic numerical modelling for sustainable innovation" (20229P2HEA), CUP: E53C240022 80006. This work has been funded by the European Union - NextGenerationEU under the Italian Ministry of University and Research (MUR) National National Centre for HPC, Big Data and Quantum Computing CN_00000013 - CUP: E13C22001000006).

References

1. Carissimo, N., D'Ambrosio, R., Guzzo, M., Labarile, S., Scalone, C.: Forecasting in shipments: comparison of machine learning regression algorithms on industrial applications for supply chain. In: Lecture Notes in Computer Science (including subseries Lecture Notes in Artificial Intelligence and Lecture Notes in Bioinformatics), vol. 13957, pp. 462–470. Springer, Heidelberg (2023). https://doi.org/10.1007/978-3-031-36808-0_33
2. D'Ambrosio, R.: Numerical Approximation of Ordinary Differential Problems - From Deterministic to Stochastic Numerical Methods. Springer, Heidelberg (2023)
3. Di Giovacchino, S., Higham, D.J., Zygalakis, K.C.: A hierarchy of network models giving bistability under triadic closure. Multiscale Model. Simul. **20**(4), 1394–1410 (2022)
4. Higham, D.J., Kloeden, P.E.: An Introduction to the Numerical Simulation of Stochastic Differential Equations. SIAM (2021)
5. Guglielmi, N., Scalone, C.: An efficient method for non-negative low-rank completion. Adv. Comput. Math. **46**(2), 31 (2020)
6. Guglielmi, N., Scalone, C.: Computing the closest real normal matrix and normal completion. Adv. Comput. Math. **45**(5–6), 2867–2891 (2019)
7. Kagawa, S., Suh, S., Kondo, Y., Nansai, K.: Identifying environmentally important supply chain clusters in the automobile industry. Econ. Syst. Res. **25**(3) (2013)
8. Kagawa, S., Okamoto, S., Suh, S., Kondo, Y., Nansai, K.: Finding environmentally important industry clusters: multiway cut approach using nonnegative matrix factorization. Social Netw. **35**(3), 423–438 (2013)
9. Andreotti, E., Edelmann, D., Guglielmi, N., Lubich, C.: Constrained graph partitioning via matrix differential equations. SIAM J. Matrix Anal. Appl. **40**(1) (2019)
10. Andreotti, E., Edelmann, D., Guglielmi, N., Lubich, C.: Measuring the stability of spectral clustering. Linear Algebra Appl. **610**, 673–697 (2021)
11. Fiedler, M.: Algebraic connectivity of graphs. Czechoslov. Math. J. **23**(98), 298–305 (1973)
12. Matsushima, S., Kagawa, S., Nansai, K., Xue, J.: A comparison of deflation methods for carbon footprint calculations using Japanese data. Econ. Syst. Res. **36**(3) (2024)
13. Nansai, K., Kagawa, S., Suh, S., Inaba, R., Moriguchi, Y.: Simple indicator to identify the environmental soundness of growth of consumption and technology: eco-velocity of consumption. Environ. Sci. Technol. **41**, 1465–1472 (2007)
14. Nansai, K., Kagawa, S., Suh, S., Fujii, M., Inaba, R., Hashimoto, S.: Material and energy dependence of services and its implications for climate change. Environ. Sci. Technol. **43**, 4241–4246 (2009)
15. Newman, M., Girvan, M.: Finding and evaluating community structure in networks. Phys. Rev. E **69**, 026113 (2004)
16. Newman, M.: Fast algorithm for detecting community structure in networks. Phys. Rev. E **69**, 066133 (2004)
17. Shi, J., Malik, J.: Normalized cuts and image segmentation. IEEE Trans. Pattern Anal. Mach. Intell. **22**, 888–905 (2000)
18. Milstein, G.N., Tretyakov, M.V.: Stochastic Numerics for Mathematical Physics. Scientific Computation, Springer-Verlag, Berlin (2004)

Implementation of Multiple Multiplicative Inverses Modulo 2^w Using Intel AVX-512 Instructions

Daisuke Takahashi$^{(\boxtimes)}$ (iD)

Center for Computational Sciences, University of Tsukuba, 1-1-1 Tennodai, Tsukuba,
Ibaraki 305-8577, Japan
daisuke@cs.tsukuba.ac.jp

Abstract. In this paper, we propose an implementation of multiple multiplicative inverses modulo 2^w using Intel Advanced Vector Extensions 512 (Intel AVX-512) instructions, where w is the bit width in the integer arithmetic operations. The proposed 52-bit implementation is based on a combination of Newton's method with quadratic convergence and a variant of Newton's method with cubic convergence. For multiple modular multiplicative inverses, the proposed 52-bit implementation using Intel AVX-512 instructions is up to approximately 9.95 and 1.92 times faster than a 64-bit implementation based on an inclusive scan using Intel 64 instructions and a 64-bit implementation based on Newton's method using Intel AVX-512 instructions, respectively, on an Intel Xeon Platinum 8468 processor.

Keywords: Modular multiplicative inverse · Newton's method · Intel AVX-512 instructions

1 Introduction

The modular multiplicative inverse is widely used in fields such as computational number theory and cryptography. The modular multiplicative inverse can be computed using the extended Euclidean algorithm, but Newton's method is more efficient when the modulus is a power of two [1–3,5,6,10,11]. An effective algorithm is presented for computing multiple modular multiplicative inverses for the same modulus [2].

We consider the computation of multiple multiplicative inverses modulo 2^w, where w is the bit width of the integer arithmetic operations. Such computations appear when computing Montgomery multiplications [12] for multiple moduli and exact divisions [9] for multiple divisors.

The multiple multiplicative inverses modulo 2^w are expected to be computed faster when vector instructions are used. Intel Advanced Vector Extensions 512 (Intel AVX-512) [7] is a 512-bit vector instruction set. In this paper, we propose an implementation of multiple multiplicative inverses modulo 2^w using Intel AVX-512 instructions.

O. Gervasi et al. (Eds.): ICCSA 2025, LNCS 15650, pp. 375–384, 2025.
https://doi.org/10.1007/978-3-031-96962-1_27

Algorithm 1. Newton's method for modular multiplicative inverse a^{-1} mod 2^{64} [11]

Input: a such that $0 < a < 2^{64}$, $2 \nmid a$
Output: $x = a^{-1}$ mod 2^{64}
1: $x \leftarrow \{(3a) \oplus 2\}$ mod 2^{64}
2: **for** i **from** 1 **to** 4 **do**
3:    $x \leftarrow x(2 - ax)$ mod 2^{64}
4: **return** x.

```
uint64_t invmod64(uint64_t a)
/* Compute x = a^-1 mod 2^64.
   Requires 0 < a < 2^64 and a mod 2 != 0. */
{
  uint64_t x;
  int i;

  x = (3 * a) ^ 2;
  for (i = 0; i < 4; i++)
    x *= 2 - a * x;

  return x;
}
```

Fig. 1. Modular multiplicative inverse of 64-bit integers.

The remainder of this paper is organized as follows. Section 2 describes the modular multiplicative inverse. Section 3 presents the implementation of multiple modular multiplicative inverses using Intel AVX-512 instructions. Section 4 presents the performance results. Finally, Sect. 5 presents the concluding remarks.

2 Modular Multiplicative Inverse

The modular multiplicative inverse of an integer a is an integer x such that $ax \equiv 1 \pmod{N}$. A necessary and sufficient condition for the existence of the inverse of a modulo N is that a and N are coprime (i.e., the greatest common divisor $\gcd(a, N)$ is 1).

Algorithm 1 shows Newton's method for modular multiplicative inverse a^{-1} mod 2^{64} [11]. Here, $(3a) \oplus 2$ is the correct multiplicative inverse modulo 2^5 (5 bits) [11], where $\oplus$ denotes the exclusive OR operation. Since Newton's method has quadratic convergence, four iterations are sufficient to obtain a^{-1} mod 2^{64}. 64-bit unsigned integer operations are performed with modulo 2^{64}, so there is no need to explicitly calculate the remainder divided by 2^{64}. Algorithm 1 requires nine multiplications, four subtractions, and one exclusive OR operation. Figure 1 shows the modular multiplicative inverse of 64-bit integers based on Algorithm 1.

Algorithm 2. Multiple modular multiplicative inverses [2]

Input: $0 < a_1, \ldots, a_k < N$
Output: $x_1 = a_1^{-1} \bmod N, \ldots, x_k = a_k^{-1} \bmod N$
1: $b_1 \leftarrow a_1$
2: **for** i **from** 2 **to** k **do**
3:    $b_i \leftarrow b_{i-1} a_i \bmod N$
4: $q \leftarrow b_k^{-1} \bmod N$
5: **for** i **from** k **downto** 2 **do**
6:    $x_i \leftarrow q b_{i-1} \bmod N$
7:    $q \leftarrow q a_i \bmod N$
8: $x_1 \leftarrow q$.

Algorithm 2 shows an algorithm for computing multiple modular multiplicative inverses [2]. This algorithm requires only one modular multiplicative inverse (on line 4) and $3(k-1)$ modular multiplications. Therefore, it is faster than computing the modular multiplicative inverse k times when the modular multiplicative inverse requires more than three times the computational cost of the modular multiplication [2]. Lines 3 and 7 of Algorithm 2 contain an inclusive scan that can be vectorized and parallelized.

Figure 2 shows the vectorized multiple modular multiplicative inverses of 64-bit integers based on Algorithm 2. In this program, the first and second for loops include an inclusive scan that can be vectorized using the `#pragma omp scan inclusive` directive supported since OpenMP 5.0. The function invmod64() shown in Fig. 1 is called to compute a 64-bit modular multiplicative inverse. It is also possible to compute multiple modular multiplicative inverses of 64-bit integers by executing Algorithm 1 multiple times, rather than using Algorithm 2.

3 Implementation of Multiple Modular Multiplicative Inverses Using Intel AVX-512 Instructions

The Intel AVX-512 is a 512-bit vector instruction set with several extensions that can be implemented independently. Intel AVX-512 implementations require only the Intel AVX-512F (Foundation) core extension. The Intel AVX-512DQ (Doubleword and Quadword) instruction set [7] supports the vpmullq instruction, which calculates the lower half of the product of two 64-bit integers. The Intel AVX-512IFMA (Integer Fused Multiply-Add) instruction set [7] supports the vpmadd52huq and vpmadd52luq instructions, which multiply 52-bit unsigned integers, produce the high and low halves of the result, respectively, and add them to 64-bit accumulators. Intel provides intrinsics [8] to facilitate the use of Intel AVX-512 instructions.

The vpmadd52luq instruction requires fewer cycles than the vpmullq instruction [4]. In this case, since Newton's method has quadratic convergence, it is faster to compute the first three of the four iterations in Algorithm 1 using

```
void minvmod64(uint64_t *x, uint64_t *a, uint64_t *q, uint64_t *b)
/*  Compute x[:] = a[:]^-1 mod 2^64.
    Requires 0 < a[:] < 2^64 and a[:] mod 2 != 0. */
{
  uint64_t tmp;
  int i;

  b[0] = a[0];
  tmp = b[0];
#pragma omp simd reduction(inscan, *:tmp)
  for (i = 1; i < VLEN; i++) {
    tmp *= a[i];
#pragma omp scan inclusive(tmp)
    b[i] = tmp;
  }

  q[VLEN - 1] = invmod64(b[VLEN - 1]);
  tmp = q[VLEN - 1];
#pragma omp simd reduction(inscan, *:tmp)
  for (i = VLEN - 1; i >= 1; i--) {
    tmp *= a[i];
#pragma omp scan inclusive(tmp)
    q[i - 1] = tmp;
  }

#pragma omp simd
  for (i = VLEN - 1; i >= 1; i--)
    x[i] = q[i] * b[i - 1];
  x[0] = q[0];
}
```

Fig. 2. Vectorized multiple modular multiplicative inverses of 64-bit integers using inclusive scan.

52-bit unsigned integer operations and the last iteration using 64-bit unsigned integer operations. The Intel AVX-512IFMA instruction set does not support the fused multiply-subtract (FMS) instruction. In the calculation of $2 - ax$ in Algorithm 1, $-a$ can be calculated by subtracting a from 0 in advance and then using the fused multiply-add (FMA) instruction.

Figure 3 shows the vectorized multiple modular multiplicative inverses of 64-bit integers using Intel AVX-512 intrinsics. This program iterates Algorithm 1 VLEN (vector length) times on a vector a[:] of 64-bit integers.

The __m512i data type shown in Fig. 3 is supported by Intel AVX-512 intrinsics. The __m512i data type can hold 64 8-bit integer values, 32 16-bit integer values, 16 32-bit integer values, or 8 64-bit integer values. In this program, the intrinsics _mm512_set1_epi64(), _mm512_load_epi64(), _mm512_sub_epi64(), _mm512_xor_epi64(), and _mm512_store_epi64() correspond to the Intel AVX-512F vpbroadcastq, vmovdqa64, vpsubq, vpxorq, and vmovdqa64 instr-

```
void vinvmod64(uint64_t *x, uint64_t *a)
/*  Compute x[:] = a[:]^-1 mod 2^64.
    Requires 0 < a[:] < 2^64 and a[:] mod 2 != 0. */
{
  __m512i a64, neg_a, three, two, x52, x64, zero;
  int i, j;

  zero = _mm512_set1_epi64(0);
  two = _mm512_set1_epi64(2);
  three = _mm512_set1_epi64(3);

  for (j = 0; j < VLEN; j += 8) {
    a64 = _mm512_load_epi64(&a[j]);
    neg_a = _mm512_sub_epi64(zero, a64);
    x52 = _mm512_xor_epi64(_mm512_madd52lo_epu64(zero, three, a64), two);
    for (i = 0; i < 3; i++)
      x52 = _mm512_madd52lo_epu64(zero, x52,
                          _mm512_madd52lo_epu64(two, neg_a, x52));
    x64 = _mm512_mullo_epi64(x52, _mm512_sub_epi64(two,
                          _mm512_mullo_epi64(a64, x52)));
    _mm512_store_epi64(&x[j], x64);
  }
}
```

Fig. 3. Vectorized multiple modular multiplicative inverses of 64-bit integers using Intel AVX-512 intrinsics.

uctions, respectively. In addition, the intrinsics _mm512_madd52lo_epu64() and _mm512_mullo_epi64() correspond to the vpmadd52luq and vpmullq instructions, respectively. If the vector length VLEN in the program shown in Fig. 3 is not divisible by 8, a remainder loop is required.

We propose a combination of Newton's method with quadratic convergence and a variant of Newton's method with cubic convergence for the modular multiplicative inverse $a^{-1} \mod 2^{52}$, as shown in Algorithm 3. Here, a is the correct multiplicative inverse modulo 2^3 (3 bits) [6]. To obtain $a^{-1} \mod 2^{52}$, it is sufficient to use a variant of Newton's method with cubic convergence twice and Newton's method with quadratic convergence once. Algorithm 3 requires eight multiplications, four additions, and three subtractions. The total number of operations in Algorithm 3 is greater than that in Algorithm 1. For a processor with FMA and FMS instructions, Algorithm 1 requires four FMS operations, five multiplications, and one exclusive OR operation. In contrast, Algorithm 3 requires four FMA operations, three FMS operations, and one multiplication.

Algorithm 3. Combination of Newton's method with quadratic convergence and variant of Newton's method with cubic convergence for modular multiplicative inverse $a^{-1} \bmod 2^{52}$

Input: a such that $0 < a < 2^{52}$, $2 \nmid a$
Output: $x = a^{-1} \bmod 2^{52}$
1: $x \leftarrow a$
2: **for** i **from** 1 **to** 2 **do**
3:     $t \leftarrow (1 - ax) \bmod 2^{52}$
4:     $x \leftarrow \{x + x(t + t^2)\} \bmod 2^{52}$
5: $x \leftarrow x(2 - ax) \bmod 2^{52}$
6: **return** x.

Figure 4 shows the vectorized multiple modular multiplicative inverses of 52-bit integers using Intel AVX-512 intrinsics. This program iterates Algorithm 3 VLEN (vector length) times on a vector a[:] of 52-bit integers.

The integer operations in Algorithm 3 are performed with modulo 2^{52}, but the intrinsic _mm512_madd52lo_epu64() returns the result of adding a 64-bit unsigned integer to the lower half of the product of two 52-bit unsigned integers (i.e., modulo 2^{64}). If the first argument of the intrinsic _mm512_madd52lo_epu64() is set to zero, the lower half of the product of two 52-bit unsigned integers (i.e., modulo 2^{52}) is returned. Therefore, it is sufficient to perform the multiplication of x and $2 - ax$ modulo 2^{52} using Newton's method with quadratic convergence in line 5 of Algorithm 3.

4   Performance Results

To evaluate performance, we compared the performance of the following implementations of multiple modular multiplicative inverses:

- 64-bit implementations of Algorithms 1 and 2 using Intel 64 instructions
- 64-bit implementations of Algorithms 1 and 2 using Intel AVX-512 instructions
- 52-bit implementation of Algorithm 3 using Intel AVX-512 instructions

In the 64-bit implementation of Algorithm 2 using Intel 64 instructions, vectorization was suppressed by commenting out the directives beginning with #pragma omp in the program shown in Fig. 2.

The batch size of the modular multiplicative inverses was varied from 512 to 4096. The input integer a was set to be a random odd number in the range $[1, 2^{64} - 1]$ for the 64-bit implementations of Algorithms 1 and 2, and in the range $[1, 2^{52} - 1]$ for the 52-bit implementation of Algorithm 3. Each batch of modular multiplicative inverses was executed one million times. The number of modular multiplicative inverses per second (Invmod$\times 10^9$/s) was calculated based on the average elapsed time.

The specifications of the platform used in the evaluations are listed in Table 1. The Intel Xeon Platinum 8468 processor has 48 cores. However, to focus on

```
void vinvmod52(uint64_t *x, uint64_t *a)
/*  Compute x[:] = a[:]^-1 mod 2^52.
    Requires 0 < a[:] < 2^52 and a[:] mod 2 != 0. */
{
  __m512i a52, neg_a, one, t, two, x52, zero;
  int i, j;

  zero = _mm512_set1_epi64(0);
  one = _mm512_set1_epi64(1);
  two = _mm512_set1_epi64(2);

  for (j = 0; j < VLEN; j += 8) {
    a52 = _mm512_load_epi64(&a[j]);
    neg_a = _mm512_sub_epi64(zero, a52);
    x52 = a52;
    for (i = 0; i < 2; i++) {
      t = _mm512_madd52lo_epu64(one, neg_a, x52);
      x52 = _mm512_madd52lo_epu64(x52, x52,
                            _mm512_madd52lo_epu64(t, t, t));
    }
    x52 = _mm512_madd52lo_epu64(zero, x52,
                            _mm512_madd52lo_epu64(two, neg_a, x52));
    _mm512_store_epi64(&x[j], x52);
  }
}
```

Fig. 4. Vectorized multiple modular multiplicative inverses of 52-bit integers using Intel AVX-512 intrinsics.

vectorization, performance was evaluated on a single core and a single thread. The program shown in Fig. 2 uses four arrays of 64-bit unsigned integers, so the dataset fits into the 48 KB L1 data cache for batch sizes of up to 1024. The programs shown in Figs. 3 and 4 use two arrays of 64-bit unsigned integers, so the dataset fits into the 48 KB L1 data cache for batch sizes of up to 2048.

The Intel oneAPI DPC++/C++ Compiler (version 2024.0.2) was used. The compiler options were icx -O3 -xSAPPHIRERAPIDS -qopenmp-simd -qopt-zmm-usage=high. The compiler option -O3 enables optimizations for speed and more aggressive loop transformations. The compiler option -xSAPPHIRERAPIDS generates instructions for the Sapphire Rapids microarchitecture. The compiler option -qopenmp-simd enables OpenMP SIMD compilation. The compiler option -qopt-zmm-usage=high sets the level of zmm register usage to high.

Table 2 shows the performance of the various implementations of multiple modular multiplicative inverses. For a batch size of 2048, the 52-bit implementation of Algorithm 3 using Intel AVX-512 instructions was approximately 9.95 and 1.92 times faster than the 64-bit implementation of Algorithm 2 using Intel 64

Table 1. Specifications of platform used in evaluations

Platform	Intel Xeon Platinum processor
Number of cores	48
Number of threads	96
CPU type	Intel Xeon Platinum 8468
	Sapphire Rapids 2.1 GHz
L1 cache (per core)	I-cache: 32 KB D-cache: 48 KB
L2 cache (per core)	2 MB
L3 cache	105 MB
Main memory	DDR5-4400 128 GB
OS	Ubuntu 22.04 (kernel 5.15.0-100-generic)

Table 2. Performance of various implementations of multiple modular multiplicative inverses (Invmod$\times 10^9$/s)

Batch size	Intel 64		Intel AVX-512		
	64-bit		64-bit		52-bit
	Algorithm 1	Algorithm 2	Algorithm 1	Algorithm 2	Algorithm 3
512	0.38605	0.49243	2.40270	0.37828	4.60871
1024	0.38681	0.48999	2.40460	0.34734	4.60600
2048	0.38712	0.46430	2.40560	0.38465	4.62205
4096	0.38731	0.45022	2.40201	0.33912	3.95695

instructions and the 64-bit implementation of Algorithm 1 using Intel AVX-512 instructions, respectively, on the Intel Xeon Platinum 8468 processor.

When using Intel AVX-512 instructions, the 52-bit implementation of Algorithm 3 shows a speedup that exceeds the bit width ratio (64 bits / 52 bits $\approx$ 1.23 times) over the 64-bit implementation of Algorithm 1. This is because the 52-bit implementation of Algorithm 3 uses fewer instructions than the 64-bit implementation of Algorithm 1. In addition, the 64-bit implementation of Algorithm 1 uses the vpmullq instruction in the last iteration of Newton's method, which is slower than the vpmadd52luq instruction.

The 64-bit implementation of Algorithm 1 using Intel AVX-512 instructions is faster than the 64-bit implementation of Algorithm 1 using Intel 64 instructions. This is because the Intel AVX-512 instructions calculate eight 64-bit integers simultaneously, whereas the Intel 64 instructions calculate one 64-bit integer at a time.

When using Intel 64 instructions, the 64-bit implementation of Algorithm 2 is faster than the 64-bit implementation of Algorithm 1. The computational cost of the modular multiplicative inverse on line 4 of Algorithm 2 is negligible if k is sufficiently large, and lines 3, 6, and 7 of Algorithm 2 require only three multiplications in total per iteration. In contrast, Algorithm 1 requires nine multiplications, four subtractions, and one exclusive OR operation.

On the other hand, when using Intel AVX-512 instructions, the 64-bit implementation of Algorithm 2 is slower than the 64-bit implementation of Algorithm 1. This is because the `vpmullq` instruction is slow, and vectorizing the inclusive scan increases the number of operations.

5 Conclusion

In this paper, we proposed an implementation of multiple multiplicative inverses modulo 2^w using Intel AVX-512 instructions. The proposed 52-bit implementation is based on a combination of Newton's method with quadratic convergence and a variant of Newton's method with cubic convergence. For multiple modular multiplicative inverses, the proposed 52-bit implementation using Intel AVX-512 instructions is up to approximately 9.95 and 1.92 times faster than the 64-bit implementation based on an inclusive scan using Intel 64 instructions and the 64-bit implementation based on Newton's method using Intel AVX-512 instructions, respectively, on an Intel Xeon Platinum 8468 processor.

Acknowledgments. This work was supported by JSPS KAKENHI Grant Number JP22K12045.

References

1. Arazi, O., Qi, H.: On calculating multiplicative inverses modulo 2^m. IEEE Trans. Comput. **57**, 1435–1438 (2008)
2. Brent, R.P., Zimmermann, P.: Modern Computer Arithmetic. Cambridge University Press, Cambridge (2010)
3. Dumas, J.G.: On Newton-Raphson iteration for multiplicative inverses modulo prime powers. IEEE Trans. Comput. **63**, 2106–2109 (2014)
4. Fog, A.: Instruction tables: Lists of instruction latencies, throughputs and micro-operation breakdowns for Intel, AMD, and VIA CPUs (2022). https://www.agner.org/optimize/instruction_tables.pdf
5. Granlund, T., Montgomery, P.L.: Division by invariant integers using multiplication. In: Proceedings of ACM SIGPLAN Conference on Programming Language Design and Implementation, pp. 61–72 (1994)
6. Hurchalla, J.: An improved integer modular multiplicative inverse (modulo 2^w). Comput. Res. Repos. (2022). https://arxiv.org/abs/2204.04342
7. Intel Corporation: Intel 64 and IA-32 architectures software developer's manual, volume 1: Basic architecture (2024). https://cdrdv2-public.intel.com/671436/253665-sdm-vol-1.pdf
8. Intel Corporation: Intel intrinsics guide (2024). https://www.intel.com/content/www/us/en/docs/intrinsics-guide/index.html
9. Jebelean, T.: An algorithm for exact division. J. Symb. Comput. **15**, 169–180 (1993)

10. Koç, Ç.K.: A new algorithm for inversion modp^k. IACR Cryptol. ePrint Arch. (2017). https://eprint.iacr.org/2017/411
11. Mayer, E.W.: Efficient long division via Montgomery multiply. Comput. Res. Repos. (2016). https://arxiv.org/abs/1303.0328
12. Montgomery, P.L.: Modular multiplication without trial division. Math. Comput. **44**, 519–521 (1985)

Author Index

The manufacturer's authorised representative in the EU is Springer
Nature Customer Service Centre GmbH, Europaplatz 3, 69115 Heidelberg,
Germany. If you have any concerns regarding our products, please
contact ProductSafety@springernature.com

Printed and bound by CPI Group (UK) Ltd, Croydon, CR0 4YY

28/04/2026

02098521-0012